N. DAK.

PEMBINA

DEVILS LAKE
FT. TOTTEN
GRAND FORKS

FT. BERTHOLD

MEDORA

BAUX

DICKINSON

VALLEY CITY
FARGO

BISMARCK
FT. ABRAHAM
FORT RICE   LINCOLN

Lake Superior

GRAND R.

MISSOURI R.

S. DAK.

COLD SPG.

SAUK RAPIDS

MINNEAPOLIS
FT. SNELLING   ST. PAUL

WIS.

FT. MEADE
DEADWOOD
FT. PIERRE   PIERRE

Black Hills

RAPID CITY
FT. LOOKOUT

MINNESOTA R.

ST. PETER

MINN

BIG SIOUX R.

JAMES R.

Lake Michigan

FT. ROBINSON   NIOBRARA

NIOBRARA R.

YANKTON

SIOUX CITY

IOWA

FT. CRAWFORD   FT. MADISON
PRAIRIE DU CHIEN

DUBUQUE   MINERAL POINT
GALENA

CHICAGO

Scott's Bluff County

NEBRASKA

CHIMNEY ROCK

SIDNEY

JULESBURG

FT. DES MOINES

IOWA CITY

DAVENPORT

DES MOINES R.

SKUNK R.

IND.

LITTLE SIOUX R.

FORT ATKINSON

COLUMBUS   OMAHA   FLORENCE
ST. PAUL   COUNCIL BLUFFS
CENTRAL CITY   BELLEVUE
GRAND ISLAND   LINCOLN   NEBRASKA CITY

KEARNEY

NORTH PLATTE

SOUTH PLATTE R.

PLATTE R.

RED CLOUD

BIG SANDY

NAUVOO

ILLINOIS

ST. FRANCIS

MARYSVILLE
GRANADA   ST. JOSEPH
ATCHISON   LIBERTY
FT. LEAVENWORTH   BRUNSWICK
ABILENE   LEXINGTON
FT. RILEY   INDEPENDENCE   ST. CHARLES   FLORISSANT
KANSAS CITY   FRANKLIN   ST. LOUIS
JUNCTION CITY   JEFFERSON CITY
COUNCIL GROVE   HERCULANEUM
DIAMOND SPRINGS   POTOSI

RADO CITY   FORT WALLACE

BENTS FORT

ELLSWORTH
SMOKY HILL R.
SALINA

DODGE CITY   HUTCHINSON

ARKANSAS R.

WICHITA   LATHAM

KAN.

PAPINSVILLE

KEN.

TURGATINE R.

CIMARRON R.

NEOSHO R.

MISSOURI

TENN.

FT. GIBSON

OKLAHOMA

CANADIAN R.

RED RIVER

ARKANSAS R.

ARK.

Mississippi R.

MISS.

GULF OF MEXICO

GEORGE ANNAND

VANGUARDS OF THE FRONTIER

JIM BAKER, MOUNTAIN MAN
From a painting by Waldo Love.

VANGUARDS OF THE FRONTIER

A Social History of the Northern Plains and
Rocky Mountains from the Earliest White
Contacts to the Coming of the Homemaker

BY

EVERETT DICK, Ph. D.

Professor of History in Union College, Lincoln, Nebraska
Author of "The Sod-House Frontier"

ILLUSTRATED

D. APPLETON-CENTURY COMPANY

INCORPORATED

NEW YORK   LONDON

1941

DEDICATED

To one whose loyalty and self-sacrifice has in a large measure made possible this volume

MY WIFE

OPAL WHEELER DICK

PREFACE

AS the first rosy tints in the eastern sky give promise of a new day, so the coming of the characters portrayed in this volume proclaimed the coming of civilization over the northern woods, the great plains, and the mountain valleys.

This work is a companion volume to *The Sod-House Frontier* and precedes it in point of the time wherein the incidents occur. The earlier work depicted the life, work, play, and general manner of living of the home-maker on the trans-Missouri plains. Long before the first settler made his humble claim shack, however, the feet of marching figures across the plains had trodden the land which the home-maker staked out to claim as his own.

It is these shadowy figures, who, because of the ravages of time, seem more phantom-like than real, whom this volume strives to bring back from the delusiveness of unfamiliarity to the certainty of reality. It seeks to discover their manner of living, their dress, food, ways of enjoying themselves, methods of labor, and their mode of life in general.

In attacking this subject, it has seemed wise to enlarge the area under consideration from strictly the plains as treated in *The Sod-House Frontier* to include the whole northern portion of the United States from the Mississippi to, and including, the Rocky Mountains.

Unfortunately the material dealing with the northern region is far more scarce than that of the central region, and for that reason many more examples and specific instances have been drawn from the latter section. In spite of this, however, an earnest attempt has been made to draw the whole picture accurately.

I pause to pay tribute to the memory of Francis G. Wickware, of the D. Appleton-Century Company. His death brings not only a deep personal loss but also a definite loss to literary circles. The last few weeks of his life were largely given over to editing this volume. His wide experience, painstaking scholarship, and conscientious industry have contributed largely to whatever literary excellence it may possess.

The onerous task of research has been made light by the state historical departments or societies of the following states: Nebraska, Kansas, Colorado, Wyoming, Utah, Idaho, Montana, North Dakota, South Dakota, Minnesota, Wisconsin, and Iowa. The Mormon Church archives were opened to me also. The Universities of Wisconsin, Colorado, Iowa, Kansas, and Nebraska extended every courtesy to me. Dr. A. E. Sheldon and his staff of the Nebraska State Historical Society have rendered courteous assistance. Miss Martha Turner and Mrs. C. S. Paine have been especially helpful. Professor Louis Pelzer made my stay at the University of Iowa both pleasant and profitable. I wish to acknowledge a measure of indebtedness to students who have pursued research projects under my directions in certain of the fields treated in this volume.

Most of all I wish to express my gratitude to the Social Science Research Council for a grant-in-aid which has made it possible to pursue the research more thoroughly and to finish the work much more quickly than would otherwise have been possible.

The curtain now rises on this variegated pageant of the forest, plains, streams, and mountains.

EVERETT DICK

CONTENTS

CHAPTER I

THE GREAT FUR COMPANIES

CHAPTER II

THE MOUNTAIN MEN

CHAPTER III

GUARDIANS OF THE BORDER

CONTENTS

CHAPTER IX

MARCHING TO ZION

CHAPTER X

CHASING THE RAINBOW'S END

CHAPTER XI

IN THE DIGGINGS

CHAPTER XII

SWIFT COURIERS OF THE PLAINS

CHAPTER XIII

LIGHTNING COMMUNICATION

CONTENTS

CHAPTER XIV

STAGE-COACH TRAVEL

CHAPTER XV

OVERLAND FREIGHTING

CHAPTER XVI

THE RAILROAD BUILDERS

CHAPTER XVII

THE FRUIT OF THE FOREST

CHAPTER XVIII

THE VANGUARD OF SETTLEMENT

CHAPTER XIX

SLAUGHTER OF THE PRAIRIE GAME

CHAPTER XX

THE LONG DRIVE

CHAPTER XXI

FREE GRASS, THE CATTLEMAN'S PARADISE

CHAPTER XXII

WITH THE WOOLLIES

CONTENTS

CHAPTER XXIII

CHARACTERISTICS OF THE FRONTIER

ILLUSTRATIONS

VANGUARDS OF THE FRONTIE

VANGUARDS
OF THE FRONTIER

CHAPTER I

THE GREAT FUR COMPANIES

AS EARLY as George Washington's administration, white men had begun in an organized way to exploit the rich fur resources of the Upper Mississippi and Missouri valleys. The British had taken over the French interests in the Upper Mississippi Valley, and the Spanish had made beginnings on the Missouri River. Nevertheless the phenomenal development in the golden harvest of furs came under American leadership. Immediately following the Lewis and Clark expedition, daring fur-traders began to farther and farther penetrate the Upper Missouri. For some years following 1800 the British influence on the Upper Mississippi was strong, but a law of 1816 excluded foreign companies and made possible the great growth of the American Fur Company. John Jacob Astor bought out the interests of the British company, reorganized the American Fur Company, and began operations in 1817. The law of 1816 was interpreted as not to exclude foreign employees, and the Americans enlisted the services of a large number of the former employees of the British. These brought with them the system that came from the old French companies.

In the early days of the fur trade a peculiar type of organization developed which in a modified form continued through the years in the Upper Mississippi Valley. The chief trader, who held a license from the government, was known as the *bourgeois*. He was all powerful, a little dictator in his domain. Immediately under him were the *commis*, clerks in training for the position of *bourgeois*. These young men lived with the master, did clerical work, and sometimes were sent in charge of expeditions to native villages or commanded subsidiary posts. Next in rank were the *voyageurs* or *engagés*, French-Canadian peasants or half-breeds, venturesome brawny lads who preferred the wild, care-free life of the wilderness and waterways to the more quiet life on the paternal acres. They signed *engagements* for three years in which they promised to obey the *bourgeois*, "to do his will, to seek his profit, avoid his damage, and refrain from trading on their own account." They performed the menial tasks of the voyagings— paddled the canoes, carried them and their cargoes over the portages, pitched the tents, supplemented the rations by hunting or fishing, and cooked the game after it was procured. At the trading-post they furnished the wood, carried the water, and packed the furs. The novices who were employed for the first time were dubbed *mangeurs de lard*, "pork-eaters," as an indication of their inexperience and inability to subsist on the coarse fare of the wilderness. The standard daily ration of the *voyageur* was one quart of hulled corn with an ounce or two of suet, tallow, or other fat. The corn, when boiled and mixed with fat, resembled hominy. From this the term *mangeur de lard*, or "eater of grease," was derived. It was equivalent to "greenhorn," and the bearer had to run the gantlet of innumerable practical jokes by the old hands who were assumed to rank much higher than the apprentices. There was not much difference between a *voyageur* and an Indian. He took his ration of flour when it was available and put it in his pocket handkerchief or hat. A three-year enlistment earned for the novices the title of *hivernants* or "winterers"—seasoned veterans who could endure the rigors of the forest.

The *voyageur* was ill requited for his arduous work of driving the heavily laden Mackinaw boat or canoe through the water and carrying immense packs of furs and merchandise over portages. His wages were not more than a hundred dollars a year and a meager outfit of clothing consisting of two cotton shirts, a pair of heavy cowhide boots, a triangular blanket, and a "portage collar," a sort of harness for carrying over portages.[1] In this manner the simple, common laborer of the northern forest fur trade fared.

The route to the remote post was sure to have rapids and falls which required the *voyageurs* to carry around these obstacles the heavy goods and not infrequently the canoe itself. Two or three pieces were carried at a time by each man. If the portage was a short one, the load was carried the entire distance before another load was taken up; but if a rest was necessary, the *voyageurs* carried all the goods to the resting point before proceeding further. A resting place was called a *posé*, and portages were almost never measured by feet or rods but by so many *posés*. By custom the distance between resting places came to be a half-mile, and hence a *posé* meant a half-mile carry.[2]

The amount of luggage the *voyageurs* were able to carry was almost unbelievable. Missionary William Thurston Boutwell of Minnesota made this observation of the *voyageurs* negotiating a portage in June, 1832:

At 4 in the morning, the men began their days work, and made 12 "poses," through mud and water in many places to their knees. A rain during the day has rendered the path much worse than it otherwise would have been. Yet the men take their keg of pork, 70 lbs. and a bag of flour, 80 lbs., and in some instances, two bags, and a keg, 230 lbs. and carry it half a mile before they rest. In a few instances, men have taken 3 bags—240 lbs. But what has surprised, and not a little amused me, is to see some of the squaws with a bag of flour, 80 lbs., a small trunk, and a soldier's knapsack on her back, wading through mud and water to her knees. Often she is seen with a bag of flour, knapsack, and a child, on top of all.[3]

[1] Bruce E. Mahan, *Old Fort Crawford* (Iowa City, Iowa, 1926), pp. 180, 181; H. H. Sibley, "Reminiscences of the Early Days of Minnesota," see *Collections*, Minnesota State Historical Society, Vol. III, pp. 245-247.

[2] Grace Lee Nute, "The Voyageur," see, *Minnesota History—A Quarterly Magazine*, Vol. VI, pp. 158-159.

[3] William Thurston Boutwell, Missionary to the Ojibway Indians, 1832-1837, *Diary*, Ms., Minnesota State Historical Society Library, p. 20.

One day the missionary recorded that they had crossed five short portages, the longest nearly two miles and the shortest one *posé*.

In the winter the *voyageurs* were frequently compelled to carry packages of fifty or a hundred pounds day after day in visiting remote outposts, returning laden with heavy bundles of buffalo robes and furs. Through cold, storm, rain, or sunshine, under all circumstances, these men with reasonably fair treatment were ordinarily cheerful, unmurmuring, obedient, and faithful to their trust.

In the autumn, after spending the summer at the headquarters of the fur company, the *voyageurs* packed up the merchandise for the wilderness posts. The day of their departure presented a picturesque scene. They were dressed in gaudy turbans or plume-bedecked hats, brilliant neckerchiefs, calico shirts, colorful belts which held knife and tobacco pouch, rough trousers, leggings, cow-hide shoes or moccasins. At the wharf there was kissing and embracing among both sexes as the wilderness travelers bade their friends good-by. *"Bon voyage! Bon voyage!"* echoed from the shore as the gaily-clad swarthy boatmen pushed off. Dipping their paddles into the water simultaneously, they slipped into the current. The leader at the same time commenced to sing in a tremulous voice and was joined by his fellows. In a moment the figures with their rhythmic motion had swung around the bend and were lost to view for another nine months. One of the songs to which the *voyageurs* kept time with their paddles, translated rather literally, ran:

> The river that we sail
>   Is the pride of our country;
> The women that we love
>   Are the fairest upon earth.
> Row, then, Row! Row, then, Row! [4]

---

[4] Nute, "The Voyageur," *loc. cit.*, p. 163.

When a lot of new recruits arrived at a post, the clerk in charge was asked to point out the most intractable and disobedient of the group, and these were immediately sent to the most dreaded points to receive discipline for their conduct. Occasionally one attempted to desert, but he was invariably overtaken by some of the company agents or by Indians and returned to do further penance for the trouble his attempted desertion had caused.

Loading their cargoes of furs at the close of the spring trapping, their boats heavy-laden, the rollicking wilderness men were off for civilization. On the return journey, with the winter's toil and hardships forgotten, the *voyageurs* became a merry crowd. Eager for the year's pay and anticipating a period of relaxation, the happy boatmen sang their French songs by the hour, keeping time with their paddles while their brawny arms drove the craft through the water. A visitor standing on the landing near the warehouse of the American Fur Company at Prairie du Chien, Wisconsin, could hear the songs ring through the forest long before the expedition appeared; and then suddenly there burst into view a little fleet of canoes, bateaux, and barges, the leading canoe gaily flying the American flag at its bow. With *éclat* and a grand burst of speed they raced up to the landing after an absence of months in isolation.

The American Fur Company in the Upper Mississippi Valley formed partnerships with tried traders who gave their time while the company supplied goods and credit. The two parties then split profits. Such a trader's organization was known as an "outfit." The well-known figures Joseph Rolette and Hercules L. Dousman headed "outfits." Rolette's division was from Dubuque, Iowa, up the Mississippi to a point above the Falls of St. Anthony and up the St. Peters River to its source.

When the Indians came to a post to trade, they were painted in their most gaudy colors. The men used red, yellow, and green to decorate their faces, and the women painted a round spot of vermilion on each cheek and a streak down the middle of the part in their hair. They brought furs, game, and other products to exchange for the trader's goods.

The whole scheme of Indian trade was based upon the personal integrity of the employer and the employed. The principal, usually located hundreds of miles away. from the scene of operations, furnished the agent or clerk with large amounts of merchandise for which he held no security but a word of honor. There was often no communication between the two for months, until the trader returned in the spring. This trusty individual made his way into the forest fastnesses and began trading with the Indians. If the vogue of a certain fur went down, owing to a whim of fashion, he knew nothing about it, and he might come out of his winter habitat to face loss because of low prices on a particular type of pelt.

In general, however, the trader set his prices so that there would be ample profit unless something very unusual happened. The net gain in the thirties, provided all collections from the Indians were made, may be illustrated as follows:

3-point blanket...............	284 per cent
1 lb. lead..................	566 " "
1 lb. tobacco................	1,166 " "
1 looking-glass..............	1,900 " " [5]

Of course, collections from the Indians were not one hundred per cent. Each autumn the trader gave the Indian credit for ammunition and whatever supplies he wanted, hoping in the spring to obtain in return enough furs to pay for the goods advanced. He gave credit according to the reputation of the Indian for honesty and for skill as a hunter. If faith was misplaced or ill fortune attended the hunter, the trader suffered losses. Nevertheless, many of these were recovered, for every time the United States made a treaty with the Indians, the traders were on hand to preëmpt a slice of the appropriation to pay the debts of the Indians to the fur company.

[5] Wilson Porter Shortridge, *The Transition of a Typical Frontier* (Menasha, Wis., 1922), p. 20.

The fur-traders were noted for their integrity. A departure from strict honesty between the principal and the clerk or trader was so rare as to be almost unknown. Dealing with a competitor was another matter, however. Any competitor was suitable prey. No scruples were felt in taking advantage of him by fair means or foul. In case of illness or distress, however, the rival party came to the rescue and afforded every assistance. A good trader likewise assisted the Indians in times of famine or sickness. He was to them a veritable ministering angel, giving until his stores were all gone. This bore fruit, for the Indians came to place unlimited trust in their patron. They consulted him about every step of any importance. Herein lies the reason why the trader had such influence with the red men that the Indian agent and the missionary had difficulty in gaining their confidence; for the influence of the trader was used for his own interest, which frequently did not coincide with that of the other whites who were attempting to benefit the Indian. H. H. Sibley of Minnesota was an example of the capable men who arose from a wilderness fur post to preëminence in statesmanship.

The section around Pembina in the Red River Valley played an interesting part in the early fur trade. In addition to furs, large quantities of pemmican and other produce were despatched from there. As early as 1808 the Red River posts sent a shipment of 3,159 pounds of maple sugar in addition to quantities of furs.

Free traders, or traders unattached to any big company, made their appearance in the Red River Valley as early as 1805, and Alexander Henry, the Northwest Company trader, complained that they were as great a nuisance to him as an organized company.

The Upper Mississippi fur trade reached its maximum in the years immediately preceding 1837, and that year marked the beginning of the decline. In the meantime a marked development had taken place in the Upper Missouri and Rocky Mountain area. In 1822 it was computed that there were a thousand men in the trade on the Upper Missouri as compared with five hundred on the Upper Mississippi.

There were four plans for exploiting the fur resources in the Upper Missouri and Rocky Mountain area. First, and most far-reaching, was the plan of organizing fur companies for the purpose of trading goods with the Indians for their furs. The second was the forming of companies which sent hunters and trappers into districts where fur-bearing animals were plentiful, to take the furs directly. The third plan was that of independent individual exploitation by so-called "free" traders, and the last was that of the individual or "free" trapper. The last two classes, free-lances in the business, bought and sold when and where they chose.

Before 1800, Manuel Lisa, a Spaniard, and Pierre and Auguste Chouteau, Frenchmen, were the principal traders on the Missouri. In 1808 Lisa organized the Missouri Fur Company. He established Fort Lisa above the present site of Omaha in 1812 and concentrated the company's activity around this post. Until 1823 it was the most important trading-post on the Missouri River. Until his death in 1820, Lisa remained the most important figure in the company. In 1819 Señora Lisa went up with him and spent the winter at the fort, one of the first women to ascend the Missouri to that point.[6]

The Rocky Mountain Fur Company, an example of an organization formed to trap as well as trade with the Indians, made its bow to the public with an advertisement in the *Missouri Republican* of March 20, 1822, for one hundred men to go into the mountains as hunters and trappers. Major Andrew Henry and General William Henry Ashley were the original partners in this concern. By all odds the strongest company, however, was the American Fur Company under John Jacob Astor, America's greatest fur-trader, which, having established itself in the Upper Mississippi Valley, absorbed the Missouri Fur Company and began operations

[6] Hiram Martin Chittenden, *The American Fur Trade of the Far West* (New York, 1902), Vol. I, Chap. VI.

in the Upper Missouri Valley in 1822. The merging of the two Canadian companies, the Northwest Company and the Hudson's Bay Company, in 1821, threw out of employment or demoted many of the minor officers such as clerks and *bourgeois*. Some of these became the best employees of the western division of the American Fur Company or "Upper Missouri Outfit," as it was known. The first permanent post established by this company was Fort Union, in 1829.

St. Louis, the starting point of all the Upper Missouri expeditions, was characterized by the frequent muddiness of its streets, the badness of its hotels, and the large floating population of trappers, traders, boatmen, and Indians. It naturally drew unto itself a cosmopolitan population. Only a short time before, it had flown successively the Spanish and French flags, and now the American frontiersman had all but overwhelmed it. Canadian French were attracted by labor opportunities or were actually imported.

Here the great companies recruited their men, and finally on the appointed day the *engagés* (for the term *voyageur* was seldom used on the Missouri) were assembled for the long trip into the wilds. Before leaving, the *engagés* and their friends had a last drunken frolic. It was difficult, indeed, to tear the crew away and get started. In 1811 Brackenridge noted that his boat put in a few miles above St. Charles while the men were gathered in from the village. Some had utilized this "last chance" to carouse at the expense of the *bourgeois*, for they were given credit by the tavern-keeper, who knew their employer would pay the bill rather than suffer delay. As soon as the last were assembled, the boat pushed off, and Manuel Lisa kept the men from thinking too deeply by encouraging them to sing songs, keeping time with the splashing oars.[7]

The crew of the keelboat in the fur trade was known as a "brigade," and the captain was called a "patron." Slowly they

---

[7] H. M. Brackenridge, *Views of Louisiana Together with a Voyage up the Missouri River in 1811* (Pittsburgh, 1814), p. 201.

wended their way along the tortuous windings of the muddy Missouri. The conventional fare of lyed corn, fat pork, and corn-meal mush was supplemented with game killed by the hunters who skirted the forests along the banks. Luttig records that on one occasion in 1812 the men gathered two hundred turtle eggs. And Brackenridge states that in 1811 duck and goose eggs were found on every sand-bar, for it was the breeding season. Plenty of the fowls were killed also.

The boats were poled or cordelled on the lower river, but on the upper river with no trees to break the wind a sail could be used. When cordelling the boat, the crew started at three or four in the morning and, working till daylight faded, made about fifteen miles a day. When the sail was used, as much as thirty-six miles was made. When two parties were proceeding up the river, the leading party left messages for the followers by "moccasin mail"— that is, they tied a moccasin to a tree and placed the missive of warning of danger, or of reassurance that all was well, in this improvised post-office.

A few decades later, when the expeditions left by steamer, the scene was equally interesting. Audubon in 1843 noted that the *S.S. Omega*, on which he had embarked, had nearly a dozen different nationalities aboard, of which the greater number were French-Canadians or Creoles from Missouri. Some were drunk and many were in a stupid state, sobering up after the farewell celebration. At the embarkation the men pushed and squeezed until they made "the boards they walked upon fairly tremble." The Indians seated themselves or squatted on the highest parts of the boat. In about forty-five minutes all were on board. The effects of the *engagés* were arranged in the main cabin, and presently Peter Sarpy, the *bourgeois*, book in hand, read off the names of those enlisted. As each man's name was called, he answered, and a clerk handed (or threw) him a blanket containing a scanty outfit of apparel of indifferent quality. Each man took his bundle and made way for the next. Audubon felt that they were ordered about like slaves. One hundred and one were present and four were missing. As the boat pushed away from the wharf, where the loafers stood, the men on board, who had congregated on the hurricane deck, a veritable moving arsenal, began to fire a sort of disorganized salute which lasted about an hour. It was renewed in a more desultory manner at every village the boat passed.[8]

The American Fur Company annually imported a number of raw recruits from Canada to serve as *engagés*. They were bound for five years under a rigorous contract at low wages, and few completed their contracts without being indebted to the firm. Thus most of them were obliged to remain with the company. There are many reports of the cruelty of the American Fur Company, which was hated by its employees. Stories persist that many an employee started for St. Louis at the end of his term of service, carrying a letter of credit for his pay, fell by the way and was reported killed by Indians. Although it is hard to believe, Chittenden felt that these persistent traditions were an indication that the company was not entirely innocent. Desertions were frequent, especially among those in debt to the company and among those of American origin. The severity of the service can be imagined from the fact that, in order to escape it, two or three men in a canoe or on horseback would start on a break for liberty through a thousand miles of wilderness infested with savage Indians.

The mouth of the Platte River was considered the line of demarcation between the Upper and the Lower Missouri, and the passing, like that of the equator on the high seas, was attended by an initiation of the *mangeurs de lard* who were going into the wilds for the first time. They were required to be shaved, unless they could compromise the matter by a treat. Much merriment ensued. The Canadian *engagés* were superstitious and sat around at night relating portentous stories. For example, it was said to be a bad omen if a crow was heard cawing at night.

[8] Maria R. Audubon, *Audubon and His Journals* (New York, 1897), pp. 455-457.

When the brigade arrived in the region where a post was to be constructed, it was necessary to select a site. Often the Indians dictated this matter, demanding that the post be established at a certain point. When Manuel Lisa arrived near the mouth of the Platte in 1812 and selected his site, all hands began cutting timber for the different buildings. Stones for the chimneys were hauled, and construction was begun in earnest. Finally, on November 19, at four in the afternoon, the great gate was hung. This ceremony was saluted with seven guns and three rounds of musketry. A tour was then made around the fort, and the structure was christened Fort Manuel. In the evening a good supper and a glass of whisky were given to the men, and afterwards there was a dance which all the ladies in the fort attended.[9] The "ladies" must have been the Indian wives of trappers and traders. Near the larger river posts a spot was selected where timber was abundant at which palisades for the fort could be made, lumber sawed, and mackinaws and canoes built. From the latter purpose this establishment received its name, *chantier*, French for "shipyard." The Fort Pierre *chantier* was about twenty miles above that post and was commonly called "the Navy Yard."

Fort Union, located on the Missouri River near the mouth of the Yellowstone, was typical of the larger posts. The stockade was 200 feet square, constructed of logs 12 inches in diameter and 12 feet long set perpendicular, with the base fitted into heavy beams 2 feet in the ground and resting on a foundation of limestone. The walls were further reinforced by crossed-beam supports on the inside, to prevent the palisades from blowing down in a severe wind-storm. On diagonal corners of the stockade there were two blockhouses or bastions 12 feet square and 20 feet high, pierced with loopholes. The various houses were built inside the enclosure. They did not adjoin the stockade but had independent walls, leav-

---

[9] John C. Luttig, *Journal of a Fur Trading Expedition on the Upper Missouri, 1812-1813*, Stella M. Drumm, ed. (St. Louis, 1920), p. 94; Fort Manuel was popularly known as Fort Lisa.

FORT UNION

From a painting by Charles Bodmer, 1833.

ing a space of about four feet between them and the palisade wall. All the buildings were covered with earth as a protection against incendiary attacks. There was only one entrance to the stockade, a double-leaved gate, about twelve feet from post to post, with a small gate 3½ by 5 feet high in one of the leaves of the main gate. This was the ingress principally used. The larger gate was opened occasionally when no Indians were in the vicinity of the fort. The houses, warehouse, and store were all about the same height as the stockade.

There were blacksmith and carpenter shops, a hay- and straw-stack yard, and out in the middle of the square a flagstaff gaily rigged, giving the establishment an inviting look to the jaded traveler, hungry and worn.

At Fort Pierre the roofs of the stores and trading-houses were attached to two of the sides. At Fort Berthold a traveler found that there was neither well nor cistern, but a large tub or cask of water was kept in all the houses that were occupied. This was for daily use as well as for fire protection. The water was carried from the muddy Missouri a short distance away.[10]

Some posts were constructed of adobes. Fort William or Bent's Fort, erected in the early thirties by the famous Bent brothers, Canadian traders, is a good example of this type of construction.[11] It was built by Mexicans, and at one time there were more than a hundred and fifty Mexicans at work on the walls, in addition to a number of Americans who cut timber for the buildings and did other work to which the Mexicans were not accustomed. Several wagon-loads of Mexican wool were imported to mix with the clay in making adobe bricks. The ground-plan was a rectangular oblong; the walls were 15 feet high and 4 feet thick. At the

[10] Rudolph Friederich Kurz, *Journal*, J. N. B. Hewitt, ed. (Washington, D. C., 1937), p. 99, footnote.

[11] Fort William, named after William Bent, the eldest of the brothers, or Bent's Fort, as it was popularly known, was eighty miles northeast of Taos, New Mexico, and one hundred and fifty east of the mountains on the north side of the Arkansas River.

southeast and northwest corners were bastions, or hexagonal towers 30 feet in height and 10 feet in diameter on the inside, with loopholes for muskets and portholes for cannon. Around the walls in the second stories of the bastions hung sabers, flintlocks, pistols, and heavy lances with long, sharp blades.

The heavy plank doors in the east wall were fireproofed by being plated with sheet-iron and studded with spike nails. Over this main gate was a square watch-tower. Above the watch-tower was a belfry surmounted by a flagstaff which proudly flew the Stars and Stripes. The bell sounded the hours for meals. The watchtower consisted of a single room like a lighthouse, with windows on every side. Furnished with bed and chair and an old-fashioned spy-glass mounted on a pivot, this room was constantly occupied by members of the garrison who relieved one another at regular intervals and kept a vigilant lookout. The spy-glass had a range of seven miles. On the west side of the fort a gate opened into the corral, and over this gate was a room 30 or 40 feet long rising high above the walls. This room was used as a billiard-room during the later years of the post. At one end was a bar across which drinks were dispensed.

The interior area of the fort was divided into two parts. The larger of the two occupied the northeastern portion of the enclosure into which the main gate opened. The outer wall formed the back wall of the living quarters. On the north side of this square were a well and a row of two-story structures, one of which housed the blacksmith and his equipment. On the south and west sides were one-story houses. On the east were the gate, the outer wall, and two-story buildings. The doors and windows of the buildings forming this court or *patio*, as the Mexicans called it, opened on the inside of the area, affording light and yet assuring the safety offered by the outer wall. Three large business rooms opened onto this *patio:* the council-room, where the Indians assembled for "talks" with the white men; a common dining-hall where the hunters, traders, trappers, employees, and visitors feasted upon the best the country afforded; and a store and supply depot. In the center of the *patio* stood the fur press. In this section the business of the establishment took place. The Indians were allowed in this area to sell their furs, buy, or barter under the supervision of the employees and under the frowning bastion cannon loaded with grape-shot. From this enclosure a passageway ran between the eastern outer wall and the one-story buildings on the south side of the *patio* leading to the wagon-yard or smaller of the two portions of the fort's enclosed area. Along the west wall of this yard was the wagon-house, strongly built and large enough to shelter twelve or fifteen huge freighting wagons such as were used in the Santa Fe trade. These made the annual trip to St. Louis bearing furs and returning with all manner of goods for the Indian traffic.

Floors at ground level were made by slightly wetting clay and pounding it solid with wooden mallets. Second-story floors were made by building a supporting platform of heavy poles, covering them with brush and hay, and then pounding down clay as in the case of the lower floors. The flat roofs were made in the same manner and covered with gravel. They furnished a splendid promenade on the moonlit summer evenings of that delightful climate. The outer walls of the fort rose about four feet above the roofs of the houses and were pierced with loopholes, forming an excellent parapet breast-high to a man standing on the roof.

On the west of the fort just outside the main wall was the corral. Its walls were eight feet high and three feet thick at the top. To prevent marauders from climbing in at night, the top of the corral walls was thickly planted with a most forbidding thorny cactus. The west gate opening into the corral permitted the stock to be driven into the fort proper in case of a dangerous attack.

Along the river there was a large garden of about a hundred acres. An irrigation ditch carried water to this fertile spot. On a rise of ground about two hundred yards southwest of the fort stood an ice-house, which was filled in the winter so that in summer it furnished a place to keep fresh buffalo tongues and other fresh meat.[12]

Colonel William Bent, a veritable combination of medieval merchant and baron surrounded by his retainers, reigned supreme at this castle. Turkeys, pigeons, and chickens, brought out at an early day, had multiplied to such an extent that they furnished an ample supply of eggs and poultry. A German traveler in 1839 found also cattle, sheep, goats, and three buffalo calves peacefully grazing with the rest of the herd. From sixty to a hundred men were regularly employed by the fort. In the spring Colonel Bent or a lieutenant led an expedition overland to St. Louis, taking furs and bringing back goods for the trade. In addition to the furs carried in this train of fifteen or twenty wagons, Bent drove herds of sheep, mules, and horses which he raised himself or procured from the Mexicans.

The return of the train from St. Louis was always a time of rejoicing. There were new dresses and baubles for the squaws, beverages for the thirsty, and little luxuries of various kinds for the isolated folk.

During the trading season trading parties composed of small groups of men left the post to visit remote tribes or bands of Indians. In the summer months, when most of the employees were absent on various errands, the fort was quiet, but in winter all the employees were present except a few traders. The mountain men also came in from their haunts, and the post came to be a winter rendezvous. Visitors were welcome and could stay as long as they liked. There was no lack of women and children, for the mountain men brought their squaws and children and the men at the fort were nearly all married to Indian or Mexican women.

Although far removed from civilization, these denizens of the

[12] George Frederick Ruxton, *Life in the Far West* (New York, 1849), pp. 189-190; Thomas Jefferson Farnham, *Travels in the Great Western Prairies, the Anahuac and Rocky Mountains, and in the Oregon Territory* (New York, 1843), pp. 34, 35; George Bird Grinnell, "Bent's Old Fort and Its Builders," see Kansas State Historical Society *Collections*, Vol. XV, pp. 39-40.

fort did not allow time to hang heavy on their hands. In the winter the teamsters and laborers spent their time playing cards and checkers in their quarters. The officers and clerks of the post entertained the important visitors at billiards or cards, and other members of the winter family sat smoking their long Indian pipes by the roaring fireplace and telling stories of adventures on the Hudson Bay, among the Blackfeet, on the prairies, or in the mountains. The visitor passing from group to group found some speaking English, some Spanish, others Indian, and still others Canadian-French.

Subjects for conversation were scarce. The only news was that carried from St. Louis on the annual trip or brought by the Santa Fe traders or an occasional visitor. The talk clung around local characters, gossip about marriages, love-making, births, deaths, the location of buffalo, or the result of an attack of the Comanches on the "meal party." The latter was sure to remind someone of a battle with the Blackfeet, the Arickarees, or the Crows.

The housekeeper and hostess for Colonel Bent was a good-natured half-French and half-Mexican woman named Chipita, who was married to one of the employees. She made the candles for the use of the post from buffalo tallow. She managed the social affairs with the skill of a modern society leader. Balls were not infrequent, where the moccasined trappers, clad in buckskin, swung the merry, laughing Indian women around in the most approved frontier "hoedown." There were some Mexicans or a Frenchman or two who could play the violin or guitar. There were love-making, coquetting, jealousy, and amorous intrigues even as in more sophisticated regions. Sometimes Chipita organized a' candy-pull. The black New Orleans molasses used in the Indian trade was boiled and pulled, providing a great luxury for the sweet-starved people at the post. A charivari to celebrate the taking of a wife by a Frenchman was recorded in 1844.

Before the Fourth of July a party was sent into the mountains a hundred and sixty miles away to gather mint for mint juleps with which to celebrate the day. Ice for mixing the drinks was at hand in the ice-house.

There was an old French tailor at the post who made and mended clothing for the men. He worked principally on buckskin, which he tanned himself. When Farnham visited the post in 1839, he met two of the Bent brothers clad like trappers in rich deer-skin hunting shirts and leggings, with long fringes on the outer seams of sleeves and legs and worked designs of colored porcupine quills on the shirts, and bead- and quiltwork moccasins. He saw Indian women promenading about the battlements in glittering slippers and long deerskin wrappers, followed by children who be-trayed their Anglo-Saxon blood.

Although a certain degree of luxurious ease was felt at a fron-tier post, it was situated on a potential volcano which might erupt at any time. There were thousands of hostile or near-savage Indians in the neighborhood, who ran off the cattle and horses, killed the herders, attacked the wagon-trains, destroyed the garden, and at times all but kept the post in a state of siege. When they might get the idea of attacking the fort themselves or be led by some white renegade no one knew, but a concerted attack by large numbers was almost sure to prove disastrous.

Nevertheless there was a measure of comfort at the fur post not readily imagined by the twentieth-century American. The windows at Fort Benton, Montana, had real glass panes. The houses were whitewashed. The furniture, though rude, was substantial and comfortable. At Bent's Fort pallets of straw were used for beds. Prairie hay probably was used at the Missouri River posts. The American Fur Company provided for more or less regular ex-press service between forts, and from fort to boat or to outposts.

Most of the posts kept a daily journal. A number of these have been preserved and give some idea of the activities within a post. At Forty Sarpy, Montana, in 1855, one day in July as many as 6 scythes were busy cutting hay and over sixty loads had been cut. On August 24, 11 barrels of charcoal were taken from the charcoal pit for the use of the blacksmith. On August 29 a freight train of 6 wagons was started for the Yellowstone River. On September 13, 2 hogs were butchered. From August 7 to 13 a crew was engaged in whitewashing the buildings. Other entries mention that the women were sweeping out the post, which apparently was done about once a month. Still others mention burning lime, hauling stone, sawing boards by hand, hauling wood, making boats, hunting for the winter's supply of meat, drying it, repairing wagons, and gardening.

Each fort had a sort of hostess house where small parties of Indians stayed. This came to be a nuisance, for the journals time after time mention that the fort was full of Indians, there were Indians hanging around the gate eating and idling about, and that it was difficult to know how to get rid of the pests without offending them. There were other visitors, too. In 1833 General William Henry Harrison's son was sent to the mountains by a fond family for the purpose of breaking him of drinking whisky. It is not known with what result, but one is tempted to liken the effort to the sending of a man to a feast to break him of eating. Then there were scientists such as Audubon, taxidermists, artists such as Catlin, royalty such as Maximilian of Wied, and literary men like Parkman. Many of these stayed a whole winter at a large post like Fort Union. Others went up the river and returned on the same boat. Among the visitors was a considerable sprinkling of foreign globe-trotters.

It was customary for the squaws to go to the fort, other villages, or the agent's house to dance. In return they expected presents of robes, knives, tobacco, or other goods. F. A. Chardon, the *bourgeois* of Fort Clark, confided in his *Journal* entry of September 11, 1835:

Had 3 dances by the Sioux squaws, had to make them all small presents, the Agent had to do likewise—some lads danced also, the Agent gave them a few knives and a little tobacco, I gave nothing—I wish ... dancing is over.

There were competing establishments at most of the best locations, and this proximity offered an opportunity for calls, dinners, and dances back and forth, for business competition was never allowed to interfere with the observance of social amenities. At Fort Union in 1850 a Saturday-evening dance found a neighboring trader and his family and people gathered in a room which had been decorated as brilliantly as possible with mirrors, candles, precious fur skins, and Indian ornaments. Edwin T. Denig, the *bourgeois*, had the hardest job of all, for he was the only fiddler and could not cease playing until everybody was worn out dancing. The scene was novel indeed, for the Indian men and women were dressed in the European mode, surrounded by Indian decorations and savage spectators in their customary dress. The Indian women had the same preference as their more civilized sisters. The cotillion was the favorite dance, and the squaws went through it with far more grace and ease than the visitor had anticipated. At another ball the same winter, given by Alexander Culbertson, the same visitor was struck with the animation, presence, and grace of Culbertson's Indian wife and with her beautiful appearance in her ball gown, fringed and valanced according to European style. At still another ball the same winter it was mentioned that the younger Mrs. Denig appeared among the dancers wearing a beautiful rose-colored ball gown in the latest fashion, direct from St. Louis.

Local travel was almost entirely by horseback, although on one occasion it is recorded that Mr. Denig, his older wife and family, and the musical instruments for a dance went in a two-wheeled cart, while the younger wife rode her pony.[13] Audubon mentioned in 1843 that cotillions and reels were danced at Fort Union to the music of an orchestra consisting of a fiddle played by Mr. Culbertson, a clarinet, and a drum manipulated by Mr. Chouteau, who played as if brought up in the army of Napoleon. These parties were almost always attended with considerable disorder, as was

[13] Kurz, *Journal*, pp. 124, 125, 126, 127, 232.

the country dance on the farming frontier. There were frequent fights, and sometimes to avert trouble those under the influence of liquor who started a row had to be put to bed. Audubon makes mention of one dance he attended which broke up at one o'clock. This was decidedly more moderate than those on the borders of civilization, where the dance almost always lasted till broad daylight.

Celebrations varied at different posts and at different times. At Fort Benton on July 4, 1855, three cannon-shots were fired at morning, noon, and night. At Fort Manuel on Christmas Eve of 1812 three guns were fired at sunset, and with the aid of a treat of whisky the post made merry. January 1, 1855, at Fort Sarpy, Montana, was celebrated with a vengeance. Many were under the influence of liquor, and when the crowd limbered up, they found that their clothing and equipment had gone on the war-path with a band of Crow Indians who had been at the post. One man found himself represented in the field by a comb, another by a coat, another by a tin cup, and still others by blankets, knives, and other articles.

An old French custom prevailing in the fifties required a man to give a present to the girl who kissed him. The half-breed girls capitalized on this. A man could not offer less than a dollar as a gift, and a visitor sighed, "Kisses are dear."

Charles Larpenteur, in charge of Fort Union in the forties, had a son born during the night. The next morning the artillery roared a salute, and all hands had a holiday with a promise of a big ball that night. Scrubbing, washing, and cooking went on all day in preparation for the big event, which was duly held.

When free traders came to the fort, it was the signal for a big celebration and debauchery in which the wily *bourgeois* in the long run got not only the furs but all the money he had paid for them.

Once or possibly twice a year a bundle of newspapers was brought to the post, and these were read and reread until utterly worn out by handling.

Hunting was the one great amusement, and in this the buffalo chase stood out preëminently. Shooting wolves from the ramparts at night was also good sport. Besides various games to occupy the attention, gambling was universal. There was no cash money, especially in the earlier years, and the gamesters gambled wages or furs. A season's catch was often gambled away in a night. A beaver was the universal unit of value, although on the books the accounts were kept in money. The beaver was worth about six dollars and was referred to as a "plus."

Pets and oddities furnished amusement and interest. At Fort Berthold, in 1850, a young grizzly bear and a war eagle were kept behind the powder-house. In the reception room was also a sort of natural-history museum, in which were displayed Indian trinkets, a stuffed Rocky Mountain sheep, a black-tailed deer, prairie chickens, and pheasants. Mr. Denig at Fort Union had a parrot which was a great curiosity. Men of all ranks and degrees were constantly laughing at the bird's remarks. Even the Indians were much interested in Polly, for although they could not understand a word of English, yet the fact that the bird spoke at all was a matter of wonder to them. At Bent's Fort a goat furnished amusement for the population. Colonel Bent had brought two out from St. Louis for the children to hitch up and drive with a cart. On the journey over the plains one was killed, but the survivor was a rugged specimen of the race and for years could be seen jumping around, climbing over the ramparts, amusing the Indians and others. George Bent also took out several peacocks, whose brilliant plumage and tremendous vanity greatly interested those at the fort.

In spite of all the social activities and amusements, time often hung heavy on the hands of the *bourgeois* and his few white assistants, especially in the smaller and more isolated posts. The Fort Benton "Journal" of 1855 has such entries as this for July before the boat arrived: "No News!" and again, "Dull about the fort. Every one crying for tobacco. No news!" Chardon's *Journal* at Fort Clark, twenty years earlier, January 27, 1836, has the same tone:

Lonesome, one single word *lonesome*—would suffice to express our feelings any day throughout the year. . . .

Eighteen days later he wrote:

Extremely lonesome and low Spirited—I hardly know how to account for it, but I have always found Sunday to be the dullest and longest day in the week—that is—the Sundays spent in the Indian Country—I suppose it is because we are apt to contrast the scene with that of civilized life—when Kin and acquaintances all assemble at the sound of the *church going bell*—Although the solemn tolling of a church bell—never possessed much attraction for me, (only so far as Served to announce the time and place—where bright eyes were to be seen.) But I could not help feeling this evening—(Whilst gazing round on this dreary, Savage waste,) That could I at this moment hear the toll of the church going bell, that the joyful Sound would repay Me for whole Months of privation.[14]

The posts were dependent on game for a large part of their living, and if for any reason the game supply failed, the prospect was far from reassuring. At Fort Clark on January 15, 1836, the hunters returned after ten days' hard traveling without having seen a single buffalo cow. The next day the men sent to haul hay returned with the report that the Indians had burned all the haystacks. The horses were turned loose to shift for themselves, possibly to starve.

At Fort Union in 1850 the fort's hunters went out only once a week, bringing in enough fresh meat to last another seven days. It was carried to the fort by pack-horses taken along for that purpose. At Fort Clark shooting and catching rats was an important post pursuit. From June 18, 1834, to August 12, 1835, the score was 1,056.

The food at a post was coarse and lacking in variety. At Fort

[14] *Chardon's Journal at Fort Clark, 1834-1839,* Annie Heloise Abel, ed. (Pierre, S. D., 1932), pp. 55, 58.

Laramie the old standard diet was dried buffalo. Often the hunters had to go fifty miles for it. As late as the fifties Colonel Bent's men seldom had flour but lived principally on meat, game, coffee, and beans. On special occasions a more elaborate menu was offered. One employee mentioned that the clerks had dried-apple pie and cream on Christmas Day by way of celebration.

The love-affairs of the fur-trader were legion. The men in charge of posts liked to marry into prominent Indian families when they were able to do so. Such a connection increased their adherents and multiplied their patronage, for their Indian relations remained loyal and traded with no other outfit. Furthermore, their association with these relatives kept them informed as to the demands of the trade and where they could find buffalo robes. Culbertson of Fort Union married an Indian princess, daughter of a leading chief. A clerk could not afford such a luxury, however, for he was on a fixed salary and no advantage accrued as the result of a marriage into royalty. The white man readily fell into the marriage custom of the Indians, which required the suitor to present the parents of the bride-to-be with one or more horses. If the price was accepted, the girl went to live with her new husband and they were husband and wife without further ceremony. Baptiste, the cook at Fort Clark, even bought a young wife on the instalment plan, making a sixty-dollar down payment. Chardon of Fort Clark in his *Journal* entry of March 2, 1838, mentioned that after six days of pouting and quarreling with each other, Newman and his wife had separated and he had started to the Ree camp in quest of another. He fervently added: "O may success attend him, in the wife line it is his third since his fall hunt."

In this instance all was well that ended well, for Newman and his wife came back from the Ree village with all difficulties settled amicably. Chardon had at least six different wives. Some traders had two or three wives at once. As a rule, parties to such marriage arrangements lived with each other only so long as it was convenient and ended the connection as readily as it was entered upon.

Occasionally, however, there was a real love-match. Such a marriage was regarded in the same light as one contracted in a more regular way in the States. When ready to retire, in spite of the inconvenience of the procedure and the social scandal, the man took his wife and family to the settlements to live. That many men loved their dusky children cannot be doubted, and it was the usual thing for the *bourgeois* to send one or more children to St. Louis or some eastern point for an education.

A source of more complications was the fact that many of the upper group in the fur trade had wives and families in the States and maintained others at their places of business. When steamer service became efficient, there was the ever-increasing and alarming possibility of wives coming up the river to see their husbands. The Fort Pierre "Letter Book" reveals such a hazard. This letter is dated January 8, 1848:

Mrs. Picotte and Mrs. Kipp have intimated to me their intention of coming up in the steamboat. I have no doubt that your lady when she hears it, will also wish to come, and as there is every probability of her doing so, would it not be well for you to dispense with the society of at least some of your present companions.

The half-breed children of these interracial marriages did not fare well as their fathers' heirs. When Jacob Halsey, a clerk of the American Fur Company, died at Liberty, Missouri, the friend who cared for him in his last hours tried to protect his half-breed offspring in their rights and wrote to the company about the children. The company, however, chose to ignore the information, and a member of the company who was chosen administrator swore there were no known relatives except a brother (also a member of the company) and two sisters. The four small sons were thus cheated out of their inheritance, and they never knew until years later that their father died leaving an estate of $45,000.

The principal business of the fur company was to get furs, and the forts kept on hand blankets, red, blue, and scarlet cotton goods, red, white, and blue beads, brass wire, hoop iron from which the

Indians made arrow-points, butcher knives, small axes, guns, powder, flints, lead, looking-glasses, copper, brass and tin kettles, vermilion and verdigris, beaver and muskrat traps, abalone shells, bridles, spurs, needles and thread.

If Fort Union may be taken as a typical example, trade began early in September. A store was built on each side of the main gate just within the walls. The space between the two stores was closed off at the far end by another set of gates, thus forming a large, strong roofless room between the stores. In the wall of each store was a trap window, or "trading-hole" as it was called, about eighteen inches square and five feet from the ground, closed by strong shutters on the inside. When a party of Indians came to trade, the inner gate was locked and Indians were allowed to enter to the full of the enclosure. The outer gate was then locked while trade proceeded. The Indians handed whatever they had to sell through the window, and the clerk threw out whatever they wanted in exchange. When the group was done trading, it was turned out and another allowed to enter. The Indians were entirely at the mercy of the traders, who at the first show of hostility could slaughter them from loopholes in the store without any danger to the traders themselves.[15]

When a competitive establishment was operated in the vicinity of an American Fur Company post, it was always referred to as "the opposition." There was almost always plenty of competition, ranging from the larger companies like the Rocky Mountain Fur Company and the Columbia Fur Company to the smaller concerns who, like minor political parties, had no real expectation of accomplishing anything themselves but hoped to embarrass the larger company into buying them out or making profitable concessions to them. Like gadflies they were ever buzzing about to annoy their large competitor. As Chittenden remarked, the whole career of the American Fur Company was one prolonged effort to exter-

[15] Verna Anne Elefson, *Indian Agencies on the Upper Missouri to 1850*, Ms., Master's Thesis, University of Iowa, 1927, pp. 28, 29.

minate the myriad pests that were always swarming about it. And here liquor entered into the trade in a prominent way. The American Fur Company always contended that it could not compete with the other companies without liquor. It was easier for the smaller outfits to smuggle liquor into the Indian country, for they were watched less closely. Liquor in the hands of unscrupulous persons was a powerful and devastating force.

When a band of Indians arrived in the vicinity of rival posts, each post tried to entice the group into its fort. In 1844 the traders were not allowed to go into the Indian camps to trade, but had to induce the Indians to come to the fort or outpost. At that time the American Fur Company posted pickets to be on the lookout for trading parties, and when the pickets made prearranged signals, the men in the fort immediately mounted and galloped out with pockets full of tobacco and vermilion, to induce the Indians to come to the company fort instead of to that of the opposition. If it was a small party, they did not wait for the consent of the Indians, but loaded the pelts onto their horses and started for the fort. If, on the other hand, the party was large and difficulty was feared, a keg of whisky was brought to treat the men. A band, consisting of a clarinet, drum, violin, triangle, and the bells on the sled, helped to win the Indians to Fort Union. When they were once huddled in the trading-room like a band of sheep, they were given more liquor to work them further into a trading mood, and they never were allowed to leave until they had been shorn completely.

So keen was the competition that rival companies sent out salesmen, as it were, to meet the different Indian chiefs and their followers and guide them into their respective posts. At Fort Union in 1834, when the Indians and half-breeds got on a glorious drunk and became uncontrollable, the trader gave the drinkers laudanum in the whisky. It put them to sleep for several hours, and they lay stretched out on the floor in every direction. Larpenteur tells of one instance in 1833 when, soon after the liquor trade started at dark, singing and yelling commenced and more than five hundred of the Indians with their squaws, all drunk, were locked up in the fort. At daybreak the spree abated, but since many went to sleep, the goods trade did not begin till afternoon. By midnight the trade was over, and early the next morning the Indians moved on. Apparently the traders believed in "making hay while the sun shone," for Larpenteur says they regularly traded all night. He was kept busy all night long turning out drunken Indians, often dragging them out by the arms or legs.

The *bourgeois*, like a politician, had to keep the good-will of his constituency, and not a few, figuratively speaking, became expert at the art of kissing the molasses-smeared faces of the babies. Larpenteur shares his secret of dealing with the Indians. He says he did not hesitate to "butter" them. On one occasion an old chief was very angry, swearing vengeance on both the fur company and Larpenteur. Larpenteur spoke of how much the white men thought of the chief's only child and predicted that this fine boy would no doubt be a chief some day. He then gave the old chief's squaw a nice *cotillion* (a piece of dress-goods, for women's wear, woven in black and white), and the old Indian was pleasant enough.

At Bent's Fort there were seven or eight traders, each of whom had especially friendly contacts with some particular tribe. Sometimes when a village of Indians camped near the post, the chief would ask for a particular trader. If it was a large village and the trade more than one man could handle, two or three were sent. When it was determined that a trader should go out, he and the chief clerk counseled concerning the trip, and the trader enumerated the goods required. These were laid out, charged to him, and packed for transportation. If the journey was over a level terrain, he used wagons; if over rough country, he used pack-animals. Sometimes dog teams and sleds were used in the north. If the trader, on arriving at his destination, found there was a large number of pelts and that more goods were needed, he sent his wagon or horses back for them. When he returned, he was credited with the furs and the goods unused.

When a trader reached an Indian camp, he went to the lodge of the principal chief; with him he stayed and under his protection he placed his goods. The chief appointed three "soldiers" to guard the trader's lodge from intrusion. These sentries could be trusted implicitly. Very soon after his arrival, the crier went about camp announcing the news of the trader's presence, what goods he had, and for what he wished to trade.[16] In opening trade a quantity of liquor was expected by the Indians, "on the prairie," as they expressed it in words or by quickly rubbing the palm of one hand across the palm of the other—the term and sign for "free gift" in Indian vernacular. As the crowd of Indians pressed around the lodge entrance and those in the rear became impatient, some large-mouthed savage who had received a portion might make his way through the throng with his cheeks distended and his mouth full of liquor to be quickly surrounded by particular friends. Drawing the face of each one in turn near his own, he would squirt a small quantity into the friend's open mouth until the supply was exhausted, whereupon he returned for more and repeated the work of distribution. Unfortunately this novel measuring cup had a tendency to leak, and soon the good Samaritan succumbed to his own generosity.

When ready for business, in the earlier days before the whites had encroached very much, the trader gathered a number of sticks, each one representing a certain article he had brought. The Indians soon became familiar with these crude symbols, and when this preliminary process had been completed, the business transaction began. An Indian, for example, would place a buffalo robe on the ground, and the trader would lay down a number of sticks representing what he was willing to give for it. The Indian dickered until he felt he was getting a fair equivalent. Finally the bargain was made. The traders claimed that the Indian was never

[16] Grinnell, "Bent's Old Fort and Its Builders," *loc. cit.*, p. 58.

satisfied but always wanted more sticks placed on the pile, and no doubt the white man, bearing this in mind, made his first offer low enough to allow for raising. The price determined upon for the first robe governed the price of all the rest for that day regardless of size and quality. What the Indians offered in trade was then placed on one side of the lodge, and the trader put what he had to offer on the other side. After prices had been set, trade went on rapidly, and soon many thousands of dollars' worth of valuable furs was collected by the successful trader.

In 1844 the Indians of a certain village in Montana sent for traders of both the American Fur Company and the opposition. Larpenteur was sent a hundred miles over the snow in the dead of winter to represent the former. He took two kegs of alcohol, buried one outside the Indian camp in a snowbank, and took the other to the village. Then he procured water and mixed the beverage. When the announcement of his arrival was made, it was not long until the whole lodge was filled with Indians. He traded for 150 fine robes that night and 30 the next day. He then sent for the "reinforcements" buried in the snowbank, and another drunk took place. He got 30 more robes and business ended, there being no liquor and hardly any robes left in camp. Thus, during weather so extreme that on the return journey a mule froze stiff standing up, the Indians traded away 210 robes which were their main protection from the deadening cold. One hundred and eighty of these were obtained for 5 gallons of alcohol on which the camp got drunk twice, and 30 were exchanged for flimsy cloth, beads, hawk bells, red paint, and hand looking-glasses. The percentage of profit in such a case was many thousand, since five-sixths or more of the liquor was water. Under the circumstances one buffalo robe would have been too much for the drinks.

To aggravate the fraudulent transaction, when the Indians became too drunk to notice the deception, a common practice was for the trader in measuring the fiery liquid to thrust his thumb or the four fingers of his hand into the half-pint cup in order to make it measure less, or even to fill the bottom of the measure with melted buffalo tallow. Besides, the more the Indians came under the influence of the beverage, the more the trader diluted it, until the last was not only diluted five to one but poisonously drugged. Alcohol or "high wine" diluted was known as "salteur liquor."

White buffalo robes were rare and were highly prized by the Indians for use in their religious rites. At Fort Clark at one time a white cow robe sold for the enormous price of six horses, and at another time two sold for sixty ordinary robes.

In the spring the *bourgeois* had to arrange for the packing and transportation of pelts to St. Louis. A press stood inside or near the fort. By means of this press the skins were packed and tied into neat bundles weighing about a hundred pounds, which were then wrapped to protect them against bad weather. There were 10 buffalo robes to a pack, 30 wolf skins, or 60 beaver skins. Marten, otter, and mink pelts were also exploited. At Fort Benton, Montana, in the spring of 1855, 250 packs were pressed in a day. That year, a comparatively late period in the fur trade, 1,020 packs of buffalo robes besides 50 packs of smaller pelts were ready for shipment by April 15. The journal entry of April 30, 1856, states that a fleet of three boats, one of which, 85 by 12½ feet, was the largest that had ever been built there, left carrying 1,540 packs. The "returns of the trade," as it was called, at Fort Union for the winter of 1838-39 left there on June 3 in eight Mackinaw boats, each containing 250 packs besides many small furs. The disagreeable features of such a trip were caused chiefly by the crew's getting whisky on the lower river and becoming unmanageable. No company would insure below St. Joseph for that reason.

In 1850 the American Fur Company in the West was organized with an agent for each of the three outfits, the Upper Missouri, the Lower Missouri, and the Platte consisting of Forts Laramie and Hall. There were two or more posts in each outfit, each under the direction of a *bourgeois* or chief clerk who received a fixed salary of $1,000 a year and a stated percentage on profits. The amount of profit or loss was determined by the business management of the chief clerk. The less a *bourgeois* had to pay for the upkeep of his fort, in salaries, and for pelts, the greater his profits were. The *bourgeois* had a responsibility as great as the commander of a frontier military post. Indeed, there was a degree of similarity between the two, for the *bourgeois* ruled with an almost military discipline. The distinctions of rank were sharp also, and the common *mangeur de lard* would no more presume, uninvited, to hold social intercourse with his *bourgeois* than would a soldier with his regimental commander. Some of the *bourgeois* in the early days, especially where British influence prevailed, wore a uniform, and there were strict gradations at the post table. The *bourgeois* controlled the policy of trade in his region, superintended all the activities of the post, and directed every move of fifty or more men far removed from any agencies of local government. He attended to all the correspondence with St. Louis and supervised the keeping of the books. His duties required not only business administrative ability, but an outstanding personality to rule the restless, adventurous white men under his command and to influence the savage Indians. These men regarded their employment as a career and stayed in the Indian country for years. Denig, *bourgeois* at Fort Union, in 1850 had been in that vicinity for nineteen years.

The second in rank was the clerk who was next in line for promotion. He was frequently in charge of the post during the absence of the chief and was often required to trade in a village or command an outpost. His duty was the most exacting that pertained to the trade, and his social rank was on a par with that of his chief. In 1850 clerks and traders who had mastered an Indian language received from $800 to $1,000 a year. An interpreter without other employment, which was seldom the case, received $500 a year, and a hunter $400. A craftsman such as a blacksmith or carpenter received $250 a year, and an assistant workman $120 a year. All employees received their board and lodging in addition to their wages. Hunters and workmen ate at a second table and subsisted on a diet of meat, biscuit, and black coffee with sugar. The clerks ate at the first table with the *bourgeois*. In addition to well selected meat, they had bread, and frequently soup and pie on Sundays. Everyone had to furnish his own bedclothes, although a clerk could borrow two buffalo robes from the storehouse.

Since many of the employees had formed connections with Indian women and had to buy more or less goods in the Indian country, there were many complaints about the high prices the companies charged. All employees were expected to buy from the company, not at cost price but at Indian trading prices. Coffee, brown sugar, and soap were each a dollar a pound, meal 25 cents a pound, calico a dollar a yard. On the average, one man wrote, prices were nine times what they were in the States. It was not surprising that many employees came out at the end of the year in debt.

What might be called the pioneer overland-mail service in the Upper Missouri Valley was that carried on by the American Fur Company as early as the thirties. The winter express, as it was called, was sent every winter to all the posts. Usually an express from the posts on the Upper Missouri started downstream before the arrival of that from below, and the two met at Fort Pierre, where they exchanged despatches. By this means communication was kept up between the house in St. Louis and the partners in the field. The posts were able to send requisitions for goods to come up in the spring, to forecast the volume of the winter trade, and to inform St. Louis as to the amount of snow in the mountains, for the navigation of the Missouri the next spring was conditioned by the mountain snowfall. Carrying this express was a matter of great danger and hardship. In the dead of winter it was conveyed on horseback between St. Louis and Fort Pierre and by dog team and sled between there and the Upper Missouri posts. The packages were wrapped with the greatest care, and only the most reliable men were entrusted with them. The carriers were not permitted to do any errands for others or carry anything else, but gave their time and effort to the express only. The chief danger on the long, lonesome journey was from the cold, for the Indians did not leave their villages very frequently in winter. When, in 1834, Joseph La Barge, later famous as a steamboat captain, carried the express to Fort Pierre, the express from the north came in the next day after he arrived. On this trip the rider took for food only a few pounds of hard bread and a few ears of corn to parch, depending on game for the rest of his fare.[17]

The overland expeditions to the fur country were of equal interest with the river expeditions. One expedition which left Missouri in 1833 consisted of 45 "enlisted men" divided into nine guards, 4 on each relief and one officer, making 9 officers in all. In charge was a clerk whose duty it was to remain in the rear and aid in adjusting loads that got out of order and to oversee the whole cavalcade. Three mules were given to each man, 2 to pack and one to ride. For the first few days the mules did a great deal of running and kicking off of packs.

A flock of 20 sheep was driven along to provide fresh meat till the buffalo grounds were reached. Some bacon and 500 pounds of corn-meal were also taken to supplement the mutton. For bedding, each man was allowed to carry only a pair of three-pound blankets—"three-point" as they were called in the fur trade, owing to the fact that three stripes or "points" were woven in the fabric to indicate its weight. With these the men had to make the best of a hard bed on the knotty bunch-grass of the plains.

The camp was pitched in the form of a circle, and at night the animals were driven into the enclosure. A number of men under the direction of an officer were stationed around the circle as a guard. To render themselves less conspicuous, they were compelled to remain immobile at their posts. It was the duty of the officer to

[17] Hiram Martin Chittenden, *History of Early Steamboat Navigation on the Missouri River* (New York, 1903), Vol. I, pp. 41-44.

cry out every twenty minutes, "All's well!" and the men were to answer with the same phrase. Should any fail to answer, it was the officer's duty to go the rounds, find the sleeping guard, and take his gun to the boss' tent. In the morning the culprit was given his punishment, which was a five-dollar fine and "three walks"— that is, he had to go on foot for three days. The usual tour of duty was two and a half hours, and it was most trying for the men, after a hard day's journey, to keep awake. Hence some poor fellow trudged along on foot almost every day.

The *engagés* were anxious to get into the buffalo country, for they were tired of sheep meat. At last they arrived and killed an old bull. There was no wood for fuel, and they had to use sunflower stalks. It seemed the pot would never boil. Finally, when the meat had cooked the proper time, the men made preparations to dish it out. Since they had no pans, the stew was dumped out on a clean place on the prairie grass, and the crowd seated themselves around the pile, hauled out their long butcher knives, opened their sacks of salt, and began to eat. The old bull was so tough they could hardly chew it, and they looked forward to finding fat cows. After a long, tedious journey across the never-ending Plains, the party reached the North Platte River near Fort Laramie where they made a bullboat and ferried their stuff over before sunset the same day.

William H. Ashley and Andrew Henry after about 1825 left the Missouri River and abandoned the old idea of using forts when they began to exploit the mountain region. In place of the fort system, the Rocky Mountain Fur Company held an annual rendezvous in the summer, at which the proprietors of the company met the trappers with St. Louis goods and received the pelts to be taken back to St. Louis. Apparently the first rendezvous was not a foreplanned arrangement. About the last of February, 1824, William Sublette and some of his companions buried some powder, lead, and other articles not needed for the spring hunt. The group agreed that if they became separated they would meet at the cache or at a navigable point on the river below (the Sweetwater) about the first of June.[18] After 1824 the idea of meeting at a prearranged place for the transaction of business became habitual. The next year the first rendezvous that met over the rim of the Rockies was held at Henry's Fork on the Green River. Besides ninety-one of Ashley's trappers there were a number of Hudson's Bay trappers who had deserted and come to trade their furs to the Americans. Thus in time the rendezvous, which had been started as a means of assembling the trappers of the Rocky Mountain Fur Company, became a kind of fur men's fair which met annually for a decade and a half. It brought together those who bought and those who trapped furs. Often the greenhorn visiting the West for the first time was there to see the sights also.

[18] James Clyman, *American Frontiersman, 1792-1881*, Charles L. Camp, ed. (San Francisco, 1928), p. 32.

CHAPTER II

THE MOUNTAIN MEN

THE WHITE MEN were not content to allow the red men to have a monopoly of fur gathering, and Yankee ingenuity came forth with more systematic exploitation of the fur-bearing creatures than that employed by the irresolute aborigines. There were two general classes of white trappers, those who signed a contract to hunt for a firm or person, and those who hunted on their own responsibility.

All the fur companies hired hunters and trappers to kill buffalo, trap beaver, and take such other furs as were worth taking. They worked at a fixed wage which was usually paid in goods at an advance in the mountains of about 600 per cent upon their cost. The wage of a trapper was about $400 a year, and that of a camp-tender $200 a year. With average success each trapper would take a hundred and twenty beaver skins during this time, worth in New York about a thousand dollars. With a group of twenty hunters there were ten camp-tenders. Horses were worth four dollars in goods at the Boston cost. With due allowance for expenses, an outlay of $2,000 would net in the neighborhood of $15,000.[1]

The leader of company trappers was called the "booshway," which was the corrupted French *bourgeois*. When they were on the march, the booshway rode at the head of the column. Near him was the lead mule on which was packed the company's books, papers, and articles of agreement with the men. Then followed the pack-animals in charge of the camp-tenders. Behind them came

[1] Hiram Martin Chittenden, *The American Fur Trade of the Far West* (New York, 1902), Vol. I, p. 6.

the trappers with a pack-animal apiece to carry their "fixens." The women and children were mounted. In safe country the caravan moved in single file stretching out nearly a mile. Arrived at a suitable camping-place, the booshway stopped and dismounted on the spot he was to occupy. The others, on coming up, formed a circle about him. The second officer came in last, to see that all were there, to assign places, and to examine the horses' backs for sore places. The horses were turned out to graze but were brought inside the ring and picketed at night. The officer of the guard called out at intervals during the night, "All's well!" and was answered in the same manner. At daylight the second officer gave the command to rise, and five minutes later the men were expected to be out of their lodges. A man then galloped off at full speed about a half-mile and looked around carefully to see whether there had been any Indians thereabout; after reconnoitering every ravine and hiding-place and finding all safe, he would gallop off in the opposite direction. If all was well, the horses were turned out to graze under the eye of a guard. After they had fed long enough, the caravan started off in the same order as before.

The word of the leader was supreme, similar to that of the ship's captain at sea. The guns and trapping equipment were kept in perfect order, and the camp equipment was inspected periodically. If the leader found some equipment in a neglected or slovenly condition, a neighbor was called and asked if he could do the job up right. When he answered in the affirmative, he was given the job and was credited with from one to ten dollars on the company books at the expense of the delinquent man.

On coming in at night, the trapper took his beaver to the clerk, who counted them and placed the number to his credit. The men were divided into messes, with four trappers and two camp-tenders to a lodge. When fresh meat was brought in, it was cut up in front of the booshway's lodge, and a passer-by was made to turn his back and call out the number of the mess that should receive each cut. Even the hunter who brought in a choice bit of meat had to take his chances with the rest. The captains did likewise in a very democratic manner.

When accompanied by their families, the trappers on breaking camp spread their lodges on the ground and deposited all their "possibles" thereon. A rope was run through the peg-holes around the outer edge and the skin was drawn up, forming a large pouch. This spherical package was then loaded on the horse with the mouth upward. When crossing a stream, the trapper tied a rope to the pouch, and it was launched on the water with the children on top and the women clinging to and swimming after it. A man with the rope in his hand swam ahead, holding onto his horse's mane, and pulled the frail little ball-like craft safely across. A camp of a hundred women and children and three hundred men could thus be taken across in an hour.

Competition was keen between companies, and it was death for a man of one company to dispose of furs to a rival association. Even the "free" trappers who had made an agreement with a company concerning the price of furs and the cost of an outfit dared not sell to any other than the one with whom the agreement had been made.

The free trapper, as the name implies, was not bound by a contract to serve with any company. There were two gradations or types of free trappers. The first type was only semifree, for he had made an agreement with the fur company whereby he was supplied with a complete outfit and engaged to sell his furs to the company at a stipulated price. The second and completely free type regarded himself as superior to any other trapper. He furnished his own equipment, hunted and trapped where he chose, traded with the Indians, and sold to the highest bidder. It was the height of ambition of the ordinary trappers to reach the level of this aristocracy of the craft. They were exceedingly vain and fond of ornaments for themselves, their horses, and their squaws, bedecking themselves with useless "fofaraw" (*fanfaron*—showy trifles, gaudy finery and other gewgaws). They were wholly improvident, fond of contests, such as racing or shooting matches, and gambling, and as a rule they squandered their hard-earned proceeds at the first post or rendezvous to which they came. Proudly independent and foolhardy, they often foolishly risked their lives, and the Indians "made wolf meat" of many, as the trappers expressed it. This was not without retribution, however, for they took scalps as readily as the Indians themselves. We may rest assured that with woodcraft equal to the Indians and fire-arms superior, at the end of the year the mountaineer had made the red man pay heavy toll.

These free trappers developed their own organizations and came and went as they chose. Sometimes a number of free trappers joined together for protection, but each man trapped for himself and sold his own furs. Sometimes a group of trappers would form a sort of communistic organization under which all shared alike in the proceeds. W. T. Hamilton mentions a company of twenty trappers who organized on this basis, selected a leader, and decided important questions, such as where to go and how long to stay in a place, by a vote in council. Everything was held in common, and the value of all furs trapped was equally divided. Not all the men could trap, for a picket had to be constantly on duty. A horse-herder had to guard the horses during the day; during the night the horses were corralled. One man took care of camp, and usually two men acted as skinners and caretakers of all the furs brought in. The remainder set traps, and all kept a sharp lookout for Indians. No shooting was permitted while traps were being set, as a shot signified Indians and brought every-one to the alert. The horses were hobbled so they could not be stampeded. When animals were lost, it was necessary to go to a rendezvous or fort and restock, and it was impossible to collect furs without horses.[2]

When, in 1823, James Clyman hired out to General Ashley,

[2] W. T. Hamilton, *My Sixty Years on the Plains Trapping, Trading, and Indian Fighting*, E. T. Sieber, ed. (New York, 1905), pp. 106-107.

one of his first duties at St. Louis was the recruiting of hunters for the mountain service. Ashley instructed him that he would be most likely to find the type of men that would be willing to go into the mountains in the "grog shops and other sinks of degradation." Ashley later made three-year contracts with his men. When men were being recruited, a house was rented and furnished with provisions for them while the force was assembled. There was plenty of bread and pork, which the men had to cook for themselves. Of Ashley's crew which pushed off from St. Louis in 1823 with the usual salute, Clyman said Falstaff's battalion was genteel in comparison. While on the lower river, the trappers each cut one or two long, straight hickory sticks for ramrods, for there was no timber in the mountains equal to hickory for this purpose. When they arrived at Fort Atkinson, just above the mouth of the Platte, several soldiers whose enlistment had nearly expired joined the expedition, replacing those who had deserted. The officers of the fort very generously supplied Ashley with a quantity of vegetables also.

The Indians along the Missouri River at times attacked with loss of life and property. Then, too, the competition of the Missouri Fur Company was very keen on the Upper Missouri. As a result, parties were sent overland to the mountains. Within two years the Rocky Mountain Fur Company was taking its supplies overland regularly and exploiting the rich fur-bearing regions without using the Missouri as an artery of travel.

Various conditions caused men to forsake civilization for the life of the trapper. A situation occurring oftener than any other, perhaps, was that of the wild youth who, after an escapade of some sort, sought refuge from the punishment or reproach imposed by society in a sojourn in the wilderness. Perhaps an illicit love-affair or the death of an opponent in a duel was the cause of the exodus from home. Many belonged to a class which would have been considered disreputable anywhere, and they naturally gravitated to a life not subject to social laws. A few were brave, hardy, independent characters who delighted in the hardships and adventures that the calling entailed. The free trappers especially were subject to no will but their own. A life of absolute liberty is apt to degenerate into license. Constant danger made them reckless and caused them to consider lightly their own and their companions' lives. It came to be almost a habit with them to shoot an Indian on sight unless he was known to be a friend. There were, however, some good, upright men who, lured by the hope of a fortune and with the pioneer instinct strong in their veins, sought the mountains for a time, intending to retire to civilization in a few years after a competence was gained. Jedediah Smith was a well-known example of a trapper of character, a deeply religious man, who prayed and fought with equal earnestness and vigor.

There were two seasons for trapping, known as the spring and the fall hunt. In summer the skins were unprime and unfit to take. The trappers utilized this off season to spend some time at the rendezvous or fort. When the weather became cold enough to make the furs prime, the trappers worked hard, letting up when the weather became so cold that the animals hibernated, the creeks froze up, and the heavy snowfall made travel difficult.

After the rendezvous a band of trappers, having organized themselves under the leadership of a good captain, slowly traveled toward their chosen trapping area. Jim Bridger regularly led a party into the Blackfoot country. In the summer of 1836 his party numbered sixty men. They moved along the Yellowstone, trapping the tributaries as they went. Bridger himself and twenty-five camp-tenders remained on the Yellowstone while the men would be gone for days on its tributary streams.

In 1830 the proprietors of the Rocky Mountain Fur Company led an unusually large party, numbering about two hundred men, into central and western Montana in the heart of the Blackfoot country. In 1844 a party of forty-three trappers found Rush River the richest place they had yet come across, and it took forty days to "hunt" that vicinity.

It was easy for a trapper isolated from his comrades on some lonely stream to fall a victim to the Indians, who would stalk him for days if necessary. Sometimes, seeing the wily redskins in the neighborhood, he remained hidden for hours or days, awaiting an opportunity for escape. In the spring of 1824, Clyman, while keeping a lookout from such a hiding-place, missed his companions, who, when he failed to return, left the country thinking that he had been killed by the Indians. He waited twelve days in the vicinity and then determined to try his best to reach civilization. Afoot and alone, uncertain whether he was on the headwaters of the Platte or of the Arkansas, with only eleven bullets, he started eastward. For days he traveled, almost overcome with loneliness. At length he found a bullboat, which gave him hope of finding a white man in that world of Indians, for Indians never made such a craft. Day after day he trudged down the stream. One day he saw men chasing buffaloes but could not make out whether they were Indians or white men. Great herds were driven across the river all around him. He shot a buffalo and dried some meat. He stayed there two or three days hoping to see a human being. Even a friendly Indian would mean relief from the terrible oppression of unbroken solitude. Two or three days afterward he went into a grove of old cottonwoods where a number of martins were nesting and was almost overcome with homesickness for civilization. He tells us: "I laid down in the shade and enjoyed their twittering for some hours. It reminded me of home and civilization." He saw a number of wild horses out on the prairie and, having heard of creasing, hoped for a ride. He killed a buffalo and made a halter from his hide, and when a fine black stallion came down to drink, Clyman shot him in the neck. He fell and Clyman quickly haltered him, but the horse, which he had hoped to capture by stunning with a grazing bullet, was dead.

He had to follow the river, for there were no springs or waterholes on the prairie. Noticing where a lodge of Indians had crossed the stream, he thought it would be a pleasure to communicate with human beings even though they were Indians, and, plunging in, he crossed the stream and found an Indian village two miles away. The Indians ran out and it seemed for a time they would take his life. They took his gun, powder, bullets, fire-steel, and flint. Finally one Indian took Clyman to his lodge and protected him. Clyman had lost his hat a year before, and as a keepsake for saving his life the warrior asked for his long hair, which had not been cut in all that time. The Indian barbered him with a dull butcher knife, returned his gun, and helped him on his way.

The grass was thick and tall, and he kept to the ridges. On the second day in the afternoon he sat down in the shade a short time and ate a few grains of parched corn which his Indian acquaintances had given him. While thus engaged he heard growling and found two badgers fighting. He aimed at one and his rifle missed fire, but he picked up some horse bones near-by and, like Samson of old, killed both animals. Striking sparks from the lock of his gun, he soon had a fire, and he skinned and roasted both animals. He made a bundle of grass and willow bark to carry his lunch. During the latter part of the night it rained, and he started out through the wet grass. The mosquitoes were so bad he could not sleep, and it was so damp he could not light a fire. He swam several rivers and at last struck a trail leading in the right direction. From loss of sleep, fatigue, worry, and isolation he got so nervous he could keep the trail only with difficulty. A number of times he fell and went to sleep, but a quick jerk brought him to his feet again. In one of these fits he noticed after traveling about a quarter of a mile that he was going back the way he had come. Turning around he trudged along for some time with his head down ... and then, raising his eyes, he saw the Stars and Stripes floating in the breeze over Fort Atkinson. He swooned away and lay unconscious he knew not how long. Finally he sat up and contemplated the scene. He made several attempts to rise but as often fell back for lack of strength. At last he managed to struggle into the post, where he was warmly welcomed and cared for. Of the experience he said: "No man ever enjoyed the sight of our flag better than I did." [3]

Every trapper had his particular method of setting traps, baiting them, and outwitting the beaver. Trappers became expert at reading "signs," as the indications of the presence of beaver were called. Some old veteran mountaineers could look at a beaver house and fairly tell how many beavers lived there and how they could be trapped most successfully. A newly felled cottonwood tree was always inspected to see whether it had been cut for food or for a dam. All tracks, runs, and slides of animals were scrutinized. Every old-time trapper boasted of the superiority of his method of operating. At night by the camp-fire there was much tall talk and argument for the superiority of one way over another. Younger members of the party learned much concerning the tricks of the trade from these animated camp-fire talks. A beaver-trap had a five-foot chain with a swivel on the end to keep it from twisting. It weighed five pounds and was valued at from twelve to sixteen dollars. Six of these were considered a full complement of traps for one man. To set a trap where there were beaver and not catch any was considered a great disgrace and on the rare occasions when he failed, the trapper never advertised the fact.

Beaver-trapping necessitated a large amount of wading in the icy mountain streams in a day before hip-boots were available. It was necessary to leave the beaver runs on the shore free from alien scents. Having found beaver cuttings, the trapper followed the "sign" along the bank until he discovered where the beaver ascended and descended the bank to gnaw the cottonwood trees. Locating this "slide," the hunter set his trap in the water beneath it and fastened the end of the chain to a stake in the bed of the stream. When caught the beaver plunged into the water for safety, and the weight of the trap drowned him. This system prevented an animal's gnawing his leg off and releasing himself.

[3] James Clyman, *American Frontiersman, 1792-1881*, Charles L. Camp, ed. (San Francisco, 1928), pp. 35-38.

A stick was tied to the trap with a rawhide string and floated downstream. This was useful in marking the position of a trap in case the animal got loose and made off with it.

Another method was to trap with bait. The end of a short stick was dipped into a little phial (often made of elk horn) of "medicine" and placed on the bank in such a position that it would be immediately over the trap which was set in the water. The "medicine" was made from musk produced by glands in the beaver itself, known as beaver castor. A string of horsehair was tied from the bait to the trap, and when the beaver was caught, it pulled the bait into the water. This was to prevent the bait from attracting other beavers and thus keep them from finding other traps waiting for them. When a trapper skinned a beaver, he always saved the musk-glands and the more edible parts, including the tail, which was considered a special delicacy. Smoke, the firing of a gun, or jarring of the ground alarmed the beaver, and for the latter reason the trapper never rode his horse near the traps.[4]

In 1838, according to Osborne Russell, in addition to a sack of beaver-traps, a trapper had a horse upon which were placed one or two *epishemores* or saddle-blankets, a saddle, a bridle, a blanket, an extra pair of moccasins, powder-horn, bullet-pouch, a belt to which was fastened a butcher knife, a wooden box containing beaver bait, tobacco-sack, pipe, implements for making a fire, and sometimes a hatchet fastened to the pommel of the saddle. From necessity and inclination the trapper adopted the customs of the Indians in his dress. Russell, in describing an expedition of 1838, said the trapper wore a flannel or cotton shirt if he was fortunate enough to obtain one. If not, he wore an antelope blanket and breeches or smoked buffalo-skin leggings. A coat was made of blanket or buffalo robe, and a hat or cap of wool, buffalo, or other skin. For socks, pieces of blanket were wrapped around his feet and

[4] Alexander Majors, *Seventy Years on the Frontier, Alexander Majors' Memoirs of a Lifetime on the Border* (Chicago and New York, 1893), pp. 125-127.

encased in moccasins made of dressed deer, elk, or buffalo skin.[5] As he rode off, his long hair hung down over his shoulders. The costume varied, with sometimes more clothing pertaining to civilization and sometimes more nearly a full Indian costume.

Apparently the hunter who stayed in the mountains year after year came to dress in the familiar buckskin costume, which he made for himself during the period of winter inactivity. The summer costume consisted of a hunting shirt with an ample tail or skirt, pantaloons, moccasins, and a hat or head-band, all of buckskin. Buckskin clothing was fringed along the seams and well decorated with gewgaws of one kind and another. The free trappers especially were noted for their vain use of ornaments and decorative work, and they spent much time working on beads, silver, and other trinkets for their buckskin clothes. Often a red bandana handkerchief or a felt hat was used for head-gear. The moccasins extended well up on the legs. Leather had to be well tanned to stand the hard usage of wading through wet snow or water when the trappers were setting traps. The worn-out trapper who settled down to comfortable sleep by the camp-fire was apt to be awakened by the shrinking leather, and woe unto the man who took his footwear off to dry, for he might not be able to get it on again. Imperfectly tanned trousers and shirts when wet also shrank and drew out of shape in the legs and sleeves, where there was the greatest pressure. It was quite the regular thing after a day of wading on the trap-line to find the bottom of the pants flaring out like a flowing skirt, and once in that shape they remained so until worn out.[6] For this reason some trappers, before the trapping season began, cut the bottoms off their breeches and substituted blanket leggings in their place. In time the leather trousers grew so slick, black, and greasy that it took close examination to tell of what they were made.

---

[5] Osborne Russell, *Journal of a Trapper, or Nine Years in the Rocky Mountains, 1834-1843* (Boise, Idaho, 1914), p. 64.
[6] Cecil J. Alter, *James Bridger* (Salt Lake City, 1925), p. 41.

Two other essentials were often carried close at hand. Around his neck the sturdy woodsman carried suspended a pipe-holder, a highly ornamented piece of squaw workmanship wrought with porcupine quills and beads and often made in the shape of a heart. Fastened to his belt was a buckskin case carrying a whetstone, for knives had to be sharp for the trapper's business, and he used his knife for everything from cutting stakes for traps and skinning the catch to eating his food.[7]

The trapper's dress was comfortable, and after having worn such a costume for years the hunter very reluctantly laid it aside. Jim Baker, a noted mountain man, went into New Mexico and decided, as he said, to try to act civilized after twenty years in the mountains. He bought a complete new outfit, and the change was so great that the members of his own party scarcely recognized him. Captain Marcy, meeting him, remarked that Baker was so metamorphosed that he hardly knew him. Baker replied that he did not know what it was called, but those store clothes did sure hurt his feet. It was not long until he was seen walking along the street in his bare feet carrying his boots in his hand. When asked why he was doing that, he replied that he supposed those store-bought clothes made him look respectable, but they hurt and made him feel like a fool. Not long afterward he laid aside his new outfit and donned his buckskins, saying, according to report: "I'll never wear any more store-bought clothes or act like a gentleman again." [8]

When the mountain men found it necessary to rid their clothing of vermin, they just took them off and laid them on an ant hill and watched the ants carry off the lice.

The life of a trapper was as variable as the weather. One day it would be all peace and harmony, with the trappers enjoying life as very few people in civilization do. The next day it would

[7] Henry Inman, *The Old Sante Fe Trail* (Topeka, 1916), pp. 259, 260.
[8] Nolie Mumey, *The Life of Jim Baker, 1818-1898, Trapper, Scout, Guide and Indian Fighter* (Denver, 1931), pp. 115-116.

be just the reverse, among hostile Indians, without food, or perhaps with their horses captured.

The forests furnished the trapper with the bulk of his necessities. For months he lived on the game he shot and from the by-products made his clothes. The buffalo was his chief reliance for food. Elk, deer, antelope, and bear were also widely used. When he left a trading-post, the trapper's supplies consisted of salt and tobacco, with possibly some flour, coffee, and sugar. Sometimes, when game was scarce, the party traveled for days with little or no food. Then it was that the common saying among the trappers, "meat's meat," became very real. Every reptile or rodent or vulture was food if the trapper could lay hands on it. The flesh of the panther was given first place for richness of meat and delicacy of flavor, followed second by dog meat. Beaver tail ranked high in mountain cuisine also, either roasted or in soup. Buffalo meat was the old reliable food, however.

Like the wild animals they trapped, these mountain men feasted and fasted as occasion offered. When a party had been without food for three or four days and a buffalo was killed, all raised a shout of delight, and the butchering was a joyous occasion. Many cut off large slices of meat with their butcher knives and ate it raw. When a buffalo was butchered, it was turned on its belly, its legs stretched out on either side to support it, and the hide split down the spine. The skin was peeled down and laid out on the ground to receive the meat. The flesh on each side of the spine was pared off. The mouth was opened and the tongue cut out. With an axe the ribs were cut and the cavity opened, the heart, fat, tenderloins, the tepid blood, and the small intestines were torn out, and the legs were robbed of their generous marrow-bones. The choice pieces were then wrapped in the green hide, loaded on an animal and transported to camp.[9] Along the animal's backbone next to the hide was a fat substance as thick as the width of one's hand and about twice as broad, thick by the backbone and tapering

[9] George Frederick Ruxton, *Life in the Far West* (New York, 1849), p. 72.

off to an edge at the outer side. It weighed from five to eleven pounds, and when it was taken off and dipped in hot grease for half a minute and hung up and smoked in a lodge twelve hours, it kept indefinitely. It was used for bread. When eaten with lean or dried meat it made an excellent sandwich, and trappers lived on the combination for months. The small intestines, or "boudins" (French, "puddings") as they were called, were a great delicacy. Covered with blood and unwashed, without further preparation they were cut in lengths and wrapped around sticks. The merry trappers held these over the fire, and when they were roasted to a crisp, ate them, both contents and casing, with great relish.

Thomas Jefferson Farnham was invited to a special banquet by an old mountain man originally from Kentucky. A buffalo had just been killed, and the Kentuckian, in the approved manner of trappers who had fasted for some days, prepared a feast. They sat down and ate until there was a reasonable presumption that they had eaten enough, but the old Kentuckian would not hear of Farnham's stopping and proceeded to expound a trapper's philosophy and habits of eating:

Our meat here in the mountains never pains one. Nothing harms here but pills and lead; many's the time that I have starved six or eight days; and when I have found meat, ate all night: that's the custom of the country. We never borrow trouble from hunger or thirst, and when we have a plenty, we eat the best first, for fear of being killed by some brat of an Indian before we have enjoyed them. You may eat as much as you can, my word for it, this wild meat never hurts one.

While talking the old hunter was preparing the next course. With his hatchet he crushed the buffalo bones and laid bare the rolls of "trapper's butter," extracting a pound of marrow. This was put into a gallon of water heated nearly to the boiling-point. The blood dipped from the cavity of the buffalo was then stirred in until the broth became the thickness of rice soup. It was rich, indeed, and made the faces of the trappers shine with grease. The visitors thought this concluded the repast, but old Kentuck cried out: "No giving up the beaver so, another bait and we will sleep." So saying he prepared the boudins for roasting, and after concluding the mountain feast by eating them, the men were ready to lie down to slumber.[10]

It was literally true that these mountain men, like half-famished wolves that have made a kill, sat around gorging hour after hour. George Frederick Ruxton attended such a feast. Yards of appetizing boudins slipped down the throats of the trappers, rib after rib was picked clean and thrown to the wolves; and when it seemed that frail human nature had done its utmost and the trappers were lazily wiping their greasy knives which had done such good service, suddenly one began to chuckle and, reaching his knife into the ashes, brought forth a pair of tongues so admirably baked, so juicy and sweet, that no persuasion was necessary to start the crowd to eating once more.

In the early thirties a party of trappers had been some time without water and food and finally reached the Snake River in a wretched state. Here it was discovered that the back of one of the mules was sore. On investigating the cause they found a large safety-pin in the blanket. The trappers were not long in bending the pin into a hook and in braiding a line of hair taken from the horses' tails. Soon the frying-pan was filled with fish, furnishing them with a welcome supper. They caught an additional supply and took them along for future use.

In cooking deer meat the mountain men sometimes roasted the head whole. After the burning logs had deposited enough embers, a hole was raked in them and the head of the deer—skin, hair, and all—was placed in this primitive oven and carefully covered with hot ashes. Sometimes it was impossible to start a fire for fear of Indians. On one such occasion an observer saw two trappers sit down on a log. One drew from the end of the blanket strapped on

[10] Thomas Jefferson Farnham, *Travels in the Great Western Prairies, the Anahuac and Rocky Mountains, and in the Oregon Territory* (New York, 1843) pp. 45-46.

his shoulder a piece of buffalo liver, which they ate raw with relish. Instead of bread they ate strips of dried fat. When subjected to the rigors of hunger a few days, trappers would go to any length to get food. First the mules or horses were killed, and in some extreme cases Indian captives were slain in cold blood and their flesh cooked and eaten.

The trapper seldom used dishes from which to eat unless it was for soup. Grasping a piece of meat, he gnawed, sliced with his hunting-knife, and threw the bones over his shoulder when done. Russell tells us that at a Christmas dinner in 1840 a number of trappers who ate in a lodge, sitting on saddle-blankets around the fire, used large chips or pieces of bark from which to eat. At a signal they drew their knives and commenced. The table conversation was concerning the political affairs of the Rocky Mountains, the state of the governments among the various Indian tribes, and the personal character of the distinguished chiefs.

Fire-making was a simple process in dry weather. Taking his flint, steel, and pieces of punk from his bullet-pouch, the woodsman pulled a bunch of dry grass, made a nest of the hay, placed the punk within it, and, lighting the punk, closed the grass over it and waved it about in the air. This caused the hay to ignite readily. For drying meat quaking aspen was the most desirable fuel because it gave off less odors to be absorbed.

Certain Indian tribes were always friendly to the trappers while others were uniformly hostile. Among still others there was the temptation for a few of the young men to try to enrich themselves by stealing furs, although the tribe might not necessarily be hostile. Trappers many times had to work for days on a military basis without a minute of relaxed vigilance. Every day and hour a lone trapper might expect an ambush. Every night the group might expect an attempted stampede or night attack. The Blackfeet were the inveterate enemies of the whites, and they carried so much prestige that whites dared not venture into the heart of their country except in large expeditions.

Most frequently the Indians hoped to dash in among the horses and stampede them, possibly killing a sentry or two and taking their scalps in the process. Ruxton gives us a picture of a night attack. As the party of trappers sat by the fire, suddenly a whizzing sound was heard, followed by a suppressed cry of pain from one of the hunters. In an instant the mountaineers had sprung from their seats and, seizing their ever-ready rifles, had thrown themselves on the ground in the darkness beyond the lighted circle of the fire. Not a word escaped them as, lying close to the ground, with keen eyes directed toward the thicket near-by and with rifles cocked, they awaited a renewal of the attack. Soon the leader raised himself and, placing his hand over his mouth, made the prairies ring with a wild Indian war-whoop. This was instantly repeated from the direction where the horse-herder was keeping the horses. Three shrill whoops in response to that of the leader showed that the guard was on the alert and understood the signal. The attack was not renewed, and after the arrow was extracted from the injured man, the party slept on their arms.

Sometimes the Indians crept in unperceived, cut some picket-ropes or hobbles and got away with several of the horses. In 1831 a party of young Crow warriors conducted a raid and three hundred horses disappeared in a cloud of dust. Sometimes, as in this case, the trappers followed the thieves and inflicted punishment on them while regaining their horses. When all the horses were lost, it meant days and weeks of tramping to get a fresh supply, and the season's endeavors were ruined. If the trappers anticipated an attack, sometimes they took the dead trunks of trees and laid up a breastwork. The Indians were wary of attacking a stronghold. Sometimes the trappers in anticipation of a battle made a sort of coat of mail by soaking in water a blacktail-deerskin coat and putting it on over their other clothes. One old trapper affirmed that it was impossible for any iron- or flint-tipped arrow to penetrate this tough protection. Ordinarily there were no pitched battles, but on occasion they did take place with considerable loss on each side. The trapper was very expert at molding his own bullets for both rifle and pistol from lead purchased at the rendezvous or post. He was also expert at handling a muzzle-loading rifle and could load and shoot four times in a minute.

When death snatched a comrade away, the burial rites were very simple. The unfortunate man was rolled in his blankets and lowered into the grave, covered with a few pieces of bark, and the grave filled without further ado. Sometimes the body was thrown into a river instead of being buried, for graves were hard to dig in winter and were often desecrated by wolves. Very little was said. Perhaps a few remarks were passed, such as, "Poor fellow! Out of luck!" Perhaps someone commented that the "old hoss" was a "mighty clever fella." This was the only ceremony. The mountain men rejoiced noisily when a lost comrade was found but said little about one who had died.

"Went under," "rubbed out," "lost his topknot," were all terms used to describe the death of a comrade. The latter term meant that the Indians had scalped him, the second that he had died a violent death, and the first meant death by any means. If a man was killed and left unburied, it was said, "They made wolf meat of him." Another expression indicating death by Indians was "They took his hair." If a man had received several wounds, he was said to be "as full of arrows as a porcupine."

A wounded man was without medical care other than that supplied by the friendly Indian medicine-men or fellow trappers. Father Pierre de Smet stated that Jim Bridger had had within four years two quiverfuls of arrows in his body, and when he was asked if the wounds had been long suppurating, he answered, "Among the mountains nothing corrupts." However that may be, Dr. Marcus Whitman in the year 1835, on his journey between the States and Oregon, took an arrow from Bridger's shoulder which had been imbedded there for several years. It was a difficult task because the arrow-head had become hooked at the point by striking a large bone. Time and time again arrows were pulled out by comrades or carved out with the ever-useful butcher knife, and the blood-flow stanched with beaver fur.

There is one instance of a trapper who had his leg badly shattered by a bullet in a drunken row. Amputation was necessary, but there was no surgeon within a hundred miles. He whetted one edge of his hunting-knife to its utmost sharpness, filed the other into a saw, and with his own hand the iron-nerved mountaineer cut the flesh, sawed the bone, and seared the blood-vessels with a red-hot iron. He pieced out his anatomy with a wooden leg and in 1866 was living in California.

A wounded man was packed on a sort of stretcher between two horses. For colds or almost any other ill the Indians used the vapor bath. The same treatment was no doubt used by the trappers, who were so closely allied with the Indians by marriage and association. This bath, which was essentially the same in principle as our modern Russian bath, was taken on the bank of a stream. The skeleton of a small house was made of willows and covered with skins. A hole was dug in the ground on the inside, and on the outside a number of stones were heated in a fire. When the rocks were sufficiently hot, the patient sat in the house while attendants passed stones and jugs of water in to him. He placed the stones in the hole, poured the water over them, and sat in the hot steam. After fifteen or twenty minutes of this, the patient emerged, dripping with sweat, and jumped into the icy water. The other remedies were simple and few. When men who had gone without food for several days killed some wolves and ate too much and became nauseated, they made sage-brush tea and drank it as a remedy.

Most of the mountain men, like others of the fur trade, took Indian wives. Some of these marriages were born of love, many of convenience, and only a few really endured a lifetime. A considerable body of the men had two or more wives at the same time, but the greater proportion had a number consecutively. As he tired of one wife or she was captured or ran away, the trapper readily found another to take her place. The finest girls, daughters of chiefs, were readily secured by the mountain men, for the free trappers especially had a marked economic superiority over the males of the Indian tribes. Their wives could dress better than the wife of an Indian and had a higher social status on account of the greater power the white man possessed by reason of belonging to the conquering race. Moreover, these native wives of white men often were treated more considerately than were the wives of the Indians, since if the white husband really loved his squaw, he was inclined to treat her more as American women were treated. Indeed, squaws frequently henpecked their white husbands in regard to the domestic economy. For the most part the wives of the free trappers displayed remarkable fidelity and affection for their husbands. Children born to such unions naturally bound the couples together, and Farnham gives this as the reason why so many trappers stayed in the mountains year upon year. These women often lived a migratory life, following their husbands from camp to camp, day by day caring for the children, making clothing, tanning skins, drying meat, and doing the other tasks of camp life. The free trapper's wife rode a gaily caparisoned horse, and she dressed in the finest goods, with ornaments of beads, ribbons, fringes, and feathers.

Some of the mountain men had real romances worthy of the story book. In the latter part of an April in the early fifties a Grand Encampment was held in Wyoming where trappers from all sections of the country gathered to dispose of their furs and procure needed supplies. Heavy snows falling for several days made tremendous drifts, so effectively blocking the trails to the camp that it was well-nigh impossible to travel. One afternoon, while a blizzard raged without, Jim Baker and some other trappers were playing cards in a cabin. Suddenly the door flew open and an exhausted trapper staggered in. When revived he said he had stumbled on a dying Indian runner who told him of some Sioux Indians down the river. The party consisted of Prince Long

Lance, his beautiful daughter Flying Fawn, and a subchief Flash of Fire. After traveling toward the encampment for twelve days, they had become snowbound and were in a desperate plight with their provisions exhausted. The Sioux prince and his household were on the verge of starvation and would die unless they were rescued at once. Jim Baker responded immediately, organized a rescue party, battled his way through twenty miles of arctic frigidity, and rescued the group. Within a few months Baker lost his heart to the beautiful, lithe, graceful Indian maiden. Flash of Fire had long loved the princess, however, and came near ending Baker's career. One evening, while Baker with no thought of danger was wooing Flying Fawn, Flash of Fire hid behind a rock about sixty feet away; drawing his bow, he was about to slay his rival, when the old prince saw his intention and loosed an arrow which killed the would-be assassin. Hearing the whistle of the arrow, the stalwart hunter turned and saw the tragedy that had been enacted. Prince Long Lance then walked over to the young couple and bestowed his blessings on the happy lovers.[11] Sometimes, when an Indian wife was supplanted by another Indian beauty, the squaw, wild with jealousy and rage, vented her fury on her faithless spouse and the new love.

The "refined trapper" after long years of bachelorhood, when he wanted to marry, went to Taos, New Mexico, to woo a dark-skinned white beauty. The advantage there over the Indian woman was that the Mexican woman combined beauty and utility, for she would work like the Indian woman. American women were at a discount in the wilderness, for they were too fine and "fofaraw." They could not make moccasins or dress skins, nor would they render perfect obedience and take a lodge-poling, which the lord and master frequently gave his beloved spouse.[12] Certain it is that American women could never have stood up under the strenuous nomadic life of the wives of the free trappers, traveling about and

[11] Mumey, *The Life of Jim Baker*, pp. 83-88.
[12] Ruxton, *Life in the Far West*, pp. 106-107.

facing hardship and danger without the least semblance of comforts —not to mention luxuries, except personal adornment on which their husbands set great store. The Indian wife took great pride in her station, considering it above that of her sisters married to Indians.

John Ball mentions an incident which gives an idea of the conditions under which these proud Indian wives lived. A certain man named Frapp, a mountain man, had his wife along with him, a thing not unusual at all. She rode horseback with the rest of the party. One day the leader stopped the group. No reason was given, but in a few minutes they heard an outcry from Frapp's wife out in the bushes to one side. Word was soon passed around that she had given birth to a child. The very next day she placed her new-born baby feet down in a deep basket hung to the pommel of her saddle and, mounting her horse, rode with the party as usual. She had another child, two or three years old, who had his own horse. He sat on the saddle with blankets wrapped around him to keep him erect, and his gentle pony was driven loose with the pack-horses.[13]

On one occasion in the forties Uncle Dick Wooton and a party of trappers descended upon Taos to get wives. Most of them managed a whirlwind courtship and were starting for the mountains, but Uncle Dick was unfortunate. He had wooed and won a damsel whose parents forbade her to wed the hunter, and he regretfully made ready to leave. Resolving to have a last visit with his lady-love, in a melancholy mood he rode up to her house. A companion, struck by a sudden idea, said, "Ho Dick! thar's the gal and thar's the mountains, shoot sharp's the word." Dick understood and was himself again. As the girl came forward to meet him, he whispered a word in her ear, she put her foot on his and was whirled onto the saddle in front of him. He struck spurs to his horse, and the elopers flashed out of sight in a moment. His

---

[13] *Autobiography of John Ball*, compiled by his daughters (Grand Rapids, Mich., 1925), p. 80.

three comrades with their rifles kept back the crowd that had gathered, and the whole party made their way into the mountains without harm. This Lochinvar system was often employed by the mountain men at this mountain town.

When the hunters returned to the bivouac after the activities of the day, a pleasant season ensued. A large fire was soon blazing, encircled by sides of elk or buffalo ribs and meat cut in slices supported on sticks. The stillness of the lonely mountain glen was often broken by peals of laughter which echoed across the canyon. Russell describes an evening camp beside a stream under mighty forest trees. The group surrounded the cheery fire, eating, drinking, and telling stories. As a trapper told a tale, the whole party listened with Indian gravity. Occasionally a listener gave vent to a "Wagh!" or a fellow participant in a particular part interrupted to corroborate the speaker's statement with "This child remembers that fix" or "Hyar's a niggur lifted hair on that spree." Every tale reminded an auditor of a similar happening under different circumstances. The "laughing part" of the story gave rise to increasing merriment, witty sayings, and good jokes until the trappers' usual gravity melted away and the canyon fairly rang with good cheer. Pipes were got out, and a little of the precious store of tobacco, mixed perhaps with willow bark or kinnikinick for economy's sake, was smoked. When the moon rose from behind the quaking aspens, all wrapped themselves in their blankets and gradually fell asleep. Only the lonely howl of a solitary wolf on the mountainside broke the stillness of the night.[14]

When one party of mountaineers met another, there was as much joy as when, after long absence at sea, friends in different crews meet in a foreign port. Greetings ran something like this:

"Ho, Bill! What, old hos! not gone under yet? Give us your paw."

Bill replied, "Do 'ee now, if hyar ain't them boys as was rubbed out on Lodge Pole a time ago!"

[14] Russell, *Journal of a Trapper*, p. 37.

"Whar's Bill Williams?"

"Gone under they say: the Diggers [a tribe of Indians] took his hair."

"Any baca in your bag, Bill? This beaver feels like chawin'."

"Seen any bufler?"

"Strong signs over the ridge."

"If we don't make a raise afore long, I wouldn't say so. Let's camp."

An unbounded hospitality reigned among them, and a stranger was certain to be welcome to whatever the mountain men had. When Farnham left the mountains, he sought to give his hosts some ammunition as a token of his regard. But for every little kindness of this kind they sought to remunerate him tenfold with moccasins, dressed skins, and other things they had. Everything, he said, was at his service, even the shirts on their backs. They always remarked as they made such offers that it was nothing, the country abounded with skins and they could have plenty more when they wanted them. When a stranger came to camp, the kindly invitation was "Sit and eat!"

While wandering about, the mountaineer ordinarily had no shelter but the sky and slept in the open air. His bed consisted of a buffalo hide with leaves or boughs underneath it when opportunity offered. A bundle of pelts or his saddle served as a pillow, and one or two blankets were his sole protection from the cold. On a rainy night, before spreading out his bed, the trapper took his knife and made a trench around it. Then, taking his rifle, pouch, and powder-bag to bed with him to keep them dry beneath the supposedly waterproof Navajo blanket, he lay down to sleep. Naturally such a bed was far from dry and comfortable. Sometimes sleeper and robe began to sink in the mud, and, wet and cold, the trapper tried to cheer himself by the aid of a fire. On a wet night in a hostile region the leader was apt to caution his sentinels, "Keep your eyes skinned, powder'll be burned afore morning."

In the lull during the dead of winter or when business demanded a considerable sojourn in one place, the trappers often made quarters. They were erected near a stream where grass and wood were plentiful. Sometimes they were made of skins thrown over an arched framework of saplings. In front was the fire, and nearby were the trapper's stretching-frames, for stretching furs, and his graining-block, a log of wood with the bark stripped off set obliquely in the ground, on which the hair was removed from the deerskins that furnished clothing for him and his squaw. A pole was laden with meats. His traps were in a convenient place, and perhaps antlers on a tree served as coat-rack. Close at hand was his best friend, his rifle, and by it powder-horn, bullet-pouch, and tomahawk. Thus situated, the trappers in their mountain home owned no man as lord, and no creature enjoyed life more fully than they.[15]

In winter sometimes a more permanent camp was built. One such habitation was made by felling several cottonwoods and forming them in the shape of a horseshoe with the entrance narrowed down to a bottle-neck. This house, or fort, as all structures were called no matter how small, was loopholed around and had a sod chimney. As time went on, such forts were built here and there, and many times the trappers made it a point to winter in them.

Sometimes the trappers had Indian lodges, which they pitched in a circle with a fire in the center. About six persons occupied a lodge. One who spent a winter in this kind of quarters remembered that in the long winter evenings the group collected in one of the more spacious lodges and spent the time till midnight in spinning yarns or in debates. This "Rocky Mountain College," as they called it, had considerable educational benefit, for a number of the trappers were college-trained. Others not originally so fortunate learned to read in this rude fireside school. Some read all the papers and books they had been able to accumulate by their contacts with the States. Men not only told marvelous stories of

[15] Rufus B. Sage, *Scenes in the Rocky Mountains* (Philadelphia, 1847), p. 288.

mountain origin, but rehearsed tales read in their youth, such as *Robinson Crusoe* and the *Arabian Nights*. Even Bunyan's *Pilgrim's Progress* was recounted as a sensational novel and enjoyed as such, although the trappers esteemed it especially for its moral values.

Trappers had a mail system on occasion. When a group was supposed to meet at a certain spot and the place was changed, a note was put in a buffalo's horn and buried at the foot of a marked tree. At other times the trappers peeled the bark from trees and wrote notes on the bare space with charcoal.

Sometimes the trapper's luggage became too unwieldly, or perhaps the horses were stolen and there was no way to carry his "fixens" or "traps," as he called various odds and ends of equipment. In such a case he was forced to "cache" his possessions. This term came from a French word meaning to hide. Sometimes caches were made in caves, hollow trees, or even in tree branches, but more commonly they were made in the ground. Two things were essential: first, the goods must be kept dry, and second, the place must be completely concealed. Sometimes these storage-places were large, containing space enough to hide a wagon. A high dry bank was selected where digging was easy and there was no danger from seepage. A round hole was made in the sod, the sod carefully laid aside, and a jug-shaped chamber five or six feet deep made underground. The dirt was placed in skins and thrown into the river to remove all trace of the cache. The pit was lined with leaves and sticks, and the goods were deposited. Then the hole was filled up and the sod laid back in place to serve as a cork for the jug. In every way possible the site was made to look as it did originally. If there was no sod, a camp-fire was built on the spot to hide the place, or animals were made to trample it into obscurity. Even with every precaution, caches were often discovered and "raised" or "lifted," in the language of the trapper, by those who had no right to the goods. Sometimes the wolves dug into the spot and exposed the hiding-place to the Indians. It was a point of honor among mountain men never to violate the cache of a rival, and this code was almost never violated. A "general cache" consisted of a number of such pits in a general locality.[16]

Of the many dangers trappers faced, one of the most trying was the severe cold and storms of the mountains. Storms rose suddenly and took the mountain man unawares unless he was cautious and experienced. Sometimes a subzero wave froze the extremities or actually took life itself. In February, 1824, Milton Sublette and James Clyman were traveling together near the summit of the Rockies. After they had cooked supper, the temperature dropped and the wind rose to a gale. The atmosphere grew colder and colder with frost flying in the air. Suddenly a gust blew their little sage-brush fire in every direction. The two men lay down on the frozen ground on a hillside, the arctic blast blowing the frost and snow into their bed at every crevice. Sleep was out of the question, but they lay in discomfort till daybreak. They then counseled on the best course and decided that Clyman was to rise and gather sage-brush for a fire while Sublette was to remain under the buffalo robe, keep his hands warm, and if possible strike fire. This calculation failed, for as soon as his hands struck the air, they became too numb to hold the steel. The trapper afterward spoke of such an incident: "If thar wasn't cold doin's about that time this child wouldn't say so." They tried to strike fire with their guns but had no better success, for lack of fuel material and because of the gale. Sublette lay down, but Clyman after a struggle saddled his own horse, determined to leave the inhospitable place. Not wishing to abandon his comrade, Clyman asked if Sublette would go if he could get his horse saddled also. Sublette thought he could not. Clyman made more unsuccessful attempts to strike a fire. When about to leave he thought of the ashes, and to his great joy he found a small coal about the size of a grain of corn, which, thrown into a handful of material, soon started a fire. Drawing

---

[16] Levi O. Leonard, personal interview, October 2, 1938; Chittenden, *The American Fur Trade of the Far West*, Vol. I, pp. 41-42, 279.

the robe around their backs, they tried to get warm, but the smoke and blaze swirled up in their faces so badly they had to give it up. Clyman saddled Sublette's horse, got him mounted, and drove him ahead. It was four miles to the timber, and seeing he was going to freeze, Clyman got off and walked, leading his partner's horse, for Sublette was too nearly gone to walk. At the timber Clyman lit a fire almost immediately, got his friend off the horse, and carried him to the blaze. Sublette lay in a state of coma, but after a time he "came to" and was as lively as ever. They roasted meat for breakfast and soon were back to normal after their close call. Such experiences were legion.

Horses often fared hardly at the hands of the trappers. They were the bone of contention between redskins and whites, and when there was danger of a stampede or of Indians' stealing horses, they were tethered. This meant little or no grass, but it was felt to be better to starve the horse and keep him than to feed him for someone else. The trapper's maxim was, "Better count ribs than tracks." Trappers moving from place to place could not carry hay, and so the horses had to find their forage along the little streams. When these were covered with snow, the trappers cut cottonwood trees, shaved the bark off, and gave it to the horses. They soon learned to like it and ate the bark off the small limbs without waiting for them to be barked. Soon they learned to bark the tree, and no other assistance was needed beyond felling the trees. Zenas Leonard tells of a party of trappers in 1831 who were marooned in the mountains for weeks. They tried to feed their horses cottonwood bark, but the horses would not eat it, and they discovered it was the bitter cottonwood. The animals became poorer and poorer until one by one they died of starvation. On this occasion the trappers likewise suffered from lack of food. Part of the group, setting out for New Mexico to procure more horses, passed through a country devoid of game and had nothing except dried beaver skins to eat for nine days. When they did kill a buffalo, the men who before appeared scarcely able to speak were soon yelling like Indians. They remained at this place four days feasting on the buffalo meat.

The rendezvous was the great occasion of the year for the trappers, and thither they wended their way in June or July. Some had many packs of beaver, some only a few; some walked in, having had their horses stolen. Indians also gathered in to trade. This was a joyous season to which the trapper looked forward for months. As group after group arrived, friends asked about other old comrades and learned the news. The whole camp was buzzing with stories of Indian attacks, furs stolen, horses taken, and of those who attended the last rendezvous but had since "lost their hair." If while two old buddies hobnobbed, someone announced that Jim Bridger had arrived at the other end of the camp, the group hastened that way, only to visit a few minutes and rush off to see some other newcomer and hear the news of the season in his quarter. Thus the first few days of the encampment were a veritable newspaper, read by all, as it were, in a mouth-to-mouth conversation.

While the trappers were waiting for the goods train from Independence, various sports were entered into. There were contests at shooting, foot-racing, horse-racing, jumping, wrestling, and other exhibitions of manly skill and strength. Sometimes the white men would shoot against the Indians, using bow and arrow or rifle. Contests of horsemanship were also held between the Indians and the whites. One event was attempting to stop ponies in full career at a mark, the one stopping nearest the mark winning. There were shooting contests on horseback. Three six-foot posts, ten inches in diameter, were put in the ground about twenty-five yards apart. The tops of the posts were squared. The rules of the contest were to ride a horse at full speed, pass the posts at not closer than ten feet, and fire two shots at each with a Colt revolver. Some of the trappers put two balls in each post, and all the contestants at least one. There were contests at riding bucking horses. One old trapper claimed that the white men almost always won in all these contests and that the Indians would give as an excuse that their medicine was not strong that day.[17] The trials of horsemanship made the camp one of the noisiest and dustiest of places.

Among the wares offered for sale were a number of Indian girls, who, with tinkling bells about their necks and in their hair, rode coquettishly about the camp on their ponies, waiting to be taken by the highest bidder.[18] On just such a scene as this the three Tetons looked down in 1828 and 1832 at Pierre's Hole at their feet. Other famous rendezvous were Brown's Hole, Green River, and Powder River. A rendezvous was always held in a valley where game was plentiful and there was ample grass for horsefeed. Another name for this high tide of the trapper's year was a grand encampment.

It must not be thought that the trappers were wholly idle at a rendezvous. Many were constantly dressing buckskin, since they made buckskin of a quality superior to that of the Indians; clothing of their manufacture would not stretch or shrink when wet. Although at one rendezvous at Brown's Hole there were two tailors, most of the trappers made their own buckskin clothes. Some were busy putting their guns and traps in perfect condition.

In the evening the music of voice and drum rang out over the prairies, the accompaniment of dancing. Sometimes the Indians treated the assembly to a scalp-dance. The Indian game of hand was played. Seated around the great camp-fires in Indian style were groups with a buffalo robe spread before them, playing card games —seven-up, euchre, and poker. There was no currency; beaver skins were the stakes and were accepted as money. When the gamblers' furs were gone, their horses, mules, shirts, hunting-packs, and even their pants were staked. The story is told of two veteran trappers who played for each other's scalps. Whether true or not, this represented the spirit of the rendezvous. Professional gamblers soon began to attend the encampment. When a man sustained a severe

---

[17] Hamilton, *My Sixty Years on the Plains*, pp. 99-101.
[18] Rufus Rockwell Wilson, *Out of the West* (New York, 1936), pp. 5-7.

MOUNTAIN MEN AT THE SUMMER RENDEZVOUS
From Francis Fuller Victor, *The River of the West*, 1870.

loss from any cause, it was customary for the mountain men to say, "There goes hoss and beaver," and certain it was that horse and beaver skins soon found their way into the hands of the gamblers. Frequently free trappers brought to the rendezvous as high as a thousand dollars' worth of furs, only to lose them in a few hours of gambling.

Finally the expected train arrived. Before 1830 it consisted of pack-mules bearing the coveted merchandise. In that year Captain William L. Sublette rolled into the midst of his fellows at the head of a train of ten wagons. He also brought two buggies and thirteen head of cattle, including a milch cow. This was the beginning of the use of wagons on the Oregon Trail. To these gatherings botanists, artists, literary men, and clergymen came occasionally, each interested in some phase of the life presented. With the arrival of the train with recruits and visitors, everyone was happy. Some received letters, some newspapers and periodicals, and others, having broken the ties with civilization, consoled themselves with a spurt of reckless spending. Some spent their money in lavish feasting, drinking, and treating. Starved for sweets, they paid two dollars a pint for sugar and drank sweetened coffee and cocoa. While out on the hunt they smoked only at night, and then sparingly, mixing their tobacco with red willow; but now their pipes were aglow day and night, with tobacco at two dollars a pound, and for a few days they lived like lords. Others, as if desiring to counterbalance their long exile from the haunts of men, sought to make up for lost time in an overdose of good-fellowship. Whisky flowed freely, and soon the trapper had squandered all his money in a long drunken debauch. Red-eyed and sadder but not a bit wiser, he proceeded to collect his "possibles," as he called his property, and, followed by his squaw, went into the wilds for another period of isolation. The Indians also plunged into a drunken orgy. Too often a rendezvous was a continuous scene of tumult, gambling, drunkenness, and fighting, but this was particularly so during the last few days.

Fist fights were numerous, and gun-play and dueling with the rifle took place. A duel among mountain men was tragic, for they were dead shots. Cases have been known where the principals killed each other. In 1829 a trapper bought a small kettle of alcohol. As it went the rounds of his friends, they were soon ready for any frolic, and one, seizing the kettle, poured its contents over the head of a tall, lanky fellow while repeating the baptismal service. Another touched him with a lighted stick, and immediately his clothes burst into flame. Some of the men sober enough to see his danger beat him with pack-saddles, but he nearly lost his life and never fully recovered from the effects of this unconventional fiery baptism in the mountain fastnesses.

In the earlier period the rendezvous lasted only a few days. Ashley in 1825 had the business so well organized that all the work was finished in two days. At the rendezvous contracts for another year were made and credit extended. Some decided to break their connection with a company and become free trappers. They spoke of themseves as "on the loose" again.

As the rendezvous became a fixed institution, however, it some-times lasted several weeks and hundreds attended. Then, too, there came into being a glorified type of winter quarters, which became known as the winter rendezvous or grand encampments. There were centers where hundreds of trappers came together to spend the winter period in congenial company and in a mild climate. Probably the largest gathering of this kind was on the present site of Ogden, Utah, where, if James P. Beckwourth can be trusted, some seven hundred trappers were joined in midwinter by twenty-five hundred Snake Indians, making a total of about three thousand two hundred persons. Finally forts were built at some of these agreeable spots, and the trappers spent their winters there sitting by the fire, eating roasted mountain sheep, laughing at merry tale and song, and mocking the wintry blasts. Such a place was the significantly named Fort David Crockett in Brown's Hole, a veritable trapper's paradise amidst the howling wilderness.

At the close of the rendezvous the mountain harvest was carried across the plains. One who saw the pack-train return said:

It is impossible to describe my feelings at the sight of all that beaver —all those mountain men unloading their mules, in their strange mountain costume—most of their garments of buckskin and buffalo hide, but all so well greased and worn that it took close examination to tell what they were made of. To see the mules rolling and dusting is interesting and shocking at the same time; most of them, having carried their burdens of 200 pounds' weight for about 2,000 miles, return with scarcely any skin on their backs; they are peeled from withers to tail, raw underneath from use of the surcingle, and many are also lame.

So long had the typical trapper lived in the wilderness and associated with the Indians that he became like them. He had the same wild, unsettled, watchful expression of the eyes and the same unwillingness to use words when a sign, a contortion of the face or body, or a movement of the hand would convey his meaning. Farnham, speaking of Joe Meek, said that in standing, walking, riding—in all but complexion—he was an Indian. In bidding Farnham good morning and wheeling away for the day's ride, Meek said, "Keep your eye shining for the Blackfeet." Hardships and exposure seem to have had their effect on the trapper's physique, for he was usually gaunt and spare, tanned by the elements, and his eye had a piercing look. He was somewhat taciturn and to the casual observer appeared gloomy and furtive. In conversation his jokes, for the most part, tended to dry wit rather than gay humor. The Indians had a universal sign language by which members of the different tribes who could not understand each other's speech could converse readily for hours. Often by way of practice trappers sat conversing by this method, and it was reflected in the sparsity of words in their conversation.

Furthermore, they developed a spoken language which was so interspersed with idioms that it was difficult for the uninitiated to understand. When speaking of a time when he was very hungry,

the mountain man expressed it, "I was wolfish." When he wanted
to say "If that's what you are driving at," he said, "If that's the
way your stick floats." Having discovered Indians preparing to
attack, the remark of one trapper to another would run something
like this: "Thar plans is plain to this child as beaver sign. They're
after our hair as certain as this gun's got hindsights." And then
as the attack began to get hot and he felt the need of taking to
cover, he remarked: "Wagh! This old hoss is goin-a cache!" If
he wished to express his entire disgust with his food, he compared
it to lean buffalo meat. For example, some trappers had raided a
Digger Indian camp and captured a few sacks of dried ants, on
which they were attempting to subsist until they could find game.
Their conversation on the prospect of finding buffalo ran something like the following: "Wagh! Here's strong bufler signs! If
we don't make a raise afore long I wouldn't say so. Them ants
is worse than poor bull." When a group of trappers found an old
friend's horse, the leader addressed his fellows: "Well, it ain't
nothin' else, it's the old boy's hoss as sure as shootin' and them
Rapahos [Arapaho Indians] has rubbed him out at last and raised
his animals. Ho, boy! let's lift their hair." A trapper's closest friend
was his rifle. Sometimes he gave it a name. A trapper in speaking
of the two partners at Bent's Fort, Ceran St. Vrain and William
Bent, said: "Bill Bent was as clever a man as I ever knowed. Old
St. Vrain could knock the hindsight off him though when it came
to shootin' and old Silver Heels [his rifle] spoke true, she did:
plum-center she was eh? Well, she wasn't nothin' else." Plum-
center evidently meant that a rifle would hit the center of the
target. When a man wanted to inform his hearers that he knew
a few things, he said: "This hoss knows fat cow from poor bull
anyhow!" If one wanted to say a certain person was extravagant,
he expressed it thus: "He flung about his dollars right smart." A
trapper who had two wives lost one when a band of Indians raided
them and took her captive; the bereft husband philosophized:
"Here's the beauty of having two 'wiping sticks' to your rifle; if

one breaks while ramming down a ball, there's still hickory left to supply its place." [19]

In such a wild life as the mountaineers led, there were some men who enjoyed unlimited freedom of speech and action, while others were the butt of everyone's jokes and ridicule. Even the leaders did not escape this democratic practice of freedom of speech. It was the special delight of the men to find some incident that might reflect on the courage of a leader and to make him aware of it at the appropriate time. Once the Blackfeet Indians waylaid Jim Bridger and several arrows pierced his horse, which reared so violently that the trapper dropped his rifle. The Indians grabbed it up, and there was nothing the old master scout could do but run. Not long after this, Bridger, in making his tour of inspection of the camp, picked up a gun and, finding it dirty, asked the Irish camp-tender, whose duty it was to keep it in shape, what he would do if the Indians charged the camp. Maloney quickly replied, "I would throw it to them and run the way ye did." This effectually muzzled the great scout for some time. It was the custom to poke fun at a fellow in an embarrassing position. Two men, for example, when a bear treed their partner, laughed heartily at him. When one was in trouble, his companions said, "Let him keep out of such a fix" or "Let him have better luck."

The adjective "old" prefixed to one's name denoted that he was an object of distinction. The tone and inflection of the voice in speaking it gave the clue to whether the distinction was an enviable one or otherwise.[20]

Not only were their talk and their mannerisms deeply affected by their contact with the Indians, but some mountain men were indoctrinated with the religious superstitions of their wives and relatives-in-law. Ruxton tells us about Old Rube who had had bad

[19] There are many splendid examples of trapper talk in Ruxton's *Life in the Far West*.

[20] Mrs. Frances Fuller Victor, *The River of the West* (Hartford, Conn., 1870), pp. 92, 93.

luck. The unfriendly Indians had stolen two of his three horses and three of his six traps, and early in the season he went to Beer and Soda Springs, an Indian sacred place, to "make medicine." Here he prayed and blew the smoke from his pipe to the four quarters of the sky to the accompaniment of his medicine words. Again, when some trappers buried a comrade, killed in an Indian battle, they followed Indian custom by putting the scalps of the dead Indians on his breast.

The effect of the trapper on the plains and mountains has never been fully disclosed. Decades before the permanent settler came, he traveled over or camped on the sites of present-day populous centers. He gave names to the great multitude of smaller streams, passes, mountains, lakes, and valleys, and to-day many towns are named after these path-breakers. The explorers after Lewis and Clark were led by men who had long since explored the regions traversed. The trapping-ground of the plains and Rockies was the training-ground for the scouts who so efficiently acted as eyes and ears of the post-Civil War armies that swept the Indians from the great open spaces onto the reservations.

CHAPTER III

GUARDIANS OF THE BORDER

FOR A CENTURY after the founding of the republic, the Indians were regarded by the Government of the United States as a foreign nation within our boundaries. The existence of this warlike race on the margins of settlement naturally called for the occupation of the borderland by troops. In addition to garrisoning posts, guarding a vast frontier line, and protecting the white settlers from the Indians, the troops had also the unique task of enforcing the treaty stipulations that protected the Indians from white aggressors. Furthermore, they were called upon to conduct exploring parties, protect trade-routes, escort surveying parties and railroad-builders, and even to build roads themselves. These duties often carried them among the Indians far beyond the frontier. For this reason the soldier stationed at a post on the western fringe of civilization or beyond was indeed a frontier figure, although he did not evolve into a peculiar type as did the trapper or the cowboy.

During the frontier period it seems that very few frontiersmen joined the Army. The enlisted personnel were often down-and-outers, adventurers, or men who for one reason or another found it comfortable to be absent from their home communities for a time. A recruit's morals were not scrutinized. Family trouble, disappointment in love, participation in riots, or irregular personal conduct involving difficulty with the law often caused the enlistment of men who proved to be the best of soldiers. Many German and Irish immigrants entered the service as a means of livelihood until they could get a better knowledge of the new language. Some of these foreigners were men of excellent education. The native-born American ordinarily hesitated to sign up on account of the small pay offered, his reluctance to surrender his individuality, and his unwillingness to submit to a system of social caste which, though inevitable in military life, clashed with his ideas of equality and democracy.

Naturally these recruits knew little or nothing about the use of firearms. Recruit training apparently consisted of marching (although pivoting by squads or fours did not come until after the Civil War), learning the bugle calls, and becoming acquainted with the handling of firearms. Skirmish drill was used by the officers of the Seventh Iowa Cavalry in Nebraska in the sixties. They deployed at from twenty- to fifty-yard intervals and rode dashing across the prairie, wheeling and rallying on the right, left, and center—all by bugle calls. They also drilled dismounted, using the same general plan. One man walking well in the rear held the horses while his comrades advanced consecutively at intervals at the call of the bugle, moved forward twenty to fifty paces, and lay down firing and loading. Everything was done at the double-quick. This drill, always by the bugle, was practised day after day until the soldiers were hardened for a campaign. These men ran for miles over the Platte Valley. At Fort Leavenworth in the fifties the cavalry trained over an area five miles square.

At Fort Atkinson[1], in 1819 the companies were divided into classes for target practice. Each man was required to shoot at a target at a distance of 50 yards offhand. All those who could put four balls out of six within four inches of the center of the target two days in succession were in Class 2. These would then shoot at a target 100 yards away. When they could place four balls out of six within three inches of the center for two days in succession, they moved up into Class 1 and practised at any distance up to the

[1] Established in 1819 about fifteen miles north of the present site of Omaha, on the west bank of the Missouri River hundreds of miles from the nearest settlement.

maximum range of the rifle. The balls were dug out of the target and taken to the chief of artillery, who remelted them to be used again.

The period of enlistment was five years, with clothes, lodging, and food furnished. The wages, which changed from time to time, were $11 a month just prior to the Civil War, with 25 to 40 cents a day extra for work done for the government. The wages of the non-commissioned officers were: corporal, $13, sergeant, $17, and first sergeant, $20. During the twenties and thirties the figures were approximately half these, and after the Civil War they were approximately one-third higher. If a soldier was careful, he could save most of his clothing allowance.

During the fifties the soldiers were paid every two months if in the vicinity of a post, but if they were on an expedition or located at a remote post, they often waited six or seven months for their pay. The paymaster endeavored to visit the isolated posts in the spring and fall. The posts furnished a strong guard for this officer as he journeyed from post to post with a large sum of money. When the paymaster visited Fort Riley in 1856, his money chest occupied a wagon and the guard rode in a second wagon drawn by six mules. The sergeant in charge of the guard rode horseback.

Strategically the ideal location for a fort was on a high bluff in the V formed by the confluence of two rivers. In 1805 Lieutenant Zebulon Pike, on his journey up the Mississippi, pointed out several such spots for forts. On one of these Fort Snelling was built, between and commanding the Minnesota and Mississippi rivers. Other important considerations in locating river posts were the proximity to good building material and fuel and the healthfulness of the surroundings.

There were several classes or degrees in garrisons. A "command" was frequently housed temporarily in tents or makeshift huts. A more permanent dwelling-place with buildings and other conveniences was called a "cantonment." Usually it was not occupied more than one or two seasons and did not possess extensive defenses. The permanent dwelling-place and defense position of troops was called a "fort." It often was walled and well protected. Especially after the Civil War, however, many forts were little better than cantonments. Their location depended on a water-supply to a large extent, and they often had little or no defenses. As an illustration of the part water played, Fort Larned, Kansas, in 1867 was besieged by three thousand Pawnee Indians who kept the soldiers virtual prisoners for a week; they might have starved the whole garrison had it not been for a tunnel from the block-house which enabled the defenders to get water without exposing themselves to the whizzing arrows.

Often a command lived in a camp or cantonment while they themselves built the permanent fort that was to be their future home. Such a temporary cantonment, occupied during the building of Fort Snelling in Minnesota, was called Cantonment New Hope.[2] Another interesting name for a camp was given to one located on the Missouri River above St. Louis, Camp Salubrity. The first military post in Kansas, established in 1818, a temporary one known as Cantonment Martin, was established as a base of supplies for the Major Stephen H. Long expedition of 1819-1820.

The establishing of Fort Madison, Iowa, one of the first posts west of the Mississippi, was perhaps typical of the building of an early frontier post. On September 26, 1808, a company of the First U. S. Infantry arrived and pitched camp. They began the erection of a cantonment at once. Cabins were built, and a low stockade was constructed as a protection from the Indians. During the winter months the men were busily engaged getting out logs from the adjacent timber for the permanent structures. Having no horses or oxen, the men drew the sleds loaded with fifteen-foot pickets for the stockade and the logs for the buildings.

As a rule, the posts on streams were built of logs. Gradually

---

[2] Fort Snelling, still occupied to-day, is located a few miles below St. Paul at the confluence of the Minnesota and Mississippi rivers.

Photograph by U. S. Army Signal Corps

AN EARLY DAY LOG CANTONMENT

the original buildings were replaced in stone or brick. These structures were shingled, plank-floored, and an order at Fort Atkinson enjoining greater care shows that as early as 1822 the windows were of glass. A sawmill and a brick-kiln were erected at this post for the construction of new buildings.

The buildings were heated by mammoth open fireplaces which, although they devoured wood in vast quantities, left the outer margins of the quarters like an ice-box. Forts built in the heart of the forest skirting a stream within a few years had used all the wood in the vicinity. Frequently the prairie posts consisted of frame buildings. The log forts often were surrounded by a stockade like the fur post. The prairie forts, however, were often wholly unprotected by walls of any kind.

Often a parade-ground with a flagstaff was surrounded by a variety of buildings of every sort. The majority of the buildings were barracks for the enlisted men. At hand were the officers' quarters and homes for the laundresses. At one side of the fort were the stables. In addition to these, there were warehouses, a hospital, a guard-house, a sutler's establishment, and a graveyard located perhaps a half-mile from the post.[3]

Obtaining water was a real problem even though the fort was located on a river, for it was often necessary to haul the precious liquid in barrels up a steep slope. In winter it was necessary to cut the ice and dip up the water with buckets in subzero weather. At Fort Sanders, Wyoming, in the seventies, water was brought to the quarters by trenches from the reservoir.

The regulations of 1841 required the men to bathe once a week and wash their feet twice each week. This ceremony was performed in half-barrels in the dining-room between supper and tattoo. By 1870 bath-houses were beginning to appear. At this period the barracks were equipped with double beds, two-tiered, made of poles or boards. Such beds, serving four men, were furnished with a bed-sack for each couple. Filled with straw or prairie

[3] George A. Forsyth, *The Story of the Soldier* (New York, 1900), pp. 102-103.

hay, this sack gradually flattened out until the end of the month, when the contents were burned and a new supply obtained.

Guard duty was especially onerous and was avoided if possible. The various sentinels at each hour cried out the time and repeated "All is well!" Finally, some night, one of the sentinels failed to respond. The corporal of the guard, sent to investigate, brought in an alarm that Indians lurking about the post had shot the guard and an attack was impending. Quickly was sounded the long roll of drums, made by rapid and long-continued beating of the drum without break or stop until the infantry was fully aroused. The assembly call on the bugle of the cavalry took the place of the long roll on the drums for the infantry, and together there was a clanking of arms as the order "Fall in," "Fall in," "Fall in," was heard on every side. The moment was one of tense excitement, and if an observer could get out in time, he would catch a glimpse of officers scurrying across the parade-ground to their commands, fastening their clothes and weapons as they ran. The women and children rushed to a prearranged place of protection. Soon all was in order, and the troops marched out to attack the enemy or hurry to their appointed places to defend the post.

The government did not furnish overshoes, mittens, gloves, leggings, or extra wraps, nor could these articles be bought at isolated posts or detachments. The men, therefore, became tailors for the time being and devised protective garments from old blankets, skins, cast-off clothing, or anything that seemed suitable to fortify them against the bitter cold.[4] Dress uniforms were not the uniform of the day under such circumstances. Even General Custer, who had the reputation of being a natty dresser, while on the Washita Campaign wore a pair of buffalo overshoes with the hair inside and a vest made from dressed buffalo-calf skin with the hair on.

Summer conditions on the Plains also brought variations in the

[4] Percival G. Lowe, *Five Years a Dragoon* (Kansas City, Mo., 1906), pp. 45, 46.

regulation uniform, and in time they effected changes in the regulations. On an expedition in 1857, Sergeant Eugene Bandel of the Sixth Infantry recorded, there were no uniforms. Every man wore a broad-brimmed hat, each of a different color; white trousers of rough material; a woolen shirt of red, green, blue, brown—of any and every color—open in front and worn like a coat; and the shoe uppers slashed wherever they chafed in marching. The arms, too, were not regulation by any means. Swords and bayonets were in the baggage wagons, and every person, whether man or officer, carried a long hunting-knife at his side, a rifle over his shoulder, and some had revolvers.[5] At Fort Laramie in 1875 the post orders permitted broad-brimmed straw or felt hats for fatigue, drill, and target practice.

The regulation daily ration prescribed by Congress in 1802 was in use until 1850. It consisted of three-quarters of a pound of pork or bacon, or one and one-fourth pounds of fresh or salted beef; eighteen ounces of bread or flour, or twelve ounces of hard bread, or one and one-fourth pounds of corn-meal; and one gill of rum, whisky, or brandy. And for each hundred rations there were four pounds of soap, one and a half pounds of candles, two quarts of salt, four quarts of vinegar, eight quarts of peas or beans, or in lieu thereof ten pounds of rice. In the year 1832 six pounds of coffee and twelve pounds of sugar per hundred rations were substituted as a beverage in place of the liquor. As a hint to the cooks, the regulations of 1841 stated that bread and soup were the principal items of diet, and that the bread should not be eaten until cold and the soup should be boiled at least five hours. The savings from an economical use of the rations constituted a company fund, which was not to be used for the commissioned officers. Privates sometimes gave two of their scanty eight dollars to swell this fund for extras for some special occasion.

When the troops were in a permanent post, this diet was sup-

[5] Eugene Bandel, *Frontier Life in the Army, 1854-1861* (Glendale, Cal., 1932), p. 124.

plemented by vegetables from the post garden. In spite of this, one soldier who served in the dragoons in the fifties said that he had lived for six months at a time on beans, rice, bread, and a little sugar and coffee, with no other vegetables and no cereals. At Fort Leavenworth at that time each man passed his tin cup to be filled with coffee from a big kettle on the table. By 1870 the mess furniture at Fort Laramie, which was pronounced good, consisted of delft plates, bowls, and knives and forks. After the Civil War, the lack of vegetables, so keenly felt on the Plains where little gardening had been done and the distances were too great to haul fresh vegetables, was remedied by the War Departments' furnishing dried vegetables. These desiccated products consisted of onions, cabbage, beets, turnips, carrots, and green peppers, steamed, pressed, and dried. They were in the form of cakes a foot square and an inch thick, pressed so hard that they weighed as much as wood. They were packed in sealed cans and were very handy to carry on a scouting expedition. The soldiers would break off a piece and nibble on it as they rode along. These vegetables swelled to such proportions when water was added that a generous piece, broken off by a novice cook, filled all the available pots and kettles in the place. They made good soup and were usable in other ways also. The regular ration was readily supplemented by game until the garrison grew heartily tired of it and wished for fresh fruits and vegetables. The men searched the forest for berries, plums, and currants, and these were preserved by the cooks. Hazelnuts, walnuts, pecans, and other nuts were gathered in the forest.

Soldiers set "trot lines" (trawl lines) and got enough fish for the officers' mess and often enough for the men. The quartermaster made a boat for the use of the fishermen in at least one post. On Christmas, New Year's, and the Fourth of July extra dinners were served. This accounted for a portion of the company mess fund. On such an occasion several kinds of game, such as deer, buffalo, bear, prairie chicken, wild turkey, pigeons, and wild water-fowl, were all on the board. Then, too, dried-apple pie and whisky punch were served. At an isolated post where liquor was unobtainable, the soldiers sometimes supplemented their feast with essence of Jamaica ginger and bay-rum bought at the sutler's store and made into a punch by adding sugar and hot water.

The man who kept a store in connection with a military post or with a regiment in the field was known as the sutler. There were many changes in the regulations regarding this office, but in general the sutler was given a monopoly of all buying and selling in his jurisdiction, for which he paid a fee. He was appointed by the military authorities and was granted the rank of warrant officer in order to give him standing with the men, although he received no pay from the government, nor was he commanded except in regard to his business. Neither could he command anyone except in defense of his person or property. His rank was higher than enlisted man and below the commissioned personnel, but in the social circles he and his wife stood with the officers and their wives. He was subject to a general court-martial for capital offenses and could be dismissed by garrison or regimental court-martial. On the march he followed the regimental headquarters, a sort of huckster or traveling store. The sutler was to be given a building at the post if there was one to spare, and if not, he was allowed to build one. On the Sibley expedition, in 1863, the chief sutler had a purser and another assistant. There were also a bookkeeper and four teamsters. The teamsters received $2.25 a day under the agreement to haul twenty-four hours or less.

A Council of Administration, consisting of the three officers next in rank to the commanding officer, was convened at least once a quarter. The junior officer acted as secretary. This group met with the sutler and went over his invoices to establish retail prices for his goods.

The commanding officer approved this price list. Sometimes, when the board did not meet promptly, the sutler had a whole shipment sold before the price was set by the Council. For his monopoly the sutler was charged ten cents ("not to exceed 12¢") a month for each man in the organization he served. On the Sibley expedition the following prices were in force: cheese, 35 cents a pound; dried beef, 35 cents a pound; chewing tobacco, $1.60 a pound; raisins and figs, 40 cents a pound; herring, three for 5 cents; and peaches, $1.00 a can.

The library also was under the care of the Council of Administration. At Fort Atkinson the baker, the library, and the school received an equal amount as a subsidy.

About 1818 the idea of farming on a considerable scale came into vogue. Practised at the various posts, it reached a high point at Fort Atkinson. This post, located at one of the most fertile spots in Nebraska, was in a good situation for the purpose. During the first years of the twenties it more nearly resembled a plantation than a fort at some seasons of the year. For example, in 1822 the following crops were raised: 410 acres of corn, yielding approximately 20,500 bushels; 49 acres of potatoes, yielding 6,000 bushels; 7 acres of turnips, yielding 1,050 bushels; 40 acres of gardens, which gave an abundant yield; and 250 tons of excellent hay. The wheat was a failure, though in the preceding year the yield was 26,000 bushels.

In a day when plows were small and crude and cultivators had not been thought of, this was extensive farming indeed. So heavily involved was the post with agricultural pursuits that an order of November 21, 1822, ran:

Every Non Commissioned officer, Musician and Private who is not necessarily employed in his company will be sent to the Corn field immediately after Breakfast, and the old Guard as soon as relieved every morning until the corn is gathered. They will carry their dinners with them & return at retreat.

Military duties were almost laid aside during times of need on the farm. Even the prisoners were dealt with kindly during the

SUTLER'S STORE AT FORT DODGE, KANSAS

From *Harper's Weekly*, May 25, 1867.

rush of work. At corn-picking time in 1821, a deserter, having voluntarily agreed to have the cost of his apprehension deducted from his pay, was freed and returned to his company for duty.

When the crop was harvested, the commissary department bought what it needed at the St. Louis contract price, and after 15 per cent of the proceeds was given to the officers, the other 85 per cent was divided among the enlisted men. In 1825 this amounted to $1,427.12½. The commandant expected his men to work during the crop season, and in the hunting season they could indulge in their favorite amusement. Numerous orders sound more like those of the overseer of a large farm than of an army officer. One decreed that no soldier or other person was to set the dogs on the hogs. Another ordered a detail to camp at the potato patch and dig the potatoes. A third prescribed the duties of the cattle-herders, and still another charged that thenceforth no hog and calf pens were to be built in the vicinity of the barracks. Again, it was directed that in the absence of sufficient cradles, sickles would be used to harvest the wheat and oats. Others pertained to maintaining fences, plowing, and shucking corn.[6] In short, the frontier fort of the Twenties was a huge farm.

Liquor was the greatest and the most persistent problem of the Army. As has been noted, until 1832 whisky was issued to the soldiers as part of the daily ration. At that time prohibition was instituted, and liquor was forbidden to be introduced into any fort, camp, or garrison by any soldier or sutler. In this same year General Winfield Scott sent from headquarters a vigorous order that:

Every soldier or ranger who shall be found drunk or insensibly intoxicated after publication of this order will be compelled, as soon as his strength will permit, to dig his grave at a suitable burying place large enough for his own reception as such a grave cannot fail to be wanted for the drunken man himself or for some drunken companion.

[6] Records of the Sixth and Rifle Regiments, Ms., see Nebraska State Historical Society Library, Lincoln, Nebraska.

There apparently was reason for this unusual order, for during the years when whisky was issued, nearly twenty per cent of the deaths reported from the Army were attributed to intemperance. The small liquor allowance, instead of satisfying the thirsty, seemed merely to whet the appetite, and the soldier went to the sutler or whisky-peddler and got more. A Fort Atkinson order of 1824 noted that "The free sale of strong draft Porter for several days has kept a great number of the regiment in a constant state of intoxication." At another time the orders stated that since the soldiers had been paid off, there had been repeated instances of intoxication even while on guard duty. In a few months' time at this post, of 136 persons tried by court-martial, 38 were found guilty of intoxication.

The prohibition order did not stop intoxication. Bootlegging continued to thrive, and whisky-peddlers did a big business. In the fifties there was a place on the opposite side of the river from Fort Leavenworth called Whisky Point. There anything and everything could be traded for whisky. Soon overcoats began to disappear from the barracks. A place of the same name, consisting of two rows of saloons and houses of ill fame, about fifteen buildings in all, was located across the river from Fort Abraham Lincoln near Bismarck, Dakota Territory, in the seventies. At Fort Des Moines in 1836 the post commander was continually irritated by the dram-shops near-by. General Gaines gave as one reason for advocating the removal of a post the nearness of the "tippling shops."

Then, too, liquor was bootlegged into the barracks or procured in some mysterious ways. During the summer and autumn of 1832 the officers at Fort Snelling in the pursuit of their duties took 172 gallons of liquor valued at $510. This was placed in the storehouse at the fort. The Indian agent wrote the Commissioner of Indian Affairs: "I am of the opinion from what I hear that the high wines, and whiskey seized by Lieuts. Vail and Greenough, and in store here will soon be of little account in consequence of loss by leakage, and the property not in charge of any responsible person." [7]

Since prohibition did not bring the desired results, controlled sale by the sutler was tried. This, too, had its grief for the commandant. At Fort Abraham Lincoln in the seventies only three drinks a day were allowed a soldier. By way of enforcing the rule, a large board was put up in the sutler's store with the names of the enlisted men upon it. It hung behind the counter where the liquor was served. Opposite each name a certain number of holes were bored, and when a man got a drink, a peg was inserted in a hole opposite his name. Another plan was to allow each man a pint of whisky when he came off guard.

Officers were only human, and they, too, liked to celebrate. They were inclined at times to wink at evasions of the regulations. A few drinks had the tendency to mellow them materially. An officer, leaving Fort Leavenworth on an expedition, wanted to take a stock of books and applied to the quartermaster for carriage of this extra baggage. That worthy was inexorable; the government regulations allowed only so many pounds, and he regretted not having the power to vary the allowance. A little later another officer applied for transportation of increased luggage. He was the possessor of two ten-gallon casks of bourbon whisky which was "so unusually fine that you must allow me to send you a sample, you can then appreciate more fully what my feelings must be at the thoughts of leaving it behind." The quartermaster was touched to the quick and generously replied: "Of course you can take it; anything in reason, my dear sir, anything in reason." [8]

Whisky was the greatest cause of punishment meted out to the troops. The commandant of Fort Atkinson in his orders of November 19, 1821, in speaking of the difference in the situation before and after pay-day, said that before everything moved on with the utmost regularity but "now the whole scene is changed. The

[7] Marcus L. Hansen, *Old Fort Snelling* (Iowa City, Iowa, 1918), pp. 142-143.
[8] William A. Bell, *New Tracks in North America* (London, 1869), pp. 28-29.

Guard House is crowded with offenders and courts-martial are constantly in session. What has caused this change? Whiskey!"

Minor offenses, such as drunkenness, unsoldierlike conduct, disobedience of orders, petty thievery, or talking back to a non-commissioned officer, were tried in a garrison or regimental court-martial. A private at Fort Bridger was fined five dollars for refusing to peel onions. Another was fined a like amount for giving liquor to the prisoners at the guard-house. A private at Fort Atkinson who left his company without permission was reprimanded by the commanding officer and denied the privilege of leave of absence for a month.

During the period when liquor was issued as a part of the ration, a stoppage of the whisky ration for a certain length of time, with diversion of the amount to the post fund, was a common punishment. At Fort Atkinson a private who "created a noise and disturbance in one of the rooms by striking with an earthern pitcher Marg. Smith a laundress" was sentenced to have his whisky rations stopped for ten days. Raiding a cucumber patch must have been more serious business than mistreating a woman, for ten days later for this offense a private was sentenced to fifteen days' solitary confinement on bread and water, to have his whisky ration stopped an additional fifteen days, and to forfeit one-half month's pay. The laundresses also were subject to military law, and for throwing a quantity of foul and dirty water in front of the quarters of Company A, Sarah Fox was sentenced to have her whisky ration taken away for a period of ten days, have it appropriated to the use of the company to which she belonged, and to be present at the promulgation of the sentence in front of the regiment at the first regimental parade.

The usual sentence of a non-commissioned officer was reduction to the ranks. Sometimes additional penalties were assessed, such as loss of whisky ration, ducking, confinement in the guard-house, or other punishment.

The following cases at Fort Atkinson are interesting as types of army misdemeanors and punishments. A private charged with slander was convicted and sentenced to stoppage of one month's pay, one month in the guard-house at night, to do the most menial police duty, and to stand on a block in the most conspicuous part of the post with the label on his cap, "I stand here for slander." Destruction of government property must have been serious business, for a private for biting a piece off a fellow private's ear, in addition to stoppage of pay and the wearing of a ball and chain, was condemned to ride the wooden horse in the center of the parade-ground from breakfast drum till guard mounting for ten days. For mutinous conduct, among other things, a private was sentenced to be ducked under the inspection of the officer of the day every morning for six mornings. This was in the month of November.

The more serious charges were subject to a general court-martial or court with wider powers than that of the regiment or post. Under its jurisdiction came such cases as desertion, sleeping on post, rioting, insubordination, mutiny, and the grosser cases of stealing and drunkenness.

Aside from drunkenness, desertion probably caused the army officers the most headaches. The soldiers at a lonely post, dragging out a weary, isolated existence with a long term ahead to serve, oftentimes grew discouraged and were tempted to leave the lonely life of drudgery behind. So anxious were they to escape that they would start out through the wilderness with five hundred miles between them and civilization.

During the years 1823, 1824, and 1825 there were stationed at Fort Snelling an average of 277 soldiers. Of these, 43 deserted in three years' time.[9] In 1831 more than one-fifth of the whole Army deserted. Probably the greater portion of these desertions were at frontier posts.

The penalty for desertion was severe. In the twenties the practice of cutting off the ears of deserters was introduced into the

[9] Hansen, *Old Fort Snelling*, p. 92.

department in which the Missouri River was located. This apparently was not very often used. Whipping was the popular method for punishing this offense. A typical sentence condemned the victim to be tied, with his hands over his head, to a stack of arms, a tree, or a flagpole, while the musicians took turns in administering fifty lashes on the bare back with a rawhide "well laid on."

This was done in the presence of the command. If the musicians failed to lay on well, an officer soundly berated them. Each blow of the rawhide cat-o'-nine-tails, made of whang leather tied in knots, cut the back, and before long the blood flowed while the poor deserter squirmed and groaned piteously. He was finally carried, for he could not walk, to the guard-house to spend from one to three months. At the end of this time his head and eyebrows were shaved and he was chased out of the camp by a squad with fixed bayonets while the drummers or buglers played "The Rogue's March."

There were variations of this general punishment, of course. When a certain private was found guilty of desertion at a wilderness post, he was furnished with thirty days' provisions, had his coat turned inside out, and was drummed out of the garrison with a straw halter around his neck.

The more serious crimes, such as desertion or mutiny in time of war, an attack on an officer, or murder, were punishable by death. As a usual thing the entire garrison was assembled to witness the execution. The culprit's coffin was brought to the place of execution, he was blindfolded, and a firing-squad shot him. Sometimes a pardon was withheld until time for the signal to fire and then handed to him; or the squad was instructed to fire over the culprit's head, and after that nerve-racking experience his sentence was revoked.

At almost all the Plains forts there was a pack of greyhounds, sometimes the property of the fort and sometimes of an officer. The Twenty-second Infantry, stationed at a fort in Dakota Territory in the seventies, owned sixty or seventy beautiful hounds.

Officers and men had much amusement running jack-rabbits, coyotes, and antelopes. Then there was hunting with the rifle. It was fun to raid a turkey roost at night and kill a few birds or to engage in a daylight buffalo hunt. At almost every post the soldiers trapped and poisoned coyotes and badgers, the hides of which they used for making gloves and caps. Soldiers often set lines and brought in quantities of fish. In a wooded region they hunted bee trees. At Fort Atkinson a soldier who found a bee tree was entitled to one-fourth of the honey, while the other three-fourths went to his company. Sometimes two chums would get permission to spend a day on leave, and, taking a lunch of sardines, crackers, raisins, or some other treat, they tramped through the woods hunting for wild fruit, such as plums or berries.

At some posts the officers had a jockey club and, laying out a track on the prairie, held highly exciting horse-races, with large amounts of money changing hands. Sometimes a dog-fight between dogs representing different units was scheduled. Frequently in such cases nearly all the money in camp, including that of the laundresses and the sutler's employees, was involved. In winter sometimes a near-by stream was dammed up or an artificial rink made by flooding, and officers and men skated. There were sleigh rides for the officers and their families. During the weeks when the snow lay too deep for drill or dress parade, some of the soldiers at Fort Bridger amused themselves by throwing a lasso. They scraped off a path, and each in turn ran along it while the others, standing in a line, tried to rope the runner as he passed. At such a season the story-tellers shone. The Seventh Iowa Cavalry had a man named Cannon who had traveled a great deal during a career in the Regular Army. He was a most outstandingly talented liar. His stories were inexhaustible, and though the yarns were ninety-nine per cent fiction, they served to ward off homesickness and lonesomeness by keeping the minds of the men occupied. The scouts like Kit Carson, Bridger, and others were full of stories and entertained the officers with tales of their adventures, among the

Indians on the Plains and in the mountains, even moving about among the enlisted men at times and spinning yarns to them.

That there was some ball-playing even at an early date is indicated by a Cantonment Missouri order of November 23, 1820, forbidding the throwing of bullets or any species of ball-playing that would endanger the windows of the cantonment. After the Civil War baseball came in as a sport, played, however, without equipment other than a ball and bat. Money was sometimes thrown at a mark, and perhaps shot-throwing was a similar game. In the seventies the forts had outdoor gymnasiums for summer practice.

Soldiers often visited the scaffolds where the Indian dead were "buried." Indians sometimes stayed in the fort overnight, and soldiers often visited the Indians and slept in their lodges. Frequently illicit relations developed between the soldiers and the Indian women. Stephen Riggs, in 1837, wrote that of the officers stationed at Fort Snelling there were but two who were not known to have an Indian woman if not half-breed children.[10] Orders had to be issued by the commanding officers barring "Indian ladies" from their daily and nightly visits to their friends in the fort.

As early as 1820 the sutler at Fort Atkinson had a billiard-table. There was also a bowling-alley there. From time to time orders were issued against cards and against gambling in general, but in spite of this both officers and men nearly always found a way to gamble with cards, dominoes, chess, checkers, and hustlecap. The latter was played by placing dollars or smaller coins in a hat, shaking it, and turning them out on the floor, one player taking "heads" and the other "tails." In the brush outside camp, in the stable, in a workshop, or in a cellar, the boys found a way to engage in the forbidden games.

Dances were frequent occurrences. A dance was always a "hop" to a soldier. Ordinarily officers and their wives did not dance with the enlisted personnel, but apparently all attended. "Soapsuds

[10] Stephen R. Riggs, *Mary and I, Forty Years with the Sioux* (Chicago, 1880), p. 24.

row" where the laundresses and married men lived, gave the men some contact with the gentler sex.

According to the regulation of 1841, four laundresses were allowed to each company. They were given quarters, one ration each per day, and were permitted to collect their money from the men's pay. In 1849 the laundry fee at Fort Kearney in the winter was fifty cents a month for men and two dollars for officers. The laundresses were given their whisky rations along with the men and sometimes became overpowered by the drink habit. At an enlisted men's hop in the kitchen of Company "I" at Fort Laramie in 1864, the women nearly all became drunk and the dance broke up in an uproar.

In sharp contrast to such diversions, a clergyman sometimes held meetings at the fort, and on one occasion a revival was conducted. A unit of the Presbyterian Church was organized at Fort Snelling in May, 1835. The men were marched to church. A story was told concerning Lieutenant-Colonel G. Loomis, commander of Fort Snelling, who was a member of this church and an enthusiastic Christian. The Sunday-morning inspection was always brought to a close at the hour for church. After inspection one Sunday, the colonel, before dismissal, asked all who wanted to go to church to step two paces to the front. Only a half-dozen responded. The ranks were closed up, and the colonel directed a good reader to read the Articles of War to those who did not care to go to church. The reading continued till long after the benediction at the church service had been pronounced. The next Sunday, when the same procedure was followed, about half of the command signified its desire to attend, and when the option was offered on the third Sunday, one can imagine the joy of the commander to see every man express a desire to go and listen to the words of life. As one writer says, Colonel Loomis did more in two weeks to fill the church with willing listeners than could have been accomplished by evangelists in twice the time.

As Professor Frederick Jackson Turner points out, the fort not only served to protect the settlers but also acted as a wedge to open the Indian country to settlement.

In the absence of government, the commanding officer of the fort often administered law in equity. If two men quarreled, he straightened out the situation. If one defrauded another, he saw to it that the matter was made right. The post commander was, in short, a despot, albeit usually a benevolent one, dealing out extra-legal decisions which were not questioned because of his superior power.

There was always a great deal of sickness at the frontier posts located on the rivers. There was somewhat less on the plains, because the climate was more healthful and in the later period more healthful food was served and greater knowledge made it easier to combat disease. The great scourge in earlier times was scurvy. This, as we now know, was caused by a lack of fresh vegetables and fruit. The never-ending diet of salt pork or beef and beans or rice was certain to bring scurvy. During the first winter at Cantonment Missouri more than half the garrison of 1,120 were sick, and over a hundred died. When such a scourge came, the only recourse at that early period was to send out hunters in an effort to get fresh meat. Usually it was successfully arrested if game was found. Raw potatoes, vinegar, or roots dug from the ground helped. In one instance a doctor made a sauce of the prickly-pear cactus which was successful in combating the disease. Malaria was prevalent at the river forts. A traveler who landed at Fort Des Moines remarked on the pale and sickly countenances of the soldiers loitering at the wharf. He was told that a short time before there was only one officer on duty out of the seven or eight stationed there.[11] During the first summer at Fort Leavenworth, out of 174 enlisted men, at one time 77 were sick with the same ailment, 65 were caring for them, and only 32 were left for duty. Cholera struck the soldiers as well as civilians. Alcoholism

[11] Louis Pelzer, *Marches of the Dragoons in the Mississippi Valley* (Iowa City, Iowa, 1917), pp. 59, 60.

was the cause of many deaths. During the seventies diarrhea and malaria continued to take the bulk of the toll. Officers who were ill were granted furloughs to recuperate.

The Indians accounted for many deaths. A cemetery at a post long since abandoned told a mute but tragic tale. Of over one hundred headboards, all but three read, "Killed by Indians." At Fort Rice, in 1871, there were three hundred graves of men with that simple story on the wooden head-markers.

When death came to the soldier, the body was placed in a coffin and carried by six men of his own rank to the cemetery, where it was interred with military honors. The drums were covered with black crape. A salute was fired over the grave, and there was solemn music by the band. Sometimes the body of an officer of higher rank was taken back East. The body of Colonel Henry Leaven-worth, who died on a campaign on the prairies, was wrapped in spices and sent via St. Louis and New Orleans to Delhi, New York. Later, when the Plains became a civilized region, his body was disinterred and reburied in the national cemetery at Fort Leavenworth. Some of the officers were kept in the Indian country a long time. When Colonel Zachary Taylor was commandant of Fort Crawford, he had been twenty years continuously in the Indian country. There he reared his four daughters, and they were married to army officers, the youngest eloping with Jefferson Davis. It was a sore trial for a mother to send her young children away to the East to be educated.

The government asked the officers to do various tasks aside from technical military duty. The doctor was required to operate a weather bureau, that is, to keep a rain-gage and make reports on the climate, the weather, and the flora and fauna—when the last killing frost occurred in the spring and the first in the autumn; the first appearance of various birds in the spring; observations on meteors, hurricanes, lightning, and other meteorological and botanical information.

Officers were ordered to survey roads, to measure distances, and to make maps of the country. The odometer, a sort of instrument attached to a wheel, which recorded distance, was used in mapping the country and measuring distances from place to place.

Much of the soldier's time, particularly after 1830, was taken up by expeditions. Some of these meant battles, others mere marches across the wilds. The earlier movements took place on the rivers. A troop movement upstream in keelboats was a laborious process. The boats were poled but had sails in case there was opportunity to use them. A code of signals was prepared: at the hoisting of a red flag or the firing of a rocket the squadron was to move; the hoisting of a blue flag meant to anchor, and so forth. Sometimes the boats kept together with intervals of from fifty to two hundred feet. The fleet started at 4:30 A.M. and at 8 or 10 stopped for breakfast on the bank, after having run five or six miles. Another like distance was run, and a stop was made at 1 or 2 P.M. Two flanking parties, one on each side of the river, were thrown out to precede the head of the column. There were twenty men in each party. At about 7:30 the fleet tied up to the bank for the night. Pickets were thrown out on the river-bank adjoining the boats. When cordelling was necessary, a group of pioneers went ahead with axes and cleared the way for the men to walk along the bank. Hunters brought in an abundance of game, fishermen caught plenty of fish, and Indians brought goods to the shore to trade. Going downstream the program varied somewhat, and often the command traveled sixty-five or seventy miles in a day. Occasionally they stopped to wash clothes. In the procession of boats the sutler's boat came in the rear of the others. Sometimes, instead of trying to keep together, each boat went its own way, after the rendezvous was appointed. When the steamboat came, it meant faster travel and more ease for the soldiers. They, however, wooded the boat and helped warp it when necessary or do anything else that needed doing.

On account of the tedious routine of inspections, roll-calls, and monotonous drills, any move was welcome. Sometimes an order

FORT LARAMIE

James Linforth, *Route from Liverpool to Great Salt Lake Valley*, 1855.
Engraved after a drawing by Frederick Piercy.

came to prepare to march on a certain date. Again, in response to a message brought by a horseman, the command was ready to go in an hour or two. They might be gone for an indefinite period or perhaps never return to that post. The equipment was always ready. If time was allowed, the property was packed. If not, a non-commissioned officer and a private or two stayed behind and packed the property and baggage of each company. In that case the small amount of luggage taken was piled on the walk in front of the quarters and was picked up by the quartermaster-sergeant.

The number of wagons and head of stock needed for an expedition is quite overlooked by the average reader as he reconstructs such a troop movement. The Cheyenne expedition of 1857, under Major John Sedgwick, left Fort Leavenworth with 300 fat cattle and, after killing some on the way, drew 150 more from the commissary at Fort Laramie. Long lines of wagons and horses also moved slowly across the prairie.

An infantry command on the march plodded along sleepily for the first few hours, but gradually it awakened and a hum of talk and laughter arose. A regular pace was struck, and soon the distance between the marching column and the wagon-trains began to widen. During the ten-minute rest period given every hour the men skylarked and made merry. As the day wore on, the hum and buzz died down and the men lay on their backs in full relaxation during the rest periods. With each period that passed, it took longer for the men to fall in and to drop into the regular gait. The wagon-train drew nearer, and when the marching men, looking ahead, saw a camp-site had been selected, a thrill ran through the command. The hum of conversation started again, and the last few miles saw a sprightlier step. If it was in a country devoid of wood, the soldiers speared buffalo chips with their ramrods as they marched along and deposited them as an offering at the foot of their company cook.

The cavalry, which started a half-hour later than the infantry, passed the weary footmen and was already on the camp-ground.

As the wagon-train approached, the cooks jumped down, gathered sticks, and had a fire started before the tent walls were up. In the meantime a wood detail went after fuel. When a savory aroma floated through the air, there were many inquiries concerning the progress of supper. Soon the men lined up, received their food in their mess pans, and ate wherever they cared to go.

Sometimes large tents were carried, but often after the Civil War the "pup tent" or "shelter-half tent" was used. With this arrangement two men carried the halves of the small tent, which were buttoned together and made into a tent at night. The men commonly said that the name "shelter-half" was a good name, for it sheltered only half of a tall man.

On a clear night on the prairie the men often lay for hours looking up into the starlit sky, enjoying the awe-inspiring sight of the heavens and talking to one another in low tones. A camp at night on the plains was a beautiful sight. The many camp-fires cast their radiant glow, and when the embers had died down and sleep had overtaken the weary soldiers, the moonlight showed the lines of wagons and rows of tents. All was silent save for the soft footfalls of the sentry and the rattle of a halter-chain as a mule searched for feed or a cavalry horse on the picket line restlessly pawed the ground.

At two or three o'clock in the morning, oftentimes, "first call" sounded, and in a few moments lights appeared. The cooks and teamsters had been busy with their preparations to feed man and beast even before the bugle call. Shortly after first call reveille blared out, and after a brief interval breakfast was served. The luggage of all kinds except the tents was loaded on the wagons. At a given signal the waiting camp-guard struck the tents and loaded them. It was the work of a few minutes, and at the blowing of assembly the column formed and was on its way as the broadening light in the eastern sky gave promise of the rising sun.[12] The sleepy soldiers paid small heed to the beautiful Plains sunrise as

[12] Forsyth, *The Story of the Soldier*, pp. 160-167.

they tramped along in the morning hours. As the blazing sun rose in the sky and its rays beat down relentlessly, the heat was often intense, and the terrible fog of dust raised by the marching column was almost stifling, especially to those not in front. For this reason the leading company each day was placed in the rear the next day. Often the recruits overloaded themselves on starting, but as they marched along, they began eliminating part of the load until the trail was strewn with discarded articles.

When in a hostile Indian country, the soldiers were forbidden to fire a gun. Obedience to such an order was more than frail humanity could stand, and on the march the men often took a shot at buffalo or elk in spite of the orders to the contrary. One day when General Sibley was looking and the cavalry dared not shoot, a deer ran into the marching column. The men tried hard to kill him with their sabers. When elk and buffalo meat came into camp, frequently the explanation was that the animal had been killed with a saber or that it had snagged itself. There was a common saying that the cavalry had their sabers trained so they would kill at forty rods. An elk, wounded previously, was actually despatched with a bayonet. Hunters who became lost from the command were notified of the whereabouts of the column by the discharge of rockets.

There were diversions en route. On the Sibley campaign the marchers passed a large swamp filled with thousands of frogs which fell a prey to the expert sabers and bayonets of the soldiers. Some expeditions had a seine and caught great quantities of fish. The men played horseshoes when in camp for any length of time. Some of the men in the Sully expedition had prayers together each evening.

The length of the day's march depended on the conditions encountered. An expedition from Sauk Rapids, Minnesota, to Fort Pembina in 1849 started its day's tramp at six in the morning and was in the mire every few hundred yards, struggling through it thirty-four times before six that evening. They traveled sixteen and a half miles in a large arc to avoid an impassable morass and at night had progressed eight miles from the morning camp. Every man had to get into the mud and water waist-deep, and men were sent forward constantly to make "coss bridges" or hay causeways across bottomless quagmires. In order to get the wagons over, it was lift, tug, and push day after day. The Sibley expedition experienced much inconvenience and suffering as a result of the wet weather in the earlier weeks; then the weather turned dry, and for days they suffered from heat, dust, and lack of water. A member of the expedition in his diary says of June 23, 1863:

Hot fatigueing day. Dust till you can't rest. March 14 miles. Much bad water. Grass is drying up. This country since we left yellow medicine is almost barren plain.

The heat was so intense on a few days that marching was halted temporarily. A member of the Sully expedition a year later noted in his diary that it was so dusty on June 12 that the butchers could not kill beef, and the command had to go without it. Neither could food be cooked on account of the oppressive dust. On a dry march of this kind even the dogs suffered much from the heat and lack of water.

On an expedition the soldiers collected a large number of specimens and pets. In 1857 a man caught a fawn, and the company attempted to raise it on the milk of one of the officers' mares. Pet elks, eagles, hawks, a badger, a wolf, jack-rabbits, horned toads, and other pets or stuffed animals were accumulated in the course of a campaign. As the expedition neared the fort, men and officers looked forward to letters and newspapers from home and a winter of relaxation by the fire. In later years duty was not over then, for freight and emigrant trains were protected in midwinter, railroad construction gangs had to be guarded, and for a time in the sixties troops of cavalry, scattered along the overland telegraph, acted as linemen as well as guards.

The slang phrase of the frontier soldier for Indian in the sixties was "abbri-goin," possibly a corruption of aborigine. A tall lean person was called "Shanghai" or "Shang" for short. Canister charge for a cannon, consisting of a large tin can fitting the bore of the gun filled with iron balls, was called "canned trouble." The men nicknamed their officers. Oftentimes these names, although not elegant, carried real affection with them. Colonel Snelling was called "the Prairie Hen." He was quite bald, and what little foliage he had was red. Zachary Taylor was called "Old Rough and Ready" or "Old Zack."

The actual Indian punitive expedition, which was rare, was a more serious matter than the ordinary march or escort duty. The women of the post saw their husbands and brothers ride away into a great ominous prairie silence unpenetrated by telegraph and broken only by an occasional despatch. Such an expedition began on May 17, 1876, at Fort Abraham Lincoln. At seven o'clock in the morning the officers' wives kissed their husbands as they left the quarters for the last time. A snappy drill marked the final preparation, and the married men took their final leave of their families. On "Soapsuds Row" wives and children stood with tears in their eyes waiting for the long column to start. Children played war with handkerchiefs and colored cloth on sticks. Then the regimental band struck up "Garryowen," the Seventh Regiment's own tune. The cavalry moved off under the dashing Custer. Then followed the infantry, the scouts, the pack-train, the artillery, and the supply-trains, forming a column over two miles long. As the beloved members of the expedition moved off in a cloud of dust, there drifted back as a last parting message the air from the band, "The Girl I Left Behind Me." Custer and the gallant Seventh Cavalry marched into the unknown—their doom at the Little Big Horn.[13]

Anxiously from week to week the well-nigh deserted fort awaited news from the Indian country. The women attended the regular Fourth of July ball at the fort, little suspecting the terrible tragedy

[13] Edna La Moore Waldo, *Dakota* (Caldwell, Idaho, 1936), pp. 190, 192.

that had taken place nine days before. For two days before the news arrived, however, a fearful depression had hung over the fort. Men and women moved about anxiously, nervously straining their eyes for the expected messenger. There was ominous whispering and excitement among the Indian police. Moccasin telegraph had apprised them of something entirely unknown to the whites. Their joyous actions convinced the observing that no good news was in store. Men would have given anything to know what was behind the scenes. Finally, on the morning of the sixth, the steamer *Far West,* the supply ship for the expedition, arrived with a cargo of wounded men and news of the greatest single catastrophe of the American Army in the annals of Indian warfare, the extermination of Custer and his command. The boat had traveled a thousand miles in fifty-four hours, the best time ever made by an Upper Missouri River steamer. The Battle of the Little Big Horn left twenty-six widows at Fort Abraham Lincoln. It was many months after the death of Custer before the post lost the gloom that enshrouded it on that July day.

The frontier soldier, although not a true, distinct frontier type, yet took on certain frontier characteristics from his contacts with the Indians and their environment. He accepted the Indians as associates, married into their tribes, or cohabited with them. In battle he often took scalps as they did.

CHAPTER IV

THE INDIAN AGENT

PROMINENT among the earliest problems of the new government under George Washington was that of establishing machinery to maintain a proper relationship between the United States and the Indian nations within its boundaries. Since the Indians constituted powerful warlike groups on the western borders and called for the intermittent attention of military men, the War Department was naturally given control of Indian relationships. Thus, if punishment was needed, it was meted out by the same hand that gave gifts or in other ways dealt with the sons of the forest.

Next in rank under the Secretary of War was the regional superintendent, who was usually the governor of a territory and carried the Indian work as one of his varied duties. This arrangement was weak and unsatisfactory from several angles. In the first place, with territories quickly becoming states, there were frequent changes and shifts in the headquarters and personnel of superintendencies. Territorial governors were often political appointees who formerly lived in the East and knew nothing about Indians. Once in a while there was a clash and misunderstanding as to whether a particular tribe was within the jurisdiction of one superintendent or another, since one tribe might inhabit two territories.

The next officer under a superintendent was an agent. Originally a subagent was appointed to assist the agent. In time the subagents were given stations of their own, and there was no difference in the two positions except the matter of rank and salary. Whereas the superintendent was in charge of a vast region with numerous tribes, the agent or subagent lived with a certain tribe or in a center where he could have easy access to two or more tribes in a given vicinity. The agents and subagents were usually frontiersmen themselves, such as fur-traders, trappers, missionaries, or discharged army men. In the last analysis they were the most important figures in the Indian service. Indeed, their contact with the Indians was more intimate than that of any other group except the traders and trappers. Under the direction of the agent or subagent were the interpreters, who were usually former traders, trappers, or in many instances half-breeds. Other minor employees such as blacksmiths, teachers, or farmers were provided frequently.

On July 9, 1832, Congress created the office of Commissioner of Indian Affairs. This official functioned at the capital under the direction of the Secretary of War until the Act of Congress of March 3, 1849, authorized the creation of the Department of the Interior. One of the chief functions of the Secretary of the Interior was to direct Indian affairs. The Commissioner, however, continued to function in the new cabinet set-up.

In 1816 there were fifteen agents and ten subagents employed. The salaries of agents ranged from $600 to $1,200 a year, and those of subagents from $300 to $819 a year. In the region with which this volume is most concerned, the Indian superintendent, by act of Congress in 1822, was located at St. Louis with a salary of $1,500 a year. In 1851 his salary was increased to $2,000 a year.

According to the law of 1832, the salary of the interpreter was $300, and men of Indian descent were to be given the preference. They were appointed by the agents, one for each tribe, and confirmed by the Secretary of War. The same act provided for a salary of $480 a year for blacksmiths, with an additional $120 if they furnished their own shops. Farmers, teachers, and mechanics, appointed by the Secretary of War, were to receive salaries ranging from $480 to $500 a year.[1]

---

[1] The author is indebted to Ruth Augusta Gallaher's series of articles on the Indian agent in Volume XIV of the *Iowa Journal of History and Politics*.

In the earlier years the Indian service was somewhat over-shadowed by the "factory system." This, a system of government-owned trading-posts, was urged by Washington as a means of winning the friendship of the Indians, weaning them away from the British influence which was so strong, and helping the Indians by honest dealing. A law of 1796 established two factories, and subsequent laws provided for six more. In 1806 Congress made provision for a superintendent of Indian trade who had charge of the factories. Fort Osage, on the Missouri River, and Fort Madison, on the Mississippi, served the trans-Mississippi region. The latter post was destroyed during the War of 1812.

The factory stocked the usual line of goods sold by the private fur-trading establishments. At first the chief demand included blankets, axes, knives, kettles, indigo, fishhooks, trinkets, guns, and ammunition. As the tribes became more civilized, they wanted tin cups, cow-bells, frying-pans, shirts, yard goods, and side-saddles. The plan was to operate much as private traders did, that is, to trade goods for furs, skins, and feathers at rates which would make the factory self-supporting. The reasonable prices for goods thus offered by the factory was expected to induce the Indian to trade with the government and to win his friendship.

The great error in the whole plan was in licensing traders to compete with the government trading-posts. The factories were forbidden to extend credit except under very pressing circumstances and were not allowed to sell any liquor to the Indians. Furthermore, the factor, as the government trader was called, was not permitted to go into the Indian country to engage directly in the trade, whereas private traders extended credit and followed the Indians about, taking raw furs in payment. Worst of all, they used liquor as a trading enticement to win the Indian away from the factory. Naturally the fur companies fought the factories, and since the factor was a more important figure in the eyes of the Indian than was the agent, thereby relegating him to an unimportant status, the latter also favored the abolition of the system.

Moreover, many of the agents had been Indian traders or were still interested in the fur trade, which provided another reason for fighting the factories. The combination of these powerful interests was too strong for the system, which had no interested party fighting for it, and accordingly it was abolished in 1822. The influence of the agents was immediately magnified.

The work of the agent in earlier days made him a true frontier figure. Often he was sent into the depths of the wilds. When John Sanford was appointed subagent to the Mandan villages in 1826, he was stationed 1,050 miles from Council Bluffs and 2,500 miles from Washington, in the very heart of the wilderness. In such a situation the agent was outside the military protection of any government fort, and it was necessary to protect himself against the Indians in case of an uprising. Maximilian, Prince of Wied, in writing of his journey up the Missouri, described the Sioux Agency at Fort Lookout, as it was called, as a square of about sixty paces surrounded by palisades twenty or thirty feet high, made of the trunks of trees squared and placed close together. Within the enclosure the dwellings were located close to the stockade. Two rival fur-trading establishments stood near-by.

When George Catlin toured the West, he found the Indian Agency at Bellevue, near the mouth of the Platte, a "lovely" place. He said: "It was a pleasure to see again, in this great wilderness, a civilized habitation; and still more pleasant to find it surrounded with corn-fields, and potatoes, with numerous fruit-trees bending under the weight of their fruit—with pigs and poultry and kine." The buildings at this agency were constructed by the Missouri Fur Company and later purchased by the government for the use of the agency.[2]

Naturally an agency was a considerable establishment. In addition to the dwelling of the agent and his office, there were warehouses for the storage of goods, a blacksmith shop, farm buildings

[2] George Catlin, *Letters and Notes on the Manners, Customs, and Condition of the North American Indians* (New York, 1841), Vol. II, p. 12.

BELLEVUE, MAJOR DOUGHERTY'S POST
From a painting by Charles Bodmer, 1833.

of the farmer, a school-house, homes for the interpreter, teacher, farmer, and blacksmith, and a council house. When near a fort, as agencies often were, the enclosing palisade wall was not necessary, and neither was it in use among the more civilized Indians of later days. As a matter of fact, the Indian agent was always safe if the Indians were sober. Even when the agent was absent, his wife and family were never molested in any way.

While life in an isolated place was less attractive than that on the edge of civilization because of its loneliness, it had its compensation, for the agent's duties were less difficult than where the two races came into direct contact.

The ideal Indian agent was a diplomat, representing his government in the best possible light to the group with which he was placed. He was their "father," as they called him, and represented the "Great Father," the President, at Washington. In the very early days it was one of the chief duties of the agent to win the confidence and allegiance of the tribes to the United States and destroy their fealty to Great Britain. The British, as a means of cultivating the loyalty of the Indians, had presented British flags and medals to the chiefs. One of the big tasks of the agent was to give out presents, take up British flags and medals, and distribute American medals. At the same time he endeavored to persuade the Indians of the might of the United States, which was once weak but had become mighty and powerful. In this the agent sometimes enlisted the services of the artillery, to drop a few shells and duly impress the children of the forest with the almost supernatural power of the Great White Father who had many such machines.

Another way of impressing them was to send a delegation to St. Louis or even to Washington to visit the Great Father himself and see the stupendous cities and inventions of the whites. A delegation of this kind from beyond the Mississippi was the chief Big White and his associates who went back with Lewis and Clark on their return to civilization.

The agent also visited with the innumerable delegations who came to see him and held powwows with them in the council house. On such occasions presents were given the chiefs and the whole party was fed from the storehouse. From May 28 till June 29, 1821, Major Lawrence Taliaferro at St. Peter's Agency, near Fort Snelling in Minnesota, gave away to Sioux and Chippewa chiefs and head-men $2,227.74½ worth of goods. Among these gifts were six hundred needles, four gross brass finger rings, two dozen fine combs, ten pounds Chinese vermilion, powder, lead, five hundred gun flints, thirty-six shot-guns, eight dozen fire steels, twenty-four dozen butcher knives, two gross looking-glasses, brass kettles, iron kettles, scissors, and many other articles.[3]

Major Taliaferro left what are probably the most voluminous, as well as the most valuable, journals of Indian relations in the trans-Mississippi-Plains area. By means of these the historian can reconstruct the activities of this remarkable man day by day. During the third quarter of 1821 he gave the following presents to influential chiefs:

August 4—1,000 pounds tobacco to Flat Mouth @ .12½ $125.00
August 28—10 pounds vermilion to Keyah @ $2.50 ...... 25.00
September 11—6½ dozen boxes of combs to Kokomo 6.81
September 19—31 yards scarlet cloth to Little Crow @ $4.00 . 124.00

On June 2, 1817, he gave four gallons of whisky and a large present to visiting notables. On June 7 he made a long talk to the little chief of Big Stone Lake to root out the British influence. He made him a "handsome present." Again he was engaged in issuing forty rations of bread and pork to poor and helpless men and women of the Sioux tribe.

Taliaferro records going through endless ceremonies and talks in the council house, giving out flags and medals and taking up British medals and flags. When an Indian chief lost his medal, he

---

[3] Lawrence Taliaferro, *Journal*, Ms., Minnesota State Historical Society Library, June 30, 1820.

received another from the agent. The medals apparently had the likeness of the Great Father on them, since some were called Madison medals and some Monroe medals. There were three sizes of each, signifying different degrees of honor. Taliaferro gives the following speech made by an Indian on January 28, 1828, upon giving up a medal:

My Father—I have your heart to wear, and that is enough for me. I present to you a medal given to me by the British. I do not wish to wear it.

The agent's duty sometimes called him away from the agency to make long journeys through the wilderness, visiting tribes or bands of Indians and holding talks with the chiefs. When the agent was at home, the agency was open for business every day but Sunday. Even on that day the American flag was run to the top of the pole in front of the office. When a chief died, it was customary in the period before 1850 to send presents to the family and gifts for the burial. For example, when the war chief Anoketo died in 1826, Taliaferro sent a three-point blanket, three yards of calico, one pair of leggings, and six or eight yards of London gartering to cover the body. He also despatched carpenters to make a coffin.

A receipt, yellow with age, in the papers of Agent Joseph Street, who was located in Iowa, records that on March 18, 1842, the carpenter received $31 in full for procuring plank, making a coffin, and hauling the body of Wapello from Skunk River to the Sac and Fox Agency.

In carrying out the general policy of keeping the fur trade for Americans, foreigners were forbidden to operate in the Indian country. Any foreigner found trading in the Indian region without a permit was subject to a fine of $1,000.

A second duty of the agent was governmental. He punished Indians who committed depredations on the whites, by requiring the chief of the tribe to give up the culprits or pay damages out of funds coming to the tribe from the government. If his demands were not complied with, punitive measures were taken, for troops were at the command of the agent.

A third function was to protect the Indians from white encroachment. The agent had the duty of preserving the integrity of the Indian territory for their use. He licensed traders, who could operate only at the location that the license specified; gave permits to whites to travel in the Indian country; prevented liquor from being taken into the Indian country; prosecuted whites for crimes committed against Indians, and served claims for damages done to the red man. This was among the most difficult of the agent's functions, especially with tribes in close proximity to the westward advancing line of settlement. The frontiersmen were self-reliant, usually lawless, and utterly intolerant of any authority working in favor of the Indians and against the whites. Their motto was, "If the land is fair, let us go over and possess it." Again and again white intruders invaded the Indian lands and remained in spite of warnings of the agent to leave. The agent was supposed to be supported by the Army, but usually political influence was strong enough to prevent its use, and the squatters kept their toehold until a treaty extinguished Indian ownership and opened the land for settlement. Occasionally, at the command of an agent, troops removed settlers time after time. They were sometimes obliged to burn the cabins and other property of the intruders in order to evict them. This always appealed to the frontier public as a pitiful case of persecution and had its political repercussions. The rights of the Indians guaranteed by treaties were overlooked.

Then, too, the frontiersmen did not hesitate to poach on the game preserves of the Indians. In one case, in 1840, a party of seven went on a hunting expedition in the Indian territory in Iowa. They camped near the boundary until the Indians started for the agency to receive their annuities. The whites knew when the annuities were due and that during the absence of the Indians was the only time it was safe to poach, for a white man caught hunting on their lands was considered a lawful prize. When all was clear, the hunters moved into the rich hunting-ground. In a grove of old oak-trees, many of which were hollow, they found sixteen bee trees within a square of a half-mile. They also found plenty of meat. While they were encamped, curing meat, straining honey, and trying beeswax, an Indian rode into camp and left hastily, evidently to summon reinforcements to stop the party. The wary whites took the hint. Hitching up their oxen and horses hidden in the brush, they hastily loaded their wagons, after dark built a big fire as a ruse, and pushed with all speed toward the boundary line. They successfully crossed it about daybreak. The loot of which they had despoiled the Indians consisted of eight barrels of strained honey and quantities of deer and elk meat.

The most difficult of all duties of the Indian service was to prevent the importation and sale of liquor to the Indians. Try to stop it as the agents might, the traders always managed to get the fiery liquor into the Indian country. In an attempt to put more authority behind the ruling, an act of Congress was passed on July 9, 1832, prohibiting the introduction of ardent spirits of any kind into the Indian country for any purpose whatever. Agencies began to search all boats on the Mississippi and Missouri rivers. So thoroughly and energetically was the law enforced that the flow of liquor was greatly lessened. Prince Maximilian of Wied could scarcely get a permit to carry a small amount of alcohol to preserve his natural-history specimens. Nevertheless, while this was taking place, liquor was being bootlegged into the Indian country in great quantities. Pack-trains took it by the keg to the mountains.

In 1832 William L. Sublette was given permission to take 450 gallons of whisky to the mountains for the use of his boatmen. He was compelled to give bond that he would sell none to the Indians. The whole transaction was a sham, however, for he traveled overland all the way to Pierre's Hole and never expected to employ a boatman on the trip.

Almost every steamboat, in spite of thorough search, carried liquor. Many ingenious means were used to smuggle the illegal goods into the trading-posts. Some steamers loaded the liquor onto wagons below the agencies and forts along the rivers, carried the goods overland to some point above the point of search, and loaded them again after the inspection had been passed. In other instances tricks were used to divert the attention of the inspector while the liquor was moved about. At one time an ex-Methodist minister who was the inspector at Bellevue was determined no liquor should escape him. When a boat arrived, a number of barrels purporting to be flour were unloaded. Each barrel was marked P. A. S., and the inspector supposed it to be flour for Peter A. Sarpy, the trader. The search of the boat was duly made and no liquor found. On some pretext, however, the boat tarried until evening and under cover of darkness reloaded the barrels and proceeded upstream.

Later laws made the penalties more and more severe, and more vigilant inspection tended to dry up the source of supply. Kenneth McKenzie, in order to circumvent the law, procured corn from Iowa and had it shipped up the Missouri River to Fort Union where he distilled corn whisky. It was not long until the agent at Leavenworth learned of it and broke up the brilliant scheme. McKenzie was forced to leave the Indian country, and had it not been for the powerful intercession of Senator Thomas H. Benton, the American Fur Company might have lost its permit to do business.

It is interesting to note that in the early forties the American Fur Company, which had hitherto used liquor copiously, became a strong advocate of prohibition. Apparently opposition traders were using it with effect, and since it was easier for the small outfit to elude detection, the company favored prohibiting it altogether. Since the company was well represented from top to bottom in the Indian service by ex-fur-traders, this policy was carried out to the advantage of the great concern. Major Drips, a past employee of the fur company, was selected as a special agent to enforce the law. He was a faithful agent, traveling widely even in winter.

It was the duty of the Indian agent to enforce treaty stipulations, superintend the payment of annuities, take a census, compile lists of Indians to whom payments should be made, and to supervise the development of civilizing media for which treaties often called, such as schools, farming instruction, gifts of equipment, and blacksmith service.

Annuities had their origin in promises to pay a certain yearly sum to the Indians in return for relinquishing lands or rights. Sometimes the Indians agreed to move and give up lands long occupied, or perhaps they agreed to a common use of certain lands with the white man. The first general treaty with the tribes of the Upper Missouri, signed at Fort Laramie in 1851, provided that the sum of $50,000 should be paid for a right of way across the Plains for immigrants and for the building of railroads.

In earlier times the annuities were paid in money. This was easier for the government, but the Indians profited little. In September, 1830, Agent Joseph Street paid $3,000 annuity to the Winnebago Indians. This was done in the presence of two other white men, the agent giving the Indian men the amount allotted to each family. He urged them not to spend their money for whisky but to save it until cold weather, when they would need clothing for themselves and their children. By the late afternoon of the next day the local trader had $2,300 of the $3,000. The Indians had, in exchange, some blankets, cloth, many trinkets, and much whisky. The year before, when the annuities were paid in goods, each chief and warrior had three blankets and each woman and child had three suits of clothes. In addition to these personal possessions, each band had seven or eight kegs of powder and such a large amount of tobacco they had to leave some of it at the agency. Because of their improvident management the government authorized the agent to ask the Indians how they wanted their annuities the next time, whether in goods or money.

At first the goods were given to the chiefs of the various bands, who divided them among their followers; but this was not satisfactory since sometimes there were quarrels over the distribution of the bulk materials, such as flour, powder, lead, and tobacco. In 1834 the Omahas and Otoes were so ill behaved that half a barrel of flour was wasted in a quarrel over the distribution. At a distribution among the Chippewas in the forties the chiefs of the several bands each bore a number of sticks representing the number in his band, and the goods were allotted and distributed by bands. Of course, there were disputes, and these had to be settled by the agent. When the Indians became more civilized, a census was taken and an annuity roll made up like a pay-roll.

Joseph A. Paxson, a Quaker missionary physician attached to the Winnebago Agency, mentioned that when the census was taken in 1869 and Indians were found without names, the whites gave them the names of people they knew in the East. When beef was issued there, the cattle were placed in an enclosure and shot by an Indian. They were then cut up, weighed, and given to the different families.

At Red Cloud and Spotted Tail agencies the chief and subchief were told how many cattle they were to have. They then "cut out" the number, and the warriors had a mock buffalo chase on the prairie. Those wild Texas cattle made a very excellent substitute for buffalo. The tongues, by the way, were sold to the trader, who shipped them east for sale as buffalo tongues.

When money payments were made, there was a roll with the names of the heads of families and the number in their families. When the Indian received payment, he made an X in lieu of his signature. The Sac and Fox receipt roll for 1841 bears the name of Keokuk, who had a total of eight in his family and received $142.60. Nase-e-wus-kuk, the eldest son of Black Hawk, had four in his family and accordingly received only $71.30.

The annuity system was open to much abuse. Agency goods sent up the river on the fur-traders' boats were often stored in their warehouses, mixed with those of the company. When payment was in goods, it was easy for an agent to conspire with the fur-trader, allowing him to sell half the annuity goods while the other half was given out. In the end the two, who possibly had formerly been good friends in the fur trade, split the proceeds.

In June, 1863, when the agent for the Indians along the Upper Missouri in the Dakotas unloaded only two-thirds of the annuity goods at the distribution point at Fort Pierre, the Indians, who were not deceived, followed the boat for six hundred miles, kept it in a state of perpetual attack, and sought to destroy the boat or kill the passengers and crew. Their efforts were futile, however. The goods were unloaded at a fur warehouse far up the river and did not come out until buffalo robes and furs were given in exchange.

Colonel William Bent, in giving his testimony concerning the famous Sand Creek Massacre, stated that when S. G. Colley, the son of the Cheyenne agent, came out to that country the year after his father became agent, his sole possessions were thirty or forty cows, but within two or three years he had accumulated from twenty-five to thirty thousand dollars. Much of this was made by selling annuity goods.

A remark attributed to Horace Greeley is to the point in this connection. When asked how an Indian agent receiving $1,500 a year could save $40,000 in four years, he replied: "It is above my arithmetic." Chittenden was doubtful whether the tribes along the Missouri received more than half their annuity money between the years 1850 and 1870.

Sometimes contractors drove a herd of cattle to an agency and obtained a receipt for them, and then drove part of them elsewhere and sold them. At one time a herd of eighteen hundred cattle destined for the Grand River Agency was culled just before they reached the agency, and four hundred of the best beeves were cut out and sent to Sioux City to be sold. When the herd reached the agency, four hundred head of the cattle were run before the counting officer twice. This graft of the contractor at the expense of the Indians was possible because of poor facilities for handling the cattle.

As early as 1806 the first agent in Iowa was instructed to teach the Indians agriculture and domestic manufactures. He was by precept and example to encourage the growing of vegetables and fruits. He was to establish a nursery to supply the chiefs with fruit-trees, garden seeds, and plants. As soon as practicable he was to be furnished with a blacksmith who was to mend guns, axes, and hoes, and as soon as possible he was to introduce plows. Schools were provided also, but frequently these were under the direction of missionary societies. The more promising Indians who completed elementary-school training were sent to the Choctaw Academy in Kentucky at government expense.

It was difficult, however, to get the Indians interested in agriculture. According to traditional custom, it was the man's business to hunt and the business of the women to do what little farming was done. To take up the hoe or the plow was considered degrading, and a man who would do such a thing was thought to be effeminate. The Indians almost invariably refused even to haul annuity goods or carry them from the boat to the storehouse, although at times some carrying was done by the squaws. The bucks were glad to have the government farmer put in the crop and the squaws cultivate it.

At the Whetstone Agency in Dakota, in 1869, with great difficulty a board fence one and a half miles long had been built. Trees had been felled and hauled to the sawmill and made into boards; the cedar posts had been rafted down the river, and a very fine fence was the result. The agent warned the Indians to protect it, for it would be needed to save the crops of corn and wheat in the spring. During a blizzard the agency employees were not out for four days, and when they did go out they found that the squaws, with the knowledge of the bucks, had torn down most of the fence and used it for firewood. It was easier to do this than to carry fuel from an island a half-mile or more away. When the loss of the fence was mentioned to the Indians, they did not seem at all depressed; no doubt they thought they could take a chance on another fence's being built of green cottonwood in the spring so it would be dry enough to burn by the next winter. At any rate they lost no tears over the destruction of their property.

A little later the idea was put forth that if the Indians were furnished with machinery it would encourage farming. In accordance with this philosophy a large number of new wagons were ordered from the factory for the Indians. When they came, a whole acreage was covered with the dismounted parts. After the greatest difficulties, the Indians, who knew nothing about machinery, succeeded in assembling the wagons and hooked their ponies to them. Then ensued a hilarious celebration as the bucks rode about the prairies with their families in the shiny vehicles. But soon tiring of their new playthings, they began trading with the white settlers, and before long every settler in the community had a new wagon which he had secured for a mere trifle. Likewise where suits were issued the whites fell heir to them shortly.

Contact with the whites had brought certain diseases which decimated Indian tribes. The most feared was smallpox. In 1832 Congress appropriated funds to vaccinate the Indians. Army doctors and Indian agents were ordered to use every possible means to persuade the Indians to be vaccinated. Evidently few submitted, for in 1837 a terrible scourge on the Upper Missouri wiped out thousands. The steamboat *St. Peter's* carried the smallpox into the region. The crew tried to keep the Indians away lest they catch the infection, but the aborigines thought it was an attempt to cheat them of their annuity goods. As a result of contact with the boat the plague was carried to the various villages and began its deadly work. Its ravages spread alarm throughout the Indian country. The Indians, dumb with terror, appealed to the Deity and the whites to do something. The victims died by hundreds, and the disease spread with frightful rapidity. At the Mandan villages the bodies were thrown in piles over a cliff, and a sickening stench pervaded the atmosphere for miles. Of the fifteen hundred to two thousand persons, only thirty, mostly boys and old men, survived. The country presented a scene of utter desolation, with tents still standing but no smoke rising from the camp-fires, nothing to interrupt the fearful silence.

A further duty of the Indian agent was to settle intertribal disputes, and even to help settle disputes within a tribe when so asked by the disputants. In June, 1826, the Chippewa and Sioux, who were almost continually fighting, met in council at the mouth of the St. Peter's River under the influence of an agent. With three flags flying, the tribes were drawn up in line a hundred and fifty yards apart, singing the peace song. About twenty braves of each nation advanced with their arms and accoutrements and halted about ten paces from the other party. The braves then slipped forward and quickly and gently pressed each other's sides above the hips, shook hands, and the whole assembly fired a salute, after which the peace-pipes passed between the tribes. Making such a peace and keeping it were two different things, and from time to time young braves, anxious to prove their mettle, broke over and attacked parties of the other tribe. It was then the duty of the agent to obtain delivery of such marauders to the fort, where they were kept pending punishment.

In 1869 the Winnebago Indians conducted a trial in which they arraigned one of their own number for drinking, which was a crime among them. In such a trial the agent and his men had important parts to play. The doctor at the reservation acted as judge in this case, and the agent, or someone appointed by him, examined the witnesses. The prisoner sat at the center of a circle of men who acted as a jury. A chief, acting as prosecuting attorney, made an eloquent speech. In this particular case the young man had bought whisky at a wood-yard from the mate of a steamer. After careful deliberation, the jury arrived at the simple verdict: "Go and sin no more!"

Finally, the Indian agent gave aid and hospitality to white people in need in the Indian country. In short, he was to the United States Government what fingers are to a blind man. He was both the medium of perception and the means of execution. He was a dual character in that he was often the only source of information concerning the Indians reaching Washington, and at the same time he represented Washington in the wilderness.[4]

From time to time, when the government desired to wring further concession from the Indians, councils were held for the purpose of drawing up treaties. In most of these treaties the Indians gave up their lands and agreed to move farther inland before the surge of westward migration.

Certain self-interested groups, hovering like vultures awaiting a kill, always wanted a treaty signed. The fur-traders saw their business vanishing with the intrusion of the whites and the disappearance of game. Their credit system often involved large sums of money, and these debts, owing to the communistic ideas of the Indians, were considered tribal obligations. Consequently it became customary at each treaty signing for the traders to present their claims for payment out of the money paid to the Indians by the United States.

There was so much fraud in these accounts that the regulations of 1838 provided that any claim against an Indian tribe had to be submitted with proofs to the agent, who questioned the Indians. If they admitted the justice of it, he made a formal demand on the tribe for payment. If they refused, the agent sent a report to the Commissioner of Indian Affairs. If he decided the claimants were entitled to redress, the amount was taken out of the next treaty payment, and the Indians were informed that this was the decision of the Great Father on the case.[5] The half-breeds also were usually favorable to a treaty. The government customarily gave them a

---

[4] Alban W. Hoopes, *Indian Affairs and Their Administration* (Philadelphia, 1932), pp. 28-29.

[5] Charles Lowell Green, *The Indian Reservation System of the Dakotas to 1889*, Ms., Master's Thesis, University of Iowa, 1928, pp. 24-25.

donation for their good offices in acting as "go-betweens" for the Indians and the government officials.[6]

The treaty councils followed a general pattern. The Indians were summoned to gather at a certain point at a specified time. The superintendent, with some assistants or a group of commissioners especially appointed for the occasion, usually represented the United States, although in the case of less important treaties an agent sometimes represented the government.

A council at Fort Atkinson on July 4, 1825, began with a meeting of the commissioners with the chiefs at the council place at eight o'clock. The purpose of the council was explained at that time. At three the chiefs invited the commissioners over to their camp and partook of a dog feast, consisting of thirteen well-done dogs boiled in plain water in seven kettles. The beverage was Missouri River water brought up in the paunches of buffalo, which gave it a disagreeable taste. Skins were used for seats. On a row of buffalo chips lay the peace-pipe. Chief Standing Buffalo presented the stem of the pipe to a commissioner and lighted it with a coal of fire. It was then passed along the line. The ashes were knocked out on the buffalo chips and the pipe refilled occasionally. At the Fort Laramie council of 1845 howitzers were fired to open the ears of the Indians to the white man's words, and sky-rockets were sent up as messages to the Great Spirit to evidence that the Indians had listened.

Two important councils were held in 1851, culminating in treaties with the respective tribes. One of them, at Traverse-des-Sioux, was described by a visitor named La Duc. On the prairie receding from the river the commissioners had their cluster of six tents. At a short distance there had been prepared a council house consisting of a number of benches placed in front of a rude platform and a desk of rough boards. The whole was shaded by an arbor of poles covered with boughs of trees. Near-by the half-

[6] Verna Anne Elefson, *Indian Agencies on the Upper Missouri to 1850*, Ms., Master's Thesis, University of Iowa, 1927, pp. 80-81.

PAWNEE COUNCIL

From a painting by Samuel Seymour, artist with the Long Expedition.

breeds were camped with their families, and with them were the Indians who had come in contact more familiarly with the whites. The remaining bands pitched their conical lodges on the high ground away from the river for a mile or more up and down the stream. A very wet season made traveling difficult, and the bands came straggling in. The commissioners were there on June 30, but not till July 18 did the council start. The Indians were not particularly anxious to begin, since they were regaled on government provisions during the entire period. They spent their time in dancing, singing war songs, playing Indian ball, and fighting sham battles. On one occasion the plains Indians living away from the river put on their cavalry suits and, grasping limbs of bushes covered with rustling leaves, mounted their horses and charged the lodges of the other bands, simulating a Comanche attack. They were received at each encampment with a volley of blank cartridges. Wheeling swiftly from one band to another, they finally swept down in front of the commissioners' camp singing a wild song, a terrible disquisition on scalps. The behavior of the Indians was all that could be desired, however.

Finally, on July 18, the commission firmly refused to wait for other bands and began the council. For five days there ensued "big talk" with a great deal of ceremony and procrastination on the part of the Indians. It was several days before they would assent to anything less than extravagant terms. At last they agreed to the final terms on July 23. The treaty provided for the sale of all the territory in Iowa and all in Minnesota east of the Red and Big Sioux rivers with no northern boundary specifications. A tract of land was to be set aside as a reservation, and schools, mills, and farms were to be established. The Indians were to receive $1,665,000.[7]

As a result of problems arising from the opening of the Oregon and Santa Fe trails, a council was held at Fort Laramie the same year to obtain the permission of the Indians for roads and posts in their territory and to preserve peace among the tribes. Congress

[7] Green, *The Indian Reservation System of the Dakotas*, pp. 27-32.

on this occasion appropriated $100,000 for the expenses of holding councils with the wild tribes of the prairies.

The defects of Indian control were shameful. The spoils system controlled appointments, and fitness and experience received little consideration. There was more or less friction between the agents and the military men after the Indian service was placed in the Department of the Interior. There was a total absence of a fixed method of procedure, and business was conducted in a haphazard fashion. Too often agents were traders. Manuel Lisa throughout his term as subagent during the first two decades of the nineteenth century traded with the Indians. This was not nearly so serious, however, as the practice later became when annuities were issued and the agents worked hand in glove with the fur companies. Larpenteur said that had the agents been ever so well qualified for their work, they could not have done it well because once in the Indian country they were entirely under the influence of the fur company and could not help themselves. Corruption and graft were so rife among Indian officials that during the nineteenth century the appellation "Indian agent" was another term for grafter. The frequent changes due to the spoils system did not alleviate the matter. Red Cloud expressed his idea of the situation thus:

I don't see why the government changes our agents. When one agent gets rich at his trade of looking after us and has about all he wants, he may stop his stealing and leave us the property which belongs to us if he keeps his place.

Under President Grant in the sixties a policy was inaugurated of turning Indian control over to the religious bodies, with the superintendent and agents in a given district chosen from a particular sect. In Kansas the Quakers held sway. They held religious meetings for the Indians and treated their position much as a pastorate. In the fall of 1869 the Kansas *State Record* remarked upon the fact that the new Quaker agent to the Pottawattomies, Joel H.

Morris, knelt in prayer among them after his first conference with the tribe. The paper continued:

This is decidedly a new feature in Indian Councils. It has generally been understood that Indian agents are always ready to *prey*, but we venture that there are not many, if any, persons now living in Kansas, who ever saw an Indian agent kneel in the midst of his charge, and ask for the blessing of Heaven to rest upon them.

Even the religious men did not entirely exclude graft, for they lacked in experience what they made up in moral quality, and in some cases even moral fiber was worn threadbare under repeated wear and tear.

From out the noisome atmosphere of pollution of the old-time Indian service, it is refreshing to find honest, incorruptible agents emerging. The outstanding ones were Major Lawrence Taliaferro of the St. Peter's Agency in Minnesota and John Dougherty at Council Bluffs. The latter had been there since 1819, and when he was appointed agent in 1828, he could speak thirteen or fourteen native dialects. He was one of the most capable, as well as trustworthy, men in the service. His report of 1837 gave mute testimony to the incessant struggle he had to carry on against the fur-traders. He felt that so long as the traders were allowed to reside among the Indians the efforts of the agent to better their condition would come to naught.

Major Taliaferro was equally courageous and incorruptible. Added to that, he is especially interesting to the historian on account of the voluminous records of his work over a period of years. When during a severe winter the Indians were starving, he exhausted the government stores and then used his own means to satisfy their hunger. In 1827 he stated that in eight years he had spent $1,196.75 of his own money because the public funds were inadequate to fulfil the pressing needs. After he retired, a group of Sioux chiefs visited him in Washington. Little Crow, the spokesman, said:

My old Father; we love you; we respect you. . . . Since you left us a dark cloud has hung over our nation. . . . We failed to get a friend in anyone like you; they all joined the traders. We know your heart, it feels for your old children.

He himself made the honest statement:

I have the sad consolation of leaving after twenty-seven years—the public service as poor as when first I entered—the only evidence of my integrity.[8]

The Indians often became very fond of an honest agent who treated them kindly. In 1842, when the Sacs and Foxes made a treaty with the United States, they had written into it the provision that the land at the agency on which their late agent Joseph Street and their former chief Wapello were buried was to go to Mrs. Street. The Indians agreed to buy the agency buildings from the government for $1,000, and the government gave a section of land surrounding it to the widow for a home. She was to select the land, and there in nicely kept graves the Chief and his "Father" sleep to-day, associated in death as in life.[9]

[8] Taliaferro, *Journal*, No. 2, 1821.
[9] Joseph Street Papers, Ms., Iowa State Historical Library, Des Moines.

CHAPTER V

THE MISSIONARY

FROM THE TIME the first colonists arrived on the Atlantic seaboard, the settlers carried on missionary efforts for the Indians in the back country of the English colonies. Missionary zeal had waxed and waned from time to time until the Civilization Act of 1819 gave a new impetus to missionary activity, which continued until the removal policy of the thirties caused its decline. The act set aside an annual appropriation of $10,000 for the civilization of the tribes adjacent to the frontier settlements. It authorized the President to appoint suitable persons to teach the Indians and instruct them in agriculture. It was understood that these appointees were to teach religion, although it was not so stated on account of the fact that Congress is forbidden by the Bill of Rights to pass religious laws. The President rather than Congress was to direct the recipients of government support.[1] An act of 1802 had previously provided for the erection of schools and teachers' residences and for tools and implements in suitable quantities.

Immediately following the passage of the Civilization Act, in 1820, a delegation of Osage visited Washington asking for missionaries. This request from savages who had traveled two thousand miles to petition President Monroe for a mission station appealed to the people. The United Foreign Missionary Society responded, and from the more than one hundred volunteers a mission family of forty-one persons was selected, consisting of twenty-five adults and sixteen children. There were in the group ministers, a physician, a mechanic capable of manufacturing ma-

[1] Martha L. Edwards, "Government Patronage of Indian Missions, 1789-1870," *Edwards Papers*, Ms., Wisconsin State Historical Society Library.

chinery and doing blacksmith work, a carpenter, a millwright, a
wagonmaker, a shoemaker, and two farmers. The women were
teachers, musicians, and seamstresses. The leader was known as
the superintendent. The group was consecrated at a special church
service in New York and started for Pittsburgh on March 5, 1821,
amid fond good-bys and the singing of farewell hymns. Churches
along the way received them and paid their way a given distance
or raised money for the expenses of the mission. At Pittsburgh
the group hired two keelboats and started down the Ohio.

Before they started, rules were drawn up for the entire party—
crew and missionaries. Among other things, profane language and
liquor-drinking were forbidden. The boatmen were to have fifty
cents a day and provisions from the mission on the prairie back to
St. Louis. The group was cordially received along the way, and
donations of money and goods were raised at the various towns.
At Marietta old General Rufus Putnam met them and butchered
an eight-hundred-pound ox which he sent on board. Shortly beyond Louisville a child was born, but both the child and the mother
died.

On Sunday the missionaries always rested and held religious
services. If they were not in a town, their services were held at the
boats, and often a few from the shore joined them. They even
stopped some passers-by, convinced them of the impropriety of
traveling on Sunday, and invited them to stay and worship with
them. When they reached the Mississippi, the journey upstream
to St. Louis was extremely difficult. In spite of grueling work they
reported an advance of only seven miles on May 10.[2]

At St. Charles, Missouri, the governor met the group to bid
them God-speed on their way into the wilderness. A St. Charles
minister addressed the Throne of Grace, and they took leave by
singing a touching farewell song. The city gave an offering of a
hundred dollars.

[2] Doris Denton, *Harmony Mission, 1821-1837*, Ms., Master's Thesis, University of Kansas, 1929, pp. 10-14.

Finally, in August, just six months after leaving Pittsburgh, they arrived at Manuel Lisa's trading-post near where Papinville now stands. The first arrivals reached the mission site, on the Marais des Cygnes River about six miles above its junction with the Osage, near the western boundary of Missouri, in November and put up tents. They then built ten cabins, sixteen feet square and seven feet apart, in a row. To the rear of the cabins was the kitchen, and behind that the common storehouse. The cabins had puncheon floors. Holes bored in the walls and in posts supported poles on which prairie hay was spread for beds. There was no glass for windows. This mission named Harmony was one of the earliest missionary enterprises in that isolated region.

Not all missionaries left with the spectacular send-off this group received. The experience of William Thurston Boutwell, missionary to the Ojibways, is an interesting example of the problems faced by a couple entering a new field. He chose Leech Lake, about two hundred miles above St. Peter's, Minnesota, as his place of labor. He expected help from the American Board of Commissioners for Foreign Missions, but as it did not come he helped himself. He married Hester Crooks, a half-breed daughter of one of the heads of the American Fur Company, who had been educated in the mission school at Mackinaw. His honeymoon was spent in traversing the Northern wilds between Fond du Lac and his chosen field of labor. After a tedious journey of forty-three days by land and water, exposed to the elements, they arrived at the mission site on October 9, 1832. He did not have a gallon of corn, rice, or anything for winter except four hogsheads of flour and eighty or ninety pounds of pork. He had himself and his wife and a hired man and his family to feed. There was not a sign of a house. He built a birch lodge and then sent the hired man to fish for the winter's food. Boutwell, in the meantime, shouldered an axe and with the aid of another man cut and helped to carry on his back the logs for a house. In five weeks he had about six thousand small fish drying on a scaffold before his door. These formed the principal part of their diet that winter. In December they left the lodge for a log cabin. It was a palace to Boutwell, although he had neither chair, table, bedstead, nor stove. The windows, made of deerskin, admitted a very imperfect light, scarcely sufficient to enable one to read. Some missionaries were fortunate enough to have window glass. The typical mission home was built of logs with hewn-board floor, a few articles of crude, home-made furniture, and a fireplace in which to cook.

By the thirties the missionaries traveled to their fields in steamboats. Samuel Pond, in the Indian country, instructed his brother Gideon to come by deck passage instead of cabin since it was only one-third the cabin fare. On arrival in the field it was often a task to prepare a dwelling-place. Sometimes the Indian agent or trader gave the newcomer a shelter until he was able to build one of his own. The problem of food was no small item.

One of the first tasks the missionary faced after he had a shelter was to learn the language of the natives. Sometimes it was possible to study with an interpreter at the agency or trading-post, or at the factory, as was the case of the Harmony Mission. Sometimes, however, the missionary had no other means than to go into the lodges of the aborigines and listen to their talk and learn their ways.

Samuel Pond found living with the Indians very disagreeable but felt it his duty. The Indians hunted lice on their bodies, and cracked and ate them, considering them a great delicacy. He said, "Their cooking etc. does not very well accord with a yankee woman's idea of neatness."

Some men found great difficulty in learning the language. Missionary Thomas S. Williamson wrote that it was slow work at best: "It will be years before I can preach in Sioux, but I can manage to get along very well with them." The unmarried missionaries learned the language faster than the married ones, for they sometimes made their homes right with the Indians for months at a time, whereas the married men lived in their own homes. The

Pond brothers, who were single at the time, learned the Dacotah language very rapidly.

Missionary Boutwell among the Ojibways found himself unable to accept the invitation of a squaw to eat with the family because up until breakfast time the squaw and several of the children had been busy cracking lice. When he returned to his tent, he found lice on himself, and killed ten or fifteen which had found their way onto his body. He stated that the missionary had to be very careful and practice much reserve in visiting the lodges lest he lay himself open to slander or give occasion for evil speaking, since the men were mostly absent. Immoral white men were accustomed to visit the lodges and seduce the women with ribbons, jewelry, and trinkets.

The natives were hospitable—in fact, too much so. When Reverend Joseph Kerr arrived at a Wea village, at the first lodge a bowl of sweetened broth and bread of cracked red corn was set before him. After he had eaten, a town crier took him to another tent where he ate buffalo meat. In this way he was taken to six places where he was expected to eat. He was soon completely stuffed with food, none of which was very palatable.

Different ways were used to win the confidence of the natives. Sometimes an Indian official would introduce the missionary. Henry R. Schoolcraft, on an expedition to the Ojibways, introduced Boutwell and urged on the Indians the importance of learning to cultivate the soil and having schools for their children. The missionary then preached to them by means of an interpreter. Later Boutwell created an interest by becoming chummy with the children. This proved an entering wedge to the hearts of the adults, for they were very indulgent with their children and were inclined to listen to their whims. One missionary related that when he went among the lodges, the children ran screaming in terror as though he were a bear. It was not long, however, until they had largely overcome their fear, and his lodge was filled with boys from morning till night, hanging on his knee, on his shoulder reading or singing, while a few of the more timid lay flat on the ground at a safe distance, looking on. The hearts of the elders were won through this contact.

One of the great difficulties the mission workers encountered was that the Indian dialects had no words to express much that the good Christians wished to say. Many abstract terms had no counterparts in the Indian language, and the most common figures of speech had no meaning in the strange tongue. As Missionary Stephen Riggs put it: " 'The Lamb of God,' an expression perfectly at home in our ears, is exceedingly strange to a Sioux."

If a doctor were among the mission group, he could relieve distress and soon win a place in the hearts of the Indians. Missionary Ayer, located near the Yellow Lake trading-post in Minnesota in 1833, made it a point to spend a considerable portion of the day reading and singing to the Indians in their own language. Notwithstanding the bustle incident to trading, he found time to talk to little groups of four or five up to a dozen. With the aid of infant cards he was able to interest them an hour. In the evening he was able to gather a considerable number to a meeting. The aborigines seemed to take a special interest in songs sung in their own language.

Great difficulties faced the missionary in his attempts to influence the natives. They clung to their manners and customs, and changes were made very slowly and with great effort. Ridicule was the supreme opposing weapon. Children would not come to school because of the ridicule of older boys. An Osage Indian who had long attended school and who understood English could hardly be persuaded to speak a word of it before the Indians for fear of the tyrant ridicule. Girls in the Delaware School did not want to learn English for they said if they spoke it people would call them "old white folks." The same power prevented Indian boys from doing work.

Polygamy was another gulf between the Indian and the acceptance of Christianity. Many tribes followed the custom of plural marriage, and this presented a real problem for the missionaries to solve. Stephen Riggs of Minnesota mentioned that in several cases two wives of one man had been admitted to church membership because the missionaries could not adopt a rule that would exclude either of them. Later a man so blest applied for membership, pleading he had married in ignorance and logically citing the examples of Solomon, Jacob, and David. The missionaries did not see eye to eye on the question. Finally it was worked out satisfactorily, and no man having more than one woman was admitted to church fellowship. Nevertheless, the operation of the rule brought hardship, for homes were broken up and women had to find new homes. Father De Smet told of one poor man who hesitated as to which of his wives he should select. The elder, seeing his irresolution, said to him: "You know how much I love you, and I am also certain that you love me, but you cherish another more; she is younger than I am. Well, remain with her, leave me our children, and in that manner we can all be baptized."

The traders, always inimical to civilization since it was against their interests, worked against the missionary. One trader made the statement that it was a loss to him of five hundred dollars whenever an Indian learned to read and write. They talked against school and learning to read. Efforts to improve the conditions of the Indians often hurt the traders' business, thus increasing their normal antagonism. The Indian agents were often close allies of the traders, and their skulduggery naturally made them enemies of the missionaries who sought to protect the government's wards.

The Missouri group of Catholic missionaries had its beginning in 1823, when Bishop Dubourg, located at St. Louis, persuaded a community of Jesuits in Maryland to move to Florissant, Missouri, near the spot where the Missouri empties into the Mississippi. The Sisters of the Sacred Heart were already located there. The Maryland party, consisting of seven Flemish novices, three lay brothers, and three Negro families, left Baltimore with two wagons to carry the luggage and a light wagon in which the travelers were to ride when they were too tired to walk. The lay brethren and novices led the way on foot, followed by the wagons. They cooked their own food and camped by the wayside at vacant cabins or farm homes. After eighteen days they reached Wheeling, West Virginia. Since their resources were too limited to purchase a boat, two scows were acquired and lashed together forming a make-shift boat. At the mouth of the Ohio the goods were loaded on a steamer, and the party walked the two hundred miles across Illinois to St. Louis, through marshes, often up to their waists in water, and seldom finding shelter in an inn or farm-house. On reaching their destination they found one large room with an attic above it. The gable-roof was so low, however, that people could not stand erect in this upper room. A short distance away stood two mud-plastered log huts with clapboard roofs, rough-hewn slab doors and latch-strings hanging on the outside. The dark, stuffy attic became the dormitory for the novices. The floor, which served as bed, was softened by a truss of straw covered with a buffalo robe. One of the two outhouses, which had served successively as chicken houses and pigpens, was transformed into a study for the novices and a community refectory. The other was used as a machine shed and sleeping-quarters for the slaves. Although few Indians were near there so late in the season, an Indian school was established. The Sisters of the Sacred Heart taught the girls and the young scholastics taught the boys. Father De Smet was principal of this seminary. The school was as useful as a training-school for the teacher as for the pupil. The teachers studied the characteristics and traits of the Indians.[3]

Father Pierre Jean De Smet is the best known of the Catholic missionaries of this period, and yet, as Garraghan points out, he was not a typical Jesuit missionary. He never lived for any considerable time with the Indians; he never learned to speak any of

[3] Arthur Thomas Donohue, *A History of the Early Jesuit Missions in Kansas*, Ms., Doctor's Thesis, University of Kansas, 1931, Chap. II.

their languages. He was rather a publicity man, traveling, learning of the needs of the Indians, organizing the work, promoting it, raising money, and securing workers to man the staff. As a founder of missions he was the most conspicuous in the nineteenth-century movement in behalf of the Western Indians. The typical Jesuit, however, lived among the Indians, spoke their language, and devoted his life to their religious and economic welfare. The Catholic missionary had the advantage over the Protestant on account of his celibacy. He was not hindered by home ties. It took less to support him, and there was fifty per cent less chance of sickness taking him from the field. There were no children to send east for an education or tempt him to abandon his work for this purpose.

Father Nicolas Point, who was located near Fort Benton, Montana, in the forties, lived with the Indians in their native habitats, shared with them their distresses and discomforts, ate with them their daily bread, followed them in their hunts, and gave himself to be spent in ministering to their needs.[4]

Father Jean-Baptiste Genin traveled through Minnesota and North Dakota with the Teton Sioux, enduring the hardships and poverty incident to that life. He had a mission flag, a snow-white banner with a blood-red cross in the center. The Indians adopted Father Genin's ensign as their nation's flag. In 1868, on a bluff on the south side of Devil's Lake, Father Genin erected a cross. The bluff is the exact shape of a heart, and the mission was known as the Sacred Heart. Once a year he journeyed to that spot, held mass, baptized infants, and received those of proper age into the Church. He was often seen in the hay-field pitching hay, or at the work-bench plane in hand, dressed in his robe.

Some of the other Jesuit missionaries must have differed with Father De Smet on the manner of working for the Indians. Father

---

[4] Gilbert J. Garraghan, "Nicolas Point, Jesuit Missionary in Montana of the Forties," in James F. Willard and Colin B. Goodykoontz, editors, The Trans-Mississippi West (Boulder, Col., 1930), pp. 43-56.

De Smet baptized hundreds, apparently without long periods of instruction. At the Laramie council of 1851 he baptized 1,133 children of the various tribes, and 1,586 during the succeeding two months. On the other hand, at about the same time Father Point stated that he could have baptized many, but that their desires were not sufficiently imbued with the true principles of religion. Apparently he did not even baptize children unless there was some danger of death from sickness or a reasonable prospect of their being reared as Christians. Father Van Quickenborne, among the Kickapoo Indians, wrote to his superior: "It is one thing to come to the Indian mission and another thing to convert the Indians."

Often when the missionary moved in among the wild Indians, the untutored children of the forest were very curious and intensely interested in every move on the part of the missionary family. Many had never seen a white woman before, and in accordance with Indian custom they walked right into the house and made themselves at home. They looked at the woman's clothes, felt of the cooking utensils, and thoroughly examined everything about the premises. The missionary family was continually under observation. These simple, childlike savages even wanted to watch the missionaries undress and go to bed and dress again in the morning.

After breakfast the mission family had prayers with the few who cared to attend. There was work then for both the man and his wife, to care for the sick and visit among the lodges. When the missionary had won the confidence of the Indians, they entrusted him with a host of duties. He took care of their things while they went on a hunting-trip. He helped the agent or did some of his work when that official was absent. In fact, he almost took the place of an agent in villages away from the agency, buying things for the Indians and looking after their welfare. In addition to this work, there were often near-by whites to be reclaimed to the church, and he had the task of general supervision of the mission

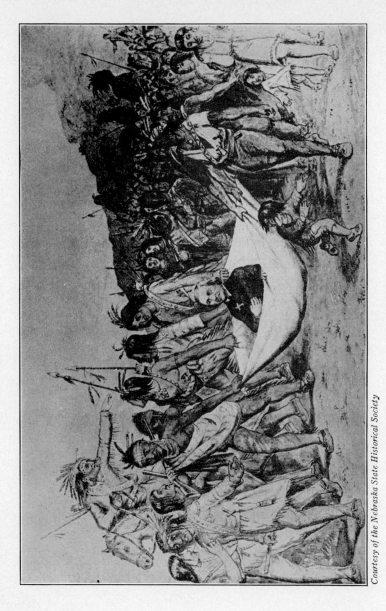

THE MISSIONER'S WELCOME

Father De Smet Welcomed by the Indians.

plant. By precept and example the missionary tried to encourage sewing, cooking, and the cultivation of crops. Isaac McCoy, the well-known Baptist missionary, was especially firm in his contention that candidates for the Indian missions should be of the type who liked to do manual labor. If the missionary hired his work done, it only confirmed the Indian in his ideas that labor was disreputable.[5]

Samuel Pond described a day in a missionary's life for his mother:

It is now sabbath morning but a sabbath morning here is not like a sabbath morning in Washington. One Indian has been here to borrow my axe another to have me help him split a stick—(another now interupts me. He wants to borrow a hatchet) another has been after a trap which he left with me, another is now before my window at work with his axe, while the women and children are screaming to keep the blackbirds out of their corn. Again I am interupted by one who tells me that the Indians are going to play ball near our house today hundreds assemble on such occasions. What a congregation for a minister of Christ to preach to! But alas! so far as I know the "glad tidings" of salvation never sounded in the ears of a Dah-co-tah; yet I cannot but hope that some will be gathered into the fold of Christ even from among this wild and savage nation.

One of the chief activities at a mission station was the conduct of a school. From 1819 until 1832 education was largely in the hands of the missionary societies. The societies appointed certain persons among their number to teach, and the salary due the individual for this work went into the hands of the mission. The funds under the act of 1819 were thus in reality a subsidy to the missionary societies. In 1832 the Secretary of War announced the policy of distributing the Civilization Fund in such a way as to educate the Indians but grant no part of it to the support of missions. The regulations required a separation of school and mission

[5] Isaac McCoy, *Remarks on the Practicability of Indian Reform, Embracing Their Colonization* (New York, 1829), p. 55.

accounts in the annual reports. The regulations of the next year required agents accompanied by Army officers or others to visit the Indian schools annually. This attempt to secularize control of education failed to make any change in the practical working of the schools. When the Indian service looked for teachers, there were none to be found in the Indian country, and the authorities had to appeal to the religious groups. During the thirties and forties government coöperation with the missionary societies remained similar to that in the twenties.

School was often begun in an Indian lodge or a room in a log hut which was used until a building was erected. For various reasons it was difficult to secure the attendance of the pupils, and the authorities, as an attraction, were accustomed to give the boys and girls their dinner every day. Sometimes they were coaxed to attend by offers of cakes, sweetmeats, or raisins. On one occasion the Indians at a mission in Nebraska went on a strike for white bread. Missionary Jerome C. Berryman had ninety primitive, untaught Kickapoo children, not one of whom understood a word of English, nor had they so much as seen a book. He soon discovered that it was an impossible task to teach such a large number one at a time, and he rigged up a box-like apparatus with letters in it. This was placed at the front of the room, and by pulling a string over a pulley the teacher was able to present the letters of the alphabet one by one at an opening provided for the purpose. The school was divided into classes of reasonable size, and each group formed in a semicircle in front of the machine. The teacher took his seat at a convenient distance and exhibited each letter singly at the opening. Within two days all knew their letters. In general, the subjects taught in these day schools were reading, spelling, writing, arithmetic, plain sewing, and knitting.

Owing to the migratory habits of the Indians, they often were not near the mission except during corn-growing season in the summer. Even during the latter part of the season older children were kept out of school to keep the blackbirds away from the corn-fields. In the autumn came the buffalo hunt, and perhaps the Indians wintered away from the mission. Even if they returned after the autumn hunt, attendance at the day school was intermittent, and the home influence often outweighed the civilizing work of the school. As a solution to this problem, boarding-schools were urged.

Often during the forties and fifties the treaties with the Indians made provision for manual-labor training-schools. An allowance of $75 per year for each pupil was granted from 1856 until the Civil War. In 1863 the Friends Shawnee Manual Labor School, because of increased prices due to the war, made an agreement with the Shawnee tribe setting the figure at $31.25 per student for each quarter of the school year. Owing to the good crops in 1867, the school made a thousand dollars. In 1850, when the Friends Shawnee School was at its height, there were in attendance 56 Indians of both sexes between the ages of eighteen and twenty-four. That year the big boys had been employed splitting rails and doing other farm work. Sixty acres had been cleared of brush, and 550 rods of fence had been made. Six hundred bushels of wheat and oats had been threshed, 100 fruit-trees set out, 84 pounds of wool spun, 42 yards of linsey-woolsey woven for blankets, a large number of pairs of stockings and socks knit, and 230 garments made up, besides other garments taken in and made for whites and Indians.[6]

The Methodist Shawnee Manual Labor School, in Kansas near the present site of Kansas City, had 600 acres in cultivation with grist- and sawmills. There were 100 students in attendance from half a dozen neighboring tribes.

Because they were unused to restraint at home, school discipline proved irksome to the pupils and a real task for the teachers, especially out of the school-room and in the winter when the children could not play out-of-doors. A roomful of lively children,

<hr>

[6] Rayner Wickersham Kelsey, *Friends and Indians, 1655-1917* (Philadelphia, 1917), pp. 150-157.

jabbering in an unknown tongue, was trying indeed to the teachers. At the Delaware Mission, in Kansas, the teachers wanted to get away from corporal punishment as much as possible and resorted to ingenious methods of discipline. To keep the little ones from annoying one another, they sometimes pinned aprons over their heads, blindfolded them, or tied their hands behind them. If they talked too much, a chip was placed between the teeth. Quarrelsome boys were made to stand on the two- or three-foot stumps around the house, living statues adorning the grounds.

When the children came to the boarding-school, the induction procedure was rigorous. The lady in charge of this matter at one mission asked if the applicants had had a bath before they came. If they answered in the affirmative, she examined their ears. If they did not stand inspection, she put a wash-boiler of water on and they were given a bath. A few from civilized homes came clean and dressed neat and tidy. Others were given a clean outfit of clothes, were bathed, and had their heads looked over. This latter process was known to the boys as "buffalo hunting." In order that none of the game might escape and that the hunting might be easy, the hair was kept short and the heads were subjected to an inspection every morning but Sunday. Both boys and girls liked to braid their hair and plait it with gay ribbons. The loss of this ornamentation was a great sacrifice indeed. One day a young woman fresh from the East was watching while a veteran missionary combed out a child's hair. The newcomer finally said to her companion, "Do you ever get lice in your hair?" "Certainly," replied the veteran. "We never pass a term without them." The young woman thought to herself, "Can I ever come to this?" [7]

When the children came to school at the Harmony Mission in Missouri, they were given names of patrons or friends of the mission. The rules called for the teacher to start the boys to work

[7] Clara Gowing, "Life Among the Delaware Indians," see Kansas State Historical Society *Collections*, Vol. XII, pp. 185, 186.

at sunrise and after an hour's labor allow a recess until eight o'clock. They were then to labor until the school session opened. In the afternoon they were to labor one hour in addition to their school work. The teacher was to keep a record of the manner of labor, with the idea of offering premiums for punctuality and faithfulness.

There were many hardships for the missionary to endure. Sometimes there were long journeys to make. Missionary Boutwell, on a journey with the Indian agent during the summer of 1832, mentioned in his diary that he traveled 16 hours a day in a cramped position with wet feet and legs and amidst "musketoes" in hordes. From time to time a portage had to be negotiated on foot. The entry for July 13 mentions that they took all their effects on their backs and to begin with entered a swamp. These occasional low places were so low, he said, that "a man only finds bottom when he finds himself to his middle in mud." Father Christian Hoecken, missionary to the Pottawattomies in western Iowa, wrote:

Many a time I was lost in the immense prairies, was obliged to ride from morning until night, and from one day to another without rest or nourishment. I have at times been so much as fourteen days without sleeping. Often have I tarried in the midst of winter in a tent without fire, and with no other bed than a blanket and my saddle for a pillow. Sometimes on rising in the morning, I would find the ground frozen to my back.

One missionary traveled on foot one year about three thousand miles. At one time Father De Smet wrote he had to live on acorns and wild roots for over a month.

One can hardly picture the extreme loneliness and privations of the bride who left her New England home to give her life to the work of carrying the Gospel to the Indians. Mrs. John Gill Pratt bore seven children in the wilderness with no medical aid or care other than what her husband could give on such an occasion. She remarked, however, that the "sacrifices and inconveniences were forgotten by us when we considered the great object for which we lived and labored—the conversion of the Indians and their advancement to civilization."

Father Van Quickenborne wrote from St. Mary's Mission: "We live here as it were, out of the world." Father De Smet, among the Pottawattomies near Council Bluffs, gave expression to the same feeling of loneliness:

We who are at the end of the world ... look forward to letters as a real treat. If you only knew the joy they bring, I am sure every one of you would give us this consolation and support, for after reading our letters we are filled with renewed zeal.[8]

Sometimes three or four Indians would gather around Mrs. Pratt's fireplace before she was dressed in the morning. Among some tribes the Indians begged or stole everything they could lay their hands on. At the Lac Qui Parle Mission, in Minnesota, a woman came to beg clothes, and when she was gone the paring-knife had disappeared. A towel hanging on the wall would be tucked under the blanket of a woman, or a girl would sidle up to a stand and take the scissors. When one family was all alone, sometimes it was unsafe for the man to go away and leave his wife for fear she might come to harm. The wild young men occasionally became very arrogant and quarrelsome. In 1839 the Otoes became so ugly while Mr. Merrill was away that his wife, the hired man, and some neighbors locked themselves in the cabin at night and awaited in alarm an expected attempt to murder them.

The five-year-old Sandy Lake (Methodist) Mission was completely broken up by lawless Indians led by a half-breed who boasted he would drive all the missionaries out of the country. The Indians, stirred up by traders and in a half-drunken state, broke the window-panes, shot the domestic animals, poisoned one of the children, threatened the family, struck the missionary, and kept the mission family in terror and suspense for days. Finally the

[8] Frank Anthony Mullin, "Father De Smet and the Pottawattomie Indian Mission," see *Iowa Journal of History and Politics*, Vol. XXIII, p. 212.

strain and worry from the danger grew so great that they gathered up what few possessions they could take in a canoe and abandoned the station. Making their way to a neighboring station, they were thankful, indeed, to find a haven of refuge.[9]

Of all the problems of the missionary, whisky was the worst. The Indians who had never been in close contact with the whites did not drink. It was the universal testimony of missionaries that the low class of white men debauched the Indians and caused their degraded condition. After they had once got a taste for liquor, they would sell anything they owned for the sake of a drunken orgy. At first the Cheyennes would not touch liquor, but white traders persuaded them to drink a little of it diluted with sugar and water, and in a few years they were a tribe of drunkards. When the Otoes succeeded in trading a pony for five gallons of whisky, they had a spree in their village as long as it lasted. Four reliable men of the camp were selected as soldiers. Their duty was to keep every gun, knife, arrow, and other weapon out of reach. Should anyone become dangerous, he was to be tied fast to a tree until he became sober. In order that the liquor might be evenly divided, it was measured out. The tribe had no measuring cup, and so one man with an average-sized mouth served as measure. He filled his mouth with liquor and emptied it in a cup held by one of the men. It was then served to one of the circle. This was kept up until the entire quantity had been consumed. Unfortunately the measuring mouth leaked and the owner got dead drunk, so another was selected. When enough of the group sobered up to ensure safety, the four soldiers were given their share. The next day the women celebrated while they consumed their portion. They presented a far more disgusting scene than the men. Nearly all of them went on the war-path and pulled hair and bit one another to such an extent that nearly all had to be tied. The missionaries tried their best to put an end to these debauches. They

[9] Samuel Spotes to David Brooks, October 30, 1855, Akers Mss., in North Dakota State Historical Society Library.

preached against liquor, organized temperance societies, secured signatures to temperance pledges, and in every conceivable way fought the evil.

Among the Pottawattomies Father F. Verruydt organized an antiliquor brigade. A little later his charges at the Sugar Creek Mission, in Kansas, passed stringent blue laws anticipating the later Kansas prohibition disposition, forbidding drunkenness, libertinism, and card-playing. Shortly afterward the tribe built a prison to punish offenders. In spite of all efforts, however, the missionary fought a losing fight against the unscrupulous men who furnished the liquor and against the appetite of the primitive race.

There were a few unmarried missionaries of both sexes among the Protestants. These occasionally married in the Indian country. Boutwell, as has been mentioned, married a half-breed girl from one of the mission schools. Women missionaries had plenty of offers of marriage from Indian chiefs, and occasionally one married an army officer or employee of some business concern on the frontier.

Along the Kansas border in the thirties and forties missionaries got together in a sort of interdenominational convention to discuss mission work. This gave an opportunity for the lonely mission workers to associate with those of their own kind, forget their isolation for a time, and return to their work with renewed vigor. Friendships were formed at these gatherings, and now and then visitors from another station would call. On one occasion a certain Brother Fuller from the Union Mission near Fort Gibson visited Harmony, and after a whirlwind courtship of five days he and Sister Howall were married. The bride mounted a pony behind her new-found husband, and they started on their honeymoon over the prairies to their future home. Threatened by a heavy rain that night, the groom made a bridal chamber of a blanket spread in the form of a shed over which were placed leaves from a sycamore tree. With a large fire in front of this shelter, they seated themselves and after offering up thanksgiving to God sang hymns.

For their evening meal they roasted meat on sticks and ate it with their fingers.

In some instances groups of Catholic sisters became missionaries to the Indians. When four Sisters of the Sacred Heart came to the Sugar Creek Mission in July, 1841, Indian messengers met them a day's journey away, telling them the whole tribe was assembled to greet the holy women of the Great Spirit. The next day the tribe met them and escorted them to the church, where a reception was held.

The missionary often identified himself fully with the frontier in dress. Far from markets and with little or no cash to buy clothing made in the East, the missionary found it the most natural thing to wear apparel made of skins, similar to that of the Indian. The diary of Missionary Samuel M. Irvin reveals that he spent three days making a buckskin coat. He wore buckskin pantaloons also.

It was hoped that the Indians could be induced to settle down and till the soil. Eastern people sent fruit-trees, vines, and seeds of all sorts. The missionary planted these and also raised domestic animals. Reverend Jotham Meeker, while attending to his many duties, found time to make beehives and transfer the bees from bee trees to his hives, thus starting one of the earliest apiaries in Kansas.[10] The St. Mary's Mission among the Pottawattomies in 1851 had a wood cathedral and two schools, one for the girls in charge of the community of the Sacred Heart and the other for boys. This mission was in the fifties a center of scientific farming. The superintendent was in reality director of a bonanza farm, a breeder of live stock, the introducer of new machinery, and a contractor selling hay and beef to the Army. He also served as a sort of county agent in adopting the latest farming methods and disseminating them to the neighborhood. He ordered clubs of the best farm journals for himself and others.

[10] Jotham Meeker, *Daily Journal*, September 10, 1832–January 4, 1855, Ms., Kansas State Historical Society Library, Vol. I, pp. 106, 108, 127, 166.

At times there was pleasant coöperation among the denominations, but at other times there was considerable friction and jealous zeal was displayed. Some missionaries were sent out by individual denominations, some by associations of an interdenominational character, and occasionally a self-supporting missionary appeared in the field. The Pond brothers, converted in a revival at a small town in Connecticut, resolved to give their lives to Indian work. Arrived in the Indian country, they carried their resolution into effect by becoming independent missionaries for a time. Later the American Board of Commissioners for Foreign Missions gave them appointments.

There was a wide variation in salaries, some missionaries receiving during the thirties and forties from three to four hundred dollars a year, while others worked for their room and board. Oftentimes friends in the East sent boxes of clothing and food-supplies to a mission, designating what was to be kept by the mission family and what was to be given to the aborigines. In 1844 Jotham Meeker received what he estimated to be thirteen hundred dollars' worth of goods, of which two hundred was to be kept by his family.

Sometimes the missionaries made trips through the East soliciting money and arousing interest in missions. Thomas S. Williamson wrote that he had begged nearly enough money to have some books published in the Dacotah language. Frequently the missionaries wrote articles to be published in Eastern church papers, telling about the work and particularly calling attention to special works of grace. When an Indian gave up his pagan treasures, such as his ear-braid or necklace, or cut off his scalp-lock as a sign that he was giving up the war-path, the trophies were sent East.

Education was really needed among the Christian people in the East, as there was abysmal ignorance of conditions in the West. Even the mission authorities were woefully uninformed as to the problems confronting the missionary in the field. To illustrate this point, one candidate was told that, because of the lack of a definite plan, upon moving into his new field he was not to build a home but should rent a tenement till definite plans went through. One can well imagine the awakening of a new missionary who tried to carry out these instructions upon arriving in the wilds hundreds of miles from the nearest white habitation except that of an occasional fur-trader or Indian agent.

Sickness, especially the ague, was rife on the whole frontier. Of the forty members of the Harmony group not one escaped. Two died, and at times there was not one person well enough to write in the mission journal. Missionary Irvin had to pull two of his wife's teeth, a trying ordeal but inescapable as they were miles from any dentist.[11]

As soon as the missionary mastered the language and started a school, the next thing was to get some books in the language of the Indians. Translation was drudgery. After Stephen Riggs had finished translating the Golden Rule, "Whatsoever ye would that men should do to you, do ye even so to them," he said it was far too difficult for the Indians to grasp. If it were paraphrased according to their economy they could understand it: "You don't want anyone to rip your tent nor kill your hog, and so you must cut up no one's tent nor kill anyone's hog." Jotham Meeker did the first printing in Kansas in 1834, and by means of this new system of writing, which could be used with any language, he was able to publish literature for a number of the tribes. In 1835 he issued 6,600 pieces of literature in seven languages and a monthly newspaper called the *Shawanoe Sun*.[12]

The continual and irrepressible force exerted on the Indians to push them ever westward was a death-blow to the fruitful development of missions. As long as the domain of the Indian was a good hunting-ground untouched by settlement, he could not be persuaded to settle down to the humdrum business of farming. But

[11] Samuel M. Irvin, *Diary*, Ms., Kansas State Historical Society Library, January 28, 1841.
[12] *Baptist Missionary Magazine*, Twenty-Second Annual Report, June, 1836, p. 130.

at the moment settlement drew near and it seemed the Indian would be obliged to take up agricultural pursuits, the white people removed him to a new untamed region, leaving the mission station, which had taken years to develop, standing amidst the land that was quickly settled by white people. Within five years after Harmony Mission was founded, the Osage Indians whom it served were moved farther west so that the nearest boundary of their reservation was more than fifty miles from the mission. Often the missionaries moved with the Indians, setting up new stations and repeating the former process with indifferent success. For this reason and others, many stations were abandoned. The Presbyterians established and abandoned not less than five mission stations between 1819 and 1836.

It was hard, indeed, to distinguish between white men, and somehow in the back of the savage mind lurked the idea that at heart the trader and the missionary were of the same mold. Then, too, it was a bit hard for the untutored savage to appreciate the type of generosity of the white race which offered him the consolation of its religion in exchange for the hunting-grounds of his ancestors.

The missionary had an important part in settling the country. The civilizing influence that he exerted on the red man reduced the wild tribes to comparatively harmless "tame Indians" and opened the way for the home-seeker. Furthermore, the continual propaganda for mission funds, together with the information concerning the climate and the fertility of the soil, furnished by the needy missionary, proved to be excellent ammunition in the hands of speculators and others interested in booming a region soon to be opened to settlement.

CHAPTER VI

THE SOURCE OF BULLETS

AMONG the other rich resources of the United States were lead deposits. This metal, of greater importance to the pioneer than gold itself, was to be found along the Mississippi River in two general regions. The Missouri mines were located about sixty miles southwest of St. Louis and the Fever River mines were located on the Upper Mississippi in the region where the present states of Iowa, Illinois, and Wisconsin adjoin. From this metal Galena, Illinois, and Mineral Point, Wisconsin, get their names. Dubuque, Iowa, is named after an early lead miner.

The Missouri lead region was the first of the two to be worked by Americans. As early as 1719 a Frenchman by the name of Renault organized a company to exploit these mines. Leaving France in that year with two hundred artificers and their tools, he proceeded to Santo Domingo, where he purchased five hundred slaves, and arrived at the lead area in 1720. He opened up the mines of Potosi and St. Francis. He remained in the wilds for some years, returning to France in 1742. The greater part of the workmen returned with him, and the slaves were sold.[1] About 1720 M. La Motte, acting under the authority of the Company of the West, discovered the famous La Motte mine.[2] Then for a time little was done with the mines, but about 1779 the Mine a' Burton was discovered. These early mines were very crudely worked. Not more than fifty per cent of the lead was extracted from the ore by means of the open log furnace, and the lead ashes

[1] Henry Rowe Schoolcraft, *View of the Lead Mines of Missouri* (New York, 1819), pp. 15-17.
[2] *Ibid.*, p. 167.

145

were thrown away. Nevertheless some of the lead used by the patriot army during the Revolutionary War no doubt came from that region.

Great improvements were made at the turn of the century when Moses Austin, later a founder of Little Rock, Arkansas, and an opener of Texas to American colonization, arrived in the lead region from the lead mines of Wythe County, Virginia, and, obtaining a Spanish grant, began to work the Mine a' Burton. In 1798 he erected a reverberatory furnace. He sank the first shaft for raising the ore and introduced other improvements. In 1799 he erected a shot-tower and also began the manufacture of sheet lead.[3]

Shortly after the American purchase of Louisiana the interior parts of the country were explored, and several rich discoveries of large bodies of lead ore near the surface brought riches to the discoverers and fame to the region. This attracted to the country a large number of floaters, many of whom were the most abandoned characters. The mining area soon became the scene of every disorder, depravity, and crime, and a rendezvous for renegades. Many of the mines were discovered by these questionable characters, and soon strife arose over discoveries and claims.

Custom established certain rules among the miners which minimized the number of disputes. According to these rules, a person making a discovery was entitled to claim the ground for 25 feet in each direction from his pit. This gave him a plot 50 feet square. Other diggers were allowed only 12 feet square, which was just enough on which to sink a pit and throw the earth out. Each man measured off his plot, and though he might not begin digging for several days, the others respected his rights. The miner was then allowed to dig straight down, but he was not allowed to run drifts horizontally which would break into or undermine the pits of others. If a claimant abandoned a mine as worthless or unprofitable, he had the right to go onto unoccupied

[3] *Ibid.*, p. 19.

ground and begin anew. His abandoned mine was then open to the claim of a second occupant, who through greater industry or persistence sometimes struck rich bodies of ore.

Not many years after the purchase of Louisiana, in order to serve the public interest and remedy the irregularities practised in the region, Congress passed a law reserving all lead mines, salt springs, etc., that should be discovered on the public lands after the passage of the act. This act, however, was not adequately enforced.

When the noted Indian agent Henry R. Schoolcraft visited the region on an exploring expedition in 1819, he reported that the mining territory occupied a district between the waters of the St. Francis and the Meramec about forty miles west of the Mississippi River and sixty miles southwest of St. Louis. The mining area, according to Schoolcraft, was about one hundred miles in length and about forty in breadth. At that time about forty mines were being worked. Although the depression of 1819 had caused a decrease in employment, there had been employed prior to this date a thousand men in Mine a' Burton alone.

The method of raising ore and the processes employed in separating the metal were extremely simple. Pickaxe and shovel were the only tools used for excavation. A drill, rammer, and priming-rod were the simple additional devices used when blasting was necessary. Having determined on a spot for digging, the miner measured off his plot of ground and, throwing out the earth, gravel, and spar, sank his shaft as deep as possible by hand. A practised hand was able to pitch the dirt clear out of the pit from a depth of twelve to fifteen feet. Below that an ordinary windlass and bucket such as were used for well-digging were employed. The finding of an occasional lump of ore or a body of spar encouraged the miner to continue digging to a great depth. If all signs failed, however, he reluctantly abandoned his pit and began at another place. Some miners in searching for ore took notice of the lay of the land, the trees, and the outcroppings, but in general there was the greatest disposition to trust to blind luck and pure chance in stumbling upon ore rather than to any scientific formula or the use of any knowledge of geology.

Naturally this type of work called for labor, and slavery was apparently introduced into the region at an early period of the American occupation. Many of the slaves became expert blacksmiths, carpenters, and other skilled craftsmen.

When sufficient ore had been raised for smelting, the next process was that of separating the spar and cleaning all extraneous matter from the galena, the native sulphide in which the lead was combined. Small pickaxes with delicate points were used to detach the tiniest particles of adhering spar. The larger masses were then broken up and all the lumps of galena brought to a fairly uniform size. It was desirable that they should be about the size of a man's two fists, or about fifteen pounds in weight. If some of the lumps were too large, the heat for driving off the sulphur could not operate equally. If they were too small, there was a waste in smelting.

The ore was processed in what was known as the log furnace. It was of very simple construction, consisting of an inclined hearth surrounded by walls, with an open top and an arched opening for the admission of air at the bottom of the lower end. The whole structure was built of stone for from fifty to sixty dollars. The largest item in its cost was the wages of the mason, who could not be hired for less than two dollars a day in that region. The furnace was always built on the slope of a hill, and two were usually built together in order to utilize one wall in common. Then, too, a double-eyed furnace could be tended by the same number of hands required for a single one.

In charging the furnace, oak logs were rolled into it and split logs were set up around the sides. Ore was dumped in until the furnace was full. About five thousand pounds was put in at a charge. Then more logs were piled on until the ore was completely covered with wood. It took three hands to man the smelter—

one to cart wood during the daytime, the other two to relieve each other alternately every twelve hours at the furnace.

When all was ready, the fire was lighted at the arched mouth, and the ore was heated gradually. It was kept at a moderate roasting heat for twelve hours while the sulphur was eliminated, and then the heat was raised for the purpose of smelting the ore. The whole process was completed in from twelve to twenty-four hours more. Wood was added occasionally as the process went on. At a certain spot in the back wall a sharp iron bar was driven and when it was withdrawn the molten lead flowed into a large iron pot. It was then laded into iron molds yielding pigs of lead of about fifty pounds each. A high degree of skill was necessary to get the best results. The correct amount of fuel and the proper regulation of the draft were highly important. The furnaces more expertly operated extracted a much higher percentage of lead than the others.

When the furnace had cooled, it was cleaned out and the whole operation was begun again. About fifty per cent of the lead was recovered at the first smelting. A considerable proportion of the ore for one reason or another did not get processed properly. Small pieces often dropped down between the logs and failed to get roasted thoroughly. Other lumps were too large and failed to be desulphurized or were melted together into a slag. This residue, known as the lead ashes, was put through yet another process in what was called the ash furnace.

The ash furnace, also built of limestone at a cost of about a hundred dollars, would run one blast of from fifteen to thirty days. During this time it would turn out from sixty to ninety thousand pounds of lead. The lead ashes were reckoned to yield a further fifteen per cent of metal, which, added to the first smelting, made an average recovery of sixty-five per cent.[4]

Lead in the pig sold for $4.00 a hundredweight at the mines in February, 1819. It brought $4.50 on the Mississippi River, $5.50

[4] *Ibid.*, pp. 103-104.

at New Orleans, and was quoted at $6.00 at Philadelphia. This was an extremely low figure, accounted for only by the fact that it was at the depth of the panic of 1819.

Division of labor early appeared, and the merchants began to buy ore (from those who chose to dig) and smelt it in quantities. The miner received $2.00 for every hundred pounds properly cleaned. The ordinary hand raised that amount on the average each day.

The lead was hauled in carts and wagons the thirty to fifty miles of abominable road to Herculaneum and St. Genevieve on the river. In the vicinity of Herculaneum there were three shot-towers where shot was made by letting molten lead drop from a cliff overlooking the Mississippi River. At that point the limestone bank of the river overhangs slightly at the top. On this overhanging bank a building was constructed, the lead was melted in an iron pot in the upper part of the building, and the liquid was poured through a sieve made by punching holes the size of the shot desired in a copper pan. The globules of metal hardened sufficiently during the drop to keep their shape. At the foot of the cliff was a cistern of water which caught the shot and cooled them. One man could cast from four to five thousand pounds in a day, but to polish this amount required nine days. This finish was achieved by putting a quantity of the shot in a wooden vessel or barrel, fixing it on a shaft, and turning it by a crank. The friction of the shot against one another converted them into perfect spheres.

A village of some thirty buildings had sprung up at the mines by 1819. In its attempt to be cultured, this wild, straggling frontier community had laid off a tract of forty acres in the center of the mining district for a grand county-seat, named it Potosi, and erected a court-house decorated with Grecian columns of the Doric order. Manufacturing of products other than lead was beginning. Tan-yards, flouring-mills, distilleries, salt-works, sawmills, and a powder-mill had begun crude operations in the lead region.

In St. Genevieve in 1817 there were three hundred and fifty

houses, an academy, and eight or ten stores. The walls of the larger proportion of the houses were made of mud and were whitened with lime. The region was not in very good repute in the eyes of travelers, who reported that the workmen were continually engaged in brawls and quarrels and the proprietors were frequently at odds. Nearly everyone carried a concealed dagger— sometimes two, one in the bosom and another under the coat— while others had a brace of pistols in the girdle at the back. A traveler named Schultz was astonished on more than one occasion when he saw a dagger fall out of the bosom or out of the girdle while the owner was dancing with a lady. The ladies did not betray any uneasiness at this sudden and unexpected exposure of "murderous and assassin-like weapons." Even during court session everybody was armed, some with pistols at the back under their coats, and nearly all with dirk knives "peeping from their bosoms." According to an observer, even the judges on the bench had their pistols and attaghans by their sides.

On one occasion, when one of Daniel Boone's salt-boilers who had risen to some political prominence appointed a justice of the peace and was asked what qualifications the appointee had for the position, the budding statesman gave the all-sufficient answer that his protégé was handy with a gun.

One of the leading amusements of this wild, half-savage wilderness population was shooting at a mark with rifles and pistols. These weapons were forged by hand by a backwoods blacksmith and his two slaves.

Lawyers, medical men, merchants, officers in civil and military authority, and Indian traders all played cards and bet liberally. At St. Genevieve one ball followed another in the winter social season, opening at candle-lighting time and lasting until ten or twelve the next day. Mary Eastin, in a letter to her father dated from St. Louis on September 28, 1816, stated that at Mrs. Peebles' tavern "everyone pays $1.50, and is admitted to eat tough pancakes and dance as long as they please."

Schoolcraft reported in 1819 that the government had not derived any lease money from the land that had been reserved by law a dozen years or more before. In true frontier style the miners had dashed into the region, squatted on the reserved government land, and proceeded to exploit it. The more responsible men had not bothered about leasing land because the short-period lease did not allow them time to equip the mines and realize anything from the investment before the lease terminated and jeopardized their possession. On Schoolcraft's recommendation, apparently, an official was stationed at the lead mines to supervise the leasing of the ore-bearing lands, to collect the royalty and in general to look after the government's interests.

In the meantime the Fever River or Upper Mississippi mining region had begun to attract attention. As early as 1690 lead deposits had been discovered on a tributary of the Mississippi by a Frenchman named Nicholas Perrot. It is supposed that his discovery was on the site of present-day Dubuque. At any rate, the principal center of mining activity from 1788 to 1810 was the Dubuque mines on the west bank of the Mississippi, nearly opposite the line separating Illinois from Wisconsin. Here Julien Dubuque used their friendship to gain a powerful influence over the Sac and Fox tribes who owned the Upper Mississippi lead region. In 1788 he obtained from the council of the tribes permission to dig lead in the district where Dubuque is now located. He hired the Indians to dig the ore and disposed of the lead at St. Louis. When Zebulon Pike passed that way on his tour of exploration in 1805, Dubuque told him the mines produced from twenty thousand to forty thousand pounds of lead a year. The wily Frenchman must have hidden the true amount, however, for in 1811, the year after Dubuque's death, the Indians, without his direction, sold to the traders five hundred thousand pounds of lead which they had produced in the Dubuque mines.[5]

[5] Joseph Schafer, "The Wisconsin Lead Region," *Wisconsin Domesday Book* (Madison, Wis., 1932), p. 28.

For a number of years the Indian women scooped out the lead ore from near the grass-roots with stone picks, bone spades, wooden shovels, rifle barrels formed into crowbars, and an occasional white man's tool. Others worked the old mines of Dubuque, carrying baskets of ore out of the pits on inclined walks. This they either smelted themselves in crude log furnaces such as the primitive furnace of the white man or bartered to the traders for goods.[6] The Indians did not enjoy their monopoly indefinitely.

During 1826 and the years following there was a boom in the lead-mining business. A large number of men rushed into the Upper Mississippi region. Whereas in 1825 there were 100 men in the Fever River district as compared with 2,000 engaged in the lead business in Missouri, by August, 1826, there were 453. In 1826 the production of the Upper Mississippi mines was 428 tons as compared with 1,343 tons for the Missouri mines. In 1829 the Upper Mississippi mines had far outstripped Missouri, producing 5,957 tons to the latter's 1,867 tons.[7]

In Iowa, as previously in Missouri, the miners met in 1830 and decided how much land a miner could claim. These earlier comers were a bit more generous with themselves than the Missouri rules allowed. They voted each miner the right to hold an area of ground 200 yards square by working the claim one day in six. The rules furthermore provided for an arbitrator elected by the whole group to settle disputes between claimants. His award was to be final when the claimants sought his services. This was some improvement over the custom of 1819 in Missouri, where dueling was the regular thing in the mining regon. The French language was spoken exclusively in many areas. In strange incongruity with their rough and terrible ways, a large percentage of the people in the lead-mining regions belonged to one or other of the religious bodies. The Methodists were the most numerous, al-

---

[6] *Ibid.*, pp. 33-34; Henry Rowe Schoolcraft, *Summary Narrative of an Exploratory Expedition to the Sources of the Mississippi River in 1820* (Philadelphia, 1855), pp. 172-173.

[7] Schafer, "The Wisconsin Lead Region," pp. 30, 36, 37.

though there were many Baptists, and the French were uniformly Catholic. A few years saw great improvement in the decorum and refinement of lead-mining society, but even so, judged by present standards, the men were half-wild denizens of the mines or tenders of smelters, toiling day and night by the light of the flaming furnaces in the little island of settlement surrounded by the virgin wilderness.

The rush of miners into the Upper Mississippi lead region was similar to that into Missouri, with probably more zest because there was a good demand for lead. In many instances men struck rich veins yielding thousands of dollars. Ore was found practically on the surface. Often excavations from three to forty feet deep offered rich prizes. Not infrequently a vein was opened on the side of a hill, a cart backed in, and the mineral shoveled up or wheeled out onto level ground. In valleys and at the foot of cliffs, float mineral was often found in paying quantities. This is what the Indians most often dug.

When a miner struck it rich, he went to St. Louis, or even to Louisville or Cincinnati, and lived on the costliest wines and foods. At this time, when a gold watch was a rare thing, these half-savage men exhibited their primitive character by buying gold watches. Some of the speculators who bought and sold "leads" and thereby made fortunes went off on wild orgies of celebration and led a fast existence for a time. Such men seemed to have a mania for collecting gold watches, some carrying a string of eight or ten. An observer said he heard of one man who had twenty-seven at one time, each with a costly chain, and worth altogether from five to six thousand dollars. In the end these celebrators came back to the mines in rags and with eyes black and faces swollen. That was called being "busted." They went to work, perhaps struck another lead, and once again, with pockets full but no wiser from the former experience, they started off to celebrate once more.

This crude pioneer group holds a place all its own in the annals of the frontier. Although an industrial pursuit, lead mining was truly a frontier episode, for, in the words of William J. Petersen, "fully a decade before the northern half of Indiana and Illinois began to receive settlers, lead miners formed an island of population far beyond the fringe of settlement."

CHAPTER VII

THE ROMANTIC ERA ON WESTERN WATERS

AMONG the outstanding characteristics of the American frontier was that it always advanced most rapidly along waterways. Accordingly the trans-Mississippi streams were the scenes of the earliest thrusts of settlement into the wilderness. Long before the shores were occupied by agrarian settlement, strange craft manned by stranger crews plied up and down western streams under the crudest of frontier conditions. The boatmen formed a distinctive Western type. The canoe, pirogue, bateau or barge, flatboat, bullboat, mackinaw, and keelboat each served in its place before the coming of the steamboat in the first quarter of the nineteenth century.

The simplest western craft was the canoe. This boat, made of birch bark, was a familiar sight on the lakes of the north country, but it was not used much on the trans-Mississippi waters owing to the absence of birch and because the frail craft was no match for the turbulent rivers. The typical river canoe was a dugout made from a cottonwood, walnut, or cedar log from fifteen to twenty feet long and three or four feet in diameter. Such a craft possessed strength and lightness. It required a crew of three, two to propel it with paddles and one to steer. It was universally used for local business and was the most generally employed of all the river craft. It was often used for express messages downriver and occasionally carried freight. Bear oil was an item freighted in canoes on the Missouri. Fats were scarce in St. Louis, and as bears were plentiful on the river above, much bear oil was carried down and used as a substitute for lard. Casks were not available in the wilderness, and since bear oil readily filtered through skin receptacles, the trappers resorted to carrying the commodity loose in the canoe. When the dugout was made, two transverse partitions were left to reinforce the sides of the craft. These were water-tight, and the bear oil was poured into the center compartment of this makeshift tanker, which was covered with a skin drawn tightly over the top and fastened to the sides of the boat. Honey taken from the many bee trees of the forest was carried in the same manner.

In 1811 John Colter descended from the headwaters of the Missouri River to St. Louis in one of these boats in thirty days. Sometimes a square sail was hoisted in the middle of the canoe for use in an aft wind only, since any other would be likely to capsize it.

The pirogue was made of two canoes built in the shape of flatirons with sharp bows and square sterns. These were fastened together some distance apart and floored over with planks or puncheons. The cargo, placed on this deck, was covered with skins. The craft was about thirty or forty feet long and six to twelve feet wide. It had the advantage of being almost impossible to capsize, owing to the broad base formed by the canoes which were placed well apart. The pirogue was propelled upstream by oars or pulled with a rope by men on shore, and was steered by an oarsman who stood on the stern. A square sail also was used in going upstream when the wind was in the right direction. Sometimes a large canoe with square stern was called a pirogue.[1]

The bateau or barge was a flat-bottomed boat clumsily constructed in the shape of a huge box with the square ends given enough rake to prevent impeding headway. It measured from fifty to seventy-five feet in width. Although principally a downstream craft, when taken upstream it was propelled by pole, oar, sail, and line (rope to the shore).

On the Mississippi and its tributary rivers of Iowa and on the lower Missouri the flatboat was used. It has been called the "friend

[1] Hiram Martin Chittenden, *History of Early Steamboat Navigation on the Missouri River* (New York, 1903), Vol. I, pp. 92-94.

of the pioneer," for it provided an outlet for the little produce the early settlers had to trade for the necessities of life. It was often built on his farm by some enterprising pioneer who mustered a crew from the vicinity and undertook to carry the produce of the neighborhood to the market on the river below. Sometimes a group of neighbors associated themselves in a coöperative marketing enterprise. The flatboat was similar in construction to the barge and often had a tent or some other protection built over the perishable goods. Perhaps a pen of pigs, fat steers, or teams of horses gave weight to the clumsy, unwieldy craft, which, with a crew of two or three, drifted ever toward the sea. At night the crew tied up, preferably at an island for better protection, and at the first streak of daylight were on their way once more. At St. Louis, or more likely New Orleans, the produce was sold at the market and the boat itself was sold for fuel or for building material. It is said there were several small towns in the vicinity of New Orleans in the period before the Civil War that were built almost entirely of the lumber from dismantled flatboats. The crew returned to their homes on foot or horseback as a rule, dodging as best they could the outlaws that infested the way, ready to rob them of the returns of their produce.

The backwoods boy who made such a trip as this to the big city with its many sights was more to be envied in the neighborhood and had a bigger story to tell than a man who had been abroad a century later.[2]

As late as the summer of 1870 timber was rafted down the Otter Tail and Frazee rivers in Minnesota to McCauleyville, where some forty flatboats or scows were built and floated down the Red River to Winnipeg.

On the shallow waters of the tributaries of the Upper Missouri the bullboat was used to transport furs downstream. This is not to be confused with the small round single-hide boats the size of a

[2] Seymour Dunbar, *History of Travel in America* (Indianapolis, 1915), Vol. II, pp. 271-272.

tub or larger used by the Mandan Indians. It was about thirty feet long, twelve feet wide, and only twenty inches in depth. The framework was made of willow poles tied together with rawhide. Cross poles tied to gunwales on each side kept the craft from spreading out of shape. This skeleton, constructed without a nail or peg and exceedingly strong, was covered with a continuous sheet of rawhide made from the skin of the buffalo. When the material was all sewed together, it was thoroughly soaked in water, stretched as tightly as possible over the framework, and laced to the gunwales. When the hide dried, it was as tight as a drumhead. The seams were then pitched with a mixture of buffalo tallow and ashes. The bullboat was probably the lightest craft ever built that could transport the cargo it carried. Two men could easily turn it over, and yet it could be loaded with from five to six thousand pounds of furs. The draft of the boat when placed in the water in the morning was about four inches, but as the hide became soaked during the day, it increased to as much as six or eight inches by night. The disadvantage of the craft was that it had to be unloaded every evening when camp was pitched and drawn up on the bank in an inclined position, bottom side up, to dry. If this precaution were not taken, the bullboat, becoming water-logged in a few days, began to rot and leak and was entirely unserviceable long before a voyage of any length was completed. This type of craft was manned by a crew of two, who guided and propelled it on its way downstream by means of poles.[3]

The Mackinaw boat or mackinaw was imported into the West from the Great Lakes. It also was a flat-bottomed vessel made entirely of timber. Before nails were available, the lumber was fastened together with pegs. The boards were sawed by hand, and the boats were sometimes as much as fifty feet long and twelve feet wide. The prow was sharp and the stern square. The keel had about a thirty-inch rake from the bow and from the stern to the

[3] Chittenden, *History of Early Steamboat Navigation on the Missouri River*, Vol. I, pp. 96-101.

bottom. The central part of the boat was partitioned off from the bow and the stern, and between the two water-tight partitions the cargo was loaded and piled up in a rounded form three or four feet above the gunwale, which was low in the middle of the boat. In the bow were seats for the oarsmen, and in the stern an elevated one for the steersman. The crew of five was comprised of four oarsmen and the man at the rudder, who was in charge and was called the "patron." The mackinaw ran fifteen to eighteen hours a day and traveled seventy-five to a hundred and fifty miles. Like the flatboat, it was intended for a single trip downstream with its fifteen tons of freight.

Another craft, known as a yawl, was a flat-bottomed rowboat used in connection with larger boats, such as keelboats or steamboats, for messenger service or short trips.

Of all the craft of any size on the frontier before the era of the steamboat, the keelboat was the most important. It alone of the larger vessels ran both upstream and down. For this general service it was built long and narrow with as little bottom surface to cause friction against the water as possible. From sixty to seventy-five feet long and fifteen to twenty feet wide, it was constructed with a keel from bow to stern. It had a capacity of fifteen to twenty tons, a draft of thirty inches when empty, and it cost from two to three thousand dollars. Keelboats were often built at Pittsburgh, Pennsylvania, by skilled workmen after the most approved plans of the day. The craft was fitted with what was known as a cargo-box, or cabin, which occupied the entire body of the boat except about twelve feet of deck at each end. The cargo-box, whose walls, rising from the hold, slanted inward somewhat, was covered with a slightly convex roof. Running on each side of the cargo-box and around the outer edge of the deck was a narrow walk, which gave the boatmen a complete open circuit of the boat.

Nearly all of the methods of propulsion known to navigation before the advent of the steam-engine were used on the keelboat. About one-third of the length of the boat back from the bow was

KEELBOAT

From a painting by Charles Bodmer, 1833.

a mast rigged with a square sail. When there was sufficient wind in the right direction, the sail alone was used. At other times the boat was towed by men on shore, by means of a line running through a pulley attached to the top of the thirty-foot mast and fastened to the bow so that it could be laid out or drawn in at pleasure. A crew of from twenty to forty men walking in Indian file along the bank pulled on the thousand-foot line attached to the boat. The pilot, or "bosseman" as he was generally called on the Missouri River after the manner of the French boatmen engaged in the fur trade, stood on the bow directing the cordelle men, and with a pole he kept the boat off the shore. The patron, or master of the boat, stood at the rudder on the stern, manipulating it by means of a long lever from the rear of the cargo-box. Cordelling, as this process was called, was the main reliance for motive power up a stream. Fifteen miles a day or even more could be accomplished by this means. If the nature of the bank permitted, horses were sometimes used to tow the boat short distances. Sometimes when an obstacle prevented the men from walking along the bank, the cordelle was made fast to some object beyond and the boat was moved forward by pulling on the line. This process was known as warping.

When trees, tangled underbrush, crumbling banks, or impassable objects prevented cordelling, the crew had to resort to poling. The pole was made of ash wood. On the upper end was a ball or knob for the hollow of the shoulder to push against, and the lower end had a wooden shoe and spike to be placed against the bottom of the river, which prevented the pole from going too deep. A large keelboat required a crew of eighteen for poling. Eight men on each side of the boat took their places on the narrow walk forward. At the command of the patron the men would set their poles and, with their shoulders against the knobs, stooping over so low that they could almost touch the deck with their hands, proceed to "walk" the boat ahead. After walking the length of the boat in this stooping position, at the command "Raise the poles" the men would quickly pull up their poles, run back to the bow, and repeat the operation. It was one continual round of grueling work requiring great muscular strength and stamina.

Just aft of the mast was a pair of heavy sweeps, one on each side of the boat, and at the forward part of the cabin were places for six oars, three on each side. The seats for the rowers were on the inside of the cabin. When the water was too deep for poling, resort was had to the oars. It was frequently necessary to cross from one side of the river to the other, and the oars were used in that event also. Both oars and sweeps were active on the down-stream trip.

On account of the heavily timbered banks, the sail could scarcely be used on the Mississippi and the lower Missouri, but above the mouth of the James River, in present South Dakota, the hundred square feet of sail often gave sufficient power to make headway even against the swift-flowing upper river. No doubt the crew literally prayed for wind. Most of the journey upstream, however, was by means of cordelling, with a goodly portion of poling and rowing thrown in. It was a slow, laborious task at best, and it required most of the season to reach the Upper Missouri from St. Louis. In the spring of 1811 two keelboats, competing craft in the fur trade, raced from St. Louis to the mouth of the Yellowstone, 1,790 miles. The principals were Manuel Lisa and W. P. Hunt, a partner of John Jacob Astor. Hunt had wintered near the present site of St. Joseph, Missouri, on the Nodaway River. On April 2, a month after Hunt went up the river, Lisa left St. Louis, and on June 11 overtook his rival about half-way to the Yellowstone. For sixty-one days he had made an average of eighteen miles a day. This was considered the most remarkable voyage of its time, and it was never beaten on the Missouri by a keelboat.

At this day, when labor has reached a degree of independence unthought of a century and a quarter ago, men could not be persuaded to endure the rigorous toil and hardships of the first decades of the nineteenth century. At daybreak the patron's horn called the crew to the cordelle, and the order of the day from that time till dark was push and pull through sunshine, rain, and storm. Half-bent the boatmen toiled in the water and out, over rocks, through brambles and brush, first on one side of the river and then on the other, pulling against the swift current day after day for six long months, until at last the glistening snows gave assurance that they were nearing their goal.[4]

John C. Luttig, the fur-trader, gave a picture of the tribulations of a particularly troublesome day on the Missouri River in 1812:

Started at 6. in the Morning went ½ Miles but were stopt by hard head wind and Current...started about 1 Mile took the Cordell the Boat swung and went down the River like the Wind in full Speed, leaving all hands on shore, the few, the few which were on Board landed the Boat opposite to our last nights Lodging, our hands came on board made a new start, but night overtook us, got on a sand bar and were very near lost running against a Sawjer had to cross again to the North Side, the other Boat came to close swept by the Current we unshipped our Rudder, run against a tree and brocke her mast, this ended this doleful Day camped at 11. oclock at night distance 1½ Mile...

A quarter of the time that was consumed going up was sufficient to return downstream in the autumn.

Many of the boatmen on the Missouri River were French, St. Louis Creoles, a hard-working, obedient, cheerful, light-hearted, and contented group of men. After an arduous day's toil, they would dance and sing around the camp-fire as though they had been resting during the day and, refreshed, were ready to begin work.

The boatmen's exceedingly plain fare, consisting of pork or game, lyed corn, and navy beans, with no bread of any kind, was cooked at night for the next day on a stove on top of the cargo-box. The stove was set in a shallow box filled with ashes or gravel

4 Philip Edward Chappell, *History of the Missouri River* (Kansas City, Mo., 1911), pp. 56-64.

to protect the cabin roof from fire. The baggage of the men was stored in the front of the cabin, where there was a place for anyone who was sick to lie down. Otherwise the crew slept on the ground wherever the boat was tied up for the night.

On the Mississippi River the keelboatmen probably were largely drawn from the American backwoods hunters, and even on the Missouri before the fur trade reached its peak, there was a generous sprinkling of these men. They were not meek and obedient as were the Creoles, but were wild, unrestrained, and individualistic in the extreme. As a result of the circumstances of their hazardous occupation, they developed a definite frontier type.

In addition to whirlpools, snags, rapids, and other natural hazards of the river, there was constant danger from Indians and outlaws. These factors, together with long absences from civilization in the wilderness, tended to develop a hard and lawless set of men. Richard Edwards wrote that they were "as desperate a set of vagabonds as ever bore the seal of humanity." By an imperative law among themselves they were idlers while on shore, where their chief amusement was shooting at a mark, dancing, fiddling, engaging in rough frolics and fist fights. They frequently played severe and dangerous practical jokes upon one another. With the rifle ball at long distances, they would cut the pipe out of the hatband of a fellow boatman, or unexpectedly upset the cup of whisky that might at lunch time be resting for the moment on a fellow's knee.[5] True it is, they brought rifle marksmanship to perfection. Their deadly aim counted heavily in the Battle of New Orleans. The weapon that had been their companion as hunters was retained in the new vocation. It was always within reach when they were working pole or oar, and a venturesome deer or bear was struck down with unerring aim. In spite of their precision in shooting, their bravado and foolhardy displays of skill sometimes brought trouble. Mike Fink, most famous of the backwoods river-

[5] John C. Van Tramp, *Prairie and Rocky Mountain Adventures, or Life in the West* (Columbus, Ohio, 1866), pp. 96-97.

men, at one time from a great distance shot the protruding heel off a Negro so the victim could, as he explained, "wear a genteel boot."

Occasionally at some landing several crews came together and tried their mettle against one another. When things seemed to be moving along peacefully, perhaps some bellicose fellow, after the manner of a game-cock, would jump onto a conspicuous place and in the spirit of braggadocio roll up his sleeves and utter a challenge. One such speech has been recorded:

I'm from the Lightning Forks of Roaring River. I'm *all* man, save what is wild cat and extra lightning. I'm as hard to run against as a cypress snag—I never back water. Look at me—a small specimen—harmless as an angle worm—a remote circumstance—a mere yearling. Cock-a-doodle—doo! I did hold down a bufferlo bull, and tar off his scalp with my teeth but I can't do it now—I'm too powerful weak, I am.

I'm the man that, single-handed, towed the broadhorn over a sand-bar—the identical infant who girdled a hickory by smiling at the bark, and if anyone denies it, let him make his will and pay the expenses of a funeral. I'm the genuine article, tough as bull's hide, keen as a rifle. I can out-swim, out-swar, out-jump, out-drink, and keep soberer than any man at Catfish Bend. I'm painfully ferocious—I'm spiling for someone to whip me—if there's a creeter in this diggin' that wants to be disappointed in trying to do it, let him yell—whoop hurra!

Such an arrogant challenge was sure to be followed by a primitive backwoods rough-and-tumble fight, in which biting and gouging were legitimate and both victor and vanquished sometimes lost an eye or a portion of an ear or nose.[6]

The first steamboat to run on the Missouri was the *Independence,* which left St. Louis on May 21, 1819, and ran up as far as Franklin. In September of the same year the *Western Engineer* steamed up the river as far as the present city of Omaha, and in the summer of 1820 it was the first to ascend the Mississippi,

[6] C. B. Spotts, "Mike Fink in Missouri," see *Missouri Historical Review,* Vol. XXVIII, October, 1933, pp. 4-5.

going as far as the Des Moines Rapids. This vessel was constructed for an engineering corps which was to explore the West, and it was named the *Western Engineer* in honor of this group. It was designed with the idea of scaring the savages. There arose from its bow an ingenious figurehead fashioned in the shape of a serpent with its head painted black and its tongue a fiery red. The steam escaping from the exhaust was released through this reptilian head, and at intervals its passage created loud wheezing noises and gurglings like the expiring groan of some imaginary sea monster of the long ago. The noise, heard for miles, together with the looks of the creature, filled the natives with terror.[7] The *Virginia* steamed to the mouth of the Minnesota River in 1823, establishing thereby the practicability of navigating the Upper Mississippi by steamboat.

During the decades of the twenties and thirties, the steamboat was largely occupied with the fur trade, and the boats were small, crude, freighting vessels taking trading goods upstream and returning laden with great quantities of furs and hides. Provisions for military posts and goods for Indian treaties and annuities were also carried. The transfer of soldiers from one post to another, the removal of Indian tribes, and the carriage of government explorers also formed important items of traffic during those years. Added to these was the minor business created by Indian delegations visiting Washington or St. Louis, visitors touring the Indian country, missionaries going to or from their posts of duty, the children of those in the Indian country going to school in the East, or others incidentally traveling between the wilderness and civilization. Another source of tonnage on the Mississippi, and indeed by far the most important for some years, was the lead-carrying business from the Dubuque-Galena-Mineral Point area.

As the years passed and emigration into the trans-Mississippi region rose to flood tide, passenger boats multiplied in numbers and increased in size and quality. Since migration ran from east

[7] E. W. Gould, *Fifty Years on the Mississippi* (St. Louis, 1889), pp. 153, 154.

to west, the Missouri reaped the lion's share of this great expansion in business, but the settlement of Iowa and Minnesota greatly increased the traffic on the Mississippi also. The great rush on the Missouri began in 1849, when thousands of gold-seekers sought transportation from St. Louis to the outfitting towns along the Missouri. Soon shipbuilding responded to the demands of traffic, and in the fifties floating palaces were built.

The typical passenger steamer in the heyday of steamboating was about two hundred and fifty feet long, with a thirty-five- or forty-foot beam and a hold six feet deep. It had a full cabin capacity of from three hundred to four hundred people and a freight capacity of from five hundred to seven hundred tons. The boat was well proportioned, symmetrical, trim, and speedy, and she kindled enthusiasm in the breast of the boatman as she sat on the water like a swan, a living thing ready to respond to her crew. Between the two tall smoke-stacks with ornamental tops was usually suspended some gilt letter or device. The *F. X. Aubry*, named for the famous Santa Fe Trail rider, which plied the Missouri during the fifties, bore on her hurricane-deck the figure of a man on horseback riding at full speed. Unlike an ocean vessel, much of which is submerged below the water-line, a river steamer was built flat and drew only three or four feet of water; thus it was almost entirely above the surface and had a much larger appearance than its actual dimensions and tonnage substantiated. But the mammoth craft were the life of the river traffic.

Some of the finer boats had tramways and little flatcars in the hold to aid in stowing away the hundreds of tons of freight. On the main deck were the machinery and boilers, the latter consisting of six or eight horizontal cylinders under which was located a fire-box enclosing a huge fire. Two large smooth-running engines furnished the motive power to turn the immense paddle-wheels, one on each side of the boat. Some boats were propelled by stern-wheels. Around the machinery was a large space reserved for an overflow of cargo. Oftentimes highly inflammable materials stowed near the boilers endangered the craft. A considerable space was reserved for huge ricks of wood used for fuel.

On the saloon deck above was the cabin of the boat. The long, narrow saloon, flanked on either side by staterooms, was painted a dazzling white with gilded ornaments and scrollwork. The floors were covered with the softest of Brussels carpets. About three-fourths of this space was known as the gentlemen's cabin but was also used for the dining-room. In the rear, farthest removed from the engines and more luxuriously fitted, was the ladies' cabin, which was shut off from that of the men by glass doors. Only those men who were friends or acquaintances of ladies on board were allowed entrance to the ladies' cabin. Above the saloon deck was the hurricane deck, which sometimes was used for an overflow of cargo. On this was the "texas," a cabin occupied by the boat's officers. It was said that in early years, when cabins were few, it was customary to name them after the states. Since Texas was much the largest and was built on the others, its name was given to this large cabin on the hurricane deck. Finally the custom of naming the cabins for states died out, but the officers' quarters still kept their name of the "texas." Surmounting all, over the texas was the pilot-house, highly ornamented with glass windows on every side.

Such a vessel cost from $50,000 to $75,000. The crew consisted of a captain, two clerks, two pilots, four engineers, two mates, a watchman, a lamplighter, a porter, a carpenter, and a painter. Then there were a deck crew of about forty men and a cabin crew of about twenty, generally colored. There were also four cooks, a steward, two chambermaids, a barkeeper and his assistants, and a barber. In the entire crew there were from seventy-five to ninety persons.

The captain received from $250 to $300 a month, clerks $125 to $250, mates $100 to $250, engineers about the same as the mates. The absolute czar of the boat, however, was the pilot, who received twice as much salary as the captain. He decreed whether to run at night or tie up. He had to have a remarkable memory and know the river night and day like a book. He had to carry in his head the location of every snag, wreck, sandbar, crossing, chute, and landmark along the bank, and at night he could verify his sense of location by the reverberation of the whistle from the bluffs along the river.

The pilots formed one of the early monopolies of labor through their association, known as the Pilots' Benevolent Association, which controlled the number of apprentices who were allowed to learn the trade. In this way they kept the number of pilots down to a minimum and unwittingly helped to kill the goose of river steamboating that laid the golden egg. Often boats sought a pilot when only one was available, which was his cue to act very independent and to demand exorbitant wages, since a boat could not leave without a pilot licensed by the United States Government.[8]

On one occasion the *Post Boy* steamed into St. Louis on her way to Leavenworth. As usual, it seemed to the harassed captain, only one pilot was available. In this case it was Pilot Joe Oldham who came to the levee bedecked with diamonds, wearing patent-leather shoes and a silk hat, and shielding himself from the sun with a gold-beaded silk parasol. He demanded $1,500 for the trip. The captain remonstrated, saying that the sum was more than the boat would make, to which Oldham merely shrugged his shoulders. "Well, talk fast, Captain," he continued, "I won't stand here in the hot sun fifteen minutes for fifteen hundred dollars." The captain ground his teeth in rage but saw there was nothing to do but pay the price or lie in port, so he said: "All right, I'll consent to be robbed. We're all ready to start. Come aboard." "But I'm not ready," quoth the independent pilot. "Just call a carriage and send me up to my rooms for my baggage." Once on board, he was efficient, making the round trip in nine days.

On another occasion the captain of a boat sought the services of this same noted despot, and when he would not make a trip for

[8] Chappell, *History of the Missouri River*, pp. 81-84.

less than a thousand dollars, the captain tied up his boat and sought other help. After several days' idleness, when no other pilot appeared, the captain decided to give in to the old tyrant and told Oldham he would pay his price. "Well, I can't accept now, Captain," the pilot replied roguishly, "I'm going to a picnic this afternoon." All manner of entreaty failed to move him, and to the picnic he went. Under such circumstances the captain was helpless, for he could not move until he had the services of a licensed pilot.

The barkeeper was an important personage on the boat. He would not stoop to the common work of mixing drinks, but employed help to do that while he circulated among the crowd assisting the professional gamblers to fleece the passengers, for which he received a fat commission. After making "a winning," the gamblers disembarked before public censure was aroused against them, but the barkeeper remained with the boat.[9]

The rivers were very treacherous and difficult to navigate. The Missouri was somewhat more troublesome to negotiate than the Mississippi since it was constantly changing its channel. The editor of the *Sioux City Register* voiced a common sentiment that "of all the variable things in creation the most uncertain are the action of a jury, the state of a woman's mind, and the condition of the Missouri River." Sandbars were made and the channel changed radically in one flood. As a result of this characteristic, the channel was often divided into a number of small channels or "chutes" and "crossings," where the channel crossed from one side of the stream to the other. Sometimes the stream ran fairly straight, but often it meandered. At the Grand Detour in South Dakota the boat traveled thirty miles around a huge horseshoe where the neck of land was only one and one-half miles across. It was customary for passengers to disembark at this point and go hunting while the boat went around. Several hours could thus be devoted

[9] Joseph Mills Hanson, *The Conquest of the Missouri* (Chicago, 1916), pp. 19-23.

to pleasurable diversion in an otherwise monotonous journey. The most dangerous points were the bends, and they accounted for most of the accidents.

In crossing a sandbar the pilot would select the most promising chute and proceed by the trial-and-error method. One of the deckhands was kept at the bow on the forecastle sounding the channel. In case no channel was found by direct trial, the pilot went out in a yawl and sounded the entire river over the shallow portion, sometimes spending hours in diligent search for the deepest water. Having settled on the best place, he began the long, laborious task of getting the boat over it.

In response to the pilot's jingle of the bell, the vessel drove forward under a full head of steam. One passenger said his great boat writhed and twisted, and the hurricane deck rose up and down in waves, moving slowly on until the bar was cleared. The hulls were so pliable that they would bend five or six inches without material damage.

If the vessel moved more and more slowly, finally coming to a dead standstill, warping was tried. If there was a tree on the bank, a line was made fast to it and the other end was slowly drawn in by the capstan. By this means the boat was pulled over the bar. If there were no trees, the order was "Plant a deadman!" This consisted of digging a hole three or four feet deep on the prairie and burying a log with a line attached to the middle to serve as the fixture to be used in place of a tree for warping. So the boat pulled itself out of the mud by its own bootstraps.

When the boat rested too solidly on the bottom for the warping method to work, "sparring" was tried in an attempt to dislodge it. The spars were two poles like masts shod with sharp iron points, held erect, one on each side of the bow; when the boat stuck, the ends of the spars were lowered to the river-bed. By means of block and tackle operated by a small donkey-engine, commonly called the "nigger," the front end of the boat was raised a foot or more off the bottom. The paddles were then put in motion at full speed, and with luck the vessel was jumped over the bar. The order to start the engine was, "Go ahead on the nigger."

If the craft could not be "grasshoppered" over the sandbar, the crew was "blue" indeed, for "double tripping" was the last resort. This was the simple process of lightening the boat by unloading half the freight on the bank, steaming over the bar, unloading the other half, returning for the first half, passing over the bar again, loading up and proceeding.[10] Sometimes the passengers were requested to get out and walk in order to lighten the boat for the passage of rapids or sandbars. One passenger remembered a trip in 1862, on the far Upper Missouri, when two hundred passengers, walking in the rain and mud, helped cordelle their boat over a rapids. He remarked: "We were a sorry looking lot of first-class passengers when we filed on board the boat, after playing canal horse in the rain and mud." Sometimes as many as half a dozen boats at once would be stuck on a crossing within a short distance of one another. There they kept pushing, pulling, warping and sparring, day and night until the crossing was made. The hissing of steam, together with the jangle of the bells and the cursing of the mate, rendered the scene animated and interesting to the passengers, but anything but pleasant for the crew. Instances were not uncommon when one or two days were consumed in getting a boat over such an obstruction.

Trees along the banks in the timbered section caused much difficulty. The changing river ate the banks away and brought large trees tumbling into the channel. These, lodging here and there, formed three dangerous menaces to the river boat: sawyers, planters, and snags.

A "sawyer" was a large tree whose roots rested on the bottom and whose top pointed downstream. The current gave it an up-and-down motion, and if it were in the proper position, it was sure to force its way through the bottom of the boat. Sawyers

---

[10] Captain DeWitt Clinton Poole, *Among the Sioux of Dakota* (New York, 1881), pp. 25-27,

which did not reach within two or three feet of the surface were called sleeping sawyers; these were the most dangerous, for they could not be seen. "Planters" were similar, but were firmly set, having no motion. "Snags" were small trees or limbs of large trees sticking up in the river and might either be fixed or have motion.[11]

Mark Twain, in speaking of the troubles of the boat on which he traveled from St. Louis to St. Joseph in 1861, said: "The boat might almost as well have gone to St. Joe by land, for she was walking most of the time, anyhow—climbing over reefs and clambering over snags patiently and laboriously all day long."

The average river steamer burned about twenty-five cords of hardwood or thirty cords of softwood in twenty-four hours' steaming. On the Lower Missouri and on the Mississippi, hardwood was obtainable at the numerous wood-yards. From St. Joseph northward, however, hardwood became scarce, and cottonwood and willow were burned. Above Sioux City wood-yards were infrequent, and often the crew had to get wood from drift piles or cut it themselves. This latter was unsatisfactory because green wood did not burn well. A wise captain going up in the spring had his crew cut wood to dry for the downward trip in the fall.

Those who operated the wood-yards were known as wood-hawks. The malaria, or fever and ague as it was called, had a terrible hold on these people on the Lower Missouri and the Mississippi. A traveler on the Mississippi near St. Louis in 1834 said: "I have landed about twenty times and I did not see a single family where the fever and ague had not chased the native color from their cheeks."

On the Upper Missouri by the sixties wood was available most of the way to Fort Benton. The venturesome nomadic wood-hawks who braved the dangers of Indian attacks naturally received high prices for their dry wood. The wood-yards acted independently

[11] Henry Rowe Schoolcraft, *View of the Lead Mines of Missouri* (New York, 1819), pp. 223-224.

of one another, and the price of fuel depended on the supply, the location, and the kind and quality of the wood. On account of the perils of their trade, the wood-hawks sometimes built forts for protection. One such stockade, consisting of two log cabins with a horse stable in between and a palisade around the whole area, was found at Tough Timber, Dakota. The wood-choppers who owned it spent part of their time hunting and supplied mackinaws and steamboats with fresh meat. Their yard was located on a heavily timbered bend of the river.

Although they knew the wilderness like a book, wood-hawks were a bit shy in an atmosphere of greater civilization. Captain Grant Marsh in 1869 encountered X. Beidler and "Liver-Eatin'" Johnson near the mouth of the Musselshell, bought wood from them, and, as was customary, took them on board and entertained them while the boat proceeded on its way. It so happened that it was the captain's birthday, and the cooks, who had procured ice at a trading-post, served ice-cream for dinner, a rare luxury indeed in the wilderness. Neither of the wood-hawks had ever seen any before, and its astonishing frigidity on a warm day aroused their suspicions, though Beidler was averse to admitting his ignorance. Johnson was less backward and whispered an inquiry as to where that stuff came from. "Shut up, you fool," growled Beidler, bravely swallowing a spoonful of the cream. "It comes in cans."

Profitable though the wood business was, with the product selling for not less than eight dollars a cord, the isolated wood-hawks took their lives in their hands. They were harried and hunted like beasts of the forest. Between 1867 and 1869 nearly a third of the men so employed between Fort Benton and the settlements were killed. The log of the *Bertha* for August 5, 1868, recorded, "Found seven woodchoppers and their dog murdered at a woodyard at Round Butte." [12]

[12] Harold E. Briggs, *The Settlement and Economic Development of the Territory of Dakota*, Ms., Doctor's Thesis, University of Iowa, 1929, Vol. II, pp. 368-369.

Sometimes when steamboats were racing, the captain in the lead would buy up all the dry wood in order to delay his competitor by compelling him to burn green wood, cut his own, or waste time in hunting and bargaining. Sometimes a flatboat loaded with wood was taken in tow and the steamer was wooded while in motion.

When the Indians realized the money to be made in wood, the more work-brittle of their number went into the business and made themselves a considerable profit. At a time when, on account of severe Indian hostilities, wood was scarce and it was dangerous for a crew to cut it, Captain Joseph La Barge equipped a boat with a sawmill and took along a yoke of oxen. When he needed wood, he swung out a stage, drove the oxen ashore, dragged a few logs on board, and sawed them up at leisure en route.

Wooding at one of the yards was always an interesting time for the passengers. When the whistle blew for a yard, the mate went through the crew's section and among the poorer passengers to roust out the workers. He accosted each with, "Do you carry wood?" There were three classes of passengers. The first had bed, food, and did no work; the second, known as deck passengers, provided their own provisions and bedding and did no work; and the third class had no bed or food and worked. If the mate was not satisfied when a passenger told him he was not in the third class, the passenger was obliged to show his ticket. Most of the wood-carrying passengers were foreign immigrants.

When the boat ran her nose into the bank, it was the usual thing for the captain and the wood-hawk to dicker and bargain, using a good many hard words and entering into much contention. Finally, when the bargain was made, about forty or fifty well-drilled Negro roustabouts, dressed in fancy shirts of rainbow hues, formed an endless procession out among the trees and back onto the boat, carrying huge loads of wood, with mechanical regularity. There was often good-natured competition among them as to which could carry the biggest load. The working passengers and anyone else who might be interested in hurrying the process along, or who, tired of the monotony of the journey, desired a bit of exercise, joined the wood-carriers. Apparently most of the passengers got their exercise otherwise, however. One traveler remembered that their firearms made the woods ring with their pop! pop! at every conceivable object. Athletic contests, with the standing broad jump in popular favor, were the rule. Sometimes the contestants used weights, throwing them backwards while in mid-air, when the counteraction of the weight pushed the jumper several feet farther than was possible in the regular jump.

Meanwhile, as the wood-carriers marched to and fro, the mate entertained the listener with a running fire of exhortations, such as, "Oh, bring them *shavings* along!" "Don't go to sleep at *this frolic!*" and by swearing oaths of such monstrous proportions that the observer wondered whether he was really profane or merely trying to be ridiculous. Finally the last load was carried, the passengers were gathered in, and slowly the boat backed away from the bank and proceeded on her way.

Because of the extremely dirty water used, a steamboat had to lay up occasionally and have its boilers cleaned. A traveler on the way to the Montana gold-fields remembered that while this was going on, the passengers built a great bonfire in the woods on the bank and spent the long evening in games and singing.

The boat usually stopped at night unless the trip was urgent or there was bright moonlight. In the summer, however, daylight was interpreted to mean about eighteen hours out of the twenty-four, for the run was begun at three in the morning and continued until nine at night. The crew was divided into four watches to enable the members to get sufficient sleep. The late-evening and early-morning runs were often the most successful, for the water was usually calm. When a strong wind on the Upper Missouri prohibited running for several hours at a time, the captain employed this period of otherwise enforced idleness in cutting wood.

As compared with stage or immigrant train, travel by boat was very pleasant. There was room to walk about, beds were provided, and regular meals were served in style. The passenger was protected from the elements and the hard usage of overland travel and enabled to while away the time in association with companions. One excursionist of 1840 found in the saloon of her Upper Mississippi steamer a book in which the passenger was invited to write his name, place of residence, whither bound, and his politics. Whether this was an official registry or merely a social formality designed to cultivate good-fellowship and promote acquaintance among the passengers the lady did not state. She recorded, however, that the rules of the boat were printed on a piece of pink satin, framed, and hung against the wall of the cabin. Among other rules noted were these: Gentlemen were forbidden to go to the table without their coats; no one was to pencil or otherwise injure the furniture; no gentleman was to lie down in a berth with his boots on; gentlemen were not to enter the ladies' saloon without permission from them.[13]

While a trip of several months must have been tiresome, yet there were many happenings to break the monotony. There was the ever-changing scenery of bluffs, forests, and prairies. In the springtime the soft zephyrs wafted to the passenger the aroma of thousands of flowers and the songs of innumerable birds. Beavers at work felling trees and great flocks of wild-fowl furnished interesting sights. Now and then on the upward journey, as Mackinaw boats from the upper river were met, passengers sent letters by them to be mailed at the towns down the river. When the railroad building westward connected with river points, passengers received mail at the rail towns. Often the passengers disembarked and walked across country, meeting the boat at the end of a long circuit like that of the Grand Detour already described. Such tramps were enlivened by hunting and shooting at a mark. Indeed, passengers often hunted from the boat's engine deck, shoot-

[13] Mrs. Eliza R. Steele, *A Summer Journey in the West* (New York, 1841), pp. 155-156.

ing at the acres of wild-fowl or a stray deer or bear along the bank or a luckless buffalo which had attempted to swim across the stream. Sometimes, with so many shooting indiscriminately, it was necessary to elect officers and adopt "safe and sane" regulations. Live stock also was driven across the short cuts occasionally, to give the animals exercise and allow them to garner their own food instead of having it served on a platter, so to speak, in their stalls. Sometimes a man lost on such expeditions caused some delay and excitement.

The pilot-house was a favorite resort when the conditions of navigation would permit. The pilot was always an interesting person. When in a proper mood on an easy stretch of river, he would regale a group of listeners with stories of his exploits, in reality an accumulation of stories he had heard through many years, which, however, were new to the newcomer and could be used with impunity by the raconteur to create a halo about himself as hero.

Some of those floating palaces of the fifties and sixties had steam calliopes which played popular tunes of the day when approaching or leaving a town. The listener was charmed to hear "Old Folks at Home," "Gwine to Run All Night," or "Oh! Susanna" reverberating from the hills and forests on a summer evening. There were a string orchestra and often a band on board, and dances were frequent. The first trip of a boat up the river in the spring was the signal for a ball at each of the ports where it stopped for the night. Often when two boats were in the same vicinity for an evening, they were lashed together and the passengers enjoyed the opportunity of a wider circle of association. Dancing took place in one cabin while the talkers and listeners gathered in the cabin of the other. The men's cabin of the *Red Wing*, a Mississippi River boat of 1847, is said to have been arranged so that the men could indulge to their heart's content in their favorite pastime of chewing tobacco with the unrelenting, merciless spitting of which Mrs. Frances Trollope spoke with such disgust. Operations centered around the two stoves, where the chewers sat as silent as statues. For their convenience a hole had been cut in the floor and the carpet cut away around it.[14]

During the gold-rushes and when emigrants were flocking into the West to make new homes, the boats were literally jammed. The staterooms would not begin to accommodate the cabin passengers, and all the available mattresses were spread out on the cabin floor. When there were not enough for all, there was a general rush to "stake out claims for the night." After fussing and kicking up a general uproar, those who were without beds finally calmed down and allowed the more fortunate to sleep. Another rush occurred at meal-times, when three hundred passengers had to be fed with table room for only seventy-five. Resourceful single men secured the services of ladies to accompany them to meals, thus assuring themselves places at the first table.

The day began at 6:30 with the ringing of a gong. The passengers arose and went to the wash-rooms, where they made their ablutions in the murky river water. The beds were removed from the cabin floor, and a table running the length of the cabin was spread. At seven the breakfast gong sounded. As a rule the food was excellent, far better than the travelers were accustomed to at home. At dinner the captain, like a medieval baron in all his glory, stood at the head of the table carving, with a colored steward to assist him, while a troop of twenty colored waiters, as well drilled as soldiers, trotted up and down the long tables bearing heaping dishes of food. There were roasts, stews, and broils of fresh meat and game. There were rich pastries, jellies, cakes, ices, fruits, and nuts. Solton's immigrant handbook warned the overland traveler against overeating the rich food on the steamboats. When passenger traffic increased, each steamer while in the Indian country had a hired hunter who left the boat about mid-

[14] William J. Petersen, *Steamboating on the Upper Mississippi* (Iowa City, Iowa, 1937), pp. 361, 362.

night and scoured the river-bank for game. When he found a deer or antelope, he hung it up in a conspicuous place, whence it was brought in by men in the yawl when the boat came along.

The water of the western river was always muddy—at times so thick that an egg was rendered invisible in a glass of it; if a glass was left standing, as much as half an inch of sediment precipitated. Casks of water were dipped and allowed to settle a few hours, when it became clear as crystal. Westerners preferred it straight from the river, however, feeling that the clear water was insipid. Those who were too particular could get something stronger than river water at the boat's bar.

There was all manner of fun on board a steamer when there was a lively crowd. On a boat in 1859 were a large number of Pike's Peakers traveling second class. The rules forbade these deck passengers to go up on the cabin or hurricane decks. This prohibition seemed arbitrary to them, and they organized themselves into a pure democracy, drew up a code of laws, elected officers, and established a kangaroo court. The cabin passengers were quite as anxious to go below and see the Pike's Peakers as the latter were to go up and see the ladies. In accordance with their principles, the Pike's Peakers passed a law declaring it a trespass for a cabin passenger to come onto the lower deck and fixing a penalty of not less than one dollar or more than five. The minute a "cabby" stepped on the deck, he was seized and tried before the Kangaroo Court of the Missouri River. He generally took it all in good part and paid his fine. The first man was so pleased with the joke and entered into it with such enthusiasm that through his machinations the Pike's Peakers got almost every male on the cabin deck into their clutches before the game was over. When this source of gain and fun ran dry, snoring was declared "disturbing the peace with malice aforethought." Many unsuspecting persons were arrested who up to that time had thought themselves pretty decent fellows, only to have their friends testify that they had been in the penitentiary, had been convicted of chicken-stealing or other deviltry. The fines collected were spent for cigars and furnished nearly enough to supply the travelers throughout the voyage.[15]

Near the bow end of the boat was a gambler or two with a large number of gold and silver watches, earrings, and other jewelry, each piece displayed on a numbered square on an oilcloth. For fifty cents one could throw the dice for one of these articles. According to the gambler, there were no blanks; a player was *certain* to get an article worth twice what he paid for it and was liable to draw a gold watch worth a hundred and forty dollars. A player advanced and threw the dice and drew a pair of earrings which the gambler claimed were worth three dollars and a half (actual value about a dime). Others stepped up and won prizes. One man won an ivory-handled bowie-knife and a silver goblet in two throws, and the gambler complained that at that rate they would break him; he declared, however, that he was not the kind to back out but would continue. He then gave the man five dollars for his knife and goblet. This encouraged the others, who crowded up anxious to share in the apparent spoil. The repurchase was a master-stroke, for half-dollars fell like rain, bringing the gambler a rich harvest. The secret of the business was that the really valuable articles were upon figures the dice never exhibited, and on the others there was a profit of three or four hundred per cent. Often the ship's clerk, barkeeper, or other employee was in alliance with the gamblers, helping them fleece the flock of unwary ones. Poker also was played all the time, and men who lost all their money put watches and other jewelry in the jack-pot. At the other end of the boat perhaps there was a prayer-meeting in full sway.

Some captains would not allow gambling on board. There is on record at least one instance where a captain, who had caught gamblers beating an old man, pulled up to a lonely shore on a dark

[15] Jesse L. Pritchard, "To Pike's Peak in Search of Gold in 1859," *The Trail*, September, 1911, pp. 8, 9.

night with the rain pouring down and made the gamblers walk the gang-plank into a dense forest miles from any habitation.

When the cholera epidemic was rife on the western rivers, sometimes so many of the crew died that the boat had to tie up and wait until a new crew could be mustered. If a deck passenger died in those troublous days, the ship's carpenter hurriedly made a rude wooden box and the boat was run alongside the bank; a shallow grave was dug and the body hastily buried, unmarked, there to remain until the shifting current, swirling and cutting, carried the earthly remains down toward the ocean. It was not uncommon to see part of a coffin denuded to the view of the passer-by. One captain said there was a spot below Kansas City where he had buried eight cholera victims in one grave. He declared he could easily name a hundred vicinities along the Missouri where he had buried the dead, and he ventured the guess that if all the forgotten graves were located, there would be enough to make the shores of the Missouri one continuous cemetery from its mouth to its source. Many strangers whose friends never knew of their fate occupied those nameless graves of bygone years. In 1849, when the people of the town would not allow the boat to land because of their terror of the cholera scourge, the *James Monroe* was abandoned a mile below Jefferson City.

By 1860 the freight trade on the Missouri had reached enormous proportions. In 1859 a larger number of vessels left St. Louis for the Missouri trade than for both the Upper and the Lower Mississippi. After the gold discoveries in Montana in the sixties, the traffic on the extreme upper river jumped to an unbelievable figure. Prior to 1864 there had been six steamboat arrivals at the levee of Fort Benton, Montana. The trade reached its peak in 1869 when forty-two boats unloaded at the landing. The wharf was literally jammed with a dense mass of bales, boxes, barrels, and goods of all descriptions. Every warehouse in the place was filled to the fullest capacity, and every available building and space in private dwellings was requisitioned to care for

FORT BENTON

Head of steam navigation on the Missouri River.

the tremendous volume of freight. A total of 4,823 tons of freight was reported discharged there in 1868.[16] Albert D. Richardson estimated in 1865 that 60 per cent of the goods brought into the gold-camps came by the Missouri River, 20 per cent by overland freighting from Missouri, Kansas, and Nebraska, and 20 per cent overland from California. Every necessity of life, from food to mining machinery, was sent up the river to the gold-fields.

As a rule it required over a month to steam from St. Louis to Fort Benton, although Captain Joseph La Barge established the record of going to the mouth of the Yellowstone and returning to St. Louis in twenty-eight days, in spite of spending several days doing the business of the American Fur Company at the various posts. The freight rate from St. Louis to Fort Benton was 12 cents a pound, and the cabin fare was $300. Although the insurance rate was 6½ per cent for side-wheel boats and 8 per cent for stern-wheelers, the profits were great. In 1866 reported profits of some of the boats were: the *St. John*, $17,000; *W. J. Lewis*, $40,000; *Peter Balen*, $65,000. In 1867 Captain Joseph La Barge cleared over $40,000 on the trip of the *Octavia*. In the same year Captain Grant Marsh with the *Ida Stockdale* made a net profit of $42,594 for her owner, which was nearly twice the boat's own value. In 1866 with the *Luella* Captain Marsh transported 230 miners and $1,250,000 in gold-dust, the most valuable cargo ever carried down the Missouri River.[17] In the sixties, in addition to the steamboat passengers downstream from Fort Benton, it was estimated that 200 other boats and 1,200 passengers left annually, arriving at St. Louis in ten days or less.

When they were leaving the lower river, the steamboat hands often celebrated in some fashion or other. A passenger on the *Henry Adkins* mentioned that the boat stopped at Brunswick, Missouri, and the boys went ashore in the evening for a last spree

---

[16] *Contributions*, Montana State Historical Society, Bradley Manuscript, Book II, Vol. VIII, p. 129.

[17] Hanson, *The Conquest of the Missouri*, p. 80.

before entering the upper river. By the light of dawn next morning there appeared certain souvenirs of the night's frolic. The characteristic signs and emblems of various establishments of the town appeared on deck. Here was a barber's pole, there a huge boot, yonder a big wooden watch, and still beyond was a saddle. The captain put these ashore at the first port and gave orders that they be returned to their owners.

Sometimes steamers were organized into a line with packets running regularly. Such a line was the St. Louis and St. Joseph Union Packet Line established in 1858. It had twelve first-class boats which made regularly scheduled trips and provided every luxury in order to win the favor of the public. Every boat was a "floating palace," and every courtesy was extended to the patrons. Every dish of the season was offered by the stewards, and the finest assortment of imported wines was served. These de luxe boats had a piano in the cabin, a bathroom, and a nursery. Nothing was left undone to make them deserve the term "elegant." At the other extreme, there were the so-called "wild boats," which were mere transients running at irregular times.

Racing was an evil which grew naturally and, far from being deprecated, was often encouraged by the passengers, because of the natural desire to see their boat triumph over a competitor. When a captain found himself immediately behind a rival who was picking up all the passengers and freight while he was left with no traffic, naturally he was tempted to overtake his competitor, even at the risk of a possible explosion. In such cases any combustible at hand was used to increase the steam-pressure. Pitch, lard, butter, or grease of any kind was fed to the fiery monster. Sometimes fat pork and sides of bacon were thrown into the fires. So intense was the excitement that now and then the engineer tied the safety-valve down. The passengers often crowded the deck, urging the crew to greater exertions. Of course, such a proceeding was hazardous in the extreme. The most disastrous explosion on the Missouri River occurred at Lexington, Missouri, on April 9, 1852, when the captain of the *Saluda* ordered the steam-pressure to be raised beyond the limits of safety. Nearly all the officers were killed. The number of lives lost was never known, although about a hundred bodies were recovered. Most of the passengers on the crowded boat were Mormons on their way to the starting-point of the overland trek to Utah.[18]

Although navigation on the Mississippi in the Civil War era can hardly be classed as a frontier development, it is noteworthy that the river above St. Louis saw a great increase in traffic during the war. In the first few months hundreds of Southern refugees went northward and thousands of troops were carried southward. When armed conflict began, wounded soldiers were moved northward. In the spring of 1862 steamboats made regular trips to Iowa ports, bringing about three hundred sick and wounded at a trip. Twice during one week in the autumn of the same year the *Fanny Bullitt* arrived at Keokuk carrying 700 patients. In December, 1862, the records showed that 7,396 sick and wounded soldiers had been brought by steamboat from the South to Keokuk.

The life of a river steamer was short. Barring accidents, which were many, and from various causes, the boat was expected to last from eight to ten years. The depreciation was estimated at ten per cent the first year and twenty-five per cent each year thereafter. On account of the many wrecks occasioned by snags, explosions, ice-jams, and fire, the mortality rate of river steamers was much higher than otherwise might be expected.

There remains to glance at the steamboat traffic on the Red River of the North. The first boat, the *Anson Northrup*, named after the owner, was placed upon the river in response to a $2,000 bonus offered by the St. Paul Chamber of Commerce in the spring of 1859. At its height the Red River traffic supported two lines of boats. One of these, the Red River Transportation Company, in 1875 carried 24,500 tons of freight and 7,690 passengers. The

[18] Chittenden, *History of Early Steamboat Navigation on the Missouri River*, pp. 124, 125.

other carried between fifty and sixty thousand tons of freight. On October 30 of that year the steamboat *Cheyenne* passed Grand Forks having in tow twelve flatboats loaded with coal, flour, grain, and merchandise. The boats ran between North Dakota points and Fort Gary (Winnipeg), Saskatchewan. This traffic declined rapidly, however, until in 1880 the larger boats had been taken off the river.[19] In 1866 the Hudson's Bay Company sent 1,600 packages of goods through the United States via St. Paul and the Red River to Winnipeg.

The crew of a steamboat had a lingo all its own. The *Silver Lake* had been forced to tie up to the bank for the day on account of high winds on November 13, 1872. The same fate befell her the following day. The log read: "Still choking a stump." From morning till night the conversation of the officers, especially, dwelt upon navigating conditions, with such remarks as "the river is high" or "the river is low," "the river is rising" or "the river is falling," "the river is two feet higher" or "the river is one foot lower." The small engine, as we have seen, was called "the nigger." Boats were measured by the number of boilers they carried, just as in later times automobiles were rated by cylinders. For example, reference was made to "a two-boiler boat" or "a four-boiler boat" without reference to her length, breadth, or tonnage. A "reach" was a straight piece of river.

The famous pen-name Mark Twain came from the procedure of measuring the depth of the river preparatory to negotiating shoal water. A man in a small boat, sounding the channel, was accustomed to cry out, "Mark one!" or "Mark twain!" to indicate the fathom mark reached.

Romantic and heroic as was the pioneer navigation of the western rivers, it could not last. The railroads building westward cut off the traffic section by section, leaving river transportation to die a lingering death, a dramatic chapter closed forever.

[19] Briggs, *The Settlement and Economic Development of the Territory of Dakota*, Vol. II, p. 390.

CHAPTER VIII

CARAVANS OF THE GREAT AMERICAN DESERT

IN THE ROSTER of the historic highways of America none is more famous than the Santa Fe Trail. The reports of golden trading opportunities that Lieutenant Zebulon M. Pike carried back from New Mexico in 1807 spread in Missouri. Although the imprisonment of the Robert McKnight expedition of 1812 dampened the ardor of the Yankee traders, by 1821 they were ready for another attempt to open trade with the Spanish. The New Mexico trade as it was finally opened, however, was an adjunct to the American fur trade.

The *Missouri Intelligencer* of June 25, 1821, contained a proposal by William Becknell under the head of "An article for the government of a company of men destined to the westward for the purpose of trading for Horses and Mules and catching Wild Animals of all description." His scheme as outlined was thereafter known as the "first article" and was important in the organization of the Santa Fe trade. Every man was to fit himself for the three months' trip with horse, rifle, ammunition, and clothing. He was to furnish an equal part of the fitting out of the trade and to receive an equal part of the product. If the company consisted of thirty or more men, it was thought ten dollars a man would suffice to purchase the necessary merchandise with which to trade. It was distinctly understood that all were to share alike. There was to be no division of the profits until the party returned to the Missouri. Every man upon joining the expedition was to put up fifty dollars as surety that he would go. This was to be forfeited in case he withdrew unless he was prevented from making the journey by reason of some unavoidable accident. Every eight men should have a pack-horse, an axe, and a tent for shelter, and Becknell proposed "for the good order and regulation of the company that every man shall be bound by an oath to submit to such orders and rules as the company when assembled shall think proper to enforce." Signers to the number of seventy were to be received, and on August 4 every man wishing to go was to meet at Ezekiel Williams' on the Missouri River about five miles above Franklin.

Information is rather meager on the organization of the company but apparently the party was finally made up of from twenty to thirty men, and it was to be a trapping as well as a trading expedition. They left Franklin on September 1, 1821. Josiah Gregg, in his classic *Commerce of the Prairies*, says that Becknell went out to trade with the Indians and, having fallen in with a party of Mexicans, was readily persuaded to accompany them to New Mexico.[1] Although the company had a trifling amount of merchandise, they realized a handsome profit, and on their return to the United States they reported the results. Common calicoes and bleached and brown domestic goods, for instance, sold for as high as two and three dollars a Spanish yard (33 inches). The news of this success spread, and a larger group was ready to go in the spring of 1822 with a larger amount of goods. The journey that year was accomplished without mishap.

Captain Becknell's journey of the following year was far different, however. With about $30,000 worth of goods and about thirty men, Becknell, who was an excellent woodsman of the daring American type, resolved to pioneer a direct route from the Arkansas River and shorten the distance appreciably. The adventurers little realized the terrible trials that awaited them in the uncharted desert ahead. Wth no instruments other than perhaps a pocket compass and the starry heavens to guide him, Becknell led the little band across the arid plains toward the Cimarron River. After two days' march the scanty supply of water in the

[1] F. F. Stephens, "Missouri and the Santa Fe Trade," see *Missouri Historical Review*, Vol. XI, pp. 291-294.

canteens was exhausted. The sufferings of man and beast had become so acute that the men in a desperate effort to save themselves killed their dogs and cut off the ears of their mules and drank the blood. This only aggravated the thirst of the sufferers, and in frantic despair they scattered to the four winds, feverishly hunting for water. Time and time again mirages appeared with their tantalizing visions of green trees and life-giving water, only to recede beyond reach. At last, not suspecting they were near the banks of the Cimarron, the party resolved to try to get back to the Arkansas. No doubt they would all have perished in this attempt had not fortune forestalled it. A stray buffalo direct from the Cimarron with its paunch filled with water was despatched by a member of the party, and the contents of its stomach was a temporary fountain of life. One man said afterward that nothing ever passed his lips which gave him such exquisite delight as his first draught of that filthy beverage. This providential relief pointed the way of salvation for the party. Some of the strongest went to the river and with full canteens hurried back to the assistance of their comrades, whom they found prostrate on the ground unable to proceed further. Finally the whole party was revived enough to get to the river. They were then content to follow it west and down into New Mexico.[2]

The first trading attempts were carried out by means of pack-trains. The Americans probably obtained their information on expert packing from the Mexicans, who were masters of the art. A pack-saddle was a nearly square pad of leather stuffed with hay. It lay across the mule's back with an equal area on each side. When an animal was being saddled, a sheep-skin was laid next to the back to prevent chafing. Over this was placed a saddle-cloth, and the pack-saddle over that. The saddle was cinched tightly, and during the process the animal grunted and groaned as though he were being cut in two. To the uninitiated this seemed very cruel, but it was necessary and was really a help to

[2] Josiah Gregg, *Commerce of the Prairies* (New York, 1845), pp. 22-24.

the animal during the day's work. The firmer the saddle the more comfortably the load rode.

The load was generally about three hundred pounds. It was placed on the mule with skill and despatch by two packers who stood one on each side of the animal. If the load was a single package, it was set on top, but if in two packages, they were fastened together with ropes and allowed to balance themselves on either flank. A rope was then thrown over the load and under the mule's belly and drawn as tightly as possible. Over the pack a square cloth was fastened to protect it from rain. A refractory mule was sometimes blindfolded until the load was set. Packers were very skilful; they could lift to the mule's back a load which would ordinarily be considered impossible to move and pack him in five minutes.

A caravan of pack-mules numbered from fifty to two hundred and traveled from twelve to fifteen miles a day. The march was made without stopping for noon, because if a pack-mule was allowed to rest he would lie down, and when he did so he was not able to rise again without a desperate struggle which badly strained him, sometimes ruining him. When the caravan first moved off, the loads were so tight the mules could scarcely wiggle, but soon the weight settled down and the girts, from time to time, had to be tightened. The packers were kept busy adjusting packs as the march proceeded. They were constantly shifting, losing their balance, falling off; and sometimes saddle, pack, and all swung under the mule's belly, an accident which necessitated stopping and repacking. When the caravan arrived at a camping ground, the pack-saddles and their loads were arranged in regular order, with the covers on the loads and a ditch dug around the whole to carry off the water in case of rain. After a few days each mule came to know his own load, and at loading time he would step up to it and wait to receive his pack.

Discipline in a mule caravan was severe. Every man employed had certain duties to perform. The night herder kept the mules from straying too far in their effort to gain their only subsistence, grass. Each herd had a bell-mare which was led by the cook. The mules followed her implicitly and appeared to respect her as a colony of bees does its queen. When the bell-mare was taken away, they seemed bewildered and lost. There was about one man for each eight mules in the train. These Spanish pack-train employees worked for a few dollars a month and the coarsest fare.[3] Probably the early trains were operated by Spanish methods.

In the summer of 1824 the first wheeled vehicles were taken over the trail when about eighty traders, taking between $25,000 and $30,000 worth of goods, traveled to Santa Fe. A portion of the company used pack-trains, but there were about twenty-five wheeled vehicles—one or two road-wagons, two carts, and the rest Dearborn carriages. They brought back $180,000 in specie and $10,000 in furs for their enterprise.

The early traders for a period of years were mere peddlers as compared with the later big interests. These adventurers crossed the prairies in detached bands, with individuals rarely carrying more than two or three hundred dollars' worth of goods. By 1830 larger amounts of capital found their way into the trade. During the earlier years the traders left from Franklin, Missouri, but as settlement moved westward and navigation of the Missouri River improved, it became advantageous to start from Independence, Missouri, at the most southwesterly bend of the lower river. To this point of annual departure about the first of May gathered "the prairie adventurer whether in search of wealth, health, or amusement."

Independence soon became a busy place. Here were purchased supplies for the journey and many of the oxen, horses, and mules. Most of the wagons used in the early trade were manufactured at Pittsburgh, although before long St. Louis furnished the bulk of them. Wagon manufacture was begun at Independence, and

---

[3] Colonel Henry Inman, *The Old Santa Fe Trail* (Topeka, 1916), pp. 55-58; Gregg, *Commerce of the Prairies*, Chapter IX.

in 1845 (even before the gold-rush of 1849) there were seven wagon-wrights' establishments there.[4]

The ordinary supplies for each man for the journey consisted of about fifty pounds each of flour and bacon, ten of coffee, twenty of sugar, and a small quantity of salt. Beans, crackers, and a few other items were sometimes taken but were considered non-essentials. The chief food was buffalo meat, which was to be found within two or three hundred miles of Independence.

In the beginning of the trade, horses were largely used, but as mules became available, they drove their half-brothers out of commission except for riding purposes. About 1830, however, it was discovered that oxen could perform about as well as mules, and soon approximately half the trains used mules and half oxen. Neither animal usually was shod, and the oxen had a tendency to become tender-footed. Sometimes the drivers resorted to the expedient of manufacturing "moccasins" of green buffalo skin for them. These served well in dry weather but were soon worn out in wet weather. Sometimes the hooves of the mules became very smooth and they slipped on the dry grass as though treading on ice.

Loading the wagons was a rite almost religious in its care and precision. Great ingenuity was exercised by the packers, who so expertly arranged the goods that after the journey of eight hundred miles they were found in perfect condition. In the earlier days smaller wagons drawn by eight oxen or mules were used, but in later years a larger vehicle bearing five thousand pounds' burden and pulled by ten or twelve animals came into vogue. Canvas sheets were placed over the bows and down the sides of the wagon bed to prevent the rain from blowing into the cracks and spoiling the merchandise. Gregg recommended also that a double top be placed on the wagon, with wool blankets between the two canvas sheets. This not only rendered the top dry but

[4] James Joseph Webb, *Adventures in the Santa Fe Trade, 1844-1847*, Ralph P. Bieber, ed. (Glendale, Cal., 1931), p. 129, editorial note.

enabled the trader to smuggle the blankets through the unreasonable customs in New Mexico.

Independence was the starting-point also for trapping expeditions and expeditions on the Oregon Trail. Since many of the animals to be used were wild and "unbroken," there took place on the prairie near Independence a carnival in connection with the taming and training of the motive power. An English observer found around the wagons groups of tall, stalwart Missouri teamsters busily engaged in preparations for the start to Santa Fe. They were greasing the wheels, smoothing the ox-bows, fitting or repairing harness, or overhauling their own kits. He said they were dressed alike, with a pair of "homespun" pantaloons tucked into heavy boots reaching nearly to the knee. A broad leather belt about the waist held up the pantaloons and supported a strong butcher knife in a sheath. The upper part of the body was clothed in a coarse checked shirt, with a fur cap on the head.[5]

Among the others waiting on the prairie for the start were usually a number of pale-faced invalids who were looking for health. The prairies had a reputation for hygienic benefits. Josiah Gregg himself went west for his health and made his first journey to Santa Fe in 1831 on the advice of his doctor. He started in a buggy too ill to ride horseback, but before the end of the first week he saddled his horse and rode him. By the time the buffalo country was reached, he was as anxious as anyone to take part in the fun. His health was restored, and becoming interested in the trade, he made eight trips across the Plains.

The days of preparation were wearisome indeed, with the many details, the consultations, the annoying delays. Finally a group was ready to go. The multitude of vexatious worries incident to preparation was forgotten. The drivers thrilled at the prospect of moving out upon the journey. Throwing aside restraint, they cracked their whips in exuberance. Even the mules seemed to catch the spirit of the moment and pricked up their ears. The best

[5] George Frederick Ruxton, *Life in the Far West* (New York, 1849), p. 66.

of feeling and harmony prevailed everywhere. Gay good-bys and witty repartee made their rounds, and with optimism and good cheer the white wagon-train disappeared over the rolling green prairie. Sometimes owners or travelers waited at Independence a few days and, driving on at a rapid pace, overtook the travelers.

The traders were accustomed to travel in little groups to Council Grove, a hundred and fifty miles southwest, where the first ones waited for the later comers and a general rendezvous took place. Between Independence and Council Grove there was no danger from Indians and the stock was not guarded at night. This in some ways was the very time a watch was most needed, for there was a greater tendency for the cattle to stray. There were often rains and storms to create a panic; moreover, the cattle were not used to the trail. Later on the season was dry, and after traveling for some time the stock began to feel attached to the caravan much as a herd of milch cows would regard a farmyard as their home.

In a wet season the dashing rains drenched the traveler, and vivid lightning and tremendous thunderclaps struck terror in the hearts of those unaccustomed to the Kansas electric storm. In 1845 it rained so incessantly and the prairie became so soft that the route was almost impassable. Wagons mired down, wagon hounds broke, and there were unloading, doubling of teams, and reloading in order to get out of the veritable quagmires.

The drab, cloudy, gloomy weather that year all but discouraged the stoutest-hearted. Sometimes it rained two or three times a day. From sleeping on the wet ground, the men's clothes and blankets were hardly ever dry—indeed, they had so little chance to dry that two or three times they became flyblown and maggoty. It took thirty days instead of the usual fifteen to get to Council Grove that season. In 1831 this rendezvous consisted of about one hundred and sixty acres of timber on the Neosho River without a building. Some years later a little trading center grew up there.

At Council Grove it was customary to effect a permanent organization for the passage through the territory inhabited by the wild Indians. For some little time on the road before that point was reached the political pot had been boiling. There were candidates for the captaincy with partisan adherents who electioneered for them in typical American fashion. The election was conducted by ballot in the most democratic way. The captain's powers were not defined by any written instrument and hence were limited. It was his duty, however, to direct the order of travel during the day and select the camping spot at night.

After the captain was chosen, the company was divided into watches. If the caravan was large, it was apportioned into eight watches, each of which was under a sergeant of the guard appointed by the captain. Each sergeant drew his watch by lot, and each watch stood guard duty a quarter of every other night. If the caravan was small, it was divided into only four watches, and each stood guard a quarter of every night. The early expeditions were attended by a minimum of Indian animosity. Soon, however, individualistic frontiersmen who believed there was no good Indian but a dead one acted on the principle, bringing down the wrath and hostility of the Plains tribes on the traders. This rashness imperiled all travelers and made necessary a strict nightly guard. The guards did not walk boldly erect on a beaten path like a sentry on post, but in order to avoid the sharp eyes of marauding Indians, who would be sure to pick off a figure in bold relief, they stood or crouched motionless among the stock, watching for any moving spot on the horizon. Everybody dreaded guard duty but it was inescapable. No one could furnish a substitute, and the more severe the storm the more necessary it was to be on the watch. No one was exempted from this duty unless he could show good proof that he was physically disabled. Even the hangers-on, or "wanderers," had to take their turn although they had no part in the trade. There were always a number of these predecessors of the twentieth-century hitch-hikers along. The wanderers, amateur tourists, and idlers spent their time amusing themselves.

The hospitable traders never turned them away from their meals.

If the company was large, the captain divided it into four divisions and appointed a lieutenant to each. It was the duty of these men to ride ahead and inspect every creek and ravine, select the best crossings, and superintend the "forming" of each encampment, as it was called.

There was a medley of arms and dress. At times a cannon or two were dragged along. The Missouri frontiersman preferred his rifle and contemptuously referred to the double-barreled fowling-piece of the more urbanized men as a "scatter gun." The more erudite among the latter argued for the greater effectiveness of this weapon when loaded with buckshot in a night Indian attack. Pistols and knives of every description gave the travelers the appearance of a band of brigands. The city merchant wore a coat with a large number of pockets for carrying extra articles; the backwoodsman wore buckskin or linsey hunting shirt; the farmer dressed in blue-jean coat; the wagoner donned flannel-sleeved vest. In addition to these there was a variety of other costumes.

The time spent at Council Grove was utilized in cutting timber for axletrees and other wagon parts. This was the last point where good timber could be obtained for repairs. The timbers were tied under the wagons and sometimes were carried all the way to Santa Fe and back.

At last, when the final preparations had been made, the captain gave the order, "Ketch up! Ketch up!" Immediately the camp became a scene of light-hearted activity. The woods resounded to the yells of the joyous travelers. Wagoners flew to harnessing up their mules, racing to see which would be the first ready to start. Drivers halloed, log chains rattled, bells clanged, and angry imprecations were hurled at stubborn beasts. Soon some quick and lucky fellow gave the first cry, "All's set." This was followed by similar cries from wagon after wagon. Sometimes a teamster had a hard time getting a stubborn mule in place. Finally, when the cry from the last driver came, there was a response from all quarters, "All's set," and the captain commanded, "Stretch out!" This was followed by a cracking of whips, the trampling of hooves, and the rumble of the wagons. From headquarters then came the order, "Fall in!" and the wagons fell into line and strung out on the plain with the eyes of every man set like flint toward Santa Fe.[6]

Where the terrain permitted, and especially in the Indian country, for the sake of better protection the train traveled in four columns abreast. At night in the earlier years the camp was formed in a hollow square, each division constituting a side of the resulting corral, in which the stock was enclosed when necessary. In later times an oval corral was made.[7] All camp-fires were built outside the enclosure, and the sleepers made up their meager beds of a couple of blankets or a buffalo skin and blanket on the prairie and looked up into the vaulted skies until slumber closed their eyes.

Not far beyond Council Grove was Diamond Spring. Early travelers had planted some mint roots at this spring, and later comers made juleps from the abundant supply of mint, passing a vote of thanks to the public benefactors who planted the herb.

At some of the mud creeks the wagons would stick and it was necessary to "double out," that is, take the team from another wagon to pull the distressed one out. Then the company paused, cut willows or grass, threw them into the slough, and covered them with dirt, forming a causeway over which the other wagons could pass safely. In crossing small streams the precipitous banks often made it necessary for fifteen or twenty men to grasp a rope tied to the back of the wagon and allow the vehicle to roll slowly down the steep place.

On this part of the journey there was much talk of the buffaloes

[6] Gregg, *Commerce of the Prairies*, Chapter III.

[7] Alphonso Wetmore, "Diary of a Journey to Santa Fe, 1828," *Missouri Historical Review*, Vol. VIII, p. 181; Thomas Jefferson Farnham, *Travels in the Great Western Prairies, the Anahuac and Rocky Mountains, and in the Oregon Territory* (New York, 1843), p. 15.

that would soon be seen. The "greenhorns" were anxious to try their hand, and the veterans bantered them, offering to eat the horns, hooves, etc., of any buffalo the newcomers brought into camp. When James Webb went back to camp after shooting his first buffalo, his comrades could hardly be convinced that he had killed one, and finally suggested that it was probably a poor old bull that could not get out of the way. That evening the captain of the train went to Webb's mess and asked for volunteers to sit up with a man. When asked who was sick, he said he wanted a group to sit up with Webb; he declared he was afraid the lucky hunter would be so excited he would keep the camp awake all night, and he needed someone to talk on a different subject and calm him down.[8]

Before long the train arrived at the Arkansas River. It was no small job to cross this stream safely with a hundred tons of freight. The Arkansas was about a third- to a half-mile wide with rapid current and quicksand bottom which was continually shifting. When a stream was reached in the evening, it was customary to ford it and camp on the far bank. This was because a sudden storm might cause the stream, especially if small, to rise sufficiently to hold up fording it for several hours and thus delay the travelers.

In crossing the Arkansas, if the water was fairly high, the trader had to lift his load and place timbers on the bolsters, raising it as high as he dared and still avoid turning the wagon over. This elevation kept the cargo above the water.

Before the train started across, a careful survey was made to ascertain the shallow and deep spots, for the shifting bottom would leave a deep hole where the day before had been shoal. The wagon was given a double team, and with a large number of men on each side to steady the cargo and to lift to keep the wagon from turning over in a deep or rough place, the team was meandered across, the driver picking the best footing and shallowest depth. James Webb recorded that in fording the Pawnee River

[8] Webb, *Adventures in the Santa Fe Trade*, pp. 48-54.

in 1844 one wagon capsized in the stream bottom side up in deep water. All hands jumped in, and within two or three hours they succeeded in getting the goods and wagon onto the farther bank. Then two days were spent opening the goods, spreading them on the ground to dry, repacking, and loading once more. One trader remembered that nearly an acre of ground was covered with goods while a cargo was drying out.

Sometimes it was necessary to build a bullboat to ferry the goods across. More often a wagon box was made into an improvised scow for this purpose by calking it and stretching raw buffalo skins on the outside. The empty wagons were easily taken over and the goods reloaded. Such a process was long and laborious, however, delaying a train a week or ten days in transporting from seventy-five to a hundred tons of freight.

On reaching the Arkansas River some caravans chose to strike across an arid stretch of fifty miles to the Cimarron. Others, preferring the less hazardous route, followed the Arkansas to the mountains and then turned down into New Mexico. The desert route, although allowing the saving of a hundred miles, was always dreaded and often avoided. Such a trip across the desert was called a "water scrape." The evening before embarking on this arid plain, which at the time of Gregg's first journey in 1831 was unmarked, the captain's voice sounded above the sundry camp noises, "Fill up the water-kegs." This warning was usually most fitting, for the inexperienced among the travelers had little idea of what was to follow. Often they were careless about keeping filled the five-gallon cask which was part of the equipment of each wagon. The cooks, too, were busy cooking up bread and other foods sufficient to last for two days.

This portion of the trip was known as the *Jornado* and was feared and remembered by all. The intense suffering of the animals often caused trouble. When water was discovered after a "water scrape," it was almost impossible to keep them from dashing into it to quench their burning thirst. In the mad rush a wagon was sometimes overturned or other damage done. The Cimarron and other southwestern rivers in the summer season sometimes dry up completely, and water is procurable only by digging in the sand. Under such circumstances the party dug wells and obtained water for the stock and themselves.

Toward the end of the route rough and rocky roads were encountered. The wheels, which were completely dried out by this time, began to loosen up. The spokes were loose in both hub and felloe. It became necessary to drive pegs along the spokes in the hubs and bind them with buffalo hide. Sometimes the wheels became so loose that the tires fell off on the ground. Since, in the early days at least, no forge was carried, the method of tightening tires most commonly used was that of driving strips of hoop iron around the wheel between the tire and felloe. During a halt a dozen wheels might be undergoing repairs at once, with such a clatter that a visitor might imagine himself in a shipyard.

The severe military discipline that was attempted failed miserably among the individualistic frontiersmen. The rank of captain, high-sounding enough, was really but little more than nominal. Every proprietor, small or great, was apt to assume as much authority as the captain himself and start issuing orders without so much as consulting the commander. The latter was expected to command, was blamed for every failure, and yet had no real authority. Then, too, the guard, vigilant at first on reaching the Indian country, soon grew careless and slept or watched as their inclination might direct.

The culinary equipment and tableware of the Santa Fe traders consisted of a skillet, a frying-pan, a sheet-iron camp kettle, a coffee-pot, and a tin cup for each man. When the cooking was finished, the food in frying-pan and kettle was set on a grassy clump while the men surrounding it seated themselves on the ground. There they cracked jokes and in jovial mood proceeded to gnaw the meat from the bones held in their greasy hands, with a relish begotten of life in the open which far surpassed that experienced in homes of greater luxury in the settlements. Coffee was considered an indispensable beverage. Seldom did the wagoner fail to fill his huge tin cup a second time with this steaming liquid even under the broiling noonday sun.[9]

During the first part of the journey, for nearly a month, the food consisted principally of salt provisions, varied with small game or an occasional luckless antelope which fell into the traders' hands. Major Alphonso Wetmore records that on June 7, 1828, his group caught fish and picked strawberries. Two days later for breakfast they had wild-goose eggs with their bacon, and at noon they made turtle soup from a soft-shelled turtle which had been picked up.[10] When a buffalo was killed, however, there was a joyful revel as the men gathered around the meat and devoured huge quantities of the juicy roasts.

The travelers were none too careful about washing and bathing, and hence nearly all of them got lousy before they reached Santa Fe.

When the train was still about two hundred miles from Santa Fe, "runners" were despatched to enter the city before the caravan. They left in the night in order to elude any lurking savages who might be waiting to attack them. The runners were usually proprietors or agents who went to procure and send back provisions, to rent store space, prospect for sales, and make "arrangements" with the customs officers.

Near the end of the route the organization, never any too robust, expired. Then it was every man for himself until the weary, wayworn, but sprightly travelers reached the city. Gregg said that the entry into Santa Fe was

truly a scene for the artist's pencil to revel in. Even the animals seemed to participate in the humor of their riders, who grew more and more merry and obstreperous as they descended towards the city. I doubt, in short, whether the first sight of the walls of Jerusalem were beheld by the crusaders with much more tumultuous and soul-enrapturing joy.

[9] Gregg, *Commerce of the Prairies*, pp. 55, 56.
[10] Wetmore, "Diary of a Journey to Santa Fe," *loc. cit.*, p. 186.

The arrival of the traders was the high day of the year and aroused the drowsy little adobe town to economic and social activity. The Americans had prepared for their triumph the night before, and now with clean faces, combed hair, and wearing their best Sunday suits, these adventurers, with all the romance that attended the arrival of travelers from a far country, made their grand entry with *éclat*. The wagoners had tied new lashes to their whips, and as the cry "Los Americanos! Los Americanos!" rang out, fully aware of the dark-eyed beauties among the spectators, they vied with one another in the dexterity with which they flourished their rawhides and handled their teams.[11]

The goods had first to be got through the customs. This was an aggravating and wearisome process. The duties were high and the officials corrupt. The Americans accordingly resorted to every possible device to escape paying the duties. Governor Armijo for a time charged five hundred dollars a wagon no matter how large or how small the vehicle was. As a result the traders used very large wagons, and just outside of Santa Fe they reduced them to the minimum, destroying some and loading their cargo on the remaining ones. False bottoms enabled the traders to hide their gold and get it out of the country without paying the export duty. In some places it was said to be customary to split the duty three ways and divide it among the customs officers, the government, and the traders.

When the goods were placed on the market, there was a real boom. Stocks in the stores were renewed, new styles and newer goods were offered. Business among the tavern and restaurant keepers took a sudden spurt upward. Social life blossomed out also. Every night there was a fandango, orderly and without moral reproach unless the Americans turned it into a battle-ground. This is just what happened frequently.

The wagoners and other employees feasted, drank, and spent their time enjoying this Arabian-night world while the traders

[11] Gregg, *Commerce of the Prairies*, pp. 110-111.

sold their goods in Santa Fe or the neighboring towns. Sometimes a merchant took his goods for another trek far inland. As a rule, however, he disposed of them at Santa Fe, and laden with furs or wool and carrying gold or perhaps driving donkeys and mules, he joined with his fellows in forming a caravan bound for Missouri.

In the earlier days the profits were large. In 1823 Major Stephen Cooper led a company of thirty men with an investment of about two hundred dollars each. They returned with four hundred jacks, jennies, and mules, furs, and miscellaneous articles. Perhaps this was the beginning of the mule business which was destined to make Missouri famous.

The company of 1824, comprising 81 traders with an investment of between $30,000 and $35,000, left Vernon, Missouri, on May 16 with 156 horses and mules and 25 wagons, including some carriages and carts. They returned to Franklin, Missouri, on September 24 with $180,000 in gold and silver and $10,000 in furs. At first nearly all the travelers who made the trip were investors or proprietors. Gradually the number of proprietors in proportion to the whole decreased. In 1825 there were 90 proprietors and altogether 130 men in one trip. In 1843 only one man out of eleven was an owner of goods.[12] The era of centralization had come, and another fifteen years found large freighting companies carrying the goods very much as was done in the Platte Valley.

In the earlier times some men entered the trade with a few hundred dollars and with good management after a few years retired independently wealthy. James Webb with six hundred dollars of borrowed money went into the Santa Fe trade as late as 1844. Shortly after he commenced business, he had his life insured and assigned the policy as security. With this little start, credit, and good partnerships he was able to amass a comfortable fortune and retire seventeen years later. His stock in 1844, similar

[12] R. L. Duffus, *The Santa Fe Trail* (New York, 1930), pp. 81-84.

to that of other traders, consisted of dry-goods, notions, and hard-ware. The largest item was dry-goods. It included:

black cloth; striped, plaid, and black and white calicoes; white cambric, cotton, pongee, silk, fancy and blue plaid handkerchiefs; bleached, and plaid muslins; blue, and brown drillings; bleached sheeting; red pongee; bonnet ribbons; plaid silk shawls; women's white cotton hose; hickory shirts; and satin jeans. Among the notions were: cotton thread, black sewing silk, hooks and eyes, ivory combs, coat buttons, plain, and gilded vest buttons, needles, "London pins," and suspenders. Brass nails, iron spoons, scissors, pocket knives, butcher knives, saw files, padlocks, tacks, hoes, and spades comprised most of the hardware.[13]

The wages of drivers and packers were from $25 to $50 a month and found.[14]

Compared with more modern mercantile enterprises, the Santa Fe trade was small indeed. Viewed in its larger aspects, however, this movement holds an important place in the development of the Plains. It illustrates the ingenuity and resourcefulness of the American frontiersman. Furthermore, it penetrated the Indian country which was being set aside for the red man's permanent home and foreshadowed the failure of this policy before it was much more than instituted. It thrust a spear-head of American expansion toward the heart of the Mexican territory, and in due time the United States flag followed the trade.

Before the idea that the prairies were a desert—the Great American Desert—had more than been established by Pike and Long, the travelers to Santa Fe began to see the possibilities of permanent homes and agricultural pursuits along the route. To-day iron rails have followed where the patient mules and oxen made their weary way. The passenger amidst the comfort of the stream-liner accomplishes the eighty-day trip of yesterday in less than twenty-four hours.

[13] Invoices in Webb Mss., quoted in Webb, *Adventures in the Santa Fe Trade,* p. 82.
[14] Duffus, *The Santa Fe Trail,* p. 135.

CHAPTER IX

MARCHING TO ZION

THE ANTAGONISM of the frontier toward the Mormons, which manifested itself in outbreaks of mob violence from time to time, led to the determination of the Church of Jesus Christ of Latter-day Saints to move beyond the borders of civilization to a new Zion. These outbreaks at Nauvoo, Illinois, became so serious and bitter that in the dead of winter, on February 6, 1846, the first company of exiles crossed the Mississippi on the ice, not knowing where they were going. That night they camped in the snow, sleeping in their wagons, and in the morning there were nine new babies in camp. It was intended that each family of five persons should have one good wagon, three yoke of cattle, two cows, three sheep, one thousand pounds of flour, twenty pounds of sugar, one rifle and ammunition, a tent and poles, from ten to twenty pounds of seeds, twenty-five to one hundred pounds of farming tools, cooking utensils, and bedding. Many families were driven out, however, with almost nothing.[1]

The Saints camped at Sugar Creek, about nine miles from Nauvoo, for the remainder of the month of February. During this period there was much travel back and forth between the camp and the town, for the purpose of disposing of property and purchasing equipment for the journey. Gradually others joined the camp. Great sacrifices of property were made. Orson Pratt, one of the Twelve Apostles, owned a dwelling and two lots adjoining the Temple Square in the business section of Nauvoo which he says was considered worth $2,000 before the exodus. He had to accept for this real estate the small sum of $300 in

[1] Christopher Layton, *Autobiography* (Salt Lake City, 1911), pp. 26-27.

property at a high valuation or leave it unsold. He was offered four yoke of oxen with yokes, three chains, one wagon, and eight pounds of superfine flour.

While encamped at Sugar Creek the exiles were organized for the march. All men of families were organized into companies of tens, fifties, and hundreds. A commissary, a historian, and a clerk were appointed for the camp. The spare men were organized as pioneers and police. The pioneers were to go ahead and prepare roads, look out for camp-grounds, dig wells when necessary, and ascertain where hay and corn could be purchased for the horses. The police were to form a day and night guard. After dark no one was to leave the camp without the countersign or approach the guard abruptly. Every captain of ten was to keep one man on watch every night. One man was designated to receive, preserve, and dispense to the owners all lost property found. When Brigham Young, the leader, wanted to see the brethren together, a white flag was hoisted. When the captains were wanted together, a blue or colored flag was raised. Every detail was arranged for the orderly march into the unknown.

The winter was uncommonly severe, and the snow was so deep that paths had to be made with staves between the wagons and the tents. Great log fires were burning all through the camp. The exiles slept on the ground, but Patty Sessions wrote that on February 16 it was very cold and the wind blew so hard she could scarcely get near the fire for the smoke. Her family suffered much, for they had no tent.

Conditions of extreme hardship existed at this time because of the lack not only of food and clothing but also of teams and wagons to continue the exodus. Several families were entirely destitute and had to depend on their neighbors for charity. Yet camp life on Sugar Creek was quite novel and pleasant compared with what was to follow. The band played every evening, and by the camp-fires a fiddler played while the young people formed a cotillion or French four by the blazing logs. The band was organized to travel together. Many declared they had never suffered so much from the cold as they did in that winter camp, but this musical organization did much to gladden hearts and keep spirits from drooping.

On March 1 about noon the emigrants broke camp, and soon nearly four hundred wagons were moving toward they "knew not where." Snow still covered the ground but winter was breaking; the frost had begun to leave the ground, and the caravan all but foundered in a sea of mud. To add to their distress, it rained incessantly and the roads were impassable. Then, too, the teams were weak and poor, for they had been living on browse—buds and twigs of trees felled for this purpose. The diaries record innumerable broken axletrees and wagon hounds, attesting to the terrible condition of the bottomless roads.

As they moved along, the emigrants were obliged to sell their feather beds for corn. Crockery, cooking utensils, and everything that could possibly be spared were turned into provisions. The responsibility on Brigham Young was so great that he became a mere shadow of his former self. His coat, which would barely meet around him before he left Nauvoo, lapped over twelve inches. But even under such circumstances those from neighboring communities who visited the camps reported the emigrants cheerful, happy, and contented.

The leaders responded to the occasion and organized the multitude efficiently. Some were to repair wagons and make new ones out of the old, manufacture chairs, barrels, tubs, churns, baskets, and other such goods to be traded in the settlements for provisions. Parties of workmen took contracts for splitting rails, moving dirt from a coal-bed, and like tasks, receiving their pay in provisions or cash. Two elders were sent to Ohio and other parts of the country to solicit aid and to invite rich Gentiles to contribute to the needs of the Saints and assist them on their westward journey. About six hundred dollars was raised in this manner. These arrangements resulted in supplying the emigrants with an abundance of food and traveling facilities. The people of Iowa were very sympathetic toward the Mormons. The men were given employment, many Iowans visited the camps, the band was invited to play at every settlement, and they were generously recompensed.

The camp program was so well arranged that a tent city was raised in a few hours' time and many real conveniences were enjoyed. The camp was large and spread over a wide territory. Two ladies who visited a friend in another part of the camp one evening lost their way and had to be guided to their tent by the friend's husband. On March 9 the camp was laid out in the form of a half hollow square.

The caravan was often delayed by freshets and had to wait for three weeks to cross Shoal Creek near the Chariton River. During the first month they advanced only about one hundred miles. Helen Mar Whitney wrote of the dreary muddy march of April 2:

Some of our experiences during those days could not be written, neither could time erase them from my memory . . . the road lay over a prairie, and the earth being soft and inundated with a previous rain all that could were obliged to walk to favor the poor animals. Our feet would sink into the deep mud at every step, and some of us came near being minus some shoes. As for umbrellas, they were rare articles, and we had the cold, pitiless rain beating down upon us all the way, till we were chilled and shaken with the cold . . .

At a location which they named Garden Grove, the emigrants paused and made some improvements for those who would follow. A number of log cabins were built, and a group was left to cultivate the ground and prepare a stopping-place for the travel-weary Saints to come. The main body moved forward to another halting point which they named Mount Pisgah. All hands went to work, some breaking the sod, some preparing the soil for planting, and others splitting rails and fencing a big field. This was all done in one day, and that evening there was singing and a dance. The places where such improvements were made were called "traveling stakes of Zion."

At a party at Mount Pisgah the problem was how to light the building. Finally ingenuity suggested a way. Turnips were hollowed out and the rind scraped very thin. A short candle was placed in each of these cup-like holders, and the light shone through the translucent rind. They were placed around the walls and suspended from the ceiling. The subdued lighting was pronounced a real success and helped to make the guests forget that they were homeless.

The weather continued rainy, drenching the travelers on the road, and in camp the mud was ankle-deep in and around the tents. The travelers were obliged to cut brush and limbs of trees and throw them on the ground in order to keep their beds from sinking in the mire. On April 9, on account of the muddy roads, many wagons were unable to reach the timber and suffered much because there was no fuel for fires. On May 2 Patty Sessions wrote: "It has rained continuously for six days, and my bed has been wet all the time. Today I got my bed out to dry for the first time."

On the 16th of May Eliza R. Snow went to an outdoor quilting party. After the work was done, the ladies took tea with the mistress of the quilting. The simple refreshments were served in a tent around a table made of bark supported by poles resting on crotched sticks.

When the laundering was to be done, the boys hitched up the teams and took the girls to a neighboring stream, where they fished while the girls washed. Either they took a picnic lunch or the boys returned to the camp and brought a warm dinner. The moving multitude made a thrilling picture indeed to one of the leaders, who said he stopped his carriage on the top of a hill in the midst of the rolling prairie. "I beheld the Saints coming in all directions from hills and dales, groves and prairies with their wagons, flocks, and herds, by the thousands. It looked like the movement of a nation."[2]

On reaching the Missouri River in the vicinity of the site of the present city of Council Bluffs, the emigrants camped on the eastern bank while they built a ferry-boat and began ferrying the great multitude over. Night and day this work continued for months, and still the crossing was not completed until late in the season.

When the van of the emigrants arrived in the Missouri Valley, they found ripe strawberries, and after eating all they cared for, they filled all their buckets with the luscious fruit. Peter Sarpy, who ran a trading-post at Bellevue, gave a ball in honor of the Mormons which was a delightful affair. It was the first time the emigrants had any use for the better clothes packed away in their chests since they left Nauvoo. Sarpy's people were nearly all Indians or half-breeds. An Indian girl, the daughter of Chief Le Clerc, was the belle of the evening. She had been educated in a western city, was dressed with good taste, and was quite an accomplished coquette.

Sarpy also gave the Mormons the job of bringing about ninety thousand pounds of buffalo robes and furs from Grand Island, about two hundred and twenty miles west. Forty wagons with three yoke of oxen to the wagon were required, and the Saints received $1,000 in cash, some provisions, and a horse.

It had been the design of the leaders to leave the main body encamped in temporary settlements while the leaders, with a select band of pioneers, hastened on to the Rocky Mountains that season, but word came to the headquarters on the Missouri that a recruiting officer had arrived at Mount Pisgah with a requisition for five hundred men for service in the United States Army during the Mexican War. It was customary at the larger camps

[2] Matthias F. Cowley, ed., *Wilford Woodruff, Fourth President of the Church of Jesus Christ of Latter-day Saints, History of his Life and Labors, as recorded in his Daily Journal* ...(Salt Lake City, 1909), p. 250.

where the emigrants stopped a few days to make large arbors or boweries of poles, brush, and wattling. These were used as council houses, for religious services and conferences. In one of these boweries, where the ground was tramped firm by the worshipers, a farewell ball was held for the Mormon Battalion on their last afternoon with their friends. Old faded gowns of cotton, pierced ears without earrings, hands without finger rings, and men's watch-pockets without watches gave evidence of the sacrifice of expensive ornaments and attire as a part of the hardships of exile. There were no refreshments, but a spirit of brotherhood prevailed. At sunset they had a song, and an elder asked the blessings of Heaven on all as they separated, some to go on a three-thousand-mile march, facing unknown hazards, while the others were to remain in the camps.

The Mormons were in a pinched economic condition that summer. Colonel Thomas L. Kane from Fort Leavenworth met two teamsters who had traded a Missouri squatter some silver spoons and a feather bed for wagonloads of corn. They asked the colonel for something to eat, and when they were refused, they said grace and made a lunch before him from the softer of their ears of corn, eating the grains from the cob as horses do.

After the leaders had crossed the Missouri and while they were searching out a location for the winter on the west side, a large number of emigrants were encamped on the east bank, scattered along the Missouri and its tributaries for twenty-five miles. They were cutting hay, building cabins, and preparing for winter. Those west of the river, with Brigham Young at their head, pitched a temporary camp at a place known as Cutler's Park. The first day after the decision was taken to camp at this point, a place for holding meetings was made. A stand and seats for three hundred people were drawn up. The camp was pitched upon some hills which encircled a cool spring. Squares were laid out, and as the wagons arrived, they took their positions along the four sides in double rows, forming hollow squares and leaving room between squares for streets. The tents were also pitched in rows at intervals between the wagons. The stock was enclosed in high fenced pens without the camp, and the streets were covered with leafy arborwork and kept scrupulously clean, forming shaded cloister walks.

While occupying this temporary camp the pilgrims built permanent homes for the winter on the river bottom. About three miles northeast, where the town of Florence is now located (about six miles north of Omaha, Nebraska), the winter camp was established. It was called Winter Quarters. The town-site was laid out in blocks of 20 by 40 rods. Each block contained 5 acres and was divided into 20 lots. The city as laid out occupied about six hundred to eight hundred acres. About the first of October workers began to converge on that point, and soon hundreds of men were busily engaged chopping down trees and sawing logs. Like magic a city rose from the wilderness. Within two months there were 538 log houses and 83 sod buildings. Wells were dug and yards built for the stock. Blockhouses, breastworks, and a stockade were built after the custom of the frontier to protect the dwellers from the Indians.

Most of the houses were 12 by 18 feet and were made of logs. Many were roofed by splitting oak timber into boards or shakes and anchoring them in place with weights, as was customary in the wooded regions, but many others had the typical sod-house roofs of the Plains. These were made by laying willow brush over the pole rafters, covering this with hay, and placing a layer of sod or soil over all. The log houses were daubed on the inside with mud. Fireplaces and chimneys were made of sod. Some of the houses were true sod houses, and in one of these Brigham Young lived. There were a few dugouts on the sides of the hills. These were simply square holes in the ground, the walls on three sides being formed of earth, the front of logs or sod, and the roof of sod. House doors were made of puncheons, and the floors were largely earth. Helen Mar Whitney's turf fireplace chimney smoked and drew so poorly that at the end of a month the brethren brought some bricks down from the debris of old Fort Atkinson and built her an excellent chimney.

The dirt floors were covered with pieces of carpet or canvas that had survived the wear and tear of the journey. Curtains were made to divide the cabins into rooms. The furniture, such as cupboards and bedsteads, was made to order and attached to the house. Chairs, tables, and stools were also made from the forest, although there was an occasional rocking-chair, a relic of better days.

The church organization was not neglected. A tabernacle was provided, and the city was divided into twenty-two wards with a bishop over each. The departure of five hundred men in the Mormon Battalion and a hundred and forty for pioneer service weakened the camp in man-power and entailed sacrifices. When the homes were being built, it was no strange thing to see the women hauling logs or mixing and carrying mud for the chinking and daubing.

The various activities common to any well regulated community were carried on. About the middle of December several schools were started. On January 12, 1847, a dancing-school had four hundred pupils. So great was the patronage that two sections were run. Classes met from ten in the morning until three in the afternoon and from four in the afternoon until nine at night.

The town was well supplied with workshops, and there was a water grist-mill with machinery costing $8,000 and one or two horse-power mills. The water-mill was not ready for use until far into the winter, however, and many makeshifts were used. Some of the Saints ate their wheat boiled, others ate their corn on the cob or made hominy, while some boiled the corn in the ear until it was soft enough to be grated. Many pieces of tin were converted into graters. Coffee-mills were laboriously used to grind cereals, but they did little more than crack the grains. A spring-pole with a pestle attached to it was used to pound grain, and the finer particles were sifted out for flour while the coarser were used for hominy. Naturally there was great anxiety for the completion of the mill. The price of grain doubled in border counties of Missouri as a result of the location of the Latter-day Saint's camp.

The regular diet was corn-bread, salt, bacon, and a little milk. John Young said that mush and bacon became so nauseating that to swallow it was like taking medicine.[3] As a result of such a diet day after day with no fresh meat and no vegetables, black scurvy appeared. The symptoms commenced with black streaks running up the nails and pains in the ends of the fingers or toes, together with inflammation. Poultices of raw potatoes on the affected parts were used to combat the disease. The pain was so excruciating that the victim welcomed death. As early as December 20 almost one in ten were sick. Again and again mournful little parties proceeded to the burial-ground to lay to rest the victims of the scourge, until it began to look as though all would be sleeping on the hill before spring unless fresh food could be obtained.

Brigham Young, like an able field-marshal, was everywhere—now at the bedside of the dying, next in his carriage flying to the scene of a priarie fire, aiding to extinguish it, and in a calm voice directing in the crisis. Constantly he was giving counsel, and again he was the leading spirit in a social evening, for he fully realized the need for social diversion in the face of such trying times. On January 23, 1847, there was a celebration and dance at the Council House. President Young was there and told the assembly he would show them how to go forth in the dance in an acceptable manner before the Lord. He then knelt and prayed to God in behalf of the meeting, asking God's blessing on those present and dedicating the meeting and house to the Lord. At the sound of the music he led out in the dance. Thirteen days later a party of "Silver Grays" was held at the Council House during the day and evening. In attendance were all the old people who could be found in the camp. In the afternoon a band circulated through

[3] John R. Young, *Memoirs of John R. Young, Utah Pioneer, 1847* (Salt Lake City, 1920), p. 41.

the camp in a carriage, playing "The Bride and the Bridegroom Accompanying." Stag-parties were held, and members of the band went around in a sleigh serenading various people.

Brigham Young recommended the women to keep their gold rings and silk dresses instead of disposing of them for necessities, and proposed that they manufacture willow baskets and the men make washboards and tables with which to carry on a trade with the Missourians for grain and other commodities needed. The women also spun their wool and knitted stockings. Deer and elk skins were procured and leggings made for the men.

The widows, of whom there were seventy-five, and the needy were cared for by the brethren. Phineas Richards was placed at the head of a committee to fish in the river and thus provide food for the destitute. Boatloads of fish were caught and distributed.

Even in the midst of the hardships and difficulties of that winter spent on "Misery Bottoms," as Winter Quarters was sometimes called, the leaders of the church were preparing and planning for the general migration which occupied the next twenty years. A general epistle to the church directed the Saints in the British Isles and other Atlantic countries to emigrate as speedily as possible.

In the spring a band of pioneers led by Brigham Young himself, whom they appointed lieutenant-general, prepared to go to the Rocky Mountains and locate a new Zion. In case they did not find a place, they were to plant a crop and arrange another camp which should serve as a base for a further westward march. This body, officially known as the Pioneers, gathered on the Elkhorn River and, after a week of preparation, left on April 14, 1847, with 73 wagons, 143 men, three women, and two children. It was a matter of considerable trial for the men to leave their families behind for a separation of months. Elder Erastus Snow called his family together and, like a patriarch of old, laid his hands on the heads of his wives and children and blessed them before departing on that thousand-mile journey into the unknown.

At the beginning of the journey the captains of the Saints made the laws by which the company was to be governed on the way to their new home. The more important rules were as follows: The bugle was to be blown at five A.M. Every man was to rise, pray, attend to his team, get breakfast, and be ready to start by seven. Each extra man was to travel on the off side of a wagon with his loaded gun on his shoulder. The drivers were to have their guns where they could lay hands on them immediately. Every man was to have his arms ready for instant use. A halt of about an hour was to be made at noon. Prepared food would be eaten, and the column would move forward without loss of time occasioned by cooking. The camp at night was to be drawn up in a circle, with the horses inside, when necessary, and the tents on the outside. The horn was to blow at 8:30 P.M., when everyone except the night guard was to return to his wagon, pray, and be in bed by nine o'clock. All fires were to be out at that time. Very little interval was to be allowed between the wagons, which were to travel in two columns. No man was to leave his post or the camp without orders from his captain. The rear was to be brought up by the guard with the cannon. It was the business of this group, also, to see that nothing was left behind.

When the party entered the buffalo country, an advance-guard was thrown out to keep the cattle separated from the buffalo, which sometimes was quite a problem. Part of the day was spent in military tactics and drill. This had a double purpose, disciplining the men for defense and consuming the energy which might have made them restless. On Saturday evening they pitched camp and remained over Sunday. At the beginning of the journey the horses were fed on cottonwood trees, with only two quarts of corn daily as a ration; but for five hundred miles the country was so devoid of vegetation that finally the stock was fed the grain, flour, and biscuit provided for the Pioneers themselves, while they subsisted on game and fish. A small group was assigned the task of seining fish in the lakes and rivers they passed, and others took a wagon and hunted buffalo, hauling the meat to the line of march.

Among the travelers was an elder by the name of William Clayton who tied a piece of red flannel on the rear wheel of a wagon and counted the number of revolutions in a day. By measuring the wheel he was able to compute the number of miles traveled daily.[4] Detailed notes were taken and landmarks and physical features recorded. This information was later used to produce the Mormon Guide Book. William Clayton and Orson Pratt subsequently devised an odometer, an ingenious device consisting of cog-wheels made of wood, which registered the distance traveled, and enabled them to tell how far they had gone.

Over part of the route guide-boards were put up every ten miles. From time to time members of the party left letters for the following emigrants. Sometimes they were placed inside a board slotted with a saw, sometimes in a buffalo skull hung on a post, or a message was even written on the skull itself. Eliza R. Snow in the party following mentions their finding on July 14 a buffalo skull on which had been written: "All well, feed bad, are only 300 miles from W." It was dated May 9. At one time the Pioneers met traders returning from Fort Laramie to Council Bluffs and sent letters back by them.

A leather boat, called the "revenue cutter," was mounted on wheels like a spring wagon and was used for the double purpose of crossing streams and hauling buffalo meat to camp. Candles were made from the buffalo tallow. Howard Egan records in his diary that they burned beautifully and that he was "writing by the light of one now" (May 16, 1847).

At some streams the vanguard of the Pioneers built bridges, at others they tried rafting their goods over. In one instance in Wyoming, when several wagons were tied together, the plan ended in disaster with a loss of wagon boxes and their contents. At one place a hundred and ten miles west of Laramie a ferry was built, and a crew of about ten was left to run the ferry, take

[4] William Clayton, *William Clayton's Journal* (Salt Lake City, 1921), pp. 136-137.

Gentile emigrants over at the rate of a dollar and a half a wagon, and come on with the next party of Saints. In a little over a week they earned about four hundred dollars in provisions at Fort Laramie prices, besides taking their own wagons over.

Mountain fever delayed the Pioneers materially, for in less than a week half the party were stricken. Finally President Young ordered those who were well to go on ahead while he and the other sick remained a few days in camp.

The advance group went into the Salt Lake Valley and began immediately to plow, prepare the soil for putting in a late crop, and initiate the first irrigating that was ever done in Utah by white men. A few days later the rest of the party marched into the valley, and the Pioneers made their official entry on July 24. When Brigham Young saw the valley he said, "This is the place." Clara Decker Young said that when she heard it she wept, "for it seemed to me the most desolate in all the world." One week later, on July 31, they had plowed more than fifty acres and planted most of it, in addition to building houses for themselves.

On August 20 messengers were despatched with horses and pack-mules to meet the next group that was on its way. They were to ascertain who were in the party, what stores were being provided, and, if possible, return to the Salt Lake Valley before the Pioneers set out for the camp on the Missouri.

At Winter Quarters, in the meantime, all those able to travel prepared to follow for the unknown destination to be selected by the Pioneers. The second party left in June under the leadership of Parley P. Pratt and John Taylor. This expedition was known as the First Immigration and comprised 1,553 people with about 560 wagons. They traveled in several divisions and reached the Salt Lake Valley that fall. The Pioneers, after laying out the town and making plans for the new settlement, left a third of their number and started east to spend the winter at Winter Quarters and look after the emigration. Brigham Young with 108 men began the return trek. When the Pioneers met the First

Immigration about 300 miles east of Salt Lake at the Upper Crossing of the Sweetwater, a great celebration was prepared. On a grassy spot surrounded by a dense growth of bushes, tables were improvised, snowy table-cloths and dishes were brought out of trunks. An abundance of game, together with food kept packed away for special occasions, made a sumptuous feast. This was followed by dancing and speeches. A number of the Pioneers met their families there and turned back to Salt Lake City.

During the summer and winter other emigrants from Illinois moved in and occupied Winter Quarters. In the summer of 1848 three expeditions, the first led by Brigham Young himself, set out for Salt Lake. This migration, totaling 2,417 people and 792 wagons, left Winter Quarters deserted. The Indian agent had ordered the place evacuated, and the few Saints who remained moved to the east side of the Missouri, leaving the improvements for the most part to the Indians.

The town of Kanesville, Iowa, later to be known as Council Bluffs, was built up and populated by the Mormons, and the region roundabout was preëmpted and cultivated with the purpose of forming a base for the westward march. Four thousand acres were planted to wheat, corn, potatoes, and vegetables. There was enough food for two years for the community, but they expected to feed the animals in the trains for the mountains and help the immigrants from England when they came. As these settlers got ready to go to the Valley, they could sell their preëmption rights and homesteads to help start homes in Zion.

Annually for the next twenty-one years hundreds of emigrants left from some point on the Mississippi or the Missouri River to cross the Plains to the promised land.[5]

[5] The routes and starting-points used during the different years were: 1848, from New Orleans via river boats up the Mississippi and Missouri to Winter Quarters; 1849-1852, traveled the same route but landed at Kanesville and started across the Plains from there; 1853, up the Mississippi to Keokuk and by wagon to Kanesville; 1854, up the Missouri to Westport (now Kansas City) and across the Plains via the Oregon Trail; 1855, the route was the same as the year before except the emigrants landed at Atchison, Kansas, and started from

Their manner of marching did not vary materially from that adopted by the Pioneers. The wagons often were driven two abreast, and sometimes five or six abreast in a region where Indian attacks were feared. The organization consisted of companies of hundreds, and these were subdivided into fifties and tens. Each of these units had a captain, and over all were a president and two counselors. In making the divisions friends and relatives were placed in the same units. At first the hundreds tried to keep together, and each such group camped in a circle at night; but since a breakdown in one ten held up the whole hundred, smaller units were later allowed to travel independently.

The long tramp under the hot sun was almost unendurable, especially for the women and children. Women were not infrequently in a delicate physical condition but did not ride unless unable to walk. Some days the dust was suffocating, and on others the rain poured down pitilessly. Storms blew the tents down at night, and the wind blew dust and sand into the cooking. Sickness was especially hard. Since the caravan could not stop and rest from the toil of the journey, the patient lay in a wagon and bounced along ten hours a day.

In spite of privations the women carried on courageously. Mary Rich wrote:

We did not grieve or mourn over it; we had some very nice times, when the roads were not so bad. We would make the mountains ring with our songs, and sometimes the company got together in a dance of an evening on the grass. We rejoiced, instead of mourning, that we were going to the Rocky Mountains, where we would be free to live our religion and be acknowledged as wives.

Mormon Grove, 4½ miles west; 1856-1858, they disembarked at New York, Boston, and Philadelphia, traveled by train to the end of the line at Iowa City, where they took up their overland march; 1859-1863, Florence (old Winter Quarters) was used as a starting-point again; 1864-1866, the new town of Wyoming, forty miles south of Florence, became the starting-point; from 1867 on the emigrants traveled by rail to the termini and on by wagon. In 1869 the railroad reached Ogden and put an end to the overland trek after twenty-three years.

The outdoor life seemed materially to benefit some, for she recorded: "I had never had very good health, until I started on that trip."

Mary and another wife of Charles Rich walked and drove two wagons over the latter part of the journey. When she arrived in the Valley, her once long dress had been worn to knee length from walking in the brush. At night around the camp-fire the women prepared food and ministered to their children. Sunday was a busy time, for the washing and baking were done that day. Sometimes on a week-day a company would stop a day to pick berries, hunt, wash, repair wagons, burn charcoal for the blacksmiths, and make tar for wagon grease.

The manufacturing processes were carried on during the journey from Nauvoo to Salt Lake City. A witness said that before 1850 he had seen a repeating rifle made by a mechanic from scraps of old iron and inlaid with the silver of two half-dollars, under a boiling sun in a spot where the average height of the grass was above the workman's shoulders. He had seen a cobbler in the twilight hunting for a lapstone with which to finish a pair of shoes. He had seen cloth of which the wool was sheared, dyed, spun, and woven during a progress of over three hundred miles. Another witness testified that

it was a pretty sight to watch them starting off for the day's march; great numbers of women and children walking in advance gaily, the little ones picking flowers, the boys looking for grapes or plums if there were trees near, and the mothers knitting as they went: all seemed willing to endure hardship, looking upon the journey as a pilgrimage to the promised land, where they should have rest.

The organization, government, and response to leadership of the Mormon migration were remarkable. Whereas, in almost every case among the other overland travelers, companies were continually quarreling and breaking up into smaller units, the Mormons in the vast area without administration governed themselves.

When a quarrel arose, the unit stopped and counseled about the matter, settled it, and moved on amicably. When two young men intruded on a dance, they were tried before the bishop's court. A man who challenged another to a duel was expelled from the camp. Thievery, cutting tent-ropes, and passing counterfeit money were rebuked and the perpetrators threatened by Brigham Young.

In the year 1849 a plan was inaugurated to help the poor among the European Saints to come to America. It was called the "Perpetual Emigrating Fund for the Poor." During the first year over five thousand dollars was raised for the purpose.[6] The plan was for the immigrant to pay back the amount loaned as soon as he was financially able to do so. The fund would continue indefinitely to revolve and to grow if all were faithful in paying their debts. Unfortunately some did not repay the loans, and the fund became depleted. This was one reason for the experiment with hand-carts. A carrying company was established also, which furnished wagons at the starting-points in the East.

The machinery for conducting the immigration was complete, efficient, and free from corruption. When a ship was chartered to bring a group, the passengers were usually under the charge of an elder from Zion who was returning to America. Two men of the prevailing language were chosen to coöperate with him, and the three were known as the president and two counselors. At each place where there was a break in transportation, elders were stationed to protect the group from financial exploitation and to provide comforts and efficient service. At the starting-point for the overland trek was an immigration agent with great warehouses of supplies and implements. He provided the required number of wagons and the equipment needed for each summer's migration. Men from Zion took charge of the immigrants on the march to Salt Lake Valley. In 1866 nine sailing-vessels brought as many companies across the Atlantic, and the church trains that year

[6] Minutes of the General Conference of the Church of Jesus Christ of Latter-day Saints, Sept. 6, 1850, *Deseret News*, Salt Lake City, Sept. 14, 1850.

numbered 459 wagons and 3,315 draft animals. Thousands of yards of canvas was bought each year and stored for wagon covers and tents.

Of all the transportation schemes on the Plains, one of the most interesting was the use of hand-carts in the Mormon migration. The plan was proposed by Brigham Young, who was also responsible for the design, and during a period of four years ten companies, totaling almost three thousand persons, used these vehicles in their tramp across the Plains.[7] The Perpetual Emigrating Fund had become exhausted, and the desire was to bring the maximum number of immigrants west at a minimum cost. It was argued that a hand-cart company could travel farther in a day than ox-wagons and would save the expense of wagons and teams. It was felt that the teams roused the Indians' sense of cupidity and exposed the travelers to greater danger. Then, too, stock was a continual worry. It had to be constantly guarded, and lost stock, frequently hunted, caused irksome delays.

It was in 1856 that hand-carts were first tried out in a large way. That year four companies, known as the Hand-Cart Brigade, moved across the Plains. The hand-carts were two-wheeled vehicles the width of a wagon with a box about three or four feet long balanced on the axle and a handle with a long cross-bar with which to balance and pull the cart. The whole thing was made without iron except for the tires. The wooden hub turned on a wooden axle, and that the flimsy vehicles held up as well as they did, often carrying four or five hundred pounds, is astonishing. The axles wore through and the carts had to be tied together with rawhide before the journey was half done. Some of the immigrants made bows and erected canvas covers to protect the loads from the weather. At the beginning there was a shortage of carts, holding up the starting of the journey until too late in the season. Many of the carts toward the last were made of wood insufficiently

[7] Leroy R. Hafen, "Hand-Cart Migration Across the Plains," in James F. Willard and Colin B. Goodykoontz, editors, *The Trans-Mississippi West* (Boulder, Col., 1930), p. 104.

cured and did not stand up under the grueling journey over the sun-baked Plains.

There were supposed to be one tent and four hand-carts for each twenty persons. The typical company had about five hundred persons with from five to seven wagons and fifty beef cattle and cows. The better equipped companies had from 125 to 150 carts. The Christiansen Company, of 1857, with 544 persons divided into four divisions with a captain over each, had only 68 hand-carts, four wagons, and one cow. The wagons carried the provisions. The Martin Company, of 1856, was provisioned for sixty days. Most of the carts carried a hundred pounds of flour besides the personal baggage and tents. Each person was allowed only seventeen pounds of baggage. Many of the immigrants had brought the choicest of their furniture, souvenirs, and other personal property. A great deal of this was left at Iowa City. Great heaps of books and other valuables were left on the camp-ground. Again at Florence they had to leave behind all except the bare necessities.

Some of the later companies of 1856 did not leave Florence until August. The Martin Company, though warned that the season was too far advanced to attempt the 1,031 miles, were anxious to go on and take the risk. They left on August 25. The enthusiasm of the immigrant to get to Zion was well illustrated in 1857 in the case of a Swede named Hulberg who had a wife and two children. The wife was thought to be too frail to make the trip and was asked to remain at Florence. The disappointment was more than they could endure. After his company had gone about fifty miles, Hulberg rejoined it, having hauled his children and his wife most of the way in a hand-cart, driven on by an irresistible desire to reach Zion.

A semimilitary program was carried out. All items on the program were announced by bugle call. Rising, breakfast, public-worship, strike-tents, march, dinner, halt, pitch-camp, supper, public-worship, and retiring calls—all were sounded on the monotonous bugle. Every call was some well-known air which soon be-

MORMONS CROSSING THE PLAINS, 1856

came very hateful to the weary marchers. Often on the march they sang the "Hand-Cart Song" of six stanzas. The chorus ran:

> Some must push and some must pull
> As we go marching up the hill
> As merrily on the way we go
> Until we reach the Valley Oh.

The way of the cart traveler was hard. One man remembered that his father and older brother formed the wheel team and a younger brother and sister were the lead team. The mother pushed and a seven-year-old trudged along by her side. In the cart on the luggage for a time lay the baby, between one and two years old, but the child was unable to endure the rigors of the trail, and a little grave was dug on the lone prairie to receive the wasted form. A sieve was placed over the quiet little face, the sod returned to its place, and the sorrowing mother again took her station at the cart. Sometimes there were so many sick the four wagons of the company were filled.[8]

At least one company lost a large number of its oxen which had been hauling the equipment. The group was obliged to burn or abandon a large portion of its blankets and other equipment which soon were to be sorely needed on the autumn mountain journey. The rest was loaded on their overburdened carts.

Walking over the plain was a great promoter of an appetite. One man mentions that the prescribed ration was never enough. He felt as though he could eat a rusty nail or gnaw on a file. His hunger continued all day long and every time he awoke at night.

Even in the face of this experience some of the companies had to begin cutting down the ration. In 1856 the Martin and Willie companies, having started late, were caught in the mountains by snow-storms. Short of provisions, they were enfeebled by the privations; death began to take its toll and multiplied until it was neces-

[8] J. M. Tanner, *A Biographical Sketch of James Jensen* (Salt Lake City, 1911), pp. 24-25.

sary to appoint a burial squad. Death became commonplace; people were actually known to have sat on a corpse to keep warm until the body grew cold. Two men, partners, were pulling a cart together when one begged the other to let him drop down by the side of the road and die. Thinking it would revive his mate to rest a while, the man stopped, and his companion lay down on the ground. In ten minutes he was dead.

One of the relief party said:

The train was strung out for three or four miles. There were old men pulling and tugging at their carts, many of which were loaded with sick wives and children. We saw little children, six and eight years of age, struggling through the snow and mud. As night came on the mud and snow froze to their clothing.

On the day the Willie Company went over South Pass, fifteen persons died of exposure and want. Some pulled their carts all day and died in the night. Hearths served three purposes: first, a fireplace; second, a warm sleeping-place after the ashes were swept away; third, the easiest place in which to dig a grave to bury the night's dead.[9] In the midst of the mountain snows the company camped. When finally the relief party arrived, the emigrants had had nothing to eat for forty-eight hours and were freezing and starving to death. Food was given out and wood hauled from the neighboring hills. Help was too late for some, however, for nine died that night. This company lost one-sixth of its numbers on the Plains from cold and starvation.

Nevertheless the hand-cart experiment was not entirely a failure. The difficulties in 1856 were due to the fact that the suffering companies started two months too late. The first companies that year arrived in Salt Lake City after having traveled the fourteen hundred miles from Iowa City in nine weeks and had fewer deaths than normally occurred with wagon-trains. Some days they traveled

[9] John Jacques, *Salt Lake Herald*, 1879; *Journal History of the Church, 1846-1850, Handcart Companies*, Ms., Church of Jesus Christ of Latter-day Saints Library, Salt Lake City.

from twenty-five to thirty miles, which was twice the average of ox-teams. In the year 1859 a train went from Florence to Salt Lake at a cost of $22.30 per person.

The grueling hardships of the tramp, together with an increase in stock in Utah and the discovery that teams could make the round trip from Zion in one season, caused the hand-cart method to be abandoned, and with the completion of the iron bonds between the East and West the picturesque overland migration came to a close.

Little can be added to the evaluation of Katherine Coman: "It was, taken all in all, the most successful example of regulated immigration in United States history." [10]

[10] Katherine Coman, *Economic Beginnings of the Far West* (New York, 1912), Vol. II, p. 184.

CHAPTER X

CHASING THE RAINBOW'S END

THE OVERLAND TRAIL which frayed out like a rope at its eastern end, with starting-points at the various Missouri River towns from Kansas City, as it is now called, north to the mouth of the Platte, was bound into a unit near Fort Kearney, Nebraska, and ran along the Platte to the mountains in Wyoming. In the western part of that State and in Idaho it again divided, one branch leading to Oregon and the other to California.

The first travelers over the eastern end of this highway were the trappers and fur-traders who, in order to avoid the hostile Indians on the Missouri River, struck directly across the prairie with their goods for the rendezvous. Captain William L. Sublette was the first to use wheeled vehicles on this route in 1830.

In 1841 the first band of emigrants set out from the Missouri border for California and Oregon, and by 1843 the so-called Oregon Trail had become well enough established that more than a thousand moved over it in the early years. Joel Palmer, who traveled up the trail in 1845, tells us that a large body of three thousand emigrants paused for organization on Big Soldier Creek in Kansas. According to the arrangements, two chief officers were to be elected, a pilot to act as guide and a captain. That year one candidate offered to guide the party for five hundred dollars in advance. Another offered to do the work for half that amount with a small sum down and the balance at Vancouver. The latter candidate was elected. A host of lesser officers were also elected— lieutenants, judges, sergeants, and so forth.[1] But a number of dis-

[1] Joel Palmer, *Journal of Travels over the Rocky Mountains to the Mouth of the Columbia River*, R. G. Thwaites, ed. (Cleveland, Ohio, 1906), pp. 11, 39-43.

appointed candidates were unwilling to abide by the will of the majority and manifested such a spirit of insubordination that it was mutually agreed to break the group into three companies with separate officers, though the chief officers elected in the first place were to continue to hold the supreme offices. An attempt was then made to collect enough money to ensure the wages of the pilot. Only about one hundred and ninety dollars of the sum promised could be obtained. Some refused to pay, and others had no money. Each of the three companies took its turn in leading the train for a day. Henry Howe records that in 1846 a company of 288, which organized on May 12, had split twice, making three divisions, by June 2.

When he left behind the restraint of civilization and entered a pathless prairie which knew no law or order, the worst side of man's nature revealed itself. In time of sickness men sometimes deserted their companies, leaving them to die; or at the period of a stampede they disregarded their solemn promise to aid their fellow-travelers in time of distress and drove off, leaving them with insufficient animals to pull their wagons. In the many disputes which arose, hard words were often followed by bloodshed. In some instances perpetrators of capital crime were haled before a hastily summoned people's court, given a brief, though fair, trial, sentenced, and summarily executed.

Jesse Applegate, who led a band of emigrants to Oregon in 1843, described the government drawn up by his organization. A council composed of the ablest and most respected fathers of the migration exercised legislative and judicial authority. As a rule the council was called into session on the days when the group did not travel. On one occasion he recorded a special session called to deal with a dispute which did not admit of delay. In this instance the controversy related to a young man who had agreed to do a man's work on the journey for his board and bed.

When such a dispute was to be settled, the council resolved itself into a high court from which there was no appeal. The offending and the aggrieved parties appeared before the body. Witnesses were examined, and the parties represented themselves or had home legal talent to represent them. When these proceedings were over, the judges, without being in any way cramped by technicalities, decided the case according to its merits. Justice was thus efficiently and promptly administered without any monetary cost. Judgment executed largely by public opinion was not always carried out, however, due to division among a party with resultant splits.

According to one traveler, the camp was aroused at sunrise by the sound of a bugle. After breakfast the cattle were caught up and there was a scene of hurry and confusion, with oxen bellowing and men and women hastening here and there about the final preparations to break camp. On the trail a train of fifty wagons and one hundred and fifty people with numbers of loose stock would string out a mile. At noon the travelers stopped for an hour's "nooning." The pilot, by considering the terrain and estimating the speed of the wagons and the walk of his horse, was able to go ahead and locate a camp-site at the proper distance. Proceeding with a band of "pioneers," he prepared the road and selected a camp-ground perhaps an hour in advance of the main column. When the caravan arrived, the path-breakers had little wells dug and other preparations made for the night camp. A day's travel amounted to about twelve to fifteen miles. In 1846, when the travelers had gone approximately one hundred miles, they were overtaken by an express from the frontier post-office bringing the last papers and letters they expected from the States until they reached the Pacific.

In good weather life on the emigrant trail was often pleasant. The camp with its huge covered wagons, white tents, and blazing camp-fires lighting up the prairie presented a charming picture. Children played about, and here and there groups of men and women gathered around the fires, talking, laughing, and singing as night settled down.[2] Often the travelers stopped over Sunday.

[2] Henry Howe, *In the Principal Countries of the Globe, Travels and Adventures of Celebrated Travelers* (Cincinnati, 1857), p. 301.

ON THE ROAD TO OREGON
From a painting by W. H. Jackson.

For the most part the time was spent in hunting, fishing, washing clothes, baking, and ironing, although a minister often held meetings and the more religious could have spiritual food. Those not so inclined obliged the worshipers by ceasing their fiddling. Some played cards, read novels, or in other ways amused themselves.

Nevertheless the continual travel day after day bore heavily on the women—the eternal grind with its dust, dirt, and lack of the finer conveniences that women appreciate. Such things as baths and toilet facilities were almost unknown. Childbirth in the rough surroundings was hard, indeed, without the care so much valued under the circumstances. On June 26, 1851, a company from Peoria, Illinois, stopped a few hours at North Skunk River while Mrs. Jeemes Taylor gave birth to a fine baby. Her husband, upon proudly viewing the heir, inquired: "Do you feel able to go on, Sally?" "Oh, yes, Jeemes, I feel pretty pert. I reckon you'd better hitch up the steers." And with this brief pause for hospitalization the proud husband hooked up and the onward march to Oregon was resumed.

All of the fundamental procedures of life in the old home continued. There were social good times, love-making, marriage, birth, and death. One traveler recorded that in one camp a wedding took place, and at another a mile and a half distant a boy was buried by torch-light, while at a third in close proximity a child was born. In less than a month after the first party left civilization in 1841, a romance had developed to such a point that Elder Joseph Williams felt constrained to marry the couple on the Platte River, as he said, "without law or license, for we were a long way from the United States." [3]

In 1846 one hundred miles east of Fort Laramie there was a log cabin, the winter headquarters of trappers, which served as a sort of post-office for the emigrants. Those a few days or weeks ahead left letters here for their friends coming shortly afterward.

[3] Joseph Williams, *Narrative of a Tour from the State of Indiana to the Oregon Territory in the Years 1841-1842* (New York, 1921), p. 34.

The walls in 1846 were covered with advertisements and notices of lost cattle and goods. Letters also were left with entreaties to the passers-by to deliver them if their routes would permit. All in all the point was one of great interest to the pilgrim. Fort Laramie was the next oasis in the desert affording the traveler a few comforts such as a trading-post could offer. After the emigrants had been on the Plains a month, they were all so sunburnt from exposure and their attire was so carelessly worn that the casual observer would scarcely have recognized a trace of civilization about them.

The natural flow of population westward to Oregon and California had gone its tranquil way for nearly a decade when the discovery of gold at Sutter's mill near Sacramento inoculated the country with the most virulent case of gold fever it has ever had. As a consequence the little rivulet of humanity trickling westward each season became a mighty torrent flowing from the Missouri River to California. With this new development the tempo of travel was speeded up, and men strained every nerve as they pushed resolutely forward to the land of promise, anxious to reach the rainbow's end before someone else had removed the pot of gold.

During the winter of 1848-49 the eastern states literally seethed with excitement over the possibility of riches for every person who could reach California. Men sat around the stoves in the general stores talking and dreaming of the wealth to be had for the trip. Meetings were held in lodge halls, and organizations were formed for mutual aid in making the long, dangerous journey. The excitement spread like a contagious disease, and man after man announced to neighbors and friends that he had decided to go west.

Of the many companies formed to travel to the gold-fields the Jefferson County, Virginia, Mining Company was a typical example. Eighty men joined the company, contributing $300 each, which was the customary sum paid by members of such organizations. Each man was given a rubber sack with the company's marker on it in which to carry his clothing. The company left Charleston on March 3, 1849.[4] The Granite State Mining Company, numbering twenty-nine members paying the same fees as the Jefferson County Company, made arrangements to travel to California with the Mount Washington Company. As the names indicate, both of these were from New England. Companies from the East often went west by train and boat to the Missouri River and obtained special rates by buying a block ticket for the entire group. Those who did this, for the most part, arrived at Independence or St. Joseph by river steamboat in April or May. Many unattached emigrants joined in the mad rush, however, and from the Great Lakes region of the Old Northwest, companies, little groups, and individuals drove their covered wagons across Iowa and waited patiently to cross the Missouri River by the ferry-boat at Council Bluffs. One company spent a month and four days in crossing Iowa. The rush of business was so great that the ferry, working at full speed, was days behind when Sarah Royce and her husband arrived. A snow-white city of covered wagons congregated and waited turns. As the wagons arrived, each was given a number, and while waiting for their numbers to be called, the emigrants amused themselves by visiting each other's camps and whiling away the time as best they could.

On reaching the west side of the Missouri, various individuals and small groups proceeded to organize into a traveling company of their own. Resolutions were adopted and officers elected. The following set of resolutions, drawn up on the west bank of the Missouri on May 6, 1850, is representative of hundreds during the gold-rush of 1849 and the decade of the fifties:

Whereas we are about to leave the frontier, and travel over Indian Territory, exposed to their treachery, and knowing their long and abiding hatred of the whites; also many other privations to meet with. We consider it necessary to form ourselves into a Company for the

[4] Edward Washington McIlhany, *Recollections of a '49er* (Kansas City, Mo., 1908), pp. 9-11.

purpose of protecting each other and our property, during our journey to California.

Therefore Resolved, That there shall be one selected from the Company, suitable and capable to act as Captain or Leader.

Resolved, That we, as men pledge ourselves to assist each other through all the misfortunes that may befall us on our long and dangerous journey.

Resolved, That the Christian Sabbath shall be observed, except when absolutely necessary to travel.

Resolved, That there shall be a sufficient guard appointed each night regularly, by the Captain.

Resolved, That in case of a member's dying, the Company shall give him a decent burial.[5]

As a rule, companies which started with optimism and the best of resolutions began to disintegrate before many days. Disagreements over one thing or another caused division after division. One of the most fruitful sources of dissension was the provision for resting on Sunday. In their anxiety to reach the gold-fields a large portion of the group was likely to be determined to travel on the day of rest. Often the more pious travelers felt obliged on this account to part company with their less particular associates. In the absence of the restraint imposed by formal government, men were prone to give vent to unbridled anger, and frequently quarrels between individuals resulted in a company's dividing into two partisan groups. It seems unlikely that many of the organizations that left the East remained intact until California was reached.

Apparently the physical rigors of the journey, added to the mental strain, wore on the nerves until even trivial matters appeared of great consequence, causing the destruction of friendships or business contracts. Even the women felt the urge to break through the conventionalities and let the more savage qualities of

[5] Lorenzo Sawyer, *Way Sketches, or Lorenzo Sawyer's Overland Journal* (New York, 1926), p. 19.

their nature assert themselves when the coffee-pot began to leak and the daily routine grew unbearably monotonous.

One man and his wife had such a violent quarrel that they cut their wagon in two, made a cart of each part, and equally divided their team, each taking a yoke of oxen. Out there on the Plains, without judge, jury, lawyer, or fees, they had a divorce.

Two men who had prepared an outfit together at Independence frequently quarreled over the traveling and camping arrangements. At Chimney Rock one of the company suggested that they fight it out and be done with it. The mere suggestion was enough. Each drew his knife, and they closed in fierce and deadly combat. In a short time one fell and expired almost immediately. The other, fainting from loss of blood, was carried to the shade, where he died within an hour. At set of sun, with the grim irony of fate, they were laid side by side in the same unhallowed grave, never more to disagree.[6]

With the first rush of gold-hunters the towns along the Missouri River experienced a tremendous boom. St. Joseph, Independence, and Council Bluffs, which had been mere villages, became outfitting towns, doubling and trebling in business and population overnight. Even St. Louis profited enormously by this large increase in business. As soon as the Missouri River was open to navigation in the middle of February, 1849, the adventurers began to stream into St. Joseph from all of the more northerly states. The landing was a scene of the greatest animation. The town was packed so full of people that tents were pitched around the outskirts and on the west side of the river in such numbers that it seemed the city was besieged by an army. Every house lot became a stable and brought in money for the owner. Prices rose by jumps. Corn, formerly fifteen cents a bushel, rose to a dollar. Ham, which before had brought from three to seven cents a pound, sold for twelve cents, and butter rose from eight to twenty-five

[6] John Steele, *Across the Plains in 1850* (Chicago, 1930), p. 67.

cents. Oftentimes bread could not be had at any price.[7] The most extravagant dreams of riches engrossed the emigrants, and they were anxious to be on their way. They had visions of returning with fifty thousand dollars, and there went up from around the camp-fires the popular song of the Forty-niners sung to the tune of "Oh! Susanna":

> Oh, California, that's the land for me,
> I'm bound for California with a washbowl on my knee.

The outfitting towns showed enterprise and in a few weeks were ready to cater to the needs of the overland travelers. There quickly appeared on the shelves every conceivable kind of goods which either bore the brand "California" or were offered especially for use of the traveler. Under an advertisement head of "For California" was described a large variety of meats hermetically sealed in cans and guaranteed to keep for five years in any climate. "California bacon" was packed in boxes or small bales and was a marked improvement over ordinary salt pork of the time. So unexpected was the avalanche of buying that the shelves of St. Joseph mercantile houses were emptied, and the proprietors had hastily to replenish their stocks from the stores lower down the river to tide them over. In 1849 the Phœnix Mutual Life Insurance Company was organized at St. Louis primarily to insure going to California. The premiums were calculated at the regular life rates with an extra charge of 2½ per cent of the principal amount insured on account of the hazardous nature of the undertaking.[8]

At Independence in 1850 every state in the Union except Delaware and Texas was represented by a delegation of emigrants to California. Many of the adventurers brought a part or all of their equipment with them on the steamboat, putting only the finishing

[7] Rudolph Friederich Kurz, *Journal*, J. N. B. Hewitt, ed. (Washington, D. C., 1937), p. 46.

[8] John P. Minier, Jr., *St. Louis as an Outfitting Center in 1849*, Ms., Master's Thesis, University of Iowa, 1937, pp. 42, 49, 74, 150, 151; Walker D. Wyman, *The Missouri River Towns in the Westward Movement*, Ms., Master's Thesis, University of Iowa, 1935, p. 42.

touches on their outfitting at the Missouri River points of departure. Many bought live stock at these points, however. The standard equipment consisted of a covered wagon pulled by oxen, horses, or mules. In front the white-duck top had flaps, and in the rear there was a "pucker string" drawing the top taut. A sheet-iron cooking stove hung on the rear of the wagon, although in some cases this spot was occupied by a keg of whisky, a sheet-iron gold-washer, or other mining equipment. The interior of the wagon was loaded with provisions and bedding. Some overland travelers carried tents for sleeping purposes while others slept in the wagons. Many wagon covers had names on them, such as "Badgers," "Hoosiers," "From Suckerdom," "From Pike County, Missouri," "Ho! for California—if you get there before me, say I'm coming," "Pilgrim's Progress—Traveling Edition," "Rough and Ready," and "Gold Hunter." [9] The Jefferson County, Virginia, Company took two wagons with sheet-iron beds fashioned into boats. When the train arrived at a stream that could not be forded, these boats were used to ferry the goods of the whole party across. Some companies felt it more desirable to adopt the pack-train mode of travel. It was argued that such equipment would enable a group to travel fast and light, without the hindrance of heavy wagon traffic, and thus reach the gold-mines quickly.

The Mount Washington Mining Company of Boston and vicinity required its mess to undergo a rigid physical examination. They took a doctor along as a member of the company, and an old spring wagon was rigged up for an ambulance. They used a pack-train, and although they did not leave the Missouri River until June 10, which was considered dangerously late, they made good progress, arriving in California about October 1. With the company well mounted, one man rode the bell-mare, and the pack-mules followed. [10]

[9] Alonzo Delano, *Life on the Plains and Among the Diggings* (New York, 1857), pp. 71, 72.

[10] R. C. Shaw, *Across the Plains in Forty-Nine* (Farmland, Ind., 1896), pp. 18-20, 28, 34.

Breaking mules for pack-trains was trying work. Many of the animals were young and had never had on a halter, much less a saddle. The men tied sacks of sand on them and drove them about, hoping to break them in this fashion, but on the second trial they seemed as wild as ever. The vicious animals would bite, kick, and strike with their fore feet.[11]

A pack-train found it difficult to carry a stove. At their stopping-places they dug a hole in the earth on the side of a river-bank or an incline, which served for a stove and makeshift oven.

Almost every kind of team or vehicle was to be seen on the road. Among the more unconventional modes of travel were numbered push-carts, wheelbarrows, and even hikers. One man with a push-cart hauling his meager supplies stayed one night with a company. The next morning he was invited to swing his cart on the back of a wagon and ride with them. He declined, saying he could make better time on foot.

In 1850 a company known as the Wisconsin Blues was camped on the east side of the Missouri at Council Bluffs awaiting an opportunity to cross the river. John Steele, a lad eighteen years old, and two companions were among the group. One day, when young Steele had gone to buy provisions, his two partners got into a quarrel and sold out the common property of the three. When he returned, he found himself afoot without any hope of redress and had to camp with the other emigrants. After thinking the matter over he decided to go to California anyway, and, buying a knapsack, he placed in it his scant wardrobe, some pilot bread, dried beef, ammunition, a quantity of paper for a diary, a small pocket Bible, and a few toilet articles. Over this he strapped a blanket, and on top of all was a light frying-pan. He had a brace of pistols, a hunting-knife, and a tin cup at his belt, and, shouldering his rifle, he started on the trail for California. At night he stayed with someone who had a tent or sleeping space in a wagon. Each eve-

[11] Kimball Webster, *The Gold Seekers of '49* (Manchester, N. H., 1917), pp. 34-37.

ning Steele took the stationery from his pack and by the light of the camp-fire jotted down the happenings of the day, and thus handed down to us one of the most interesting and informative records of the overland trip in 1850.[12]

In 1853 John Fuller contracted to transport one hundred men to California and board them en route for $100 each. Each man was to do his share of guard duty and to place himself wholly at Fuller's command.

Some who were anxious to be on their way started as early as the first of April, taking an extra wagon or two loaded with corn and oats to feed the animals until the grass was high enough for forage. When the grain was used up, the wagons were abandoned; the wood was used for fuel and the metal portions left. This procedure gave the travelers a start of one hundred to two hundred miles ahead of the rush. Those in the lead had the advantage of good pasturage adjacent to the ideal camp-sites, while later comers found the whole terrain depastured and had to drive away from the route to find forage. Then, too, the thoughts of gold urged the seekers on lest later comers find all the good mining locations preëmpted by the early arrivals. As a rule the travelers left between April 15 and May 30.

The migration of 1849 was a deluge which all but swamped the ferries. H. Egan wrote under date of May 31, 1849:

Eight miles east of the head of Grand Island; today we have passed where the St. Joseph and Independence road intersect this road; there is one continual string of wagons as far as the eye can extend, both before and behind us; . . . This evening there are twenty-nine camps in sight, numbering from fifteen to forty wagons in a company.[13]

Another traveler, who spent a day in camp guarding the oxen and watching the mass of humanity pass by, confided to his diary:

[12] Steele, *Across the Plains in 1850*, pp. 27-34.
[13] H. Egan, "Correspondence from the Plains," *The Frontier Guardian*, Kanesville, Iowa, 1849.

I did not realize until today how great was the tide of emigration. The trains passed our camp like the flow of a river, and I suppose the line extends from Iowa to the Rocky Mountains.

Still another traveler wrote: "It would appear from the sight before us—that the nation was disgorging itself and sending off its whole inhabitance." [14]

It is estimated that the lead-mining area of southwestern Wisconsin lost a quarter of its population. Property in the region declined in value to a fraction of what it had been, such was the rage for disposing of it and going to the gold-fields. By a check on the ferries and Fort Kearney and Fort Laramie records, it has been estimated that eight thousand wagons, eighty thousand draft animals, and between twenty-five and thirty thousand people passed over the trail in 1849.[15]

As this endless white-topped column rolled slowly along, a multitude of horses carrying riders pranced by, and crowds of men moved forward on foot. In truth, the whole array looked like a mighty army on the march. The migration of 1850 was even larger, however.

The year 1849 and the early fifties were cursed by an epidemic of the Asiatic cholera. It apparently was brought to New Orleans by boat and thence up the Missouri River. The disease took a heavy toll of the travelers. Many deaths occurred on the river steamers, and near the river deaths were numerous. Farther out on the Plains there were fewer cases, and the scourge ceased by the time the Rocky Mountains were reached. Young people often died within a few hours. Old people would live as long as five or six days. From forty to fifty per cent of the victims died. One man in 1849 wrote: "Almost every camp-ground is converted into a

[14] Jesse L. Pritchard, "Diary of a Journey from Kentucky to California in 1849," *Missouri Historical Review*, Vol. XVIII, p. 545.
[15] Steele, *Across the Plains in 1850*, Introductory Note by Joseph Schafer, p. xix.

burial-ground, and at many places twelve or fifteen graves may be seen in a row."

So great was the fear of the dire disease that sometimes the victims were deserted. In one instance a mess of eight men was stricken. They had two wagons and a good outfit and had been associated with a large company. When the cholera appeared, their fair-weather friends were frightened away. A passer-by found two in their graves, three sick, one watching them, and two watching the teams.[16] Little time was spent in obsequies. One man passed about noon an encampment where there were three men. One lay sick inside a tent where he could look out upon his companions digging his grave. About four o'clock the two men in their spring wagon drove past the observer. Their companion in the meantime had died and been buried.

When the dread death struck, a feeling of gloomy foreboding pervaded the camp. The natural feeling was: Who will be next? If a death occurred in the night, the long, weary hours dragged on until daylight came, when the sorrowful survivors sewed the body of their companion in his sheet or blanket and lowered it into the grave which was dug a short distance from the trail. Then came the work of cleansing the wagon, washing the bedclothes, and sunning everything.

The end-gate of a wagon was shaped into a headboard, and the immigrant's name and the date of his death were burned in or smeared on it with tar axle lubricant.[17] Soon there was a path running out diagonally from the trail to the grave and another from the grave to the trail. These were made by people who walked out to see who was buried there. A woman buried at South Pass had been remembered in a more elaborate way than most of the departed. Her friends built a pen of cottonwood poles around her grave and placed her rocking-chair, which bore her name, to

[16] Wilbur Earl Keeling, *Cholera Epidemics of the Fifties*, Ms., Master's Thesis, University of Iowa, 1933, pp. 6, 10, 13, 29.

[17] Gilbert L. Cole, *In Early Days Along the Overland Trail in Nebraska Territory, in 1852* (Kansas City, Mo., 1905), p. 31.

mark the spot. William Lobenstein in 1851 passed the grave of an emigrant on which lay a live dog, a faithful servant howling out the token of his sympathy for the one resting beneath the sod.

A traveler who went out in the early dawn to catch his horse noticed something sticking out of the grass. Upon investigation he discovered a newly-made grave with this inscription on the headboard:

Our only child
Little Mary

Somewhere in the multitude ahead were the empty arms and grief-stricken heart of a mother who mourned a precious loved one sleeping on the lonely prairie.

Granville Stuart said that in 1852 his party drove as fast as they could in order to get through the terrible region of death, where they were seldom out of the sight of graves. One day they met a young woman with her four children from two to seven years of age. Her husband had died three days before, and she was trying to return to her relatives in Illinois. When sickness or an accident occurred, a doctor could often be found among the traveling neighborhoods. Gilbert Cole mentioned seeing a covered wagon with a doctor's shingle on the side.

In the years 1849 and 1850 a large number of adventurers became discouraged and returned to their homes. The fear that the route would be depastured by the great multitude with its numberless head of live stock, the dread of Indian attacks, the horror of the cholera, and plain homesickness, often induced by the terror occasioned by death, caused many to obliterate the golden air-castles that had lured them from their homes. Some who had traveled two hundred miles west of the Missouri River turned back, saying they had seen enough of "the elephant." [18] J. H. Benson wrote in his diary on May 13, 1849:

[18] No doubt this saying originated with the showing of a famous whitewashed elephant by P. T. Barnum in his circus. Hence "to see the elephant" was equivalent to allowing one's self to be "taken in" or hoaxed.

A few minutes ago a man came into camp on horseback going back home. He had been over 100 miles out from here. He assigned no reason except he was homesick. Some of the boys told him he would go home and go to plowing corn. He said he was not particular about what he did so long as he got home.

One man mentioned buying a horse from a pilgrim who, having traveled seven hundred miles, had "seen the elephant and eaten his ears" and was on his way back home.

By 1850 a number of streams had been bridged or furnished with ferries by the Mormons or others. In 1849 a man from New Orleans stopped at the North Platte River and established a crude ferry consisting of three canoes lashed together. It would transport one wagon at a time. Each company furnished its own rope, performed all the labor, and paid five dollars per wagon for the use of the catamaran. Its owner, an enterprising man, sent his family on with the promise of overtaking them, and he remained there coining money with his business.

The most dreaded crossing on the entire trip was that of the South Platte near where it unites with the North Platte. One traveler mentioned that on the morning before the crossing there was little joking. "Once started, never stop," was the solemn admonition. Two men cut willow sticks and, wading across the river, stuck them into the sandy bottom to mark the ford. The first hoofs and wheels to strike the water, he said, sounded dirge-like. Every man except the drivers waded alongside the horses to give assistance if need be. Scarcely a word was spoken during the entire crossing, which occupied twenty-five minutes. In describing the ordeal he said that

the nervous strain had been terrible, and at no time in our journey had we been so nearly taxed to the utmost. One man dug out a demijohn of brandy from his traps and treated all hands, remarking that "the success of that undertaking merits something extraordinary." [19]

[19] Cole, *In Early Days Along the Overland Trail in Nebraska Territory in 1852*, pp. 33, 34.

The trains moving westward were really traveling neighbor-hoods. Members got acquainted with one another, visiting on the road by day and around the camp-fires at night, much as they had visited neighbors in the old home. They spent the evenings pleas-antly talking of the road over which they had just passed and conjecturing what it would be like on the morrow. There were good story-tellers, good singers, and in almost every company was a wag who cracked jokes to the merriment of the whole company. There was seldom a company without a fiddle, and nightly the musicians sat on a wagon tongue fiddling. Often the women from other trains came to visit and gathered about the fire, seated on water-kegs. "Old Dan Tucker" and "The Arkansas Traveler" were two favorite tunes. Often the young people gathered on the prairie grass under the starry skies and tripped it "on the light fantastic toe" with as much hilarity as though in a luxurious ball-room.

Some of the companies had bands. On the evening of May 15, 1850, somewhere in Nebraska, a company camped a few rods from the quarters of the Birmingham Company. After supper its band marched out from the camp and was met by the Birmingham band. The two joined in military order and, like the army of Joshua at Jericho of old, marched several times around the Birmingham camp. The Birmingham people cheered the visitors heartily. After playing several tunes the bands retired in good order to their respective camps.[20]

Hymns and religious songs were sung in camp, also. A general favorite was

> I'm a Pilgrim and I'm a stranger,
> I can tarry but a night,
> We are going home to Heaven above,
> Will you go?

---

[20] Leander V. Loomis, *A Journal of the Birmingham Emigrating Company*, Edgar M. Ledyard, ed. (Salt Lake City, 1928), pp. 15, 16.

Popular songs were sung often. The young folks would make the prairies ring with "The Girl I Left Behind Me."

Other interesting ways were found to spend the evenings pleasantly. One writer mentioned that a candy-pull helped pass the time. Another wrote that after the company had traveled sixteen miles, a foot-race was got up in which many of the younger members participated. Another recorded a horse-race in which a man bet fifty dollars on his little grey horse.[21] Three-quarters of a mile was measured off on the prairie and the race was on. Still another traveler wrote: "This evening after supper the most of the boys went out and after choosing sides took a whooping game of ball, until time to take in our horses."

Sometimes a few hours of diversion were enjoyed when Indians came to visit the camp. They brought skins, robes, or moccasins to trade for the goods of the travelers. Then, too, they furnished amusement for the gold-hunters.

In spite of these relaxations, the pilgrims lived a narrow, circumscribed life. Their thoughts, hopes, fears, and anxieties all centered about the train, the health of the company, grass and water for the stock, fuel for cooking, and the dread of Indians. Their lives scarcely extended beyond the moving cloud of dust that enveloped them on their westward way. Day in and day out the monotonous tramp continued with scarcely a break.

Many of the men in their eastern homes had been well dressed and clean shaven with well-groomed hair. After a few weeks on the trail their uncombed locks, unshaven faces, and ragged clothes identified them as having changed from a civilized to a semi-civilized status. Unwashed, sunburnt, and clothed in old, greasy buckskin coats, the treasure-seekers portrayed a different world. Women riders had discarded their silks, satins, laces, flounces, and pantalets for riding-habits made of dark-brown denim that pro-

---

[21] Henry J. Coke, *A Ride over the Rocky Mountains to Oregon and California* (London, 1852), pp. 109-110.

tected them somewhat from the sun and wind. Mounting their ponies, they often rode far ahead of their own train or several miles back, visiting and learning the caravan's news.[22]

The outstanding error of the gold-hunters of the year 1849 was that of overloading. Great quantities of goods, tents, provisions, and mining tools and equipment of all kinds were packed into the wagons or on animal-back to be wearily dragged or carried across the Plains and over the mountains.

By the time the pilgrims reached Grand Island, they were beginning to seek ways of lightening their loads. One traveler noticed an advertisement at Fort Kearney offering one hundred pounds each of flour, bacon, and dried beef for fifty cents a hundred. The next day he saw two feather beds that had been thrown away, and meat and beans were strewn along the trail. On June 1, 1849, an emigrant wrote in his diary: "This was a day of scenes of abandoned property; items too tedious to mention; stoves, blacksmith tools, wagons, cooking utensils, provisions of every kind were strung along the road." For the next month the travelers found quantities of discarded goods. All the camp-grounds near Fort Laramie were literally covered with wagon irons, clothing, beans, bacon, pork, and provisions of almost every kind left by the advance emigrants in an effort to increase their speed. Some buried lead and marked the place, hoping to have someone recover it later. One company ruthlessly cut a foot off·the length of each of its wagons and piled the excess provisions along the road.[23] Crowbars, miners' washing machinery, log chains, and even rifles, revolvers, and expensive guns were broken and thrown away. As a rule provisions were rendered useless by the ones who abandoned them. Sugar had turpentine poured on it; flour was emptied and scattered on the

[22] Sarah Raymond Herndon, *Days on the Road Crossing the Plains in 1865* (New York, 1902), p. 18; Delano, *Life on the Plains and Among the Diggings,* p. 77.
[23] Randall H. Hewitt, *Across the Plains and Over the Divide* (New York, 1906), pp. 253-254; McIlhany, *Recollections of a '49er,* pp. 21, 22; Delano, *Life on the Plains and Among the Diggings,* p. 63.

ground, and clothes were torn to pieces. There were a few exceptions where foodstuffs were left in good order with instructions to the finder to help himself.

Parties traveling ahead often wrote messages to friends on buffalo skulls and shoulder-blades or even on human skulls. Such notices gave information about advance trains or contained a personal note. Everyone read the bone messages scattered along the way, and sometimes a postscript was added. Besides thousands of these bone letters, sometimes news for the public was left on a prominent spot. A notice on a board read: "Look at this—look at this! The water here is poison, and we have lost six cattle. Do not let your cattle drink on this bottom." A company, on camping along a shallow stream bordered with timber, found posted on a tree:

Notice—we camped here on the tenth day of May. Jim Lider went up the creek to hunt deer and never came back. We found his dead body two miles up the creek after two days' hunt, his scalp, clothes, gun all gone. The Pawnees did it. Look out for the red devils.[24]

Water was sometimes hard to find. On the whole, later comers fared better in this respect than earlier travelers, for they used the wells which had been dug in the sand or in a slough and had filled with water. The old reliable diet was bacon, beans, and coffee. This was supplemented by bologna and crackers in the early part of the journey and by game and fish as opportunity came to procure them. Flapjacks and bread cooked in a Dutch oven supplied the breadstuffs. Wild onions, currants, strawberries, gooseberries, and plums gave a welcome addition of fresh "stuff" to the diet otherwise wholly lacking in green food.

Considerable difficulty was caused by the oxen's becoming sorefooted. Sometimes the animals had to be abandoned or butchered. Sometimes rough boots were made and fitted over the hooves. This device allowed the hoof to be treated with grease and tar and protected it from sand and sharp stones. In 1852, near the mountains

[24] Shaw, *Across the Plains in Forty-Nine*, p. 46.

in Wyoming where shoes became a necessity, a man sat by the road with a bushel basket of horseshoe nails, selling them for 12½ cents each. One traveler recorded his anger at this holdup but forthwith paid ten dollars in gold for eighty nails.

By means of Mormon guide-books which could be purchased at Kanesville, Iowa, travelers on the route north of the Platte River were able to tell exactly how far they had traveled and where they were.[25]

The Fourth of July was usually celebrated appropriately with the flying of flags, firing of guns, shooting at a mark, foot-races, horse-races, singing, and dancing. Sometimes the Indians joined in the celebration.[26]

The overland migration with its long wagon-trains continued to flow through the fifties and sixties until the Union Pacific brought the luxury of train travel to the westbound traveler. In the meantime several more gold strikes encouraged heavy migrations to the different gold-fields.

In 1858 gold was discovered at the foot of the mountains in what was then the western part of Kansas. During the following five years several strikes were made in Montana. These finds brought about a repetition of the California gold-rush of ten years before.

When the news of the Colorado discovery arrived in the Missouri River towns, excitement ran high. Hundreds left that fall and winter. John J. Ingalls wrote to his father on December 22, 1858:

The Pikes Peak fever rages furiously here, and parties are organizing in all parts for emigration early in the spring. They are getting up a company here, in which they agree to transport and feed persons to the gold-bearing region at the moderate price of $50 per head.

[25] William Edmundson, "Diary Kept by William Edmundson, of Oskaloosa, While Crossing the Western Plains in 1850," see *Annals of Iowa*, Vol. VIII, p. 518.
[26] Jerome Dutton, "Across the Plains in 1850," see *Annals of Iowa*, Vol. IX, p. 467.

A letter written by General William T. Sherman at Fort Leavenworth on April 30, 1859, stated that steamboats by twos and threes each day were arriving loaded with people for the new gold region. The streets were full of emigrants buying provisions and equipment, and all around the town were little encampments preparing to go west. A new daily stage west to the mountains had started, and General Sherman estimated that twenty-five thousand people had actually gone.[27]

The same excitement prevailed at each of the river towns. For months Omaha looked like a military establishment, with tents crowding vacant lots and covered wagons everywhere. Every newspaper on the Missouri River expressed absolute confidence that rich mines existed and boosted its own town as an outfitting place. Rivalry ran high between the different outfitting towns. Each claimed to be the terminus of the shortest route, the least dangerous route, the most healthful route, or the route that had the best roads and water. Articles and statements by individuals who had been over the road appeared in the papers as propaganda for particular towns.

All sorts of vehicles were used in this rush. As early as March, 1859, the Brownville, Nebraska, *Advertiser* mentioned a man who had come from Minnesota pulling a sled laden with a few provisions. A few days later, one of many knapsack travelers, in addition to his knapsack, had a ham of meat on his back for food. He left with the full intention of tramping over the five hundred miles of prairie to the mines. So great was the excitement that children only thirteen or fourteen years of age started with meager supplies for the gold-fields, but parents overhauled the little adventurers. A man from Pennsylvania loaded all his camping outfit, provisions, and blankets on a wheelbarrow and traveled about a hundred and fifty or two hundred miles of the distance across the Plains. Although footsore and weary, he was making good time

---

[27] This stage line over the Smoky Hill route was given up after a short time and the equipment moved to the Platte Valley route where it operated thereafter.

when a party from Oskaloosa, Kansas, overtook him. He was willing enough to abandon his mode of travel and swing his wheelbarrow behind one of the wagons.

In several instances wind-wagons were tried. One man reported having overtaken such a vehicle about ten miles west of Kansas City. It had four wheels, each about twenty feet in circumference. The carriage was about nine feet across and had a body like an omnibus. It was designed to carry twenty-four passengers. Rigged with a very large sail, schooner style, it plowed right along through the mud but cast anchor in a deep ravine where the wind failed to fill the sail. The captain of the three-thousand-pound craft stated that when it was perfected he'd bet he could make it to the mountains in six days.[28]

A group of three men built a combination wind-wagon and hand-cart which made the trip from the Missouri River to the mountains in twenty days, equaling the speed of horse-drawn vehicles. Eleven men rigged up the running-gear of a buggy without the body and loaded it with tools and provisions. An observer recorded that at the beginning, at least, the leader had a fine cloth coat, a stovepipe hat, and patent-leather boots. There were many hand-cart companies. All sorts of other vehicles were used— Conestoga wagons, buggies, spring wagons, sulkies, children's wagons, and even baby-buggies. The *Rocky Mountain News* reported that a man had ridden across the Plains in a little wagon drawn by two big dogs.

The famous newspaper correspondent Albert D. Richardson, who went to Denver with Horace Greeley over the Smoky Hill Route in the spring of 1859, said: "During our journey from Leavenworth we have doubtless passed ten thousand emigrants." One man who lived beside one of the trails asked a passer-by if there were any people living in the States. On being assured peo-

[28] J. P. Post, *The Trip to Pike's Peak, Diary of J. P. Post, 1859*, Ms., Colorado State Historical Society Library, p. 3; Carla Elizabeth Neuhaus, *Transportation to Colorado, 1858-1869*, Ms., Master's Thesis, University of Colorado, 1928, pp. 33-35.

ple lived there still, he replied that he "didn't allow there were" he had seen so many come west.

There were three general routes from Missouri River points to the Pike's Peak mines. The Platte was the northern route, the Arkansas the southern route, and the Smoky Hill the central route. The Smoky Hill, although the shortest from Kansas points, was the most dangerous, owing to lack of water and inferior protection from Indian raids. Consequently the Platte route, running along the line of the Overland Trail for a considerable distance, was used more than any other after the first two years.

As a matter of fact, gold had been found at Cherry Creek but in such small quantities that the grand rush was altogether unwarranted. In the spring of 1859 there was so little confidence in the mining region that there was an exodus and an accompanying economic slump. In Denver a pick sold for from ten cents to fifteen cents, and town lots and log houses were bartered for revolvers or sold for ten or twenty dollars each. Of the few men engaged in gold-mining, not a half-dozen were washing out a dollar a day.[29] The discouraging prospect, together with a scarcity of provisions, caused a panic to develop which became a stampede as men poured out of the Cherry Creek district like a routed army, traveling with every sort of vehicle and on foot. Some were begging for food, and many were cursing the ones who had brought the reports of the riches in Colorado.

By the middle of May the returning Pike's Peakers began to meet the westbound gold-hunters. The *Rocky Mountain News* of May 14, 1859, stated that a company from Leavenworth reported having met fifteen hundred wagons west of Fort Kearney going east. Many companies westward bound met those back-trailers and began to question whether they should go on or not. At first they were unanimous in their determination to move forward, but as the stream of disillusioned Pike's Peakers continued to flow by, they were infected with the spirit.

[29] Albert D. Richardson, *Beyond the Mississippi* (Hartford, 1867), p. 178.

A company from Illinois met one of the returning panic-stricken throng and was told that Hiram Wethey of Marshall, Michigan, who prospected three weeks on Cherry Creek, had offered to work for his board and even to work for one meal a day, but could not get a job and thought it best to start home. He had traveled one hundred miles with nothing to eat but corn that had passed through the cattle and been dropped on the road. Stories like this caused a company to stop and reconsider its program.[30] A few parties, dreading to face the home folks and determined to see the thing through, went ahead. Some divided, part going forward and others returning. Sometimes members of a company argued about the matter for several days. One company turned around and started back, but that night four wagons of the thirty-five changed their minds and decided to face west again. One party on separating made quite a busy little commercial village as those who turned back sold their equipment to the ones going ahead. Many threw away their equipment rather than carry it back. The Smoky Hill Valley was strewn with stoves, mining machinery, and other heavy goods. Some enterprising souls from Denver went out and hauled these goods to the mountains. So great was the recession that the same cattle that sold for from $85 to $100 the latter part of April were sold by the returning immigrants for from $35 to $50. Emigrants going out often had inscriptions on their wagons stating where they were from and that they were bound for Pike's Peak, often adding "or bust." On the way back many wrote underneath, "*Busted.*"

The discovery of gold in Montana in 1861 and 1862, although occurring during the Civil War, occasioned a rush to that region. From California treasure-seekers followed the Overland Trail to Utah and north into Montana. Some traveled eastward from Walla Walla into the territory on Mullen's Road. Many from Colorado followed the Oregon Trail to Idaho and up the same

[30] Darius H. Chapman, *Diary of a Trip to Pike's Peak, 1859*, Ms., Nebraska State Historical Society Library, May 13, 1859.

route into the gold-fields. A few moved northwest across Wyoming and directly into Montana by the Bozeman Trail. Some journeyed directly west from Minnesota across Dakota to Montana via the Fort Totten Trail.[31] The Montana rush differed from that to Pike's Peak in that a considerable number traveled almost the whole distance to the gold region in comparative comfort on Missouri River steamboats. The Society of Montana Pioneers in 1899 made an inquiry into the records of 1,809 settlers who had come to the gold-fields before 1865. Of 1,474 who gave a record of their route of travel, only 61 traveled the Dakota route, 111 came by way of the Pacific Coast, and the great bulk, 1,302, came in either by the Missouri River to Fort Benton or on the southern overland route by the Oregon Trail.

For a number of years the rush continued. General John Pope wrote in 1866:

People in incredible numbers continue to throng across the great plains to the rich mining territories, undeterred by the seasons, by hardship and privations, or by the constant and relentless hostility of the Indian tribes. Notwithstanding the unusually severe weather which has pervaded the whole region west of the Mississippi during the present winter, the stream of people crossing the great plains seems to have been nearly as continuous and determined as during the summer months. For several hundred miles along the routes ... to Colorado and Montana, the hospitals of the military posts are filled with frost-bitten teamsters and emigrants whose animals are frozen to death and whose trains, loaded with supplies, stand buried in the snow on the great plains.[32]

The Montana gold-fields also had their recession in 1865 when several hundred men left the mining region. It did not reach the proportions of a panic as did the Pike's Peak recession, however.

The Black Hills of Dakota belonged to the Indians when the first whispers of gold came to the avaricious public. These rumors

[31] Myron L. Koenig, *Fort Union as a Missouri River Post*, Ms., Master's Thesis, University of Iowa, 1933, pp. 74, 75.
[32] Harold E. Briggs, *Frontiers of the Northwest* (New York, 1940), pp. 55-56.

were established as facts when General Custer made an expedition into the region in 1874. The leading outfitting points at first were Cheyenne, Wyoming, and Sidney, Nebraska, on the Union Pacific; Sioux City, on the Missouri River and also the western terminal of a railroad connecting that point with the East; Yankton, Dakota Territory, on the Missouri River; and Bismarck, the western terminus of the Northern Pacific Railway. From these points on the south, east, and north, trails focused on the Black Hills carrying the hurrying gold-hungry throng. The United States Army tried for a time to keep the gold-hunters out of the Indian country, but the attempt was ineffectual. The most famous incident in that connection was the expulsion of the Gordon Company from the Black Hills by a troop of cavalry.[33]

The rivalry between the outfitting towns encircling the Black Hills was keen, with extraordinary claims matched by counter-claims concerning the superiority of the routes that the various towns served. Each attacked the others as presenting false claims to the detriment of all. Sidney jumped to the front in 1876 when a bridge was built across the Platte. Fort Robinson, Fort Meade, and a number of ranches were established along the trail. Soon several stage lines were operating between the outfitting towns and the mines.

This last major gold-rush within the continental United States (aside from Alaska) bore many of the characteristics of the former ones. Companies formed in the East for mutual protection. The New England Black Hills Company of Springfield, Massachusetts, found that the entire expenses for equipment and fare to Yankton were $246.24.[34] This stampede had few of the hardships incident to the grueling journey of 1849. In the quarter of a century since the California gold-rush, transportation had so improved that the gold-seeker could ride most of the way by train or

[33] Annie D. Tallent, *The Black Hills; or, The Last Hunting Ground of the Dakotahs* (St. Louis, 1899), pp. 76-95.
[34] *Yankton Press and Dakotaian,* April 27, 1876.

steamer and stage-coach. And yet some of the attributes of the former excitement held sway. First, there was the feverish anxiety to reach the "diggin's." Again, people converged upon the district in every sort of conveyance with mining tools and merchandise stocks. One Eastern company purchased a steamboat in which to travel to Yankton.[35] Again there was a rush out of the region when gold was not found in the plentiful quantities expected. Over three hundred left for Sidney in one day, according to the *Deadwood Pioneer*, which could be relied upon not to exaggerate an item that was by no means complimentary to the region.[36]

The discovery of gold led to the establishment of permanent systems of transportation and communication—the stage-coach, Pony Express, telegraph, and the railroad—opening a new era on the northern plains and mountains and leading to the coming of the permanent homemaker, the farmer, and the town-builder.

[35] *Ibid.*, April 6, 1876.
[36] *Deadwood Pioneer-Times*, August 19, 1877.

CHAPTER XI

IN THE DIGGINGS

FOLLOWING the discovery of gold in Colorado, the bearded prospector with one animal to ride, and a second to carry his tent, blankets, frying-pan, coffee-pot, and grub, together with a pick, shovel, and gold-pan, patiently and laboriously searched every promising nook and cranny in the majestic Rocky Mountains for the precious yellow metal.

Some gold-hunters financed themselves and retained the entire profits of their ventures. Others were grub-staked by men of means, and the partnership thus formed returned equal shares to the prospector and his speculative backer.

Often the prospector went his way alone, but during a gold-rush frequently several went in company. They dug holes from three to fifteen feet deep here and there over the mountainsides, washed pans of gravel from the stream-beds, and with a geological eye noted the rock formations and the lay of strata and veins. All miners prospected more or less, but there were professional prospectors who, like boys in a huckleberry patch, were always hunting a better place.

When several went in company, a division of labor was arranged whereby certain members of the party hunted, and supplied game and fish for the group. A few excerpts from a Montana gold-hunter's diary gives a picture of his work:

May 15th: We follow the river to a creek and up the creek . . . about three miles we camp for the night. The creek looks well for Gold

May 16th: Will prospect and hunt today. Gold in every pan but in small quantities, not enough to pay; hunters came without meat; bread straight

May 17th: Moved camp three or four miles and camped to prospect and hunt. Found gold, but light; no game; bread straight

May 18th: Moved camp to big bald mountain. Now for sheep; got one; all in good spirits again. . . .

May 20th: Move camp around the foot of the mountain four miles and camp again. We are in a gold country and want to find where it comes from. . . .

May 22nd: Will stop and dry some meat so we will not run short again.[1]

One version of the Gregory discovery of gold in Colorado says that at the time when the panic took hold of the population of the Cherry Creek region in Colorado, John H. Gregory and two other men, about the first of May, 1859, took two mules loaded with provisions and went to the mountains. They finally pushed up Clear Creek to the spot where Central City now stands. Noticing a ridge with outcropping indicating gold, Gregory washed a pan and got a dollar's worth. The party took about ten or fifteen dollars' worth of gold back to Denver. This led to a stampede to Gregory Gulch, as the discovery was named. It yielded the first gold in paying quantities in Colorado.

The first important discovery in Montana was made in the summer of 1863. William Fairweather and a group of associates were prospecting, some near camp and others farther away. Fairweather took the horses over the creek and on his return said there was a piece of projecting rock over there they ought to try, to see if they could get enough money to buy a little tobacco. Taking a pan, pick, and shovel, he and Robert Vaughn went across to investigate it. Fairweather dug up a panful and Vaughn went to wash it. While he was busy, Fairweather scratched around in the bed-rock with his butcher knife and exclaimed, "I've found a scad." Vaughn, who had the pan half washed down, replied, "If you have one, I have a thousand." The first pan weighed about two dollars and thirty cents. They washed three pans before dark and

[1] Henry Edgar, *Journal,* see *Contributions,* Montana State Historical Society, Vol. III, pp. 136-137.

made over twelve dollars. The next day altogether they obtained about a hundred and eighty dollars. Thus was one of the richest gulches in the world discovered. The party decided to call it Alder Gulch from a clump of alders growing on the bank. They undertook to keep the discovery a profound secret, as many others attempted to do; but in due time they had to have provisions, and when they went to Bannack and bought supplies, the miners suspected they had discovered something in the vicinity. They protested that they were merely going prospecting, but the type of tools they were taking belied the statement, and a large crowd followed them for three days. The mob of miners finally threatened to hang the Fairweather party if they did not divulge their secret. An agreement was made whereby each of the discoverers was to have two hundred feet, three locations, and all the water privileges. The crowd was then led to the discovery.[2] In a short time a large portion of the population of Montana was drawn to the spot in a mighty stampede to this richest placer deposit in the history of gold mining. Virginia City sprang up overnight and in less than two years had become a city of ten thousand and the principal center in the territory.

"Stampedes" were common, and usually were wild-goose chases. A prospector would come in and tell a few cronies of a find. They would attempt to sneak out of camp before day, but a crowd was on their heels, each man trying to be the first at the new strike in order to get the best claim. If the story proved false, the stampeders went back to camp with as little publicity as possible, anxious to avoid becoming the butt of the jokes of the other miners. In one case twenty men with kettles, frying-pans, blankets, and tools followed a miner around for two days, heedless of his statement that he was hunting a stray hog until he came in sight of the porker. When a crowd had been fooled and left in an angry mood, they were said to have "a big disgust on." Sometimes discolored

<hr>

[2] George Aux, "Mining in Colorado," Ms., *Bancroft Manuscripts*, Colorado State Historical Society Library.

GREGORY, COLORADO, GOLD DIGGINGS

From Albert D. Richardson, *Beyond the Mississippi*, 1867.

water in a stream caused a stampede to a point above, where miners were suspected of washing out gold.[3] Day laborers, merchants, and freighters joined in the rush. The first man who arrived in a new camp with a train was sure of a fortune, for he was besieged for supplies, and prices soared as the crowds of miners sought equipment.

When the miners got to work, the scene in Alder Gulch was a lively one indeed. The multitude of men passing and repassing never seemed to stop shoveling and wheeling dirt for a moment. They reminded the onlooker of bees around a hive. The ground, with its great deep holes and high heaps of dirt, was literally turned inside out. In the early days of this rich camp a miner who failed to wash a hundred dollars in a day was regarded as either very unfortunate or very indolent.

By placer mining was meant separating loose gold from the dirt in which it had settled as a result of erosion. In some places the magic metal was in the form of minute flakes called colors; again, larger particles like grains of wheat were found. Occasionally a lump called a nugget was uncovered. The gold was separated from the dirt by washing, the technique being to give the pan of gravel and water a whirling motion which carried the lighter materials over the sides and allowed the heavy metal to settle to the bottom. When the larger particles of gold were washed out, the finer were separated from the remaining sand by amalgamation with mercury, a phial of which the miner carried. Later the gold and quicksilver were separated again by heating the amalgam in a retort.

This crude individual method eventually gave way before labor-saving devices. The rocker, or cradle, was simply a large box so built that the water and gravel could be rocked or shaken in it until the lighter, coarser material had been separated from the gold. From this developed the "long tom," which added a separate riffle-box to catch the fine particles of metal. A still faster

[3] Luella Fergus Gilpatrick, *A Sketch*, Ms., Montana State Historical Society Library.

method was the sluice, which was a trough made of three boards about ten or twelve feet long through which water was run rapidly. Cleats were nailed across the bottom to hold the gold when it settled. Six to eight lengths of these sluice-boxes were often used, making a continuous or stepped inclined trough seventy to a hundred and twenty feet long. The gold-bearing gravel was shoveled in at the top, and at the lower end a man shoveled out the material that was too large to go through a sieve located there.

Water was obtained either by diverting it from a stream by the use of flumes or by pumping it to the patch claims. When neither means was practicable, the "pay dirt" was wheeled, carried, or hauled to the water. In the Black Hills of Dakota in 1877 miners dragged the dirt on raw hides down the hillside or carried it in gunny-sacks to the water. A man named Stedman and his two partners carried their dirt a half-mile, and up to September 1 had secured $2,000 for their pains that season.[4] Sometimes, where water could be diverted easily from a swift-flowing stream to patch claims, a sort of crude hydraulic mining was practised, using the force of the water to wash the gravel from the hillside claim down into the sluice-box. All of these operations went under the general name of "placer" or "gulch" mining. With such large-scale devices a number of men worked together. On Saturday came the "cleanup," which meant taking out all the gold that had been accumulated in the sluice-boxes during the week and processing it ready for disposal.

Sometimes a number of men were working partners, but soon some budding capitalist got enough gold-dust ahead to be able to hire newcomers to work for him. When there was need for water away from the stream, a ditch company would be formed. Usually capital for such an enterprise came in from the outside. This was what happened at Gregory Gulch, and furnishing the water proved to be a better business for its stockholders than mining. The lumber business also was fostered by the need for

4 *Black Hills Pioneer*, Deadwood, Dakota Territory, September 1, 1877.

sluice-boxes. At first the boards were whip-sawed, but soon water-power sawmills were set up, and thus lumbering was among the first industries in the mining region.

Placer or gulch mining paid good wages for a time at least, but soon the source of the loose gold was traced to "leads" or "lodes" in the hillsides. The ore there was rich but only partially disintegrated, and it had to be crushed before it would yield its treasure. The first device used for this purpose was the primitive Spanish *arastra*, a mill consisting of a circular space paved with hard stones. In the center was a post to which was fastened a sweep. A team of oxen hitched to the sweep dragged a large granite boulder over a quantity of the gold-bearing rock known as quartz, which, kept wet, was ground between the stones. Water-power was used on the improved "rasters," as they were called.

Soon the decomposed surface ore had been worked, and the inner rock was too hard for the "raster." Crude stamp-mills were then made by fastening stamps onto a wheel in such a way that the ore fed into the machine was churned into particles by the heavy weights descending upon it. These in time were replaced by factory-made stamp-mills for crushing the quartz. In the operation of one of these machines, according to Albert D. Richardson, the gold-bearing rock was first broken with sledge-hammers into pieces the size of apples. It was then fed under the massive iron stamps weighing from three to eight hundred pounds and rising and falling sixty times a minute. This powerful machine, which made the very building tremble, crushed the hard rock to a pulp and made it possible to separate the precious metal from the refuse. Within fifteen months after the discovery in Gregory Gulch there were sixty of these mills and thirty "rasters" in operation.

In exploiting the lodes, shafts were sunk and drifts or tunnels were driven at right angles to the shaft. Ore was wheeled to the shaft and hoisted to the surface by means of a "whim" or windlass. Thus within a short time after a gold discovery there was an evolution from placer mining; the individual, working in informal combination, was displaced by a corporate body which mined the deep deposits by means of expensive machinery, submerging the common man and replacing his haphazard free-lance operations with systematic thoroughness. Lode mining made possible year-round operations, whereas placer mining meant a short season of work with a long winter of inactivity to use up the summer's gain.[5]

There was much bartering of claims and much dishonesty in selling them. A smooth-talking, mild-mannered, accommodating individual would offer to sacrifice a gold mine to the newcomer at a low figure. He would "salt" the claim before taking the prospective buyer onto it and invite him to take samples himself. Salting was done by distributing gold-dust in the sand and gravel, a favorite way being to load a shot-gun with gold and fire it into the dirt. Tradition says that when Horace Greeley visited Colorado in 1859, a crowd of miners had effectively used an old shotgun on a partly worked mine, giving the outer layer the richness of Ophir. When Greeley arrived, they showed him some of the gold they had just panned out of the dirt. He called for a shovel and a pan and, after having been instructed in the use of the latter, rolled up his sleeves and went down into the pit. Soon his efforts brought good results. He was encouraged to try again, with an equally gratifying outcome. Then, gathering up the dust in a bag, he is reported to have said: "Gentlemen, I have worked with my own hands and seen with my own eyes, and the news of your rich discovery shall go all over the world as far as my paper can carry it."[6]

There was much speculation in mines. Some were sold outright, and others were sold for a certain sum with the provision that the seller should receive a specified portion of the production. California interests paid $400,000 for three or four mines in the Black

[5] Lynn Irwin Perrigo, A Social History of Central City, Colorado, 1859-1900, Ms., Doctor's Thesis, University of Colorado, 1936, pp. 51-55.

[6] "Pike's Peak or Bust," Washington Post, April 25, 1909.

Hills in 1877. Many claims were staked out just for the purpose of selling them to dupes in the East. In the fall of 1863 a grand boom in the sale of Colorado mines began. Almost everyone sought a hole in the ground that he could attempt to palm off on someone else as a mining prospect. Some men owned from fifty to one hundred and fifty claims for speculation purposes. A few were perhaps good, but many were worthless. If they could get valuable down payments of money, teams, or other property, they never worried about the next payment. Credulous or gambling people in the East were swindled out of literally millions of dollars in Colorado mines. Hundreds of telegraph messages costing from $50 to $300 each passed between Central City and New York. The work of the county clerk and recorder of Gilpin County so multiplied that a large force of extra helpers had to be employed day and night to keep up the records of claims, deeds, and abstracts of title. According to the *Denver Post*, the net income of the county recorder (who was paid by fees) as returned to the Federal income-tax collector was at the rate of $40,000 a year during this frantic gambling in mines. In the mad rush titles were in many cases defective, and purchasers were never able even to find the hole in the ground for which they had paid good money. The boom lasted about six months and collapsed flat in the spring of 1864.

Over a hundred companies were organized in the East and in Colorado, not to mine, but to speculate in the big boom. A considerable degree of folly in building mills and attempting to work mines accompanied the swindling. Travelers who visited the vicinity following the Civil War found great mills and other abandoned property covering the Colorado hills and gulches in the mining area.

Some of the names given the various gulches were interesting. In the Black Hills, Bear Gulch, fully ten miles long, is fed by Shirt Tail, Saratoga, Nigger, Hungry, Two-Bit, Centennial, and Bob-Tail gulches. Many were named for states, others for battles of the Civil War, and still others for generals, statesmen, or early miners in the region.

Soon the tent camp of the miners gave way to more permanent dwellings, and towns sprang up without planning on these gulches. For example, Helena, Montana, arose along the sides of Last Chance Gulch, Virginia City along Alder Gulch, and Bannack on Grasshopper Creek. The boom town was composed of shanties of every description—evergreen lean-tos, sage-brush huts, shelters made of blankets, potato sacks, and wagon covers, and various kinds of holes in the ground. Chimneys were made of whisky barrels.

A primitive permanent habitation was the brush-and-pole house which was the mountain counterpart of the prairie dugout. A hole sloping back into the side of a hill was roofed with poles laid close together, covered with evergreen boughs and topped with about nine inches of dirt. The dirt was put on in two strata: the layer next to the boughs was worked into a mortar before being spread on, the upper was composed of loose earth patted down. This roof was warm and tight for winter and cool for summer. The one defect was that it would not stand a long-continued rain. When soaked through, it leaked for days.

The next improvement was the old-fashioned log cabin, usually about 12 by 14 feet in size, with eaves projecting. It had the same dirt roof as the brush-and-pole shack, for this was the roof universally used in the mining country. Enough whip-sawed lumber was procured for a door and window-frames, but it was too precious for use as a floor, and hence clay had to suffice. When women came to dwell in these houses, certain refinements had to be added. Floors had to be put in and the inside lined with calico or other cotton cloth. This was dipped in alum water to give it fireproof qualities. Even homes built later were not plastered but were ceiled.

Beds were fastened onto the log walls, and the people slept on hay, with blankets to cover them. Chairs, tables, and other furni-

Jorud Photo Shop, Helena, Montana

LAST CHANCE GULCH

ture were made of poles from the forest with the bark still on them. Chairs were sometimes seated with hay rope. Raw hides on the floor sometimes served for carpets. In 1864 in Bozeman, Montana, brooms of broom-corn sold for five dollars, and women used greasewood and willow-twig brooms which answered the purpose of sweeping a dirt floor very well. A woman of Bannack, Montana, who paid fifty cents a pound for her nine-pound flat-iron stood it in front of a fire in the fireplace to heat it. This made ironing a tedious, intermittent process, but there was little of it done in a mining-camp. A man in the Black Hills, craving a washboard, took a two-foot length of pine log, split it, and hewed out a slab a foot wide. With a pencil he marked lines across it, and with a saw and pocket-knife notched out a fairly effective washboard. At least it was good enough to be used for practically three eight-hour shifts for the next few days in the camp. Inside of the miner's cabin were to be seen tin cups, kettles, pans, shovels, and various other kinds of equipment here and there about the place.

To pass the winter evenings in the mining-camp the miners read old newspapers and books, played checkers and chess, held lyceums, and had debating clubs, and in one instance, at Black Hawk Point, Colorado, a singing-school of thirty-two robust miners was organized. One of the members reported that they literally made the tin dishes on the cabin shelf rattle. Cards, of which euchre and poker were the favorite games, were played everywhere. The deck of cards got so soiled and black that a king could not be told from a jack without close examination.

Central City, Colorado, may be taken as an excellent example of a camp which blossomed out into a mining town. The houses were built on the mountainside with little regard for order. Bayard Taylor said of it and the other towns in Gregory Gulch:

The whole string of four *cities* has a curious, rickety, temporary air, with their buildings standing as if on one leg, with their big signs and little accommodations, the irregular, wandering, uneven street, and the bald, scarred and pitted mountains on either side.

The main street of Central City ran up the gulch, and there was only one cross street as late as seven years after gold was discovered there. The streets were so narrow that two teams could scarcely pass abreast, and persons on the narrow sidewalk were always being spattered with mud. There were no gardens and no shade-trees, for the earlier settlers had in short-sighted fashion completely denuded the immediate environs of the town. Because of the crowded ravine, many of the houses were built in terraced rows on the sides of the hills. One observer said that a man could sit on his door-step and look down on the roofs of the houses below.

The hill at Deadwood Gulch was so abrupt that wagons were let down by cables tied to the rear axle and run around a tree. Main Street was so narrow that if two bull trains were in town at the same time, it was difficult for either to unload goods.

Virginia City was a city of confusion. Piles of goods mingled with dirt and rubbish were dumped wherever space could be found and soon settled into the snow and mud. Clampitt tells us that:

Every particle of ground covered by canvas, boards, or baked mud was crowded to suffocation. Into sleeping houses, 20 x 30, were jammed 150 to 200 beings each night, at a dollar a head. Three hundred sleepers nightly filled the chief hostelry with the euphonious name of Hotel de Haystack. From attic to the earth beneath they lay in solid ranks, like winnows in the fields of sickled grain.

Some of these cities became fixtures and later widened their streets, organized their building programs for permanency, and put up brick and stone buildings. The great majority of them, although buildings might improve, were merely mining-camps which lapsed into coma when the mines became unprofitable and died a lingering death, always buoyed up, however, by the hope of new discoveries or increased prices for ore. A good example of a boom town which faded was Custer City in the Black Hills. In the spring of 1876 it had nearly six thousand people. Discoveries in Deadwood Gulch started a stampede in which a thousand people left in a day, and within a short time there were less than a hundred inhabitants. Two years later there were fifty-seven people in the place.

The stores were of the general-merchandise variety, carrying everything from drugs to mining tools. In 1860 at a Colorado mining-camp a place consisting of three small tents arranged together bore a sign advertising a saloon, store, boot and shoe shop, bakery, and barber shop. The visitor upon entering found as a background two tables, on each of which was a pack of cards; along one side was a tray of pies, cakes, and bread, and on the other a barber's chair. At the entrance hung boots, moccasins, mittens, and a number of signs, one of which read "Milk for sale!"[7] Advertising was vigorous if not elegant. At Russell's Gulch a storekeeper, having received a fresh supply of goods, hung out a white-cardboard placard lettered with charcoal:

> Just arrived.
> A right smart of bacon!
> A good many molasses!
> A power of dried apples!
> You bet!

Sunday in the mining-camp brought a change of occupation if not rest. After the cleanup, at a rather early hour a procession of miners began to file past the cabins, almost staggering under loads of worn implements which were deposited at the blacksmith's tent to be sharpened or repaired for a renewal of activities the next day. Steadily for two or three hours this procession moved down the gulches, until the narrow streets and cramped business-houses were crowded. Purchases were to be made for the coming week, the mail was to be got, and the hard-working miner paused a few hours to be with the crowd, to drink or enjoy the pleasures of the variety of amusements offered. At Helena, Montana, a year

[7] Perrigo, *A Social History of Central City, Colorado, 1859-1900*, pp. 84, 85, 89, 107.

after the gold discovery, Sunday was the busiest day in the week. The street spaces were blockaded with men and merchandise, with wagon- and pack-trains waiting near-by for a chance to unload. Auctioneers were crying sales in the streets with a lively trade, saloons were crowded, hurdy-gurdy dance-halls were in full blast, Mexicans were attempting to ride wild mustangs which were rearing, jumping, kicking, and bucking in the effort to unhorse their riders. On a near-by level spot horse-racing ensued. The saw and the hammer were busy all day long. As one man stated, Sunday was much different from that of his early education in New England.

Of religion there was almost none. Many, no doubt, salved their consciences as did James Morley, who on July 19, 1863, wrote in his diary:

Sunk drain ditch one hundred and fifty feet and turned creek three hundred feet. Thinking of wants of loved ones at home, it seems no sin, in this savage country, to exert oneself on their behalf, on Sabbath.

Alexander Majors attended a service in a muslin building in Helena in 1866, but the blacksmith's hammer next door and the auctioneer's bellow in the street all but drowned out the voice of the preacher and nullified divine instruction. A miner recorded, "Good society and morals were strangers to this country." Even the banks were open on Sunday until after some years the mining town began to take on Eastern ways. When the first death occurred in Custer City, Dakota, in 1876, that of a youth suffocated by a cave-in, there was no preacher in town, and a two-hour canvass of the community was unable to find a professor of religion among three hundred and sixty people. Worse still, a close search failed to disclose a prayer-book or Bible. Lawyers, doctors, the reporter, were besought to "say a few words at the grave to be Christian-like," but none could do it. Said the mayor, "We want to put the poor boy away kind o' Christian-like, not like a dog." Finally a girl came with a small Bible, the only one in town.

The mining town, although less refined than that of the farming community, was not entirely devoid of cultural agencies. Churches, schools, and lodges, although appearing a little more tardily than on the agricultural frontier, were established within a few years. The *Montana Post* of Virginia City indicated that by October, 1864, the Episcopal, Methodist, Congregational, and Presbyterian churches were active. The first Methodist church edifice in the territory was built of split logs with a dirt roof and windows of white muslin cloth. Bishop Daniel S. Tuttle of the Protestant Episcopal Church reported that while in Montana he held services in saloons, stores, or other buildings, often using a dry-goods box for a pulpit. The membership of the mining-camp churches was never very large, but those who attended the services were generous. When the collection plates, often gold-pans, were passed, the miners took out their buckskin pouches and put in a pinch of dust. The earliest educational projects were subscription schools which charged a dollar and a half a week tuition. The Masons, Odd Fellows, and Good Templars organized within a few years after a "strike." They became an active factor in the social life of the camp, sat up with their members who were sick, and took charge of funerals.

One of the first things the mining town clamored for was mail service. Denver for many months had to send a rider two hundred miles to Fort Laramie, the nearest post-office, for mail. In 1859 a mail service across the Plains was inaugurated, and with the price of delivery from Laramie eliminated, postage was cut in half. Letter postage cost twenty-five cents. Emigrants usually took about a month to cross the Plains, while the stage made it in eight days, and hence the first thing the newcomer did was to go to the post-office. When the stage came in, two long queues of men lined up in front of the two windows and waited patiently for their mail. The carriage fee was payable at the receiving end, and some of the miners got to playing tricks on the officials. A man would receive a letter, read it, bring it back to the office denying it was his, and collect a refund. The officials soon caught on to this swindle and offered to open the letter and read a portion in order to determine whether it belonged to the claimant. Some amusing incidents occurred in this connection. On one occasion the letter began by informing the recipient that his wife had been "acting up" ever since he left. He stopped the agent, fully satisfied that the letter was his. Another missive informed the addressee that his brother had been hanged in Iowa for stealing horses. He also claimed the letter without further public reading.[8]

By far the larger portion of the inhabitants of a mining-camp were young men from twenty-five to thirty years of age. There were a few respectable women, but most of the weaker sex were dance-hall girls and prostitutes. The absence of the restraint that a settled, orderly community with women and homes has upon a man accounts for much of the program carried on at the mines.

The sports tended toward the brutal and were always accompanied by betting. The following examples selected from a wide range are typical. At Central City, Colorado, in November, 1862, a dog-fight was held in a theater with bets of one hundred dollars a side. At Virginia City, Montana, two years later, a Mexican projected a bull-fight. It was backed by others and on the appointed day was attended by a crowd. It was not very popular with the miners, however, for the bull and the matador experienced their rages at different times. When the animal finally got into a fighting mood, his antagonist climbed the fence and became one of the spectators temporarily. At last the bold matador got an axe and essayed to hack off the bull's horns. The crowd vetoed that mode of warfare as a foul against the bull. Finally, in an attempt to get their money's worth, the crowd called for dogs and set them on the bull. But this was not a success either, and after watching the baiting for a time, the crowd walked away

[8] William Larimer and William H. H. Larimer, *Reminiscences of General William Larimer and His Son William H. H. Larimer* (Lancaster, Pa., 1918), pp. 101, 176, 177.

feeling that no one was hurt except the spectators themselves who had got "bit." At other times two bulls were placed in a ring and fought. A Montana bull-fight of this kind drew two dollars each from a large crowd. In this case also the spectators felt they had been cheated, for the two bulls were old stags that had pulled goods across the Plains and did not have any fight in them. Cocks were armed with steel spurs and fought before cheering, betting miners.

At Denver, in 1860, from six to eight hundred people gathered and watched a duel wherein the acting governor, S. W. Bliss, killed Dr. S. Stone, a member of the legislature and judge of the miners' court. The Virginia City miners were the recipients of their money's worth on January 7, 1865, when a prize-fight began at twenty-four minutes before two and lasted until daylight was failing. One hundred and eighty-five rounds, fought in that many minutes, failed to bring any decisive results, and the spectators called for the combatants to stop. The referee pronounced it a drawn battle, the ring money was divided, and the bets were called off.[9] These fights were oftentimes between representatives of neighboring camps and heavy betting resulted. The rings were sometimes very primitive. For a championship fight between the representatives of Virginia City and Bannack, a level spot among the hills was selected and a corral built. The ring was made in it. No weapons of any kind were allowed even outside the enclosure.

Not all the diversions were of the gory, brutal type, however, for soon there were ten-pin alleys, billiards, and shooting galleries, all attended by betting and competition. It was not uncommon for someone to challenge all comers to a championship series at chess, checkers, or other game.

The mountain cities had long winters with heavy snowfall, and sleigh-riding and coasting became very popular sports. Not only the boys but the whole town, preachers, bankers, lawyers, and schoolma'ams, were at the slide on every manner of coasting de-

[9] *Montana Post*, Virginia City, Montana, January 17, 1865.

vice, from improvised sleds made from dry-goods boxes to well-designed racers. The citizens of Black Hawk, Colorado, hauled their sleds up the hill on horse-drawn vehicles and coasted a mile and a half over a rough winding road in three minutes. In many mountain towns all travel in the winter was on runners. Even the hook-and-ladder vehicle for fire protection of the town was placed on a bob-sled.

Dancing was a universal pastime. As early as 1864 Dan Rice's Circus was making the rounds of the mining towns. Theaters were soon established and troupes came in from the East. Bell-ringers, sax-horn players, magicians, ventriloquists, singers, phrenologists, and lecturers made the circuit of the mining-camps. A correspondent of the *New York Tribune* in 1866 attended the Virginia City theater and reported that $1.50 admitted one to a hall holding two hundred and fifty persons, with a rude little rear gallery, long wooden benches, a large wood stove, an orchestra of four, five tallow candles for footlights, and a green cambric drop-curtain. Several children and a dog ran about the floor during the performance, and some in the gallery amused themselves by throwing apples over the heads of spectators to their friends below. Most of the audience carried Navy revolvers. The beautiful diction of the play was rendered in a manner, surmised the *Tribune* correspondent, that the author could scarcely have survived had he been there to hear it. At Deadwood the first variety theater, the Bella Union, had seventeen curtained boxes facing the stage. The log building was furnished with seats made of wooden slabs fastened to stakes driven into the ground. It had the first piano in the Black Hills. The instrument was hauled from Bismarck by bull train, the trip taking nearly two months. General admission to this crude theater was $2.50 and reserved seats $5.00.

When a man wanted to leave the region, he offered his property at auction in the street. This practice, together with that of leaving wagons standing in the street, faced Virginia City with a problem equal to the parking problem in a modern city. An ordinance forbidding any wagons to stop on Main Street and eliminating auctions in the street was passed but was not enforced without considerable remonstrance. A livery-stable in that city raffled off all its horses and vehicles as a means of closing out in 1865.

Water was a problem in a mining-camp. Those who lived along the stream in the gulch could take their water from the cold mountain supply, but those who lived on the hillsides had a long and steep carry. Consequently wagons hauled water around town, selling it at fifty cents a barrel or ten cents for five gallons. A barrel or keg in the kitchen was used for storage purposes. In Custer City, Dakota Territory, a well in the center of town furnished water for the whole "city." At first firewood was chopped in the back yard, but soon all the beautiful trees were cut down and it was necessary to go miles for fuel.

In the Black Hills some of the cities had a degree of planning. At Custer City, the first town in the region, a town-site company was organized and the site plotted. With the aid of a compass and picket-rope the surveying was finished, and the first plat was made on a piece of birch bark twelve inches square. The blocks were divided into lots and numbered from one to twelve hundred. Tickets bearing these numbers were drawn from a box by the miners. Rapid City was begun in a very similar way.

City institutions were primitive indeed at first. There was no undertaker in Denver during the second year, and the bodies of nine men killed in an accident were taken to the Methodist Church where the ladies of the town prepared them for burial. At a funeral in a mining town the coffin was placed in a quartz wagon and, accompanied by friends, proceeded slowly up the gulch to the cemetery on the mountainside. There was, however, a hospital in Denver at an early date, and, to judge from the rough times, it must have been as well patronized as any other institution in the town.

Under favorable circumstances miners made money readily and spent it freely. The universal currency was little pieces of gold from the retort or gold-dust, and it was carried about in little buck-skin bags. When a purchase was made, the miner opened his pouch and handed it to the merchant, who took out enough to pay for the goods. In small purchases the buyer might be penalized to the extent of twenty-five per cent. Close change was not customary, though every business man had a pair of scales on his counter with weights from a few grams to an ounce. Coins and paper money were seldom seen. Any article from a wagon to a newspaper was purchased with the gold-dust currency. Some miners were very careless and carefree with their treasure. Sometimes they played quoits with nuggets or dropped precious bags down in a corner as negligently as one would a bundle of old clothes. At Virginia City, Montana, every morning the little boys swept the floor of one of the business houses, took up the dust on shovels, and washed it out. Sometimes they realized five dollars for their day's work. Other miners used great care in placing their gold in a safe belonging to some place of business. Space in safes was at a premium. Merchants of a camp met and decided upon a price for gold as a standard. The price at Deadwood in 1877 was $20 an ounce.

Prices of commodities and services varied but were always high. In 1876 at Deadwood men sat on logs at the saw-mill with money in hand waiting for lumber to construct buildings at a price of $70 a thousand. In the sixties in Montana a game of billiards, a gallon of milk, and a shave all cost the same—one dollar. A bath at the barber shop cost $2.00. A place to stay at a hotel was $4.00 a day. Sixteen pounds of hay for a bed cost $1.28. The lower story of a stone block 35 by 70 feet in Virginia City rented for $400 a month. In Colorado women washed clothes for $3.00 a dozen. The regular interest rate in Denver in 1859 was 25 per cent a month.

The miner was likely to wear a badly battered felt hat, blue or red flannel shirt, buckskin or butternut pants, high-top moccasins or boots with wool socks turned down over his footwear. After they had been in the mountains a time, the prospectors and miners often patterned after the trapper and wore buckskin. The *New*

York Tribune correspondent, Albert D. Richardson, described the crowd that gathered to hear Horace Greeley at Gregory Gulch in June, 1859, as a motley gathering of men with long, unkempt locks, shaggy heads, and tanned faces, having bowie-knives and revolvers hanging from their belts. Some were reclining on the ground, some sitting upon stumps and walls of unfinished buildings, and still others perched in trees. The presiding officer occupied a log instead of a chair, and one of the speakers was clad in a full suit of buckskin with long fringes. A woman writer in 1876 thought that the Chinese laundry must have its prices entirely too high, judging from the looks of the clothing of the men she met.

The meeting of the second Territorial Legislature of Colorado, in 1862, indicated something of the dress and customs of the time. George Crocker, a brilliant lawyer, and his fellow-member from California Gulch walked a hundred and fifty miles over the snowy range, across South Park and down through the mountains to Colorado City, each carrying a blanket in which he slept beside the trail when night overtook them. When Crocker walked up and laid down his blanket at the door of the House of Representatives, he possessed no other clothes than the ones he wore at the sluice-box in the gulch. He had on a blue flannel shirt, trousers patched with buckskin, an old boot on one foot and a brogan on the other, and an old slouch hat that he had slept in, the brim partly gone. His face was blackened by the smoke of camp-fires and furrowed by perspiration, his eyes hollow with fatigue and hunger, his feet blistered from walking, and his hair tangled and yellow with dust. The next day he was elected Speaker of the House and made an eloquent speech which would have done credit to a polished Eastern statesman.[10]

Prospectors and early miners found game for food, but soon the game was driven out by population, and the frontier diet became staple—bacon, beef, bread, and coffee. Potatoes and dried peaches

[10] Irving Howbert, *Memories of a Lifetime in the Pike's Peak Region* (New York and London, 1925), pp. 72-73.

or apples were luxuries. The beef often came from old oxen that had pulled the other goods out there and was extremely tough. When a group was working together, the men took turns at doing the cooking, each man serving a week. Let an enterprising individual start a bake-shop and his pies and cakes were disposed of readily. It seemed just like home to those starved miners to get a change from their crude cabin fare. When flour was scarce, brown wrapping-paper was used for crust, and pies sold at "four bits" a slice, four slices to the pie. When paper was scarce, it was too valuable to use for wrapping, and the butcher gave the customer a pointed stick to put in the meat and carry it home. At the Montana mining-camps California grapes were sometimes brought in, packed in barrels in wine, and coaches from Salt Lake City brought in peaches which the Mormons were producing. They sold at from twenty-five to fifty cents each.

A shortage of provisions due to a snow blockade or other cause sent prices soaring sky-high. On one such occasion the people of Virginia City staged a flour riot, set reasonable prices, and brought an end to the corner in foodstuffs.

Gambling was a universal and inveterate habit of the miners. Some of the most luxurious places in the new mining towns were given over to that business. The Denver House, the erection of which was begun in January, 1859, was a good example of a typical gambling establishment. It was thirty feet wide and nearly a hundred feet long, built of cottonwood logs with a slanting skeleton roof covered with canvas. There were no glass windows in Denver at this time, and the window openings were covered with cotton cloth. The building was originally intended for a hotel, and it continued to function in that capacity in a limited way although the principal activity was gambling. On the inside there was no ceiling and the floor was of earth. Canvas nailed on frames seven feet high served as partitions to divide the space. The front area was occupied by a bar for the sale of strong drinks and by a dozen gambling-stables at which experts in their line presided. Several well-dressed individuals whom Henry Villard saw hanging around town, taking them for men of means waiting for a chance to make a respectable use of their wealth, now appeared in this part. Next to the bar-room came another space enclosed by canvas partitions where the meals were served. Immediately behind it were six apartments for sleeping purposes, divided by the same fragile walls, set off on either side of a passage. Outside at the end of the building under canvas was the kitchen. There was no furniture in the building except the gambling and other tables and benches and chairs made of rough wood; bedsteads made of the same material were without mattresses or pillows. The guest furnished his own buffalo robe or blankets in which to sleep. In the passageway were barrels of water at which the guest filled his tin wash-basin, and after using it he emptied it on the floor.[11]

Gambling was carried on night and day, and the clink of the money, the rattle of the dice, and over all the cry of the three-card-monte dealer accompanied by the oaths of the players created such a din that the guest could not sleep in the back room. Now and then some dissatisfied customer with a little too much Taos lightning (whisky, some of which came from Taos, New Mexico) fired a few shots at random. The canvas-covered windows were used as exits in such a case, the occupants leaping out like frogs. An orchestra performed on one side of the building, but its tunes were interrupted time and time again by trips to the bar for liquor. After a while the music became mechanical. There was little money in town, and the gamblers lay in wait for the greenhorns. Lack of money did not altogether prevent gambling, however, for Richardson saw the probate judge of the county lose thirty Denver lots in less than ten minutes one Sunday morning, and the county sheriff pawned his revolver for twenty dollars to spend in betting at faro. The gamblers, he noted, were entertain-

[11] Henry Villard, *Memoirs of Henry Villard* (Boston and New York, 1904), Vol. I, p. 123.

ing in conversation, had curious experiences to relate, and showed a keen insight into human nature. They were open-handed and charitable. More money could be raised for a widow and orphans in less time in a gambling-house than in any other place.

The hurdy-gurdy house competed with the gambling establishment as soon as a mining town began to flourish. One of these houses in Custer City, Dakota Territory, in 1876 was described as a long building comprising the following apartments: first, a bar- and gambling-room; second, the dance-hall; third, sleeping- and dining-rooms for the dance girls and boarders; and still farther back the kitchen. As a rule, at one end of the dance apartment was an orchestra of three or four fiddlers and at the other a bar.

The miners bought dance tickets for one dollar each. One-half of this went to the girl and one-half to the proprietor. At Virginia City, Montana, the proprietor, who with a revolver at his belt dealt faro at a table in the front, assured a *New York Tribune* correspondent in 1866 that his daily profit averaged $100 from the dance-hall. The girls, known as hurdy-gurdies, sometimes made as much as $25 a day. Favorites received many "gifts" in addition to that. Sometimes the hurdy-gurdies were dressed in uniform, but more often they dressed according to individual taste in the gayest colors and most extreme styles. Some outfits of gay ribbons, kids, silks, and laces represented seven or eight hundred dollars. Some of the most highly favored of these butterfly sirens invested with merchants and bankers thousands of dollars in gold and received more in a week than a well-educated girl in an Eastern city could earn in two years.

The miner with sun-browned neck, bearded face, long black hair hanging down beneath his wide felt hat, and a big cigar in his mouth made his way into the hall and bought his ticket. At the command by the prompter, "Take your partners for the next dance!" he approached the women's bench and invited one of the girls to dance. Once launched in the dance, our hero bounded off, rising and falling to the rhythm with clumsy movements and growing enthusiasm. As the dance progressed, he grew more excited, and only the long practice of his fair partner kept her from being swept off her feet. With practised foot and easy grace she kept perfect time to the music and rounded out her part as gracefully as a swan. At the close of the dance the miner treated his partner at the bar. Obviously other services were at his disposal at a price. In the dance-hall were to be found judges, members of the legislature, and everyone except the minister. Gray-haired men were to be seen there, dancing sometimes while their wives sat at home, perhaps far away, blissfully ignorant of the proceedings.[12] The *Montana Post* of Virginia City commenting on this situation in 1864 stated that it was nearly impossible to find seven-eighths of the able-bodied males of the town without going the rounds of the dance-halls.

The self-government of the miners is a good example of the ability of Anglo-Saxons in the absence of government to form regulations and bring order out of chaos. The miners in Colorado brought with them knowledge of the operation of claim clubs and the preëmption law in the agricultural sections and of the mining regulations in vogue in the lead mines and in California, and in 1859 and 1860 these laws were rounded out to a large extent into permanent form. The miners in a given region met and drew up a constitution defining the boundaries, giving a name to the district, as it was called, and passing laws and regulations for its government. These varied somewhat, but in general they allowed a miner one claim and only one by discovery although he could buy others and hold them. At first it was customary to give a discoverer two claims, but this was discontinued. Preëmptions of 100 by 40 feet for building-lots and mill-sites 250 feet square were allowed. In 1866 the right of preëmption of mineral lands according to local miners' rules was finally recognized by Congress,

---

[12] Thomas J. Dimsdale, *The Vigilantes of Montana* (Helena, Mont., 1915), pp. 11-14.

and land-offices were opened up some time later. A president and a secretary or recorder were elected by ballot for one year. Voters had to be sixteen years of age and have a residence of ten days in the district. Some districts would not allow a lawyer to practise in their courts. Common law was used, and no technicalities were allowed to defeat the ends of justice.

There were three kinds of trials. The first was before a judge. The president of the district acted in this capacity, and when the evidence was presented by the two parties to a dispute, he listened and decided the case as equitably as he knew how. The second type of trial was by a board of arbitrators. One man was appointed by each of the litigants, and they appointed a third. If they could not agree, the judge appointed the third. The third type was trial by jury. Twelve men were appointed by the judge, and each litigant struck off a name until only six remained. In some places an appeal to a court with a jury of twelve was allowed. In such a case this was final, but in most districts an appeal to a general assembly of all the miners in the district was final. The judgment and costs were charged to the loser. The judge and referees received five dollars for their services.

The president, recorder, and one other man appointed by the president acted as a probate court and decided concerning the disposition of the effects of a deceased miner. The only debts collectable were those contracted after the debtor's coming to the gold-fields, and in some places gambling and liquor debts were not collectable. Twenty dollars' worth of tools, bedding, and clothes were exempt. Notice of meetings had to be posted ahead of time. Requirements for a quorum were low. In the Snowy Range in Colorado only five were required. At Gold Lake the miners succeeded in getting through an annual tax of one dollar for each claim, which was to be used for road-making. The secretary received a fee for recording the claims, and a glance at the list of fees leads one to believe the officers were well paid for their work. When territorial laws became operative, claim number three was left vacant on each lode and was recorded free of charge for the benefit of schools.[13]

In the Black Hills there were three districts in the vicinity of Deadwood, and not content with one claim, some of the first comers had claims in each district. Newcomers, among whom were many old, experienced miners, rebelled. They called a miners' meeting between Deadwood and Gayville, and as both parties were armed with rifles, bloodshed was imminent. The newcomers led by a belligerent one-eyed miner wanted to cut down the size of claims. At that time 900 feet crossways of a gulch from rim-rock to rim-rock was allowed the first discoverer, and strips 300 feet wide for each new claimant. The old miners would not concede the point, and since no one was particularly anxious to die, a compromise was reached whereby every claim had actually to be worked or be forfeited. The selfish holders thus lost, or sold at a low figure, two of their claims.

It was but a step from deciding civil actions to trying criminal cases by the mining-district machinery. When a man in Colorado named Davis shot a man named Roulan, although not seriously, in an argument over the latter's wife in 1861, the culprit was sentenced to have half his head shaved, receive fifty lashes, and be expelled from the mountains. The prisoner was taken to the scene of the crime and tied to a tree; five men gave him the lashes on his bare back while eight hundred or a thousand shouted, "Lay it on harder." The woman was given twenty-four hours to leave the mountains.

Sometimes a justice of the peace and a sheriff or constable were elected to handle the criminal cases in connection with the mining-district government. A thief was more certain of punishment than was a murderer in some places, for public opinion often regarded shootings as justifiable, but never thievery. Then, too, men were compelled to regard stealing as a serious offense since there was no

[13] *Rocky Mountain News*, Cherry Creek, Kansas Territory, May 14, June 11, 1859.

place where the individual could keep his gold-dust and other property secure from burglary. The only alternative was to make theft terribly unsafe. The day of a trial was a general holiday when the miners from the whole gulch gathered to see that punishment was meted out. In Montana for reckless conduct a man was banished a hundred miles from the mountains. At the same time one found guilty of manslaughter was banished six hundred miles from the mountains with three hours to leave.

Closely akin and merging into mining-district justice on the one hand and lynch-law on the other was the people's court. It was an extralegal tribunal organized by the people for the purpose of giving an immediate and speedy trial. A president elected by the populace appointed a judge or associate judges, a clerk, and a sheriff who appointed his deputies. A jury of twelve citizens was impaneled, and the court was ready for action. In a case in Denver in 1860, a man killed another at 2:00 P.M. At nine the next morning the court commenced organization, and at two in the afternoon began the trial. Witnesses were examined, the attorneys summed up the evidence, the jury brought in a verdict of guilty of first-degree murder, and the judge sentenced the prisoner to be hanged on the following day. A committee of twenty-five citizens took charge of the condemned that night. The next morning a scaffold was built at the scene of the crime, and at four that afternoon he was hanged, barely fifty hours after the crime was committed. A variation of this type of semi-lynch rule occurred when the populace acted as jury. When the evidence was in, the judge took a vote on whether or not the prisoner was guilty. When the judge could not tell whether the sound of the ayes or the nays was the stronger, it was necessary to have all the ayes stand on one side of the road and the nays on the other, or, as was done in a Montana trial, have those in favor of conviction pass between two objects (wagons in this case) while a count was taken. In this instance a number were caught passing through twice. There were serious objections to the people's court on several counts. First, the rogue population became so large that it intimidated honest witnesses and officers. There was dishonesty in the vote, as exemplified above. A rogue's vote nullified an honest man's vote. Many could not hear what was going on in the inner circle and voted from prejudice.

The jury system was better, but it also was subject to criticism. Some friends of a man on trial in Denver slipped whisky in to the jury, and its mellowing influence helped to establish the absolute innocence of one killer.[14] The thing that caused the greatest concern among respectable people was the fact that the underworld had the upper hand.

After a mining town had grown to some size and its riches had attracted vultures of all sorts from all quarters, rough times ensued. The *Rocky Mountain News* of February 29, 1860, carried this statement:

> We are curious to know how long this reckless and promiscuous firing of pistols, cutting, and stabbing will be permitted. . . . Drunken men frequently firing pistols right and left, totally indifferent as to whom or what they hit. On Sunday evening last, while standing at our door in the space of less than half an hour we witnessed two street quarrels, entirely distinct, in both of which pistols and knives were drawn.

In September the editor again called attention to the times:

> There is hardly an hour in the day or night that the sound of pistol and gunshots, in all parts of the city, is not heard. Each man seems to fire off his arms at pleasure, let it annoy or alarm whom it may.

With plenty of liquor and a general wild, unrestrained spirit, it is little wonder that numerous homicides occurred. In order to bring about a semblance of peace and quiet, a vigilance committee was formed. One hundred and fifty of the leading citizens got together in an attempt to run the rascals out. In some way the evil characters got word in advance of every move of the vigi-

[14] J. J. Thomas, "In the Days of the Overland Trail," *The Trail*, Denver, Col., May, 1910, p. 7.

lantes. Some members were playing into the hands of the underworld and a smaller committee of only ten of the most trustworthy members was formed within the larger group. Within a few months Denver became almost as quiet as any Eastern town. It was found that many of the new arrivals were from Helena, and at Helena many of their worst crooks were from Denver. An exchange of officers was arranged whereby two detectives from Denver went to Helena and Helena sent two to Denver. Shortly after the two arrived in Denver, two Helena desperadoes hove in sight. Upon being identified by the Helena officials, they were taken into custody and marched to the starting stand at the racetrack, strung up without ceremony, and left there as an example. This was the signal for the immediate exodus of questionable characters, and the ones left behind were handled satisfactorily.[15]

At Virginia City, Montana, the situation had got more seriously out of hand than in Denver. Henry Plummer, a desperado quick on the draw, had got himself elected sheriff of both Virginia City district and Bannack. He gathered around him deputies as bad as himself, and they became the leaders of one of the West's most noted bands of road-agents, as stage-coach robbers were called. Since Plummer worked from the inside as leader of the robbers who lived in a gulch and sallied out to assail the coach, they had a perfect arrangement. When there was gold on the coach, it was robbed, and when there was no gold, it passed in safety. The secret of this was that the sheriff put a special mark on the coach when it carried money. These bandits pounced upon lone travelers as well as upon stage passengers who offered a fair prospect of gain. By the discoveries of bodies of victims, confessions of murderers before execution, and reliable information sent to the vigilance committee, it was found that one hundred and two people certainly were killed by this gang of road-agents in various places, and it was believed that scores of others who mysteriously

---

[15] Asa F. Middaugh, *When Denver Was Young and Tough*, Ms., Colorado State Historical Society Library, pp. 12, 13.

disappeared after starting with sums of money for various destinations also met death by the same hands.

Finally, one of the agents, George Ives, was captured and tried by a people's court in Alder Gulch. The jury consisted of twenty-four miners. The judge sat in a wagon, and the jury sat in a half circle by a big log fire, for it was cold. Hundreds of men stood around the circle during the trial, which lasted two or three days. It was a battle royal between the upright citizens and the lawless element, both there, armed and determined. The jury brought in a verdict of guilty and fixed the death penalty. Ives was hanged two hours later. Before he was strung up, he made a confession, exposing the whole organized band of robbers. To the utter surprise of all, Henry Plummer, the sheriff, was leader of the band. This was kept secret from the public, and a vigilance committee was organized immediately. Plummer and his two deputies were taken from their beds and hanged before they knew their crimes were discovered. There were over thirty in Plummer's gang whose names were known to the vigilance committee, and they were followed by the vigilantes until all but two had been executed.

The miners, like other frontiersmen, were tolerant in many ways, but they were intolerant of the Chinese, compelling them to pay discriminatory taxes and in some places forbidding them to work in the mines. At times race riots broke out, and the "Mongolians" were mistreated and compelled to leave the diggings.

The early miners, like other frontier figures, developed a language all their own. Not a few of them had left North or South in order to escape the Civil War. Some deserted and others evaded service. There was in the diggings a large sprinkling of people from war-torn Missouri. This had its effect upon the language in use. The special correspondent of the *New York Tribune* reported a conversation on the street in which a lounger was defending as correct the rural Southern phrases "we'uns" and "you'uns." A bystander inquired, "Are you a grammarian?" "Which?" was the bewildered reply. "Are you a grammarian?" he repeated.

"Why no," retorted the budding rhetorician, "I'm a Missourian!"

A mining region was always known as "the diggin's." The term "dust" was always used for money; for example, the statement was made, "He wanted to buy, but he couldn't raise the dust." The prospector who found a good claim was said to have made "a lucky strike" or to have "struck it rich." The faintest particles of gold in the earth were spoken of as "the color." A miner said of a man he had tried out in various positions and found utterly worthless, "I have panned him out clear down to bed-rock and I can't even raise a color." A "lead" was a rock formation in which one might expect to find gold. A miner said of the *New York Tribune* to its correspondent: "I have read it ever since I was a boy and can't possibly do without it, though now and then it strikes a lead which don't pan out well." In the "diggin's" every-one talked of "feet," "claims," "dust," and bets were made and drinks paid for in "ounces" or fractions thereof. A green lad who bought a mine which had been salted and who had been beaten out of all his money went to an old miner who seemed very friendly and poured out his tale of woe, expecting sympathy. The miner responded something like the following: "Why, you dad-gasted fool, a Digger Ingin would a knowed thar wan't no gold in that ar kind of ground. You are too green to be runnin' loose here by yourself and ought to have a gardeen. Pack your blankets and git back to the States, whar your friends can take care of you, if such a condemned eget [idiot] as you has friends." Some terms which are in common use today were unknown in the East then. A "square" meal was used in its present sense. "Shebang" meant any structure from a hotel to a shanty. An "outfit" was a general term meaning anything one might happen to have from a complete stamp-mill to a toothpick, a suit of clothes, a revolver, a twelve-ox team, or a velocipede. The term "you bet" as an affirmative response was used almost continuously everywhere.[16]

[16] *New York Daily Tribune*, February 3, 1866, p. 4; James F. Rusling, *Across America* (New York, 1874), pp. 65, 74.

Nicknames were regularly imposed to distinguish between the Bills and Toms. There were Fat Bacon Tom, and Sour Dough Bill. These names were given in the best of humor and rarely did anyone offer any remonstrance. One man was named Stove Pipe Sam because he went to the blacksmith shop to get a stovepipe rigged up and thereafter the blacksmith identified him by that handle. Gulches sometimes were dubbed in the same way: for example, Tin Cup Gulch, where someone washed gold with a tin cup; Frying Pan Gulch, after washing gold in that culinary implement; and Dead Man's Gulch, which was so named because the Indians annihilated there a whole party of white men. Whisky was called tanglefoot, forty rod, lightning, tarantula-juice, strychnine, and like names describing its qualities.

Men stood by their friends. Friendship was a defensive and offensive alliance. An insult offered a man's "pardner" was resented by both. The miners tenaciously held to their rights. Their philosophy was, "You may drive your stakes where you please, only don't try to jump my claim or I'll go for you sure." This principle operated in love, law, mining,—in fact, regulated the miner's every move. He worked hard, and after all expenses were paid, the average miner had little more than experience to show for his labor and risk. When a need for charity was presented, he was generous to a fault.

The individual gold-hunter's short day soon drew to a close, and in the lengthening shadows of his eventide were to be seen rising on the ashes of his camp-fire the great mills, smelters, and industrial plants of giant corporations. Shortly he found himself faced with the choice of becoming a mere cog in this industrial machine or returning to the old home in the East with the accumulation of his mining years. The institutions of civilization soon transformed the rough mining-camp into homes, cities, and commonwealths.

CHAPTER XII

SWIFT COURIERS OF THE PLAINS

FAST COMMUNICATION has always been sought by man. From the epoch when swift runners bore the news throughout Greece, through the time when couriers carried messages across the far-flung Roman Empire, until the radio began magically to annihilate space, man has been willing to pay the price for speed in communication. The last of the agencies depending solely on flesh and blood for a vast stretch over the never-ending Plains, in speedy transcontinental communication in the United States was the famous Pony Express.

Naturally the people of California, isolated three thousand miles from the nation's capital by a vast territory, much of which was uninhabited, wanted closer contacts with the East. Senator W. M. Gwin of that state on one occasion in the fifties rode to Washington on horseback accompanied part of the way by B. F. Ficklin, superintendent of the Russell, Majors & Waddell freighting company. The two men talked at some length about the famous ride of Francis Xavier Aubry, who rode the eight hundred miles from Santa Fe to Independence in five days and thirteen hours in 1853. Thus during the tedious hours of an overland trip were the first seeds of the Pony Express sown. Senator Gwin later interested William H. Russell of Leavenworth, one of the partners in the freighting firm, in the project, and they brought it to fruition. Russell kept the plans for the express secret, and when all arrangements had been made, it was announced in the *New York Herald* and the *Missouri Republican* that the service would begin on April 3, 1860, when at 5 P.M. the first courier would leave St. Joseph, Missouri. On the same day at almost the same hour (4 P.M.) an eastbound courier was to leave San Francisco.[1] The plan called for despatch of this pony mail from each end of the line once a week, every Tuesday. A short time later an improvement in the service brought semi-weekly mail.

A project such as this required a huge sum of money as capital and a vast organization of men, horses, and material equipment of all sorts. First of all, in some places along the old California trail, roads had to be made. This was especially true beyond the mountains in Nevada, where willow switches were cut and made into corduroy roads.

Since Russell, Majors & Waddell already had a monthly mail route from Independence to Sacramento and possessed many well stocked stations, less difficulty than would have been the case otherwise was experienced in inaugurating this most romantic chapter in the history of American transportation. New stations had to be added, however. Eighty riders were hired, between four and five hundred horses purchased, and two hundred men for station-keepers and attendants were recruited. Hundreds of tons of grain and hay had to be forwarded to the 190 stations along the line.[2]

The Pony Express riders were many of them mere lads selected for their light weight, endurance, bravery, coolness in time of danger, and their resourcefulness under all circumstances. For the most part they were products of the frontier able to ride and shoot *par excellence*. Few if any weighed over 135 pounds, and many, used to roughing it on the Plains, were peculiarly fitted to stand the exposure and fatigue incident to the successful prosecution of the project.

The stations were located ten, fifteen, or twenty miles apart depending upon the terrain, the water-supply, and other conditions. The ride between two stations was known as a stage. At

[1] Frank A. Root and William Elsey Connelley, *The Overland Stage to California* (Topeka, Kans., 1901), pp. 106-107.

[2] Alexander Majors, *Seventy Years on the Frontier* (Chicago and New York, 1893), pp. 184-185.

each station the keeper had a horse ready for the next stage. After riding several stages, the horseman gave the mail-sack to another rider who waited impatiently to take the precious messages to the end of his ride. The first horseman, after his 40- to 125-mile ride, rested and visited with the station-keeper until the rider from the opposite direction rode in, when he went flying back to his home station. The ride on some of the longer shifts was grueling even for a horseman accustomed to long hours in the saddle. Moreover, if accident or sickness disabled the relief rider, the tired courier had to ride his fellow's course also. Perhaps his comrade had been killed by Indians, or was so badly wounded he could not ride, or had been thrown by a misstep of his horse in the inky blackness of night. The situation had to be met, and with only a moment's pause the rider was in the saddle and posting along over the strenuous course. Unless an emergency arose, each rider rode his own round only once a week. In order to keep down weight, the courier's arms, originally including a carbine, were limited to a pair of revolvers and a knife. The saddle, bridle, and pouch used for carrying the messages were made of the best quality of leather, were strong and durable, and their combined weight was only thirteen pounds. In some places where the stations were close together, the stage was traversed at a steady gallop, making it at the rate of twenty miles an hour.

The saddle was a skeleton with little or no padding, and the leather mail-sack, known as a *mochila* (from the Mexican), was thrown over the saddle. It consisted of a leather blanket about four feet square to which was sewn in each corner a pocket about nine by twelve inches. A hole in the front slipped over the saddle-horn. When the rider mounted, he sat on the *mochila* and two of these pockets were in front of the rider's legs and two behind.[3]

Three of the pockets were locked at the beginning of the journey and were opened at only four or five points (at the forts and

[3] W. R. Honnell, "Pony Express," see *Kansas Historical Quarterly*, Vol. V, No. 1 (February, 1936), pp. 68-69.

PONY EXPRESS RIDER CHANGING HORSES AT ONE OF THE STATIONS

From a painting by W. H. Jackson.

Salt Lake City) by postal officials who had keys; but the fourth, known as the "way" pocket, was opened and closed en route by the station-keepers, who had a key for it. In it was also kept the way-bill or time slip on which was recorded the time of arrival and departure of the rider at the more important stops and at the end of his relay. The weight was evenly distributed among the pockets. All messages were required to be written on the thinnest onion-skin or tissue-paper obtainable, and when the package of about two hundred letters was made up, it was wrapped in oiled silk to prevent soaking when the speeding riders swam the many streams which at times were raging torrents. Not more than twenty pounds of mail was allowed for each rider, and this maximum was rarely reached.

Two minutes were scheduled for the change of mount, but so skilful did the riders become that they regularly made it in about fifteen seconds. The schedule between St. Joseph and San Francisco was ten days during eight months of the year and twelve days for the other four months.

A considerable portion of the westbound rider's feathery burden consisted of telegrams which had come by wire to St. Joseph and there been transcribed on tissue-paper. Before the Pony Express was started, a telegraph on the western end had been built across the Sierras and telegrams from there were carried eastward; similarly they traveled in the opposite direction from the western terminal on the eastern end as the telegraph crept westward up the Platte River. The building of the telegraph did not immediately put the Pony Express out of business. In fact, business increased, for the telegraph-builders used this fast service for communication between their various gangs of workmen. The stations at the ends of the line bore a rich harvest of telegrams to be carried between the terminals of the telegraph as the gap narrowed. The fast pony mail did not cease even after the transcontinental telegraph was completed, but continued another month. At times after the Civil War broke out, New York newspapers printed special issues on tissue-paper carrying the latest war news for California.

According to Alexander Majors, the riders received for their arduous duty from $120 to $125 a month and keep, although it is said that a few received as high as $150 for riding long relays or through extremely dangerous regions infested with fierce Cheyennes and Comanches. In addition to this, from the time of the firing on Fort Sumter a bonus was given by the California business men and public officers to the Pony Express company to be distributed among the riders for carrying the war news with the utmost speed. In 1861 the sum of $300 extra was collected for the riders for bringing to Sacramento a day earlier than usual a bundle of papers containing news of a big battle. Stationmen received from $50 to $100 a month.[4]

The postage rate between the Missouri River and California was $5.00 in gold per half-ounce at first. This was later reduced to $2.50 and still later to $1.00. Even after this reduction, no doubt, bulky love-letters were at a minimum. Sometimes the official and business mail was heavy, and the receipts were enormous, amounting to as much as a thousand dollars on some days. The United States Government required that a letter be enclosed in a stamped envelope bearing ten cents postage for each half-ounce. One employee remembered having affixed as many as twenty-five one-dollar "pony stamps" and twenty-five of the regular government stamps on a missive. A letter of this kind thus cost $27.50. In 1860 Great Britain and China were at war, and the British Government communicated with its Far Eastern squadron via the Pony Express, saving days in transportation time. The "pony" charges on some of these documents were as much as $135.

Even with this tremendous income, the company lost a large amount of money. One writer on the subject estimates that Russell, Majors & Waddell lost at least $100,000, and another places the loss at a quarter of a million. Alexander Majors declared that the

---

[4] Majors, *Seventy Years on the Frontier*, p. 85.

amount of business was not sufficient to pay one-tenth of the expenses, to say nothing of the capital invested.

The mounts used on the Pony Express were not ponies but sizable horses larger and faster than Indian ponies. If the horse was fresh, it could outrun an Indian mount. Majors said that these horses were mostly half-breed California mustangs, which, like their Moorish ancestors brought over from Spain, were alert, wiry, and as tough as buckskin. Captain Levi Hensel, who had a contract to shoe the horses on the eastern end of the Pony Express and stage lines, said that the horses Johnny Frey and Jim Beatley used to ride on the eastern end were imps of Satan; in order to shoe them it was necessary to throw them, put a rope around each foot, stake them out, and have one man on the head and another on the body while he trimmed the hooves and nailed on the shoes. Though utterly helpless, the spirited animals would squeal and bite all the time Hensel was working on them. He said it generally took half a day to shoe one of them, but on the road they never seemed to get tired. These fleet tough California horses of Mexican strain were particularly sure-footed and safe for mountain travel.

A definite time schedule was kept, and the stock-tender knew when to expect the riders. At first the rider carried a horn on which he gave a blast to warn the station-keeper to have his horse ready. As a rule, on dashing up to the station at the end of a stage, the courier found the relay agent on the lookout and waiting with a fresh horse saddled. Stopping abruptly, the rider made it the work of but an instant to dismount and throw the *mochila* over the saddle of the waiting horse. In a moment he was off again with the speed of the wind. The agent unsaddled the horse, watered him, and lariated him on a plot of pasture. The best of care was given these horses. Grain and hay were shipped from the Missouri River at tremendous freight costs. The agent always had a drink ready for the rider—water in summer, coffee or tea in winter.

Mark Twain on his trip to Nevada observed the Pony Express in action and described his experience as follows:

We had had a consuming desire, from the beginning to see a pony-rider, but somehow or other all that passed us and all that met us managed to streak by in the night, and so we heard only a whiz and a hail, and the swift phantom of the desert was gone before we could get our heads out of the windows. But now we were expecting one along every moment, and would see him in broad daylight. Presently the driver exclaims: "Here he comes!"

Every neck is stretched further, and every eye strained wider. Away across the endless dead level of the prairie a black speck appears against the sky, and it is plain that it moves. Well, I should think so! In a second or two it becomes a horse and rider, rising and falling, rising and falling—sweeping toward us nearer and nearer—growing more and more distinct, more and more sharply defined—nearer and still nearer, and the flutter of the hoofs comes faintly to the ear—another instant a whoop and a hurrah from our upper deck, a wave of the rider's hand, but no reply, and man and horse burst past our excited faces, and go winging away like a belated fragment of a storm!

So sudden is it all, and so like a flash of unreal fancy, that but for the flake of white foam left quivering and perishing on a mail-sack after the vision had flashed by and disappeared, we might have doubted whether we had seen any actual horse and man at all, maybe.

As the humorist said:

No matter what time of the day or night his watch came on, and no matter whether it was winter or summer, raining, snowing, hailing, sleeting, or whether his "beat" was a level straight road or a crazy trail over mountain crags and precipices, or whether it led through peaceful regions or regions that swarmed with hostile Indians, he must be always ready to leap into the saddle and be off like the wind! He rode . . . by daylight, moonlight, starlight, or through the blackness of darkness just as it happened.

The dress of the express rider corresponded to his flying career but was dictated somewhat by the frontier surroundings, the arduous task, and the severe climatic conditions. Some on the eastern end are said to have worn red-flannel shirts and blue trousers. The usual costume was a buckskin shirt with cloth trousers. Some of the men wore a full buckskin suit with the hair on in cold or rainy weather.[5] Mark Twain, in describing a summer costume, said that the rider's clothes were thin and close-fitting. He wore a "round about" and a skullcap and tucked his trousers into the tops of his light-weight boots. Leaving and entering St. Joseph the horse wore silver-mounted paraphernalia for display purposes and the rider wore embroidered leggings and huge silver-plated spurs. These were left on the ferry-boat, however, and over the prairie the rider sped unhampered by tinsel trappings.

During the freighting season, when mile after mile of great covered wagons, sometimes three or four abreast, formed an endless parade, the pony rider was obliged to turn out and ride over the rough ground in order to pass the lumbering trains. One freighter mentioned that many of the pony riders, in spite of their oath renouncing swearing, blessed them in true Western style under such circumstances. The express rider's life was not all hardship, however, for a station west of St. Joseph called Cold Springs Ranch was kept by a homesteader who had three young, good-looking, vivacious daughters who baked cookies, pies, and other good things to eat and handed them to Johnny Frey when he went by.

The nature of the country to be traversed between the Missouri River and the Rocky Mountains was varied and often difficult. On the prairies there were many ravines, gullies, creeks, and rivers to be crossed. On the high plateau there were parched stretches of sand and alkali, the dust from which was caught up and driven across the landscape, making travel all but impossible for the flying horsemen. Through the mountain region the trail wound over high passes, along giddy heights, through rugged canyons and gorges. The daring rider was often subject to dangers such as snowslides, roaring mountain torrents, blizzards, and storms, not to mention

[5] Alvin F. Harlow, *Old Waybills: the Romance of the Express Companies* (New York, 1934), p. 227.

the danger of losing his way on the trackless prairie. For hundreds of miles the trail crossed a country not only uninhabited but at that time thought to be desert seemingly incapable of cultivation. There were only three military posts on the route between the Missouri and Salt Lake City. For hundreds of miles only the weather-beaten station-houses and the occasional overland stage-coach broke the monotony of the dreary ride.[6] Hostile Indians occupied large sections of the route, and the rider started on his relay with the unnerving possibility that he might encounter an Indian ambush in some lonely canyon or other isolated spot. The high plains and mountain stretches were especially hazardous.

Many famous rides have been recorded. The first riders were scheduled to leave San Francisco and St. Joseph, the termini of the far-flung route, at almost the same moment amidst a gala celebration. As a matter of fact, the rider scheduled to leave St. Joseph at 5:30 did not get started until 6:30 because the train bringing the mail was an hour late as a result of delay east of the Mississippi, although the train across Missouri had made a record run, averaging more than fifty miles an hour. In reality the first rider from San Francisco rode only to the river, where a boat carried the mail to Sacramento. At that city a substantial sum had been raised to celebrate this glad occasion which was the signal for California's liberation from isolation. Thousands of people came in from neighboring mining-camps and farms, all business was suspended for the occasion, floral arches were built, cannons boomed, brass bands played, and speeches helped to make the day one of the most brilliant ever celebrated on the Pacific Coast up to that time. At the appointed signal, at 2:45 A.M., a spirited mount bore the waiting rider eastward. St. Joseph also was in gala attire, with flags floating in the breeze, bands playing, and a general air of celebration prevailing. Billy Richardson, an ex-sailor mounted on a fleet-footed horse, started at the sound of the firing of a cannon and, dashing down the street, received the mail-sack

[6] Root and Connelley, *The Overland Stage to California*, pp. 113-115.

at the office without a moment's delay and rode onto the waiting ferry-boat, while the largest crowd that up to that time had assembled on the Missouri River looked on. Arriving at the other side, he galloped into the golden sunset on that third day of April, 1860.

On this first trip one boy lost his way in a canyon of snow, wasting precious hours wandering in search of the trail. Finding his way once more, he pressed on with vigor. Another was overwhelmed in the Platte River. His horse was drowned, but by good fortune the rider was able to swim ashore bearing the precious *mochila*. With all possible speed he "footed it" to the next station, where he mounted and hastened on his way.

J. G. Kelley's most thrilling adventure on the Pony Express route was a narrow escape when a camp of green emigrants fired on him. When he took them to task for this, they excused themselves by saying they thought him to be an Indian.

The newspapers of the time give us an insight into the dangers of the trail as day in and day out, in winter's blizzard and summer's heat, these wiry youth swung along in the saddle traversing plains, mountains, deserts, and roaring streams. The hazard attending these grueling rides is revealed in the newspapers of the sixties which chronicled such items as these:

The pony expressman has just returned from Cold Springs driven back by the Indians.

The men at Dry Creek have all been killed and it is thought the Robert's Creek Station has been destroyed. Eight animals were stolen from Cold Springs Monday.

Bartholomew Riley died last night from a wound received at the Cold Springs Station on the sixteenth of May. Just arrived from the Indian battle ground at Pyramid Lake, tired, as he was, he volunteered to ride to the next change then a distance of eighty-five miles, where he received the wound of which he died.

Six Pike's Peakers found the body of the station-keeper horribly mutilated, and all the animals missing at Simpson's Park.

These incidents indicate that the life of the lonely stock-tenders and station-agents was little less heroic than that of the riders themselves. Not only were they ready with a change of mount when the fagged steed galloped up to the station, but many times they actually rode when the regular rider was ill or had been killed by the Indians.

On numerous occasions the riders were chased, but seldom were they overtaken. At one time, however, an expressman was scalped, but his horse escaped bearing the letter-bag, which was afterward recovered out on the Plains, and the letters were sent on to their destination. The Indians became so hostile at one time and stole so much stock that it was decided to stop the Pony Express for at least six weeks and to run stages only occasionally during that time. While the express was suspended, a party of stage-drivers, express riders, stock-tenders, and ranchers, well mounted and armed, went into the Indian country in search of stolen stock. They attacked an Indian camp, stampeded their horses, and four days later returned to Sweetwater Bridge. The expedition had been a grand success, and the event was commemorated by a big celebration in the usual manner. When these festivities ended, the stages and the Pony Express again began running on time.

One of the noted rides was that of R. H. Haslam, known as Pony Bob, who, while carrying the news of the election returns of 1860 through Nevada, was waylaid by the Paiutes. After a running fight of several miles, he got away. A flint-tipped arrow struck him in the mouth, knocking out five front teeth clean and fracturing his jaw. Another arrow went through his left arm. He pulled this one out, and although his arm swelled up to an astonishing size and was extremely painful, he took the election news through to the end of his run. Remarkable as it may seem, he rode one hundred and twenty miles in eight hours and ten minutes on that trip, riding thirteen horses.[7] Sam Hall, while

[7] R. H. Haslam, "Haslam's Thrilling Ride with Returns," *Denver Post*, February 14, 1905.

riding at a dead run over the trail to Willow Springs, was unfortunate enough to have his horse step into a badger hole which threw horse and rider in a pile. Hall's foot got caught in the stirrup, and the horse dragged the helpless rider two hundred yards across the plain before the shoe was jerked loose, leaving the boy lying on the barren plain with blood running from his mouth and nose. Reviving, he followed his galloping horse back to the station.

What was said to be the longest ride on record was made by William F. Cody, later known as Buffalo Bill. After riding the seventy-six miles of his own division, he found that the man who was to relieve him had been killed in a drunken brawl the night before. There was no one to send in his place, so without more than a moment's rest Cody galloped on over the next eighty-five mile division through a dangerous country, arriving at every relay station on time and accomplishing the round trip of 322 miles back to Red Buttes without any untoward incident.[8]

The first eastbound mail arrived at St. Joseph in exactly ten days. As additional stations were put in, shortening some riders' tours of duty, the time was cut down somewhat. Great rejoicing attended the first arrivals both at St. Joseph and at San Francisco. At the end of his run at Sacramento the westbound rider and his pony were taken aboard a steamer, and a fast run was made down the Sacramento River to San Francisco. Word had been sent ahead by telegraph, and although it was past midnight when they arrived, bands of music, the fire department, and great crowds met and honored the rider and his worthy steed. The fastest time made was on the occasion of Lincoln's first inaugural address in 1861, when the mail was carried through in seven days and seventeen hours.

This communication system was one of the most remarkable and romantic in the history of the American people. In all the trips

---

[8] William F. Cody, *Life and Adventures of "Buffalo Bill"* (New York, 1927), pp. 75-77.

made by the riders across the continent, totaling 650,000 miles in
the saddle, it is said that only one mail was lost. In its day this
postal system was a remarkable improvement. The time for letters
between New York and San Francisco was reduced from twenty-
three days to thirteen days. For telegraphic messages the time was
reduced to eight or nine days. The west coast benefited greatly by
the service of the fleet ponies. Civil War information was brought
to the news-starved Western people nearly two weeks ahead of the
Overland Mail and three weeks in advance of the Pacific Mail
Company's ocean steamers.

The Pony Express lasted less than eighteen months. Two
months before it stopped, the daily overland stage-coach carrying
mail was put into service. During the last few months of its existence the Pony Express shuttled madly back and forth. Telegraph
lines building both east and west daily intruded on its domain
until the gap gradually narrowed to the vanishing point. Flesh
and blood could not compete with the magic of electricity, and the
short but brilliant career of the Pony Express came to an end.
Other pony-express systems modeled on the original were operated, but none gave the regular or rapid service of the transcontinental line.

CHAPTER XIII

LIGHTNING COMMUNICATION

THE ADVANCE in speedy communication across the Plains came like a whirlwind. On September 15, 1858, the Butterfield stage line made possible the carrying of messages from the Missouri frontier to the Pacific Coast in twenty-five days. In 1860 the Pony Express cut the carrying time to nine days, but before this romantic courier system was well started, plans were laid for extending the telegraph across the vast space of plains and mountains.

On June 16, 1860, Congress passed an act "To facilitate communication between the Atlantic and Pacific States by electric telegraph." This act directed the Secretary of the Treasury to subsidize a telegraph line from the western border of Missouri to San Francisco, in an amount not exceeding $40,000 a year for a period of ten years. Bids were to be received, and the government was to award the contract to the lowest bidder.[1] The act specified the completion of the line by July 31, 1862. It also stipulated that a ten-word message from Brownville, Nebraska, to San Francisco should not cost over three dollars and that government despatches should have precedence over all other messages. The Smithsonian Institution, Coast and Geodetic Survey, and Naval Observatory were to have free use of the line during the period of the subsidy.

Hiram Sibley of New York, inspirer and promoter of the act, secured the contract with its subsidy in the latter half of September, 1860. Sibley was president of the Western Union

---

[1] Lucius S. Merriam, "The Telegraphs of the Bond-Aided Pacific Railroads," *Political Science Quarterly*, Vol. IX, No. 2, p. 187.

Telegraph Company and soon brought his associates into the mammoth undertaking. He sent the general agent, J. H. Wade, to California by steamer via the Isthmus of Panama. He also sent Edward Creighton to survey a route to California for the line. On November 18, 1860, Creighton left Omaha by stage and, making observations en route, at length arrived at Salt Lake City, where he interested Brigham Young in the project. He then rode a mule to California where he met Mr. Wade. Wade forced the California telegraph companies to consolidate with the California State Telegraph Company. This company then formed a separate corporation known as the Overland Telegraph Company, incorporated by the State of California with a capital stock of a million dollars, to coöperate with the Western Union by building the western end of the line. In the meantime the Western Union incorporated the Pacific Telegraph Company, under the liberal laws of Nebraska Territory, to take care of the eastern end.

Creighton was given the task of building the eastern end of the transcontinental line. He had built much telegraph line east of the Mississippi and from 1851 to 1859 had been general agent of the Western Union Telegraph Company.[2]

According to the terms of agreement between the Overland Telegraph Company and the Pacific Telegraph Company, the former was to build east to Salt Lake City and the latter was to build west from Brownville, Nebraska, to meet it. The company that arrived at Salt Lake City last was to pay the other $50 for each day it took to fulfil its agreement after the other had carried out its part. Other provisions gave further advantages to the company reaching Salt Lake City first, thus forming an incentive to speed.

The Pacific Telegraph Company was not incorporated by Nebraska Territory until January 11, 1861, and in the meantime W. H. Stebbins of the Western Union had been busy building a

[2] P. A. Mullens, *Biographical Sketches of Edward Creighton, John A. Creighton, Mary Lucretia Creighton and Sarah Emily Creighton* (Omaha, Neb., 1901), pp. 13-15.

line west from Omaha on the north side of the Platte River. He reached Fort Kearney in time to receive at that point the news of Lincoln's election. During the spring of 1861 he was busy building on to Julesburg.[3]

When the great transcontinental line was begun in the spring of 1861, the builders on the western end were only four hundred miles from Salt Lake City while the eastern end had about twice as far to go. Creighton set the first poles on his end of the line on the Second of July at Julesburg. It was believed to be an impossibility to finish the undertaking by July 31, 1862, the time specified by Congress. The race was on, however, and so energetically did Creighton push his end of the construction that in less than four and a half months he had completed his line to Salt Lake City. His company drew the $50 a day for four days before the western line reached Salt Lake City and closed the gap, making transcontinental telegraphic connection a reality on October 24, 1861.

By all odds the most difficult task in building the telegraph over the Plains and the Rocky Mountains was that of transporting the building materials. Creighton divided his construction force into two crews. One, under W. H. Stebbins, started east from Salt Lake City, and the other, under Creighton himself, headed northwest from Julesburg. The crews were divided into three trains, one to dig the post-holes, a second to cut the poles and set them, and the third to string the wire on the poles.

Creighton's equipment was of the very best. He had seventy-five strong wagons, a supply of good tents, cooking-stoves, and all the necessary utensils for such an undertaking. The camp larders contained "the best food that could be conveyed over the plains and mountains." A large herd of cattle, including a number of milch cows, was driven along to supply food.

Usually there were ten men in the party digging the holes. The

[3] The author acknowledges his deep indebtedness to Carlyle N. Klise, whose master's thesis, *The First Continental Telegraph* (Ms., University of Iowa, 1937), written under the direction of Professor Louis Pelzer, has been used extensively in the preparation of this chapter.

men strung out along the line, each digging a four-foot hole. When the last man on the string finished his post-hole, he walked to the front about a third of a mile and dug another. Thus the digging line moved quickly forward. Two teams distributed the wire, insulators, etc. About six men nailed the brackets on the poles and raised and set them. Four men and one team strung the wire and put it on the poles. One man followed, where necessary, trimming off the tree branches that touched the wire.

It was the duty of a teamster to move camp and aid the cook. In the late morning he helped the cook load the wagon with the cooking outfit and tents, then drove to the place where the furthermost men would quit for the day, and established there a new camp for the night. After he had unloaded the cooking utensils and tents and helped the cook get started on the supper, he drove back and picked up the men farthest in the rear and brought them to camp for the night. The men nearest at hand, in the meantime, walked to camp, pitched the tents, washed, cleaned up, and ate supper. The cook plied his trade early and late. At daylight he was busy preparing breakfast. Soon the men had despatched this early meal, and those farthest behind mounted the wagon and were driven to their posts by the teamster. In the meantime the cook boiled and baked and fried, skilfully preparing the noonday meal. Before noon the parties in the rear had gone beyond the camp, and as the wagon passed the men at work, the cook and the teamster distributed the noontime food.

In the evening the big tent was the scene of all manner of fun. Henry M. Porter, who had a part in this epoch-making enterprise, recalled that every evening mock court was held. A trumped-up charge would be brought against some culprit, and a regular trial would continue with interest until bedtime. The teamster presided, and on account of the nature of his service he was nicknamed Judge Doolittle. Since he did not labor with spade, axe, or tamper, this title the men thought appropriate. All of them, however, were nicknamed some outlandish name. Among other titles were "Sorrel Top," "Curley," "Limber Jim," "Dutch," "Greasy," etc. A lone stranger passing the work line was asked all manner of silly questions as he ran the gantlet of the workmen.[4]

At the outer end of line a transmitting station, known as an "outer station," was set up in the construction camp. In this way communication between Omaha and the construction crew was maintained. This proved very valuable in bringing up materials at times. In one instance when Creighton ran short of wire he had a supply sent to the mountains by the Overland stage, at great expense but in time to avoid delay on construction work.

Hundreds of head of oxen and mules were used in conveying the materials to the line. Scores of wagons carrying from 3,500 to 4,500 pounds each transported the wire, insulators, tools, and provisions. Many stretches along the way were barren of trees for poles. In one instance poles had to be hauled two hundred and forty miles over the roadless plains. The canyons near Cottonwood Springs, in western Nebraska, furnished red-cedar poles which were used for miles. In the mountains pine-trees were obtainable. Contractors distributed the poles and wire in the field at the points where they were to be used. Brigham Young, who had been enlisted in the project by Creighton, contracted to haul and erect poles east of Salt Lake City.

The companies took advantage of the public enthusiasm attending the completion of the telegraph and charged excessive rates. For the veritable flood of messages sent over the line the first week they charged a dollar a word between California and Missouri. Later, rates were reduced to five dollars for the first ten words and forty-five cents a word thereafter. A new precedent was set also in charging for the date and the place from which the message was sent. The newspapers objected both to this new regulation and also to the rates, which were in disregard of the three-dollar rate from the Missouri River to California set by the

[4] Henry M. Porter, *Autobiography* (Denver, 1932), pp. 18, 19.

law of Congress authorizing the telegraph. The telegraph companies paid little attention to this complaint, however, since the country was at war and Congress was too absorbed in war problems to bother about telegraph rates.

The line through Nebraska, which the company had said, when getting an appropriation from Congress, would cost $250 per mile, had in reality been constructed at an expense of $67 per mile. The men who organized the companies that built the first line made enormous profits as a result of their shrewdness and financial daring. Only fifteen per cent of the original capital of the Pacific Telegraph Company had been raised by subscription. By March 15, 1863, capital stock was increased to $3,000,000 and distributed among the stockholders. Good business during the war years rocketed shares from 18 to 85 cents on the dollar. Edward Creighton had been permitted to take $100,000 of the original stock in order to induce him to superintend the difficult Rocky Mountain construction. When the capital stock was tripled, he sold a hundred thousand shares for $85,000 and still was shareholder to the amount of $200,000. His financial interest in the transcontinental line "was eventually more than a million dollars."

The telegraph was a great benefit to everyone concerned. During the stirring war times the newspapers on the Pacific Coast were able to give the news of the bloody battles nine days sooner than by means of the Pony Express and twenty-five sooner than by the Overland Mail. Business men in Denver and other mining towns were kept posted on prices in border towns from which their supplies were freighted. Freighters kept in contact with prices on the Missouri. In one instance, in 1863, a firm made five thousand dollars by means of the telegraph. The company had a large consignment of whisky and other spirits on the way across the Plains when Congress imposed a tax on liquors in the East. The news was received by the train at a station west of Fort Kearney, and when the cargo was sold in Denver, the tax was added to the price. The

THE PONY EXPRESS MEETS THE TELEGRAPH

From a drawing by W. H. Jackson in *Harper's Weekly* November 2, 1867.

difference went into the pockets of the firm instead of the government, of course.

As late as April 12, 1858, a newspaper correspondent mailed a letter from Fort Leavenworth, Kansas, stating there would be no telegraph built across the uninhabited plains. He gave four reasons for his conclusions:

1. Poles would blow down as a result of wind-storms, and the wires would break under the heavy fall of snow and the formation of ice.
2. Prairie fires would burn the poles.
3. Buffaloes would rub the poles down.
4. The Indians would cut the poles and destroy the line.

The first two difficulties did not prove serious. Only occasionally did storms and winter weather interfere with the operation of the telegraph. Prairie fires likewise were not of great consequence. The buffaloes, however, were a much more difficult problem to handle. In almost treeless regions the poles made ideal places for rubbing. Someone got an idea that this could be stopped by placing sharp spikes in the poles at the proper height. The plan was tried but proved to be a grand failure. The buffaloes seemed to enjoy the new scheme. To them it offered an improved comb which most efficiently scratched through their long, shaggy coats and reached the itching points on their tough hides.

At first the Indians caused very little trouble. Numerous different stories were told in explanation of this. Henry M. Porter stated that when the line had been built twelve miles west of Fort Kearney, the Indians felt this new development was going to interfere with their country and began to object. They built some fires around poles set in the ground and burned them down. Immediately the telegrapher sent a message from the "outer station" to Fort Kearney for help, and before the Indians had left the spot, the soldiers arrived and arrested them. From that episode the Indians got the idea that there was something mysterious and supernatural about this new device of the white man. Porter said the Indians threw a cordon of scouts along the bluffs and kept the buffalo and other game out of the Platte Valley all summer.

Another story stated that Washakie, a Sioux chief, was invited to talk over the wire from the telegraph office at Fort Bridger to Winnemucca, the Paiute chief at Smoky Valley, Nevada, five hundred miles away. They were urged to remember just what each one had said. Then, by means of the Overland stage, one traveled east, the other west, and the two doughty warriors met at a mid point in Utah. When they compared notes, they were convinced their messages had been carried almost instantaneously over five hundred miles of space. Word of this experience spread among the Indians and created a profound respect for the wires.[5]

Still other stories record instances of Indians' holding the end of the wire while an electrical storm gave the venturesome redskins a hearty shock. In some other cases the shock was an artificial one concocted by the telegraph employees to duly impress the red men.

For these reasons the Indians had a wholesome deference for the solitary wire stretching away across their hunting-grounds. In two or three years, however, this awe commenced to wear off, and they began to tear down the wires. One cause of the change of attitude was the fact that the movement of troops was definitely connected with the telegraph, so the Indians vented their displeasure on it. The stations, which oftentimes were located in the Overland Mail depots, were also the objects of attack by the Indians who were seeking rich loot. Each station was stocked with from four to six horses. The larger stations had many more. One raid in the later sixties netted the Indians two hundred horses. In order to evade pursuit by troops the wily red men tore down the telegraph line.

One June afternoon in the sixties the telegrapher at Bitter Creek noticed that his station was being surrounded by about a hundred Indians. The raid was wholly unexpected and found the two

[5] Robert Lardin Fulton, *Epic of the Overland* (San Francisco, 1924), pp. 62, 63.

women and five men with an armament consisting of three muskets, one of which had no lock, the second had a tube missing, and the third had no ammunition to fit it. The operator had a derringer in good order, the only gun in good condition in the place. The Indians, however, did not attack but contented themselves with burning poles. The operator sat at his post reporting the procedure to Salt Lake City. His principal report repeated many times that trying afternoon was: "There goes another pole." Finally communication with the west closed. The line to the east remained in order for another half-hour, when it, too, ceased to function. The operator did not go out on the line until after dark, when the Indians had gone. After riding nine miles he found the break. The raiders had cut down four poles and carried away about a mile of wire. It took him two days to repair the break since he had no help. After that, raids were frequent all summer. The agent reported having had to fight his way into the station no less than seven times that season.

Sometimes white desperadoes raided the station, robbed a stage, or committed other misdeeds and destroyed the line in order to make good their escape. At one time employees of the Overland Mail Company whose pay was in arrears took collection into their own hands and, seizing stock and other company property, escaped northward to the mines. Naturally such an escapade was accompanied by cutting the telegraph line.

In 1865, when a detachment of the Seventh Iowa Volunteer Cavalry was stationed at Julesburg, Colorado, one of the duties of the unit was to keep the telegraph line in repair. Captain Eugene Ware reported that at twelve o'clock one night his troop of cavalry started west to repair the line which had been torn down by a recent Indian attack on the town and vicinity. The men were detailed by fours. Number four held all the horses. Numbers one and two had picks, and number three had a shovel or a spade. It was found easier to dig out the old stump of a pole than to dig a new hole. The men drove their picks into the snag and with the aid of the spade pried it out. When the pole wagon came up, they put a pole in and tamped it down, and then the order was: "Mount! Forward! Gallop! March!" The four horsemen quickly rode past the other men and found the first available stump. There were six sets of fours, besides wagoners and guards out on each side protecting their comrades. Following the pole-setters were the pseudo-linemen stringing wire.[6]

The work of the operators located in lonely spots along the line was far more dangerous than that of the men within reach of military protection, and heroic indeed was the operator at an isolated station who held down his job and added that of line repairman to his other duties. The operator was required to test his apparatus at certain intervals; if he found no current, he was instructed to wait fifteen minutes, testing occasionally during the time. If he still found no current, he was to saddle his horse and prepare to go in search of the trouble. Thirty minutes was allowed for this. When all was ready he was to test again and then if the line was still dead, he was to follow it into the uninhabited wilds, hunting for the break. Often an operator had to cover a radius of fifty miles on either side of the station.

In order to facilitate the service, ranchmen along the route were hired to help keep the line in repair where there were no stations or operators. Such line repairers were to make tests at seven and eleven in the forenoon and at three in the afternoon. Tests were to be made quickly in order not to disturb transmission over the line. At the testing stations the wires could be disconnected and tested from either direction. Brass plates with a brass button were attached to the wire. When the button was turned, the current was broken, and by applying one damp finger to the wire and a second finger to a ground wire the rancher could tell whether the line was broken or not. If no shock or electrical sensation was felt, he knew the line was broken. In that case the rancher was to wait

---

[6] Eugene F. Ware, *The Indian War of 1864* (Topeka, Kans., 1911), pp. 533, 534.

fifteen minutes, testing occasionally during that time. At the end of thirty minutes, if there was still no current, after connecting the line he was to ride forth in search of the trouble.

Sometimes the line was out of order for days before the break was found. On one such occasion, after workmen had failed to find a break, a closer search resulted in the discovery that the wire had been cut and a short splice of buckskin used to connect the two metallic ends.

When the Civil War activities of the Confederates broke the line across northern Missouri, the Western Union interests built a line across central Iowa. The company, to obtain aid in the project, asked the various towns for subsidies in order to secure the benefit of the telegraph. Des Moines, for example, was asked for $3,000. When a vote was taken the proposition was rejected, but finally the amount was raised by popular subscription on the promise that forty per cent of this amount was to be returned to the subscribers in service over the telegraph.

Soon this transcontinental line was so busy, it was necessary to run a second wire on the poles to handle local business. This was known as the "way line," in contrast with the other, the "through line." It connected with the through line where there were stations on the latter. One operator recalled that in the early days of the telegraph profanity was quite customarily transmitted, especially during the building of the Union Pacific Railway.

An interesting side-light on the speed of transcontinental trains of that day is seen in the many telegraphic orders handed to the engineers. A common telegram to freight engineers and conductors was: "Increase your speed to fifteen miles an hour to recover time," and to passenger crews: "Increase your speed to twenty-four miles an hour to recover time."

The transcontinental telegraph was pushed through a forbidding, unsettled wilderness by shrewd, energetic leaders and hardy, courageous workmen. It was truly a magnificent step in the westward march of empire.

CHAPTER XIV

STAGE-COACH TRAVEL

ORDINARILY stage-coaching could hardly be classified as a pioneer activity since there was no need for stage lines until a country was settled. The area west of the Missouri River was different, however, in that the peopling of the Salt Lake Valley and the discovery of gold at various points created little islands of settlement which soon called for a transportation service through a wild region where frontier conditions existed to the superlative degree.

As early as 1849 the United States Government responded to the call for a faster mail service across the Plains. Starting from the bend of the Missouri River, one line ran across Kansas to Santa Fe, and another, beginning at the same point, ran northwest in a circuitous route to Salt Lake City.

The Santa Fe line was initiated in May, 1849, on a twenty-one-day schedule. The equipment on this line consisted of a few mule teams, some Murphy spring wagons, and harness. Three men made the trip, driving from four to six mules and taking two extra for use in case of sickness or accident. The wagon was stacked high with corn, but before long the mules had eaten enough to leave room under the cover for the "mail boys" to sleep. At Council Grove, Kansas, was a station with changes of mules, and at Fort Union, New Mexico, was another where the spring wagon was left and a stage-coach taken thence into Santa Fe. The party carried two pouches of mail: one, the "through" pouch, which was not opened en route, and the other the "way" pouch, which carried mail for the places along the way. At the few small settlements on the eastern end of the route the wagon stopped and the driver would yell, "Mail!" One of the carriers then took the way sack to a house and emptied the contents on the floor, where the little group pawed over them and claimed their own.

Often the mail-carriers met other wagons, for the contract called for a weekly mail. When two parties met, it was always customary to go into camp together and have a feast. The principal question was whether any Indians had been seen, and then there was an exchange of the latest news at either end of the line. Early in the morning they arose and each wagon went on its way.

Traveling in the winter was the hardest. Many mornings the men awoke to find themselves covered with snow. At night they pointed their wagon tongue toward their destination, and in the morning all they had to do was to rise and shake the snow off their beds, feel for the wagon tongue, and know they were headed directly toward Santa Fe, or Independence, no matter how the snowstorm might have changed the looks of the country. Crossing a stream in winter was a trying experience. Often the ice was not thick enough to hold up a team and wagon. The mules were the best judges of this matter. If the ice was too thin, the men took axes and cut a passage through the ice wide enough for the mules to swim or wade. The men who did the cutting found dry clothes in the wagon, but wading icy water in winter's frigid atmosphere was no picnic. If the mules would not venture onto thick ice, the men threw them down, tied them one by one, and dragged them across the stream.

When they reached Santa Fe, there was a shout, "The eastern mail! The mail boys!" If they arrived on schedule, they had a one-week lay-over in Santa Fe. This was a great pleasure after the hardships of the journey. They were wined and dined like princes.

By July, 1850, this line was using stage-coaches beautifully painted and with water-tight bodies intended to serve as boats in ferrying streams. Two coaches were scheduled to leave Independence the first of every month.

The line between Salt Lake City and Independence providing

monthly service was opened in 1850. This line was taken over in 1857 by a firm known as Hockaday & Liggett and was run about the same way as the Santa Fe line. Their coaches used the same teams for several hundred miles en route. Every few hours they stopped, allowed the teams to graze, and drove on. The firm had only a few stages, light, cheap vehicles, and no stations along the route.

In 1858 the first Missouri-California overland stage line began to run via the Southern Plains route between St. Louis and San Francisco, a distance of 2,729 miles, on a twenty-five-day schedule. This was three days faster than the voyage by ocean steamer and was considered a great improvement over water transportation. However, this route, forming a giant semicircle, was too long, and when the South lost the preponderance of power about the time of the Civil War, the line was changed to the Northern Plains, at which time it becomes of interest for this volume.

The first daily mail service was put in operation in May, 1859, by the Leavenworth and Pike's Peak Express Company and ran up the Smoky Hill River in Kansas. It was expected to make the trip from the Missouri River to Denver in from ten to twelve days. Stations for relays were projected along the line, and every ten days a freight and provision train was to leave Leavenworth to supply them. The stations, located every few miles, were housed in tents, with the expectation that permanent buildings would be erected as soon as possible. The rush to the Colorado mines did not prove as lucrative as was expected, however, and before the business was well started the company was reorganized under the management of Russell, Majors & Waddell. Taking over the semimonthly Hockaday & Liggett line which ran up the Platte from St. Joseph to Salt Lake City, they combined the two lines under the name of the Central Overland California and Pike's Peak Express Company. The new line left from Atchison and after 1861 ran coaches daily, making the trip to Denver in six days, to Salt Lake City in ten days, and to California in nineteen days.

After the Civil War broke out, the mail contract was transferred from the southern route to the Central Overland, which became known as the Overland Route. The firm was unable, however, to make a daily service pay even after a mail contract should have placed the business on a profitable basis.[1]

The losses incurred by the Pony Express venture amounted to approximately $200,000 and placed the company on shaky financial ground. From time to time the concern was forced to borrow money, and in March, 1862, the line was forced to the wall. Ben Holladay, who had loaned the company over $200,000, bought it at auction. From this time on, though officially the Holladay Overland Mail and Express Company, the concern was popularly known as the Ben Holladay Line and its chief owner was popularly called Old Ben. In many ways the line was a pattern for the other lines that were established from time to time and finally formed a network over the West. For this reason its operations may be portrayed as a typical stage and mail service.

There were a general superintendent of the line, an attorney, and a paymaster. Under the supervision of these were three division superintendents, one between Atchison and Denver, one between Denver and Salt Lake, and the third on the reach between Salt Lake City and Placerville. Each of these had charge of three smaller divisions which under his superintendency were supervised by division agents, one for each two hundred miles. The division agent was an important individual, for he had charge of all the property in his division, looked after the stock, bought the hay and grain, hired the employees, and kept up the stations. His position was one of trust, and a level-headed driver was selected for the place at a minimum salary of $100 a month and keep. The general superintendent resided in New York and went over the line about every three months. Mr. Holladay made the trip once or twice a year in his special coach. In addition to these employees, there were

[1] LeRoy R. Hafen, *The Overland Mail, 1849-1869* (Cleveland, Ohio, 1926), p. 227.

several stock-buyers, nine messengers, seventy-five drivers, twenty blacksmiths, a number of harness-makers, several carpenters, and about one hundred and fifty stock-tenders. Root and Connelley estimated the cost of the entire equipment together with the expense of operating the line the first year after it went into daily service at not less than $2,425,000.[2]

The stations averaged about twelve and a half miles apart. They were of two types: the smaller were called "swing stations," after the term "swing" which meant the middle pair of horses in a team of six; the larger, about every third one, were known as "home stations." At the swing stations only a stock-tender was located. On the Platte in western Nebraska these stations ordinarily were nearly square in shape and were built of hewn cedar logs procured in the canyons south of the Platte. The roofs were made of poles, brush, hay, and earth. In the mountains the stations were sometimes built of stone. The station at Rock Springs, Wyoming, had walls of stone with loopholes every 12 feet. It was 60 feet long and 25 feet wide.

The typical building consisted of one to three rooms, with a stable and corral. The home stations were two or three times larger than the swing stations, had sheds, outbuilding, and other conveniences. In the vicinity of Denver the buildings were made of rough sawed lumber from the mountains, very plain, with the boards nailed vertically on the frames. Few west of Marysville, Kansas, were weather-boarded, and many through Nebraska were built of sod adobes with clay roofs. Small windows in the thick sod walls served the double purpose of letting in light and providing portholes from which to fire in case of an attack. Houses and barns were usually connected by high sod walls, and often a corral was enclosed by walls of the same material. All these walls were pierced with loopholes. Some stations had sod bastions on the corners like a fort.

[2] Frank A. Root and William Elsey Connelley, *The Overland Stage to California* (Topeka, Kans., 1901), p. 77.

HAT CREEK STATION

A hundred and fifty miles east of Denver was located one such station which had a special provision for escape from the Indians. In the fireplace at one end of the cabin a broad flat stone concealed the opening of an underground passage or tunnel which extended from the station to the bottom of a ravine fifty yards away. This was large enough for the easy passage of a man, and the outer end was cunningly concealed behind a mass of tangled brush.[3]

The stock-tenders who lived alone and kept bachelor quarters at the more isolated swing stations led a lonely life. For ten or fifteen miles in every direction the prairie stretched away without a break in the monotony. Here for twenty-four hours of each day the station hand dwelt in fear for his life from Indian attack and in painful solitude broken only by the brief stop of the daily coach each way or a chance conversation with a passer-by. A stock joke among stage hands had its setting in such an environment. According to the story, at the dinner hour one day in 1864 a weary pilgrim in making his toilsome way along the trail stopped at the station for a drink of water and a rest. In harmony with frontier hospitality the stock-tender invited the stranger to eat with him. "I don't care if I do," quickly responded the anticipating pedestrian as he took his place at the table. The host cut off a helping of fat pork and asked the guest to pass his plate. "Thank you," replied the visitor, "I never eat it." "Very well," returned the host, "Just help yourself to the mustard." It so happened that fat pork and mustard made up the entire list of edibles in the house at the time, and the station hand had offered his best. Word of this incident was passed along the line, and thereafter if a bill of fare was a bit lean or a person refused to partake of a certain dish, someone was sure to speak up: "Help yourself to the mustard."

The furniture of one of these stations was scant and crude. A few rude beds, some three-legged stools, a table, a fireplace, and in the corner a stack of arms and ammunition completed the fur-

[3] John J. Beitleman, "An Attack on the Stage Stations," *The Trail*, June, 1929, pp. 5, 6.

nishings. At the most westerly station on the Sweetwater the walls
of the room were decorated with plates taken from various magazines and illustrated papers. Besides the station, at the headquarters
of each division were coach and repair shops, as well as blacksmiths
and harness-makers whose duty it was to travel from station to
station on one continuous round of horseshoeing and repairing.
Mark Twain, who stopped for a meal at one of these stations,
described it as follows:

The station buildings were long, low huts, made of sundried, mud
colored bricks, laid up without mortar. . . . The roofs which had no
slant to them worth speaking of, were thatched and then sodded or
covered with a thick layer of earth, and from this sprung a pretty rank
growth of weeds and grass. It was the first time we had ever seen a
man's front yard on top of his house. The buildings consisted of barns,
stable room for twelve or fifteen horses, and a hut for an eating room
for passengers. This latter had bunks in it for the station keeper and a
hostler or two. You could rest your elbow on its eaves, and you had to
bend in order to get in at the door. In place of a window there was a
square hole about large enough for a man to crawl through, but this had
no glass in it. There was no flooring but the ground was packed hard.
. . . In a corner stood an open sack of flour, and nestling against its base
were a couple of black and venerable tin coffee-pots, a tin teapot, a little
bag of salt and a side of bacon. By the door of the station keeper's den,
outside, was a tin wash-basin, on the ground. Near it was a pail of water
and a piece of yellow bar soap, and from the eaves hung a hoary blue
woolen shirt, significantly—but this latter was the station keeper's
private towel.

The humorist noted that the station men wore pantaloons of
coarse homespun, into the seat and on the inner side of the legs
of which ample pieces of buckskin had been sewed. These patches,
designed as a protection to the wearers when they rode horseback,
gave the trousers a picturesque half-blue and half-yellow color.
The breeches were stuffed into boots, the heels of which were ornamented with large Spanish spurs which jingled at every step.
The keeper wore a huge beard and mustachios, an old slouch hat,

a blue woolen shirt, no coat. From a sheath at his belt hung a long navy revolver and from the top of his boot protruded a horn-handled bowie-knife.

Within the course of a few years a number of "ranches" were established along the route. Captain Eugene Ware mentioned that in 1864 a ranch or two adjoined most of the stage stations in Nebraska. At that time in the vicinity of Fort Cottonwood there were ten of these ranches within twenty-five miles. The term "ranch" had a slightly different meaning from that which later came to be applied in the same region. It is true that many of the "ranchers" raised cattle and some had a number of herders, but many also ran eating-houses, sold merchandise, and, not least, retailed a variety of ill-famed whisky. Nearly all trapped and traded for pelts with the Indians. When new stations were added to the stage establishment in later years, these ranches apparently were selected sometimes as stations. As a matter of fact, the Overland Mail Company owned only about half of the stations in use along its line. The telegraph also often established its office in a ranch building.

Jack Morrow, a tall, raw-boned man with a few notches on his gun, lived with his Indian wife on a typical "road ranch." He ran an establishment which was the legitimate predecessor of the twentieth-century tourist camp. The ranch house was two and a half stories high and sixty feet long, constructed of red-cedar logs. The top story was divided into rooms for sleeping-quarters, and in addition to these there was a row of pilgrim quarters where the travelers could sleep on the floor and do their own cooking. It was said that Morrow got his start by stealing a large quantity of government goods from a train with which he was employed and absconding with it.[4] An establishment such as this at Council Grove on the Santa Fe Trail, although larger than the ordinary road ranch because that was such an important point, sold over $12,000

[4] Eugene F. Ware, *The Indian War of 1864* (Topeka, Kans., 1911), pp. 97, 141.

worth of whisky in two years, an estimated $200,000 worth of merchandise, and $15.20 worth of Bibles. One of the leading lines of business of the road ranch was to purchase sore-footed oxen for from $25 to $35 each and after keeping them thirty to sixty days sell them back to the freighters for from $100 to $125 each.

Overland stage-drivers and stock-tenders of the sixties were infested with lice. They slept for years on ticks of prairie hay, and years on end their blankets were not washed. Furthermore, a bath was an almost unknown process to many of them. In warm weather, when the vermin multiplied rapidly, it was customary for the men to imitate the trappers and spread their underclothing and blankets in the morning on an ant-hill. The ants were very fond of lice. In the evening, the "washing" done, they brought them in minus every grayback. For a time there was rest—until the eggs hatched and another "wash day" was necessary.

The advertisement of the Overland Mail Company in 1864 stated that meals averaged sixty cents, but at many places they were quoted much higher by travelers. A dollar or a dollar and a half was not unusual. Some passengers, indignant at such prices, bought up a quantity of crackers, cheese, herring, bologna, and other eatables and did not take a single meal at any of the twenty eating-stations between Atchison and Denver. West of the Little Blue there was no butter but plenty of beans, bacon, hominy, sorghum, and on the western plains an abundance of buffalo and antelope steaks. Mark Twain in describing the fare at one station said the food consisted principally of bread and bacon with a concoction of tea which the landlord called "slum gullion," taken without sugar or milk. Twain felt certain that the one who nicknamed that brew was inspired. The passengers paid a dollar apiece for this lean meal.

The coach stopped twice a day for meals, forty minutes each time. At the eating-stations in the mountains someone spent considerable time hunting and furnished fresh game for the guests. One who made many trips over the route said that for dessert on this line it was dried-apple pie from Genesis to Revelation along the Platte. Finally some one wrote the following poem which was passed up and down the Eastern Division:

> I loathe! abhor! detest! despise!
> Abominate dried-apple pies;
> I like good bread; I like good meat,
> Or anything that's good to eat;
> But of all poor grub beneath the skies
> The poorest is dried-apple pies.
> Give me a toothache or sore eyes
> In preference to such kind of pies.
>
> The farmer takes his gnarliest fruit,
> 'Tis wormy, bitter, and hard, to boot;
> They leave the hulls to make us cough,
> And don't take half the peelings off;
> Then on a dirty cord they're strung,
> And from some chamber window hung;
> And there they serve a roost for flies
> Until they're ready to make pies.
> Tread on my corns, or tell me lies,
> But *don't* pass to *me* dried-apple pies.

Some of the eating-stations were indescribably filthy, and at one such place a passenger who had not roughed it much on the Plains began making disparaging remarks about the food. The proprietor, who was standing behind the guest, spoke up:

"Well, sir, I was taught long ago that we must all eat a peck of dirt."

"I am aware of that fact," hastily responded the passenger, "but I don't like to eat mine all at once."

Mark Twain felt that the stock-tenders and station employees in general were of a very low order of humanity—in fact, little better than desperadoes. Nevertheless a job such as they held required nerve and stability, for at their isolated stations on the lonely plains they were beaten by relentless winds in spring, baked by a sweltering sun in summer, chilled by frigid blizzards in winter, shut out from the world for weeks at a time, the monotony broken only twice a day by the coaches bound in opposite directions.

Quantities of hay had to be obtained from ranchers along the way who cut the wild prairie grass with the newly imported machine, the mower. This hay cost from $15 to $40 a ton. Freight was very high, making the cost of grain exorbitant. Great wagon-trains were kept busy furnishing the stations with horse feed and supplies for the stock-tenders and others located along the line. Sometimes a coach would carry a number of sacks of shelled corn from a home station to the neighboring swing stations. Stock and station agents were not to sell hay or grain to the passer-by. A correspondent of the *New York Tribune* tried to buy some hay and corn. The station agent replied that he was forbidden to sell forage. "But," said he, "if you will take it forcibly, I guess your party is the strongest." So, assuming the most ruffianly and fierce looks, the correspondent took it, paid for it, shook hands all around, and went away.

In spite of their isolation the denizens of the stations managed to find means to while away the time. Between coach arrivals they contrived to visit their neighbors. Many times they traveled thirty-five to fifty miles to a dance, going and coming on horse-back or on the stage. During the emigration there was a continual stream of emigrants flowing past the station day in and day out, with a large circle of camp-fires near-by at night. At Rock Springs station, in Wyoming, an enterprising stock-tender made money watering emigrants' horses at ten cents a head.

In December, 1865, coaches were run over at least three different routes at the eastern end. The Western Stage Company operated two lines having as starting-points Omaha and Nebraska City which converged with the Holladay line at Fort Kearney. The problem of furnishing stock for a long stage route was a difficult one. When Holladay in May, 1864, got the contract from the government to carry the mail from Salt Lake City to Virginia City, Montana, he set about with all the vigor and resources of his organization to get the line in operation by the dead-line date of July 1, for every day's delay after that date cost him a penalty of $500. It was a seemingly impossible task, but one of his lieutenants hastened to Missouri, selected his supplies, and with a train of two hundred mules, ten lumber wagons, and thirty coaches made the return trip at top speed. On June 2 the train crossed the Platte at Julesburg and, leaving the stage line, took the old California route through Fort Laramie, arriving at Salt Lake City on June 29. Next day the coaches were running toward Virginia City four hundred and fifty miles away.

The Northwest Express Stage and Transportation Company, which was started a decade later when gold had been discovered in the Black Hills, was an example of pioneering enterprise. It ran from Bismarck, North Dakota, at the end of the Northern Pacific Railway, to the new mining region. There was no road, not even a human habitation between Fort Abraham Lincoln on the Missouri River near Bismarck and the Black Hills. Rough stations of native lumber or sod were built along the route. The first outfit of seventy wagons left Fort Abraham Lincoln in March and ran into a blizzard in which several men lost their lives. Light wagons went ahead to mark the route with mounds. Tents were used for the first stations while the buildings were going up. Passengers were soon carried to the Black Hills in thirty-eight hours.

The coach universally used in the West was known as the Concord coach, being made in the city of that name in New Hampshire. It had an arching roof with a railing around the outer edge. In front was the boot where the driver sat with his feet braced against the footboard. Behind his feet were a sack of tools, the treasure-box, a water-bucket, buffalo robe, and perhaps some mail. At the rear was another boot, a sort of projecting platform covered by a leather curtain. This was used to carry the baggage, express, and mail also. An overflow of packages or mail was carried on top. A waterproof curtain covered the exits of the coach, also protecting the passengers from rain and cold wind.

Two seats inside, facing each other in the front and in the rear, were provided with cushion backs and seats for the comfort of the traveler. Between these in the middle of the coach was a seat with a broad back of thick leather which could be removed. Three persons could sit on each seat. It was a case of first come first served in buying the tickets, at which time a particular seat was reserved. The lucky persons took the back seat, the next fortunate the front seat, and the middle seat was left vacant unless traffic was heavy and the traveler was in a hurry.

The whole structure was mounted hammock fashion on heavy leathers attached to rocker springs which made it a grand swaying vehicle. Swinging like a palanquin, it is said to have been the easiest-riding vehicle of its time for traveling over all kinds of roads. The fore-and-aft as well as the lateral motion was described by passengers as not unlike the swell of the ocean. The vehicle was painted in shining colors, red being the one most mentioned. Sometimes a seat which would accommodate three persons was constructed a little above and just behind the driver on top. These places in addition to the nine inside and one in the boot with the driver and the messenger made a total of fifteen riders when the coach was loaded to full capacity. Frank Root, a messenger, said he once made a trip from Denver to Atchison when there were fourteen passengers besides himself and the driver, and they pulled into Atchison on time. On one of the Black Hills lines a decade later the coaches were given names such as "Deadwood," "Kittie," "Dakota," and "Medora."

On the Holladay lines the express messenger accompanied only the special express coaches which left once a week. The line between Atchison and Placerville, California, was divided into three express runs: Atchison to Denver, Denver to Salt Lake City, Salt Lake City to Placerville. The messenger was in charge of the coach and, as Mark Twain said, was the "conductor" or "legitimate captain of the craft." He had charge of the treasure and other valuables carried, checking on a waybill every item as it passed out of or came into his hands. He took his life in his hands, for the treasure was a great temptation to bandits.

The messenger rode the entire length of his run, approximately six days and nights without sleep except such as he could catch while driving along. His place was on the box with the driver; armed to the teeth and warmly dressed, he was presumed to keep that place at all times. In practice, on safe stretches he often curled up in the boot behind the driver's feet and, pulling down the leather curtain for protection, slept snugly in his buffalo robe for hours. He also slept an hour at a time while sitting by the driver on the box. At the end of his run he had a few days' rest before starting out on another strenuous tour of duty. When Frank Root arrived at Denver after his first "run" from Atchison, he went to bed and slept so soundly that it was twenty hours before anyone could rouse him.

A little later an express messenger accompanied every coach and his run was cut to a division. He timed the drivers, delivered all mail and express, and on lines where the company owned the eating-houses, he collected the money there. Express was carried from Atchison to Denver at the rate of one dollar a pound.

The driver fully realized his importance as a bearer of the United States mail and showed his authority like a king. "Clar the road! Git out of the way thar with your bull-teams!" was often his salutation on meeting or passing a freight train. If the bull-whacker did not comply, the driver did not hesitate to run into the ox team, swearing until the very air was vitriolic. A passenger remembered one such instance when the irate teamster returned the compliments in the shape of a bullet which whizzed past their ears as they whirled away.[5]

All classes were found among the drivers, from college graduates to desperadoes. Some professional men of ability such as doctors and lawyers, men who later rose to places of prominence

---

[5] James F. Rusling, *Across America, or The Great West and the Pacific Coast* (New York, 1874), pp. 42-43.

when the West grew up, served as drivers. They handled the "ribbons," as the lines were called, with skill, and they could crack the whip with such dexterity and accuracy as to flick a fly off the lead horse without touching a hair. Although talkative enough when off duty, they were inclined to be taciturn on the box. It seemed to be a professional code that when mounted with lines in hand they should not talk.

There were many strange names and nicknames among the roll of drivers, such as Whisky Jack, Heenan, Happy Jack, Rowdy Pete, Waupsie, Tough Cuss from Bitter Creek, Rattlesnake Pete, One-eyed Tom, Fiddler Jim, Arkansas, Long Slim, and Fish Creek Bill.

There were several first-class singers among the drivers, and often while riding over the trail in the still hours of the night they sang feelingly old favorite songs. Many played musical instruments and when off duty entertained one another at night in that fashion. They had few perquisites, but among others was that of getting furs, principally beaver skins, and selling them to travelers. Although when sitting on the box the stage-driver was as proud as a peacock, as a rule these men were kind, sympathetic, and accommodating.

They formed a close attachment for the horses they drove back and forth on their tours of duty. They took pride in keeping them in good condition so they would look well when the inspector examined them. The driver fairly worshiped his whip, although he seldom struck an animal. He almost regarded it as worth its weight in gold, and could hardly be persuaded to lend it even to his most intimate friend. Some mounted the stock with silver decorations.

The drivers had a lingo all their own. When driving into a town with a flourish, the driver pulled up on his handful of lines with: "Whoa-a there ye whipper snappers!" At table his wants were made known in a conversation something like this: "Pour me out a mule's ear full of coffee, for I'm as thirsty as an old toper." "Sam, hand me a slice of sowbelly as long as your arm." "Bob, flip one of them sockdologer slapjacks down this way." "Jake, waltz some of that petrified army hardtack over here." "Boys, save me a few crumbs, for I'm hungry enough to eat a jackass and chase the driver." Captain Ware said the stage-drivers were as rough and jolly a lot of men as he had even seen. The whole dinner, he said, was loud and uproarious with profane pyrotechnic. When the drivers were off duty their conversation was of horses, drives, wild rides, and Indian fights.

Once a day two coaches met. At first there was a tiny cloud of dust, so small no one could tell what it was, although each driver was alert for he knew at what point he was due to meet the other coach. Before long the vehicle had been identified, and quickly the two coaches drew up alongside each other. After a brief exchange of the customary "Howdy!" an inquiry concerning the news, a joke or two, and "Give me a chaw of tobacker" or "Want a swig of tarantula juice?" with a crack of the whip over the leaders the two coaches sped in opposite directions, one toward the Pacific and the other toward the Missouri River.

There was a general professional custom for the drivers not to drink while on duty, but once in a while one did get drunk on the job. F. A. Root said he had seen drivers so drunk he was anxious for fear they would tumble off the coach, but he never had seen one so full he could not hold the reins and whip, drive around a curve, or make a sharp turn as skilfully as a sober man. When such lapses occurred too frequently, however, the man was relieved of his duties, put on the black-list, and never rehired again.[6] It was against the rules to have whisky at the stations, but the drivers and stock-tenders knew that it could readily be procured at a neighboring ranch. As one road rancher said, he might run short of the "luxuries of life" but he would never be caught without the "necessities."

When the coach was some distance from the station, the driver let out a yell, "Ah-whooh-ah!" which to a new hand sleeping in

[6] Root and Connelley, *The Overland Stage to California*, pp. 274-275.

the front boot seemed the most horrible noise he had ever heard. This was done to awaken the stock-tender so that he might have the horses out, and also to awaken the relief if it was time to change drivers. Sometimes a bugle was sounded at the distance of a mile or half a mile from the station.

The horses—usually six on the western portion of the line—were changed at every station. The driver sat in his place, never relinquishing his lines. The stock-tender unhooked the traces on the lead team first, then pulled the lines on the lead team through the terrets and tied them up. This procedure was repeated with the swing team and then with the wheel team. The driver did not get down till the wheelers were unhooked.

The stock-tender then drove out the fresh teams. The animals were trained like fire-horses and readily stepped into their respective places. A change was regularly made in four minutes. At the home stations, usually located twenty-five to thirty miles apart, the drivers were changed also. Sometimes, however, a driver drove fifty or sixty miles, covering this distance and return every other day. At these change points the coach was greased. At first castor-oil was used, but later a special order came through to use "patent dope." Once, along the Little Blue River, one of the front wheels on a coach stuck and refused to turn. The axle was found to be sizzling hot, and the wheel could not be removed until it cooled. The passengers held up the axle while the driver took off the wheel and examined the spindle. It had not been greased at the proper station and had to be doped in some way before they could go farther, but there was no dope in the coach. The driver thought of wrapping grass around the spindle with the hope that it would run part way to the next station and that by repeating the process they could get there all right. Suddenly one of the passengers thought of a piece of cheese he had in his carpet-bag, and some of it was sliced off. It worked efficiently.[7]

The drivers sped over the same territory every day and got

[7] *Ibid.*, p. 92.

to know the country like a book. Even the blackest night did not daunt them. For endurance, mules were preferred, but horses were chosen for quick, brisk work. In sand or on other heavy roads a "spike" team was used. On the eastern end of the line this consisted of five mules in place of the usual four horses. One mule was hooked up in the lead of the other two teams. Most of the teams were matched. There were spans of beautiful white, jet black, bright bay, iron gray, and chestnut.

Crossing rivers was not a light task. Fortunately by this time ferries had been built on most streams. One company provided a "sand wagon" for crossing the Platte at Fort Kearney. It was built high out of the water. The driver left the coach on the bank, put the baggage, mail, and passengers on this wagon, and took them across to a waiting coach on the other side. Five-inch tires on the wheels prevented it from sinking into the quicksand.

When westbound passengers reached the end of their railroad journey at Atchison, some, like Mark Twain and his brother, were surprised to learn they were allowed only twenty-five pounds of baggage each; they had to unpack their trunks, dig out the most pressing necessities, and repack them in a small bundle. Excess baggage cost a dollar a pound to Denver. Sometimes, after the seats were all sold, a person with money who wanted to get to the gold-fields on business in a hurry would offer a big bonus to a passenger for his preëmpted seat. Sometimes a group would charter a coach and travel as an exclusive party. Often they had a few cases of beverage that could not be obtained en route and celebrated in high style. They were usually provided with pneumatic pillows which they would inflate to promote a comfortable sleep at night. Fat persons always had anything but a pleasant time, but their traveling companions suffered likewise. All were glad to jump out of the coach every ten or twelve miles, to run around and limber up a bit during the interval while teams were being changed. Sometimes the driver made the mistake Luke Vorhees did on the Black Hills line when he lost a lady passenger who had got out at a station. He did not even realize his loss until he reached the next station. When he started back after her, he met the chivalrous boss of a wagon-train who was bringing the woman on horseback.

There was no sleep for the passengers the first night or two as they sat bolt upright bumping along over the prairie; but before they had traveled many days they could settle back from a lurch of the coach and go to sleep in a remarkably short time. If a traveler cared to do so, he could "lay over" and get a night's rest in the pilgrim room at a station, but even so he would have to ride at night when he boarded the coach again. There was no chance of riding in the daytime and sleeping at night, for there was only one coach each way a day.

When the traveler began his journey in the spring, it was a delightful ride indeed across the corner of Kansas to the Platte Valley. The coach rocked gently over the smooth, broad roadway beaten by the hoofs of thousands of animals. The curtains were rolled up, and the passengers viewed the vast stretches of verdant prairie which surged like waves of the sea. At intervals this illimitable ocean of green was broken by a small stream along whose banks grew elm and cottonwood trees.

Later in the summer the trip was not so pleasant. The sun beat down on the coach mercilessly. The hot winds all but seared the panting passengers. Clouds of dust entered the openings of the coach and added to the discomfort. In some places the dust was four to six inches deep, and it was a marvel how the eyes of the drivers ever stood it. On the coach Mark Twain and his brother took, since there were no women passengers and none at the stations, they stripped to their underclothing, riding in cool splendor all day long and dressing at night in order to keep warm.

The passengers tried many schemes as a matter of diversion. Sometimes they shot at antelopes, coyotes, jack-rabbits, or even buffaloes. These denizens of the wild were comparatively safe, however, for they were hard to hit from a moving coach. The buffaloes were so numerous on the Smoky Hill route in 1859 that the coach in which Horace Greeley rode was overturned by the animals and he received a severe cut on the knee which crippled him for several weeks.

In nice weather passengers would sometimes lie flat on top of the coach and sleep there. To keep from being jolted off in crossing a rough spot they tied themselves on with a rope or strap. Card-playing and gambling were common forms of amusement. One stage messenger mentioned that during the Civil War when money was cheap he had seen passengers' games where the ante would be nothing less than five dollars. Soon passengers who had lost money complained to the company that they had been cheated; the company tried to stop the practice, but it was impossible to enforce any antigambling edict. Many of the passengers provided themselves with appliances for lights on the trip. Although these were not much more than the old-time tallow-dip candles, they served the purpose admirably. Sometimes there were good voices on board and the evening was made pleasant by the songs of such passengers.

A ranchman remembered boarding a coach on the way from Cheyenne to Deadwood and finding a drunken companion who reminded him that it was Sunday and that the day should be celebrated. The ranchman reluctantly agreed, and the tipsy passenger proposed to bet a gallon of whisky he could sing more hymns than his new friend, so they shook hands on the bargain. The rancher sang "Shall We Gather at the River," and the other rendered "A Charge to Keep I Have." Upon concluding he mumbled, "Zalmighty dry work tryin' t' keep Shunday, pardner, le's take a drink." This done, the rancher continued by singing, "From Greenland's Icy Mountains," and his companion rendered "I Hunger and I Thirst." Out of deference to the song the cowman consented to take another drink. This continued for over an hour, but finally the rancher was driven to singing popular songs, patriotic airs, or snatches of anything he could think of while the other sang hymn after hymn in startling succession. Finally the challenger dropped into a snore and slept until late the next morning, when he offered to pay the bet, saying, "I sure thought I was the chief as a hymn whooper, but you beat me as easy and done it so hard it would appear to the undersigned you must have spent most of your life setting stop on a Sunday School organ. The gallon is yours and the cost mine." When the cattleman told him he had been obliged to sing many songs not found in a hymn-book, the challenger was a good sport and replied: "Deadwood gets to sell two gallons, and one of them's yours!"

During a political campaign or on the Fourth of July an orator could almost always be found to orate to the "large and respectable audience." There were often good story-tellers who spun their yarns in profusion. Root remembered a party of half a dozen college boys on their vacation. They were on a lark and were ready for anything. The stage crew soon found there was no species of scrape or college deviltry unknown to them. Talented speakers and singers, they gave evidence of religious training but were indifferent to its influence and were impishly sacrilegious. With sanctimonious faces they proceeded to conduct an old-fashioned revival meeting. First of all they joined in singing an old-time Methodist hymn. "Parson Jones" then offered prayer and preached a brief but able sermon. "Elder Brown" gave out a hymn in which the "congregation" joined. A fervent prayer by "Deacon Smith" was followed by experiences from "Brother Obadiah" and "Brother Hezekiah," who told how good they felt and how glad they were to be there. When these exercises were drawing to a close, "Brother Johnson" suggested that one of the most important parts of the program was likely to be overlooked: he had a burden to pass the contribution box, and he exhorted the "brethering" to "shell out" liberally to pay his back salary and liquidate a long-standing church debt. Substituting his hat for a plate, he passed it around without getting a cent, whereupon, looking into its vacant space, he fervently returned thanks for getting his hat back. He then gave out a hymn beginning "Oh, what a wretched land is this that yields me no supply." Other exercises and drinking followed, and the meeting ended in an old-fashined carousal, with black eyes, bloody noses, and other visible results of a drunken fray. At length the young blades sank into a drunken sleep. When one by one they awoke, they looked at each other in amazement, for it was almost impossible for any of them to recognize the bloody, disheveled heads of his companions. After they had eyed one another with anything but sanctimonious countenances, one broke the silence with an old familiar scriptural passage: "Behold, how good and how pleasant it is for brethren to dwell together in unity."

The travelers were not completely out of touch with the world, for after 1861 they could drop into the telegraph office generally found at the stage station and read the press telegrams giving the war and other news. The stages the travelers met from day to day brought newspapers with news which, though often old, was at least reading-matter.

Miners coming out of the gold-fields after a successful season were often in a mood to celebrate. One such passenger on the Oliver & Company stage line between Helena and Virginia City, Montana, stopped at a stage station for breakfast. Seeing four weary miners rolled up in their blankets on the floor, he dragged each one out by the collar with the command: "Get up and take a drink with me; if any of you don't like it, I will fight him afterwards, but you must drink first!" The astonished sleepers woke with a start, rubbed their eyes, responded to the invitation with gusto, and returned to their blankets.

Now and then a passenger stopped at a road ranch and got his canteen filled. The liquor retailed at these places was of very dubious character. In western Nebraska, between Cottonwood Springs and Alkali Lake, the keepers of a ranch had placed a board across the tops of two barrels to give the inside of the building the appearance of a store. Across this board was sold a decoction made of tobacco, poisonous drugs, alcohol, and water, some of the vilest liquor ever sold to drinkers. At one place between Julesburg and Denver, in the shadow of the Rockies, where a passenger asked for whisky, he was not a little astonished to be told that he would have to wait for a few minutes as the "whisky" unfortunately had frozen in the barrel the previous night and was being thawed out.

Carrying mail was one of the most important functions of the stage lines. Without the lucrative contracts of the Post Office Department long-distance staging could hardly have been long continued. The letters were carried in leather pouches and printed matter in canvas sacks. The amount carried varied with the times. When Mark Twain rode from St. Joseph to Carson City, Nevada, the coach carried twenty-seven hundred pounds, or three days' delayed mail. The fore and hind boots were full, and the fore part of the inside was piled up to the roof and back far enough nearly to touch the knees of the three passengers. When a woman sought a ride a short distance along the route, one of the three had to ride with the messenger and driver while the woman took his place inside. When the coach broke down, part of the mail was unloaded and left on the prairie to be placed in charge of the stock-tender of the next station. Perhaps the slogan of the Post Office Department, "The mail must go through," was correct for letters, but often large quantities of government documents were not treated so kindly. One man said they were very useful to make a sort of corduroy road through a swale.

The Overland Mail was important not only to California but to British Columbia, Australia, and New Zealand, for the route shortened mail transit to these countries by days. Millions of dollars, quantities of priceless documents, and valuable packages were handled. The number of pouches carried west on the coach six times a week ran about as follows: San Francisco, two; Sacramento, one or two; Virginia City, and Carson City, one each; Salt Lake City, one or two; Denver, two. Besides there was a way pouch opened at the few post-offices along the route. In spite of the magnificent service rendered, there were many complaints. An observer at Valley City, Nebraska, in 1865 said that when the mail-pouch was dumped on the floor, he had never seen such a lot of dilapidated letters. He picked up a photograph of an elderly lady and could not find the envelope from which it had escaped. A great many letters were past saving, and if the owners had been there, he said, they could not have deciphered the address or contents since they were only a mass of pulp. He reported that the postmaster gave as the reason that old, leaky pouches had been sent to the West when the very best should have been provided. All the letters that could be recovered were carefully handled and spread out to dry, yet they would reach their destination in a very disreputable condition. Often in the West during this period people preferred to send anything from letters to valuables by Wells-Fargo Express. The United States Government would not allow such carriage of mailable matter unless the package bore a stamp, but people preferred to put a stamp on the missive and send it by express anyway. In some instances the express company stamped the package, allowing for this cost in fixing the rates.

Naturally the vast amount of treasure carried out of the mountains by the stage-coaches was tempting to men who were inclined to attempt to obtain money without working for it. At first, stage robberies were accomplished so easily that holdups became almost habitual and it was almost impossible to get gold out of the hills. In Montana the authorities were in league with the bandits, which complicated the situation. As a rule, the road-agents, as the robbers were called, were polite enough and shed no blood so long as their demands were complied with. Often, through someone on the inside of the stage organization or through allied observers at the gold-field, the bandits knew about how much money was to be shipped, who the passengers would be, and what they were carrying. The Sydney, Nebraska, *Telegraph*, in giving the story of a typical robbery in July, 1877, stated that the gang was well organized, having one man assigned to hold the team and a second to "cover" the passengers, who were ordered to stand with their backs to the guard with hands in the air. A third was to search the passengers for money and jewelry from hats to toes of boots. If a passenger attempted to look around, his ardor was cooled by a threat to blow the top of his head off. The captain in the meantime acted as a sort of extra guard and directed the work. The stage was next searched, the treasure-box wrenched open and spoiled of its contents, and the mail rifled. Finally the captain gave the passengers a lecture, leaving them to go on their melancholy way while the bandits went back to Deadwood or Rapid City to prospect for gold in their peculiar manner. These holdups became so frequent that a Deadwood paper, in 1877, said:

We have again to repeat the now hackneyed phrase "the stage has been robbed" three miles below Battle Creek. Four masked men took over the treasure box, robbed the passengers, and rifled their baggage, and after taking a drink all around and wishing the passengers and driver a pleasant journey, they packed their booty on their horses and started off at a loping gallop.[8]

At first the treasure-box was made of heavy leather or oak boards, strapped with iron, and padlocked. Later on light iron safes were carried, but these were unequal to the occasion. When holdups in the Black Hills became so numerous, passengers going out of the Hills with gold-dust or other valuables entrusted them to the express companies for carriage in their special treasure coaches. To meet the situation the express companies lined the treasure coach with steel, making it bullet-proof, and provided it with portholes so that guards on the inside with the box of bullion at their feet could stand off the ordinary gang of road-agents. As much as $140,000 was transported in one load by one of the treasure coaches.

Finally, in order to protect these coaches, scouts on horseback were employed to ride the lines on dangerous spots at night. This greatly lessened the danger of holdup, but the famous Canyon Springs robbery occurred even after this precaution had been taken.

[8] Harold E. Briggs, *The Settlement and Economic Development of the Territory of Dakota*, Ms., Doctor's Thesis, University of Iowa, 1929, Vol. II, p. 451.

The robbers by strategy got possession of a stage station and used it as ambush, taking the driver and guards by surprise when they were preparing to change teams. The safe, which had been guaranteed to withstand the roughest treatment possible for twenty-four hours, was pried open and looted before rescuers came.

One day in July, 1865, a coach left Virginia City, Montana, with seven passengers and a large amount of treasure in dust and gold bars. The passengers, all hardy miners and mountaineers, with a view to protecting their hard-earned wealth from the attacks of road-agents, had armed themselves with double-barreled shot-guns loaded with buckshot. These resolute men took turns at sitting at the windows with guns ready for instant use. The driver and another man, afterward found to have been one of the robbers, were on the driver's seat. At a wild spot in the Port Neuf Canyon this man cried, "Boys, here they are." The passengers fired at what appeared to be the gun barrels of the robbers, protruding from behind the willow trees. This volley was answered by one from the willows at which four passengers fell dead, one was mortally wounded, and another was wounded three times but feigned dead when a robber advanced to give him a final shot and thus escaped death. One alone was uninjured and escaped in the bushes. The driver had purposely driven his charge into this deadly ambush and shared equally with the robbers. He left the employ of the company immediately and departed from Salt Lake City. Avengers were on his trail, however, traced him to Denver, and watched his every move until the evidence of his crime was secured and a vigilance committee performed the last grim ceremony at the famous oak by the waters of Cherry Creek one morning before sunrise. Of the eight robbers who took $70,000 in gold, not one except the driver was ever punished.[9]

From time to time Indians caused much trouble, going so far occasionally as to stop traffic entirely. In 1862 in the Rocky Moun-

---

[9] John W. Clampitt, *Echoes from the Rocky Mountains* (Chicago, New York, San Francisco, 1889), p. 81.

tains east of Salt Lake City service was disrupted, and when Captain Robert T. Barton made a trip along the route in April and May he found things in a deplorable state. On May 8 he wrote: "All the stations this side of Green River look as though they had been deserted in a hurry." Between Dry Sandy station and Pacific Springs station, a nine-mile stretch, he saw a great deal of paper mail scattered along the road. This was supposed to be the contents of two sacks that were found on the road empty. Some mail had been burned at one place. At Ice Springs they found the station in a terrible state, with mailbags cut open and the contents littered about the premises. Many envelopes, torn open, which evidently had contained letters, were found scattered around. There were twenty-two sacks of locked mail, eight of them cut open and rifled, and a large amount was thought to have been taken. Two or three Wells-Fargo checks were found. At Split Rock station two men had been killed and one escaped. Halfway between Three Crossings station and Split Rock two mail-coaches had been attacked; six of the seven men were wounded, the mail was burned, the animals were taken, and the horses cut up. Thus the expedition found the stations all along that part of the line. On April 2 of that year two coaches were attacked on the Sweetwater. In defending themselves, according to one of the party,

Everything that could afford protection, mail sacks, blankets, buffalo robes, etc., were thrown out of the coaches and from the front boots, and were placed upon the north and south sides between the coaches, against the wheels and along the east side of us, behind which we barricaded ourselves. . . . The bullets pattered like hail upon the sacks that protected us.[10]

Again in 1864 Indian depredations reached the pitch where all traffic was stopped between Latham, Colorado, and the Missouri River, although this time the line was clear between Denver and Latham and Latham and California. On August 7 of that year the Indians executed what was evidently a prearranged plan and

[10] Hafen, *The Overland Mail*, p. 245.

about noon attacked every stage station from Big Sandy to eastern Colorado, stopping all stage and mail service. The last stage to bring mail from the east for some time arrived at Latham at three in the morning of August 15, and it was five days overdue. In the days following, mail and passengers continued to arrive from the west until there were between fifty and seventy-five passengers held up at Latham and many tons of mail. While waiting the passengers formed a military company for self-defense and drilled on the prairie. They did guard duty nightly.

It was difficult to find sleeping-quarters for so many. From fifteen to twenty men slept on the floor of a single room—lawyers, bankers, doctors, professors, mechanics, and miners. Sometimes they were packed in as closely as sardines, and when the hard floor induced someone to give the order "Turn over," all had to move in concert. Finally, on September 24, after six weeks, the blockade was raised and the accumulated mail began to move eastward. The passengers had to wait until the mail had gone out. The first coach that left for the east carried forty-one pouches, filling the front and rear boots and the whole inside. This load of nearly a ton was followed by others until the mail had been cleared and the passengers could be started on their way. On September 28 the westbound mail which had been lying at Fort Kearney during the Indian Embargo began to move. Stages had been unable to run either east or west of that point.

To keep the mail moving after this experience, the Army was called into service. Soldiers were stationed along a three-hundred-mile stretch, and a mounted escort of from six to ten cavalrymen accompanied each coach east or west. These squads were posted at various stations, guarded the stage to the station where the next escort was located, waited there until the stage from the opposite direction came through, and accompanied it to their home station. This did much to remove the danger from Indians.

One of the most remarkable fights ever put up by a stage-coach in the annals of the Plains was that which occurred one day in

June, 1867, near Fort Wallace, Kansas. The coach carried a driver, one soldier, and five passengers. Attacked by a hundred mounted Sioux and Cheyennes, the whites made the best resistance they could with their rifles and kept the Indians at a distance while the driver put his horses to their utmost speed. Every man on board except one was seriously wounded or killed. At last the vehicle with its bleeding and dying passengers and crew reached the shelter of Big Timbers station, and the Indians retired without having taken a scalp.

Aside from the loss of human life, these raids did great monetary damage to the stage line. From 1862 to 1865 over five hundred and fifty head of live stock were run off or killed, dozens of stations were burned or damaged, and quantities of hay and grain were destroyed. Root and Connelley place the losses for those years at $375,839.72.

In many respects Ben Holladay was one of the most remarkable men of his time. As a transportation king he rivaled a Hill or a Harriman of a later day. He had been on the frontier a number of years and knew how to rough it, and having a brilliant talent for organization together with capacity for leadership that could get things done, he welded, under circumstances unsurpassed in difficulty, a far-flung transportation system. For his own use he had a special coach with the unusual comforts of coil springs, a bed, a writing-table, and an oil lamp with reflector so he could read papers and make notes in the coach at night, and he swept across the plains with the dazzling brilliance of a meteor. He created as much excitement as a railroad magnate with a special train a few years later. At one time Old Ben made a fast trip from Folsom, California, to the Missouri River. At every station the agents had their orders to have fresh teams ready. When the long grind day and night was over, it was found he had made it in twelve days and two hours, beating the regular schedule by five days. This was the quickest trip ever made with a vehicle across this stretch before the railroad was built.

THE BEN HOLLADAY OVERLAND COACH AT KIMBALL'S, 1867

At the height of his career, in 1866, Holladay employed 700 men and drove 1,500 horses and mules, not to mention the hundreds of oxen that pulled freight wagons used to supply the 250 way-stations he operated. His 3,300 miles of stage lines represented the greatest system then operated under one management in America. In November, 1866, anticipating the completion of the Union Pacific Railway, the great stage king sold out to Wells, Fargo & Company for $1,800,000. This deal gave Wells, Fargo control of all stage lines west of the Missouri River.

It is difficult to generalize on traffic rates and salaries of stage workers because of the change in the value of money during the Civil War. In the midst of the war, however, the fare from Atchison to Denver was $75; to Salt Lake City, $150; to Placerville, $225; to Virginia City, Montana, $210. Transient way fares were from 12½ to 15 cents a mile. The wages of the employees at about the same time were: drivers, $40 to $75 a month, depending on length of service and the danger involved on a particular run; stock-tenders, $40 to $50; carpenters, $75; harness-makers, $100 to $125; division agents, $100 to $125; and messengers, $62.50 and meals free on the road.

The Overland Mail, which would seem slow indeed in our day, was a fast transportation system in its time. The schedule of more than nineteen hundred miles in from seventeen to twenty days meant over a hundred miles every day winter and summer, muddy roads or dry, rain or shine. The coaches made good time on the rolling prairies between Kearney, Nebraska, and Atchison, Kansas. Often much time was made up on this stretch going east. F. A. Root remembered a trip from Big Sandy to Thompson's in southern Nebraska when a four-horse team pulled nearly half a ton of mail and fourteen people fourteen miles in fifty-two minutes, or at the rate of sixteen miles an hour, a remarkable feat.

Such a success was the Overland Mail line that "Overland" became the word of the day. People bought Overland hats, Overland boots, Overland coats, and even Overland eggs.

CHAPTER XV

OVERLAND FREIGHTING

BY THE FIFTIES a group of isolated communities beyond the Plains were calling for goods produced in the area east of the Mississippi. New Mexico had been served in a meager way before the Mexican War by the Santa Fe trade. After 1848 a vastly larger commerce flowed over the historic trail to Santa Fe. The California population induced some freight, although most of the wants of that section were met by ocean transportation. Salt Lake City was served from the Missouri River but largely by the Mormon church organization itself. The event that was to awaken the great freighting business between the Missouri River and the Rocky Mountains was the Mormon War of 1857. When the United States Army was despatched to Utah, quantities of supplies had to follow the expedition. Gold discoveries in Colorado, Montana, and Idaho increased the volume of freight during the sixties.

This vast freighting business, which reached its crest about 1866, for the most part ran from the Missouri River up the Platte Valley like a silver cord. The strands of the eastern end of this cord ran westward from Independence, Leavenworth, Atchison or St. Joseph, Nebraska City, Omaha, and a number of smaller intermediary points, uniting in the vicinity of Fort Kearney. The Western end also separated into strands which led to different points in the mountains. In addition to this main artery of freight transportation, there were shorter freighting lines between railroads or rivers and other points. A large amount of freight was hauled across Iowa before that gap was bridged by the railroad. In Montana quantities of freight were carried between the highest navigable point on the Missouri River and the mining towns, and from points around the Black Hills lines later converged on the mining towns there. Stretching across Minnesota, connecting the Mississippi and the Red rivers, ran the famous Red River cart line. But the route from the Missouri River up the Platte to the Rocky Mountains was by far the most important, and will engage most of our attention in this study.[1]

The great activity in freighting came in 1858 with the Mormon War. The government gave large contracts to the big freighting companies. Among these was the firm of Russell, Majors & Waddell. Alexander Majors, who was the principal figure in the concern, had built up a large freighting business on the Santa Fe Trail and was able to serve the government with his organization.

Russell, Majors & Waddell began operating from Leavenworth, but becoming convinced that the route was shorter from Nebraska City, Majors transferred the main eastern base to that point. As one of the conditions for this move, he demanded that Nebraska City enact a prohibition law as a protection to the morals of his men. He required each employee to take an oath that he would neither drink nor swear while in the employ of the company. Then he gave each man a Bible to carry on his way. It was his aim to send the boys home better men morally than when they entered his employ. Other freighters were not so particular, and in spite of all the precautions of Alexander Majors, Nebraska City became a rather wild town in a few years.

When Majors' firm selected Nebraska City as an eastern base in the fall of 1858, he purchased 138 lots for building sites and a general headquarters. Over five hundred hands were soon at work constructing the base, at an expense of more than $300,000.[2] The town catered to the freighters, providing a park with benches

[1] For much valuable data in this chapter I acknowledge my indebtedness to a former student and present colleague, F. E. Bresee, who at my suggestion wrote his master's thesis on the topic of freighting. See Floyd Edgar Bresee, *Overland Freighting in the Platte Valley, 1850-1870*, Ms., Master's Thesis, University of Nebraska, 1937.

[2] *Nebraska City News*, Nebraska City, Nebraska Territory, May to August, 1858.

and a speaker's stand for meetings. Religious services for the freighters were held there in favorable weather.

Nebraska City was but one of Majors' eastern bases. Horace Greeley in 1859 observed:

> But Russell, Majors & Waddell's transportation establishment, between the fort and the city, is the great feature of Leavenworth [Kansas]. Such acres of wagons! Such pyramids of extra axletrees! such herds of oxen! such regiments of drivers and other employees! No one who does not see can realize how vast a business this is, nor how immense are its outlays as well as its income. I presume this great firm has at this hour two millions of dollars invested in stock, mainly oxen, mules and wagons. (They last year employed six thousand teamsters, and worked forty-five thousand oxen.)

Great warehouses were built to house the perishable goods brought up the river by steamboat. Spacious wharves and levees were constructed to receive the merchandise, and great quantities of it were left there under cover of tarpaulin until loaded for the overland journey.[3] The big wagons were being loaded constantly, in fair weather or foul, and large trains lumbered through the streets creeping westward to the expansive prairie beyond. In spite of this activity, freight piled up and congestion grew. From May to November of 1860 there were 232 steamboat arrivals at Nebraska City, landing 9,280 tons of freight.

Although the large companies are better known, a host of smaller concerns and individuals were carrying quantities of goods. One man wrote of the late fifties:

> Every person almost in this neighborhood, who could master a vehicle, went into the freighting business; and for most of the ventures a fine profit was returned. From a capacity of one to three, six or eight yoke trains, carrying from one hundred thousand pounds to over half a million, down to a one mule cart the means of transportation was supplied in almost every conceivable style.[4]

[3] Charles E. Young, *Dangers of the Trail in 1865* (Geneva, N. Y., 1912), p. 20.

[4] Augustus E. Harvey, *Sketches of the Early Days of Nebraska City, Nebraska Territory, 1854-1860* (St. Louis, 1871), p. 20.

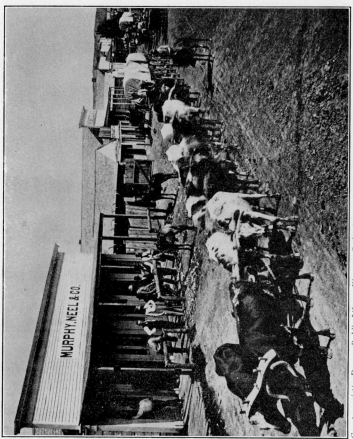

BULL TRAIN AT BENTON, MONTANA

A visitor to a freighting town in those days saw

... huge freight wagons on every street, at every corner; there are hundreds of oxen and mules attached to them. ... There is heard the lumbering of these "prairie schooners," the bellowing of oxen, braying of mules, cracking of long lariats [whips] which for me is a show of itself, to see the dexterity with which the drivers use them. There is the hollowing—yelling—of teamsters, mingled with more oaths than I ever heard before in all my life together. ... "Everybody for himself." And the people rush up and down the streets in utter forgetfulness apparently, of everything but *rushing*, rushing right on— not much matter where.[5]

At Atchison, one man reported, newcomers were confronted by outlaws and wild men well supplied with revolvers and fond of drink. In the evening at the tavern he and his companions were forced to join in the "beastly carnival" of the lawless bands of degenerates. Sleep was out of the question until the early hours of morning. Hideous blasphemous language, howls of pain, and the noise of revolvers were heard all night. The same conditions were reported at Council Bluffs.

Much preparation was necessary in order to get a wagon-train started westward from a base. Large numbers of wagons had to be purchased and oxen bought. Of the latter, the Cherokee and Texas steers were the wildest and yet the most efficient when once broken. These were almost as wild as buffaloes, and during the breaking process large numbers of the townspeople would go out to watch the spectacle on the prairie adjacent to the town. The freighters branded their oxen on the hip with a letter about three inches high. As a rule the last initial of the owner was used. This marking was done by snubbing the steer's head to a wagon wheel and pressing the sizzling-hot iron through the hair into the flesh.

A corral for breaking the cattle was made by a circle of forty or fifty wagons chained together. When a couple of these wild creatures had been lariated and tied to wheels, the yoke was put

[5] C. F. Bentley, "Freighting in 1866," see *Proceedings and Collections*, Nebraska State Historical Society, Vol. I, Second Series, pp. 46-47.

on them and they were allowed the freedom of the prairie to run, jump, bellow, or break their necks, as they sometimes did. Many times a team of six yoke of oxen left the Missouri with all but the leaders consisting of these half-broken wild steers. The yoke was left on them day after day until they became subdued and tame. At first it took a dozen men to hook them up, and it was a strenuous job to drive such a team.

The driver, upon choosing a new wagon, would sometimes daub a name in huge letters on the white cover. Some names observed were Constitution, Excelsior, President, City Hotel, The Republic, and Old Kentuck.[6]

From three to five tons of freight were loaded into the mammoth wagon, depending upon the stowage. The skilled packers balanced weight and bulk with the large variety of goods in a most efficient manner. To prevent cargo spoilage by water entering the wagon box while fording a stream, the canned goods and other non-perishables were placed at the bottom, and sugar, crackers, flour, salt, and beans on top. Just before a train left, it was not unusual for the head of a freighting concern to call the men together and address them on the subjects of duty, honor, fidelity, courage, morality, and discipline. The citizens of the town often attended such a farewell meeting. When the train returned after weeks or months of labor, fatigue, and hardship, sometimes a pleasant social hour was arranged for the men. On this occasion, whether held in a local hall or grove or at a freighter's house, the story of the trip was heard and the faithful men were commended for their fidelity to duty. Refreshments were served and an air of good-fellowship prevailed generally.

A standard train, known as a "bull outfit," consisted of twenty-five freight wagons and a mess wagon. The latter carried the food and the odds and ends needed for repairs en route, such as spare tires, spokes, jacks, and sometimes a forge. Occasionally trains of as

---

[6] William Chandless, *A Visit to Salt Lake* (London, 1857), p. 19; P. J. De Smet, *New Indian Sketches* (New York, 1895), pp. 79-80.

many as fifty or a hundred wagons were made up. There might be some extra wagons, such as a reserve mess wagon, office wagon, workshop wagon, and others. A train of less than twenty-five or twenty-six wagons was known simply as an "outfit." The driver of a six-yoke team and wagon was known as a wagoner, but he was nicknamed a "bull-whacker," or "mule-skinner" if he drove mules. When mules were employed, one line only was used to drive the team. Most of the motive power, however, was oxen. Although slower, they lived and throve on the grass along the way, while grain had to be hauled for horses or mules. Horses were used least of all, although a light mess wagon was pulled by them sometimes.

Alexander Majors discovered that, when properly driven, oxen would make two round trips to Denver, two thousand miles, in a season, and subsist on forage along the way. This discovery saved a great deal, for before that time cattle at the end of the trail had been sold for meat and the wagons were almost given away. At Salt Lake City, for example, hundreds of wagons that had cost $175 were sold to the Mormon authorities for $10. Many of these were purchased for wreckage, and the iron was wrought into nails.

The "leaders," or leading team, were a well-broken Texas yoke, and if possible the "wheelers," or those nearest the load, were experienced animals. The "swing" oxen, although wild, were held in check by the old front and rear guards. Six yoke or twelve oxen were the usual number used, although some freighters employed as many as ten or twelve yoke on a wagon. Several extra oxen were driven along as reserves, making in all from 320 to 330 head of cattle in a regular bull train.

The wagons used in this business were for the most part the Murphy and the Espenshied made in St. Louis and the Studebaker of South Bend, Indiana. The axles were of wood, but the iron skein fitted into an iron thimble in the hub of the wheel. Tar was used as lubricant, and the tar-bucket, which hung on the rear end of the coupling or reach pole under the wagon, had to be applied often, on account of the fine sand and dust that was lifted and deposited on the axle at every turn of the wheel. This "greasing" was done at the regular stops, when by the aid of jacks and tools the big linch-pin which held the wheel was pulled and the wheel removed for the purpose.

In addition to what spares extra wagons might carry, each wagon had strapped to its running-gear an extra tongue, one or two extra yokes, and a like number of axles. Each wagon carried a water-keg, fastened on the side and filled at every watering place. A chip-sack also hung on a hook on the side of the wagon. This was filled with buffalo or cow chips during the day and was ready for the evening camp-fire.[7]

For success in an enterprise involving the safe-keeping and carriage of the thousands of dollars' worth of merchandise in a train, discipline and a faithful crew were necessary. The individual in charge of a train, corresponding to the captain of a ship, was the wagon-master or wagon-boss. He had to be courageous, firm, and genial. The harsh, unsympathetic master always had trouble with his men. The word of the boss was law. Every move on the part of the train was subject to his will. As a rule, he carried a gun or two and stood ready to enforce his decisions and quell mutiny. He selected camping sites, directed the fording of streams, chose watering places, gave orders to start in the morning and halt at night, and directed the repair of a wagon or the treatment of an accident.

It was his task, also, to guard the goods from theft on the part of the crew, as well as from Indians and white renegades. It was not uncommon to find that in a cargo of whisky there had been a tremendous loss from leakage between the Missouri River and the Rocky Mountains. Had they been able to talk, a gimlet and

[7] Frank A. Root and William Elsey Connelley, *The Overland Stage to California* (Topeka, Kans., 1901), pp. 304-308; Alexander Majors, *Seventy Years on the Frontier, Alexander Majors' Memoirs of a Lifetime on the Border*, Colonel Prentiss Ingraham, ed. (Chicago and New York, 1893), p. 144.

some straws in possession of the thirsty freighters could have told some interesting tales. Strange as it may seem, some barrels, when opened at their destination, were found to contain a mixture of half whisky and half Platte River water. The story is told that Jack Morrow, the successful road rancher already referred to, got his start when, as a member of a freighting crew, he emptied a large number of boxes of powder and substituted sand in its place. He deserted with his loot, readily sold the powder for a high figure, and established his famous ranch.

The second in command was known as the assistant wagon-boss. He rode at one end of the train while the wagon-master rode at the other. When they were in a hostile Indian country, the job of these men was not a coveted one. The advance rider was sometimes attacked suddenly and wounded or driven back to the protection of the train. These men were mounted on fast riding animals, usually mules.

The officer third in rank was the commissary, who was a sort of business manager for the train and issued provisions. In some cases the wagon-boss acted as commissary also. A messenger boy, mounted on a pony, carried messages from the wagon-boss to the assistant or elsewhere as directed. On occasion he rode from one train to another bearing messages. Buffalo Bill did his first work in this capacity while a mere lad. Later he advanced in the ranks of Russell, Majors & Waddell to driver, and still later to wagon-boss. The rank and file comprised one man to each wagon, but wise freighters sent along at least one extra driver as a substitute in case of accident or sickness. Other members of the crew were a cook and a herder to drive the extra animals. Every man was expected to do his work without ostentation or complaint.

The bull-whackers ranged from twenty to forty-five years of age. They were described as wearing broad-brimmed hats, red or blue flannel shirts, and pants that were tucked into the tops of high-legged boots. A bowie-knife (in scabbard) protruded from a boottop or hung from a bullet-filled belt which also supported a pistol or two. An additional piece of ordnance in the form of a rifle or shot-gun was carried.[8]

The symbol of authority of the bull-whacker, however, was the bull whip. Its stock measured from eighteen inches to three feet in length. The lash was from fifteen to thirty feet long, made of braided rawhide, and tapered from several inches in circumference six feet from the stock to a "ribbon-like thong" near the end, to which was fastened a buckskin popper.

Each man was furnished with a pair of blankets. One of the tricks of the trade was to steal them from one's fellows. This was a shameful exploit but was not considered dishonest, for all the blankets belonged to the employer anyway. Various methods were used to guard against the loss of blankets. Marking them with thread was useless, for the rascal who purloined them would pull out the thread. One plan for branding the precious protective cover was to rub gunpowder into the blanket in some sort of design and then set fire to it. This mark it was impossible to eradicate.

There was little sickness, for the active life in the open air ensured a maximum of health to men in their prime. The wagon-boss, however, had under his charge a medicine chest with simple remedies such as Epsom salts, calomel, and laudanum. Bottles were numbered, and the directions on the inside of the lid of the chest advised the impromptu practitioner to give number one for a certain ailment and number three for another species of complaint.[9]

Lieutenant Eugene Ware, who was stationed at various military posts along the overland route during the Civil War, made this observation concerning the freighters: "They were a class... that liked fun, enjoyed freedom, despised luxury, and took no note of danger or privation; and they were not of the dumb and

[8] John Bratt, *Trails of Yesterday* (Lincoln, 1922), p. 51; Majors, *Seventy Years on the Frontier*, pp. 243-245.
[9] Wilbur Earl Keeling, *Cholera Epidemics of the Fifties*, Ms., Master's Thesis, University of Iowa, 1933, p. 37.

stupid class of society. Many were educated, some of them were gifted."

The same officer told of an experience with a telegraph-pole train which had pushed rapidly across the Plains with poles to repair breaks in the line. When it reached Fort Sedgwick at ten o'clock in the evening, it was ordered to rest two hours and move right on. This order was received with such a volley of oaths and protests as Ware had never heard before. The profanity, he said, was terrible, especially that of the wagon-boss, whose remarks "had a sublimity that no unprofessional wagon-boss could hope to excel." "He had," reported the by no means inexperienced Army man, "a collection of compound adjectives that equalled anything I had ever heard."

In 1858 the first train of the season left Nebraska City on May 20. The departure of a train was picturesque indeed. With the wagon-master in the lead, like a colonel at the head of his regiment, there followed the long line of white-topped wagons on the green prairies, stretching out a half-mile or more in a winding procession. In the rear followed loose animals driven by the day herder, and behind him came the assistant wagon-boss. Just outside of Nebraska City a little boy, Joy Morton, in the late summer sold apples by the trail—one of the earliest roadside stands and the last chance to buy apples.

The first day out was usually a trial to all concerned. The half-broken steers often ran here and there without much control. If the prairie was smooth, all was well, but if creeks and rough ground lay before the train, the drivers whose teams went on a rampage were frequently in for trouble. The first train in which John Bratt was an employee had two wagons upset, and at the end of the day only a mile of the trek toward the Rockies had been covered. William Chandless' first attempt at bull-whacking ended in the oxen's tying themselves in a double knot, every steer having his feet over the chain, with most of the yokes upside down.

Often at the beginning of the trip the train traveled but three to five miles a day. After the oxen had become seasoned a bit, the average day's travel was from twelve to fifteen miles.

At the first appearance of the new day, about 3:00 or 3:30 in the morning, the night herders rode in and awoke the wagon-master. He got up and went around pounding on each wagon to rouse the men. Then, mounting his horse, he helped corral the animals.[10] When they were in the corral, the wagon-master commanded, "Roll out! Roll out! Cattle in the corral!" As the drivers began their day, the night herders turned in to sleep. Next came the command, "Yoke up." The wagon-master, his assistant, and the extra men guarded the gaps in the corral while each man found his team. Yoking up usually required about thirty to forty-five minutes, although Alexander Majors claimed that his men could finish the entire task of yoking the teams, driving them out of the corral, and hitching them onto the wagons in the record time of sixteen minutes. He gave all credit for this amazing time to thorough discipline.

The process of yoking up was especially difficult during the early days of the trip. One can imagine the bull-whacker running around in the semidarkness among three hundred head of cattle, with an ox-yoke over his left shoulder, a bow in his right hand, and the key in his mouth. Once he had identified a lead ox and placed the bow over his neck, he led him to a wagon wheel and chained him there. Taking the other bow, he found the mate of this ox and yoked him with the other. The wild ones gave still more trouble, for it was necessary to lariat and tie them in order to get them lined up. This accounted for the practice on the first part of the journey of merely unhitching the half-broken teams and allowing them to graze in the yoke.[11]

Finally, when one bull-whacker after another had got his team

[10] George P. Marvin, "Bull-Whacking Days," see *Proceedings and Collections*, Nebraska State Historical Society, Vol. V, Second Series (1902), p. 227.

[11] D. P. Rolfe, "*Overland Freighting from Nebraska City*," see *Proceedings and Collections*, Nebraska State Historical Society, Vol. V, Second Series (1902), p. 282.

"YOKING UP"

From a water-color sketch by W. H. Jackson, July, 1866.

yoked up, driven out of the corral, and hitched to his wagon, the order came, "Pull out." At once there floated through the air a chorus of "Get up Black, Go 'long Brandy, Gee Buck, and Wo-ah Sandy!" It was the ambition of every wagon-master to get his train on the road ahead of all the other trains camped in his vicinity.

Oftentimes the white-covered wagons formed a line stretching out on the prairie as far as the eye could see. In the summer season two, three, four, or even more trains were constantly moving along the trail within sight, some going east and some west. Naturally the clouds of dust were stifling. As a rule the bull-whacker walked on the left-hand side of the wagon, but if the direction of the wind enabled him to avoid the dust, he changed sides. The dust arising from a train could be seen on a clear day for twenty miles, and a dweller near the trail stated that when the wind was favorable, the *pop, pop, pop* of the bull whips could be heard two miles away long before sunrise. The lash of the whip was coiled and thrown around and over the head, then it was allowed to shoot right out and was brought back with a quick jerk of the stock. The result was a crack like a revolver shot. When directed against an ox that was not pulling as he should, it made "him hump up and almost go through his yoke."[12] Seldom did a driver strike an ox, however. A well-directed popper would nip the hide like a knife and draw blood every time. The old-timers used to offer to bet a newcomer that if he would stoop over, the expert could take a piece out of his trousers without breaking the skin. Needless to say, the newcomers were none too trusting of their new-found friends.

The train proceeded about six or eight miles during the cool hours of the morning, and about nine or ten o'clock the corral was formed, the steers unyoked, driven to water, and herded in a place where there was plenty of good grass. Then the men took

[12] William H. Jackson and Howard R. Driggs, *The Pioneer Photographer* (Yonkers-on-Hudson, N. Y., 1929), p. 22.

their first meal of the day. After the meal followed a rest period. When there were no oxen to shoe, wheels to fix, tires to tighten, or wagons to grease, the men spent their time in various ways. Some went fishing in a near-by stream, some tried their hands at buffalo or antelope hunting, others washed or mended clothes. They played freeze-out poker, using plug tobacco cut up into cubes. Some wrote letters to be mailed at the fort or Overland Mail station, some read books or magazines, and still others braided whips.[13]

In the middle of the afternoon the oxen were yoked up and driven a distance approximately equal to the morning drive. About sundown the wagon-master would ride to the center of the location he had selected for the camp. The leading team would turn to the right and make a large half-circle. The second team would turn to the left and make a similar half-circle. These two wagons met at the far side of what was to be the corral and, stopping twenty or thirty feet apart, formed the gateway. The teams following turned right and left alternately. Each wagon was driven close to the wagon ahead, with its inner front wheel against the outer rear wheel of its predecessor. This scheme allowed the wagon tongues to rest outside the circle. Any gaps were closed by stretching log chains across them. The corral thus formed was all-useful. It was a yard in which to hold the cattle for yoking up; it gave protection from the sweeping prairie storms; in case of an Indian attack the cattle could be driven within the shelter of this improvised fort and the big wagons formed a defense for man and beast.[14]

The favorite time for an Indian attack was in the morning while the oxen were being yoked. During the confusion and distraction the Indians hoped to catch the train unprepared. In the evening, as the train was going into camp was another moment of opportunity. When the corral had been formed, the oxen were

[13] William Francis Hooker, *The Prairie Schooner* (Chicago, 1918), p. 38.
[14] W. W. Cox, "Reminiscences of Early Days in Nebraska," see Nebraska State Historical Society, *Transactions and Reports*, Vol. V (1893), p. 75.

unhitched, driven to water, and brought back into the corral alongside the wagons to which they belonged. Here they were unyoked, and the equipment was placed in order preparatory to hitching up the next morning.[15] The animals were then turned out to graze, and the men were free for the problem of making camp within the circle of the wagons.

Each man had chores to do. One man carried water, another dug a fire trench, and if an insufficient amount of fuel had been gathered, one or two from each mess sought an old freighters' camp and soon had an ample supply of cow chips. Along the lower Platte driftwood was "fished" out and hung under the wagon until it dried and served as a reserve.

If no train cook was carried, each mess of six to ten men elected one of their number to be cook. He was excused from all duties in camp except the cooking and the care of the cooking utensils. Each mess was supplied with several six-gallon water-kegs, perhaps a sheet- or cast-iron stove, and at least an oven. Then there were skillets, bake pans, iron kettles, coffee-pots, a coffee-mill, a frying-pan, and a big combination dish and bread pan. Sour-dough bread was made by cooking the dough in a skillet. Sometimes the skillet full of dough was covered with a lid and buried in a heap of live coals for fifteen minutes. When the loaf came from the oven, it was temptingly brown and palatable, but when cold only the cast-iron stomach of a hungry bull-whacker could stand it. Flapjacks, beans, crackers, and molasses supplemented the standard fried bacon and coffee. The eternal dried-apple pie was the dessert two or three times a week. Each man had his own dishes, consisting of a tin plate, cup, knife, fork, and spoon. When the cook's announcement, "Grub pile!" sounded, the hungry freighter lost no time in getting his share of the crude but substantial food. The menu was varied by game, by watermelons and chickens stolen as opportunity offered, and by milk bought from the road

[15] H. T. Clarke, "Freighting—Denver and Black Hills," see *Proceedings and Collections*, Nebraska State Historical Society, Vol. V, Second Series (1902), p. 300.

ranches. When the meal was over, each man washed his own dishes and made them shine with a gunny-sack and ashes.[16]

The camp-fires were made inside the corral. The camping ground of a freight train could be distinguished from that of an emigrant train by the number and size of the camp-fires. The former had a few large fires and the latter a profusion of smaller ones.

When the evening meal was ready, the night guards ate while a couple of the wagoners relieved them at the ox herd; then they took charge of the oxen until yoking time the next morning. The herders had no other duties than to care for the animals while the train was in camp. They spent about ten or twelve hours a day at the task, dividing it about equally between night and day herding. If the herders had experienced a hard or long night, two of the bull-whackers were detailed to do the day herding. In the day-time the herders slept in the wagons as they moved along.[17]

After the evening meal came a time for song and stories. The men who had been among the Indians on the cutting edge of the frontier had the tallest tales to tell. Veterans of many an overland trip attracted attention by their experiences. As the group sat around the buffalo-chip fires, gazing into the dying embers, some-one led in singing the familiar songs of the time. One song peculiar to the freighters, composed, no doubt, by a Russell, Majors & Waddell driver, was entitled "Root Hog or Die." A fragment is given here:

> I'll tell you how it is when
>   You first get on the road;
> You have an awkward team and
>   A very heavy load.
> You have to whip and holler, but
>   Swear upon the sly.
> You're in for it then, boys,
>   Root hog or die.

[16] Marcellus Pugsley, "A Plains Adventure of an Iowa Man," see *Annals of Iowa*, Vol. X, p. 138.

[17] Cass G. Barns, *The Sod House* (Madison, Neb., 1930), p. 200.

> We arrived at Denver City the
> Twenty-first of June
> The people were surprised to
> See us there so soon.
> But we are good bullwhackers,
> On whom you may rely,
> We go it on the principle
> Of root hog or die.

Another song sung by the freighters, miners, and others on the Overland Trail was entitled "Betsy from the Pike":

> The wagon broke down with the tear of bull-crash
> And out of the end-gate rolled all kinds of trash;
> A small volume of infantry clothes done up with care
> Looked remarkably suspicious, though all on the square.
>
> . . . .
>
> Says a miner to Betts, "Won't you dance along with me?"
> "Oh, I will that, old hoss, if you don't make too free;
> But don't dance me hard, for I'll tell you the reason why,
> Dog-gon you, I'm chuck-full of alca-ho-li." [18]

Another favorite trail song of the sixties was "Joe Bowers." And, of course, "John Brown's Body" was everywhere extremely popular throughout the Union states and was sung with spirit around the prairie camp-fires.

A considerable amount of more or less good-natured wrangling concerning who was going to do the camp chores took place among the members of a mess. One freighter recorded such a verbal battle around a camp-fire:

> "Now give us another drink of coffee."
> "All gone, woodpecker."
> "Well, some water then."
> "Not a drop left. . . ."
> "Oh, here's a nice state of things," cries one of our cooks, "how are

[18] This song, said to have been composed by an orchestra leader of the Denver House named Jones, was very popular in the sixties. It was a historical poem relating the adventures of a traveler en route to California and was sung to the tune of "Villikins and His Dinah."

we to get breakfast, and not a drop of water to do it with? Whose turn is it?"

"Oh, I went for water this evening," cries one.

"And I for wood," cries another; and that great shirk, Moran slips away to his waggon.

"Oh, well, if none if you'll go it's no affair of ours," says the cook, "we can do as well without coffee as the balance, can't we Tom (to his sub)? I know No 2 mess'll give us a drop."

"Call me up first thing, and I'll go," says Howard.

"No, we've had plenty of that; you'd have had no breakfast this morning, if some one hadn't lugged you right out. Won't anyone go?"

"I'll go," says Dutch John, the most willing man in camp.

"It's too bad Dutch John should have to go, he brought wood and water both this evening," says another, but never offers to go himself.

The men as a rule slept on the ground under a wagon with a rubber sheet and a buffalo robe for mattress and a pair of blankets for covering. In cold weather a driver sometimes would sleep with one of his oxen, or if the beast would not lie still, the bull-whacker made his bed on the warm spot left by the animal's body. A driver's diary entry for July 30, 1855, read: "Slept very badly; rough bed, and cold too." Poor though the sleeping accommodations were, they were alluring to the tired bull-whacker when his turn came to go on watch, for in addition to the herders there was a camp guard with three or four men on duty all night long regardless of weather conditions. Each mess took a full night's guard, dividing into two shifts which went on duty the first half and the last half of the night. The camp was constantly on a war footing, and in times of great danger all guards were doubled. Even in the day-time, in hostile country, scouts were sent ahead of the train and the wagons were kept close together. At night Indians sometimes slipped up and despatched a herder and drove off or stampeded the herd. With their motive power gone, the freighters were left helplessly stranded on the prairie.[19]

The roads were often very good running across the firm sod

[19] C. B. Hadley, "The Plains War in 1865," see *Proceedings and Collections*, Nebraska State Historical Society, Vol. V, Second Series (1902), p. 278.

of the level prairie, but in other places there were soft-bottomed sloughs or creeks to cross. These obstacles required doubling or trebling up: that is, the oxen of two or three wagons were hooked onto one, each wagon being pulled across by the composite team.

Sometimes the wheels sank nearly to the hub in sand or mud. When a wagon once stopped in such a place, it took tremendous force to move it. In this situation the team was swung around with the leaders back by the wheelers. The leaders' heads were then turned to the front and the long line of oxen started on a run. When their full weight was finally thrown on the wagon, it usually moved forward. Sometimes the tongue was broken in this maneuver and there was need for the extra one carried under the wagon. When steep slopes were descended, the rear wheels were locked and the wagon was allowed to slide down the incline.

Rough, rocky roads and the hot, dry atmosphere were hard on wheels, and they sometimes lost their tires. The difficult process of setting them was accomplished in a very ingenious way. The tire was placed on the prairie, covered all the way around with cow chips, and these were set on fire. A thickness or two of heavy duck was placed on the circumference of the felloe to increase its size. This canvas was wet when the hot, expanded tire was put into place. More water was quickly poured on the tire and felloe to prevent burning of the canvas and to shrink the tire to a tight fit. The job seldom had to be done again on the same trip.

In the interest of making their county-seat, Nebraska City, the most attractive starting-point for overland traffic, the people of Otoe County, Nebraska, voted $20,000 in bonds at ten per cent interest to build the bridges over the streams on the "air line" or "cut-off" between Nebraska City and Fort Kearney. In order to mark the trail, a furrow was plowed the entire distance from Salt Creek (a few miles south of the present city of Lincoln) to the Platte River.

Most freighters ran their trains seven days a week. The few who ordered the train to rest on Sunday did so with the understanding that the layover was dependent on locating the camp where good grass and water were available. The wagon-masters usually managed not to have their trains fulfil these conditions and thus evaded the rule. It took a bull train from twenty-eight to forty-five days to reach Denver from the Missouri River. A train spent seventy-five days between the Missouri River and Salt Lake City.

In the late sixties Indian hostilities on the Plains became very pronounced. All trains passing a government fort were required to have a sufficient number of men to cope with the redskins. The post commanders generally felt that a hundred men were necessary. Sometimes a train laid over a few days at a post, waiting for other trains, repairing equipment, or resting under the protection of the Stars and Stripes. The little fort on the prairie represented civilization, intercourse with people of their own kind, and an opportunity to buy a few things at the post trader's store.

When enough men and wagons were assembled, the post commander organized the group and empowered the captain to keep the train together and to report any insubordination to the post commander nearest the point where it occurred. The most dangerous foes were the half-breeds and squaw-men who combined the knowledge of the white man with savage cunning. Bands of plundering Indians ambushed their victims and stampeded the cattle.

A special type of freighting was the driving of stock across the Plains. As early as 1853 Dr. Thomas Flint drove a herd of over two thousand head of sheep, oxen, cows, and horses from the States to the west coast. He had fifteen men in his crew. After being herded for a couple of weeks, the stock got accustomed to the scheme and at night would gather around the camp much as stock will become used to a barnyard on a farm.[20] Every year for a number of years the Gibson family of northwestern Missouri drove cattle across the Plains. In 1852 cattle were $10 or $15 a head in Missouri and they sold for $150 a head in California. Consequently, many were driving herds to the west coast.

[20] Thomas Flint, *Diary* (Claremont, Cal., 1924), pp. 1, 25, 28.

When they were leaving Missouri, great difficulty was experienced in getting the animals out of the brush country. J. W. Gibson mentioned that on the day his party were ready to start in 1854, about fifty neighbors were on hand to see them go. These men on horseback helped them get the cattle out of the brush and onto the prairie. The herd of six hundred head was handled by a crew of twenty employed men, with two wagons of provisions pulled by four yoke of oxen to the wagon, and thirty-two head of horses and mules. Thirty men in all accompanied the train.[21] Probably a number of them worked their way to the land of gold. Arrangements were frequently made whereby the drover furnished a horse to ride and the food for the overland trip and the man helped herd the cattle in exchange for his expenses en route.

On the trail a few leaders among the cattle were always in the forefront setting the pace. The animals got such a travel habit as was hard to break when they arrived in California. After grazing for a time in the morning, the leaders would start off across the range with the rest following. In a few days, if not watched, they would march clear out of the vicinity.

In 1863 a man with two boys drove a flock of over five hundred turkeys across the Plains to Denver. He had a wagonload of shelled corn drawn by six horses and mules. The turkeys were purchased in Iowa and Missouri. The birds ate grasshoppers along the way and at night roosted all over the wagon and on the ground around it. The boys had an easy time as long as the wind was favorable, but when it came from the west, it was almost impossible to drive the fowl. The flock arrived in Denver with a loss of only a few birds. No doubt thousands of miners blessed the man who had the nerve and patience to bring for their use this choice meat from civilization.

A new country lacks many things, and among the scarce commodities were cats. Apparently in the mining-camps the mice and rats almost ran away with the provisions, and cats were in great

21 J. W. Gibson, *Recollections of a Pioneer* (St. Joseph, Mo., 1912), p. 87.

demand. In 1876 a freighter between Cheyenne, Wyoming, and the Black Hills, in response to the call for cats in South Dakota, passed the word around among the boys in Cheyenne that he would give twenty-five cents for any cat brought to him regardless of pedigree or looks. He built a crate and took it full of cats to the mines. When he stopped on the street of Deadwood and began business, not a cat sold for less than $10 and good Maltese brought $25 each. The records contain other instances of cargoes of cats' being freighted to the mining-camps.[22]

There was very little freight in the mountains to be carried east. Some freighters helped pay expenses on the way back by taking miners and their baggage for a fare of ten dollars. Hundreds of such passengers, known as pilgrims, were carried. The freighters guaranteed twenty-five miles a day, and in the winter they stopped at night at a pilgrim house in connection with one of the stage stations. There the passengers cooked their food on a sheet-iron stove and night after night slept on a frozen floor for ten cents a head. Hides and furs were a common cargo, and some lumber was hauled from the mountains for building forts and perhaps a few houses along the Overland Trail.

Empty wagons going east were often "trailed"—that is, two, three, or even four wagons were fastened behind one another and pulled by one team. Indeed, in the sixties and seventies it became customary to trail wagons even when loaded. During the Black Hills freighting period an outfit known as a "jerk-neck team" came into being. With this the freighter drove a team of horses or mules on one wagon and led a second team and wagon from the tail of the first. The rear end-gate of the first wagon was protected from the tongue of the following one by a bump-board. When oxen were used, they were hitched to the leading wagon and short-tongued trail wagons were hooked behind it.[23]

[22] Jesse Brown and A. M. Willard, *The Black Hills Trails*, John T. Milek, ed. (Rapid City, S. D., 1924), pp. 432-433.

[23] Charles O. Armstrong, see *Reminiscences*, Ms., North Dakota State Historical Society Library.

In the Black Hills freighting, ten yoke were hitched to three wagons, designated the lead, the swing, and the trailer wagon. A similar type of freighting was carried on between the head of navigation on the Missouri at Fort Benton and the mines.

Some winter freighting was conducted at times, especially the carrying of perishables. On December 15, 1876, a train of ninety-six yoke of oxen and thirty wagons loaded with eggs, butter, flour, and pork left Yankton for Deadwood. The eggs were wrapped in paper and packed in oats in paper-lined barrels to prevent freezing and breakage. A month later on the Cheyenne River a severe blizzard overtook the train. Snow piled as high as the wagons. The foreman was up all night during the coldest weather knocking the frozen breath from the bulls' nostrils so they would not smother. The party finally placed improvised runners on the wagons and got to the mining towns. Eggs sold for a dollar a dozen, and the other goods brought exorbitant prices.[24]

"Quick freighting" was done with horses and mules the year around, and grain was stored at stations here and there along the way for horse feed. Hay was purchased from the road ranches. Oftentimes the freighters received from eight to fifteen cents a pound for carriage from the terminal points to the Black Hills. A man who purchased his own goods and carried them to the gold-fields was known as a "shot-gun" freighter. Many farmers and small freighters hauled butter, eggs, dressed hogs, sausages, and lard.

The economics of freighting varied with the status of the currency, the demand for goods, the competition, the attitude of the Indians, the class of freight, and the time of year. A standard price was one dollar for each hundred pounds per hundred miles.[25] The rate between the Missouri River and the Rocky Mountains

[24] Lawrence E. Olson, *The Mining Frontier of South Dakota*, Ms., Master's Thesis, University of Iowa, 1931, pp. 90-92.

[25] Harold E. Briggs, *The Settlement and Economic Development of the Territory of Dakota*, Ms., Doctor's Thesis, University of Iowa, 1929, 2 volumes, Vol. II, pp. 453, 457.

varied from four or five cents a pound in 1862 to ten cents a pound during the Indian War of 1864.

A man hauled apples from the Missouri River to Denver in 1865 and received $20 a bushel for them. Two Germans who could not speak English decided to go into a shot-gun freighting business. They filled their wagons with cans of fresh oysters at Omaha, poured water into the wagon beds, and froze the whole load into a solid lump. They each hauled all that two mules could pull, and in order to hide from the Indians traveled at night. Their adventure must have been successful, for they were selling the oysters at $10 a gallon on the trail fifty miles west of Julesburg.[26]

An example of a shot-gun freighter who started in a small way was Henry M. Porter. He went to Achison and purchased some farm wagons, procured some unbroken mules in Missouri, and despatched an outfit as soon as he could break the mules and get his equipment ready. Each week he started a train of five wagons for Denver. The last train he took himself. On the way out he met the first outfit coming back. Thus he kept them going for several years. At the end of the first year he found he had sold over $300,000 in goods and made $75,000. He felt this was marvelous for an inexperienced man.

In 1864, when there was a stampede from Colorado to Montana and Porter knew there would be a big demand for wagons for the gold-seekers, he bought one hundred new farm wagons and the same number of yoke of oxen. He loaded the wagons with groceries and despatched them to Denver in April. The long line of shiny new wagons caused a sensation in Denver, and they sold like the proverbial hot cakes. Porter cleared $16,000 net.[27]

The wages of the freighters varied from time to time, but in the late fifties Russell, Majors & Waddell paid their men a dollar a day and keep. By 1865, one freighter says, the wages were $70

[26] Eugene F. Ware, *The Indian War of 1864* (Topeka, Kans., 1911), pp. 537-539.
[27] Henry M. Porter, *Autobiography* (Denver, 1932), pp. 24-29.

to $75 a month for drivers, for wagon-masters twice this amount, assistants $80 a month, and night herders $60 to $70 a month. Mule-skinners received ten dollars a month more than bull-whackers.

On at least two occasions steam locomotive tractors were tried in the overland freighting business. On July 4, 1860, the Overland Steam Wagon was tested at Atchison. It seemed to work satis-factorily and, gaily decorated with flags, sped through the streets at an unheard-of speed. Unfortunately the driver lost control of the monster, twenty feet long, and it crashed through a store. When it was tried on the prairie, even while stationary its tre-mendous weight caused it to sink into the mud, and the scheme was given up.

Two years later a Prairie Motor was landed at the Nebraska City wharf from the steamboat *Omaha*. It was made more road-worthy than the first locomotive. The wheels were ten feet in diameter with a tire eighteen inches wide. The vehicle could carry enough wood and water to run four hours at the rate of four miles an hour. It was planned to travel to Denver and back in a few days' time, hauling twelve to fifteen tons of freight. On its maiden trip the Prairie Motor breezed down a Nebraska City street at the rate of eight miles an hour, greeted by the cheers of the citizens of the outfitting town lining the streets. But the ma-chine broke down in the hills a few miles northwest of Nebraska City, and thus ended the attempts to use steam in the overland freighting business before the era of the railroad.[28]

Still another type of freighting in the northern region was that used between Pembina, Dakota Territory, and St. Paul, Min-nesota. Joseph Rolette of the American Fur Company in 1843 started a line of Red River carts between these two points. By 1858 the number arriving at St. Paul in a year had increased from a small beginning to six hundred. The business amounted

---

[28] Carla Elizabeth Neuhaus, *Transportation to Colorado, 1858-1869*, Ms., Master's Thesis, University of Colorado, 1928, pp. 35-37; Root and Connelley, *The Overland Stage to California*, pp. 430-431.

to $180,000 in 1857. The distance from Pembina to St. Paul was about four hundred and fifty miles, and a regular trail was established between the two points.

A Red River cart was made entirely of wood and rawhide. Not even the tires or linch-pins were made of metal. The two wheels were about five feet in diameter, and the felloe three inches wide. There were four spokes in each wheel, set at right angles to one another at the hub, which was well built. The felloes were joined by tongues of wood, and a crude form of rawhide, known as "shaganapi," was used for tires. The box frame was fastened together by pegs also. The whole cart was made with an axe and an auger and was worth fifteen dollars.

Such a vehicle, equipped with a pair of shafts, would haul as much as a thousand pounds, although generally not over six or seven hundred constituted a load. It was usually pulled by one ox, although at times two were hitched in tandem to the lubberly vehicle. The harness used to hitch the animal to the cart was made of broad bands of buffalo hide. The axles were never oiled, and in motion each wheel had its own particular squeak. A caravan made up an orchestra which could be heard for miles on a still day.[29] A large number of carts often traveled together as a company, divided into brigades consisting of ten carts each and manned by a crew of three men. The company was in charge of a guide who was given great authority. At one time a train of five hundred carts left St. Paul laden with goods for the Canadian Northwest.

An observer who saw a train of a hundred and fifty carts bound for St. Paul from Pembina in 1858 said that a cloud of murk was seen long before a cart was visible, and then slowly the seemingly endless caravan emerged from a thick pall of dust. Each driver in this case was in charge of five or six carts. The driver flourished his whip over the lead animal, and the ox next in line who was tied to the cart in front was obliged to follow. The train left

---

[29] A. W. Graham, "Diary," entry of July 8, 1869, in Grace Lee Nute, "New Lights on Red River Valley History," *Minnesota History Bulletin*, Vol. V, p. 569.

Pembina in early June, as soon as there was sufficient pasture, and arrived at St. Paul early in July, averaging thirty days for the trip. At night they camped at a spot where wood and water were obtainable. They drew up their carts in the form of a corral and placed sentinels to guard against Indian attack. On the long trip the men subsisted on game and pemmican, a concoction of dried buffalo meat pounded into shreds, stuffed into a bag made of buffalo hide, and covered with melted tallow.

The drivers were half-breed Indian and French Red River men. They presented every hue from fair skin and light-brown curls to the swarthiness and straight black hair of the Indian, with every intermediate shade that amalgamation would produce. Their dress consisted of a uniform costume of coarse blue cloth with an abundance of brass buttons, showy red-flannel belt, and jaunty cap.[30] The train carried loads of furs to St. Paul and took back tea, tobacco, alcohol, hardware, and other manufactured goods.

Overland freighting was a gigantic business. From April 25 to October 13, 1860, the Russell, Majors & Waddell establishment at Nebraska City carried 2,782,258 pounds of goods, using 5,687 oxen, 515 wagons, and 602 men. This was only one of a number of large concerns, not to mention the other outfitting points of the same company and the hundreds of smaller companies and individuals. In 1860 an eastbound traveler reported 1,830 heavily loaded westbound freight wagons between Denver and Fort Kearney. For miles the road was lined with the great ships of the prairie.[31]

This great business, killing on animals and fraught with hardship and danger for men, could not compete with the railroad. As the lines crept westward from the Missouri River and eastward from California, the freighters hauled their burdens from the end of the rails, until finally the gap was bridged and the romantic days of the bull-whackers and mule-skinners were gone forever.

[30] "The Red River Trail," *Harper's New Monthly Magazine*, April, 1859, pp. 602-620.

[31] *Huntsman's Echo*, Wood River Center, Nebraska, Oct. 26, 1860.

CHAPTER XVI

THE RAILROAD-BUILDERS

LIKE THE STAGE and the telegraph, the railroads as a rule came as a part of the civilization that was ever pushing westward behind the frontier line, but the earlier transcontinental lines were drawn across vast unsettled spaces by the magnet of population on the west coast and in isolated gold-fields. It was this that led to the building of railroads through thousands of miles of uninhabited plains and mountains where there was no permanent settlement and no traffic anticipated for years to come.

Since the Union Pacific was the first, it has remained the outstanding and typical example of a railroad built before the frontier came. As early as 1850 railroad conventions looking toward a Pacific railroad were held, and many men with prophetic eyes were talking of replacing the old overland wagon-train with the railway. But hardly half a dozen men in the country, perhaps, anticipated building a transcontinental line connecting the Missouri River and the Pacific Ocean within the short space of twenty years.

The Civil War hastened the beginning of construction. Military necessity, the dictator in wartime, seemed to require that the western part of the Union be connected with the East. Over the vast intervening space there came rumors of a separate Pacific republic, and then, too, the isolated Pacific coast was an extremely weak link in the American defense scheme. Congress, callous to voting large sums by reason of the Civil War expenditures, passed the Union Pacific bill giving the company a charter and large land and money subsidies. Likewise within the next few years the Kansas Pacific and the Northern Pacific were chartered with generous grants. The Union Pacific, since it was a special protégé of the National Government and was completed first, had all eyes upon it, and information concerning its building is much more abundant and colorful than for later lines.

In such haste was the Union Pacific begun that it was pushed across Nebraska before a railroad had been built across Iowa to make an eastern connection. And it had made the junction with the Central Pacific completing the line from the Missouri River to the Pacific Ocean before a bridge was built across the Missouri River to complete the actual connection at Omaha. All the first rails, engines, and cars had to be shipped on river boats up the Missouri or taken to pieces and hauled in wagons across Iowa.

Ground was broken near Omaha on December 2, 1863, but the actual grading was not begun until the spring of 1864, and only forty miles of track had been laid by January 1, 1866. In fact, the road was ready to start and had no place to go. No exact line had been decided on, and during the year 1865 the engineers began surveying the route west of Columbus.

A party of surveyors under the direction of Division Engineer Edwards set out from Omaha on August 2, 1865. He had fifteen men including assistants, teamsters, and cook. His train consisted of several covered wagons drawn by horses and mules. One contained food supplies, cook's utensils, a sheet-iron stove which was lashed up behind the wagon with stout cords when the party was on the march, and the tableware, consisting of tin plates, tin cups, knives, and forks. The remaining wagons were occupied by surveying tools, arms, ammunition, personal effects of the men of the party, and five good-sized white-duck wall tents. A party of this kind, numbering usually from eighteen to twenty-one men, with a hunter added when it was expected to live largely off the country, comprised the usual number of civil engineers, rodmen, flagmen, chainmen, axemen, besides a cook, teamsters, and herders.

In the preliminary surveys in open country a party would run from eight to twelve miles of line in a day when all preparations had been made. On location, in the same type of country, not over three or four miles would be covered, and in mountainous country generally not more than a mile. For surveys on the treeless plains, it was necessary, before starting, to cut a wagonload of stakes to be hauled along from day to day.

With the first streak of dawn the camp was astir and camp-fires were blazing in the dim light of the morning. The cook, up long before the others, had to prepare a lunch for the surveyors as well as to cook breakfast. After the horses had been fed at the troughs on the back of the wagons, breakfast was eaten, and soon the surveyors were out at work. Engineer Edwards' party followed a program of having the camp move parallel with the surveyors rather than follow on the line. After breakfast the cook and herders did the camp duties, taking down the tents and loading up the baggage; then they moved forward along the stream parallel to the line for about ten miles and pitched camp again at a good site where wood and water were available. When the surveying party returned at night, all was ready for them. Sometimes, especially when the party on the line did not get started for camp before dusk, it was difficult for them to find it in the dark. The men at camp would light signal fires of brush to give the camp location, and these were always hailed with delight. Surveyors rode to the line in a wagon containing the stakes, instruments, and the lunch. Sometimes men took turns at doing the cooking. At night each man spread his blankets on the ground, placed his loaded gun in his bed by his side, his loaded revolver at his head, and his cartridges in his hat, ready to go into action at a moment's notice.

Beyond Fort Kearney a military escort was furnished. Part of this cavalry squadron scouted the country every day, sometimes going three or four miles from the line and often bringing back game of various kinds strapped behind their saddles. The rest of the escort remained in the vicinity of the camp to protect it. At night a guard was detailed, and the tread of the sentinels with their carbines gave the surveyors a feeling of security.[1] Even so the Indians were successful occasionally in making a flying assault on a party of engineers, killing some and driving their stock away. Such an attack took place on the Kansas Pacific at Monument Station in western Kansas on May 20, 1867. Fortunately the engineers lost only their horses in that raid.

The Union Pacific surveyors stayed in the field during the winter of 1865-66. Sometimes their nights were most disagreeable. With snow on the ground, the tramping of feet in the tents soon reduced the footing to a muddy slop. Brush was cut and placed on the floor to keep the sleepers out of the mire. Sometimes the tents were blown down in a storm, and morning found the men, after a sleepless night, hovering around the camp-fire with their eyes red and swollen from the smoke which was whipped about by the wind. The crew did not work on Sunday, and the men spent the day reading, writing letters, washing clothes, and sleeping. Locating the route of a track which was to be a permanent fixture was no small task. Twenty-five thousand miles of exploratory reconnaissances and fifteen thousand miles of instrumental lines were run.

Behind this vanguard of the railroad-builders came the graders. The contracts for grading were left to politicians who subcontracted them to private individuals or companies. The grading contractor took his wagon-train, men, horses, and tools to his particular section of the line and located a headquarters. A little village was established, made up of a motley array of tents, covered wagons, and dugouts. The latter were sod houses half above ground and half below. They housed from two to six men and were a good protection against Indian attacks.

The work of the grading gang was done largely by plows, scrapers, and teams, supplemented by shovel and wheelbarrow. Long plank walks were built for · runways, and perspiring men like ants on an ant-hill wheeled great loads of dirt and dumped

[1] A. N. Ferguson, *Diary, 1865-1869*, Ms., Union Pacific Museum, Omaha.

them. When rocks were encountered, hand drills and black powder, or occasionally nitroglycerine, were used to dislodge the stones, which were in great demand for culverts and bridges. When the road was being built the fastest, three thousand men were busy grading at top speed to keep ahead of the rails. The graders worked as much as two or three hundred miles ahead of the track and graded about a hundred miles in thirty days when the terrain was level. All the supplies had to be hauled hundreds of miles, and even water had to be brought in by wagon-train at some places. A good-sized army of freighters and teamsters was required to supply the graders. The statement has been made that it cost more to haul the supplies than to do the actual grading.

Bridge gangs worked from five to twenty-five miles ahead of the track. They made sod houses for themselves and sod stables for their horses, or they sometimes occupied houses built by the graders. Heavy materials and all of the provisions had to be hauled for miles. The overland stage and the overland telegraph were helpful auxiliaries along part of the line where they ran parallel. By means of the stage, men at the grading-camps or with the bridge-builders far out beyond the rails could reach the end of the track occasionally. The telegraph gave instantaneous connection with headquarters. The Union Pacific built telegraph lines of its own at the same time the track was laid, and they were used incessantly between Omaha and the "end of track."

While the grade was being built, all was activity at headquarters at Omaha. In August, 1866, nine sawmills owned by the company and more than a dozen hired ones were busy making lumber. A million brick were laid in constructing the Omaha terminal yards between September 16, 1865, and January 27, 1866. Many steamboats were owned and others were chartered to bring materials up the river. At that time twelve thousand hands were employed on the road in one way or another.

For sixty miles below and a hundred and fifty above Omaha the banks of the Missouri were being depleted of timber by hundreds of men in the tie-camps preparing the 2,640 cross-ties needed for each mile of the line. The plans called for rafting the ties cut above Omaha down the river to the terminal city. Since hardwood was so scarce, it was determined to use cottonwood ties for the most part, with only four of hardwood to each rail. To obtain the hardwood ties a large part of the oak and walnut trees of the Missouri Valley were sacrificed. The cottonwood ties were burnettized, which cost sixteen cents a tie. This was a treatment with zinc chloride which was supposed to render them rot-resistant, but in this expectation the officials were disappointed, for the impregnated ties were little or no better than the untreated ones. Tie-camps were established in the canyons of the bluffs along the south bank of the Platte in southwestern Nebraska, and when the supply of timber was depleted in eastern Nebraska, quantities of red-cedar ties were ready for use. The ties had to be hauled by wagons and distributed along the grade. Some were shipped by rail to the "end of track" and hauled from there. Others were freighted from the west to meet the westward-moving track.

It was customary for all railroads to establish a construction headquarters near the head of the rails and maintain it until the track had been laid a hundred miles or so farther on. Then it was moved to a new location.

On the Union Pacific the immense task of supervising the contract for laying the thousand miles of track and for doing most of the grading beyond central Nebraska fell to the Casement Brothers, Dan and Jack.[2] Among the other difficulties encountered was the fact that all of the construction material and supplies, with the exception of the ties on the western end, had to be sent from Omaha over a single-track road.

Bringing up supplies at maximum speed and at the same time keeping the empty trains going back for more was a problem calling for organization of the highest order. Furthermore, foodstuffs, tools, rails, cars, and even the locomotives, as previously men-

[2] Edwin L. Sabin, *Building the Pacific Railway* (Philadelphia, 1919), p. 74.

tioned, had to be shipped up the Missouri River by boat or taken to pieces and hauled over a wide stretch of Iowa in wagons. A seventy-ton stationary engine for the shops at Omaha was hauled one hundred and fifty miles across western Iowa by ox team. When the North-Western Railway finally closed the gap and built a terminal at Council Bluffs, there was still a few miles' haul to the river and ferriage. For some time, when the Missouri was frozen over, locomotives and cars were taken across the river on tracks laid on the ice.

The building of such a railway might be likened to the thrust of a great army into the enemy's territory. Supplies and materials were collected at Omaha and held awaiting orders to despatch them to the front. Train after train pushed up to the line of battle, bearing hundreds of tons of iron and thousands of ties. Near the scene of action were side-tracks lined with cars loaded with supplies, and yet other switches filled with empty cars to be exchanged for the loaded ones and taken back to the base.

Since the track-layers advanced a mile or more a day during the summer months, no stationary town could long serve them; hence they did not live in the terminal town, but dwelt in long sleeping-cars which moved westward day by day, following across the Plains the still iron serpent they had created. When these rolling homes were crowded, beds were made on top and hammocks slung underneath. Tents were used, too, when there was a shortage of space. Some construction lodgings were built on three flatcars like a dwelling-house with windows and doors. One was fitted as a dining-room, another with a kitchen at one end and a reception room at the other, and the third contained berths. These were run upon a temporary track; the middle car was placed crosswise of the track, the truck wheels removed, and the other two cars were brought against its opposite sides, forming a cross. The Casement brothers' famous portable quarters comprised four large boarding-cars, each eighty feet long, two for sleeping, one for eating, and the fourth for cooking. Besides, there were attached to their camp a general store, a drinking establishment, a butcher's car with quantities of beef, and two bakers' cars, one containing flour and stores and the other the ovens.

The track-layers rolled out of bed early on a boarding-train, washed in tin basins, ate a hearty breakfast, and got out on the job promptly—placing ties on the grade, carrying rails, and spiking them down. At noon an hour was allowed for a heavy dinner. Great steaming pitchers of coffee, pans of soup, and platters of meat, potatoes, and other vegetables, together with canned fruit and pie, constituted the bounteous meal eaten from metal plates. There was little time or inclination to talk. After a period of relaxation, during which they smoked and rested in their bunks, the men were again rousted out on the line. Work ceased about five o'clock, with an hour of relaxation before supper. The supper hour was more leisurely. After the meal some returned to the bunk-cars, where the air was soon blue with smoke and the atmosphere murky with masculine talk; others preferred a game of horseshoes in the open air, or a swim in the near-by stream, if such there was. Thus the workman spent his waking hours—hard work and long hours—and for reward received $2.50 a day, which was considered superlative wages for a common laborer at a time when the prevailing wage in the farming sections of Missouri was less than half that.

A great majority of the workmen were Irish, and the Union Pacific construction songs give evidence of it. One was entitled "Poor Paddy, He Works on the Railroad." Another favorite ditty was:

> Then drill, my Paddies, drill,—
> Drill, my heroes, drill—
> Drill all day, no sugar in your tay,
> Workin' on the U. P. railway

Another ran:

> The Great Pacific Railway for California hail;
> Bring on the locomotive, lay down the iron rail.[3]

[3] Glenn Chesney Quiett, *They Built the West* (New York, 1934), pp. 37, 38.

Some of the bosses in charge of various operations kept a good supply of magazines of the best type, which were available to such of the men as cared for reading. Newspapers were published under the head, "End of Track." Sometimes these were printed in box-cars. One on the Kansas Pacific was called the *Railway Advance*. When the construction crew moved, the paper followed.

The workmen who visited the terminal points to spend a little time wore high boots, with pantaloons tucked in the legs, and a flannel shirt with no tie except a black handkerchief. The majority had on a belt from which was suspended a gun about a foot long. All wore either full whiskers or a mustache.

There was a great demand for laundering, and the workmen were ready to pay almost any price to get it done. Mr. and Mrs. C. W. Wells opened a laundry in a tent when the line was building near Julesburg. They had all the work they could do in spite of the enormous rates they charged. Their price, as Mr. Wells later stated, was whatever their consciences would allow, and their consciences were exceedingly flexible at that time; but no one complained. They charged ten cents apiece for small articles such as a handkerchief or a sock, twenty-five cents for colored or flannel shirts, and fifty cents for white shirts. Wells remembered charging one man eleven dollars for washing and ironing goods which he carried home in his arms. He noted, however, that wash water cost a dollar a barrel, and since other things were in proportion, the prices were not so unreasonable as they seemed. Then, too, he excused himself on the ground that they should have had something extra on account of the numerous insects they had to wash out of the clothes brought to them.

When General Jack S. Casement took charge of track-laying, he revolutionized the system and in a short time had the work moving with great rapidity. He had in his track-laying gang between two hundred and fifty and three hundred men, and for months they laid an average of a mile and a half a day. During the spring of 1869 they averaged two miles a day seven days a week, working every hour of the day that light made possible. The biggest day's work was eight miles.

Casement's system, which was reduced to a science, was founded on having each car of rails loaded at Omaha with a certain number of rails and the exact number of chairs and spikes required to lay them. General Jack's brother Daniel took charge of this work at Omaha. When the train arrived, the boarding-cars were pushed as far as possible toward the end of the track and a carload of rails unloaded behind them. The boarding-cars were then drawn back, and about forty rails with the proper number of chairs and spikes were loaded on a small car and hurried to the end of the track by horse power. Here a man put a check under a wheel, bringing the load to a stop at once. On each side of the car were rollers to facilitate dragging off the iron rails. Before the car had well stopped, a rail was dropped on the rollers, and twelve men, six on each side, grasped it. At the near-military commands, "Up! Forward!" they raised and carried it to the proper location. Then came the command, "Ready! Down!" and it was lowered into place. Meanwhile the same process had taken place on the other side of the grade, and in thirty seconds the railroad was twenty-eight feet nearer the Pacific Ocean. Before the clang of the dropped rail had ceased to reverberate, willing hands pushed the car forward over the loose rails and repeated the operation, moving as fast as a man ordinarily walked. Behind the car followed a man dropping chairs and spikes. Others followed tamping the earth under the ties, and last came the bolters. The moment one rail car was empty, it was tipped off to one side while a second was drawn up to the end of the track. A young Jehu, riding his horse at a gallop, then pulled the first car at the end of an eighty-foot rope back to the rail dump, where it was quickly loaded to go up to the front again. Every few minutes the long, heavy train behind sent a puff from its locomotive and, pushing the boarding-cars and cars of rails, caught up with the work.[4]

[4] William A. Bell, *New Tracks in North America* (London, 1869), p. 491.

By this system the track was laid with astonishing rapidity. Forty carloads of rails were required for every mile. Between June 8 and July 16, 1870, the Kansas Pacific laid seventy miles, or an average of a little over two miles a day.

As the pioneer railroad moved westward into the mountains, a brisk rivalry grew up between the Central Pacific building east from California and the Union Pacific building west from the Great Plains. This stimulated the officials of the companies to greater speed and eventually to bitter competition. No meeting place had been designated, but each road expected to build beyond the point where they eventually did join. As a consequence, the two companies had grading gangs working parallel and built grades side by side for two hundred miles in Utah and eastern Nevada, each hoping to lay its rails first, build its road as far as possible, and collect the mileage subsidy from the government. Toward the last, before the roads met, the Union Pacific worked three eight-hour shifts a day. By the light of huge bonfires of sage-brush an army of workmen toiled all night like ants. In 1868 cold weather caught the builders in the Wasatch Mountains, but winter was not allowed to delay the work. Grading and track-laying went forward in the snow and ice. General Grenville M. Dodge, chief engineer of the Union Pacific, said at one time he saw a construction train, locomotive, track, and all, slide off an icy embankment into a ditch. Men wearing heavy overcoats worked on cuts and tunnels at a time when the ground was frozen solid. Track-laying which should have cost only $600 a mile was said to have cost $1,500 on this account. The last few days before the two railroads joined saw the fastest track-laying in the history of railroading in the United States. Each of the two competing roads went forward at an average rate of five miles a day. The largest trackage laid in any one day by the Union Pacific was eight miles, but the Central Pacific with its great army of Chinese workers, when nearing the completion of its line close to Promontory Point, Utah, surprised everybody by setting a record of ten miles.

The Indians viewed the progress of the first railroads across the Plains with alarm. To them it meant the disappearance of the buffalo and the loss of their chief means of livelihood. It was natural, then, that before the railroads had built two hundred miles into the Plains, Indian attacks should occur. Often there would be no difficulty for a considerable period, and then an epidemic of attacks would break out which kept the builders in a continual state of war for months. It was literally true that the workers built the Kansas Pacific and the Union Pacific with a pick in one hand and a gun in the other. The tie-cutters, graders, and track-layers actually were marched to their work, and having stacked their arms, they worked with them at hand ready for instant use. Most of the employees on the construction of the Union Pacific were veterans of the Civil War on one side or the other, who, after four years of camp and military life, had found their old habits and associations disrupted and drifted west to take up work similar to what they had been doing during the war. Among the superintendents, managers, and bosses was a liberal sprinkling of military titles. There was plenty of arms and ammunition, and it was boasted that General Casement's track-layers at a moment's notice could be changed into a battalion of infantry. On the occasion of an attack at Plum Creek, General Dodge led a rescue party of twenty men, all strangers to him, and when he gave the command to deploy as skirmishers, he said they went forward as steadily and in as good order as he had seen the veterans climb the face of Kenesaw Mountain under fire.

Those who faced the greatest peril were the surveyors. Their work could be done only by stringing out, which made them particularly vulnerable. Many of them were killed and scalped while on the line with transit and chain. During construction stock was run off by the hundreds, cars and stations were burned, and graders, track-layers, tie men, and station-builders were forced to sleep under guard and to work practically under arms.

On May 20, 1867, General Dodge wrote to General William

T. Sherman giving the following facts about recent Indian attacks:

1st   They struck us this side of Sedgewick and cleaned out two of our sub-contractors of everything they had, and scared the workmen out of their boots, so they abandoned the work and we cannot get them back.

2nd   They struck one of my engineering parties on Lodge Pole and took one pair of mules, and notified them to leave, pulling up all our stakes, etc.

3rd   They attacked our tie men in the Black Hills and drove them off the Cheyenne, burning up their traps, etc., and also cleaned out one small party on Laramie Plains.

4th   They attacked Mr. Brown's engineering party, on the 14th at Rock Creek, killing one of his men, Mr. Stephen Clark of New York, taking his stock; and also killed one of the escort, and took part of their stock. While pitching into us, they burned the stage station called Fairview.... We can not hold our men to our work unless we have troops.... Our station men will not stay at the tanks and stations, twenty miles apart, unprotected.... My engineering parties are driven into Sanders, Wyo. and General Augur says it is now impossible to increase their escort, and they are working in the worst Indian country you have got.... I tremble every day for fear of a stampede. Have smothered all of recent attacks and kept them out of the press. Augur and myself only know it, but should our men get at the real truth they will stampede. Stage agents, telegraph men, emigrants, tie contractors, and railroad men of all descriptions out there are pressing for protection, and while Augur feels the importance of giving it, how can he if he moves all his mounted men three hundred miles north.... I say nothing to anyone else, because I am determined to go through to Crow Creek if we have to abandon everything else, no matter what the Indians do. Unfortunately, I am sick, have been for two weeks confined to the house, but my presence up there will give confidence to a portion of our men. If we can hold our men to it, we will be in Sedgewick in June. I am looking every day to have them burn our ties distributed up Pole Creek. We have been placing them on every half mile, 1,300 in a place, and if disposed, they could do us irreparable damage.

The determination and grit of General Dodge, the genius of the building of the Union Pacific, are seen in the above letter written in closest confidence to a trusted friend. General Sherman was astonished at the speed with which Dodge was pushing the railroad through. When, about the first of the year 1867, he wrote General Sherman giving his plans for the building of 286 miles through a mountainous region in eight working months, General Sherman, a man used to doing big things himself, answered on January 18: "It is almost a miracle to grasp your proposition to finish to Fort Sanders this year, but you have done so much that I mistrust my own judgment and accept yours."

During the building of the road through the mountains, the Indians at one time determined to wreck a train by stretching a rawhide lariat across the track with thirty braves on each end. Needless to say, they were an astonished crowd of Indians when they saw with what ease the engine pulled the rope through their scorched hands.

In the summer of 1867 the Indians attacked the line of communications, striking at Plum Creek, Nebraska. The section men had been working during the day of August 7 and left their tools alongside the track. When the men left, the Indians, who had been watching them from the islands of the Platte River, took the tools, pulled out the spikes, and raised the rails to a height of two or three feet. Then they took down the telegraph wire and tied blocks of wood to the rails. When the telegraph ceased to function, the operator at Plum Creek sent the section men out to locate the trouble. The hand-car with seven men ran onto the blocks and jumped the track, and the Indians surrounded and killed three of the crew. The other four made their escape in a running fight. About that time a freight train came along and ran into the trap. The engineer and fireman were killed immediately, but the conductor ran back and stopped a second train, which backed into Plum Creek. In the meantime the Indians plundered the cars of the wrecked train, taking all kinds of merchandise, set the cars on fire, and had a big dance and frolic on the prairie, which was lighted by the flaming cars. The next morning a party of men put a flatcar in front of an engine, got aboard with plenty of arms and ammunition, and ran up to the wreck. They found some of the Indians riding around in circles with bolts of calico tied to their horses' tails, and others enjoying themselves around two barrels of whisky. They chased the Indians away and found coffee, sugar, and dry-goods of every description scattered around on the ground. There were boots with the tops cut off—the Indians put the tops around their legs but would not wear the bottom part—about three carloads of merchandise was recovered.

Until the Union Pacific had built out about two hundred miles, Omaha was the local as well as the general headquarters. Subsequently, at intervals as the rails advanced, a new local headquarters, known as the terminus, was established. For a time it flourished, and then, as the road moved west, in a few weeks or months a new town was built at the end of the track. Officially, then, the "end of track" did not creep steadily forward like a snake, but instead progressed by jumps like a giant measuring-worm, hesitating and then reaching out rapidly in another stride. The rail service extended only to the terminal town, and only construction trains went beyond to the actual end of the track. At the terminus the stage-coaches of Wells, Fargo & Company, successors to Ben Holladay, met the trains, and California travelers broke their journey, taking the stage-coach across the gulf between the ends of the two railroads. Naturally, such a terminal point was a busy place and grew to some proportions with a population of about ten thousand.

The first of these terminal points was Kearney, then North Platte, both in Nebraska, followed by Julesburg, in Colorado. Then came Cheyenne, Wyoming, completing the list on the Plains. Beyond the first range of mountains the terminus halted at half a dozen other points. These "roaring" towns were known by various terms, but owing to their propensities for crime, "Hell on Wheels" was the appropriate general name for end of track. Such a town blossomed and flourished in all its wickedness for a

END OF THE UNION PACIFIC TRACK NEAR ARCHER, WYOMING, 1867

short time, and then, when the next terminus was laid out, almost
the whole population pulled up stakes and moved to the newly
designated site. Sometimes the move was made before the railroad
reached the new location, for the old terminal was much farther
from the actual end of the track than the new one.

At Julesburg the rougher element, which composed nine-tenths
of one of these moving towns, figured that they were far enough
west to be beyond the reign of law and order. A group of gamblers
"jumped" the land that General Dodge had set aside for shops
and defied the local railroad officials. Dodge ordered General
Casement to return to Julesburg and restore order. Three weeks
later, when the Chief Engineer visited the town, he inquired,
"Are the gamblers quiet and behaving?" "You bet they are, General. They're out there in the graveyard." General Casement had
descended on the town with a hundred seasoned soldiers and wiped
out the lawless ringleaders.[5]

When it became known that Cheyenne was to be the terminus
for the winter of 1867-68, the site on the prairie named by General
Dodge in honor of the Cheyenne Indians jumped almost immediately from an uninhabited wild to a town of four thousand, even
before the railroad entered. All manner of buildings sprang up,
from dugouts and tents to buildings of stone. The same crowd
of gamblers, saloon-keepers, dance-hall women, and hangers-on
that had moved along with the end of track were there fighting
over town lots. Lots sold by the railroad for $250 were being re-
sold at $3,500. Everything was booming. A store building 55 by
25 feet, built of rough lumber from Denver, was erected in forty-
eight hours. The whole town, with banners, a brass band, and
speeches, swarmed out to meet the first passenger train on November 14, 1867. So was born Cheyenne, which the boomers were
pleased to call the "Magic City of the Plains." Before spring
this winter headquarters numbered a population of ten thousand,

[5] J. R. Perkins, *Trails, Rails and War, the Life of General G. M. Dodge*
(Indianapolis, 1929), pp. 201-202.

and business of all degrees from legitimate to the lowest and most unseemly was going at full blast. Every form of gambling device ever invented was coining money for its operators, and even legitimate merchants were garnering wealth at the rate of $30,000 a month. In April a thousand grading teams and five thousand graders and track-layers, more or less the worse for the winter of life in the glare of the big city, left Cheyenne to resume their toilsome way toward the setting sun. A few weeks later "Hell" was loaded on wheels and proceeded to the next temporary headquarters. Immediately Cheyenne simmered down to a quiet, moral little town of fifteen hundred, and it was fortunate at that, compared with some of the other end-of-track towns which have been almost forgotten.

If, by way of example, one of the "roaring towns" must be selected, perhaps Benton, Wyoming, is as good as any. Located on the intermountain plateau on the edge of the red desert seven hundred miles from Omaha and three hundred miles from Salt Lake City, it became the terminus in July, 1868. As far as the observer could see on the alkali plain around the town, there was not a green tree, shrub, or spear of grass to be discovered. The alkali dust was ankle-deep in the streets and so light and volatile that it made ghosts of the passers-by. Almost everybody was dirty and many were filthy. Water, indeed, was high—a dollar a barrel or ten cents a bucket, for it was hauled from the North Platte three miles away—but this was hardly accounted for by the demand for baths. Twenty-three saloons and five dance-halls were busy by night. The cry of the monte dealer rose incessantly: "Watch the ace." Dancing continued all night, and the place fairly reeked with the vilest of sexual commerce. As Edwin L. Sabin said, Benton was the stage terminus, railroad terminus, and the terminus of many a life. Human life was the only cheap article in Benton. Samuel Bowles, an eye-witness, said of this end of track: "Like its predecessors, it fairly festered in corruption, disorder, and death, and would have rotted even in this dry air, had it outlasted a brief sixty-day life." When the roaring town moved on, there was little left to mark the spot except some mud chimneys, piles of tin cans, and about a hundred nameless graves. Not a stick, brick, or shingle remains to indicate its site.

At Bear River City, in Wyoming, a pitched battle occurred between the law-abiding and the lower element, numbering about a thousand on each side. Three thugs were hanged for murder, and in reprisal the town was attacked on November 9, 1868, by the "toughs." They burned the jail and sacked and destroyed the paper that had been particularly outspoken in its denunciation of the lawless element. They next attacked the stores, but by that time the forces of law and order had got organized and badly defeated them in the battle that ensued. The toughs made an undignified retreat, fifteen of their number lying dead in the streets. Bear River City soon died, leaving no indication that a town of several thousand had stood there. Many of the buildings in the moving towns were portable, with collapsible sections numbered so that their canvas, frame, or steel parts could be fitted together snugly in a short time.

Of all the terminal towns, Ellsworth, Kansas, on the Kansas Pacific, was one of the wildest. Guns were fired indiscriminately, and crowds filled with vile whisky yelled like drunken wild Indians at all hours of the night. It was an impossibility to sleep until nearly daylight, when the drunken revelry in a measure died out. For ninety-three consecutive days there was one or more homicides in the town or the immediate vicinity—one hundred altogether. It was a common saying in the terminal towns that they had "another man for breakfast this morning."

The Irish employees of the Union Pacific were the best of workers, but surrounded as they were by a rude environment, they were inclined to succumb to the wiles of whisky. One time a prominent Irish gang boss died and his camp proceeded to give him a funeral in good old Irish style. The body was placed in a rude coffin and loaded into a two-wheeled cart drawn by a mule.

The bed of the cart was too short to admit the full length of the long coffin, and a considerable portion of it projected outside. After considerable drinking, the group started off, with the cart leading the long procession, toward the cemetery two miles away over undulating hills covered with sage-brush. When they arrived at the desolate graveyard, there were further long-drawn-out ceremonies with much drinking A dissension arose as to who was to speak, offer toasts, and so forth, which ended in a free-for-all fight. While this was going on, the mule, unattended, became impatient and started for camp across country. The sun went down, and the crowd returned to camp, to find the mule there with the empty cart. It was a great mystery where the corpse was. One morning a horse-herder found the coffin at the bottom of a gulch, where it had rolled three hundred feet from a precipice above. It was several days before the funeral ceremonies could be completed.

There was little religious atmosphere in the railroad-building camps. Sunday was a wide-open day with every entertainment going full blast. On the line of the Union Pacific, however, an attempt was made to bring religious opportunities to the workers. Father Ryan, a Roman Catholic priest, was stationed at Columbus, Nebraska, for a time and did a valuable work. His parish extended as far west as the gangs were working, and he is given much credit for his aid in the building of the line. He was a man of commanding appearance, dignified, and yet kind and loved by those who came in contact with him. He knew the moral weaknesses of men and spent the greater part of his time ministering to the needs of the construction crews. He would make his way out to the furthermost grading camps and back, saying mass, holding services, and conducting rites. He settled many disputes in a country where there was no law. Father Ryan had his own attack on the difficult problem of liquor; singling out bad characters and hard drinkers, he signed them up to a non-drinking pledge for such a time as he thought they could hold out without violating it. When he found a guilty man, he went right after him to reform him. He carried a revolver and presented an appearance entirely in harmony with the times.[6]

The last few weeks of construction work were marked by feverish haste. Finally, on May 10, 1869, the two lines met at Promontory Point, Utah, where two engines, one on the Union Pacific tracks and the other on the Central Pacific, ran up pilot to pilot. In an appropriate ceremony, the last tie, made of polished California laurel, was placed, and a silver spike, representing Nevada, and a last one of gold, representing California, were driven. By means of a wire attached to the golden spike, the telegraph carried the strokes of the hammer to the waiting continent.[7] Governor Leland Stanford, of the Central Pacific, and Thomas C. Durant, of the Union Pacific, then shook hands, symbolizing the fact that henceforth there was one transcontinental railroad and one American people.

The business of the railroads the first few years was enormous for the times. The *Bismarck Tribune* on July 11, 1873, called attention to the fact that the Northern Pacific, in less than four weeks after opening a station at Bismarck, had received twelve hundred tons of freight.

The passenger cars were of the platform type, with four-wheel trucks, hand brakes, and link-and-pin couplers. They were lighted with candles and heated with wood stoves. The influx of settlers into the West taxed the new railroads to the uttermost. Emigrant cars were arranged with slat seats and the passengers furnished their own bedding. These cars were equipped with cooking stoves at one end so the travelers could make coffee and cook meals. With the primitive link and coupling pins, the cars gave such a lurch when starting that a passenger had to be an acrobat to keep his feet.[8] Old passenger cars from Eastern railroads and box-cars were

[6] William Brown Doddridge, *Reminiscences*, Ms., Leonard Collection, University of Iowa.

[7] The laurel tie and spikes were removed immediately and became museum pieces.

[8] E. R. Tuttle, "Tales from Old Timers," *Union Pacific Magazine*, July, 1926, p. 6.

pressed into use. Steps were placed on the sides of these converted box-cars, and windows cut in the walls.

The operation of the trains was a dangerous pursuit. Freight brakemen were supplied with wooden coupling-sticks with which to lift and guide the link when making a coupling. This club was carried in a scabbard attached to a belt worn about the waist. Before the day of air-brakes the control of the train was entirely in the hands of the crew. On descending grades it was slowed down from the rear by setting the brakes on the cars. When they were covered with snow or sleet, it took considerable agility to run along the roofs setting brakes. At first there was no caboose on the freight train, but a flatcar at the rear carried a tarpaulin for the crew in case of rain. When the caboose came in, a little later, each one was an arsenal. Even the engineer's cab was supplied with rifles.

Every twelve or fifteen miles was a station with section house, woodpile, and other buildings. Station houses were equipped with rifles and had cellars and loopholes for more adequate protection from the Indians. At various points water-tanks and wood-yards were located. Some of the isolated watering places were lonesome indeed, and it was with the greatest difficulty that the railroad company could get anyone to tend the water-tank. In the period of greatest danger from Indian attacks the water-pumper traveled on a train, and the train stopped several hours while he pumped the tank full. At first the pumping was done by horse power, but later these lonely water stations were equipped with windmills for this purpose. At certain points crews were kept busy cutting wood for the locomotives as well as for the stoves in the coaches that used this type of fuel. At Columbus, Nebraska, in 1867, there was a wood-yard a half-mile in length with thousands of cords of wood.

Because of the isolation, dangers, and hardships, it is not surprising that the men who would engage in operating a railroad under such conditions were little short of desperadoes. Far removed from the refining influences of society, they, like the

ACROSS THE CONTINENT
From the lithograph by Currier & Ives, 1868.

Courtesy of the New York Historical Society, New York City

trapper, buffalo hunter, and Indian fighter, almost invariably resorted to drink and moral laxity. Some were men of high character, but others were criminals of the most hardened type. Many were not known by their true names, and inquisitiveness on the part of a stranger was an invitation to gunplay.

There were no rules against drinking. In some instances the superintendent went to a saloon with the conductor and engineer of an outgoing heavy passenger train and they had a drink around. Unbelievable as it may seem at this time, the first rule upon the subject was that no man should be permitted to start on his run if it was known at the time that he was too drunk to go. Whisky was on almost every engine, baggage-car, and caboose.

Every train carried a telegrapher who served also as brakeman or baggageman. When it ran onto a siding, this operator connected with the telegraph line and got in contact with headquarters.

Trains traveled slowly. In the sixties passenger trains were allowed to travel nineteen miles an hour and freight trains nine miles an hour. Company officials frequently traveled on a sail-car ahead of a train, inspecting company property and attending to other duties. It was no trouble to keep ahead.

The scheduled time between Omaha and Kearney, 190 miles, was 16 hours and 10 minutes, and the fare was $19 or 10 cents a mile.

Crude though these beginnings were, the construction and operation of a railroad over the vast unpopulated plains and mountains was a stupendous achievement. The railroad did more than bind the Atlantic and the Pacific together. It paved the way for the population of the "Great American Desert."

CHAPTER XVII

THE FRUIT OF THE FOREST

NATURE endowed our country with remarkably rich natural resources. Not least among these were the incomparable forests which covered a large portion of the continent. One of the richest pine regions of America lay in the upper Mississippi Valley in the states of Minnesota and Wisconsin. As early as the thirties the conquest of the forests of this region began, and lumbering takes its place as one of the frontier industries along with mining and ranching.

In the earlier days the logger paid no attention to the ownership of the land or the timber. Like the grasses on the Plains a generation later, the forest was open range, and first come first served was the rule. It was argued that squatters who cut the timber on these uncared-for lands were conferring a benefit upon the United States Government, for they were opening the country for settlement and cultivation and were the true vanguard of civilization. The squatters argued, furthermore, that they were pioneers occupying the public domain under an endowed right as citizens inheriting their interest in the government.

The United States officials, learning of this wholesale theft in the name of patriotism and natural rights, sent timber agents to investigate and report regarding the exploitation of the natural wealth of the public domain. Steps were then taken to stop the widespread appropriation of these resources of the nation.

This opened the way for the speculator. Enterprising citizens of Maine, profiting by their past experience in the lumber business and sensing the unprecedented opportunity in logging on this new frontier, hastened to buy extensive tracts. They allowed them to lie until the increasing population of Iowa, southern Minnesota, and the other treeless prairies to the south and west should create an almost unlimited demand for lumber. Then they began operations on a big scale.

The logging outfits of the early squatters were small. A logger was accustomed to make a dugout of a large pine log, load it with provisions and blankets for a several weeks' cruise, and in this craft follow up the streams, noting the timber on either side. On and on he went until he found a location with enough timber on both sides convenient for hauling to occupy a winter in cutting. There a lumber camp was established. Martin Page said that his crew of fifteen men and two yoke of oxen, "got out" about one million feet of lumber each winter in the fifties with one of these small outfits. In the spring it was customary for each camp to "drive" its own logs downstream. The supplies for the preliminary operations, building the camp, and preparing for winter were taken up in boats, but the real operations did not begin until the streams were well enough frozen to allow hauling on the ice, for there were no roads open to the pineries in those early days. Usually it was planned to send the oxen "down the river" before the ice went out in the spring, since it was difficult to get them out over the Indian trails which were in many places swampy and miry when spring opened.[1]

Arrived at the scene of operations, the crew proceeded to build the camp. The "State of Maine" lumber camp, which became the typical frontier type, had but one building about thirty by forty feet with side walls scarcely two feet above the ground. The walls were built of logs, and the roof was made of shakes covered with evergreen boughs or clay. The building was so low inside that for one-third of the width it was impossible for a man to stand erect. The door was at the south, and in the center of the building was an enclosure a foot high and about eight feet square filled with

[1] Martin Page, "The Days of the 50's," *The Daily Telegram*, Eau Claire, Wis., February 24, 1916.

stone or sand. Here was built the fire. In the roof above this open fireplace was the smoke-hole, a large square opening which was supposed to allow the smoke to escape. To facilitate this purpose, shakes split from pine logs were put up under the roof around the opening, extending down in such a way as to form a large wooden funnel to catch as much of the smoke as possible. For further assistance to the draft, sometimes a mud and stick chimney was built on top of the roof, but in most camps this was dispensed with. In some places a hole in the roof eight feet long and three feet wide sufficed without a funnel. The open fire served for heating, part of the cooking, and even lighting, for there were no windows in the low sides of the building.

Along one side of the room was a field bed extending the full length of the building. The men slept with their heads toward the low side walls. Between the logger's feet and the fire at the foot of the bed was a long flat beam called the "deacon's seat." This was one of the unique institutions of a lumberman's camp. On it the logger mounted upon stirring out of his neighborly bed after the night's rest. Here he sat to dress, and again at night it was his last stepping-place before he crawled under the covers. In a jolly row the lumberjacks sat on it before the blazing fire telling stories and cracking jokes to while away the time of the long winter evening. On this seat the logger made his bargain with the boss and received his pay. When in after years his mind turned back to those logging days, the "deacon's seat" occupied a central place.[2]

At the end of the building opposite the door was a projection containing a stove and a pantry. This was the domain of the cook. Across the same end, but not set apart by a partition, was the dining-room, furnished with some rough wooden tables and benches made of split logs. Here the meals were served. Around these tables, during spare hours when the men were not in bed, they sometimes spent their time smoking and talking. In this

2 "The Minnesota Pineries," *Harper's New Monthly Magazine*, March, 1868, pp. 409-423.

"STATE OF MAINE" LOGGERS' CAMP

From *Harper's Weekly*, May 7, 1870.

apartment was to be found a grindstone, much used by the men in keeping their tools in shape but never mentioned by a recruiting officer for the lumber camp. Many hands, when hiring out, never suspected it was part of their duty to keep their axes in order. There, too, was a wash sink, a water-barrel, and various other items of equipment. On one side of the low room was the wood supply and general stowaway.

Near the central log fire hooks and wires were arranged on which to dry wet clothes. A visitor to a Rum River camp in 1867 was given a buffalo robe and allowed to sleep by the fire. Looking up toward the roof, he thought he was in a stocking factory or a moccasin store because of the countless footwear hanging around the roof in the vicinity of the fire. The next morning all were gone, only to reappear again in the same spots at night. The apparel of the logger included heavy socks and rubbers, a mackinaw, and a wool cap.

The so-called field bed, as we have seen, extended the entire length of the building along one side, allowing about two feet for each man. Usually the bed consisted of a plentiful supply of small spruce or hemlock boughs with a log at the head for a pillow, or longer boughs without the log were sometimes used. Often, however, the men folded up their coats and used them for pillows. The entire bed was covered with a single bedspread two inches thick. The men slept "spoon-fashion," all lying on the same side. When one got tired of lying in one position, he would shout, "Spoon!" and everyone would turn over.[3]

Now and then before dozing off some witty fellow would crack a joke which caused a laugh to roll around the whole camp. Once in a while one whose supper of salt pork had created a thirst slid out of bed, went to the water-barrel in the corner, slaked his drought with its ice-cold contents, and, returning, wedged himself into place again. Soon the whole layer was wrapped in sleep born

[3] *Ibid.;* James Holden, "Early Camp Life Reminiscences," *The Daily Telegram,* Eau Claire, Wis., November 10, 1916.

of hard physical labor in the open air. Sheets were unknown, and the men slept in their clothes.

There was little daylight, but that was immaterial, for the lumberjacks were rousted out long before sunrise, were at work by daybreak, and were kept at work until darkness halted operations at night. One veteran lumberjack felt there was too much regimentation in the old-time logging-camp and expressed his criticism in these words:

The work was hard, the management stupid, and its ways beyond knowledge. In general, the governing idea seems to have been mechanical. To arise at a specified time, whether work was to be done or not; to load in food as one would fire a boiler, and at night to herd bedward as one would turn off the steam—this seemed to be all the philosophy there was in the enterprise. A choreboy, usually about 60 years old, awakened everybody with a cow-bell and his piercing voice, liberally applied. In dead of winter the choppers, so urged forth, would reach the woods before there was light enough to work. Then they would light a fire and sit on a log until the day would dawn.

The camp was divided into squads for the labors of the day. One group, the teamsters, hauled the logs; another, the choppers, felled the giant trees; a third, the sawyers, sawed the trees into logs; a fourth, the swampers, prepared the roads. In the fifties the loggers were very particular in their selection of logs. A tree with a lump or bunch on the bark, indicating an inward defect, was rejected. Old-time scalers became very expert at detecting hidden imperfections by outward appearances. At that time the trees were felled with a double-bitted axe by expert choppers who commanded the best wages in camp. Martin Page received $75 a month for this work in the Chippewa Valley. When the tree was down, the choppers, if they escaped alive and unhurt, sprang upon it and began to trim off the branches, working up the tree. In the earlier days the "State of Maine" system was used, in which the trunk was "go-deviled," or dragged whole, on the snow or by means of a sled to the river-bank and cut into logs there.

Within a few years it became the custom to fell trees with a double-cut saw instead of an axe since it was quicker and more economical. This work required swift judgment and sure knowledge. Two men worked together. When they had decided which way they wanted the tree to fall, they took their axes and cut a gash on that side. They then began to saw on the other, using wedges to make the tree fall according to plan. One danger was that when the tree was about half sawed through, the trunk might crack vertically from the bottom up. If this was not stopped at once, the tree would be ruined and the men's lives greatly endangered. The first warning of such an occurrence was a slight sound from within the trunk. Instantly the woodsman who knew his business would cry, "Crack! Whip the saw!" The saw was then swung around to one side or the other and the sawing continued. Sawing on the sides, if executed in time, stopped the splitting. Another danger presented itself when the tree fell. Sometimes it did not fall in the direction planned; sometimes it struck another tree and the trunk was thrown forward or twisted to one side in an unexpected direction. If the forest giant, weighing tons, ever struck the lumberjack, it meant almost certain death. Casualties were numerous.

When the preliminary crackle of breaking wood foretold the fall, the sawyer cried, "Timber-r-r! Down the line! Watch out!" This warning gave the nimble loggers an opportunity to get out of the way while the gigantic trunk crashed through the trees, stripping branches off its neighbors as it lunged to the ground, making the very earth tremble.

When the tree was down and trimmed, the sawyers did their further work. Two men stood on opposite sides of the trunk and, grasping the upright handles of the crosscut saw, drew it back and forth with an easy regular motion, neatly slicing the mammoth trunk into sixteen-foot logs.

The cut logs were loaded onto a sled with the aid of oxen and a log chain. This was hazardous work also, and many men were crushed. Four logs made a bob-sled load to snake to the landing. Then came the next dangerous task, piling them to await the spring thaw, when the stream would rise and take them "down the river."

When the men returned to the camp at night, tired, cold, and hungry, the cook had a steaming-hot supper ready for them. The staple diet consisted of pork and beans. A cook was judged by the quality of his beans, which were baked by the bean-hole method, calling for preparation that was little short of a ceremony. On one edge of the fire a hole about two feet in diameter and about the same depth was dug. A fire was kept burning in this pit until the surrounding soil was thoroughly heated and the hole well filled with good live coals. In the meantime a quantity of beans that had been soaked for twenty-four hours were taken out of the vessel and scalded. With the coolest deliberation, akin to ritual, the cook then selected the right kind of onion and placed it in the bottom of an iron pot. Beans were added until the pot was filled to within six inches of the top. Slices of fat pork were laid across the beans, and a quantity of molasses was poured over all. The pot was then sealed and placed on a nest of coals in the center of the hole. Live embers were packed around and over the pot, and the fire was built over it and kept burning for twenty-four hours. Literally bushels and bushels of beans were consumed in the logging-camps.

Occasionally there was salted codfish, a quarter of fresh beef, or some fresh pork. Sometimes the management was able to trade some flour or tobacco to the Indians for deer meat, but usually the deer were poor and unfit for food during the winter season. There was plenty of flour for bread, and the cook made gingerbread and fried cakes for dessert. Molasses was plentiful, as was tea.[4] Although there was no great variety and the food was plain, it was wholesome and there is little evidence of sickness in the camps.

The tableware was of tin. The cutlery was certainly not silver,

[4] Charles Edward Russell *A-Rafting on the Mississip'* (New York, 1928), pp. 51, 52, 60, 61, 62.

but it was all that was needed, for if the cook neglected to give someone a fork, he readily substituted his jack-knife for it. Every lumberjack carried a knife.

After supper the lumberjacks took turns at the grindstone, which they kept in action all evening getting their axes in shape for the next day's work. Some mended the clothes that were the worse for contact with a pine knot. Some sewed their moccasins with sinew of the deer procured from the Indians. If there were any papers, they were read and reread. Some of the men played euchre or old sledge. During this period of relaxation the woodsmen solaced themselves by smoking what one man has termed probably the worst tobacco ever developed from jimson weed, burdock, and old rope. It was called "Scandihoovian brand," and its sale was one of the perquisites of the employers. Bill Nye said the reason they called this tobacco Scandihoovian was because when it was smoked in Wisconsin folks could smell it in Scandihoovia.

During the long evenings after the camp had been made ready for the winter and the establishment was snug and warm, the crew worked out various means of entertaining themselves. Each one had to contribute a part to an evening's program. He had to sing, tell a story, speak a piece, or whistle. If he was unable to do any of these, he had to put a pound of tobacco in the "poor box." That pound kept him out of trouble for a month, when he had to repeat the performance by way of paying a forfeit.

A game that was often played was known as "hot back." A man stooped over blindfolded with his head in a hat and one hand on the small of his back, while others formed a circle around him. One of the men standing in the circle would hit the hand of the victim, and he would guess who it was. If he guessed right, the striker traded places with the blindfolded one. This game had its variations, one of which was called "hot bottom," wherein the lumberjacks gave the victim a resounding whack on the seat of his pants to the loud laughter of the rest of the crowd.

Another pastime was called "shuffle the broque." In this game the men sat on the floor in a circle. Each man raised his knees, and a rubber, mitten, or other suitable article, known as the "broque," was passed around under the archway of knees. A man stationed in the center of the circle was "it" until he found out who had the broque. When he had his back turned, someone would hit him with the broque and quickly pass it on to a neighbor. When the man in the middle discovered the broque, the man in whose possession it was detected was required to take his post in the center of the circle.

A fiddler was as useful in a lumber camp as was an ox-driver, and the wise boss saw to it that he had a fiddler when he made up his crew. On Saturday nights the boys had a "hurrah." For this a stag dance was the customary program. A number of these sons of toil were designated ladies, and a bandana handkerchief tied around the arm indicated that for the evening *he* was a *lady*. There were no feminine guests to lend a touch of refinement to the scene of gaiety, and soon the place was in a tremendous uproar.

The songs of the lumberjack, like those of other frontier figures, were often plaintive and portrayed the loneliness and hard and hazardous life of the woods. A tenor was a welcome addition to a crew, and among the songs he was apt to sing was this:

> A lumberjack's life is a wearisome one.
> Although some say it's free from care,
> Its swinging an axe from morning to night
> In the forests wild and drear.
>
> Or sleeping in the bunkhouse dreary
> While the winter winds do blow;
> But as soon as the morning star does appear
> To the wild woods must we go.

Or perhaps the tenor sang:

> The rapids they were raging,
> The waters were so high;
> Says the foreman to Swan Swanson,
> "This jam we'll have to try."

Swan Swanson answered like a man,
"That's what I aim to be,"
But while he spoke the jam it broke
And Swanson he went through.[5]

From the "deacon's seat," through the tobacco smoke so thick it could be cut with a knife, there proceeded another specimen of folklore in the form of "logger's lingo," myths, tall yarns, and ghost-stories. There were tales of cruisers' adventures, of warfare between rival camps, of records hung up by camps or individuals. There were stories of ghosts who inhabited the dark and gloomy forest. There were yarns about strange animals. One such animal, angry at man's intrusion in the woods, lived in a hollow tree and dropped large limbs on the passers-by. The hoop-snake remained abroad all winter, rolling about with its tail in its mouth. When it stuck the poison barb of its tail into the handle of a peavey, the timber swelled so that Paul Bunyan, the great hero of the lumber-jacks, cut a thousand cords of stove wood from it. The French-Canadians, a superstitious people, had originated some of these stories, and they were greatly magnified and embroidered by the Scandinavians and other nationalities who came later. A logging-camp was often a strange medley of nationalities.

No work was done in the camp on Sunday, and those of the men who remained sober did their laundering, which primarily consisted of washing their shirts. A large lard can was placed over an open fire out-of-doors, and the men took their turns at boiling and scrubbing their clothes. Some cut each other's hair, and some even shaved, although most of the men allowed their beards to grow till spring. When these tasks were over, the time was passed in games of horse-play and hazing the newcomer in one way or another. A favorite joke to play on a "greenhorn" was to send him to the cook to borrow the bean-hole or to the camp office to

[5] From *Upper Mississippi: A Wilderness Saga*, by Walter Havighurst, copyright, 1937, and reprinted by permission of Farrar & Rinehart, Inc., Publishers. The writer is indebted to this volume for much of the lore of the Northern Woods.

obtain a "round turn." The devil-may-care lumberjacks laughed heartily as the greenhorn went from place to place seeking the alleged tool. The terms were drawn from woods slang for well-known activities or objects. A "round turn," for example, was a circular track where teamsters turned around at the end of the haul. A "push" or "big push" was a camp foreman. A "gazebo" was an ordinary hand. "Flaggins" was a dinner in the woods. The "wanigan" was the camp commissary where the men bought everything from tobacco to clothing. "Logging berries" were prunes. The "turkey" was the duffle-bag in which the hand carried his belongings. The "nose bag," as the name would indicate, was a haversack for carrying cold lunch.

In the seventies and eighties certain fairly well defined changes took place in the logging business. Great lumber companies, such as the International Company, the Northwest Company, Weyerhaeuser, and others, operated in the great North Woods. Each of these sent a man, known as a timber-cruiser, through the unexplored forests. With a hundred-pound pack of supplies and equipment on his back, he went far inland, fifty miles or more from the nearest settlement. With a pocket compass and by counting his steps, he located himself fairly accurately and took note of the different species of trees and their quality. At the close of the day, after building a fire, he jotted down the observations which were to form the basis of his report to his company, noting the terrain, the running water, swamps, the kinds of timber, and how many thousand board-feet an area would produce. The timber-cruiser was to the lumber industry what the prospector was to the great mining companies, the scout whose information opened the rich natural resources to exploitation of capital. On his camp-sites grew large logging-camps and, later on, cities.

In the boom era a lumber camp housed a hundred men who would cut several millions of feet of pine during the five-months season when the ground was frozen. The old "State of Maine" camp gave way to the more elaborate camp with its bunk-house,

A COOK SHACK OF THE SEVENTIES

cook-shack, shop, commissary, company headquarters, and stable. The old fare of beans and salt meat gave way to fresh meat, quantities of mashed potatoes, whole stacks of pancakes, pitchers of syrup, pans of prunes, dried peaches, rice pudding, and rows of apple pies. The men ate of this bountiful repast quickly and silently and stalked across the crunching snow of the camp yard to the bunk-house, which had changed with the years. There were now double-decked bunks. The buildings were heated by drum stoves and lighted with kerosene. Pictures from the *Police Gazette* and other magazines sometimes adorned the walls.

The cook, to do violence to nature, was the "king bee" of the camp. He was well paid and fed his men exceedingly well on the allowance of thirty cents a day per man. It was necessary to bake, stew, fry, broil, and roast great quantities of meat and vegetables to assuage the appetites of men who had worked hard all day in subzero weather and had generated unbelievable capacities. The cook's assistant was known as the "bull cook" or "cookee." Often such a man had been injured when a load of logs overturned or he had been struck by a falling tree and afterward was able only to help in the cook-house. He tended the fire, carried water, peeled potatoes, and washed the dishes. It was his duty to call the men, and entering the bunk-house with his five-foot horn or ringing a cow-bell, he walked up and down the bunk rows creating a din such as not even the soundest sleeper could sleep through. He supplemented his musical achievement with, "Roll out! Tumble out! Daylight in the swamp!" A volley of hob-nailed shoes sometimes followed this summons, but his next was more welcome: "Come and get it! Breakfast on the boards." Soon the men were in the cook-shack stowing away pancakes, hash, and beans and washing them down with scalding-hot coffee. The teamsters had an even longer day than the other members of the crew, for they had to feed and groom their horses before the other lumberjacks were up and care for them after work ceased.

With a larger crew more ground was covered in a given period, and "the works" gradually crept farther from camp. At noon the bull cook in a box-sled with numerous pots and pans of piping-hot food drove along the "tote road" to the scene of activities. There he built a fire, and after giving his dinner-horn a blast that could be heard five miles in the clear, still air of the frozen north, he uttered a half-human, half-wolf cry: "Ye-ow! 'S goin' to waste!" The men needed no second invitation but swarmed around the brush fire, where, in spite of the blaze, beans froze on their plates and tea on their whiskers.

New methods of getting the logs to the stream appeared in the new era also. The Michigan lumbermen introduced the ice road. With this system every evening "road monkeys" drove tank sprinklers along the trail to ensure a heavy coating of ice in the ruts made by the sleds. Great loads of logs which would make thirty thousand feet of lumber moved along the ice trace. The drivers each had an assistant, known as the "hay man," who threw hay or sand on slopes to check the speed of the loaded sled as it descended.[6]

The camps in the earlier years had from fifteen to twenty-five men and paid from forty dollars a month for experienced skilled woodsmen to thirty or thirty-five dollars a month for others. The lumberjacks received their keep in addition to this, which was a drawing card used by the recruiter in persuading men to sign up for the winter at a job where there was no boarding-house bill to be met.

When the winter's work of felling the trees and snaking them to the stream was over, the task of the logger was only fairly begun. In the early days everyone drove his own logs. When the spring thaw came and the water rose, the logs were started on their way downstream to the sawmill. It was comparatively simple at that period to float the winter's crop downstream. There was little difficulty in a man's getting his logs mixed up with his neighbor's, for neighbors were few and far between. In those early times the

---

[6] Havighurst, *Upper Mississippi*, Chap. XVIII.

owner simply made a "bark mark" on all logs with an axe. He made all his driving equipment, which was crude indeed, right in camp. Several dugouts were made from large pine-trees for the purpose of conveying the supplies which were taken with the logs and crew on the drive down the stream. The crew consisted of lumberjacks who continued with their boss on this work at a higher wage. Sometimes there were tents for the crew, but usually there were not. The ordinary shelter in stormy weather consisted of a blanket stretched across a pole, as in the keelboat business. The cook's boat, known as the "wanigan," followed the drive; four times a day it pulled to the bank, and the cook spread his table and blew his horn, which resounded through the woods bringing the hungry loggers to their baked beans. At night the men slept on shore near the "wanigan."

When the rivers became crowded with logs, it was necessary for the owner in addition to cutting the "bark mark" to stamp the ends of his logs with an iron stamp. These end stamps were known as the general log mark, and each logger had his mark recorded, much the same as brands on the cattle range were recorded later. Over two thousand of these marks were recorded in distinct and different characters. A double X was the mark of the Weyerhaeusers, and an I K that of Ingram & Kennedy.

The pick of the logging crew combining hardihood, strength, and daring were hired to "drive" the logs. When the thaw came, the lumberjacks laid aside the axe and saw and took up the peavey, cant-hook, and pikepole. They discarded their low rubbers and put on calked boots that would not slip when they stepped from log to log in the water during the drive. They exchanged their heavy wool pants for overalls. When the ice was out of the river, the crew proceeded to the landing and began "breaking" the rollways. Suddenly with a tremendous splash the great pile of logs plunged into the flood and the drive was begun.

For the next few weeks the streams were crammed with thousands of logs floating at all angles and giving the impression of the greatest chaos. As they raced downstream, sometimes something stopped the lead logs and the great mass of trunks would grind and twist, finally piling up in a jagged crush. The driving crew with iron-tipped pikepoles guided the unorganized mass, riding the logs, running here and there, removing obstructions, and doing feats of bravery as they dashed over waterfalls, down rapids, and through sluiceways. Sometimes they missed their footing and slipped into the ice-cold flood. Perhaps their only inconvenience was that of working in wet clothes. Again, when a driver lost his footing, he might be crushed by the mass of crunching, grinding logs.

Sometimes in spite of all precautions a jam occurred. This consisted of literally acres of logs "freezing" into a solid mass which would not move. The crew then searched for the key logs that were holding the vast pack. A skilful driver could punch a log and free the whole lot. A jam at one time blocked the Mississippi above Brainerd, Minnesota, for sixteen days and was finally broken by five charges of dynamite. During the drive a second crew brought up the rear, pushing the stranded and water-logged timbers into the current.[7]

Sometimes these drives led to a sawmill. At first the logs were sawed by a crude "muley saw," but this was replaced by the buzz-saw whose rotary blade could cut twenty times as much lumber. But not all logs were taken to a near-by sawmill. Some were taken to the rafting booms. As early as 1831 logs were rafted down the Chippewa River, and from this small beginning the great rafting industry grew.

A bayou or estuary with a sluggish current was ideal for raft-building purposes. When the logs came helter-skelter into this slough, they were assorted into booms according to the marks they bore. It took a keen eye to identify the marks as they swept along,

[7] William H. C. Folsom, "History of Lumbering in the St. Croix Valley, with Biographic Sketches," see Minnesota State Historical Society, *Collections*, Vol. IX, pp. 291-324; Daniel Stanchfield, "History of Pioneer Lumbering on the Upper Mississippi and Its Tributaries, with Biographic Sketches," *ibid.*, pp. 325-362.

but the sorters were specialists. The logs were placed side by side and lengthwise of the stream. At each end of each log holes were bored. A birch limb was laid across the logs and a binding withe of split burr-oak was bent over it to form a huge staple. Then pegs were driven into the holes to hold the staple secure. A section of logs thus fastened together was known as a "string." In forming it, care was taken not to put side by side logs of the same length, but to break the joints and so make the string as strong as possible to keep it from tearing apart as it went around bends. Each string extended the length of the raft, and at each end of a string was a great sweep-oar. A raft with ten oars at either end was a ten-string raft. One observer saw a fifteen-string raft which covered more than three acres and looked like a vast field afloat. When the raft had been constructed, the boom that had held the logs was opened and the raft slid out upon the river and down its muddy reaches toward the mill.[8]

Rafting on the St. Croix River was very difficult because it was necessary to get through the St. Croix Lake where there was almost no current. Sails were tried as motive power, but all too often the wind blew the wrong way for days. Rafters tried both rowing and poling, but neither worked very well since the raft was large and unwieldy and the water in many places too deep for poling. The solution finally hit upon was to take an anchor with a rope about a half-mile long in a skiff, go out ahead and hunt a place where the bottom could be touched, drop the anchor, and have all hands pull on the line until the raft was up to the anchor. After a number of these grueling hauls, with the program continuing with two crews day and night, the raft was finally got through. Sometimes the anchor would stick in the mud and it took both crews hours to get it up.

As time passed, division of labor appeared. The logger no longer rafted his own logs but hired a raft pilot to drive the logs for him to some downstream point. Sometimes pilots worked by

[8] Russell, *A-Rafting on the Mississipp'*, pp. 78-79.

the month, by the season, or by the trip, the owner of the logs paying all the expenses; but others had crews of their own, paid all their expenses, and ran the rafts under a contract of so much per thousand feet.

When the logs arrived at the sawmill and were cut into lumber, it too was made into a raft. The mill was located somewhat above the river-bank. By means of a roller track, the sawed lumber was run from the mill down to the rafting-shed on a lower level. There, on a balanced movable platform, it was fitted into a frame or heavy crate to form a solid mass of lumber sixteen feet wide, thirty-two feet long, and from twelve to twenty inches deep. Some layers were laid crosswise to tie the whole together. The crate was made of two-by-twelve grub plank, and sides and ends were held solidly together top and bottom by heavy two-inch hickory or oak pins. Such a unit was known as a "crib." When it was completed, the platform was tipped up, allowing the crib to slide gently into the water. There were usually three of these platforms to allow the lumber to be separated into three grades. A number of cribs were fastened into regular strings by strong couplings of plank in front and rear and also crosswise. A raft of three strings, each ten cribs longs, was typical for the Chippewa, and from one hundred and twenty to one hundred and sixty cribs were not unusual in a raft on the Mississippi. After the raft was finished, lath, shingles, timbers, and pickets were piled on the lumber cribs. These were known as the "top loading."

In the middle of each crib at each end of the raft, one for each string as on the log raft, was an immense oar. The handle was made of a small tree-trunk eight or ten inches in diameter and thirty feet long. The blade was made of a plank twelve inches wide and two inches thick at one edge and one inch at the other, which was fastened to the butt-end of the handle with wooden pegs. When properly mounted the oar was nicely balanced and swung freely.

A load of sand was thrown on the middle of the raft, and on it the cook built his fire. By the fifties tents were provided for the crew. The crew of a ten-string raft consisted of a pilot, a cook, and twenty lusty oarsmen. The ten best men took their places at the bow and the other ten pulled at the stern.[9]

As early as 1842, Stephen Hanks, a cousin of Abraham Lincoln, took to St. Louis a lumber raft twenty cribs in length and six cribs wide (120 cribs), roughly 640 by 100 feet. The business was new on the Mississippi at that time. The first lumber raft had been run down to St. Louis only three years before, and some of the tricks of the trade were still to be learned. No one dared to run at night, for to guide a raft through those twisted channels by daylight was all anyone wanted to undertake. In tying the monster up for the night, a heavy rope attached to the raft was wrapped several times around a tree. When the rope tightened up, sometimes it pulled the tree out by the roots, and sometimes the rope broke and flew through the air a perilous missile. Hanks invented a mooring device, to be built on the raft, which enabled the crew to tie one end of the rope to a tree on shore, hold the other end until it became taut, then slacken and ease it until the raft was brought gradually to a stop. This scheme was soon adopted on all rafts.

Indians sometimes swarmed over the raft at night, demanding whisky, threatening, and brandishing weapons. Snakes also were a vexation. If the raft tied up before sundown, old rafters aver that snakes were sure to come on board. Then, too, the dense swarms of mosquitoes nearly blinded the crew.

In a narrow place in the river great skill and hard work were required to keep the raft off the rocks. When a raft did go aground, it was necessary to uncouple the cribs and get them off the best way possible. Sometimes in the narrows or at rapids the raft was split and the two halves taken through separately. At some places there was a rapids' pilot who did nothing else but guide rafts over a bad stretch.

[9] Patrick Gunn, "Lumbering in the Chippewa Valley," *The Eau Claire Leader*, Eau Claire, Wis., April 12, 1916; Walter A. Blair, *A Raft Pilot's Log* (Cleveland, 1930), pp. 34, 35.

As time passed, the lumber-rafting crews put up a small shanty for cooking, some little low dog-houses for sleeping-quarters, comfortable bunks, and a floor, for there was plenty of lumber. There was an abundance of plain food as a rule, but when supplies did run low and the pilot's credit was not good, the men managed to forage off the country very efficiently. Hen-roosts, pigpens, and even calf-yards suffered. On one such occasion, when the rafters were very hungry one morning, a farmer missed a fat two-year-old heifer after the raft had passed his farm. After a long, hard row in a heavy skiff he overtook the suspected party. The dressed beef lay on the logs near the center of the raft covered with canvas, and when the irate husbandman approached it, the pilot mournfully accosted him with, "My friend, I'm glad to see you, I'm in big trouble. My crew are all afraid of me." "How so?" "Well, you see," he responded, "that white thing down there?—Smallpox, one of my best, the cook. I stay and work with him all night but tain't no use. Now, my friend, you look like a brave man. I want you to help me take him ashore and bury him." In the twinkling of an eye the old farmer was gone, almost fallen in the river in his haste to get away.

The rafting crews soon gained an unenviable reputation. They got drunk at any time opportunity offered and defied superior authority. Upon their arrival at St. Louis they were paid off and returned on the steamboat. Sometimes in season there would be several raft crews on each steamer. They freely patronized the bar, and the red liquor soon got in its work. Then there was much fighting on the lower deck, to the annoyance of crew and deck passengers. The carousal lasted until the rafters arrived back in Minnesota broke and were glad to go to work on another raft. The pilot took passage in a cabin.

A Wisconsin lumberman who in the early days ran his lumber to St. Louis estimated the loss by breakage in passing the rapids at five per cent or one-twentieth of all the lumber run over the rapids. In the forties the price for rafting lumber from Minnesota to

St. Louis was $3.00 a thousand feet, and $3.50 for logs, with 25 cents a thousand for lath and shingles carried as freight.[10]

After the Civil War the practice of towing rafts was begun, and soon hundreds of the blunt-nosed raft-boats were pushing their loads ahead of them. It took great skill to avoid the islands and sand-bars and to follow the often narrow and sinuous channel. In negotiating the sweeping bends with the great structure, it was sometimes necessary to loosen the cross-lines and allow the raft to bend itself into the shape of the channel. A skilful pilot could twist a raft into a C or an S in "making" a difficult narrow channel. Famous raft pilots received $500 a month.[11]

The lumberjack was a child of the forest. He might grumble at his hard lot while in the woods and swear he would never sign up again, but after going "down the river" and spending his winter earnings in carousal, by autumn the call of the forest was in his veins. When the word went out that the big companies had their swampers and surveyors in the woods preparing for the winter's cut and were engaging crews, the lumberjacks, clad in new mackinaws, crowded around the recruiter eager to sign up to work thirteen hours a day in weather twenty below zero. And shouldering their heavy "turkeys," they were off again for the great woods "up the river."

[10] C. E. Freeman, "Menomonie: Is Set Back in 1846," Ms. in Minnesota State Historical Society Library.
[11] Havighurst, *Upper Mississippi*, p. 192.

CHAPTER XVIII

THE VANGUARD OF SETTLEMENT

IMMEDIATELY in advance of the vast tide of settlement which inundated the virgin lands marched the surveyor with compass, chain, flags, and stakes. The Commissioner of the General Land Office at Washington had general charge of the public domain, and under his supervision on the frontier were land districts comprising the land now included in a state or sometimes in two states. The surveying of each district was in charge of a surveyor-general. From time to time, as Congress appropriated the money for surveying the land, the surveyor-general let contracts for surveys within his district. Such an arrangement was drawn up between the surveyor-general and the contractor, who was known as a deputy United States surveyor. The covenant included a legal description of the land to be surveyed, an agreement about the methods to be followed in the work and the making of plats, notes, and description of the land, together with a guarantee of the amount of pay. The surveyor furnished guaranties in the form of bondmen who would forfeit their bonds if the work was not completed or was poorly executed.[1]

About three hundred different individuals and firms did surveying in the present state of Minnesota. Many of these had a number of contracts at different times, swelling the whole number of contracts to double the number of individual contractors.

The deputy surveyor took an oath that he would faithfully discharge his duties, and all the members of his party likewise swore that they would do their work truthfully and accurately. On

---

[1] Dwight Agnew, *The Government Land Surveyor as a Pioneer*, Ms., Master's Thesis, University of Iowa, 1938, p. 9.

account of difficulties in transportation and communication, surveyors in isolated districts were empowered to swear in their assistants. An oath written in the front of the book of field notes kept by the surveyor was sworn and signed by the different employees.

The deputy surveyors were drawn from many sources in civil life, from newspaper editors and physicians to farmers. Moses K. Armstrong, delegate to Congress from Dakota, held a contract to survey land in the Missouri Valley. Many of the deputies secured their contracts by political pull, and the political support of the party in power was a paramount factor in the selection of the man, although at this date it is hard to see the connection between one's views on national politics and his fitness for surveying in the western wilderness. The following letter now found in the Nebraska state surveyor's office illustrates the type of recommendation no doubt received by the surveyor-general many times:

We recommend to your favorable notice Mr. J. L. Cozad of East Cleveland. We know him to be an experienced, practical, surveyor and engineer of high standing; perfectly responsible; and in every respect worthy of your confidence and esteem. He is a warm supporter of the administration. By letting him a contract, you will confer a favor upon a large circle of his democratic friends, as they feel assured that through him the department will be well served.

The business of the deputy surveyor involved a certain amount of capital and an efficient organization. When the coveted contract was secured, he ordinarily was miles from the land to be surveyed. It was his first task to buy equipment, hire assistants, and journey to the field of operations.

Among the surveying instruments and tools required were one solar compass, one chain, eleven tally pins, two marking tools. For note-taking and clerical work there were needed ink, pens, pencils, field-books, mapping and writing paper, India rubber, and "mouth glue." In a prairie country the surveyor traveled to his place of labor in a wagon, or occasionally in Dakota Territory, as in the case of Moses K. Armstrong, in a Red River cart. In a wooded region pack-horses were used to carry the instruments and provisions. Sometimes, in the lake country, boats were the means of transportation to the scene of work. The camp equipment included a large tent for the surveyors and a smaller one if packmen were used to carry equipment and supplies. William A. Burt, inventor of the solar compass, enumerated the necessary articles as six Mackinaw blankets, two dozen boxes of matches, four tin pails made to fit into one another, and two "half-round" cans which would fit inside the pails, together with fourteen tin basins, three light frying-pans, two tin pepper-boxes, one meat knife, and two mixing cloths (for mixing bread) made of heavy cotton drilling one yard square. In addition to the above culinary equipment, each member of the crew had a knife, fork, spoon, and a "soldier's drinking cup." Besides there were such miscellaneous articles as needles, awls, thread, twine, small cord, and tacks for mending boots.

The members of the party wore wool hats at all seasons. The trousers were large and durable. A light coat was furnished with waterproof pockets for the protection of notebooks and other papers. A large silk handkerchief was tied around the neck and ears as a protection against mosquitoes and flies in infested regions. The boots were larger than those ordinarily worn, and the uppers were protected by the sole which projected a quarter of an inch around them, preventing the bushes and thorns from tearing and lacerating the upper part of the boot. Hobs in the soles prevented the wearer from slipping. The flagman wore a red-flannel shirt in order that he might be readily distinguished.

After having ridden perhaps a week or two in a jolting wagon, the party arrived in the area of its labors. Before beginning his work the deputy was obliged first to find the corner of some previous survey in order to have a starting-point. In locating this the field notes of the former surveyor or the information given by settlers often enabled the surveyor to get his bearings. Usually,

SURVEYORS' CAMP, CACHE VALLEY, UTAH

From a photograph by W. H. Jackson.

however, there were no settlers, and often Indians, buffalo, or cattle had removed the stakes and other surveyor's marks. Sometimes several days were spent in tracing lines to the starting-point of the new survey. To the surveyor with a crew of men on pay and a definite time limit in his contract, such a delay was vexatious indeed. One green deputy, after hunting for his starting-point for several hours, became discouraged and cried, "I will give any man $50 that will show me my starting point." [2]

On the prairie the camp was often made on a stream where wood and water were to be had, and the crew traveled perhaps four or five miles to their work. Sometimes the surveyor made a cache of his surplus supplies at some convenient place, lifting it when he ran low. When in a heavily timbered region, the surveyors were sometimes obliged to leave their pack-horses behind and for several days at a time pack all their provisions and bedding on their backs. In such country a number of packers had to be hired in addition to the regular surveying crew. The portage-strap sometimes used for packing was made of leather and was ten or twelve feet in length. The middle portion was two feet long and three inches broad in the middle, tapering each way. At the ends of this broad strap were secured leather thongs which were tied around the pack to be carried, and the broad part was placed over the forehead or chest. Other types of carries also were used to transport the packs, which weighed from seventy-five to a hundred and twenty pounds each.

The deputy and his crew worked from sunrise till sunset summer and winter. With the earliest rays of the dawn they were up and taking their breakfast, and they were early on the line ready to utilize every moment of daylight, since, as one deputy complained, the solar compass could be used only about ten hours each day.

The number in the crew varied with the task in hand. In running the section lines within a township a crew of five men was

[2] *Ibid.*, pp. 17-37.

regularly used. There were the compass man with his instrument, the flagman in his red shirt carrying his rods and flags, two chain-men with their tape, chain, and tally pins, and the axeman with his axe. In the prairie country the axemen were really moundmen, carrying shovels instead of axes, although often retaining the old name. In densely wooded country more axemen were necessary. Other workmen were added in difficult terrain.

Often each man carried his own lunch, and at noon, when a fire was made, the little group sat about the cheering blaze, broiling meat and eating a simple meal. After a brief pause they were at their work once more.

Such a crew could survey a township six miles square in from five to ten days, if no ill luck befell it. A larger crew was used for more important lines, and often extra men, hunters, guides, and packmen, were employed.

In a timber country the boundary corner was to be marked by a tree if one was found at the exact spot. If not, a stone or stake was set and its position indicated by reference to trees adjacent. The description of these, with their distances from the stake, was to be recorded in the field notes.

In a prairie country, stones were to be used if they were to be had in the region. For a township corner a single rock was to be set at the exact corner and a mound of stones raised near-by to identify the place more readily. The section and quarter-section corners were marked by single stones with notches on the side ac-cording to a given code which indicated the exact quarter-section bounded.[3] Since much of the prairie was devoid of stone, the rules provided that a quantity of charcoal could be buried a foot deep at a township corner, a post set, and a mound thrown up around the post. This charcoal to-day marks the spot of the long decayed

[3] As a barefoot lad trudging down the dusty roads of Allen County, Kansas, with a school bucket on his arm, the author remembers these stones set in the middle of the road every half-mile with unfailing regularity. They had rug-gedly resisted the road-grader for a half-century at that time but have since succumbed to road-makers who have clad those quiet country by-paths with hard surfaces, removing completely these old markers of long ago.

post. The township corner posts were to square four inches, and the mile and half-mile posts were to be three inches when squared.[4]

Wood of the most durable variety available was to be used, and the post was to be inserted in the ground in the reverse position to its growth in the tree, since experiments had shown that this tended to prolong the life of the marker. According to the official manual of the fifties, the hole was to be dug two feet deep and the post tamped in with dirt and stone if possible. The township posts were to protrude from the ground at least three feet, and on their squared sides numbers were burned or cut indicating the township and section and red chalk applied to the cut. A mound of earth three feet high at township corners and two and one-half feet at other corners was heaped up around the post so that it protruded only ten or twelve inches above the mound. The earth for the mound was procured from trenches dug with reference to the points of the compass and the quarter-sections marked. After the mound was finished, sod was to be placed on it with the hope that it would grow over the mound and permanently preserve it. The southern boundary of Kansas was marked with a conical mound two feet high every mile, and every sixth mound was four feet high. A stake in the mound had a letter K on the north side. The manual also recommended that the surveyor in making mounds plant the seeds of some tree, fruit-trees adapted to the region being preferred. It was hoped that in time these corners would be marked by clumps of useful trees.

It was allowable to drive charred stakes instead of setting corner posts, and hence these were often used. Before the running of lines was begun, while some of the party hunted the starting-point for the new survey, others cut a quantity of stakes along the stream and piled them in a rick. A fire was then built on one side of the rick to char the points of the stakes. When they were charred sufficiently, water was poured on to stop oxidation. These

---

[4] Apparently there were variations in the required size of posts and manner of setting them. The figures given are those of the manual used on the Plains in the fifties.

stakes could be driven with a maul, which saved hours of time formerly used in digging post-holes. The stake, if charred properly, made a satisfactory permanent marker. In time the post decayed, but the bit of charcoal was left in the ground. Those seeking exact corners nearly a hundred years later can locate them roughly by the difference in the soil in the trenches where the original dirt was removed, and then by careful search can find in the soil the charred bit of wood which is impervious to decay.

When a corner fell in a ravine, lake, or other inaccessible place, a "witness corner," that is, a mound with charcoal, etc., was to be placed near-by and a notation made in the field notes as to where the corner should be with reference to the "witness corner." The field notes of Charles A. Manners, who held contract 109 in the Kansas-Nebraska area, illustrate this point:

Corner in a drain (course N.E.) as the corner could not be permanently established in its true place, I therefore point 100 links on the line East of the true corner, where I set a post in a mound and deposited a charred stake as per instructions for a "witness corner" to section 32 and 33 T 9 N. R. 6 E.

The field notes were very important in the work of the surveyor. The manual called for a description of the land's surface, whether level, hilly, or rolling; the kind of soil; the kind of timber, if any; the trails or roads; the lakes or ponds; the bottom land and its drainage; the improvements; coal beds and other minerals; the cataracts, waterfalls, precipices, caves, stone quarries, fossils and natural curiosities, springs of water, and many other items are mentioned. To the celebrated surveyor William A. Burt goes the credit for the discovery of iron ore in the Lake Superior region.

The field notes were taken in rough draft on the line during the day, and at night by the light of the camp-fire the surveyor expanded these hasty jottings into the book of field notes which at the conclusion of the contract were deposited with the surveyor-general of the district.

The deputy, by means of his compass and the aid of his flagman, determined the course of the line. Before 1835 lines to be laid on the true meridian had to be run by observation on Polaris in a country underlain with minerals, since the magnetic compass was useless on account of the deflection of the needle in the presence of mineral deposits containing iron. In cloudy weather a week would sometimes go by without so much as a chance to observe the stars. In 1835 William A. Burt invented the solar compass, which was a valuable addition to the instruments used in the past. It made observations in the daytime possible, but even this instrument was limited in that it could not be used in cloudy weather or at night. It proved a godsend in the iron region in Minnesota, however, where sometimes the iron deposits caused the needle of the magnetic compass to point a few degrees to the south of west. Sometimes even with this device parties were held up weeks waiting for sunshine.

The task of the chainmen was to measure the distance along the line and inform the compass man when forty chains or a half-mile had been traversed so a stone or post could be set. To ensure exact measurement eleven tally pins about a foot in length were used. One end was pointed and the other end had a loop in which pieces of red cloth could be tied to make the pin readily visible.

Every precaution was taken to avoid mistakes in counting the number of chains. When the two chainmen started measuring, the forward chainman carried the pins. Sticking one in the ground at the starting-point, he successively inserted them at his end of the chain as the measurements were taken. When the last of the pins had been stuck, he cried "Tally!" This cry was repeated by the after chainman, and both registered the distance by slipping a thimble, button, ring of leather, or something of the kind on a string worn for the purpose, or by some other convenient method. The rear chainman, who collected the pins as he passed them, then came up, and having counted the pins in the presence of his mate in order to double-check against loss, he took the forward end of the chain and proceeded to set the pins as before. Thus the chainmen alternated, with one at the forward end on the odd tallies and the other on the even.

Accuracy required that the measured line approximate an air line as nearly as possible. It was necessary therefore always to measure with the chain level. Precautions were taken also to stretch the chain to its utmost tension and to ascertain by dropping a plumb-bob the exact spot where the tally pin should be stuck. A chain of two poles (thirty-three feet) was used on rough ground, but on uniform ground a four-pole chain was used. All measurements were indicated in terms of the four-pole chain of fifty links, however. With this sixty-six foot chain each tally represented 220 yards, and four tallies made a half-mile. Each day the surveyor was required to measure the chain and adjust it by a measure of the standard chain he was required to possess, and he had to turn it in to the surveyor-general for inspection when the contract was fulfilled.

The men were less accurate in the afternoon than in the morning, and therefore some deputies had their camps so arranged that the men could take dinner and rest in camp during the heat of the day. This ensured more reliable work.

The surveyors were sometimes absent from civilization all summer when on a big job. In spite of this they managed to while away the time in a fairly enjoyable manner. W. A. Richards, who surveyed the northern boundary of Wyoming in 1873, in his journal entry of September 16 described his camp as a good specimen of a surveyor's camp. It was a bivouac of boughs in the woods with a roaring fire of pine logs before it. There was heavy timber all about the little party. On one side the mules were tied up for the night. On the other side were their packs. A dressed deer ornamented a tree near-by, and the boys were sitting around the camp-fire having their regular evening game of euchre. There, in the shadow of the giant trees of the forest which had seen the trapper come and go, the tired surveyors, forgetting the seemingly insurmountable difficulties of the day, took a smoke both from the wood fire and from their pipes. The deputy wrote out his field notes and some who kept diaries posted them to date by the light of the fire.

Sometimes the men read books, packed long miles for the purpose. Richards carried copies of *Harper's Weekly* with him. He recorded having read *Martin Chuzzlewit*, *Tom's Vindication*, and *Nicholas Nickelby* during the summer's work.

Sometimes an emigrant train crossed the path of the surveyors and they enjoyed a social evening together. The Wyoming-boundary surveying party spent the evening of May 27, 1873, in that manner. Among other amusements they voted one man the handsomest male in the crowd and a lady presented him with a cake. Emigrant trains, troops of soldiers, or hunters in many cases formed the only contacts with the outside world, giving the surveyors papers and carrying their letters to friends in civilization. The records show that when two surveying parties came together as their lines became adjacent in Nebraska, one party invited the other to take supper with them and celebrate as a result of the "good closing" they had made.[5]

Often the men took turns at cooking. Bread-making was one of the chief tasks. The canvas mixing cloth was spread on a blanket on the ground. Flour was poured on it and a hollow in the flour was filled with grease. Salt and soda dissolved in warm water were added and the mixture stirred until it was of the proper consistency to knead. The dough, when formed into loaves, was baked in the frying-pan.

From all indications, dried beans, rice, and salt pork were the staple foods, supplemented with onions and potatoes, together with some dried apples, tea, coffee, and maple sugar. Game and fish often greatly enriched the otherwise plain fare, but the old staple frontier diet of mush and molasses, corn-bread, and salt pork did duty frequently.

[5] W. A. Richards, *Diary Kept by W. A. Richards the Summer of 1873*, Ms., Wyoming History Department Library.

In the land of the evergreen trees, beds were made of fir boughs, shingled over one another a foot deep until a man's weight would not bend them down to the hard ground, thus forming a natural "inner-spring" mattress. On the prairie, sacks of prairie hay, the proverbial "prairie feathers," kept the surveyor's weary bones from striking the uneven tufts of prairie sod. On many nights a portion of the crew spent hours taking an observation. Others each night were detailed to guard the camp from hostile Indians.

The men did not shave from the time they left civilization until they closed their work. Then by way of celebrating they cut their facial foliage before returning to the friends back east.

The surveyor encountered many difficulties. On the prairies as a rule little surveying was done in the winter months since it was almost impossible to set stakes and build mounds in the frozen ground. The problems there were largely the result of the scarcity of wood and water. Sometimes water had to be hauled for miles, and stakes likewise had to be brought great distances. Prairie fires sometimes wrought havoc. W. E. Harvey, near St. Paul, Nebraska, suffered great loss from this cause. On July 31, 1872, while the cook went to the river for water, the grass caught fire and burned all the bedding, clothing, and much of the provisions, but the surveyor saved the ultravaluable field notes. He was obliged to go to the fort and buy blankets and borrow a tent and wagon. A letter from Harvey to the surveyor-general three months later stated that he had been obliged to cease work because the burned prairies offered no subsistence for his stock. John McNevin in December, 1854, wrote that three men had quit him, leaving his outfit idle two weeks while he journeyed to the settlements to procure more help.

Crossing streams was an extremely difficult and nettling task. Surveyor Blair H. Matthews in surveying a mile and a half near the Missouri River crossed a prairie creek twenty-five times. The stream was skirted by a narrow belt of timber, chiefly oak, elm, hickory, walnut, and an entangled underbrush of hazel and vines.

One can scarcely imagine the difficulty attending such a task. Moses K. Armstrong, surveying the south line of Dakota, wrote: "I am quite sick with a cold from wading so much in mud and water."

Surveyor W. A. Richards, while surveying the northern Wyoming line, spent days working on rafts or bridges in order to cross the streams. In one case the timbers for a raft had to be carried three-fourths of a mile. It took seven days to cross the swift-flowing Snake River. A raft would not suffice on account of the rapid current of the stream, and canoes were constructed for the purpose. Surveying down the sides of rugged canyons and across mountain ridges brought its hardships of climbing mountains and fording icy streams. Richards' pack-train floundered through the marshes and tangled willows in an almost impossible slough in an attempt to follow the surveyors on the line, who, of course, followed a "bee" line wherever possible over creek, canyon, hill, and swamp. Once Richards recorded that:

The little black mule fell down a hill and landed heels up against a fallen tree—and if that had not stopped her, she would have gone into the stream in [a canyon].

Two days later he wrote:

Old Jim tipped over on a side hill but did nothing worse than smash a water pail which is bad enough in this country. We are all tired and wet tonight.

The marshland and lake region of Minnesota and parts of Iowa and Dakota could best be surveyed in winter, when the frozen country, impossible to traverse in summer, was readily traveled. Sometimes, beneath the piles of snow, an unfortunate surveyor struck an unfrozen bog or air-hole in the ice and sank in to the waist.

Surveyor Barrows and his party spent the whole winter of 1837-38 in the field in Iowa, living in a canvas tent and losing but three days on account of rough weather. They returned to Davenport on the first of April, having been absent about five months and a half, and during all this time Barrows had not slept in a house and had scarcely seen a white man except his own company.

In the summer heavy rainstorms and electric storms, which are remarkable for their severity on the Plains, wrought consternation at times even when no actual damage was done. On the night of June 8, 1857, the southern Kansas-boundary surveying party experienced one of these awe-inspiring prairie storms. The rain beat through the heavy marine-duck tent, saturating bedding and personal property. Peal after peal of thunder, like tremendous artillery reports, sounded from midnight until three A.M., and the whole surface of the prairies was illuminated almost continuously with a yellow light which gave the air a pronounced odor of sulphur fumes.

The correspondence in the offices of the surveyors-general, some of which has been preserved, gives many a graphic story of the troubles of the surveyor in the field. Since the contract was for a fixed sum, it was to the advantage of the deputy to finish his survey as quickly as possible, but letter after letter records the difficulties of the work and seeks an extension of time for the completion of the contract. Deputy M. McManus, lately from Sangamon County, Illinois, surveying in Nebraska Territory, in his letter of December 2, 1855, to Surveyor-General John Calhoun set forth his tribulations.

I have got placed in the devils fix here. One of my mules broke his neck last night. We found the wretch stone cold this morning. How I am to reconcile John Cradock to it I do not know. (He as you may recollect was the owner.) The mule got his foot and hind leg over his chain and must have expired without a groan as he was hitched close to the tent and we heard no noise. . . . Altogether I have had the "devils" own luck. My contract is as cranky and cross grained as a crab apple tree. I ought to have had it nearly finished by this time and I am not more than half thro'. I have met with crosses, difficulties and delays. Even at my best licks I am thinking you will have to extend me some grace if such a thing is allowed by the department.

Also in closing on the Half Breed Indian Line I fell onto what turned out to be (or seems so to me) the random line run by the surveyor. I closed on it and subsequently find the *true line* in another township with a difference of 12° 0′ in the bearing of the line.

However I am determined to get this at all hazards unless frozen to death. As it would be utter ruin to me to return. I would be irretrievably sunk in debt (which the Lord deliver me from).

He further added that he found surveying in the West a different matter from retracing old lines in Sangamon County, Illinois.

Deputy W. J. Allason, in November, 1869, felt that the surveyor-general was not sympathetic with his besetments and wrote:

You seem very anxious to cause me all the trouble you can from what I hear but the lord knows I cannot see what satisfaction you can reap by taking advantage of the misfortunes of one who has nearly all he is worth in this one contract. I had to correct a mistake in my line and was hindered on account of high water and to cap the climax was burnt out. And now you are so I learn trying to get the commissioner to claim the forfeit of my bondsmen and annul my work altogether. God knows I never did you any harm by word or deed and if you cause my ruin by what may be your legal power may your future happiness and prosperity be in accordance with its justice.[6]

In the heavy timber on the northern boundary of Wyoming only two miles a day were surveyed at times. On the other hand, J. B. Crosby, who was surveying subdivisions on the Plains, stated that he was completing about a township a week.

Not the least among the surveyors' troubles were those arising from the fact that the plow often preceded the compass and squatters occupied the land when the surveyor arrived to measure the public domain. The migration into Iowa began three years before any surveys were made, and when the council of the territory petitioned the government to survey Dubuque and Des Moines counties, it was estimated there were ten thousand inhabitants in those areas. In 1859 the surveyor-general urged that the region

[6] These original letters may be found in the office of the Commissioner of Public Lands of the State of Nebraska.

at the foot of the Rocky Mountains in Colorado be surveyed, estimating that at that time the population numbered about sixty thousand.

Although as a rule settlers were anxious for a survey, there were times when the work of the surveyor was seriously impeded and occasionally held up because the surveys caused great inconvenience and even wiped out preëmpted holdings. In the earlier days so belligerent did the settlers become that the surveyors were driven from the field, and Congress was obliged to pass laws protecting them. These were invoked from time to time in later years to protect the land measures. It can readily be seen what confusion would result when claims, taken according to fancy, were later crossed by the lines of the rectangular survey. A traveler in the Missouri Valley in 1839 said that the lines ran every way, sometimes through a man's house, sometimes through his barn, and in general causing confusion on every hand.

An Iowa deputy subdivided a district on the boundary between Iowa and Minnesota in 1852. When the line was run, it was discovered that the farm of one of the squatters was partly in Minnesota and partly in Iowa and that it was divided among four townships and six sections. Sometimes a spring, mill-site, or other valuable location was divorced from a settler by a survey line and given to a neighbor, this always causing dissension and strife, sometimes resulting in bloodshed.

The Indians were another source of difficulty for the surveyors. Naturally the aborigine objected to this intrusion on his hunting-ground, for he sensed that it was an omen that in time he would lose it. The Indian agent told the Indians the surveyors were only marking the land and did not wish to occupy it. This explanation was not satisfactory, however, and the red men destroyed the markers by pulling up the stakes and scattering the mounds. They threatened the surveying parties and even attacked them, sometimes killing or driving them out of the field. It was often difficult for a deputy to keep a full crew because of their fear of the redskins. On August 19, 1871, E. C. Cunningham, surveyor-general for the area including Nebraska, wrote to a member of Congress that excepting the summer of 1870 there had not been a single season since 1863 that the government surveyor had been permitted to do his work unmolested. Plans were thwarted, work delayed, and in several instances property of government employees had been destroyed. In 1868 a party on the Republican River was attacked, their flagman killed, their supplies and equipage destroyed, and the party driven in until the next season. The same season another deputy had his teams stolen, and the Indians' threatening attitude caused him to abandon his work until the following year.[7]

The most noted attack in Nebraska, however, was that upon Nelson Buck, a surveyor of thirty-four years' experience, in 1869. A letter from him to the surveyor-general, written from Illinois, stated that he was not afraid of Indians and that he wanted a contract for adventure as well as for the monetary advantages. That letter, now yellowed with age, was the death-warrant of himself and his entire party. He and eleven men disappeared on a summer day of 1869 and were never seen or heard of again. To this day their disappearance is one of the mysteries of the Plains. Surveyor-General Cunningham's appeal must have borne fruit, for in the seventies military escorts were sent to guard the surveyors.

Faulty work was common, as might have been expected when practical men were selected without any standardization by means of examinations. If a man wanted a contract, he made his entry into the field not by a test of his skill in the craft, but by the recommendation of a powerful political connection who swore he was a warm friend of the administration. In the earlier times actual fraud had been perpetrated. In Gladwin County, Michigan, in 1815 occurred a notable cheat. It was said the surveyors surveyed that district from a hotel room. At any rate, fifty thousand

[7] E. C. Cunningham to John Taffe, M. C., August 19, 1871, Surveyors' Correspondence, Book I, Office of the Commissioner of Public Lands of the State of Nebraska.

dollars was required to resurvey the district of one hundred and fifty townships. In an effort to prevent a repetition of this kind of swindle, inspectors were sent into the field to check the work of the contractors. This reduced actual fraud to a minimum, but inaccuracies and careless and inefficient work continued. Mistakes and inaccuracies were often found by succeeding surveyors who could not make their work check with the previous survey, and they reported them lest their own work be thought inefficient. A deputy wrote of Surveyor Daugherty who had lost his wagons by Indian raids:

It looks to me as if Daugherty lost his field notes as well as his wagons and outfit and rewrote from memory. His closing distances on standard corners don't correspond with the plats furnished me sometimes by two chains in a distance of eight or ten chains.

When a surveyor's measuring chain was not accurate, the error sometimes would amount to as much as a whole section in every township.[8]

The cost to the government of surveying naturally varied with the years. According to the directions of John Wilson, Commissioner of the General Land Office, to John Calhoun, surveyor-general for the Kansas and Nebraska territories, on August 15, 1854, surveyors were to be allowed $12 per mile for base and principal meridian lines, $8.00 per mile for standard parallels or correction lines, $7.00 per mile for township lines, and $5.00 per mile for sectioning the townships. The southern boundary of Minnesota was surveyed at a cost of $124 per mile in 1852. Wages per day in the fifties ran about as follows: surveyor, $5.00; team, $3.00; five hands, $1.50 each and board.

If the surveyor or a member of his party chose to settle in the locality they had finished surveying, he was in a position to know the best land and could occupy it himself or, as many surveyors

[8] Under such circumstances quarter-sections sometimes had as little as 52½ acres of land instead of the theoretical 160 if the surveying were absolutely accurate.

did, could become a locator or "land-looker," as this agent was sometimes called. For a consideration he led the immigrant to a good piece of land and thereby benefited the settler as well as himself. An honest surveyor soon won a reputation and made a good thing of his new profession.[9]

The surveyor was among the last of that great procession of figures who moved across the stage before the coming of the actual home-making settler, and his work made possible a well organized occupation of the Plains with a minimum of friction and dispute over land holdings.

[9] Agnew, *The Government Land Surveyor as a Pioneer*, p. 72.

CHAPTER XIX

SLAUGHTER OF THE PRAIRIE GAME

WHEN THE WHITE MAN first arrived on the Plains, game was so plentiful the region was a hunter's paradise. As late as 1854 along the Missouri River, which had been a route of ever-increasing travel for fifty years, early settlers described the amount of game as immense. Acres of wild geese rose from sand-bars to form soldier-like lines in the sky. Storks, cranes, geese, swans, ducks, and all other kinds of water-fowl abounded in the greatest quantities. The prairies swarmed with prairie-chickens and quails.[1]

In certain regions, particularly where there were considerable brush and timber, wild turkeys were so numerous that their gobbling was continuous, and great sections of the timber along small creeks served as gigantic turkey-roosts. All these species became scarce with the coming of the white man, but the greatest sufferer was the passenger pigeon, which eventually was slaughtered to extinction. This bird inhabited the region between the Mississippi and the Missouri. Early settlers in Iowa spoke of the migrations of passenger pigeons as so heavy that the continued flight literally darkened the sky. Early travelers along the Missouri River stated that when they alighted on the ground they covered whole acres, and if upon trees, the limbs often broke beneath their weight. If they were suddenly alarmed while feeding in the midst of a forest, according to one observer, the noise they made in taking to the air was like the roar of a cataract or the sound of thunder. A

---

[1] Prairie-chickens and quails actually increased in numbers with the coming of the farmer with cultivated grain which furnished a greater supply of winter food, but declined again when the country became thickly populated.

flight of these birds completely denuded the country of everything that served them for food.[2]

In the eastern Plains area deer abounded from Missouri to Minnesota. They were mercilessly slaughtered by the squatters and first settlers. J. E. Scott, an early settler of Scott County, Iowa, killed one hundred deer in less than two months. He received one dollar each for them and did well financially at that figure. In the late thirties venison sold at the low price of two or three cents a pound. When deep snows with hard crusts lay upon the ground and the deer would break through, dogs were used in the hunt. When the animals were tired out or literally bogged in heavy snow-drifts, men knocked them in the head with axes like the killers in a slaughter-house.

To the west were herds of antelope. They were wary and almost impossible to shoot unless the hunter knew how. The antelope was a curious animal, and the wise hunter, upon getting close to a herd and frightening them, would stick his ramrod in the ground with a hat or some other object upon it. The antelope would come closer and closer in an endeavor to find out what the object was, and the hunter could make a kill.

On the high plains toward the Rocky Mountains great herds of elk dwelt. In the seventies a herd estimated at seventeen hundred head lived in the region of Scotts Bluffs, Nebraska.[3]

By all odds, however, the most important game was the buffalo. Originally it ranged westward from the fall-line near the Atlantic seaboard, but like the Indian the buffalo slowly receded before the white man. By the end of 1802 all of the buffalo in Ohio had been killed, and by 1810 they had ceased to range east of the Mississippi River. By 1820 the reduction in numbers was felt in the trans-Missouri area. General Stephen H. Long expressed the need for the preservation of the buffalo. In the era of the fur trade

[2] John Bradbury, *Travels in the Interior of America* (London, 1819), p. 52; Washington Irving, "Travels in Missouri," *Missouri Historival Review*, Vol. V, pp. 25-26.

[3] Lewis F. Crawford, *Rekindling Camp-Fires* (Bismarck, N. D., 1926), p. 54.

there was a common saying that the buffalo was moving westward before the white man at the rate of ten miles a year.

In 1843 Captain Nathan Boone calculated that over one hundred thousand buffalo robes were finding a market annually, and, taking into consideration the many additional animals killed for food when the hide was unfit for use as a robe, he declared, it could readily be foreseen that the buffalo would soon cease to exist on the Plains.

The naturalist Ernest Thompson Seton gave the following estimates of the numbers of the buffalo: in primitive times, fifty-five million; in 1800, forty million; in 1850, twenty million.[4]

From the period when the white man first began to penetrate the Plains area, hunting buffalo was considered a major sport. Emigrants and merchants on the Santa Fe Trail, not to mention any other white man who penetrated the wilderness, killed the buffalo wantonly for food and for sport. Often a number of animals were killed and not a tenth of the meat was used. The tongue, a piece of the hump, or a loin was taken and the rest of the carcass was left to rot. A factor which hastened the destruction of the buffalo was the decided preference of both Indian and white for the cow, both for the meat and for the robe. Except at the breeding season males and females ran in separate herds. Incredible as it may seem, an observer who visited the Upper Missouri country several times between 1850 and 1860 estimated that the bulls were ten times as numerous as the females. As early as 1860, the *Huntsman's Echo*, a paper published at a road ranch at Wood River, Nebraska, 160 miles west of the Missouri River, reported that the slaughtered carcasses lay so thickly scattered along the road that the stench was fearful.

With the completion of the Union Pacific Railway the buffalo were divided into two great herds. The northern herd ranged through the Powder River country and into Canada and numbered

[4] Ernest Thompson Seton, "The American Bison or Buffalo," *Scribner's Magazine*, Vol. 40, p. 402.

about one and a half million. The southern herd frequented the territory between the South Platte and the Arkansas River.[5]

The buffalo was a migratory animal, moving from two to five hundred miles each season—as a usual thing, although not always, north in summer and south in winter. In some places he migrated east and west, seeking the territory offering the best pasture and protection against the winter's storms. The normal thing seems to have been for the animals to travel in herds of from a dozen to two or three hundred as they fed upon the prairie.[6] Often such herds, each with its own leader and sentinels, grazed within a few yards of one another. When alarmed or when traveling, however, they united into one vast herd. An old weather-beaten animal— some plainsmen say a cow and others declare it was an old bull— acted as leader, and on the extreme outside were sentinels, which upon the first alarm ran into the center of the herd. Closer in were the bulls, forming a protecting ring around the mothers and calves.

From the time when the first white men arrived on the Plains, there was more or less buffalo hunting for sport. Noblemen from Europe, sportsmen, frontiersmen, even women, rode on the buffalo chase. One of the last of these was organized in honor of Grand Duke Alexis of Russia at North Platte, Nebraska, in 1872. General Sheridan and Buffalo Bill were among the hosts. Around the camp-fire the Grand Duke dipped his biscuit into the basin and ate without knife, fork, or plate, like the rest of the crowd, and thanks to Buffalo Bill's tutoring, he killed his buffalo.

The large numbers of buffalo attracted the attention of travelers after overland travel became common. Horace Greeley, westward bound by stage-coach up the Smoky Hill Route in Kansas in 1859, was amazed at the countless animals that darkened the prairie. He was confident that he had seen a million on May 30 of that year.

[5] E. Douglas Branch, *The Hunting of the Buffalo* (New York, 1929), Chap. VIII.

[6] Personal interview with Col. Frank H. Mayer, July 10, 1938.

With the building of the Kansas Pacific Railway across Kansas, excursions to the buffalo grounds were advertised. For ten dollars one could buy a round-trip ticket from Leavenworth to the hunting-ground. The advertisement for the excursion of October 27, 1868, stated that on the preceding hunting trip the party killed twenty buffaloes in six hours. The animals were so numerous at this time that they were frequently shot from the coaches. In such cases the train stopped long enough for the passengers to get out, examine the kill, and take the tongue and part of the hump or hind quarter. At first the engineers thought they could run through the herds of buffalo, but a few experiments taught them that the locomotive was no match for the dense masses of animals. Twice in one week Santa Fe engines were thrown off the tracks by the woolly hordes. Sometimes a train was stopped on the prairie for hours while the mighty thundering herd moved past.

While the Kansas Pacific Railway was being built, Buffalo Bill earned his sobriquet by his exploits in furnishing the construction crews with buffalo meat. As hunter he killed 4,280 buffaloes in eighteen months.

About the year 1870 a market opened in the East for buffalo hides, and soon the prairies were filled with men who began a systematic slaughter of the remaining bison.

Shortly after the Atchison, Topeka and Santa Fe Railway reached Dodge City, Kansas, it became the center of buffalo hunting in that region. Ordinarily the railway terminal towns sank into insignificance when the road built on west, but Dodge City, owing to the coming of the buffalo hunter, continued to boom until a few years later the cattle trade arrived to reinforce its prosperity. When construction on the Santa Fe stopped for a year after it reached Granada, Colorado, all the unemployed men who could get a gun and a wagon or could hire out to a hunter went buffalo hunting. As a result, during the fall and winter of 1872-73 buffalo extermination reached a high point. On November 7, 1872, the *Wichita Eagle* stated:

Thousands upon thousands of hides are being brought in here by hunters. In places whole acres of ground are covered with these hides spread out . . . to dry. It is estimated that there is, south of the Arkansas and west of Wichita, from one to two thousand men shooting buffalo for their hides alone.

One writer says the noise of the buffalo guns could be heard on all sides hour after hour, booming and rumbling as if a heavy battle were being fought.[7]

Few mining towns equaled Dodge City for lawlessness and booming prosperity in the seventies. Scores of men made a hundred dollars a day slaying the swarms of buffalo. A box of matches, a shave, or a drink of whisky was the same price, twenty-five cents. Money flowed like water, and men were equally extravagant of human life. During the first year of the town's existence fourteen men were shot. Barrels of water were placed along the principal streets for fire protection. They also served as breastworks in the gun battles that swept the streets of the lively town. Finally the city fathers decided to bring order out of chaos and commanded all comers to take their revolvers out of their holsters and pile them in a store. A resident of the town in reminiscing of those days exclaimed: "What piles there were of them [guns]. At times they were piled up by the hundred." On a hill overlooking the city was located the cemetery. Few buried there were placed in coffins, however; lumber was too costly.

An indication of the booming prosperity is seen in the fact that one of the leading mercantile and hide-buying concerns took in an average of a thousand dollars a day including Sunday. They handled every article one could mention. There was very little currency in circulation, however, and this establishment had to have from two to five thousand dollars in money sent to it every few days.[8]

Buffalo-hunting outfits worked in various-sized units. Sometimes,

[7] Billy Dixon, *Life of Billy Dixon* (Dallas, Texas, 1927), p. 81.
[8] Robert M. Wright, *Dodge City, the Cowboy Capital* (Wichita, Kans., 1913), pp. 156, 168, 171.

although rarely, a man worked alone; sometimes two worked to-gether; units of three or four were frequent, and larger concerns employed a number of men. In the latter part of the hide slaughter, companies in the towns sent out large crews.

The most popular crew, in the early days especially, consisted of a hunter, a camp-tender (cook), and two skinners. The pro-prietor of the concern usually did the hunting, furnished the equip-ment, and employed the other men. When a large number of men were grouped in the enterprise, there were usually two skin-ners and two camp-tenders to each killer. In one instance a hunter kept seven skinners busy. Colonel Frank H. Mayer stated that he supplied everything and divided the profits, he taking fifty per cent and his men equally dividing the other fifty per cent.

The minimum equipment consisted of a light wagon drawn by a team of horses or mules, axes, a shovel, a spade, a mess box, pot-hooks, a grindstone or set of whetstones for sharpening knives, a ten-gallon water-keg, a coffee-pot, bread pans, meat-broiler, camp kettles, a Dutch oven, a frying-pan, four tin plates, and four tin cups. The crew often ate with their fingers or used their hunting-knives in place of forks. Considerable flour, smaller amounts of coffee, salt, sugar, and bacon were taken. Some dried beans, pota-toes, dried apples, and a few other Western staples found their way into the larder. Vegetables were almost unknown in the diet. The chief bill of fare was buffalo meat, of course. A few personal belongings were carried in a "war bag," and some hunters carried reading-matter. A liberal quantity of poison was also provided, to be rubbed on the skins to prevent insects and smaller animals from destroying the hides.

The most satisfactory rifle was the Sharps "buffalo gun." This weapon was 50 or 55 caliber and fired a heavy charge which would kill at fifteen hundred yards. Winchester, Spencer, Henry, and Springfield guns were used also. A moderate amount of shells was purchased, and as these were emptied they were reloaded in the field. A ton of powder and lead was not unusual to take onto the range.[9] In the evening, by the light of the blazing camp-fire, fifty or sixty pounds of lead was put into a skillet and soon a good hot fire reduced it to liquid. The lead was then dipped out with a spoon, and the bullets were molded. It was a simple matter to replace the cap, fill the shell with powder, and press the bullet into the cartridge.

When an outfit went onto the range, a place in the midst of good buffalo country was selected for headquarters. Sometimes a tent was pitched or perhaps a dugout was made in the side of some ravine near the edge of a stream where water was obtainable. There in an improvised dwelling-place the crew made their home for a month or more until the buffalo became scarce, and then they moved on to better hunting-grounds.

Dugouts made by the construction gangs on the railroads were occupied by these hunters. A large fireplace gave light and warmth and furnished the cook with a place of operations. The rude shelter was crudely furnished with some old dry-goods boxes to serve as cupboards, prairie hay for beds, and ammunition boxes for seats. It was preëminently necessary to keep the powder and flour dry, and consequently these commodities occupied the driest spot.

The hunter started from headquarters at daylight for the day's kill. He took with him his heavy gun, from fifty to a hundred and fifty cartridges in his belt and pockets, a cleaning-rod, and a firing-rest made of sticks. First he picked up some dry blades of grass and, holding them high, allowed them to sift through his fingers. This was the weather-vane the buffalo hunter used to determine the direction of the wind.

Fortunate indeed was the man who located a herd of twenty-five to one hundred buffalo in an isolated hollow protected by ridges. Under cover of one of these, he could readily stalk his game and begin his deadly work. If the herd was in the open, the hunter made a bee-line toward it against the wind. If the stalker did not

[9] Branch, *The Hunting of the Buffalo*, pp. 159-160.

move to one side or the other, he could approach to within about four hundred yards before the poor-visioned creatures suspected anything. From two to four sentinels kept watch. When they became uneasy, the hunter dropped down on hands and knees and crawled through the grass. Some still hunters of Montana were accustomed to draw a gunnysack over the upper half of the body. They cut holes for the eyes and arms. This enabled the hunter to squirm through the seared prairie grass much closer to the game than otherwise. When the sentinels began to get restless once more, it was time to begin action.

By this time, if fortunate, the hunter was within two or three hundred yards, though often the distance was much greater. He then fixed his rest for the huge rifle and, estimating the distance, adjusted the sights. If the herd was moving, he shot the animal in the lead. If it was at rest, he shot the leader. The first animal was shot through the lungs; she started to run but soon stopped with two crimson streams running from her nostrils. In a short time she staggered and, lurching sideways, fell. The herd, in the meantime, alarmed by the noise of the gun, felt inclined to run, but seeing their leader hesitate, they waited for her. When she fell, the others gathered around her and, sniffing, looked on in bewilderment. Finally one started to lead the herd away, when "Bang!" went that murderous rifle again, and her leadership ended abruptly. Her fall only added to the confusion and mystery of the whole thing. The bewildered animals clustered about, sniffed, and bawled at what to them was something entirely unaccountable.[10] The plan of the hunter was not to fire rapidly, but to use strategy. One shot a minute was considered moderate shooting, but if necessity demanded, two per minute could be fired with deliberate precision. Every time a buffalo attempted to make off, it was killed. In this manner from a dozen to several score were often slaughtered before the herd became alarmed. This was

[10] William T. Hornaday, "The Extermination of the American Bison," *Smithsonian Institution Reports*, 1887, p. 466.

AMONG THE BUFFALO

From John Charles Frémont, *Memoirs of My Life, 1886.*

known as "a stand." Often the hunter shot so many times his gun grew hot.

John R. Cook, who with a partner was hunting below the Kansas line in what is now Oklahoma, told of his first experience in getting a "stand":

I now had what I had so often heard about but had never actually seen before, *a stand*. Charlie Hart, while I was with him had given me some good pointers how to manage a "stand," if I ever got one. He told me not to shoot fast enough to heat the gun-barrel to an over-expansion; to always try to hit the outside ones; to shoot at any that started to walk off, unless I thought they were mortally wounded. He said that "with an over-expanded gun-barrel the bullet would go wabbling, and would be liable to break a leg; and that would start a bolt."

After I had killed twenty-five that I knew of, the smoke from the gun commenced to hang low, and was slow in disappearing. So I shifted my position and, in doing so, got still closer. And I know that many of the herd saw me move. I had shot perhaps a dozen times, when, as I was reloading, I heard a keen whistle behind me. . . . [My partner, Charlie] was on his all-fours creeping up to me. He said: "Go ahead; take it easy; I am coming with more cartridges." He crawled up to my side with . . . [a] gun and an extra sack of ammunition for me and a canteen of water. He asked if the gun was shooting all right. I told him "yes; but the barrel is pretty warm." . . . [He told me to try the gun he had brought for a while and let my gun cool a little.] We exchanged guns, and I commenced again.

Even while I was shooting buffaloes that had not been shot at all, some would lie down apparently unconcerned about the destruction going on around them. I fired slowly and deliberately. Charlie poured some water down the muzzle of his gun; then pulled down the breech-block and let the water run out. He then ran a greased rag in the eyelet of the wiping-stick and swabbed the barrel out, leaving the breech-block open for a while, thus cooling the barrel, in order to have that gun ready for use when my own gun got too warm. . . . I laid the gun down and said, "Charlie, finish the job." He said, "No take my gun and go ahead, this is the greatest sight I ever beheld." . . . I would shoot five or six times, wipe the gun, and we would comment, in a low voice on the apparent stupidity of the herd. Some came back and stood by the dead ones. Some would hook them as they lay dead. I kept this work up for as much as an hour and a quarter, when I changed guns again. And at the first shot from my own gun I broke the left hind leg above the knee of a big bull that was standing on the outer edge of the herd about ninety yards from me. He commenced "cavorting" around, jamming up against others, and the leg flapping as he hopped about.

He finally broke in through the midst of the band and my *stand*. They all began to follow him, and I with the big 50 that I now took from Charlie, commenced a rear attack, Charlie putting cartridges in his belt which I was wearing; and with the belt about half full and several in one pocket, and a half-dozen or so in my left hand, I moved up to a dead buffalo, and got in several good shots; when I moved again, on through the dead ones, to the farthermost one, and fired three more shots and quit. As I walked back through where the carcasses lay the thickest, I could not help but think that I had done wrong to make such a slaughter for the hides alone.

In counting them just as they lay there, their eyes glassy in death, I had killed *eighty-eight;* and several left the ground with more bad than slight wounds.[11]

One hunter killed a hundred and twenty at one stand in forty minutes. Brick Bond, an old experienced hunter, an expert shot, and a reliable man, said he killed fifteen hundred in seven days. Two hundred and fifty was his largest day's kill. The claim is brought forward that he killed over six thousand in sixty days or an average of more than one hundred a day. He employed five skinners.

It took about three shells on an average to kill one buffalo. Each shell cost about seven cents. As the hunter fired, he put the empty shells in his pocket, and at the close of his killing he counted buffaloes and empty shells.

As more and more hunters entered the field, the slaughter increased accordingly. Hunters stationed along the streams met the animals with a murderous fire at every watering place. Tortured with thirst, they tried for water again and again, only to be met

---

[11] John R. Cook, *The Border and the Buffalo* (Topeka, Kans., 1907), pp. 164-167.

by the death-dealing lead of the "big fifties." Thinner and thinner grew the herds under the warlike campaign.[12]

There were well-defined rules among the buffalo hunters. When a buffalo was killed, the hunter would cut a mark on the hide to indicate its ownership. The hunter who first fired a shot at a herd thereby gained priority rights and was entitled to the control of them against all comers as fully as though he had raised them from calves. No matter how badly a party needed meat, they had to keep their distance. Any man who would deliberately pass on the windward side of a herd while another was attempting to stalk the animals was liable to hear a ball whistle uncomfortably close to his ear as a reminder of his delinquency.

If a wounded buffalo should escape from a hunter and be despatched by another, it was the property of the one who first drew blood. Two shots in quick succession with an interval and a repetition were a signal of distress, calling for immediate aid. Hospitality was unbounded, and a visitor was welcome to the best in the camp by way of appeasing his thirst with coffee or hunger with the best food, whether the owner was at home or not.[13] If an outfit camped on the head of some stream, another party would never camp above even if it had to procure water by digging in the ground for it, for this would interfere with the buffaloes' coming to water. When camps were made along a stream, they were located a mile apart. These rules were lived up to by common consent.

As soon as the skinners heard the booming of the hunter's "big fifty," they followed the sound with a wagon and a number of skinning knives. When the first carcasses were reached, the work of "peeling" began. Some skinners became so skilful at their craft that they offered to bet they could skin a five- or six-year-old bull in five minutes.[14] As a matter of practical work in the field, how-

---

[12] Carl Coke Rister, *Southern Plainsmen* (Norman, Okla., 1938), p. 11.

[13] Charles J. Jones, *Buffalo Jones' Forty Years of Adventure*, compiled by Colonel Henry Inman (Topeka, Kans., 1899), pp. 42, 43.

[14] Wright, *Dodge City, the Cowboy Capital*, p. 192.

ever, no such speed was maintained. John R. Cook says he averaged skinning twenty-two buffalo a day for forty-one days and received twenty-five cents a hide or $225.50 for the month and a half's work.

The skinners simplified their work by using a wagon to turn the carcasses. A forked stick was fastened to the hind axle of the wagon in such a way that one prong dragged on the ground. When the wagon was backed, it stuck in the ground, the arrangement holding the wagon solid and keeping it from backing up. A chain was fastened to the rear axle and the wagon driven up cornerwise to the carcass. The other end of the chain was then fastened to a fore leg. After the top side of the animal was skinned, the wagon was driven up a little at a time, raising the animal up so the other side could be skinned. Sometimes an iron stake was driven through the head of the carcass to hold it fast, and the skin, after it had been split down the belly and removed from the legs, was pulled the rest of the way off with the wagon. Sometimes more "buff," as the hunters called them, were killed than could be skinned in one day. Skinning animals left overnight was difficult, for the carcass would bloat and the hide would be stiff and tight, making the work tedious.

The hides were hauled to the camp, where the cook stretched them. This was done by staking them down on the prairie, flesh side up, with stakes about six inches long driven around the outside of the skins. They were allowed to remain from three to five days. Then they were turned every other day until they were perfectly dry. After that they were piled one on top of the other until they were stacked eight feet high. Holes were made in the edges of the top and bottom hides, and strings cut from a green hide were run through these eyelets and the pack drawn down as tightly as possible and tied. The hides were always sorted and tied up in grades, the bulls in one bale, the cows in another, and those of the younger animals in a third pile, known as the "kip pile." When the hunter finished killing, he helped with the skinning, and both he and the skinner helped with the stretching and drying.[15]

After a time the crew moved its headquarters, leaving a rick of buffalo hides on the old site. It was particularly necessary in this case to have the hides poisoned to protect them from wild animals. As a rule the hides were safe, but thieves sometimes robbed the skin-hunters of their product. When an outfit had two or three piles, they often made a deal with a hide-buyer. Agents for hide-buying companies in Leavenworth, St. Louis, or other points farther east traveled here and there buying in the field. Trains of twenty-five teams wound in and out and over the terrain from one camp to another, carrying hides to the nearest railway station. Each wagon was equipped with a rack like a hay-rack. Each team of six yoke of oxen pulled two of these wagons hitched in tandem. The lead wagon hauled two hundred hides and the trail wagon from one hundred to a hundred and fifty. A dry bull hide weighed fifty pounds, and hence a wagonload of two hundred hides weighed five tons. Such a large cargo rose high in the air like a load of hay and had to be held steady with a boom.

Sometimes when a buyer's agent contracted for a hunter's several piles of skins, a guard was hired to ride from one stack to another to see that they were not stolen. The expense of such a guard was borne equally by the buyer and the seller.

In addition to the killing of multitudes of buffalo merely for their skins, a few men established smoke-houses and small establishments where buffalo meat was prepared for market. A. C. Meyers built a smoke-house on Pawnee Fork, in Kansas, and cured meat for the eastern trade. A hind quarter was cut into three pieces and canvas sewed around it. This sugar-cured smoked meat commanded a good price in the East. Others shipped the hind quarters with the skin on. In the winter of 1873 one concern at Dodge City shipped two hundred cars of hind quarters and two cars of tongues. Buffalo meat was surreptitiously sold as beef in eastern cities.[16]

[15] Cook, *The Border and the Buffalo*, pp. 116-118.
[16] Branch, *The Hunting of the Buffalo*, pp. 153-154.

During the years 1872, 1873, and 1874, William T. Hornaday estimated, 3,698,730 buffalo were killed on the Southern Plains. Within a period of eight years, by 1880, the Southern herd was practically exterminated.[17]

The great slaughter reached its maximum on the northern Plains in the early eighties. Whole trainloads of hides were despatched from Bismarck, North Dakota, at a time, and a Dickinson, North Dakota, newspaper reported that two hundred and fifty thousand hides were shipped from that point in the spring of 1883. By the close of 1883 the buffalo had practically been exterminated on the northern Plains. The carnage was over. For hundreds of miles the country was a vast charnel-house. Great stretches of territory lay covered with the rotting carcasses which fairly poisoned the atmosphere of whole counties. The waste did not stop with the mere waste of meat. Colonel Richard I. Dodge estimated that in the early days of the hide-hunting era, every hide sent to market represented three or four and sometimes five dead buffaloes, but that this waste decreased until by 1874 one hundred hides represented only one hundred and twenty-five animals slain.[18]

The prices of buffalo hides, of course, fluctuated somewhat, but in the early seventies, at the height of the slaughter, apparently the figures were about $3.00 for choice cow hides, $2.50 for old bull hides, and $1.75 for others. There was only one white buffalo robe among the more than five million in the southern herd. Prairie Dog Dave sold it to Robert Wright of Dodge City for a thousand dollars. In order to secure a first-class robe it was necessary to kill the animal in the winter while the skin was "prime." Such a pelt commanded a premium. As a rule the skins procured on the northern Plains made better robes than those of the southern area.

[17] Hornaday, "The Extermination of the American Bison," *loc. cit.*, pp. 500-548.
[18] Colonel Richard I. Dodge, *The Hunting Grounds of the Great West* (London, 1878), pp. 130, 131.

The skinners received about fifty dollars a month, or twenty-five to thirty cents each when hired by the skin. At this rate many in a few months made enough money to establish themselves in business. On the northern Plains the hams, humps, and other choice portions were sometimes sold to buyers who followed the hunters. Cow meat sold for three cents a pound. Meat and hide brought the hunter about five dollars.

A few years after the hide-hunters had gone, leaving the prairies strewn with skeletons, the poverty-stricken homesteaders gathered up the bleached bones and sold them to eastern fertilizer factories, carbon companies, and other markets. Horns were polished for ornaments. The settlers received from seven to ten dollars a ton for these economic fragments of the great hunting orgy. Long trains of cars loaded with the bones moved eastward. At principal points along the railroad lines great piles were stacked awaiting shipment.

An observer as early as 1874, before the slaughter had ended, saw on the right of way of the Santa Fe Railway twenty miles ahead of the track from Granada, Colorado, a pile of buffalo bones twelve feet high, nearly that wide at the base, and a half-mile long.[19] In that single year the road hauled about 7,000,000 pounds of bones.

S. D. Butcher, who knew the professional buffalo hunter, placed him in a category all by himself. He said that when talking to you the buffalo hunter would invariably be scratching his leg with one hand and rubbing his side with the other elbow, as if by perpetual motion he could keep quiet what he called "buffalo mange," or, in other words, lice. At the same time he would be regaling his listener with tall stories about the number of buffaloes he had killed and his narrow escapes. In place of the buckskin hunting outfit of the trapper, he wore a coarse suit of duck, stiffened with the blood, grease, and grime incident to his business. His hair was often uncut for months and uncombed for weeks,

[19] Cook, *The Border and the Buffalo*, p. 135.

and his hands were unwashed for days at a time. Yet these men were a jolly, rollicking set, and the group included men from refined society and cultured circles.[20]

Men often earned nicknames by virtue of certain experiences. For example, when a man by the name of Jones broke the left rear wheel on his wagon, friends informed him that there was a good wheel on a broken-down wagon, an exact mate of his, on the prairie. He traveled sixteen miles and returned empty-handed with the explanation that the good wheel on the wreck was for the right rear axle and consequently was the wrong wheel. The crowd enjoyed a great deal of fun at his expense, and when he "tumbled" to the fact that the wheels were interchangeable and traveled the sixteen miles once more to get the wheel, someone hung on him the appropriate nickname "Wrong Wheel Jones," which stuck. There were at least two more Joneses in the region about Dodge City, Buffalo Jones and Dirty-Face Jones. Hunters sometimes named their guns also. "The old pizen [poison] slinger" was a favorite name. One hunter had a gun with a worn firing-pin which made it miss fire so frequently it was nicknamed "Old once-in-a-while."

At times, when hunting was slack, the hunters visited each other's dugouts, tents, or buffalo tepees. The salutation was, "Hello, Dirty Face! light and unsaddle!" The parting words on the Plains were, "So long!"

The long winter evenings passed pleasantly with story and song. There were many ex-soldiers among the hunters, and they entertained the group with endless tales of the desperate encounters of the Civil War. Kangaroo courts were popular also, with real or imaginary offenses. The penalties consisted of taking a certain number of steps away from the camp-fire and picking up a designated quantity of buffalo chips for the fire. Patriotic speeches poured forth, and popular songs were sung into the wee hours of

[20] S. D. Butcher, *Pioneer History of Custer County* (Broken Bow, Neb., 1901), p. 87.

morning. A song written at that time and sung with spirit all over the range has since become well known. The chorus ran as follows:

> Oh, give me a home where the buffaloes roam,
> Where the deer and the antelope play,
> Where seldom is heard a discouraging word
> And the sky is not cloudy all day.

Sometimes a dry buffalo skin was pegged down to the ground in a dugout or on the prairie before the camp-fire and the men danced on it, sometimes in couples and sometimes singly. The stiff hide offered good footing and resounded to jigging like a drum-head. There were always some who could play the French harp, violin, or accordion. Such a scene was picturesque indeed. With the starry heavens overhead, the camp-fire's little lighted circle was surrounded by the vast plains, silent save for the yelping of the coyote or the howl of the wolves at their abundant feast of buffalo meat.[21] The hunters were fond of shooting at a mark. When someone came from civilization with news, it was the subject of discussion for days.

The buffalo hunter took great delight in playing jokes on the "tenderfeet" or newcomers on the buffalo range. They took special delight in hazing anyone who was too talkative about his personal prowess or too anxious for an opportunity to shed Indian gore. A good example of this was the experience of a man by the name of Fairchild. He blew into Dodge City wearing a shining broadcloth suit, a plug hat, a flowered vest, and a necktie resembling a Plains sunset. Equipped with a "muley" saddle, he rode up and down the streets of the wild town attracting attention from all sides. A day or two later he was all decked out in a brown duck suit, with high-heeled boots, mammoth spurs, and a huge white sombrero. A gaudy bandana encircled his neck, and his belt was a veritable arsenal, loaded down with cartridges, a butcher knife, and a six-shooter. The crowd had induced him to purchase the

---

[21] Dixon, *Life of Billy Dixon*, pp. 115-116, 91; Cook, *The Border and the Buffalo*, pp. 178, 293.

knife for the purpose of scalping the Indians. When he got "rigged out," he evinced an overwhelming desire to shoot an Indian. He joined himself to an outfit, and from the very beginning he was eager to get into an Indian fight and bragged about what he would do to the first Indian who crossed his path. The rest of the group, knowing that such a reckless attitude was a menace to the safety of the whole party, determined to cure him of his insatiable desire to draw Indian blood. The whole party except Fairchild was in on the plan.

By good luck Fairchild had killed several antelope and began to think of himself as a mighty hunter. A turkey hunt was proposed. Hundreds of turkeys roosted in trees not far from the camp every night. Fairchild could hardly wait until dark. Some of the crowd, unbeknown to Fairchild, were sent out to build a fire near the turkey-roost, and at the appointed hour Bat Masterson, later famous as a gunman and journalist, who was at the height of his glory when getting off a practical joke on someone, was selected to go with Fairchild. Another joker named Myers was selected to help haze the tenderfoot. Bat warned Fairchild to be very cautious lest the turkeys be frightened.

Suddenly upon rounding a bend they came square up against a camp-fire. Bat frantically motioned Fairchild back into the timber, and the three held a council to determine who had built the fire. Bat insisted this was an Indian fire and urged immediate flight to the camp, but Myers argued that Bat was mistaken, that he was in a panic and actually was showing the white feather. Furthermore, he was sure Fairchild could whip all the Indians in that part of the region anyway. Bang! Bang! Half a dozen shots rang out from the direction of the camp-fire. The bullets whistled through the leaves close to their heads. Myers made a line for camp, yelling "bloody murder" at every jump in an effort to terrify Fairchild. Bat came last, firing his six-shooter until Fairchild imagined a desperate Indian fight was in the offing. Masterson yelled, "Run, Fairchild! Run for your life!" He ran like a deer, easily outdistancing his companions and coming into camp out of breath, wild-eyed, his teeth chattering with terror.

The hunters solicitously asked what was the trouble. When he got his breath, Fairchild managed to say, "Injuns!" "He must be shot," cried a mischievous hunter and, grabbing a knife, ripped the victim's shirt down the back from the collar to the tail. Another excitedly called for water and, when none was at hand, emptied the coffee-pot on his bare back. This further alarmed Fairchild, who thought he was wounded. When asked what had become of Myers and Masterson, he managed to reply, "Killed, I guess." Shortly afterward Bat and Myers came in and began to upbraid their erstwhile companion for abandoning them to the mercies of the savages. Masterton declared that the whole country was alive with Indians. Immediately there was a rushing to and fro in preparation for a desperate resistance. Some suggested that the party should set out at once for Dodge City. Fairchild warmly favored this plan. Other dauntless men favored fighting it out to the last ditch. The latter proposal prevailed, and it was decided to throw a strong cordon around the camp with the men taking turns standing guard until morning. Fairchild was placed at a spot nearest the river and warned to keep a sharp lookout lest Indians swim up the stream and shoot him. Then one by one the other men retired to the camp, leaving the victim trembling at his post. Finally, when no relief came, after a long watch, he approached the camp and heard the men laughing and talking about the trick. Then he entered in a mood to treat the whole crowd as he had threatened to use the Indians. Luckily they were too many for him. This experience cured him of his mania to kill an Indian, however, and his comrades reported that he became a good companion and hunter.[22]

The slaughter of the wild game, especially the buffalo, opened the way for permanent white occupancy of the Plains. Soon millions of cattle ranged the grasslands where the buffalo had grazed.

[22] Dixon, *Life of Billy Dixon*, pp. 124-130.

CHAPTER XX

THE LONG DRIVE

CATTLE-GRAZING is a logical frontier enterprise. The first English colonists who settled on the Atlantic seaboard brought cattle with them. It was natural that they should live on the extreme edge of settlement in order that they might graze their herds on the abundant pasture in the unoccupied wilderness beyond. Long before the Revolutionary War a narrow ranching area had developed along the cutting edge of the frontier. One of the battles of the struggle for independence was named from one of the cowpens on the margin of the wilderness where the cattle-raisers took care of their stock. This cattle-raising fringe moved slowly westward, an omen of advancing civilization. The ranching belt was restricted in size by two factors: it could not advance too far into the wilderness because of the savage Indians; neither could it move too far from the centers of population which furnished the cattleman with a market for his product. Nevertheless it was always present, but although the area varied in size from time to time, these early cattle-raisers operated on a small scale as compared with the cattlemen of the post-Civil War range-cattle era.[1]

One of the most phenomenal changes in the industrial life of the United States occurred when, following the Civil War, this hitherto narrow fringe along the border leaped out into space and spread with the magic of the Arabian Nights, until within ten years the cattle-raising area became larger than the cultivated portion of the United States.[2]

[1] E. E. Dale, "The Ranchman's Last Frontier," see *Mississippi Valley Historical Review*, Vol. X, No. 1 (June, 1923), p. 35.
[2] Everett N. Dick, "The Long Drive," see Kansas State Historical Society *Collections*, Vol. XVII, p. 34.

This revolutionary change came as a result of the building of the Pacific railroad. Huge land-grants and an ever-growing volume of travel, and settlement on the prairies led to the removal of the Indians, the systematic slaughter of the buffalo, and the occupation of the rich grazing areas by the rancher.

But whence were the cattle to come for the stocking of this mighty potential cattle empire? Texas was in readiness to supply the need. The early Spanish explorers and colonizers brought with them the Moorish horse and the long-horned Andalusian cattle. As the Spanish settlements pushed northward, cattle-raising naturally moved along on the outer edge of settlement. Some of the horses and cattle escaped from their owners, and from them grew up the herds of wild horses and cattle on the Plains.[3]

The horse imported by the Spanish was a descendant of the famous Arabian horse and through centuries of breeding in a region of little water and grass had developed a hardiness and stamina which were little short of marvelous. The Andalusian cattle were noted for their long horns and paucity of beef.

During the years prior to the independence of Texas, the cattle multiplied until there were countless wild herds which ran untrammeled and increased by leaps and bounds in that climate so favorable to the saving of a high percentage of the calves at birth.

The Americans who settled in Texas brought their cattle with them. These strains mixed with the Texas cattle but seemed to have made little change in the type of the long-horned stock. Kentucky saddle horses were also imported. Crossed with the Spanish horse, they produced a breed which was hardy, as tough as leather like the Spanish horse, and yet speedy like the Kentucky horse.

Since Texas was isolated from large markets, its cattle had practically no value. A few were used for meat and hides, but other-

[3] Philip Ashton Rollins, *The Cowboy* (New York, 1936), pp. 1-5; Clara M. Love, "History of the Cattle Industry in the Southwest," *Southwestern Historical Quarterly*, Vol. XIX, pp. 371-374.

wise they were almost a liability. As one writer stated, a man's poverty was measured by the cattle he owned.

A few Texas stock-owners attempted to get their cattle to market, but slight success attended their early efforts. To the north and west was a region populated with savage Indians; to the east the topography of the country discouraged driving, and freight rates on the steamship lines were prohibitive. A few cattlemen drove cattle both east and west before the Civil War, but these drives were sporadic and in general unsuccessful.

During the Civil War, however, the North decreased its cattle population, owing to the general destructiveness of war as well as its attendant increased consumption of meat by the voracious armies in the field. With the Texas cattle pent up by natural circumstances in a great reservoir and cattle scarce in the North, a great disparity in prices was bound to exist. While cattle in Texas sold at from three to five dollars a head, they sold for ten times as much in New York.[4]

The railroads pushing westward, now pausing at a terminus town and again reaching out rapidly, indicated the solution to the problem of marketing for Texas cattle. They must walk to the railroad. In the spring of 1866 enterprising cattlemen in the northern states acquainted with the low prices of cattle in Texas, and ambitious Texans who had heard of high prices in the North, attempted to get Texas cattle to the northern markets. Although about a quarter of a million head were started northward that year, most of them attempted to reach the terminus of the Missouri Pacific Railway at Sedalia and encountered much opposition in the settled area of eastern Kansas and western Missouri. As a result there were heavy losses, and although some took a long detour to the west to avoid the settled region, very few found a profitable market that first year of the "Long Drive."

One of the classic experiences of that year was that of Harvey

---

[4] Lewis Allen, "Improvement of Neat Cattle," House Executive Document 136, 39th Congress, 1st Session, Serial 1266, p. 691.

Ray and George C. Duffield, who went into partnership for the purpose of purchasing from one to two thousand head of Texas cattle and driving them to their home in Iowa. Early in the year they took a Mississippi River steamer to New Orleans and thence went on to Galveston. By the middle of March they were in the region west of Austin, gathering their herd and preparing for the journey to their northern home. On the first part of the drive it rained incessantly, the rivers were almost impossible to ford, and days were spent in waiting to cross streams, in separating herds which had become hopelessly mixed up, and in pulling cattle out of bogs. [Duffield kept a diary which, from the vantage-point of seventy years, reveals the inmost thoughts and trials of the harassed cattleman:

May 1st . . . Big Stamped   lost 200 head of cattle.

2nd Spent the day hunting & found but 25 Head   it has been Raining for three days   these are dark days for me.

3rd day Spent in hunting cattle found 23 hard rain and wind lots of trouble

6th . . . dark & Gloomey night hard rain Stampeded & lost 200 head of cattle . . .

9th Still dark & gloomy   River up everything looks *Blue* to me no crossing to day   cattle behaved well.

14th Concluded to cross Brazos   swam our cattle & Horses & built Raft & Rafter our provisions & blankets &c over   Swam River with rope & then hauled wagon over Lost Most of our Kitchen furniture such as camp Kittles Coffee Pots Cups Plates Canteens &c &c.

15 . . . Rain poured down for one Hour. It does nothing but rain   got all our *traps* together that was not lost & thought we were ready for off   dark rainy night   cattle all left us & in morning not one Beef to be seen

20th.   Rain poured down for two hours   Ground in a flood Creeks up—Hands leaving   Gloomey times as ever I saw . . .

22nd. This day has been spent in crossing the West Trinity & a hard & long to be remembered day to me   we swam our cattle & Horses   I swam it 5 times   upset our wagon in River & lost Many of our cooking utencils again . . .

23rd. . . . Hard rain . . . [last] night & cattle behaved very bad
—ran all night—was on my Horse the whole night & it raining
hard.[5]

Duffield started with one thousand head and ended his travels in
Iowa with a few hundred on the last day of October.

The fiasco of 1866 led to the establishing of Abilene, Kansas, as
a cattle town. Joseph G. McCoy, an enterprising cattleman from
Illinois, conceived the idea of establishing a shipping-point on the
Kansas Pacific Railway beyond the western edge of agrarian settlement. After some investigation he selected Abilene as the most
likely point for such an undertaking and began work on the project
the first of July, 1867. Within sixty days he had built a shipping-
yard which would accommodate three thousand head of cattle, an
office, a barn, had put in scales, and work was well under way on a
hotel, known as the Drovers Cottage, for the accommodation of
the Texas cattle-traders. After having settled on Abilene as the
cattle depot, McCoy despatched a lone rider across the prairie in
search of the straggling herds.[6]

The drive of 1867 was small in comparison with that of the
year before, owing no doubt to the icy reception of the cattlemen
by the farmers. McCoy prepared for a big drive in 1868. He sent
a man with compass, a flagman, and laborers to survey a direct
route from Abilene to the crossing of the Arkansas. Soon they had
a trail marked with mounds of dirt. Then McCoy put on a mammoth advertising campaign, informing northern buyers that cattle
would await them at Abilene in the summer, and notifying the
Texans that buyers would meet them on their arrival at Abilene.
This advertising, broadcast in the papers north and south, had its
effect. The number of cattle driven in 1868 was more than double
that of the year before, and the cattle trade on the Plains became
firmly established. Among the incidents of that year which helped

[5] George C. Duffield's Diary, W. W. Baldwin, ed., see *Annals of Iowa*, Vol.
XIV, April, 1924, pp. 246-262.
[6] Joseph G. McCoy, *Historic Sketches of the Cattle Trade of the West and
Southwest* (Kansas City, Mo., 1874), p. 7.

to more than quadruple the number of cattle arriving at Abilene in 1869 was that of a herd of six hundred wild Texas steers driven by M. A. Withers. He left Lockhart, Texas, on April 1. The cattle were valued at from eight to ten dollars a head in Texas and sold for twenty-eight dollars a head to an Illinois firm after having been grazed north of Abilene from the time of their arrival at that point on July 1 until fall.[7]

In the earlier years of the cattle trade, much cattle-driving was done by professional drovers who purchased herds of Texas cattle, usually on six or eight months' credit, and drove them north to market. Later, many ranchers drove their own herds or sent them up the trail under a competent trail boss.[8]

The size of the herds driven varied from under a thousand in earlier trail days to three or four thousand at times at a later date. It was found that almost as much help was needed for a small herd as for one that was two or three times as large, and as the drovers gained experience, there was a tendency to drive larger herds. An average of about twenty-five hundred was struck in time, however, since a much larger herd tended to become unwieldy to handle. If a cattle king had fifteen thousand head to drive in a given season, he divided them up into herds of about twenty-five hundred each and sent them off as fast as they could be got ready, with the parting words to the foreman, "I'll see you in Abilene!"

Sometimes these herds belonging to the same man would travel up the trail almost within hearing distance of one another, much as some trains to-day are run in sections on trunk-line railroads. In other cases the herds were sent off just as they were gathered. Perhaps a week or more intervened between the starting of one herd and the departure of the next. Often the foreman of the ranch bossed the crew of the last herd north. The ranch-owner then rode to the nearest railroad station or boat-landing and trav-

[7] Louis Pelzer, *The Cattlemen's Frontier* (Glendale, Cal., 1936), p. 45.

[8] E. E. Dale, *The Range and Ranch Cattle Industry* (Norman, Okla., 1930), p. 65.

eled to the northern market, arriving there in time to ride down the trail some distance, perhaps bringing buyers with him, and meet the first herd.

Sometimes there developed superdrovers who did nothing but contract for herds and drive vast numbers of cattle on the northern route each year. Major Seth Mabry in partnership with other men drove seventy-five thousand head of cattle up the long trail in 1875.

The Texas cattle of trail days resembled the cattle of Andalusia from which they sprang. They were often a yellow dun in color, with a bony form, long slender legs, light hind quarters, prominent backbone, high hip-bones, a long narrow face, and a thin chest. Their slender bones were covered with little flesh and still less fat. The horns were almost invariably long and sharp and many times were enormous in their diameter and spread. F. R. Waters, secretary of the Drum-Standish Commission Company, stated that the average length of horns of the Texas cattle in early days was from five and a half to six feet. The old time Texas "ranger," he declared, was about fifty-fifty on horns and the rest of him. D. R. Gordon, first station-agent at Abilene, recalled that the horns were so long that the drovers experienced the greatest difficulty in getting the animals through the car doors when shipments were made.[9] The usual weight of one of these cattle direct from Texas was from 650 to 950 pounds. There was a resemblance to a deer in the large lustrous eyes, the long pointed nose, and the fleetness of foot which tried to the utmost the speed of a horse. And yet the longhorns were of a nervous temperament and had pugnacious dispositions. Although they would run away from a horseman with the speed of the wind, if a person were unhorsed or were so unwise as to approach them on foot, they would attack him in an instant. When one of these animals got so poor and weak in the wintertime that he could not stand and had to be helped

[9] Personal interview with D. R. Gorden, station-agent on the Kansas Pacific at Abilene from 1869 to 1874, October 1, 1925.

up, he immediately attacked his benefactor, and sometimes the good Samaritan had to kill the object of his mercy in order to save his own life. It soon became axiomatic that Texas cattle were never handled on foot, and probably for that reason they were almost always handled on the prairies without a corral.

Many of the Texas cattle were wild or semiwild and had never been near a man on foot. Some were the brush cattle which grazed out on the prairie at night and in the daytime retreated to the recesses of the forest. They never had been branded and were not used to man in any way. Some actually had lived in the dark forests down toward the Gulf so long that it is said moss grew on their horns, and they were called "mossy-horned steers." As the accumulated surplus cattle began to melt away as a result of the northern drive, men made a business of capturing and branding these wild cattle and sending them up the trail, a plague to the drover.[10] In the earlier years mixed herds were driven, and there was a general understanding that the drover should accept the cattle as they came for a set price per head. Sometimes a man made a business of going about gathering up herds, getting them ready for the trail, and then selling them to a drover or northern cattleman. When a man gathered up a herd, he never failed to obtain a bill of sale from each of the ranchers who furnished him with cattle. These documents, covered with hieroglyphics undecipherable to the ordinary mortal, were the passport out of Texas and stood between the possessor of cattle and prison. They gave the brands, earmarks, and other means of identification, if any.

Let us follow a drover who proposed to drive a herd of twenty-five hundred head to Kansas. He went through the cattle country of Texas, contracting for animals here and there until he had made up the desired number. While the ranchmen were "cutting out," or separating, the contracted stock from their herds, the drover

[10] James H. Cook, *Fifty Years on the Old Frontier* (New Haven, Conn., 1923), pp. 14-25; Charles A. Siringo, *A Lone Star Cowboy* (Santa Fe, N. M., 1919), pp. 37-41.

secured his crew and equipment. He hired eight cowboys. In selecting these "trail hands" he took great care to enlist loyal, dependable men who would stay with the drover in any emergency.[11]

He then hired a man to herd the horses. Sometimes two horse-herders were engaged, one for day duty and the other for night service. A herd of riding horses numbering from fifty to a hundred was purchased. Each cowboy needed a string of from five to seven horses to ride in turn on the rigorous service of the trail. This herd was known as the *remuda caballado* or "cavvie yard," and the man who attended it was called the horse-wrangler.

Next the drover purchased a chuck wagon. This might be either a two-wheeled cart or a stout wagon, but in either case it was equipped with bows and a canvas cover. A barrel was securely fastened inside the wagon bed, usually between the wheels, and a spigot was run through the side of the wagon bed to the outside so that water could be drawn conveniently. A barrel of water could be made to last two days or more. On the back of the vehicle was the chuck box, which was divided into compartments for holding the cooking utensils. A leaf was fastened to the back of this box in such a way that it could be lowered like the old-fashioned writing-desk to form a work-table for the cook. Another important piece of equipment was the "cooney" or "caboose," which consisted of a cowhide tied by the four corners under the wagon and allowed to hang loose. Every piece of wood or dry cow chip found along the northward march was deposited in this receptacle. When the ground was wet, the supply of dry fuel under the wagon stood the cook in good stead.[12] On the front of the wagon was built a box which held all manner of odds and ends that were used in case of trouble. One of the chief items was a copious supply of rawhide. The chuck wagon was the headquarters of the outfit. In it were carried thirty days' provisions for the

[11] John Bratt, *Trails of Yesterday* (Lincoln, Neb., 1921), pp. 186-188.
[12] J. Marvin Hunter, ed., *Trail Drivers of Texas* (San Antonio, Texas, 1924), Vol. I, pp. 302, 303.

crew, the scanty personal belongings of the outfit, the papers of the trail boss or drover, and the sleeping equipment of all the hands.

A cook hired for the trip completed the outfit. A good cook was a gold-mine to a drover for he could do more toward keeping up the morale of a trail crew than anyone else. He had to be not only a good cook but an expert bull-whacker or mule-skinner as well, for some wagons were pulled by oxen while horses furnished the motive power for others. The cook often was a hard character with a record of his own. He might be either Spanish or Negro with a notch or two on his gun. He was called the "old woman" by the crew, but he certainly was no lady if he were to be judged by his language.

The crew was now complete, and the drover went to the various ranches to receive the herds he had contracted for. The various detachments were taken to a large corral and road-branded. The road brand was a special brand for the trip burned in the hair only. Applying it was often a mean job, for it involved tramping around in a muddy pen all day while the cattle were thrown and branded or run through a branding-chute as was customary later.

The time of starting from Texas depended on the part of the state from which the drive began. Herds left the Gulf as early as March 1 and the Panhandle as late as October 1. In general it was advantageous to start as early as possible in the spring because in the latter part of the season the pasture was short along the trail. The thousands of head of cattle had almost depastured the country on either side of the route. Often late in the season water was lacking at certain points. It was an advantage also to arrive at the cattle market early enough to pasture the herd on the rich northern grasses for two or three months so that they might recuperate from the journey and fatten for shipping, for slaughter on the prairie, or sale to the buyer at the cow town.

A herd composed of cattle from different ranches was restless the first few days on the trail, and it was necessary for the crew to ride night and day. Great caution was exercised to prevent a stampede or a break for their regular feeding-grounds. Sometimes a second crew was used to help for the first few days. It was the custom to drive hard during this period, some herders driving as much as twenty-five or thirty miles a day. There were several reasons for this. In the first place, it was desirable to get the cattle off their accustomed range as soon as possible as they were much harder to control there. A second purpose was to break them in to driving and tire them out by fast traveling so that at night they would be ready to lie down and rest instead of running over the country. After this period was over and the cattle were broken in, the drive per day was decreased to ten or fifteen miles.[13]

At the last town of any size in Texas, supplies for a month were laid in, for there were no large stores between there and Kansas in the seventies. Flour, bacon, and coffee were the staples stocked. Three-quarters of a pound each of bacon and of flour was allowed for each man per day. Some supplies could be procured at certain outposts along the trail.

The day's program began when the cook, who had breakfast ready, roused the sleeping cowboys at daybreak. The *remuda* was then brought to camp and the cowboys caught their horses for the forenoon. Some lariats or picket-ropes were tied together into two long lines. One of these was tied to the hind wheel of the wagon and the other to the tongue. Cowboys then held the extreme ends or tied them to stakes, forming a V-shaped corral with spread wings into which the horses were driven.[14] Each cowboy then roped his own horse. The horses got used to this rope fence and would not try to get over it. Of a trail hand's string of five or six horses, he selected the best one for night herding. This horse was supposed to be gentle, sure-footed, easily handled, have good eyesight, and possess all the other qualities of a first-class cow horse. The cowboy used the other horses of his string half

---

[13] Rollins, *The Cowboy*, p. 265. See Dick, "The Long Drive," *loc. cit.*, p. 56, for additional reference.

[14] Andy Adams, *The Log of a Cowboy* (Boston, 1903), p. 23.

a day at a time until all had been used; then he began with the first and made the rounds again.

In the early morning hours the herd would get up and graze. The cowboys guided them in the general direction of their destination as they ate. After they had grazed a few miles, they were turned into the trail and driven three or four miles. When they had drunk their fill at the first stream, they were allowed to lie down and rest during the heat of the day. The cowboy then had time to relax a little while and to change horses. In the late afternoon the cattle were driven seven or eight miles farther. They were then allowed to graze in the cool of the evening until dusk, when they were rounded up on the bed ground.

In going up the trail the duties of the hands and the mode of procedure were similar to those of a cavalry troop on the march. Each man was allowed a bed, consisting of two blankets covered with a tarpaulin, and a bag containing a few articles of extra clothing. No more than the bare necessities were allowed on the wagon. In contrast to the cavalry, there were no tents and no provisions for illness. A sick or injured man was unfortunate indeed. To die as quickly as possible or to recover speedily were the only desired alternatives, for medical aid and hospitalization were unobtainable.

Every man had his duty. On the March a herd of twenty-five hundred cattle strung out a mile or more and kindled an enthusiasm in the cattlemen akin to that inspired in the breast of the military man by sight of marching troops. Cowboy rank was indicated by the desirability of the position on the march. The two oldest hands "pointed herd"—that is, one rode on each side of the leaders and directed the herd. About one-third of the way back on each side were the two swing riders. At that position the herd was about fifty feet wide. Another third of the way back were the two flank riders, and at the rear three riders "brought up the drag." This was the most undesirable post of all, for the slow, lazy, or lame cattle gradually gravitated to this position and formed the widest portion of the column. The riders at the "drag" had their patience tried by the slow, toilsome, painful plodding of the weak and stubborn animals which desired to drop out and lie down. The green riders at this position were often enveloped by the cloud of stifling dust raised by the whole herd.[15]

In the morning the chuck wagon broke camp last and followed the herd, often accompanied by the *remuda*. They passed the cattle after a time and halted at a position indicated by the trail boss, who had gone on ahead to select a camp-site. After the noon meal, while the cattle were still resting, the cook broke camp with the foreman or trail boss leading, the chuck wagon and *remuda* following. The foreman rode ahead examining the grazing-grounds, perhaps conferring with the other trail bosses, and, returning to the moving chuck wagon, indicated the location for the evening camp. On these scouting expeditions the trail boss learned the news and thus became the newspaper for his crew.

In the late afternoon the cattle were aroused and driven forward to the new camp. In the meantime the cook had stopped, unyoked and hobbled his oxen, and prepared the evening meal. When the cowboys came up, one-half ate while the others herded the cattle on the grazing-ground. They then caught up fresh horses and cared for the cattle while the other half ate. The latter helped the horse-wrangler hobble the entire horse herd, if the boss followed that custom. The crew then bedded down the cattle by continually riding around them until they were formed into a round compact body. The crew was divided into shifts like the sentry watches of military units.

Two men keeping a short distance from the cattle rode around the herd in opposite directions all night long. If the cattle were restless, the men sang a low lullaby like a mother to her child. It was an essential part of the cowboy's work to sing. The human tones had a soothing effect on the frightened, restless animals. It

[15] Dale, *The Range and Ranch Cattle Industry*, pp. 66, 67; Lewis F. Crawford, *Rekindling Camp-Fires*, (Bismarck, N. D., 1926), p. 185.

was said that cattle would not stampede as long as they could hear the human voice. Joseph G. McCoy, founder of Abilene as a shipping town, said that many times, when he had the stock-yards full of wild Texas cattle, he sat on the fence and sang to them while a train was passing; as long as they could hear his voice above the din, they remained quiet, but if escaping steam or the whistle of a locomotive drowned out his voice, the frightened animals would stampede and tear the pens up. The cowboy sang anything from the familiar songs learned in childhood and the popular songs of the day to songs peculiarly the cowboy's own, composed and added to by the caroling night riders. Thus from trail days have originated some of the most typical folk-songs America has produced. On stormy nights it was especially necessary for the cowboy to call into action his repertoire of song, and many godless trail hands sang old camp-meeting hymns with the zest of a circuit-rider. This vocal activity was beneficial to man as well as beast, for it kept him from going to sleep and relieved the monotony of the long, lonely, dark hours.[16]

When the crew crawled into their blankets at night, each member except the cook had his night horse saddled and bridled and slept with the reins in his hand or tied within reach, ready for instant use in case of a stampede. Stampedes were caused by a variety of happenings. Packs of coyotes, herds of buffalo, the striking of a match to light a pipe, a pony shaking his saddle, or even the crackle of a broken stick was enough to frighten the herd.

In his early days as a trail hand, James Cook, for lack of something to kill time in his nocturnal circling, rode closer and closer to a sleeping black cow on the edge of the herd. Finally he touched her, and the nervous brute awoke with a snort, frightening the panicky herd. A stampede was on, resulting in injury to one man and the throwing of two others when their horses stepped into holes. Cook, playing innocent, asked what caused the stampede.

---

[16] Charles Moreau Harger, "Cattle Trails of the Prairies," *Scribner's Magazine*, Vol. XI, pp. 732-742.

A cow hand answered, "God knows!" The verdant youth kept silent, fervently hoping that no one else did.

As a rule the two herders experienced little difficulty until about midnight, barring the ever-present chance of a sudden fright. From twelve till two the cattle became restless, and it required skill to make them lie down and remain quiet until dawn. If the riders were not on the job, the herd was soon up and "drifting," that is, moving *en masse* to another position. Ordinarily the experienced cowboys, by jogging about and turning back the strays, could get the cattle to bed down once more, although they would lie on the side opposite to that on which they had lain the first part of the night.[17] In cold rain, sleet, or hail the herd drifted before the storm. Every man and the boss then rode in front of the herd in an attempt to hold the cattle back. Sometimes a herd drifted several miles in one night and when morning came was far away from the chuck wagon. The members of the crew were fortunate if they did not miss a meal or two before finding the cook. Wet, cold, hungry, and sleepless, the cowboy stuck to his post with a fidelity that was admirable in the extreme.

Stampedes occurred most frequently during a rainy season, and an ideal time was an inky-black night. A lurid flash of lightning, a loud clap of thunder—and the frightened herd was off with the noise of a tornado. The continuous bellowing, the clang of horns, and the clatter of hooves made the very earth tremble. The cowboy, awakened out of a sound sleep by the din, was mounted in a moment and riding after the panic-stricken herd.[18] It was his duty, at such a time, to ride up alongside the leaders and start them running in a huge circle, gradually narrowing it until the whole herd was turning in a solid mass. The cowboys then rode around the milling cattle, singing to quiet them.

---

[17] Homer W. Wheeler, *The Frontier Trail* (Los Angeles, 1923), pp. 87, 88.
[18] Joseph Nimmo, "The American Cowboy," *Harper's Magazine*, Vol. 73, pp. 880-884.

Many times the animals became scattered and ran in different directions. Sometimes it took several days to gather the badly scattered herd. After a stampede, the animals, even if held together, were very nervous the rest of the night and even for some days thereafter. Sometimes stampeding cattle would travel twenty or thirty miles, stopping and resting and then rapidly moving on. A herd has been known to stampede eighteen times in one night. Sometimes in a rainy season cattle got the stampeding habit and grew thin like hounds. This was caused by a handful of wild old steers that had got a chronic fright from which they never recovered. It was real economy to shoot these stampeders. Often the drover cut out a carload of them and sold them at the first railroad station he passed. They were poor, of course, and brought little, but the rest of the herd did better while waiting on the prairie for a buyer or continuing the journey. The cowboys always rejoiced to see a carload of these old trouble-makers loaded out for the packers.

The day after the stampede or stampedes the herd was counted, and if any were missing, the cowboys scoured the country for them, identifying them by the road brand or by the bills of sale. In counting the herd two men selected as counters rode on ahead and stationed themselves some distance apart while the other trail hands allowed the cattle to walk leisurely between them. The counters indicated the hundreds by tying knots in the saddle-string, or, as Andy Adams relates, used small pebbles, shifting a pebble from one hand to the other to indicate that a hundred had passed. Each called out the number on the hundred to check whether the count tallied.

Great losses were often suffered in stampedes. In addition to the actual disappearance of cattle, some animals had their legs broken, horns knocked off, or were otherwise crippled. When herds were held up by high water, or for any other reason there were a number of herds in close proximity, it sometimes took days to get them untangled after a general stampede and mix-up.

A stampede was always fraught with danger to the trail hands also. As the cowboy rode in front of the leaders to turn them, he took his life in his hand. If his horse stepped into a badger or prairie-dog hole, the onrushing herd passed over them, mangling horse and rider with the trampling of hundreds of hooves. Or perhaps in a strange country a rough place in the terrain caused the horseman to ride into a gully or canyon in the darkness in front of the panic-stricken cattle. In such a case there was a hunt for the lost comrade by the earliest light of dawn. The cowboys gathered up his mangled form, dug a shallow grave, wrapped his blanket around him, and tenderly placed him in the earth. There was no one to offer a prayer, and only an oath, meant to be reverent and eulogistic to the comrade, accompanied him to his final rest on the lone prairie. Perhaps a sentence or two of praise as to the man's virtues and faithfulness even unto death haltingly passed the lips of those rough men. Possibly a board was found to place at his head, and on this was cut or burned the dead man's name. Very likely no one in the crowd knew his right name, or who his folks were in the East.[19]

The trail hand had to expose himself to all kinds of weather. The worse the weather, the more he was needed in the saddle. Hail-storms, tornadoes, and electric storms occur in the region of the Long Drive. The electric storms were awe-inspiring, and cow-punchers relate that during one of these displays, balls of fire played off the cattle's horns and the horses' ears. Fire-balls rolled along the ground in a most spectacular way, while sulphur fumes reached the nostrils.

Since there were no ferry-boats or bridges, the cattle had to swim the numerous large rivers between the Gulf and their northern destination. The leaders were guided into the water and the lead cowboys kept the point of the herd headed right. The rest of the herd was kept moving so that no gaps occurred. If all

---

[19] Thos. F. Doran, "Kansas Sixty Years Ago," see Kansas State Historical Society *Collections*, Vol. XV, p. 500; Rollins, *The Cowboy*, pp. 271-274.

A DROVE OF TEXAS CATTLE CROSSING A STREAM

From *Harper's Weekly*, October 19, 1867.

went well, the cattle were over the river in a very short time. A herd of two thousand was got across the Missouri River at Niobrara, Nebraska, in forty-five minutes in August, 1877, which was a record for that point. In July of the same year it took five days to get twenty-two hundred across.[20]

A drifting log striking the leaders or the refusal of a horse to swim sometimes started the herd to milling in the water. This was almost sure to prove disastrous. The cattle sank almost completely out of sight, allowing only their horns and tailheads to protrude out of the water. It was risky business indeed to ride into the stream amidst that mass of horns and break up the mill.

The contents of the chuck wagon were placed on a raft. Lariats tied together were lashed on the end of the wagon tongue, and from the vantage-point of dry ground the running-gear of the wagon was pulled across. Sometimes log pontoons were tied to the wheels and the whole thing floated across.

At the crossing of the Red River in Texas, inspectors scrutinized the herds to see that every drover had bills of sale for the cattle he was taking out of the state. In the Indian territory between Texas and Kansas the red men often stopped the herds, demanding toll for crossing their domain. The wise drover cut out a few of the lame drags as a gift and pacified the Indians. Others had their herds stampeded, cattle butchered, horses stolen, and sometimes the crew attacked.

When the cattle arrived at the rail-head cow-towns of Abilene, Wichita, and Dodge City, technically the Long Drive was over. At Abilene a locator met the drover and assigned him an unoccupied grazing space where he was to remain until a sale was made. As early as June 16, 1877, the *Dodge City Times* stated there were sixty thousand head of cattle around the town. It required on an average about thirty-five days to drive from the Red River to the Kansas cow-towns.[21] Once located on grazing

[20] *Niobrara Pioneer*, Niobrara, Neb., July 26 and August 16, 1877.
[21] *Tenth Census of the United States, Statistical Report on Agriculture*, Vol. III, p. 975.

space, the cattle were sometimes herded for weeks while waiting for a buyer. If a buyer was not found soon and the owner did not decide to ship, a permanent camp was made some distance from town.

When McCoy established a shipping-point at Abilene, he said it was an insignificant dead village of about a dozen small rude log huts with only two shingle roofs in town. The business of the town, he said, was carried on in two small rooms. When the cattle trade came, business began to flourish. Bad characters, both male and female, were soon drawn there like vultures to a carcass. Saloons sprang up like mushrooms, and between every two saloons was a dance-hall. Here gathered hard, dissipated characters to engage in nights of wild orgy. Miserable music was ground out on a dilapidated organ or by a discordant band.

For days before the first herds arrived, the cow-towns had been preparing to entertain these visitors. In March, 1877, the *Dodge City Times* announced that prices had been reduced for the special trade of the cattlemen, that hotels and other business houses were preparing for their guests, and trustworthy men acquainted with all the ranges from the Canadian River to the North Platte were waiting to assist the drovers in finding the best pasture. Instead of encountering lawsuits, the cattlemen would be "treated as honored guests, fed on the fat of the land and regaled with two-bit drinks...."

The places of amusement had been preparing for the Texans. The Saratoga, according to an April news item, had been handsomely painted and grained, making it "look nobby and attractive," and a band from Kansas City had been hired for the summer. The orchestra in one establishment was grandly mounted on a platform enclosed by and tastefully ornamented with bunting. There was a general catering to the Texans. The name "Lone Star" was borne by all manner of business houses and articles for sale.

When the cowboys arrived in 1877, they found Dodge City

a town of twelve hundred residents but with twice as many people
on the streets daily. In its heyday everything was wide open,
rivaling the mining-camps and the railroad terminal towns in booming lawlessness and quiet iniquity. Gambling ranged from a game
of five-cent chuck-a-luck to a thousand-dollar poker pot. It was
not uncommon for a dark-eyed vixen or brazen-faced blonde to
saunter in among the roughs and enter into the sport with gusto.
There was in evidence the greatest abandon. Nice-looking gentlemen in the garb of the best society, the cattle-dealer with the marks
of a gentleman, the sport, the cowboy with boots and spurs right
from the trail—all mingled in one wild revel. According to Frank
Barnard of Corpus Christi, Texas, even the mayor of the city was
accustomed to indulge in a giddy dance with the girls; strutting
about with a cigar in the corner of his mouth sloped at a roguish
angle and his hat tilted to one side, he made a charming-looking
officer.

The green Texas cowboy was an easy mark for the seasoned
vendors of immorality. After he was paid off, the trail hand went
to the barber shop and got his six-months' growth of hair cut and
his sunburnt beard trimmed. Then, rigged out in a complete new
suit of clothes until his fellows hardly recognized him, he rode into
town to engage in a season of dissipation, gambling, and riotous
living. Having lived a lonely life of hardship for weeks and
months, he came to the cow-town parched and thirsty and hunger-
ing for the association of the opposite sex. All too often he threw
away his season's earnings in a few nights of debauchery. Dismount-
ing from his horse, he rushed into the dance-hall, not stopping to
divest himself of sombrero, spurs, or pistols. Once there he grabbed
a partner and entered into the merriment with zest. With his spurs
jingling at every step, pistol flapping, and his eyes lighted up with
liquor, he "hoed it down" in the most approved awkward country
style, often swinging his partner clear off the floor. Occasionally
there was a demoniacal yell akin to that of a savage Indian. After
a set the men always treated their partners. This was done time

and time again.[22] Perhaps the riotous living took another turn. One Texan went to the bar and called for a toddy. While he was drinking it, an attractive girl walked up to him, put her little hand under his chin, looked him straight in the face, and, calling him a pretty Texas boy, asked him for a drink. He felt he was getting on in the world with a pretty girl and plenty of whisky. He told her she could rest easy, for he was going to break the monte game, buy out the saloon, and keep the fair Delilah to run it for him while he went to Texas for his other herd of cattle.[23]

The daily program in Dodge City, according to the *Dodge City Times,* was:

She awakes from her slumbers about 11 a.m.; takes her sugar and lemon at 12 m., a square meal at 1 p.m., commences biz at 2 o'clock gets lively at 4, and at 10 p.m. it is hip—hip—hurrah! till 5 o'clock in the morning.

After a period of debauchery saturated with whisky, any insult, real or imaginary, was enough to cause the cowboy to unlimber his hip artillery and start dealing death. Friend and foe alike were in danger. Sometimes a cowboy went wild and shot up the town, riding into stores or saloons shooting mirrors, bottles, cigars in men's mouths, and in general causing the denizens of the haunts of amusement to find hiding-places under tables, behind counters, and in outer rooms. As a rule, however, the good-natured Texans let off steam by shooting in the air as they rode out of town.

After a fling of a few days of this high life, the Texan was ready to ride down the trail or to take his saddle and go home by rail, as was often done in later days. Some met their death in gun battles with peace officials or in a wild carnival of shooting. In Newton, Kansas, as many as eleven men were killed in one night's brawl. Certainly a cemetery was one of the first institutions needed in a

[22] McCoy, *Historic Sketches of the Cattle Trade,* pp. 141, 142.
[23] E. Douglas Branch, *The Cowboy and His Interpreters* (New York, 1926), pp. 152-153.

cow-town. In Dodge City the graveyard was significantly called "Boot Hill" since so many of the dead had died with their boots on.

By 1884 Dodge City had a cowboy band. They went to St. Louis for the cattlemen's convention that year and later to Chicago. They dressed in full cowboy costume, with white hat, red and white cotton handkerchief about the neck, leather riding-breeches, spurs, a cartridge belt, and a pearl- or ivory-handled six-shooter. The standard of the organization consisted of a splendid set of steer's horns supporting a silk banner bearing the name of the band. The leader waved a nickel-plated six-shooter for a baton.

At the height of its deviltry, in a last orgy in its waning greatness, Dodge City on July 4, 1888, put on a genuine Mexican bullfight in which twelve untamed bulls met five famous bull-fighters from Mexico.[24]

The cow-towns were no mere romantic scenes of drama, but were commercial centers where a large volume of business was carried on in a very small place. In its heyday Abilene did more than three million dollars' worth of business a year. The streets were crowded with people, cowboys and buyers hastened from the hotel to the stock-yards and back, and trainloads of cattle were loaded out. It was a small town to be known so widely, however, and newcomers were often astonished when they first saw it.

A Texan who rode into the midst of the village asked how far it was to Abilene. When told he was in the place, he could scarcely believe his informer and broke forth with: "Now look here, stranger, you don't mean this here little scatterin' trick is Abilene!" When assured it was, he answered: "Well, I'll swar; I never seed such a little town have such a mighty big name."

Cattle at the cow-towns were disposed of in one of three directions. Some, the smaller portion, were shipped east to market. Others were sold to government contractors, to be driven, often farther than they had come, to the forts and Indian reservations

[24] Pelzer, *The Cattlemen's Frontier*, p. 68.

where they were fed to the Indian wards and their guardians at the agencies scattered here and there over the Plains. Last, the bulk of them were driven to the northern territories to populate the ranches that were being opened there. Some of the latter were breeding stock which became the progenitors of the mighty horde of range cattle. Others were "pilgrims"—young stock which were grazed a year or two on the nutritious northern grass and then shipped to market. During the season herds were driven far beyond the Canadian border, a distance of twenty-five hundred miles.

The Long Drive became majestic in its proportions. In the nineteen years from 1866 to 1884 over five million cattle were driven north from Texas. It also grew important in its social and political effects. Hundreds of Texans went up the trail and remained in the North to start ranches. The southern drawl became the western drawl. This stream mingled with a migratory movement from the east. The Civil War there lost its sting as "Reb" and "Yank" came in contact in business dealings and mutual understanding.

CHAPTER XXI

FREE GRASS, THE CATTLEMAN'S PARADISE

THE VAST INCREASE in the size of the ranching area in the United States, with its phenomenal jump from a narrow belt at the close of the Civil War to an area of thousands of square miles a decade later, was an episode in the closing scenes of the frontier history of America.

The span of the range country's blossoming in all its splendor covered the period between the coming of the trunkline railroads and the closing of the range by the homesteader. It was made possible by free grass, railroads to carry the product to market, and a great cattle supply in Texas which made stocking of the Plains comparatively simple and inexpensive.

When the first cattle drives from Texas began in 1866, the drovers in delivering their herds to Indian reservations or forts learned that there was a vast area ideal for grazing purposes. Even before that date, however, the little thin line of Indian-harried road ranchers along the Overland Trail had begun ranching in a small way. Some travelers on the way to the Pacific Coast stopped en route and took up stock-raising. Others, discouraged or tired of the mines, turned back to select an inviting site they had seen on their way to the gold-fields. A notable example of the latter was the great cattle king J. W. Iliff. While many of his friends found graves at the diggings or vainly sought the fleeting mountain treasure, he operated a road ranch and in time accumulated riches in cattle-grazing on the then all but unoccupied Plains. In less than twenty years he became possessor of twenty-six thousand head and controlled a range a hundred and fifty miles long extending from Julesburg to Greeley, Colorado. It was literally a vast realm.

Some of the early cattlemen had filled hay contracts with the government forts. Some were scouts, hunters, Army men, and freighters. Later on, this group, commencing ordinarily with small capital, was augmented by big Texas ranchers, Englishmen, Scotchmen, Canadians, and men representing a large amount of capital in the East. Some of the earliest ranches in Custer County, Nebraska, were established by Texas cattlemen who wintered cattle there before shipping them east and thus became aware of the golden opportunity for ranching in that district.[1] *The Dodge City Times* as late as June, 1873, called attention to the many splendid opportunities in that immediate vicinity to enter the ranching business. Good Texas cattle, it stated, could be bought for from five to ten dollars a head, and there were many fine locations for ranches close to the city.

According to the old-time cattlemen, in the seventies and eighties cattlemen in the Bad Lands of Dakota fell into two classes: the "dogiemen" or nesters who got their cattle from the farming frontier, and the older, better-established ranchers who got theirs from western or Texas stock.

In selecting a ranch site the ranchman's main considerations were good grass and an ample supply of water. The first comers acquired possession of the water-holes, springs, and other natural sources of supply. At that time there was no thought of supplying stock from wells or by impounding large bodies of water.[2] As a consequence, a man who had possession of a spring controlled the grasslands for a distance of about six or seven miles around. A cow (the term "cow" in range parlance meant any type of cow brute; the term used to denote a herd of females was "she stuff") would not walk more than about fifteen miles a day to the water-hole and back to the outer edge of the grazing area. For this reason it was

[1] D. Robert Burleigh, *Range Cattle Industry in Nebraska to 1890*, Ms., Master's Thesis, University of Nebraska, 1937, pp. 36, 37.
[2] Walter Prescott Webb, *The Great Plains* (Boston, 1931), pp. 228.

considered unneighborly to establish a ranch closer than fifteen miles to one already in operation. In the year 1879, in the vicinity of Hat Creek, near Ardmore, Nebraska, Colonel Charles Coffee met Hugh Jackson. He told Hugh he was looking for a new location and, according to the early courtesy of the range, asked the first comer if he would like to have a neighbor. On being assured that he was welcome, the Colonel went up Hat Creek looking for a suitable place. He estimated his speed and took note of the time with his watch, and when he had reached a point fifteen miles from his neighbor, he was ready to select a spot for his ranch headquarters. There the "O-Ten-Bar" ranch and brand were born. In time the Colonel controlled twenty-two thousand acres around it.[3]

The ideal ranch extended out from the water-front with coulées or valleys affording protection for the cattle during blizzards and severe storms. There were also knolls and hillsides from which the snow was blown, providing grazing during storms when the valleys were covered with a heavy snowfall. Little or no hay was put up in those early years, and no sheds were built for winter protection. Cattle had to "rustle" for themselves winter and summer.[4]

When the rancher chose his water monopoly, he took possession of it and established a headquarters camp. Edgar B. Bronson described such a camp on Cottonwood Creek, twelve miles out of Fort Laramie, Wyoming. In a sheltered nook on the creek he dug a hole in the bank eighteen feet square, roofed it with poles, covered them with grass and earth, and made a rude stone fireplace and chimney. The one extravagance, he humorously reported, was the door. Since he lacked lumber, the door remained an unsolved problem until the "top cutter" fell and broke his leg.[5] The animal

[3] Grant L. Shumway, ed., *History of Western Nebraska and Its People* (Lincoln, Nebr., 1921), Vol. II, p. 110.

[4] Maude Ethel Felter, *The Beginnings of the Range and Ranch Cattle Business of Montana*, Ms., Master's Thesis, University of Iowa, 1924, pp. 13, 14.

[5] A "cutter" was a cow-horse used to cut out cattle or separate them from the herd. The term "top" signifies best.

was shot and skinned, and the green hide was stretched over a pole frame. The frame, when hung on rawhide hinges, left a wide crevice, but it sufficed and was the most expensive item in the house, a seventy-five-dollar door (the value of the horse) on a ten-dollar house.

John Clay wrote of one of his early camps: "We had lots of wood, a good supply of grub, a keg of whisky, lots of robes, and one bed." The few furnishings of one of these camps consisted of a pole table and stools, bedsteads of the same material with a rawhide stretched hammock-like across the frame for a mattress. On pegs above each bunk hung the firearms. Beneath the bunks was the storehouse, and near the fireplace was an improvised cupboard made of boxes. On the floor in front of the boss's bunk, perhaps, lay the tawny skin of a mountain lion. A broom made of willow twigs bound about one end of a pole served its intended purpose fairly well.

All of the old stage or Pony Express stations along the Overland Trail were appropriated by the cattlemen for their camps. The dugouts made by the railroad construction gangs or buffalo hunters were also often taken over for this purpose.

In time a temporary camp was raised to the status of ranch headquarters, with houses, barns, a corral, and machinery. The land on which the ranch headquarters was located was owned by the rancher. He often filed on a quarter-section as a homestead. Perhaps he added to the ranch holdings by preëmption or other means. Frequently areas were held by lease or even by squatter's rights only.[6] The latter were respected by the other cattlemen. But whether the land actually possessed was large or small, the working principle of the range industry was to establish the ranch headquarters on owned land controlling a water monopoly and to use the boundless unfenced grasslands of the government for pasture. A considerable area of land on the water-front was fenced to keep

---

[6] Joseph Orlando Van Hook, *Settlement and Economic Development of the Arkansas Valley from Pueblo to the Colorado-Kansas Line, 1860-1900*, Ms., Doctor's Thesis, University of Colorado, 1933, pp. 155, 156.

A TYPICAL MONTANA RANCH

From a photograph by W. H. Jackson.

out intruders, and there was also a large fenced horse pasture for horses likely to be needed on short notice.

With the coming of permanent improvements, the old cow-camp with its wholly masculine atmosphere was replaced by a ranch-house with a feminine touch as women found their way into the region. Even so, the average ranch-house was not a palace. Little more than a hut, it was built of logs or sod and covered with hay and earth. The logs were drawn sometimes a hundred miles or more from mountain canyons. The one or more rooms of the ranch-house were furnished with ordinary frontier household fixtures. In this dwelling the owner of the ranch, or in case he was an absentee rancher, his representative the foreman, resided. Perhaps fifty yards away, between the house and the barn, were the bunk-houses of the cowboys. These, also constructed of logs and covered with dirt, were arranged in a row, forming a long, narrow room with the kitchen and dining-room at one end and the bunks around the wall at the other. Along the walls were pegs where the cowboys hung their saddles, lariats, guns, wearing apparel, and other property. There was a stove or fireplace in the midst of the bunks, and a small table near-by for use in playing cards. The cook had his bunk near the spot where he reigned supreme. The dining-table near the cookstove indicated that this end of the building was both kitchen and dining-room.[7] Near the water supply was the barn. If it was a spring, often the stream was turned in such a way as to flow through the barnyard and horse paddock. Near-by was the cattle corral. Other buildings supplied various needs. Among the essentials was a blacksmith shop, where the numerous cow-ponies were shod and repairs of farm machinery were made. The number of buildings depended upon the size of the ranch, its state of prosperity, and the date. In later years ranches began to emerge from the crude frontier conditions. There might then be an ice-house, bringing a certain luxury to the ranch, machine

[7] E. Douglas Branch, *The Cowboy and His Interpreters* (New York, 1926), p. 90.

sheds for hay-making machinery, gardens, a cave, stables, a carriage house, and other improvements.

In a few instances large ranches in later years had elaborate ranch-houses. The Mudge Ranch in the vicinity of Dodge City, Kansas, in 1884 had a palatial stone ranch-house with a piazza, baths, halls, and parlors furnished with rich carpets, marble-topped tables, lounges, easy-chairs, and a piano. On the table were papers and magazines from London, Paris, and the larger cities of the United States. In this veritable palace many festive and social occasions were celebrated. Such a ranch-house with its breakfast at eleven A.M. and its dinner at seven P.M. was an exception, however, rather than the rule.[8]

Most of the ranches were comparatively small concerns. As late as 1880, when General James S. Brisbin made a detailed study of the ranching business, he found that on 126 ranches in western Nebraska and eastern Wyoming the average number of cattle was 1,358 head, with ten thousand on the largest and fifty on the smallest. The number of men on a ranch was seldom more than eight or twelve.

In time the number of cattle on a ranch increased to such an extent that the proprietor was forced to enlarge his area. He bought up the headquarters of various smaller outfits near-by. A western Nebraska record of one such holding reads:

Just east of Wild Cat mountain in the northern part of Banner County is a spring that adds its flow to that of Pumpkin Creek. This was located by a man named Brown, and the forty acres on which it was situated was sold to the Bay State (Ranch). This spring is known as the "Four-Jay-Spring."[9]

In time a large "outfit" had a number of these out ranches with buildings where a few cowboys made their headquarters. The original site with its buildings and equipment then was the "home ranch" to these out ranches. Brisbin reported that at the time of

---

[8] *Kansas Cowboy*, Dodge City, Kansas, October 18, 1884.
[9] Shumway, *History of Western Nebraska and Its People*, Vol. II, p. 103.

Iliff's death the cattle king controlled over twenty thousand acres of water-front and was fast buying more. Pierre Wibaux owned only a quarter-section of land where his "White House" was located, but he controlled all the range between the Yellowstone and Missouri Rivers north of the Northern Pacific Railway. The eighties were the era of the big cattleman. Large companies with an abundance of Eastern or foreign capital entered the business and operated by means of a salaried foreman who was perhaps an owner of one of the purchased ranches or an outstanding cowboy.

A number of women operated ranches. Mrs. Bishop Hiff Warren was credited with being the wealthiest woman in Colorado, with total assets of ten million dollars. This she made herself on cattle. These "cattle queens" hired trusted foremen to supervise the actual handling of the cattle while they managed the immense business as ably as her masculine neighbors.[10]

The work of the early-day cowboy was arduous and involved extreme exposure to the elements. Nevertheless the actual muscular effort put forth was comparatively little. During the early summer he rode on the round-up. In the late summer he helped put up a small quantity of hay for the horses. In the fall came the beef round-up and trailing the cattle perhaps a hundred miles to the railroad. Sometimes a cowboy would have the opportunity of going with the cars of cattle to Kansas City, Omaha, or Chicago, of seeing the sights afforded by the big city, and returning on a pass. Such an adventurer would amuse his fellows in the bunkhouse for days with stories of his escapades.

The winter was spent for the most part in toasting shins in the bunkhouse or in "riding the grub line." This consisted of making the rounds of the neighboring ranches, visiting a few days at each place. The hospitable ranchmen always expected any man who happened to be in his neighborhood hunting horses or for any other reason to stop for a meal or overnight. The visitor did ample justice at the table and regaled the inmates of the bunk-

[10] C. C. Post, *Ten Years a Cowboy* (Chicago, 1898), p. 416.

house with the doings of the crew at his ranch. The grub-line rider was also the local news-gatherer and dispenser as he went from ranch to ranch. Even the owner of the ranch and certainly the foreman were not averse to spending several hours listening to the happenings of the neighborhood for a hundred miles around. Riding the grub line was especially popular with the cowboy who had severed his connection with his ranch for the winter and had used up his summer's wages in riotous living at the neighboring cow-town.

[Although gambling was forbidden in the "dog house," as the bunkhouse was called, auction pitch, dominoes, checkers, a stag-dance, or music occupied many a long winter evening. Quirt-making, of which the cowboy was a master, took hours of his time. Cowboys very rarely got a letter, and reading material was so scarce that a paper was passed from hand to hand and reread until it actually dropped to pieces—it was never deliberately destroyed. So scarce was female companionship that some of the men joined matrimonial bureaus in order to have some correspondence. So heavy did time hang on their hands that after tin cans came into use, one man would hold a can while another would recite all the printing on the label, merely as a time-killing contest to see who would make the fewest errors. Stewart Edward White, the well-known novelist, while waiting for supper in a bunkhouse, lay on a bunk and looked up at the ceiling. He counted 3,620 bullet holes, made there by improvident cowboys who, while waiting for supper as he was doing, whiled away their time and squandered their ammunition shooting at flies that crawled about on the ceiling.]

When a stranger visited a bunkhouse and completely disrobed and put on a nightshirt in which to sleep, a cowboy thought he had gone completely insane. A cow-puncher was accustomed to take off only his coat, hat, boots, and spurs—and he was ready for bed.

In the spring came a hunt for the horses, to gather them in for use in the round-up. Many of the cow-ponies, having run wild for months, had to be rebroken and reminded of the lessons they had previously learned.

In later years the cowboy's life was much more filled with manual labor, which led him to lament that times were not what they used to be. There was gardening in the spring, perhaps irrigating a meadow, hundreds of tons of hay to be made for the cattle after the summer round-up, and in the winter there was a continual round of hauling hay and feeding the cattle when snow covered the grazing-lands.

The round-up was the most important single activity during the year. The first round-ups in Colorado, in the sixties, were a sort of informal coöperation between neighbors. From this developed the stockmen's associations in the seventies.[11] Perhaps the best known of these organizations was the Wyoming Stock Growers Association, which took in all of Wyoming and western Nebraska and the western part of Dakota. For convenience in carrying on the work, the vast area of this association was divided into thirty-one round-up districts. In 1884 five of these were in Nebraska, two in southwestern Dakota, and twenty-four in Wyoming. The association met on the first Monday in April at Cheyenne, made any necessary changes in districts, and set the dates for the beginning of round-ups, which depended on the earliness of the spring and were calculated to allow the cattle to shed off in order that the brands might be read more easily and the grass to become good so the cow-horses would be in good flesh. Following this meeting a broadside was put out with instructions for the current round-up.

The handbill for 1884 gave the following instructions for District 13:

Commence at the Sidney crossing, on Running Water, June 1st. Work to the head; thence to the head of Indian Creek, working down to Camp Creek, across to the S-D ranch, working all the tributaries of Indian Creek; thence to the head of Hat Creek down

[11] Ora Brooks Peake, *The Colorado Range Cattle Industry* (Glendale, Cal., 1937), p. 253.

to the O-B A R ranch, then down to the T. Fall round-up to commence October 15th. Sam Moses, Foreman; Chris Stortz, assistant foreman.[12]

There were anywhere from five to a dozen cow outfits in the territory covered by a district, and it was customary for each to send to the round-up a wagon-boss or foreman, eight cowboys, two horse-wranglers, a cook, a chuck wagon, and a bed wagon. The night wrangler drove the bed wagon in the daytime and helped the cook. Each cowboy furnished his own bed and riding equipment, but his employer furnished the saddle horses, about eight or ten to a man, with four horses or mules to the wagon, and a few extra animals. The work and riding stock thus numbered over a hundred head. Small "outfits" generally had only half a crew and depended on the representatives of ranches in neighboring districts to fill up their crews. These representatives, or "reps" as they were called, rode with the other cowboys and inspected the cattle to see if any stock from their outfits might have wandered into the district. Sometimes a large outfit sent ten or more reps to the neighboring districts. They were treated courteously, given their food, and their horses and cattle were handled. Sometimes two or three small ranches would pool their resources for the occasion and send one complete crew.[13] In the biggest round-ups of the eighties in Colorado there were sometimes as many as seventy-five wagons, about a thousand men, and six or seven thousand horses.

On the appointed day of the beginning of the round-up, the place of rendezvous presented a picturesque and animated appearance. The different outfits had their camps pitched, their wagons and tents scattered in an informal fashion. Here and there were herds of horses grazing near-by, each kept separate from the others by watchful riders. Cowboys rode from camp to camp visiting, exchanging news, and chaffing with other cowboys who lolled at full

[12] "1884 Round-ups," Wyoming Stock Growers Association handbill, Nebraska State Historical Society Library.

[13] Dan Adamson, *History of the Early Day Range Work and Customs*, Ms., Nebraska State Historical Society Library.

length on the grass at their tents. The cooks, "pot wrestlers," around cow-chip fires prepared savory meals with only such few "cooking tools" as a coffee-pot, frying-pan, camp kettle, and a Dutch oven. Foremen met together in a little group discussing how best to accomplish the two or three weeks' work before them. At dusk the horse herd of each outfit was driven into an improvised rope corral formed by willing hands. The night horses were "caught up" and staked out on the good grass. Then the men gathered at a few of the more popular camps, and there followed several hours of the singing of cowboy songs accompanied by the mouth-organ. The cowboy became exceedingly expert at playing that instrument. After a variety of entertainment, such as hoedown dances, humorous recitations, practical jokes, and other hilarity, the evening finally came to a close with two or three of the old favorite songs, such as "Sam Bass," "The Texas Frontier," or "The Texas Ranger." One by one the groups about the camp-fires dwindled away, and soon all was quiet except the crunch of the night horses eating grass or the lonely howl of a distant wolf. Now and then the silence was broken by the tinkle of a horse's bell or the singing of "Bury Me Not on the Lone Prairie" by a horse-wrangler in his effort to keep awake.[14]

At four the next morning each cook rousted out the hands of his own camp with his particular chuck call. One cried: "Chuck! Grub's up! Rise and grab a root!" Another shouted: "Chuck-a-luck-a-luck-a-chuck, come and get it 'fore I throw it out."[15]

The process of dressing was simple, consisting merely of pulling on the boots and coat and putting on the hat, since the cowboys slept with most of their clothes on. The bed, which was only a couple of blankets, was neatly straightened out, rolled up in its tarpaulin cover, strapped tightly, and tossed into the bed wagon. A hasty morning toilet, a good breakfast, and the riders rolled up

[14] "Annual Round-Up," see *Dawson Scrapbooks*, Ms., Colorado State Historical Society Library, Vol. XVI, p. 35.
[15] Personal interview with Chauncey Thomas, July 7, 12, 1938.

the tent and laid it by the wagon to be packed away by campmen, who in the meantime busied themselves with the camp chores.

By this time the horse-wrangler had driven the horses into the rope corral, and there was a race to see who could get his horse saddled first and ride away. At the beginning of the round-up this was the occasion for much fun, since the animals, fresh and frisky, exhibited considerable bucking; but their antics subsided as the round-up progressed and hard riding tended to calm down even the most spirited animal.

Now it was time to get the orders "for the circle," as it was called. All riders unattached to duty elsewhere rode up to head-quarters, where the captain, mounted, made the assignments for the day. His gruff, terse commands ran something like the fol-lowing: "Tex, you and those five men take the outer circle up Little Cedar and round up at Beaver Flats." The six cowboys "light out" on the outer circle. Then the captain ordered Slim Jim and five men to take the inner circle, "work" Red Buttes, and come in over Alkali Basin. Then he assigned another six men to "go down the river among the grangers [farmers] and see if any range cattle are down that way, and mind you don't tarry long." The latter injunction referred to a weakness of the cowboys for the farmers' daughters and the buttermilk or other delicacies served up by the homesteaders' women folks. Detail after detail was sent out, each under a leader familiar with the country to be covered. Finally the captain took a group of men who, like the others, scattered out and searched closely the territory assigned to them. This process was known as "combing the country." In due time the riders came in, bringing to the appointed spot the cattle found on the circle. Sometimes, in a region which had good grass and water, several thousand head were driven together. If very large, this "bunch" [16] was split up into smaller bunches in order to "work" it more conveniently.

[16] In some sections it seems the term "herd" was reserved for trail cattle. Smaller groups were called "bunches."

The next process was known as "cutting out." It consisted of locating a cow of a particular brand, skilfully separating it from the main herd by dashing into the "bunch," and holding it with others of that brand in a smaller body called "the cuts" or the "side herd." As the process went on, the main "bunch" grew smaller as the side herds grew larger. Cutting out was exciting work and required fast, hard riding, testing the skill of both horse and rider. This business was generally monopolized by the "top hands" and foremen, who willingly accepted the opportunity of displaying their horsemanship. The lesser lights "held" the herds, "heading" every animal that attempted to leave its fellows. It was often a matter of much surprise to "tenderfeet" or people not familiar with the process that the two herds were kept in such close proximity during this exciting business. The "wet cattle," that is, cows in milk, with their calves, were cut out first to preclude running over the calves and injuring them during the fast riding.

When all of the outfits had cut their cattle from the main herd, there were always a number of strays or branded cattle not belonging to anyone represented at the round-up. These strays were driven some distance away and allowed to run free on the range for the time being. The calves were castrated. Each outfit then put day herders on duty and grazed its cattle separately. When a foreman had gathered all the cattle in a given region, he was said to have "covered his dog." [17]

In the meantime, while the riders were "combing" the country, the cook of each outfit, with the aid of the horse-herder, packed the bedding, tents, and all equipment in the wagons, and they proceeded to the appointed place where the riders were to converge with their cattle. The riders, having ridden twenty to forty miles, quickly caught up fresh horses before beginning the work of cutting out. At noon, when "Miss Sally" called "Come and get it," each man grabbed a tin plate, cup, knife, fork, and spoon, helped himself, and then retired to the tent or outside to eat. The favorite

[17] *Bad Lands Cowboy*, Medora, Dakota Territory, September 4, 1884.

diet on the round-up was mulligan stew, composed of scraps of meat, onion, pepper, and salt; spotted-dog pudding, made of rice, raisins, eggs, sugar, and canned milk; sour-dough biscuits made by the cook; and coffee, which he roasted in a skillet and ground in a coffee-mill on the side of the chuck wagon. To this menu were added beef, beans, dried fruit, and potatoes. The "old lady" commanded the respect of all and would allow no criticism of the grub. One time, so the story goes, a tenderfoot, not finding work in any other capacity, hired out as a cook. He was as green at that job as at any other on the range, and when he attempted to cook dried apples for a pie, he filled the pot full and covered them with water. When they began to swell, he did not have free pots enough to care for his fast-increasing pie assets and was caught digging a hole in the prairie to bury his mistake.

After the noon meal was eaten, a couple of hours were spent in resting in the shade of the tents.[18] Sometimes the calves were branded on the prairie, and in that case the afternoon was spent at this work. At other times the cut-outs were taken to the ranch to be branded. In this case the crews proceeded to comb additional territory. When the cut-outs of any outfit became too numerous to be wieldy, they were "thrown" over to their own range and released.

The Spanish term for round-up is *el rodeo,* and it is from this that the modern popular form of entertainment derives its origin and name. Indeed, during the earlier days when the rodeo was work, not a professional show, it provided a social outlet for the cowboys. Here cowboys from far and wide met, swapped news, told stories, bragged about their respective outfits, sang together, and measured one another by their horsemanship. In later years sometimes a girl who rode well took her place in the round-up and, if skilful, was respected and admired by all. *The Bad Lands Cowboy* in January, 1885, spoke of fifteen-year-old Nellie Sergeant who

[18] Walter Baron von Richthofen, *Cattle-Raising on The Plains of North America* (New York, 1885), pp. 22-24.

Courtesy of the Union Pacific Railway

COWBOYS AROUND THE CHUCK WAGON

could handle the lariat and branding-iron and ride bronchos like a man.

In later years the round-up became more of a show. Often outsiders visited the camp, and the cowboys generally tried to entertain them. For example, on Sunday, June 29, 1884, a special train was run from Denver to Brush, Colorado, with a special round-trip fare of three dollars. Over fifty availed themselves of the opportunity of visiting a round-up, among whom were several writers and correspondents.[19]

The amusements at the round-up were attractive to cow-punchers, and they looked forward to this festive season for weeks. While the men were waiting for supper, there were tests of endurance and horsemanship in riding bronchos. The horses on a ranch were all named. Often the names indicated peculiarities or characteristics. For example, a clumsy one was called Puddin' Foot; a spotted one, Pinto; a fast horse, Lightning; a sure-footed one, Sure-Foot; and a grey one, Speck.

After the broncho-riding a cowboy sometimes rode a yearling steer by way of variation. Then perhaps followed a race on foot between several of the crowd. A cowboy never walked if he could help it. He would almost rather walk half a mile, however, to catch his horse in order to ride half that distance to do a chore than to walk to do the chore.

After supper some of the younger men had a frolic while the older ones sat about watching and smoking. Some were tying fancy knots, others were repairing saddles, polishing spurs or bridles, and perhaps one or two were braiding horsehairs into a fancy hackamore. All about were gestures, stories, and language too picturesque to be described in detail.[20]

Mavericks were unbranded cattle that were weaned and thus not attached to a branded mother. Hence ownership was unknown. Such animals were subject to different regulations in different

[19] Peake, *The Colorado Range Cattle Industry*, p. 259.
[20] Herbert Myrick, *Cache la Poudre: the Romance of a Tenderfoot in the Days of Custer* (New York, 1905), p. 86.

localities. In some places they were sold and the income went into the general fund of the cattlemen's association. In Wyoming, in 1883-84, the association collected the sum of $1,151 for strays and hides. In Colorado by state law the money from the sale of such animals went into the school fund.

Persons who owned only a few head of cattle hired the local association to round up their herds. The Turkey Creek Association of Colorado in 1880 charged $2.50 a head for this work.

In addition to the main round-up in June, there was the beef round-up in the fall, in which the marketable cattle were cut out and "trailed" to the nearest railroad to be shipped to market. Still later in the season came the bull round-up, when the bulls were taken off the range and kept on a bull ranch where they could be fed hay. This regulated mating and ensured summer calves instead of the risk of having them born in a snow-drift. All in all, the round-up lent more of the spectacular and picturesque to a cowboy's life than any other feature of his work.

When the cattle were branded immediately after the cut-out for the day, one cowboy roped the calf by the head and a second roped a hind foot. The ropes were wrapped around the saddle-horns, and the cow-horses, trained to the work, held the lariats taut. Cowboys then threw the calf on the ground and branded it with an iron heated in a cow-chip fire. In this case all the work was done on the open prairie. When cattle were driven to the ranch for branding, the calves were put into a corral and one by one were run into a massive chute which, manipulated by men on foot, held the animal tight while the hot iron was applied from the outside.

The medley of smells, sounds, and sights accompanying the branding was interesting indeed to the uninitiated. There were the lowing of cattle, the peculiar smell of the cow-chip fire, the bellow of pain as the hot iron seared the quivering flesh, the putrid smell of burning flesh and hair, together with the odor of sweating horses and the grime produced by the dust of the corral on the sweat-stained faces and hands.

After the cattle business got well organized, the brands were all registered at the state capitol, and there were no two alike in the same grazing area. The individual brand was advertised in a stock journal for a time and became as much the property of the man in whose name it was registered as a piece of real-estate. Brands were bought and sold. Ranches were known by their brands. For example, a ranch that had for its brand an L lying down was known as the Lazy L Ranch. When a man bought an animal, he "vent-branded" it by placing his own "vent brand" in the legal position for it. Every owner of a brand had his particular spot on the animal where the brand was to be placed. The old owner gave the new a bill of sale to protect him. The state or the stock growers association issued a brand book giving the brands, vent brands, their owners, and the places where the brands were to be placed. Theodore Roosevelt's brand was a Maltese cross, placed on the left hip of a horse and on the left hip and right ribs of a cow. His vent brand was an R.[21]

Although it would seem that the scheme of branding and recording of brands was efficient, there were many loopholes in the system which allowed cattle to assume new possessors dishonestly. It was a standing joke in the range country that the only time a man ever ate his own beef was when he dined with a neighbor. In the earlier days there was a certain easy practice about the range which allowed a man to keep within the law and still build up a herd at the expense of his neighbors. Cowboys were often paid a certain sum per month and five or ten dollars for every maverick they branded for their bosses. Many of the small ranchers got their start in this questionable fashion. The alert cowboy got a brand registered at the capitol although he might not own a single cow. Then, by watching, he picked up a few mavericks here and there and soon had the beginnings of a herd of his own.

An incident which happened just west of the continental divide

[21] Brand Book of the Montana Stock Growers (Chicago, 1886), North Dakota State Historical Society Library.

in Idaho well illustrates this point. John Haley, owner of a stage line, tried to buy some hay from a rancher by the name of Butler, but the rancher refused, saying he would need the hay for his cattle. When asked how many he had, he informed his visitors that two years previously he had begun business with a yoke of steers and one milch cow. By careful management in two years he had increased his herd to thirty-five head. The astonished stage-owner told the rancher he would like to buy his hay, but he would a whole sight rather buy that milch cow.[22]

As a matter of fact, in those days branding a man's calf was looked upon in a far different light from stealing a horse. If caught at the former, a man was supposed to vent-brand the animal and give the owner a bill of sale. If caught with his neighbor's horse, he invariably "stretched hemp" at the hands of a vigilante band. In a country where no man walked, horse-stealing was looked upon with greater reprobation than murder. Many got their man in a pistol fight and went scot-free, while the theft of a horse meant a hanging-bee if the thief was caught.

This easy legal means of enabling a cowboy to become a cowman by branding mavericks soon shaded into genuine "rustling" or cattle thievery. Rustlers carried small iron rods about on their saddles, and when they found an animal whose brand could be changed, they "ran" their brand. For example, an L or an E could be changed to a B. To prevent this type of chicanery, laws were passed forbidding any kind of irons to be carried or any brands "run." The rustlers evaded them by taking the girth ring from their saddles and using it to "run" the brand.[23]

Sometimes rustlers killed cattle, buried the hides, and sold the meat at the mining-camp or town. Later laws compelled the exhibition of the hide of any butchered animal on a corral fence or other public place for a certain length of time after killing.

The problem of rustling merged with the struggle between the

[22] C. S. Walgamott, *Reminiscences of Early Days* (Twin Falls, Idaho, 1926), Vol. II, pp. 103-104.
[23] Personal interview with Chauncey Thomas, July 8, 1938.

homesteaders and cattlemen on the edge of granger settlement where the two antagonistic types of economic development came into conflict. The irate homesteader had to watch his crops to prevent their destruction by the ranchers' cattle, and he began to shoot the despised animals which caused him so much damage. The ranchmen tried in every way to discourage homesteading by telling the settlers the country was too dry for farming or by spreading reports of Indian outrages. The ranchers also fenced great pastures on the public domain, threatening anyone who should enter these preserves. The "nesters," as the cowmen called them, becoming more numerous, cut the fences and exercised their legal right to homestead the land that the ranchers were attempting illegally to retain.[24]

Such was the background of the famous Johnson County War in Wyoming. In the winter of 1891-92 the ranchers determined to get rid of what to them was an undesirable element termed "rustlers." They hired a number of ex-sheriffs and fighting men of one kind and another and unloaded them at Casper. Thence they marched north to Buffalo and began their campaign for clearing the country of the rustlers. When the homesteaders learned of the movement, the whole granger population was aroused and swarmed in like the minute-men at Lexington and Concord. The cattlemen were surrounded by the settlers and beleaguered in a ranch-house. The besieged no doubt would have perished to a man had not one of their number escaped at night and carried a plea for help. United States soldiers were sent out to arrest the besiegers, but when the commander arrived and learned the true situation, he arrested the cattlemen instead.[25] This incident marked a turning-point in the conflict between the settlers and the big ranchers and presaged the end of the open range. A few years later came a struggle between the sheepmen and the cattlemen.

[24] See Everett Dick, *The Sod-House Frontier* (New York, 1937), Chap. XI.
[25] Frank M. Canton, *Frontier Trails*, E. E. Dale, ed. (New York, 1930), Chap. IV; Robert B. David, *Malcolm Campbell, Sheriff* (Casper, Wyo., 1932), Chaps. V-XIV.

At first the cattlemen had the best of the argument, because even the settlers coming in were cattlemen in a small way, and they controlled the local government.

Range cattle, as a rule, were shipped to Chicago, Kansas City, or other eastern markets, but a notable exception was attempted in 1883 when a French nobleman, Marquis de Mores, established a packing-plant at Medora, Dakota Territory. It ran for three years but did not prove a success.

In the earlier days the cowboys broke the cow-horses. Later, breaking horses became a specialized type of work done by a special class known as "broncho-busters" or "rough-riders." Probably not over two or three per cent of the cowboys were broncho-busters, but they had work enough to earn their pay at that job alone. Sometimes they were called upon to "take the top flight off" several bad horses in a day. Occasionally the cowboy ran across an "outlaw." The "top" could never be taken off such an animal, and he was worthless until in later years he gained a market value for exhibition purposes. Steamboat, a Wyoming horse, was one of the most famous of these outlaws. In riding a broncho it was customary to scratch, or "rake," the animal with the spurs at first so that he would buck and get the viciousness out of his system somewhat. Negroes made good broncho-busters. One of the most famous was Broncho Sam who rode anything led out to him.

Horse-ranching became a specialized business, and a few big ranches furnished many horses to the cattle outfits. A few men made good money catching the wild horses that ranged the prairies of the West and Southwest. It was customary to follow a herd of these mustangs for months, until, by getting into close enough range, the hunters could shoot the stallions and then corral the mares.[26] George Young of Sterling, Kansas, accompanied by two other men, for four months in the summer of 1877 followed a herd of wild horses over four hundred miles in a spring wagon. Finally

[26] Robert M. Wright, *Dodge City the Cowboy Capital* (Wichita, Kans., 1913), p. 82.

they corralled fifty of them, for which Young was offered thirty dollars a head. Naturally, as they were hunted, the wild horses became more wary and harder to catch. It became an all-winter task to capture a herd of these animals and required persistence and skill.

The newcomer in the range country, known as a tenderfoot, was hazed in various ways. In the first place, he was given the worst horse in the *remuda* to ride, and then all hands watched the fun. Pranks were played and jokes were cracked at his expense. If he could cheerfully endure this initiation, he was dubbed a good scout and received into the group. The cow country hated anything affected or stilted. Spectacles were particularly in disfavor as representing something artificial.[27]

Oftentimes the cowboy fraternity was augmented by those who for some reason or other found it more comfortable to move from the East onto the fringe of the westward march. Many cowboys lost their names as they crossed the intervening Plains to the cow country. Hence, as with other frontier figures, it was not good taste for a stranger to inquire about one's past. The cowboy in the presence of strangers was non-communicative, but in his own circle he talked intimately and much. The principal topic around the camp-fire at night was "hoss." Trades were made and imaginary races were run.

[Like others who lived close to nature on the frontier, the cowboy used pithy language. A word served to convey meaning often carried by a sentence. To one unaccustomed to his language the cowboy seemed violent. He swore for emphasis, for punctuation, and by way of appreciation or condemnation. His admirable repertoire of "cuss" words and sacrilegious phrases were not meant to revile God, but were mere slang and were as often spoken in endearment as in anger. His speech was full of allusions to the familiar things of life. "Clean straw" might mean just that, or it might mean a clean bed-sheet. An old-timer in admonition to

[27] T. A. McNeal, *When Kansas Was Young* (New York, 1922), p. 194.

a talkative tenderfoot would remark, "Save part of your breath for breathing." Indian sign language was known and used more or less by many cowboys.[28]

The cowboy resisted any show of sentiment. He attempted to exhibit a rough exterior under the most sentimental circumstances. A story filled with pathos told about a camp-fire brought an unbidden tear to the eye of a cowboy whose rough outside covered a tender heart; brushing it away, he remarked: "The smoke of your camp-fire got into my eyes." Sometimes cowboy clothing got pretty slick and dirty, and Pat Piper, an old cowboy, once got off a good joke on Arkansas Bob about it. Pat stopped at the latter's ranch and found the whole outfit batching. The bedding was none too clean, and after Pat had gone to bed, Bob asked if there was anything else he needed. The opportunity was too good to pass up, and Pat replied: "You might bring a shovelful of sand and throw it in the bed so I won't slip out of it."

The cowboy seldom complained, but "swallowed his trouble with his food" and saw the brighter side of a situation no matter how dark it might appear. His quiet gallantry toward women is proverbial. No matter how rough the celebration, a woman was a lady to the cowboy and as such represented an ideal for whose protection he would fight.[29]

There was a certain vanity about the cowboy which caused him to spend a large portion of his wages on equipment and apparel. His equipment consisted of a forty-pound saddle, a forty-foot lariat, a bridle, a tarpaulin, and two or three blankets. The apparel peculiar to the cowboy consisted of high-heeled boots, a big hat with broad brim, a big handkerchief for a neckerchief, chaps, (*chaparejos*), and California spurs with two-inch rowells. These articles were all of great utility on the range and were a social necessity on dress-up occasions. Even at a dance the cowboy in high-heeled boots walked across the floor with his mammoth spurs jingling at every

[28] Philip Ashton Rollins, *The Cowboy* (New York, 1922), p. 74.
[29] Branch, *The Cowboy and His Interpreters*, pp. 151, 158; Webb, *The Great Plains*, pp. 247-250.

step. Those same boots were a necessity for riding, for they protected the ankle from the certain chafing that came with wearing low-heeled shoes. The big hat was an umbrella, protecting its wearer from sun and rain. It served as a water-bucket and as a fan to start an obstreperous camp-fire. The neckerchief was tied over the face as a protection against alkali dust in driving the drags or was used to tie the broad brim of the hat down over the ears as a protection against the cold and stinging sleet. The chaps protected the rider from the brush, prevented saddle chafing, and the hairy-styled ones protected the leg of the rider when a horse fell on him.

The vanity of the cowboy often caused him to buy more ornate equipment and baubles until there arose the saying, "a forty-dollar saddle on a ten-dollar hoss." As a matter of fact, much of the cowboy's wages were spent on this outfit and on clothes. Wages depended on the quality of the cowhand, the locality, and the date. The farther north the district and the later the date, the higher the wages were. The average wage in Custer County, Nebraska, in the eighties was thirty-five to forty dollars a month. Wages for "top hands" in some places ran as high as sixty dollars a month. Cowboys were of all ages, from sixteen to sixty, but the majority were under thirty. One over that age was called an "old" cowboy.

When not on duty, the cowboy, like a care-free school-boy on a holiday, burst forth to find amusement. The cow-town furnished a welcome diversion in the autumn after the beef cattle had been trailed in. Hungry for companionship after months away from civilization, he fell an easy prey to the dance-hall girls, the gamblers, and the saloon-keepers. After he had danced and gambled and drunk awhile, he now and then set out to celebrate and shot up the town. Sometimes he would ride into a saloon and jump his pony onto the billiard-table. As a rule the business men were reluctant to stop the cowboys' fun, for they brought much business to the town, and it was deemed the lesser of two evils to allow them to go unmolested. Shooting up the town became a nuisance after a while, however, and seemed such an affront to the people of North Platte, Nebraska, that it resulted in an armed truce between the cowboys and the citizens. The townsmen punished some celebrating cowboys who went onto the range swearing vengeance and threatening to organize a force and wipe out the town. The citizens, awaiting an attack, posted sentinels and drilled daily as though for an Indian raid. Finally this armed though bloodless struggle was peacefully settled. An observer stated that the streets of Wibaux, Montana, in the eighties were literally covered with playing-cards and empty shells all the time. One of the merchants tried to build a sidewalk of empty cartridges driven into the ground but gave it up, though apparently not for want of material.[30]

The cowmen also celebrated. Cheyenne had a real cattlemen's society with fine turnouts and blooded horses to pull them. A racecourse was supported, and the ranchers jockeyed their own horses and then repaired to the club-house to "liquor up."

It was not necessary for the personnel of the cattle business to confine their recreation to the questionable amusements mentioned above. At Medora, Dakota Territory, in 1885, a gun club was organized and shooting matches were held. Each contestant put in a dollar and the winner took all. A roller-skating rink, whose equipment was more to be feared by a cowboy than the hurricane-deck of a cow-pony, was doing a big business among the cattlemen. The cowboys and citizens of the cow-town were generous. When the cow of a poor man in Dodge City, Kansas, died, public subscription made possible the purchase of another for the unfortunate family. At Medora, Dakota Territory, the victim of an accident had to have his leg amputated. A raffle was conducted to pay for his medical care.[31]

According to the *Bismarck Tribune*, the East looked upon the name "cowboy... as a synonym for lawlessness and cussedness in the most active form...." As a matter of fact, the cowboy was a

[30] L. F. Crawford, Interview with Charles O. Armstrong, Ms., North Dakota State Historical Society Library, August 6, 1929.
[31] *Bad Lands Cowboy*, Medora, Dakota Territory, February-March, 1885.

child of his environment. He was wild and unrestrained, but exhibited a fidelity to duty that is rare indeed. The cowman, although inclined to drink and gamble the returns of his business, was hospitable and strictly honest—and, contrary to the stories, he did eat his own meat. Moreover, his word was as good as gold.

As in other Western enterprise, there was a boom in the cattle business. By the summer of 1882 it was at its height, and men and capital flowed in from all parts of the country to buy ranches and herds of cattle by tally-book count (that is, the buyer accepted the count of the seller). English and Scotch syndicates had representatives in the field looking after their interests. Interest rates on money rose to two per cent a month. Promoters went to Europe selling range rights (there was no such thing, of course), carrying maps and lithographs rivalling those of the town-boomers on the agricultural frontier. By 1885 the range was overstocked, and a drought, hard winter, or blizzard was sure to bring calamity. The flood of homesteaders with their barbed-wire fences was pushing the cattlemen ever farther upon the high plains before its inundation. The hard winter of 1886-87 was the Samson that tumbled the unstable structure down onto the cattlemen's heads.

That terrible winter took an unparalleled toll of bovine life. Sleet and snow covered the grass, and the starving cattle moved from place to place feeding as best they could on sage-brush and cottonwood twigs. Gaunt, bony, skeleton-like animals, mere shadows of the well-fed range cattle of a few months before, came up to the ranch-houses and gnawed at the tar paper on the shacks till they dropped over dead. Thousands crowded into coulees and creek-beds and were frozen to death or smothered by the deep drifts. The next spring saw thousands of carcasses rotting in the more sheltered places, and a mere tithe of the vast herds of the fall before had survived. These were mostly steers. On top of that, prices declined to a low of $2.40 a hundred at Chicago for the best-fed Texas steers. Many cattlemen sold out for a song and left the country. Those who remained and the newcomers confined their efforts to raising small herds, and the sheepman began to share in the profits of free grass. The day of the cattle bonanza was gone forever.[32]

[32] Webb, *The Great Plains*, pp. 236-237; Harold E. Briggs, *The Settlement and Economic Development of the Dakota Territory*, Ms., Doctor's Thesis, University of Iowa, 1929, Vol. II, pp. 338-339; Albert Edward Culhane, *A History of the Settlement of La Plata County, Colorado*, Ms., Master's Thesis, University of Colorado, 1934, p. 29.

CHAPTER XXII

WITH THE WOOLLIES

SOON AFTER the miners occupied the mountain states, sheep-raising made its appearance along with cattle-ranching. The sheep of the West and Southwest, like the cow-pony and the Texas longhorn, had its origin in Spain. The silky-fleeced merinos of Castile, transferred to Mexico, were raised on the missions under the care of the Indian converts. They multiplied rapidly and their culture accompanied the missionary advance into Texas, New Mexico, Arizona, and California. For the most part these flocks became the source of the millions of animals that were herded on the area west of the one-hundredth meridian in the earlier years of the sheep industry.[1]

Since Colorado was on the main artery of travel and was also closer to the source of breeding stock in the Southwest, the sheep industry developed there before it did in Wyoming and Montana, the other two major sheep-raising areas of the northern Rocky Mountains. In 1880, with 1,091,443 Colorado had more than Wyoming and Montana together. The former had 450,225 and the latter 279,277. In that year alone, however, more than half as many sheep as were already in the Territory, 136,500, were driven into it. Of this number 72,000 came from California, 25,000 from Oregon, 20,000 from Idaho, and 10,000 from Nevada. The sheep industry gained some foothold in western Kansas, Nebraska, and the Dakotas, but in those areas it never equalled that of the Rocky Mountain states.[2] The hard winter of 1886 to 1887 all but dealt the death-blow to the cattle industry and enabled the sheep

[1] William Arthur Rushworth, *The Sheep* (Buffalo, 1899), p. 21.
[2] *Tenth Census of the United States*, Vol. III, p. 1104.

business to supersede it in many places. By 1890 many former cowmen had turned to the new activity, and by the early years of the twentieth century the sheepmen had secured the upper hand in such an ideal grazing country as that Gibraltar of the cattlemen, the Powder River country.

Before 1900 it was no uncommon thing for a herd to be trailed from the Pacific side of the Rockies to the corn lands of Kansas or Nebraska during a season. In the autumn they could be sold to feeders and delivered without freight charges. In 1880 a herd of ten thousand from Kern County, California, was driven fifteen hundred miles to Montana in five months with a loss of only six hundred head. The expense of the venture was 47½ cents a head, and the sheep which cost $1.50 per head in California were worth from $2.50 to $3.00 in the Smith River Valley in Montana. Such handsome profits encouraged stocking the Rocky Mountain area.

The sheep business, like the cattle business, was based on free grazing land furnished by the open range. In the earlier times there were migratory sheepmen, known as floaters or squatters, who did not possess so much as a foot of land by either purchase or lease. They moved at will, grazing their flocks wherever suitable grass was to be found.

As late as 1891 not one man in a hundred in Utah Territory had more to shelter his flock than the natural protection afforded by rocks, valleys, canyons, bushes, and trees. As A. M. Everts of Juab County wrote: "The only shelter that ninety-nine out of one hundred sheep get is God's great and glorious firmament."

In Wyoming and Montana many flocks were handled in the same way, with no food other than what the animals could rustle by pawing off the snow and retrieving the fodder themselves. This was not impracticable if the snowfall was not too heavy and if ice and sleet did not encase the precious dried grass. J. S. Woodruff of Fremont County, Wyoming, wrote: "The profits are large, and the chances simply desperate. If snow comes or a hard winter, we are helpless." Hundreds handled their flocks this way for years, with no more provision for the animals than that made in Texas. According to the census of 1880, over a period of years the loss in Wyoming and Montana averaged nine per cent. A hard winter was bound to bring disaster, however. In Meagher County, Montana, in the winter of 1879-80, out of 5,200 sheep, eighty per cent perished. That was the worst season in the history of the state until that time.

During this era the number of sheep owned by any one concern was, as a rule, not large, ranging from fifteen hundred to three thousand. There were a few outfits, perhaps one in each sheep county, which owned from twenty thousand to fifty thousand.[3] Flocks of from eighteen hundred to four thousand were handled by two men. They had a team, wagon, tent, and supplies and moved every few days. Such a grazing flock was known as a "band" of sheep. By 1900, however, the sheep business had assumed a status similar to that of cattle-ranching. The flockmaster, as the sheep-owner was called, owned or perhaps leased a quarter-section from the railroad or the state (school land). This land with its water rights was the site of the home ranch. At first the buildings were shabby log or sod huts, and the protection for the sheep was made by laying up sod walls six feet high and covering them with a pole, brush, and hay roof.

As the flockmaster increased the number of his animals, there was a tendency to divide the flock into two bands and place a man with each band, thus allowing a third man to act as a sort of connecting link between the ranch and the bands. This hand became known as the camp-tender, and he visited each herder about once a week, moving his camp, looking up lost sheep, and spying out new grazing ground. At first, perhaps the owner himself did this work. Later, as the number of sheep increased, he had a trusted employee to do it. The job involved more than performing the duties of a messenger boy. The camp-tender was something of a

[3] Ezra Carman, H. A. Heath, and John Minto, *Special Report on the History and Present Condition of the Sheep Industry of the United States* (Washington, D. C., 1892), pp. 782, 806, 810.

foreman, directing the herder in his work and reporting back to the flockmaster the condition of the band.

Since a herder accumulated many personal effects, it became no small task to strike the tent, load the accumulation into the wagon, and pitch the camp again. Furthermore, a tent was not any too satisfactory as a protection in stormy weather. As a result of these conditions, the sheep wagon evolved and became the standard by the turn of the century. This rolling home of the herder was a common farm wagon with a wide-bottomed bed covered with a rounded top of canvas. The canvas was usually of several thicknesses, making the abode warm in winter and cool in summer. A double floor also aided in insulating the domicile. Herders often lived in these vehicles all winter in a latitude where the mercury goes down to forty below zero. In the back end was a window, and in the front end a little to one side was a doorway with a door made in two halves, permitting the door to be open at the top with the bottom closed.

The visitor stepped on the wagon tongue and, grasping the sides of the door, hoisted himself into the doorway of the wagon. On one side he saw a stove with the pipe extending through the roof. Behind the stove was the dish cupboard. At the back end was a bunk built crossways of the wagon leaving plenty of room beneath for the dogs. A table on hinges could be folded up against the wall when not in use. Trap-doors, shelves, and lockers were ingeniously arranged in benches, on the walls, and in the bottom of the wagon in such a way as to accommodate the maximum amount of plunder in the minimum amount of space. These living-quarters were cool in summer, but on the coldest winter evening with a sizzling hot fire the herder could sit in his cozy wagon and laugh at the fiercest arctic blast. Through the window in the back he could look out at night and see how the sheep were behaving. A rope enabled him to open the window to any desired point. The wagon was swept out·occasionally, and, as one herder remarked, scrubbing and dusting were done every time the Republicans swept the Solid South.

Denver Public Library Western Collection

SHEEP WAGON IN SIX-MILE DRAW, SOUTH DAKOTA

An old black coffee pot, a skillet, a Dutch oven, and a few pans supplied the herder's culinary needs, and the food was served on tin dishes and eaten with iron "silverware."

The camp-tender on his visits brought the syrup, flour, potatoes, beans, bacon, canned milk, sugar, coffee, and a few other staples at the order of the herder. A full can of kerosene had to be exchanged for an empty receptacle, and in addition to the staples perhaps some fruit, garden vegetables, or other treat was brought out from the ranch. Occasionally a piece of fresh beef was supplied to break the monotony of "sheep, lamb, ram, and mutton meat" for which familiarity had bred contempt in the mind and stomach of the herder. The herder asked for all he could reasonably expect to get, and the boss ordinarily provided well for him, depending, of course, upon the generosity of the rancher. The coming of the camp-tender was a welcome event, for it meant a change in diet and the receiving of mail, including magazines and books passed around from the ranch to the various camps. Then, too, the camp-tender was a veritable newspaper, laden with news from the ranch, the neighboring ranches, the town forty miles away, and the other band camps.

Ordinarily within a month the sheep so denuded the area within a day's grazing distance of the camp that it was necessary to change its location. The shift was known as "moving camp." Moving-day even after the sheep wagon came into use was the trial of the herder's life. If he knew when the camp-tender was coming to move him, he had his possessions arranged in preparation for the trek. More often, however, while the herder was away with the sheep, the none-too-sympathetic emissary from the ranch piled the loose belongings onto the bed and, hooking the camp wagon behind his, dragged it several miles across a rough terrain. During the drive, of course, the herder had to remain with his sheep, although if near at hand he might possibly leave them long enough to help arrange the wagon for its jolting journey. When the herder arrived at his new camp in the evening, he perhaps found another crack in the mirror, the kerosene spilled on the bed, or the syrup-can with the lid off and the sticky contents spread over the adjacent objects.[4]

In the seventies an observer reported that many flockmasters were German immigrants who, after serving as sheep-herders a few seasons, accumulated enough earnings to start business with flocks of their own. Another observer in the early years of the twentieth century noted that it was a poor manager among the herders who could not save enough to start a little flock of his own in a few years. By that date much of the stigma that early attended the sheep-herding vocation had worn off, and with the decline in the cattle business in the eighties a large number of cowboys took up sheep.

The sheep-herders have been widely portrayed as morose, surly individuals whose minds were warped or dwarfed by long existence in the vast solitudes of plain and mountain. Many tales have been told of their becoming insane from the utter loneliness of their vocation. Even to this day, mention of the fact that a man is a sheep-herder is enough to start good-natured jesting and an inquiry as to whether he is "all there" or not. Arthur Chapman, who visited the sheep-raising section in northern Wyoming early in the twentieth century, reported that the personnel of the herding group measured up well with the cowboy and the ranchman. He found the stalwart sheep-herder stalking along, staff in hand, behind his band of thousands of "woollies," while in and out, with tireless feet, flitted the sheep-dogs, whipping the strays into line and scaring the stragglers into the herd. Again, when the immense herd was "feeding out" in a valley, the herder sat on an adjacent hill, idly building a miniature monument of stones with his dogs by his side for the moment. Or at sunset a visitor gazing upon the pastoral scene might have found the wagon in a valley near the silver

[4] Archer B. Gilfillan, *Sheep* (Boston, 1929), Chap. III. This little volume written by an in-service sheep-herder combines a wealth of information concerning the sheep-herder's life with a delightful humorous philosophy. Although it portrays a later period in the history of the business, conditions have changed little and the nature of sheep not at all. This work has been drawn on in large measure for this chapter.

stream. Near at hand he would have seen the herder and his dogs gathering up the far-flung edges of the band and sending the bleat-ing ewes and lambs hurrying across the stream to the camp. As the last golden rays of the setting sun lighted up the high points of the landscape, the herder, with the flock rounded up on the bed ground, wended his way to his rolling cabin to prepare his solitary evening meal.[5]

The sheepman, constantly in touch with nature, became a veritable wizard in weather prognostication from long observation of the sky and wind. He knew every nook and cranny of the graz-ing area. Every coulee and knoll held memories for the lonely herder. The ways of the wild things of the mountain and prairie were an open book to him. He could enjoy the gorgeous sunrises and sunsets, and his hours of solitude and observation of natural phenomena gave him a contemplative attitude seldom seen among those engaged in the busy activities of less isolated vocations.

By 1900 it had become the custom to run about two thousand to three thousand sheep in a band. The herd was kept along a stream in the summertime, so the sheep could have easy access to water and could lie in the shade during the heat of the day. In the au-tumn it was moved up on the table-lands, since in that season the sheep could thrive with little water. When the snow began to fall, they were grazed on the waterless plains, where they ate snow to slake their thirst.

Some flockmasters ran their bands in the mountains or foot-hills in the summer. In that case the herder carried his scant equipment on pack-animals and became an even more nomadic figure than usual. When he was along a stream, his day was divided fairly evenly into two halves by the sheep themselves. They arose early and grazed until about eleven in the morning, when they usually reached the water, drank their fill, and rested until about the middle of the afternoon. This gave the herder an opportunity to

[5] Arthur Chapman, "The Sheep-Herders of the West," *The Outlook*, Vol. 80, pp. 482-483.

cook a hot meal and rest until about three or four o'clock, when the sheep began to leave the shade for a second period of grazing. During the other nine months of the year the herder carried a lunch. In the warmer seasons the sheepman often used a horse, but during the winter months it was too cold to tether a horse on the Plains, so he was obliged to walk. In the morning the sheep left the camp about daybreak. Their caretaker had to snatch a quick breakfast, put up a little snack for a noonday meal, and hurry on foot after the band. By that time perhaps they were scattered, and he had some difficulty in getting them together. Toward evening he turned the band toward the camp and, arriving there about sundown, rounded the sheep up on the bed ground at the rear of the wagon. There they were huddled in a mass on the prairie without shelter of corral or shed, and without protection from wild animals with the exception of scarecrows set up to frighten the coyotes away. Quite frequently, when a sheep strayed from the band during the day or from the bed ground at night, a coyote, wolf, or other animal crept in and made away with it. These accidents never excited the herder or the flock-master, who allowed for a certain number of losses. When the herder carried his lunch, he usually made the evening meal the main meal of the day.

In the autumn came shipping, when the band was driven to the home ranch and the old sheep and wethers were cut out and driven to the nearest railroad, which was often anywhere from ten to a hundred miles away. Sometimes the herder had the privilege of driving the "trail bunch" to the shipping-point. In such a case he probably would stay in the town a few days making some purchases and celebrating his respite from a long period of lonely isolation.

On his return to the range, the herder enjoyed the most delightful season of the year, with pleasant weather and a small, easily controlled band. In later years in the winter the sheep were often driven to an outer ranch or even to the home ranch if the "outfit" was small. There the herder lived in the bunk house with the cowboys and other ranch hands, and in bad weather the ranch hands hauled hay for his charges while he had a comparatively light task for a few weeks. In the winter months the herder had to dress very heavily in order to withstand the cold during long hours of inactivity. In the vicinity of mountains he dared not venture out until summer without an overcoat. Many men lost their lives in spring or autumn snow-storms.

The spring of the year was a bugbear to all hands and especially to the herder, for the sheep ran like rabbits lured on by the promise of grass a little farther beyond. Some sheep-owners sheared the animals before the lambs were born. Others sheared in July. This work was done by a special crew which went from ranch to ranch doing the shearing. Until the industry was well established, the shearing was done with hand clippers, but by 1900 the flexible-shaft machine clipper was used extensively. After shearing came dipping, which was accomplished by putting the animals through a vat containing the prescribed medication of sulphur and tobacco.

The lambing season was the most difficult of all. Prairie-wolves were especially active then, and the herder had to circle the band time and again at night and on occasion fire rockets to frighten the sheep-hungry coyotes whose eyes formed a ring of flaming dots around the flock.[6]

The crew who assumed the extra burden occasioned by the birth of the lambs were known as "lambers." The band of ewes was herded as usual. There were a number of methods for caring for the lambs. One provided for the use of a lambing van. When a lamb was born, a sheep hand by means of a long hook caught the ewe and the wagon carried mother and lamb to the ranch, where they were kept together in a small flock until the ewe would own her offspring. This program was occasioned by the fact that a ewe knows her lamb only by smell for the first few days, and in a large flock she often became confused and lost her lamb or got discouraged after smelling so many and failing to find her progeny. In

[6] *Ibid.*, p. 485.

the small flock after a short time she learned to know her lamb by its voice and became more used to its scent. If a mother refused to own her lamb, she was put in a stall with it until she grew accustomed to its scent. A lamb that could not be raised by its mother for some reason or other was called a "bum," and was either killed, given away, or raised by hand at the ranch. Sometimes a mother who lost her own lamb was deceived into adopting a bum. This was done by skinning the legitimate offspring and pulling the pelt over the impostor. After a time the mother got used to the intruder and accepted it.[7]

In North Dakota the greatest enemy of the sheepman was the prairie fire. In 1891 a summary of the sheep business over a period of years showed that the losses from prairie fires were more in a year than those from several winters.

When the sheepmen began to invade the range, the cattlemen resisted their occupancy of the public lands. As the range grew more crowded and the number of sheep increased at the expense of cattle, friction vastly intensified. It was charged that sheep ate the grass so close that it died. Further, it was charged that they destroyed the range over which they travel by trampling out the grass and leaving the ground bare. In addition to this, it was alleged that the woollies left such an offensive odor on the grass and at the water that cattle refused to eat or drink after them. It was also charged that they destroyed the young trees on the forest reserves.

On the other hand, the sheepmen argued that they had as much right to the government domain as the cattlemen. The latter usually took the initiative in the fights between the two groups. In the middle nineties a violent outburst against the sheepmen took place. Raiders known as "gunnysackers," so called because they wore gunny-sacks over their heads, terrorized the sheep industry. In the first decade of the twentieth century the long-smouldering conflagration again burst forth. The "range war" in Wyoming

[7] Gilfillan, *Sheep*, pp. 103-123.

SPRING ON A MONTANA SHEEP RANCH

From a painting by Sverre Hanssen.

lasted nearly six years. Bands of armed, masked horsemen traversed the sheep country, shooting herders and owners of flocks, burning sheep-camps, dynamiting and poisoning sheep, clubbing them to death, stampeding them over precipices and leaving their mangled carcasses on the rocks below.[8]

This range war received a great deal of publicity, and to judge from the Associated Press despatches, the reader in the East would have imagined the whole industry was demoralized, the range area sprinkled with the blood of the herders, and their charges scattered. In 1903, however, E. P. Snow, the secretary of the Wyoming State Board of Sheep Commissioners, estimated the deaths in the range war over a period of ten years at not over fifty and the sheep killings at twenty-five thousand.[9]

One of the outstanding institutions of the sheep business was the dog. The well-trained dog was invaluable. He could run faster than the herder and could put more fear into the sheep. In short, he amplified and greatly augmented the ability of his master to control the band. The good dog could be managed by movements of the herder and was effective as far as he could see his master. His faithfulness was reciprocated by the herder. In addition to saving him miles of running, the dog was excellent company, sharing long periods of solitude with his human companion. The herder talked to his dog as to a boon companion, gave him the best of food, allowed him to sleep under his bed at night, and during dry herding he placed his hat on the ground and, pouring water from his canteen into the indented crown, allowed his faithful friend to drink. The dogs fought off coyotes and other wild animals and displayed intelligence as well as courage. Often two dogs were used together, for they were company for each other.

These animals, true to canine nature, were loyal unto death. In a great blizzard that smote the Red Desert in southern Wy-

[8] Harold E. Briggs, *Frontiers of the Northwest* (New York, 1940), pp. 327-337; Charles Moreau Harger, "Sheep and Shepherds of the West," *The Outlook*, Vol. 72, p. 690.

[9] E. P. Snow to the Editors, *The Outlook*, Vol. 73, pp. 839-840.

oming. William Moody and his flock were caught in its arctic grip. The sheep perished by the score, and at last the herder succumbed. His faithful dogs remained beside his dead body over a week, eating the flesh of the frozen sheep and fighting off the coyotes from their master's corpse. When a relief party found them, they were almost dead from exposure.

No wonder Big Jim Everett, ex-cowboy sheep-herder, took exception to the treatment of his dogs in a Buffalo, Wyoming, restaurant. A drunken cattleman strode in and purposely kicked one of the dogs. The cattleman was big, but Big Jim planted a blow on his jaw which sent him crashing into a corner.[10] On one occasion when a herder's dogs picked up coyote poison, the man tenderly carried them to the wagon and administered an antidote, but it was too late. With tears he mourned the loss of his devoted four-footed companions. He told a fellow herder of how the younger dog had died first. Then the herder had to go out after the sheep, and the older dog insisted on going with him in spite of all he could do. The faithful animal would struggle through the deep snow, fall in convulsions, rise, and drag himself along again after his master. Finally he fell for the last time in one fatal convulsion. It was snowing as the hardened herder looked out of the wagon door and feelingly remarked, "Well, the snow will cover them and they will rest forever."[11]

As the cattle industry was gradually displaced by the sheep business, so the sheep industry had to give way before the dry farmer, who encroached little by little upon the domain of the woollies. This movement tended to decrease the size of sheep holdings and take the business out of the frontier stage.

[10] Chapman, "The Sheep-Herders of the West," *loc. cit.*, pp. 487-488.
[11] Gilfillan, *Sheep*, p. 53.

CHAPTER XXIII

CHARACTERISTICS OF THE FRONTIER

THE FRONTIER holds the key to the interpretation of American history. Other great powers of the world have arisen on the ruins of older civilized states. As a rule these were established by the conquest of a particular people and a subsequent assimilation of the culture of the conquerors by the conquered. In contrast, in America a vast and almost untenanted area was occupied by streams of population flowing from many nations and mingling to form a united front, which over a period of nearly three centuries gradually pushed back the sparse aboriginal inhabitants. The point where civilization met savagery in this sweep of settlement over the continent we call the frontier. The frontier became something of a common denominator of newcomers from Europe and those who had been here one or more generations. The narrow belt where the aborigines and Europeans met was the nation's dawn which moved across the continent with the darkness of savagery before and the full light of civilization behind.[1] This frontier area developed certain well-defined characteristics, born of the struggle to overcome the Indians, to subdue the stubborn realities of raw nature, and to adjust to the general environment. The struggle of Europeans against common difficulties produced a common nationality, the American. Not only did the frontier itself have a peculiar state of society, but it became the leaven which leavened the whole lump and has left its effect on American society to-day.

This zone of unfolding dawn in reality was not always regular in its westward progress nor was it constant in width. Like water running across a field, population sought the easiest passage and

---

[1] This is an adaptation of Dr. E. E. Dale's definition of the cattlemen's frontier.

the most favored spots. Islands of settlement appeared here and there, and at some points the westward movement was far in advance of others. For example, in 1820 Missouri had sufficient population to be admitted to the Union while portions of western New York were still within the frontier zone. Settlement followed navigable rivers and then advanced inland, whether it were toward the west or in some other direction.

Life on the Plains and in the mountains as described in this volume for the most part portrays the vanguards of the frontier—those groups of whites who advanced well beyond the western edge of settlement of permanent homemakers. These bold adventurers often spoke of the thin line of homemakers they had left far behind as the frontier.

Among this advance-guard of whites penetrating the Indian country beyond the frontier, the type of society bred by contact between the white and red races is more clearly exemplified than anywhere else. Whether good or bad, its characteristics were exhibited in the extreme. Study of the area amply bears out the thesis of Frederick Jackson Turner that when civilization met savagery the European for the time being descended to the level of barbarism. When the trapper went into the wilds, he lived in the tepee of the Indian. The fur-trader's post was little more than an Indian stockade. The miner's or buffalo hunter's dugout was very similar to the prairie Indian's winter-quarters. On the Upper Missouri waters the trappers and fur-traders used the Indian canoe or the bullboat. When they fared forth in the woods, aside from improved weapons, they could hardly have been distinguished from Indians. The buckskin hunting suit and coonskin cap were adapted from the dress of the aborigines. The buffalo robe that was used for both mattress and blanket by nearly all classes was also an Indian institution. The dress of the cowboy, the miner, the freighter, and the logger, though not patterned so closely after that of the Indian, was governed by the wild conditions surrounding these figures as they worked.

The trappers and others in daily contact with danger grew as savage as the Indian himself. James J. Webb tells us that on the Santa Fe Trail, when the first buffalo was killed and the meat brought into camp, almost without exception the men fought over it like wolves over a kill. Buffalo hunters, trappers, and other more hardened frontiersmen, upon killing a buffalo, would crack the skull and eat the brains raw while they were yet warm. When Audubon expressed surprise at this almost incredible practice, he was informed that were he to hunt buffalo a year, he would become accustomed to eat raw brains and like them even better than "dog meat," which Audubon had previously endorsed. Often men grabbed portions of the hot raw buffalo liver and ate it with the greatest relish. Others stripped out the small intestines, broiled them with their contents, and ate them with gusto. Instances are known where trappers captured, killed, and ate Indians when they had been without food for several days.

The whites were as treacherous and bloodthirsty as the Indians. On countless occasions white men, on the general principle that there was no good Indian but a dead one, shot the first Indian they saw. Uniformed soldiers at times took scalps as trophies, notably at the battle of Sand Creek, in Colorado in the sixties, and during the Sibley Expedition in Dakota, in 1863. In 1876 the miners of Deadwood, Dakota Territory, offered a reward of two hundred dollars for each Indian scalp.

The white man's duplicity is well illustrated by an incident which occurred at Fort Brulé in 1843. A band of Indians had killed a man, and when this band appeared at the post the next winter, the traders loaded the cannon at the gate and invited three of the leaders into the fort, planning to murder them and then fire the cannon into the huddled group of their followers who were waiting just outside. It was thought the survivors would run for their lives, abandoning their horses and the furs they had brought to trade, of which the whites would then become owners. In the nick of time the Indians learned of the plot and scattered, escaping the deadly hail of death. Only three or four were killed. Alexander Harvey, one of the fur-traders, rushing out with his dirk knife, killed the wounded, scalped them, and, licking the blood from his blade, ran back into the fort and made the squaws do a scalp-dance around the scalps he had taken.

Liquor did much to degrade both the white and the red men and abetted immorality, disease, and inhumanity. Both races, indeed, were greatly harmed by the contact between the two. The orgies that followed the distribution of spirits to the Indians were almost beyond description. Even rough-and-tumble fights among the whites resulted in the loss of an eye or the mangling of an ear or nose. A trapper who had observed the association of the two races remarked that "it is easy to make a savage of a civilized man but impossible to make a civilized man of a savage in one generation."

In his contacts with the Indian the white man had little regard for the rights of the aborigines. Time after time, when the United States Government made treaties with the Indians solemnly reserving certain lands to them, the whites flagrantly disregarded these titles. In the third decade of the nineteenth century settlers moved into the lead-mine area and calmly took possession, in spite of the fact that it was the property of the Sacs and Foxes and the whites had been ordered by the Indian agent to leave the region. The nationalistic Westerners who strongly condemned South Carolina for her nullification threats at this same time saw no inconsistency in their bold defiance of national authority. In 1875, when gold was discovered in the Black Hills, the miners poured into the region in spite of a determined effort on the part of the United States forces to keep them out. In 1873, in spite of a line of soldiers on the Arkansas River, buffalo hunters organized themselves and proceeded to slaughter the buffaloes on the Indian reservation.

The frontiersman was optimistic. He believed in the country with its economic resources and opportunities. When the prospector went into the gold mountains, staying month after month, and returned ragged and empty-handed after each expedition, he never gave up. With a far-away look in his eyes he fixed his gaze upon the distant ranges and declared to the bystanders, "Thar's gold in them thar hills." The trapper who gathered pelts for a whole season and returned to his camp to find he had been robbed of his catch by the Indians felt as blue as indigo but consoled himself that he would have better luck next time.

The spirit of conquest or exploitation ran strong in the veins of these vanguards of white settlement. The resources of the country were so vast that there was no thought or care whether they would ever be exhausted. These natural resources belonged to the government, and the first whites argued they were doing the government a favor to exploit them. There was no hesitation to use the government grasslands for cattle ranches, to cut the forests in logging, to dig the lead or gold, or wantonly to destroy the multitudes of wild game. This ruthless exploitation was accompanied by the greatest waste. In earlier years in Minnesota no log was accepted with small end less than sixteen inches in diameter. The giant trees were cut only to have their tops above this measure discarded and burned. Or, worse still, burning the wasted material caused forest fires to start and destroy millions of feet of standing timber. It is estimated that in the inefficient placer-mining operations half of the gold in the pay dirt was washed down the swift-flowing mountain streams to the ocean. The buffalo was exterminated for his hide and his carcass left to rot on the Plains, a tremendous economic loss. Even the beaver was well-nigh exterminated instead of being hunted in a moderate manner and the fur wealth utilized temperately.

The Easterner was looked down upon by the Western man. In the earlier years the appellation applied to a newcomer in the West was "a green 'un," a little later a "greenhorn," and in still later years a "tenderfoot." He had to be initiated into the ways of the West, but if he stood the test as a real man, he was accepted by the group. Because of his eye-glasses and a none too robust physique, Theodore Roosevelt made a rather unfavorable impression on the range country, but once the cowmen had tested his mettle, he was received into their midst with open arms. Dressed in sombrero, chaps, and boots, he was a popular figure indeed as surrounded by his cowboys he rode to the Fourth of July celebration at Dickinson, North Dakota, in 1886.

⌈The West was godless. Often men went west because of their personal difficulties; some incident unfitted them for further residence in the more staid East. These, having exiled themselves from respectable society by some illicit love-affair, a duel, or a more serious crime, could hardly be expected to lead a pious life in the wilds. Moreover, even men conscientious and respectable in their home communities, when venturing into the wilds where all restraints were lacking and there was no association with good women, often began to slip into the irreligious ways of their environment. When Alexander Majors insisted on a program of no drinking or swearing for his freighters and gave each man a Bible, he evidently did not make much of a reformation at Nebraska City, for the freighters were known as the toughest aggregation of men to be found anywhere. In Kansas, when the buffalo hunters were clearing the plains of the prairie monarch, when the cowboys were driving their mammoth herds across the state, and when the freighters were being pushed ever westward by the railroad construction gangs, it was a common saying that there was "no Sunday west of Junction City and no God west of Salina." The towns, whether outfitting towns for the freighters and overland travelers, mining towns, cow towns, buffalo-hunting towns, or railroad-end towns, were wide open, wild, lawless communities where crime thrived and a "Boot Hill" graveyard was a necessity. ⌉

The attitude of the Western people was antagonistic toward restraint. The Santa Fe traders found it almost impossible to control their parties enough for common protection. Overland travelers were irked by the measures of United States troops who stopped their wagon-trains or stage-coaches in time of Indian hostility and would not allow them to proceed until a large number had been united into a strong force. Often, as soon as the train was out of sight of the fort, it broke up again into small parties, much to the chagrin and wrath of the military authorities. On the other hand, the travelers were continually calling for aid from the national government. They wanted and received a guard for the Santa Fe Trail. They demanded and obtained an expedition against the Indians on the Missouri River when General William H. Ashley's fur-trading expedition was attacked. They begged for guards for the freighting trains, stage-coaches, and railroad-building projects.

The "rugged individualism" of the West has become a commonplace. It was a case of "everybody for himself and the devil take the hindermost." There was no thought about the welfare of the whole country or of the group. The shrewdest, most fortunate, the strongest and most unscrupulous seized the country's vast resources without regard to waste or uneconomic practices.

Separatist tendencies made themselves apparent as soon as a group of travelers crossed the Missouri River and, leaving organized authority behind, started into a country without government. A group sometimes divided and subdivided time after time until finally two partners would divide their property and each go on his way. At the same time, in the face of danger a striking characteristic of coöperative self-sufficiency appeared. Individuals united until there was a strong organization which worked effectively. Instances of this were the bodies of Vigilantes formed at Denver and in Montana. These extralegal organizations worked efficiently to clear their regions of public enemies.

When these Americans felt hampered by the lack of legal institutions, they assembled in good Anglo-Saxon fashion and made their own laws to meet the needs of the occasion. In the mining gulches beyond the bounds of formal administration they formed a true democratic government, meeting to decide important matters and settle disputes. When there was no machinery to take care of the range industry, the cowmen formed the cattlemen's associations to govern the business. These associations worked effectively, with many features of government, until the states and territories regulated the industry by formal law.

The talk of the frontiersman seems to have been affected by his wild surroundings. It was characterized by the economy of words required to convey a clear meaning. The cowboy who, when asked for his opinion of his employer, answered, "Can't put it in words. Give me an emetic," well illustrates this point.[2] Billy Dixon, a buffalo hunter, exhibited the same characteristic when he spoke of a tenderfoot on the streets of Dodge City. This man, a newcomer from the East, wore a stylish eastern suit with white-flowered vest, a necktie resembling a Rocky Mountain sunset, and a top-hat. Billy remarked: "My first glimpse of Fairchild made me finger my sights, for he certainly looked like fair game."

Hospitality was a marked characteristic everywhere on the advance frontier. Said Billy Dixon: "Many a dark night have I looked with gladness at the distant buffalo-chip fire, knowing that around it I would find hospitable companions and lots of warmth." The latch-string hung out, whether at the trapper's tepee, the buffalo hunter's camp, the ranch headquarters, or the missionary's tent.

Perhaps the most striking characteristic of all, however, was the concept of democracy. Every man felt as good as every other. All faced the same dangers, battled together for an economic livelihood, and wore the same kind of clothes. Anyone who "put on airs" was detested by everyone else. A man might be the boss of a ranch, and yet his men did not regard him as any better than they in the social scale. Servant girls in the mining country went to the same dances with their mistresses, and cowboys married the ranch-owner's daughters and became cowmen themselves.

The short day of those bold figures in the vanguard of civilization has gone forever, but the effect of the frontier lives on. Some

[2] Philip Ashton Rollins, *The Cowboy* (New York, 1922), p. 74.

of its characteristics are good and some are bad. It is with the greatest difficulty that in a new era with new needs Americans can be persuaded to discard rugged individualism for coöperation. Nevertheless the conquest of the wilds was a stupendous adventure which miraculously transformed a population of Europeans of diverse origins into a nation of Americans.

BIBLIOGRAPHY

I. Sources

DOCUMENTS

ALLAN, LEWIS, "Improvement of Neat Cattle," House Executive Document 136, 39th Congress, 1st Session, Serial 1266.

American State Papers, Indian Affairs, Vol. II.

Annals of the Propagation of the Faith, Catholic Missions, 1839-1844, English edition, Vol. I.

CARMAN, EZRA A., HEATH, H. A., and MINTO, JOHN, *Special Report on the History and Present Condition of the Sheep Industry of the United States* (Washington, 1892).

"First Annual Report of the Bureau of Animal Industry for the Year 1884," *House Miscellaneous Document* 25, 48th Congress, 2nd Session, Serial 2311.

Fort Atkinson *Records* (Nebraska, 1819-1827), Vols. I-VI. Ms., transcription of the original records, Nebraska State Historical Society Library.

Fort Bridger *Records* (Wyoming Territory, 1884-1890), Ms., United States War Department, Adjutant General's Office, Old Records Division.

Fort Fetterman (Wyoming), Brevet Colonel Dye, Post Commander, *Special Orders No. 45,* Headquarters Fort Fetterman, July 19, 1868. Ms., Wyoming State History Department.

Fort Gibson *Records* (Indian Territory, 1834-1857), Ms., United States War Department, Adjutant General's Office, Old Records Division.

Fort Kearney (Nebraska), *Court of Administration* (Council of Administration), 1849-1856, United States War Department, Adjutant General's Office, Old Records Division.

Fort Laramie (Wyoming), *Letters and Orders,* 1849-1855. Ms., United States War Department, Adjutant General's Office, Old Records Division.

General Regulations for the Army of the United States, 1841 (Washington, 1841).

HORNADAY, WILLIAM T., "The Extermination of the American Bison," *Smithsonian Institution Reports* (Washington, D. C., 1887).

Instructions to the Surveyor General of Public Lands of the United States for those Surveying Districts Established In and Since the Year 1850; containing also, a Manual of Instructions to regulate the Field Operations of Deputy Surveyors (Washington, 1855).

LA FLESCHE, FRANCIS, and FLETCHER, ALICE, *Annual Report, Omaha Indian, Bureau of Ethnology,* No. 27.

NIMMO, JOSEPH G., "The Range and Ranch Cattle Traffic," *House Executive Document* 267, 48th Congress, 2nd Session, Serial 2304.

"Report of the Hygiene of the United States Army, A," *Circular No. 8*, United States War Department, Surgeon General's Office (Washington, 1875).

"Report of Inspector General G. Croghan," *Inspection Reports II, 1825-1829*, United States War Department, Inspector General's Office.

"Report on Barracks and Hospitals with Description of Military Posts, A," *Circular No. 4*, United States War Department, Surgeon General's Office (Washington, 1870).

Second Annual Report of the Niobrara League of New York, Protestant Episcopal Church (New York, 1875).

"Texas Cattle Trade," *House Executive Document* 13, 41st Congress, 3rd Session, Serial 1461.

United States Census Report For the Year 1880, Vol. III.

CONTEMPORARY BOOKS AND PAMPHLETS

ALDRIDGE, REGINALD, *Life on a Ranch* (London, 1884).

Another Letter from Bishop Hare to the Children of the [Protestant Episcopal] *Church*, June 9, 1874 (Yankton Agency, Dakota), Wisconsin State Historical Society Library.

BARROWS, WILLIAM, *The General; or Twelve Nights in the Hunters' Camp* (Boston, 1869).

BEADLE, J. H., *The Undeveloped West; or Five Years in the Territories* (Philadelphia and Chicago, 1873).

BOWLES, SAMUEL, *Across the Continent* (New York, 1866).

———, *Our New West* (Hartford and New York, 1869).

BRADBURY, JOHN, *Travels in the Interior of America* (London, 1819).

Brand Book of Montana Stock Growers Association (Chicago, 1886). North Dakota State Historical Society Library.

BREMER, FREDRIKA, *The Homes of the New World* (New York, 1854).

BRISBIN, GENERAL JAMES S., *The Beef Bonanza* (Philadelphia, 1881).

BROCKETT, LINUS PIERPONT, *Our Western Empire* (Philadelphia, 1881).

CARVALHO, S. N., *Incidents of Travel and Adventure in the Far West with Colonel Frémont's Last Expedition* (New York and Cincinnati, 1857).

CATLIN, GEORGE, *Letters and Notes on the Manners, Customs, and Conditions of the North American Indians* (New York, 1841).

CHANDLESS, WILLIAM, *A Visit to Salt Lake Being a Journey Across the Plains, and a Residence in the Mormon Settlements at Utah* (London, 1857).

CLAMPITT, JOHN W., *Echoes from the Rocky Mountains* (Chicago, 1889).

CLEMENS, SAMUEL L., *Roughing It* (Chicago, 1872).

COKE, HENRY JOHN, *A Ride Over the Rocky Mountains to Oregon and California* (London, 1852).

COOK, JOHN R., *The Border and the Buffalo* (Topeka, Kansas, 1907).

COOKE, PHILIP ST. GEORGE, *Scenes and Adventures in the Army: or Romance of Military Life* (Philadelphia, 1859).

COYNER, DAVID H., *The Lost Trappers* (Cincinnati, 1858).

CROFUTT, GEORGE A., *Crofutt's New Overland Tourist and Pacific Coast Guide* (Chicago, 1879-80), Vol. II.

———, *Crofutt's Transcontinental Tourist's Guide* (New York, 1871).

DELANO, ALONZO, *Life on the Plains and Among the Diggings* (New York, 1857).

———, *Pen Knife Sketches; or, Chips of the Old Block* (San Francisco, 1853).

DE SMET, P. J., *Letters and Sketches with a Narrative of a Year's Residence among the Indian Tribes of the Rocky Mountains* (Philadelphia, 1843).

———, *New Indian Sketches* (New York, [1865?]).

———, *Western Missions and Missionaries: A Series of Letters, 1844-57* (New York, 1863).

DIMSDALE, THOMAS J., *The Vigilantes of Montana* (Helena, Montana, 1915).

DIXON, WILLIAM HEPWORTH, *New America* (Philadelphia, 1867).

DODGE, RICHARD I., *The Hunting Grounds of the Great West* (London, 1878).

ELLET, MRS. ELIZABETH FRIES LUMMIS, *Summer Rambles in the West* (New York, 1853).

FARNHAM, THOMAS JEFFERSON, *Travels in the Great Western Prairies, the Anahuac and Rocky Mountains, and in the Oregon Territory* (New York, 1843).

GREGG, JOSIAH, *Commerce of the Prairies* (New York, 1845).

HALE, EDWARD E., *Kansas and Nebraska* (Boston and New York, 1854).

Hand Book of Minnesota (Chicago, 1867).

HARVEY, AUGUSTUS E., *Sketches of the Early Days of Nebraska City, Nebraska Territory, 1854-1860* (St. Louis, 1871).

HILDRETH, JAMES, *Dragoon Campaigns to the Rocky Mountains* (New York, 1836).

HILDRETH, SAMUEL P., *Contributions to the Early History of the North-West, including the Moravian Missions in Ohio* (Cincinnati and New York, 1864).

HOFFMAN, CHARLES FENNO, *A Winter in the West* (New York, 1835).

HOWE, HENRY, "Bryant's Overland Journey to California," *In the Principal Countries of the Globe, Travels and Adventures of Celebrated Travelers* (Cincinnati, 1857).

Indian Missions, The, in the United States of America Under the Care of the Missouri Province of the Society of Jesus (Philadelphia, 1841).

IRVING, WASHINGTON, *The Adventures of Captain Bonneville* (New York, 1902).

JOHNSON, LAURA WINTHROP, *Eight Hundred Miles in an Ambulance* (Philadelphia, 1889).

LANG, JOHN D., and TAYLOR, SAMUEL, *Report of a Visit to Some of the Tribes of Indians West of Mississippi River* (New York, 1843).

LEONARD, ZENAS, *Leonard's Narrative. Adventures of Zenas Leonard Fur Trader and Trapper 1831-1836*, W. F. Wagner, editor (Cleveland, 1904).

LUDLOW, FITZ HUGH, *The Heart of the Continent* (New York, 1870).

McCOY, ISAAC, *Remarks on the Practicability of Indian Reform, Embracing their Colonization* (New York, 1829).

McCOY, JOSEPH G., *Historic Sketches of the Cattle Trade of the West and Southwest* (Kansas City, Missouri, 1874).

McEACHRAN, D., F. R. C., V. S., *Notes of a Trip to Bow River, North-West Territories* (Montreal, 1881).

MANYPENNY, GEORGE W., *Our Indian Wards* (Cincinnati, 1880).

MARCY, RANDOLPH BARNES, *The Prairie Traveler*, A Hand-book of Overland Expeditions (New York, 1859).

MURRAY, CHARLES A., *Travels in North America 1834-1836* (London, 1839).

NEILL, EDWARD DUFFIELD, *Fort Snelling, Minnesota* (New York, 1888).

PARKMAN, FRANCIS, *The Oregon Trail* (Boston, 1886).

PERKINS, JAMES H., *Annals of the West* (Cincinnati, 1846).

POOLE, DE WITT CLINTON, *Among the Sioux of Dakota* (New York, 1881).

RANDAL, HENRY S., *The Practical Shepherd* (New York, 1875).

REMY, JULES, and BRENCHLEY, JULIUS, *A Journey to Great Salt Lake City* (London, 1861), 2 Vols.

Review of The Foreign Mission of the Moravian Church 1871-1872 (Bethlehem, Pennsylvania, 1872).

RICHARDSON, ALBERT D., *Beyond the Mississippi* (Hartford, 1867).

ROOSEVELT, THEODORE, *Hunting Trips of a Ranchman* (Medora, Dakota Territory, 1885).

ROSEN, PETER, *Pa-ha-sa-pah, or the Black Hills of South Dakota* (St. Louis, 1895).

RUSHWORTH, WILLIAM ARTHUR, *The Sheep* (Buffalo, 1899).

RUSLING, JAMES F., *Across America, or the Great West and the Pacific Coast* (New York, 1874).

RUXTON, GEORGE FREDERICK, *Life in the Far West* (New York, 1849).

SAGE, RUFUS B., *Scenes in the Rocky Mountains* (Philadelphia, 1847).

SCHOOLCRAFT, HENRY ROWE, *Information Respecting the History, Condition, and Prospects of Indian Tribes of the United States* (Philadelphia, 1852-57), 6 Vols.

——, *Scenes and Adventures in the Semi-Alpine Region of the Ozark Mountains of Missouri and Arkansas* (Philadelphia, 1853).

——, *Summary Narrative of an Exploratory Expedition to the Sources of the Mississippi River in 1820* (Philadelphia, 1855).

——, *View of the Lead Mines of Missouri* (New York, 1819).

——, *Western Scenes and Reminiscences* (Auburn and Buffalo, New York, 1853).

SIRINGO, CHARLES A., *A Lone Star Cowboy* (Santa Fe, 1919).

Sketch of the History of the Missions and Church of the United Brethren (London, 1844).

Sketches of the Dakota Mission, Mission of the American Board, 1873.

STEELE, MRS. ELIZA R., *A Summer Journey in the West* (New York, 1841).

TALLENT, ANNIE D., *The Black Hills; or the Last Hunting Ground of the Dakotahs* (St. Louis, 1899).

THOMAS, DAVID, *Travels Through the Western Country in the Summer of 1816* (Auburn, New York, 1819).

VAN TRAMP, JOHN C., *Prairie and Rocky Mountain Adventurers, or Life in the West* (Columbus, Ohio, 1866).

VON RICHTHOFEN, WALTER BARON, *Cattle-Raising on the Plains of North America* (New York, 1885).

WARE, JOSEPH, *The Emigrants Guide to California* (St. Louis, 1849).

WHITE, JOHN, *Sketches from America* (London, 1870).

CONTEMPORARY PERIODICALS AND NEWSPAPERS

American Baptist Magazine and Missionary Intelligencer (Boston, 1835), Vol. XV.

Bad Lands Cowboy, The (Little Missouri, Medora P. O., Dakota Territory), Feb. 7, 1884-Apr. 9, 1885.

Baptist Missionary Magazine, Vols. XVI-XVIII (Boston, 1836-1838).

Bismarck Tribune, The (Bismarck, Dakota Territory), July 11, 1873-Dec. 27, 1876.

Black Hills Journal (Rapid City, Dakota Territory), Jan. 26-Aug. 10, 1878.

Black Hills Pioneer (Deadwood, Dakota Territory), June 8, 1876, Jan. 6, 1877-Feb. 14, 1878.

Boise News (Bannock City [later Idaho City], Idaho), Sept. 29, 1863-Sept. 24, 1864.

Cheyenne County Rustler (Wano, Kansas), July 10, 1885-Oct. 30, 1885.

Christian Keepsake and Missionary Annual, The (Philadelphia), 1838.

Cold Water Review (Cold Water, Kansas), Nov. 29, 1884-Feb. 10, 1885.

Deadwood Pioneer-Times (Deadwood, Dakota Territory), 1876-1877.

Deseret News (Salt Lake City, Utah), June 15, 1850-June 15, 1851.

Dodge City Times (Dodge City, Kansas), Oct. 14, 1876-Oct. 6, 1877.

Foreign Missionary Chronicle (Pittsburgh, Pennsylvania), 1833-1850.

Frontier, The (O'Neill, Nebraska), Sept. 30, 1880-July 27, 1882.

Frontier Guardian, The (Kanesville, Iowa), Feb. 7, 1849-Jan. 1, 1850.

Frontiersman, The (Bird City, Kansas), Oct. 13, 1885-Dec. 29, 1886.

Hays City Railway Advance (Hays City, Kansas), June 23, 1868.

Idaho World (Idaho City, Idaho), Oct. 29, 1864-May 6, 1865.

Independence Messenger (Independence, Missouri), 1850.

Kansas Chief, The (White Cloud, Kansas), June 4, 1857-Dec. 30, 1858.

Kansas Cowboy (Dodge City, Kansas), June 28, 1884-Dec. 27, 1884.

Kansas Weekly Herald (Leavenworth, Kansas Territory), Sept. 15, 1854-Sept. 8, 1855.

Methodist Magazine (New York), 1822, 1832.

Methodist Quarterly Review (New York), 1835-1840.

Mining Journal, The (Black Hawk, Colorado), Nov. 30, 1863-Jan. 2, 1864.

Missionary Herald (Boston, Massachusetts), 1834-1841.

Missouri Intelligencer (Franklin, Missouri), Mar., 1824-Dec., 1826.

Missouri Republican (St. Louis, Missouri), Mar. 20, 1822-Dec. 27, 1824.

Montana Post (Virginia City, Montana), Aug. 27, 1864-Apr. 15, 1865, Nov. 3, 1866.

Nebraska City News (Nebraska City, Nebraska), May 15, 1858-Dec. 25, 1858, Jan. 14, 1860, Sept. 14, 1861, Jan. 4, 1862-July 21, 1865.

Nebraska Herald, The (Nemaha City, Nebraska), Nov. 24, 1859-Nov. 22, 1860.

Nebraska News (Nebraska City, Nebraska), Jan. 17, 1857-May 8, 1858.

Newton Kansan (Newton, Kansas), Jan. 6, 1876-June 1, 1876.

New York Daily Tribune, The (New York, New York), 1866.

Niobrara Pioneer (Niobrara, Nebraska), Sept. 22, 1874-Apr. 27, 1882.

Oakdale Journal (Oakdale, Nebraska), Sept. 23, 1873-Oct. 5, 1875.

Oakdale Pen and Plow (Oakdale, Nebraska), Oct. 5, 1875-June 5, 1879.

Omaha Arrow (Omaha, Nebraska), July 28, 1854-Dec. 29, 1854.

Omaha City Times (Omaha, Nebraska), June 11, 1857-July, 1858.

Omaha Weekly Herald (Omaha, Nebraska), Oct. 9, 1865-Dec. 26, 1867.

Paxico Courier (Paxico, Kansas), Sept. 20, 1888-Nov. 1, 1888.

People's Press, The (Nebraska City, Nebraska), Nov. 17, 1859-Nov. 21, 1860.

Pierre Free Press (Pierre, Dakota Territory), Dec. 20, 1883-Apr. 10, 1884.

Press and Dakotaian, The (Yankton, Dakota Territory), Nov. 20, 1873-Nov. 19, 1874, Apr. 16, 1876-Apr. 5, 1877.

Republican Valley Empire (Clyde and Concordia, Kansas), May 31, 1870-Dec. 31, 1870.

Rocky Mountain News (Cherry Creek, Jefferson Territory [Denver, Colorado]), Apr. 23, 1859-Apr. 18, 1860.

Sioux City Tribune (Sioux City, Iowa), Mar. 24, 1876-June 15, 1877.

Sioux City Weekly Journal (Sioux City, Iowa), Aug. 20, 1874-June 21, 1877.

Sioux City Weekly Times (Sioux City, Iowa), Jan. 1874-Dec., 1875.

Tri-Weekly Miner's Register (Central City, Colorado Territory), July 28, 1862-Dec. 8, 1862.

United Brethren Missionary Intelligence (Philadelphia, Pennsylvania), 1833-1844.

United States Catholic Magazine and Monthly Review (Baltimore, Maryland), Vol. I-VII, 1842-1848.

Western Star (Cold Water, Kansas), Sept. 20, 1884-Aug. 8, 1885.

Wichita Eagle (Wichita, Kansas), Apr. 12, 1872-Apr. 3, 1873.

Wichita Vidette (Wichita, Kansas), Aug. 13, 1870-Mar. 11, 1871.

Winfield Courier, The (Winfield, Kansas), Feb. 1, 1873-June 26, 1874.

DIARIES AND JOURNALS

ANTHONY, W. D., *Diary of W. D. Anthony July 9-18, 1860*, Ms., Colorado State Historical Society Library.

———, *Thoughts by the Wayside or Journal of Travel, Leavenworth, Kansas, to Denver, Colorado, May 2-June 8, 1860*, Colorado State Historical Society Library.

AUDUBON, MARIA R., *Audubon and His Journals* (New York, 1897), 2 Vols.

BARBER, T. M., *Diary of T. M. Barber, 1851,* Ms., Nebraska State Historical Society Library.

BELL, WILLIAM ABRAHAM, *New Tracks in North America* (London, 1870). A journal of travel and adventure whilst engaged in the survey for a southern railroad to the Pacific Ocean during 1867-68.

BOUTWELL, WILLIAM THURSTON, Missionary to the Ojibway Indians, 1832-1837, *Diary,* Ms., Minnesota State Historical Society Library.

BRACKENRIDGE, H. M., *Views of Louisiana Together with Journal of a Voyage up the Missouri River in 1811* (Pittsburgh, 1814).

BURTON, ROBERT T., *Diary* (1862), Ms., Utah State Historical Society Library.

CAMPBELL, ROBERT J., *Journal of Robert J. Campbell,* Ms., North Dakota State Historical Society Library.

CHAMBERS, JAMES H., *Diary* (Fort Sarpy, 1855), Journal No. 5, Ms., Montana State Historical Society Library.

CHAPMAN, DARIUS H., *Diary of a Trip to Pike's Peak, 1859,* Ms., Nebraska State Historical Society Library.

Chardon's Journal at Fort Clark 1834-1839, Annie Heloise Abel, editor (Pierre, South Dakota, 1932).

CLANDENING, WILLIAM H., *Across the Plains 1863-1865, Being the Journal of Wm. H. Clandening,* Ms., North Dakota State Historical Society Library.

CLARK, GEORGE T., *Diary* (April 24-July 31, 1860), Ms., Colorado State Historical Society Library.

CLAYTON, WILLIAM, *William Clayton's Journal* (Salt Lake City, 1921).

COOK, JOSEPH WITHERSPOON, Missionary to Cheyenne, *Diary and Letters of the Rev. Joseph W. Cook,* arranged by the Rt. Rev. N. S. Thomas, S. T. D. (Laramie, Wyoming, 1919).

COOK, MRS. MARY E., *Diary of Mrs. Mary E. Cook, Coming Up the Missouri River in 1868,* Ms., Montana State Historical Society Library.

COUES, ELLIOTT, editor, *Manuscript Journals of Alexander Henry, Fur Trader of the Northwest Company, and of David Thompson, Official Geographer of the Same Company* (New York, 1897).

COWLEY, MATTHAIS F., editor, *Wilford Woodruff, Fourth President of the Church of Jesus Christ of Latter-day Saints, History of his Life and Labors, as Recorded in his Daily Journal* (Salt Lake City, 1909).

DE MUN, JULES, *The Journal of Jules De Mun,* translated by Nettie Harney Beauregard, Thomas Maitland Marshall, editor, *Collections,* Missouri State Historical Society (St. Louis, 1928), Vol. V.

Diary of the Father of Mrs. S. N. Bliss (Genesoe, North Dakota), Ms., North Dakota State Historical Society Library.

EASTMAN, ENOCH M., *Diary of Enoch M. Eastman When He was Teamster with the Sibley Exhibition, 1863,* Ms., North Dakota State Historical Society Library.

EGAN, HOWARD, *Pioneering the West 1846 to 1878*, Major Howard Egan's Diary, William M. Egan, editor (Richmond, Utah, 1917).

FERGUSON, A. N., *Diary of Judge A. N. Ferguson, 1865-1869 while engaged as a Civil Engineer with a Union Pacific Surveying Party*, Ms., Union Pacific Museum, Omaha, Nebraska.

FLINT, THOMAS, *Diary* (Claremont, Cal., 1924).

Fort Atkinson: History, Journal General Atkinson Expedition, Ms., Nebraska State Historical Society Library.

Fort Benton—Journal of Daily Incidents Commencing 28th September, 1854, Ms., Montana State Historical Society Library.

GARRIOCH, PETER, *Diary of Peter Garrioch, 1843-1847*, Ms., North Dakota State Historical Society Library.

GLISAN, RODNEY, *Journal of Army Life* (San Francisco, 1874).

HARRIS, N. S., *Journal of a Tour in the Indian Territory* (New York, 1844).

HAWLEY, H. J., *Diary of H. J. Hawley* (March 1, 1860-December 3, 1861), Ms., Wisconsin State Historical Society Library.

HINMAN, S. D., *Journal of the Rev. S. D. Hinman* (Philadelphia, 1869).

HOWARD, WILLIAM, *Log of the Steamer Benton From St. Louis, Missouri, to Ft. Benton, Idaho*, Ms., North Dakota State Historical Society Library.

IRVIN, SAMUEL M., *Diary* (January, 1841-July 31, 1842), Ms., Kansas State Historical Society Library.

Journal History of the Church (1846-1850), Ms., Library of the Church of Jesus Christ of Latter-day Saints, Salt Lake City, Utah.

"Journal of the Expedition Under the Command of Col. Henry Dodge to the Rocky Mountains During the Summer of 1835," *Report of Secretary of War*, February 27, 1836, 24th Congress, 1st Session.

KELLOGG, DANIEL, "Across the Plain in 1858," *The Trail* (Denver, Colo.), December, 1912.

KENNERLY, JAMES, *Diary of James Kennerly, 1823-1826*, Edgar B. Wesley, editor, *Collections*, Missouri Historical Society, Vol. VI.

KURZ, RUDOLPH FRIEDERICH, *Journal of Rudolph Friederich Kurz*, J. N. B. Hewitt, editor (Washington, 1937).

LECHNER, G. W., *G. W. Lechner's Pocket Diary for the Year 1859*, Ms., Colorado State Historical Society Library.

LOBENSTINE, WILLIAM CHRISTIAN, *Extracts From the Diary of William Christian Lobenstine* (New York, 1920).

Log of Steamer Robert Campbell, Jr., From St. Louis to Ft. Benton, Jos. La Barge, Master (1863), Ms., North Dakota State Historical Society Library.

Log of Steamer Silver Lake (Sept. and Oct., 1874), Ms., North Dakota State Historical Society Library.

LOOMIS, LEANDER V., *A Journal of the Birmingham Emigrating Company*, Edgar M. Ledyard, editor (Salt Lake City, 1928).

LUTTIG, JOHN C., *Journal of a Fur Trading Expedition on the Upper Missouri 1812-1813*, Stella M. Drumm, editor (St. Louis, 1920).

MEEKER, JOTHAM, *Daily Journal of Rev. Jotham Meeker, Indian Missionary* (Sept. 10, 1832-Jan. 4, 1855), Ms., Kansas State Historical Society Library.

MERRILL, MOSES, "Extracts from the Diary of Rev. Moses Merrill, a Missionary to the Otoe Indians from 1832 to 1840," *Transactions and Reports* of the Nebraska State Historical Society, Vol. IV.

MÖLLHAUSEN, BALDWIN, *Diary of a Journey from the Mississippi to the Coast of the Pacific With a United States Government Expedition* (London, 1858), 2 Vols.

MORLEY, JAMES HENRY, *Diary of James Henry Morley in Montana, 1862-1865*, Ms., Montana State Historical Society Library.

PALMER, JOEL, *Journal of Travels over the Rocky Mountains to the Mouth of the Columbia River*, R. G. Thwaites, editor (Cleveland, Ohio, 1906).

PARK, LUCIA D., *Journal of a Trip Across the Plains in the Summer of 1863*, Ms., Montana State Historical Society Library.

PAXSON, J. A., *Diary of Dr. J. A. Paxson* (July 1, 1869-Feb. 10, 1870), Ms., Wisconsin State Historical Society Library.

POST, J. P., *The Trip to Pike's Peak, Diary of J. P. Post, 1859*, Ms., Colorado State Historical Society Library.

RICHARDS, W. A., *Diary Kept by W. A. Richards, Summer of 1873*, Ms., Wyoming State History Department Library.

———, *Diary Kept by W. A. Richards, Summer of 1874*, Ms., Wyoming State History Department Library.

RUSSELL, OSBORNE, *Journal of a Trapper or Nine Years in the Rocky Mountains 1834-1843* (Boise, Idaho, 1914).

SANDERS, HARRIET P., *Diary* (1863), Ms., Montana State Historical Society Library.

SANDERS, MRS. W. F., *Diary* (1867), Ms., Montana State Historical Society Library.

SAWYER, LORENZO, *Way Sketches or Lorenzo Sawyer's Overland Journal* (New York, 1926).

SCHOOLCRAFT, HENRY ROWE, *Journal of a Tour into the Interior of Missouri and Arkansas* (London, 1821).

SNOW, ELIZA R., *Journal* (February 12, 1846-May 2, 1847), Vol. I.

TALIAFERRO, MAJOR LAWRENCE, *Journal*, Ms., Minnesota State Historical Society Library.

WALL, O. G., *Diary of O. G. Wall, Co. B, 5th Minnesota Volunteer Infantry, Sibley Expedition 1863*, Ms., North Dakota State Historical Society Library.

WEBB, JAMES JOSEPH, *Adventures in the Santa Fe Trade, 1844-1847*, Ralph P. Bieber, ed. (Glendale, Cal., 1931).

WEST, JOHN, "Extracts from the Substance of a Journal during a Residence at the Red River Colony, 1820-23," *Collections*, State Historical Society of North Dakota, Vol. III.

WORD, SAMUEL, "Diary of Colonel Samuel Word," *Collections*, Montana State Historical Society, Vol. VIII.

MANUSCRIPTS

ADAMSON, DAN, *Carrie Nation and Arkansaw Bob*, Ms., Nebraska State Historical Society Library.

———, *Cattle Range of Early Days, Round Ups, etc.*, Ms., Nebraska State Historical Society Library.

———, *History of the Early Day Range Work and Customs*, Ms., Nebraska State Historical Society Library.

———, *A Short Sketch of the Life of Arkansaw Bob*, Ms., Nebraska State Historical Society Library.

"Annual Round-up," *Dawson Scrapbooks*, Ms., Colorado State Historical Society Library, Vol. XVI.

ASHLEY, S. R., *Colorado's Territorial Days, By a Pioneer*, Ms., Colorado State Historical Society Library.

AUX, GEORGE, "Mining in Colorado," *Bancroft Manuscripts*, Colorado State Historical Society Library.

BARBER, AMHERST W., *The Rebuilding of Fort Rice* (Washington, D. C., 1919), Ms., North Dakota State Historical Society Library.

BENNETT, JOHN, "Mining and Smelting in Colorado," *Bancroft Manuscripts*, Colorado State Historical Society Library.

BENSON, J. H., *From St. Joseph to Sacramento by a Forty Niner* (1849), Ms., Nebraska State Historical Society Library.

BOETTCHER, CHARLES, "The Flush Times of Colorado," *Bancroft Manuscripts*, Colorado State Historical Society Library.

BRADFORD, A. A., "History of Colorado," *Bancroft Manuscripts*, Colorado State Historical Society Library.

BROWN, JESSE, *A Messenger for the Ill-Fated Stage*, Ms., Wyoming State History Department Library.

BRUNSON, ALFRED, Sub-Agent, La Point Indian Agency, *Letter Book* (September 24, 1842-February 27, 1844), Ms., Wisconsin State Historical Society Library.

BYERS, O. P., *The Kansas Pacific Railway*, Ms., Kansas State Historical Society Library.

California and Pike's Peak Express Company, Bonding Articles (issued Dec. 2, 1861, Atchison, Kansas), Ms., Nebraska State Historical Society Library.

CASEMENT, I. S. and D. T., *Account Book* (End of Track, July 1-December 31, 1868), Ms., Union Pacific Museum, Omaha, Nebraska.

"Chance Discovery from Out West, A," (September, 1873), *Bancroft Manuscripts*, Colorado State Historical Society Library.

CHIPLEY, JAMES N., "Towns about Leadville, 1884," *Bancroft Manuscripts*, Colorado State Historical Society Library.

CHIVINGTON, COLONEL J. M., "The First Colorado Regiment," *Bancroft Manuscripts*, Colorado State Historical Society Library.

CRAWFORD, LEWIS F., Interview with Charles O. Armstrong (Grassy Butte, North Dakota, August 4-6, 1929), Ms., North Dakota State Historical Society Library.

————, Interview with C. W. Butler (Miles City, Montana, December 25, 1923), Ms., North Dakota State Historical Society Library.

————, Interview with F. E. Deffebach (Miles City, Montana, December 26, 1923), Ms., North Dakota State Historical Society Library.

————, Interview with A. W. Kingsbury (Great Falls, Montana, February 8, 1918), Ms., North Dakota State Historical Society Library.

————, Interview with Whit H. Terrell (Wibaux, Montana, December 7, 1917), Ms., North Dakota State Historical Society Library.

————, *The Medora-Deadwood Stage Line*, Ms., Nebraska State Historical Society Library.

CROSSMAN, G. H., *Letter of G. H. Crossman, late Captain of the 10th Infantry* (September 14, 1895, October 9, 1895), Ms., North Dakota State Historical Society Library.

DAVIDSON, SALLIE DAVENPORT, *Memoirs*, Ms., Montana State Historical Society Library.

DICKINSON, KARA, *The End of the Track*, Ms., North Dakota State Historical Society Library.

DODDRIDGE, WILLIAM BROWN, *An Indian Raid on the Union Pacific, 1870, at Sidney, Nebraska*, Ms., Leonard Collection, University of Iowa Library.

————, *Indians, Wagons, Clothing, Utes*, Ms., Leonard Collection, University of Iowa Library.

————, *Reminiscences*, Ms., Union Pacific Collection, University of Iowa.

EDWARDS, MARTHA L., *Edwards Papers*, Ms., Wisconsin State Historical Society Library.

ELBERT, SAMUEL H., "Public Man and Measures," *Bancroft Manuscripts*, Colorado State Historical Society Library.

"Fairfield's Survey of 1882 on Northern Boundary of Nebraska," *Field Notes*, Ms., Office of Commissioner of Public Lands, Lincoln, Nebraska.

FREEMAN, C. E., "Menomonie: Is Set Back in 1846," Ms., Minnesota State Historical Society Library.

————, "The Red Cedar River Valley and Its Early Settlement," Ms., Minnesota State Historical Society Library.

FRENCH, C. ADELIA, *Memories*, Ms., Montana State Historical Society Library.

FOWLER, MRS. W. R., "A Woman's Experience in Colorado," *Bancroft Manuscripts*, Colorado State Historical Society Library.

GILPATRICK, LUELLA FERGUS, *A Sketch*, Ms., Montana State Historical Society Library.

GILPATRICK, STEPHEN COLLINS, *Narrative 1838—for My Sons and Montana Historical Society*, Ms., Montana State Historical Society Library.

GOPLEN, ARNOLD O., *Fort Lincoln Museum Report*, Ms., North Dakota State Historical Society Library.

GUTHRIE, W. E., and WEHN, JOHN W., *A Roundup*, Ms., Nebraska State Historical Society Library.

HALLETT, MOSES, "Colorado Courts, Law, and Litigation in Early Times," *Bancroft Manuscripts*, Colorado State Historical Society Library.

HARVEY, ROBERT, compiler, *Letters* of Deputy Surveyors to the Surveyor General of the Kansas and Nebraska Territories and of Iowa and Nebraska, Ms. (Office of Commissioner of Public Lands and Buildings, Lincoln, Nebr.), 3 Vols.

HELM, W. A., "The Gate of the Mountain," *Bancroft Manuscripts*, Colorado State Historical Society Library.

HILGER, DAVID, *Fort Union in 1867, Reminiscences of David Hilger*, Ms., North Dakota State Historical Society Library.

HOWBERT, IRVING, "Indian Troubles of Colorado," *Bancroft Manuscripts*, Colorado State Historical Society Library.

HUGGINS, ALEXANDER G., *Papers* (1835-1888), Ms., Minnesota State Historical Society Library.

JOHNSON, A. B., "Good Times in Gunnison," *Bancroft Manuscripts*, Colorado State Historical Society Library.

KILPATRICK, MRS. JAMES, *Early Life in Beaverhead County*, Ms., Montana State Historical Society Library.

LEMMON, G. E., *Pioneer Stories*, Ms., North Dakota State Historical Society Library.

Letters of Commissioner of General Land Office to the Surveyor General, District Kansas and Nebraska, 1854-1857, Ms. (Office of the Commissioner of Public Lands and Buildings, Lincoln, Nebr.), Vol. I, Part 1.

LONDONER, WOLFE, "Colorado Mining Camps," *Bancroft Manuscripts*, Colorado State Historical Society Library.

———, "Vigilance Committees in Colorado," From the *Scrapbook* of Wolfe Londoner, *Bancroft Manuscripts*, Colorado State Historical Society Library.

McGREGOR, H. B., *Letter of H. B. McGregor to Señ. Cordeal*, Ms., Nebraska State Historical Society Library.

MATER, CHARLES, "Business in Leadville," *Bancroft Manuscripts*, Colorado State Historical Society Library.

MEREDITH, EMILY R., *Experiences and Impressions of a Woman in Montana 1862-1863*, Ms., Montana State Historical Society Library.

———, *Letter Written to her Father from Bannack April 30-May 4, 1863*, Ms., Montana State Historical Society Library.

———, *The Annual Buffalo Hunt of the Nez Percés*, Ms., Montana State Historical Society Library.

MIDDAUGH, ASA F., *When Denver Was Young and Tough, an interview with Asa F. Middaugh, May 18, 1923*, Ms., Colorado State Historical Society Library.

MORRILL, C. H., "Thrilling Days in Western Nebraska," *Observer* (no date given), Ms., Wyoming State Historical Society Library.

O'BRIEN, EMILY E., *Indians and Early Western Experiences*, Ms., Colorado State Historical Society Library.

———, *Personal Reminiscences of Army Life*, Ms., Colorado State Historical Society Library.

Pioneer Reminiscences, The (author unidentified), Ms., North Dakota State Historical Society Library.

POND, GIDEON H., and SAMUEL W., *Gideon H. and Samuel W. Pond Papers* (1833-April, 1840), Ms., Minnesota State Historical Society Library.

PRESCOTT, THOMAS, "Through Canon de Shea," *Bancroft Manuscripts*, Colorado State Historical Society Library.

Records of the Sixth and Rifle Regiments, Ms., Nebraska State Historical Society Library.

RIGGS, STEPHEN R., *Papers* (1843-1864), Ms., Minnesota State Historical Society Library.

ROBERTS, JAMES, *Recollections of Early Life in Dodgeville and of My Trip to California*, Ms., Wisconsin State Historical Society Library.

ROWE, WILLIAM R., *California Experiences*, Ms., Wisconsin State Historical Society Library.

RUDD, ANSON, S., "Early Affairs in Canon City" (Canon City, 1884), *Bancroft Manuscripts*, Colorado State Historical Society Library.

SEYMOUR, BENNETT E., *Reminiscences of Bennett E. Seymour, 1861*, Ms., Colorado State Historical Society Library.

Short History of Fort Abercrombie, A, Ms., North Dakota State Historical Society Library.

SILVER, SAMUEL D., "The Mines of Colorado," *Bancroft Manuscripts*, Colorado State Historical Society Library.

SLAUGHTER, JOHN, "Life in Colorado and Wyoming," *Bancroft Manuscripts*, Colorado State Historical Society Library.

SOPRIS, RICHARD, "Settlement of Denver," *Bancroft Manuscripts*, Colorado State Historical Society Library.

Story of Two Forts—Pembina, Ransom, Ms., North Dakota State Historical Society Library.

STREET, JOSEPH MONTFORT, *Correspondence of Joseph Montfort Street*, Aldrich Collection, Ms., Iowa State Historical Library, Des Moines.

Surveyor's Correspondence, Ms., Office of the Commissioner of Public Lands of the State of Nebraska, Book I.

TABOR, MRS., "Cabin Life in Colorado," *Bancroft Manuscripts*, Colorado State Historical Society Library.

THOMSON, CHARLES I., "Progress in Leadville," *Bancroft Manuscripts*, Colorado State Historical Society Library.

WALDERSON, MRS. MATTHEWS, *Mrs. James W. Mardis, A Sketch*, Ms., Montana State Historical Society Library.

WARD, HENRY R., *One Year of My Life on the Frontier, 1872-1873*, Ms., North Dakota State Historical Society Library.

WESTON, EUGENE, "The Colorado Mines," *Bancroft Manuscripts*, Colorado State Historical Society Library.

WILCOX, A. H., *Up the Missouri River to Montana in the Spring of 1862*, Ms., Montana State Historical Society Library.

WYNKOOP, MAJOR EDWARD W., *Unfinished History of Colorado*, Ms., Colorado State Historical Society Library.

AUTOBIOGRAPHY

BANDEL, EUGENE, *Frontier Life in the Army 1854-1861*, Ralph P. Bieber, editor (Glendale, Cal., 1932).

BECKWOURTH, JAMES P., *Life and Adventures of James P. Beckwourth* (New York and London, 1856).

BRATT, JOHN, *Trails of Yesterday* (Lincoln, Nebraska, 1922).

BRONSON, EDGAR BEECHER, *Reminiscences of a Ranchman* (Chicago, 1910).

CANTON, FRANK M., *Frontier Trails*, Edward Everett Dale, editor (New York, 1930).

CODY, WILLIAM F., *Life and Adventures of "Buffalo Bill"* (New York, 1927).

COOK, JAMES H., *Fifty Years on the Old Frontier* (New Haven, Conn., 1923).

CUSTER, GEORGE A., *My Life on the Plains* (New York, 1874).

DIXON, BILLY, *Life of Billy Dixon* (Dallas, Texas, 1927).

DYER, JOHN L., *The Snow-Shoe Itinerant, An Autobiography* (Cincinnati, 1890).

ELLIOTT, RICHARD SMITH, *Notes Taken in Sixty Years* (St. Louis, 1883).

GIBSON, J. W., *Recollections of a Pioneer* (St. Joseph, 1912).

HAMBLETON, CHALKLEY J., *A Gold Hunter's Experience* (Chicago, 1898).

LATHROP, GEORGE, *Some Pioneer Recollections* (Philadelphia, 1927).

LAYTON, CHRISTOPHER, *Autobiography* (Salt Lake City, 1911).

MAJORS, ALEXANDER, *Seventy Years on the Frontier, Alexander Majors' Memoirs of a Lifetime on the Border*, Colonel Prentiss Ingraham, editor (Chicago and New York, 1893).

MARCY, RANDOLPH BARNES, *Thirty Years of Army Life on the Border* (New York, 1866).

MEEKER, EZRA, *The Ox Team, or the Old Oregon Trail* (New York, 1907).

PORTER, HENRY M., *Autobiography of Henry M. Porter* (Denver, 1932).

PRATT, PARLEY P., *The Autobiography of Parley P. Pratt* (New York, 1874).

RAVOUX, AUGUSTIN V. G., *Reminiscences, Memoirs, and Lectures* (St. Paul, 1890).

READ, GEORGE WILLIS, *A Pioneer of 1850* (Boston, 1927).

RIGGS, STEPHEN R., *Mary and I, Forty Years with the Sioux* (Chicago, 1880).

ROYCE, SARAH, *A Frontier Lady* (New Haven, 1932).

TALIAFERRO, MAJOR LAWRENCE, "Autobiography of Major Lawrence Taliaferro, 1864," *Collections*, Minnesota Historical Society, Vol. VI.

VILLARD, HENRY, *Memoirs of Henry Villard* (Boston and New York, 1904), 2 Vols.

REMINISCENT WRITINGS

Books

ADAMS, ANDY, *The Log of a Cowboy* (Boston, 1903).

APPLEGATE, JESSE, *A Day with the Cow Column in 1843*, Joseph Schafer, editor (Chicago, 1934).

BARROWS, JOHN R., *Ubet* (Caldwell, Idaho, 1934).

BLAIR, WALTER A., *A Raft Pilot's Log*, A History of the Great Rafting Industry on the Upper Mississippi, 1840-1915 (Cleveland, 1930).

BRONSON, EDGAR BEECHER, *Cowboy Life on the Western Plains* (New York, 1910).

BRUFFEY, GEORGE A., *Eighty-One Years in the West* (Butte, Montana, 1925).

BURKLEY, FRANK J., *The Faded Frontier* (Omaha, 1935).

CHAPPELL, PHILIP EDWARD, *A History of the Missouri River* (Kansas City, Mo., 1911).

CLAY, JOHN, *My Life on the Range* (Chicago, 1924).

CLYMAN, JAMES, *American Frontiersman 1792-1881*, Charles L. Camp, editor (San Francisco, 1928).

COLE, GILBERT L., *In Early Days Along the Overland Trail in Nebraska Territory in 1852* (Kansas City, Missouri, 1905).

CRAWFORD, LEWIS F., *Rekindling Camp Fires* (Bismarck, North Dakota, 1926).

DELLENBAUGH, F. S., *Breaking the Wilderness* (New York and London, 1905).

DICKSON, ALBERT J., *Covered Wagon Days*, Arthur J. Dickson, editor (Cleveland, 1929).

DODGE, GRENVILLE M., "Wonderful Story of the Building of the Pacific Roads," *Trans-Continental Railways* (Omaha, Nebraska, 1889).

DOUBLEDAY, RUSSELL, *Cattle-Ranch to College* (New York, 1899).

FORSYTH, GEORGE A., *The Story of the Soldier* (New York, 1900).

FRENCH, JOSEPH LEWIS, *The Pioneer West* (Boston, 1923).

GILFILLAN, ARCHER B., *Sheep* (Boston, 1929).

GOULDER, W. A., *Reminiscences*, Incidents in the Life of a Pioneer in Oregon and Idaho (Boise, Idaho, 1909).

HAMILTON, W. T., *My Sixty Years on the Plains Trapping, Trading, and Fighting*, E. T. Sieber, editor (New York, 1905).

HANSON, JOSEPH MILLS, *The Conquest of the Missouri* (Chicago, 1916).

HERNDON, SARAH RAYMOND, *Days on the Road, Crossing the Plains in 1865* (New York, 1902).

HEWITT, RANDALL H., *Across the Plains and Over the Divide* (New York, 1906).

HILL, J. L., *The End of the Cattle Trail* (Long Beach, California, 1922).

HOBART, CHAUNCEY, *Recollections of My Life* (Red Wing, Minnesota, 1885).

HOOKER, WILLIAM FRANCIS, *The Prairie Schooner* (Chicago, 1918).

HOWBERT, IRVING, *Memories of a Lifetime in the Pike's Peak Region* (New York and London, 1925).

HOWARD, SARAH, *Pen Pictures of the Plains* (Denver, 1902).

HUNTER, J. MARVIN, editor, *Trail Drivers of Texas* (San Antonio, Texas, 1924). 2 Vols.

INMAN, HENRY, and CODY, WILLIAM F., *The Great Salt Lake Trail* (Topeka, 1926).

JACKSON, WILLIAM H., and DRIGGS, HOWARD R., *The Pioneer Photographer* (Yonkers-on-Hudson, 1929).

JAMES, WILL, *Cowboys North and South* (New York and London, 1924).

KENNEDY, GEORGE W., *The Pioneer Campfire* (Portland, Oregon, 1914).

KUYKENDALL, WILLIAM L., *Frontier Days* (Place of publication not given, 1917).

LARIMER, WILLIAM and LARIMER, WILLIAM H. H., *Reminiscences of General William Larimer and of His Son William H. H. Larimer* (Lancaster, Pennsylvania, 1918).

LOWE, PERCIVAL G., *Five Years a Dragoon* (Kansas City, Missouri, 1906).

MCILHANY, EDWARD WASHINGTON, *Recollections of a '49er* (Kansas City, Missouri, 1908).

MCNEAL, T. A., *When Kansas Was Young* (New York, 1922).

MCREYNOLDS, ROBERT, *Thirty Years on the Frontier* (Colorado Springs, 1906).

MAHAN, BRUCE E., *Old Fort Crawford and the Frontier* (Iowa City, Iowa, 1926).

MAXWELL, WILLIAM AUDLEY, *Crossing the Plains, Days of '57* (San Francisco, 1915).

MEYERS, AUGUSTUS, *Ten Years in the Ranks, U. S. Army* (New York, 1914).

MUNROE, KIRK, *Campmates, A Story of the Plains* (New York, 1891).

MYRICK, HERBERT, *Cache la Poudre, The Romance of a Tenderfoot in the Days of Custer* (New York, 1905).

OTERO, MIGUEL ANTONIO, *My Life on the Frontier* (New York, 1935).

PAGE, ELIZABETH, *Wagons West* (New York, 1930).

POST, C. C., *Ten Years a Cowboy* (Chicago, 1898).

REID, MRS. AGNES JUST, *Letters of Long Ago* (Caldwell, Idaho, 1923).

ROENIGK, ADOLPH, *Pioneer History of Kansas* (Lincoln, Kansas, 1933).

ROLLINS, PHILIP A., *The Cowboy* (New York, 1922).

ROOT, FRANK A., and CONNELLEY, WILLIAM ELSEY, *The Overland Stage to California* (Topeka, Kansas, 1901).

RUSH, OSCAR, *The Open Range* (Caldwell, Idaho, 1936).

RUSSELL, CHARLES EDWARD, *A-Rafting on the Mississip'* (New York, 1928).

RUSSELL, ISAAC K., and DRIGGS, HOWARD R., *Hidden Heroes of the Rockies* (Yonkers-on-Hudson, 1923).

SHAW, R. C., *Across the Plains in Forty-Nine* (Farmland, Indiana, 1896).

SHORTRIDGE, WILSON PORTER, *The Transition of a Typical Frontier* (Menasha, Wisconsin, 1922).

STEELE, JOHN, *Across the Plains in 1850* (Chicago, 1930).

STOKES, GEORGE W., and DRIGGS, HOWARD R., *Deadwood Gold* (Yonkers-on-Hudson, 1926).

STRAHORN, CARRIE ADELL, *Fifteen Thousand Miles by Stage* (New York, 1911).

STREETER, FLOYD BENJAMIN, *Prairie Trails & Cow Towns* (Boston, 1936).

STUART, GRANVILLE, *Forty Years on the Frontier* (Cleveland, 1925). 2 Vols.

TAYLOR, JOSEPH HENRY, *Kaleidoscopic Lives, A Companion Book to Frontier and Indian Life* (Washburn, North Dakota, 1932).

TRIPLETT, FRANK, *Conquering the Wilderness* (New York and St. Louis, 1883).

TUTTLE, D. S., *Reminiscences of a Missionary Bishop* (New York, 1906).

VAUGHN, ROBERT, *Then and Now or Thirty-Six Years in the Rockies* (Minneapolis, 1900).

WALGAMOTT, C. S., *Reminiscences of Early Days* (Twin Falls, Idaho, 1926). 2 Vols.

WARE, EUGENE, *The Indian War of 1864* (Topeka, Kansas, 1911).

WEBSTER, KIMBALL, *The Gold Seekers of '49* (Manchester, N. H., 1917).

WHEELER, HOMER WEBSTER, *Buffalo Days* (Indianapolis, 1925).

————, *The Frontier Trail* (Los Angeles, 1923).

WILLIAMS, JOSEPH, *Narrative of a Tour From the State of Indiana to the Oregon Territory in the Years 1841-1842* (New York, 1921).

YOUNG, CHARLES E., *Dangers of the Trail in 1865* (Geneva, New York, 1912).

Newspapers

ADAMSON, DAN, "Strenuous Times on Wyoming Range When the West Was in the Making," *Omaha Daily Journal-Stockman* (Omaha, Nebraska), July 20, 1928.

BARTLETT, W. W., "Reproduction of a Curious Old Bill Received Here Years Ago by Ingram & Kennedy, and Explanatory Article," in *Forestry Magazine*, in *The Daily Telegram* (Eau Claire, Wisconsin), December 16, 1924.

"Bruno Vinette Tells About Chippewa Valley in 'Fifties," *The Daily Telegram* (Eau Claire, Wisconsin), September 3, 1918.

BULLEN, C. A., "Lumbering in Chippewa Valley," *The Daily Telegram* (Eau Claire, Wisconsin), April 8, 1916.

GUNN, PATRICK, "Lumbering in the Chippewa Valley," *The Eau Claire Leader* (Eau Claire, Wisconsin), April 12, 1916.

"Hand Cart Brigade," *Huntsman's Echo* (Wood River, Nebraska), July 26, 1860.

HARSHFIELD, JOHN, "When War Broke Out on Wyoming Range," *Omaha Daily Journal-Stockman* (Omaha, Nebraska), June 19, 1928.

HOLDEN, JAMES, "Early Camp Life Reminiscences Told by [James] Holden," *The Daily Telegram* (Eau Claire, Wisconsin), November 10, 17, 1916.

PAGE, MARTIN, "The Days in the 50's," *The Daily Telegram* (Eau Claire, Wisconsin), February 24, 1916.

SMITH, WILLIAM H., "Lumbering in Chippewa Valley," *The Daily Telegram* (Eau Claire, Wisconsin), May 8, 1916.

VINETTE, BRUNO, "Early Days in the Valley of the Chippewa," *The Daily Telegram* (Eau Claire, Wisconsin), May 22, 1919.

MAGAZINE ARTICLES: REMINISCENT AND CONTEMPORARY

AMBULO, JOHN, "The Cattle on a Thousand Hills," *Overland Monthly*, March, 1887.

BAUMAN, JOHN, "On a Western Ranche," *The Fortnightly Review*, Vol. XLVII, April, 1887.

BEITLEMAN, JOHN L., "An Attack on the Stage Stations," *The Trail*, June, 1909.

BELL, W. A., "The Pacific Railroads," *Fortnightly Review*, May, 1869.

BIDWELL, JOHN, "The First Emigrant Train to California," *The Century Magazine*, Vol. XIX.

BLAKE, JUDGE HENRY N., "To Montana in 1866," *Rocky Mountain Magazine*, Vol. I, September, 1900.

BREWERTON, GEORGE D., "In the Buffalo Country," *Harpers Monthly*, Vol. XXV.

BURNHAM, J. W., "Recollections of Kit Carson," *The Record* (Fargo, N. D.), April, 1897.

CAVALEER, CHARLES, "A Pembina Story," *The Record* (Fargo, N. D.), May, 1896.

——, and MOORHEAD, WILLIAM H., "Good Old Buffalo Days," *The Record* (Fargo, N. D.), April, 1896.

CHAPMAN, ARTHUR, "The Sheep Herders of the West," *The Outlook*, Vol. 80, June 24, 1905.

COFFIN, MORSE H., "Early Days in Boulder County," *The Trail*, April, 1911.

COWAN, JOHN L., "Notes on the Fur Trade of the Rockies," *The Trail*, December, 1911.

COY, MRS. JOHN G., "Crossing the Plains in 1862," *The Trail*, November, 1910.

DARLEY, G. M., "The End-Gate of the Mess Wagon," *The Trail*, November, 1909.

EASTWOOD, COLIN S., "Construction Work on the Old U.P.," *The Trail*, June, 1910.

GALBRAITH, R. M., "He Railroaded in Wyoming in Days When Peril and Romance Merely Matter of Day's Work," *Union Pacific Magazine*, September, 1922.

GOODING, W. C., "On the Frontier," *The Record* (Fargo, N. D.), June, 1898.

GRABLE, FRANCIS O., "The Story of Fort Collins' Birth," *The Trail*, April, 1910.

GROHMAN, W. BAILLIE, "Cattle Ranches of the Far West," *The Fortnightly Review*, Vol. 34, October 1, 1880.

HARGER, CHARLES MOREAU, "Cattle Trails of the Prairies," *Scribner's Magazine*, Vol. XI, June, 1892.

——, "Sheep and Shepherds of the West," *The Outlook*, Vol. 72, November 22, 1902.

HILGER, DAVID, "A Vigilante Trial and Execution," *Rocky Mountain Magazine* (Helena, Montana, 1901), Vol. II.

LEACH, RICHARD E., "John W. Iliff," *The Trail*, March, 1912.

LOUNSBERRY, C. A., "Account of Life at Fort Abraham Lincoln," *The Record* (Fargo, N. D.), June, 1898.

———, "The Red River Valley," *The Record* (Fargo, N. D.), August, 1895.

MOODY, DAVE, "Tales of a Cow Camp," *The Trail*, February, 1910.

MUNSON, LYMAN E., "Reminiscences of a Montana Judge," *Journal of American History*, Vol. I.

PIERCE, ARTHUR E., "The First Two Years," Some Random Reminiscences of Events Occurring Prior to the Organization of Colorado Territory, *The Trail*, August, 1912, September, 1912, November, 1912.

PRITCHARD, JESSE L., "To Pike's Peak in Search of Gold in 1859," *The Trail*, September, 1911, October, 1911.

RAMER, C. W., "Experiences in Early Days," *The Trail*, November, 1910.

ROENIGK, ADOLPH, "When Bullets Sang a Hymn of Death," *Union Pacific Magazine*, July, 1931.

SLAUGHTER, LINDA W., "Interesting Sketch," *The Record* (Fargo, N. D.), May, 1896.

SNOW, E. P., Secretary Wyoming State Board of Sheep Commissioners, to the Editor, *The Outlook*, Vol. 73, April 4, 1903.

STANTON, IRVING W., "Early Days in Colorado," *The Trail*, March, 1910.

TAFT, MRS. WALTER, "Across the Plains in the Early Sixties," *The Trail*, July, 1910.

THOMAS, J. J., "In the Days of the Overland Trail," *The Trail*, May, 1910.

THOMPSON, FRANCIS McGEE, "Reminiscences of Four-Score Years," *The Massachusetts Magazine*, supplement to Vol. V, 1912.

TUTTLE, DANIEL S., "Montana Reminiscences," *Rocky Mountain Magazine*, October, 1900.

VANDERWALKER OF VICTOR, "Over the Santa Fe Trail in '64," *The Trail*, June, 1909.

WILCOX, EARLEY VERNON, "Sheep and the Forests," *The Forum*, Vol. XXXI.

WILKESON, FRANK, "Cattle Raising on the Plains," *Harper's Magazine*, Vol. 72, Apr., 1886.

WISTER, OWEN, "The Evolution of the Cowpuncher," *Harper's Magazine*, Vol. 91, September, 1895.

YOUNKER, JASON T., "The Early Pioneer Reminiscences of 1858-59," *The Trail*, January, 1910.

PERSONAL INTERVIEWS

EDWARDS, J. B. Oct. 1, 1925. Mr. Edwards was a "locator" for the mammoth herds of Texas cattle on the prairie near Abilene, Kansas, when it was a cowtown.

GORDEN, D. R. Oct. 1, 1925. Mr. Gorden was the first station-agent in Abilene, Kansas, when it was a cowtown, 1869-1874.

Leonard, Levi O. October 2, 1938.

Mayer, Frank H. July 10, 1938. Mr. Mayer was an old-time buffalo hunter. He participated in the slaughter which exterminated the southern herd.

Thomas, Chauncey. July 7, 12, 1938. Mr. Thomas is a well-known Colorado writer who in his youth was familiar with cowboy and mining life.

MISCELLANEOUS

Abel, Annie Heloise, editor, *The Official Correspondence of James S. Calhoun While Indian Agent at Santa Fe and Superintendent of Indian Affairs in New Mexico* (Washington, 1915).

Cole, Wesley, *Some of My Experiences as a Cow Puncher,* told to C. E. Gibson, Jr., a pamphlet in Colorado State Historical Society Library.

Great Union Pacific Railroad, The, Excursion to the Hundredth Meridian: From New York to Platte City (Chicago, 1867).

Handbill of the 1884 Round-ups of the Wyoming Stock Growers Association, Nebraska State Historical Society Library.

Periodical Account of Baptist Missions within Indian Territory for the Year December 31, 1836 (no author given).

Periodical Account of Baptist Missions Within the Indian Territory, 1837.

Sketches of the Dakota Mission, Missions of the American Board, 1873.

II. Secondary Works

HISTORIES AND MONOGRAPHS

Abbott, Cary, "Cheyenne: The Wild West Sells Its Atmosphere," Duncan Aikman, editor, *The Taming of the Frontier* (New York, 1925).

Adamson, Archibald, *North Platte and Its Associations* (North Platte, Nebraska, 1910).

Agnew, Dwight, *The Government Land Surveyor as a Pioneer,* Ms., Master's Thesis, University of Iowa, 1938.

Aken, David, *Pioneers of the Black Hills or Gordon's Stockade Party of 1874* (Milwaukee, 1920).

Alter, J. Cecil, *Utah the Storied Domain,* 3 Vols. (Chicago and New York, 1932).

Andreas, Alfred Theodore, *History of the State of Kansas* (Chicago, 1883).

———, *History of the State of Nebraska* (Chicago, 1882).

Banning, Captain William, and Banning, George Hugh, *Six Horses* (New York, 1930).

Bartlett, I. S., editor, *History of Wyoming,* 3 Vols. (Chicago, 1918).

Beers, Henry Putney, *The Western Military, 1815-1846* (Philadelphia, 1935).

Black, Wilfred W., *The Army Doctor in the Trans-Mississippi West,* Ms., Master's Thesis, University of Iowa, 1936.

BRADLEY, GLENN D., *The Story of the Pony Express* (Chicago, 1913).

———, *The Story of the Santa Fe* (Boston, 1917).

BRANCH, E. DOUGLAS, *The Cowboy and His Interpreters* (New York, 1926).

———, *The Hunting of the Buffalo* (New York, 1929).

BRESEE, FLOYD EDGAR, *Overland Freighting in the Platte Valley, 1850-1870*, Ms., Master's Thesis, University of Nebraska, 1937.

BRIGGS, HAROLD E., *Frontiers of the Northwest* (New York, 1940).

———, *The Settlement and Economic Development of the Territory of Dakota*, Ms., Ph.D. Thesis, University of Iowa, 1929.

BROWN, JESSE, and WILLARD, A. M., *The Black Hills Trails*, John T. Milek, editor (Rapid City, S. D., 1924).

BROWNING, JULIA ANNE, *The Frontier Settlements of the Early Thirties*, Ms., Master's Thesis, University of Iowa, 1933.

BURLEIGH, D. ROBERT, *Range Cattle Industry in Nebraska to 1890*, Ms. Master's Thesis, University of Nebraska, 1937.

BURLINGAME, MERRILL GILDEA, *The Economic Importance of the Buffalo in the Northern Plains Region, 1800-1890*, Ms., Master's Thesis, University of Iowa, 1928.

BUTCHER, S. D., *Pioneer History of Custer County* (Broken Bow, Nebraska, 1901).

CHAPMAN, ARTHUR, *The Pony Express* (New York and London, 1932).

CHITTENDEN, HIRAM MARTIN, *The American Fur Trade of the Far West*, 3 Vols., Vol. I (New York, 1902).

———, *History of Early Steamboat Navigation on the Missouri River*, 2 Vols. (New York, 1903).

COLLINS, MRS. NAT., *The Cattle Queen of Montana* (Spokane, 1935).

COMAN, KATHERINE, *Economic Beginnings of the Far West*, 2 Vols. (New York, 1912).

COY, OWEN COCHRAN, *The Great Trek* (San Francisco, 1931).

CULHANE, ALBERT EDWARD, *A History of the Settlement of La Plata County, Colorado*, Ms., Master's Thesis, University of Colorado, 1934.

DALE, EDWARD E., *The Range and Ranch Cattle Industry* (Norman, Okla., 1930).

DENTON, DORIS, *Harmony Mission, 1821-1837*, Ms., Master's Thesis, University of Kansas, 1929.

DICK, EVERETT, *The Sod-House Frontier* (New York, 1937).

DONOHUE, ARTHUR THOMAS, *A History of the Early Jesuit Missions in Kansas*, Ms., Ph.D. Thesis, University of Kansas, 1931.

DRIGGS, HOWARD R., *The Pony Express Goes Through* (New York, 1935).

DUNBAR, SEYMOUR, *History of Travel in America*, 4 Vols., Vol. II (Indianapolis, 1915).

EIKENBERRY, ALICE M., *Expeditions Up the Missouri River to 1819*, Ms., Master's Thesis, University of Iowa, 1929.

ELEFSON, VERNA ANNE, *Indian Agencies on the Upper Missouri to 1850*, Ms., Master's Thesis, University of Iowa, 1927.

FELLER, MYRLIN M., *Sioux City: A Center of Transportation 1850-1880*, Ms., Master's Thesis, University of Iowa, 1936.

FELTER, MAUDE ETHEL, *The Beginnings of the Range and Ranch Cattle Business of Montana*, Ms., Master's Thesis, University of Iowa, 1924.

FRITZ, PERCY STANLEY, "The Constitutions and Laws of Early Mining Districts—In Boulder County, Colorado," *The University of Colorado Studies*, Vol. 21, No. 1.

FULTON, ROBERT LARDIN, *Epic of the Overland* (San Francisco, 1924).

GANOE, WILLIAM ADDLEMAN, *The History of the United States Army* (New York, 1924).

GHENT, W. J., *The Road to Oregon* (New York, 1929).

GOSS, C. CHAUCER, *Bellevue, Larimer and Saint Mary, Their History, Location, Description and Advantages* (Bellevue, 1859).

GOULD, E. W., *Fifty Years on the Mississippi* (St. Louis, 1889).

GREEN, CHARLES LOWELL, *The Indian Reservation System of the Dakotas to 1889*, Ms., Master's Thesis, University of Iowa, 1928.

GRIEDER, THEODORE G., *The Influence of the American Bison or Buffalo on Westward Expansion*, Ms., Master's Thesis, University of Iowa, 1928.

HAFEN, LE ROY R., *The Overland Mail 1849-1869* (Cleveland, 1926).

——, and GHENT, W. J., *Broken Hand* (Denver, 1931).

HANSEN, MARCUS L., *Old Fort Snelling 1819-1858* (Iowa City, Iowa, 1918).

HARLOW, ALVIN F., *Old Waybills; the Romance of the Express Companies* (New York, 1934).

HAVIGHURST, WALTER, *Upper Mississippi: A Wilderness Saga* (New York, 1937).

HEBARD, GRACE RAYMOND, *The Pathbreakers from River to Ocean* (Chicago, 1911).

History of Old Pembina 1780-1872 (Larimore, N. D., 1917).

HOLT, EDGAR ALLEN, *Missouri River Steamboating 1850-1860*, Ms., Master's Thesis, University of Iowa, 1925.

HOOPES, ALBAN W., *Indian Affairs and Their Administration, with Special Reference to the Far West, 1849-1860* (Philadelphia and London, 1932).

HOUGH, EMERSON, *The Story of the Cowboy* (New York, 1908).

——, *The Story of the Outlaw* (New York, 1907).

HOUGHTON, ELIZA P. DONNER, *The Expedition of the Donner Party* (Chicago, 1911).

HUGHES, KATHERINE, *Father Lacombe, the Black-Robe Voyageur* (New York, 1911).

HULBERT, ARCHER BUTLER, *Forty-Niners* (Boston, 1931).

HUNT, MAJOR ELVID, *History of Leavenworth 1827-1927* (Leavenworth, Kansas, 1926).

INMAN, HENRY, *The Old Santa Fe Trail* (Topeka, 1916).

——, *Tales of the Trail* (Topeka, 1898).

JONES, CHARLES J., *Buffalo Jones' Forty Years of Adventure*, compiled by Henry Inman (Topeka, Kans., 1899).

KEELING, WILBUR EARL, *Cholera Epidemics of the Fifties*, Ms., Master's Thesis, University of Iowa, 1933.

KELSEY, RAYNER WICKERSHAM, *Friends and Indians 1655-1917* (Philadelphia, 1917).

KENNAN, MURIEL, *The Superintendent of Indian Affairs to 1840*, Ms., Master's Thesis, University of Iowa, 1936.

KENT, FLORENCE KNIGHT, *The Western Mining Frontier 1858-1866*, Ms., Master's Thesis, University of Iowa, 1930.

KLISE, CARLYLE N., *The First Transcontinental Telegraph*, Ms., Master's Thesis, University of Iowa, 1937.

KOENIG, MYRON L., *Fort Union as a Missouri River Post*, Ms., Master's Thesis, University of Iowa, 1933.

LIPPINCOTT, ISAAC, "A Century and a Half of Fur Trade at St. Louis," *Washington University Studies*, Vol. III, Part II, No. 2.

LOMAX, JOHN A., *Cowboy Songs, and Other Frontier Ballads* (New York, 1910).

MALIN, J. C., "Indian Policy and Westward Expansion," *Kansas Humanistic Studies* (Lawrence, Kansas, 1921), Vol. II, No. 3.

MARNER, GRACE LILLIAN, *The Range and Ranch Cattle Business in Wyoming 1870-1890*, Ms., Master's Thesis, University of Iowa, 1922.

MARTIN, SISTER AQUINATA, O. P. M. A., *The Catholic Church on the Nebraska Frontier 1854-1885* (Washington, D. C., 1937).

MERCER, A. S., *The Banditti of the Plains or The Cattlemen's Invasion of Wyoming in 1892* (San Francisco, 1935).

MERIAM, LEWIS, *The Problem of Indian Administration* (Baltimore, 1928).

MERRIAM, LUCIUS S., "The Telegraphs of the Bond-Aided Pacific Railroads," *Political Science Quarterly*, Vol. IX, No. 2.

MINIER, JOHN P. JR., *St. Louis as an Outfitting Center in 1849*, Ms., Master's Thesis, University of Iowa, 1937.

MORTON, STERLING J., and WATKINS, ALBERT, *Illustrated History of Nebraska* (Lincoln, 1906), Vol. II.

NEUHAUS, CARLA ELIZABETH, *Transportation to Colorado, 1858-1869*, Ms., Master's Thesis, University of Colorado, 1928.

O'BRIEN, THOMAS BRUCE, *The Frontier of Settlement in 1850*, Ms., Master's Thesis, University of Iowa, 1935.

OLSON, LAWRENCE E., *The Mining Frontier of South Dakota 1874-1877*, Ms., Master's Thesis, University of Iowa, 1931.

OSGOOD, ERNEST S., *The Day of the Cattleman* (Minneapolis, 1929).

PARRISH, RANDALL, *The Great Plains* (Chicago, 1907).

PEAKE, ORA BROOKS, *The Colorado Range Cattle Industry* (Glendale, California, 1937).

PELZER, LOUIS, *The Cattlemen's Frontier* (Glendale, California, 1936).

———, *Marches of the Dragoons in the Mississippi Valley* (Iowa City, Iowa, 1917).

PERRIGO, LYNN IRWIN, *Life in Central City, Colorado, as Revealed by the Register, 1862-1872*, Ms., Master's Thesis, University of Colorado, 1934.

———, *A Social History of Central City, Colorado, 1859-1900*, Ms., Ph.D. Thesis, University of Colorado, 1936.

PETERSEN, WILLIAM J., *Steamboating On the Upper Mississippi* (Iowa City, Iowa, 1937).

QUIETT, GLENN CHESNEY, *Pay Dirt* (New York, 1936).

———, *They Built the West* (New York, 1934).

ROBINSON, DOANE, "Old Trapper and His Money," *History, South Dakota*, 2 Vols. (Logansport, Ind., 1904).

ROLLINS, PHILIP ASHTON, *The Cowboy* (New York, 1922).

SABIN, EDWIN L., *Building the Pacific Railway* (Philadelphia and London, 1919).

SANFORD, ALBERT HART, *The Story of Agriculture in the United States* (Boston and New York, 1916).

SAUER, HOWARD M., *The Frontier of Settlement for 1860*, Ms., Master's Thesis, University of Iowa, 1931.

SCHAFER, JOSEPH, "The Wisconsin Lead Region," *Wisconsin Domesday Book* (Madison, 1932), Vol. III.

SCHMECKEBIER, LAWRENCE F., *The Office of Indian Affairs* (Baltimore, 1927).

SEYMOUR, MRS. FLORA WARREN, *The Story of the Red Man* (New York, 1929).

SHUMWAY, GRANT LEE, *History of Western Nebraska and Its People*, 2 Vols. (Lincoln, Nebraska, 1921).

SMITH, FRANCIS WAGER, *The Establishment and Early History of Fort Laramie, Wyoming*, Ms., Master's Thesis, University of Iowa, 1917.

STODDARD, HELEN O., *The Early History of Maquoketa, Iowa, 1838-1880*, Ms., Master's Thesis, University of Iowa, 1933.

SULLIVAN, MAURICE S., *The Travels of Jedediah Smith* (Santa Ana, California, 1934).

TROTTMAN, NELSON, *History of the Union Pacific, A Financial and Economic Survey* (New York, 1923).

VANDIVEER, CLARENCE A., *The Fur Trade and Early Western Exploration* (Cleveland, 1929).

VAN HOOK, JOSEPH ORLANDO, *Settlement and Economic Development of the Arkansas Valley from Pueblo to the Colorado-Kansas Line, 1860-1900*, Ms., Doctor's Thesis, University of Colorado, 1933.

VISSCHER, WILLIAM LIGHTFOOT, *A Thrilling and Truthful History of the Pony Express; or Blazing the Westward Way* (Chicago, 1908).

WALDO, EDNA LaMOORE, *Dakota* (Caldwell, Idaho, 1936).

WALLER, JOHN LEE ROY, *Economic History and Settlement of Converse County, Wyoming*, Ms., Master's Thesis, University of Colorado, 1925.

WARMAN, CY, *Story of the Railroad* (New York, 1898).

WEBB, WALTER PRESCOTT, *The Great Plains* (Boston, 1931).

WELLMAN, PAUL I., *Death on the Prairie* (New York, 1934).

WESLEY, EDGAR BRUCE, *Guarding the Frontier* (Minneapolis, Minnesota, 1935).

WILLARD, JAMES F., and GOODYKOONTZ, COLIN B., editors, *The Trans-Mississippi West* (Boulder, Colorado, 1930).

WILCOX, WILMA ESTELLA, *Early Indian Schools and Education Along the Missouri*, Ms., Master's Thesis, University of Iowa, 1928.

WILSON, RUFUS ROCKWELL, *Out of the West* (New York, 1936).

WRIGHT, ROBERT M., *Dodge City, The Cowboy Capital* (Wichita, Kansas, 1913).

WYMAN, WALKER D., *The Missouri River Towns in the Westward Movement*, Ms., Master's Thesis, University of Iowa, 1935.

YOUNG, LEVI EDGAR, *Founding of Utah* (New York, 1923).

COLLECTIONS

American Historical Review, Vols. IV, VI, XIII-XXV (New York, 1899, 1900, 1908-1910).

Annals of Iowa, 3rd Series, Vols. V, VI, VII, XVII, XIX (Des Moines, Iowa, 1903-1910).

Collections, Minnesota State Historical Society, Vols. I-XII (St. Paul, Minnesota, 1872-1908).

Collections, Nebraska State Historical Society, Vols. XVI-XVII (Lincoln, Nebraska, 1911-1913).

Collections, State Historical Society of North Dakota, Vols. I-VII (Bismarck, North Dakota, 1905-1925).

Collections, State Historical Society of Wisconsin, Vols. I-XX (Madison, Wisconsin, 1903-1911).

Contributions, Montana State Historical Society, Vols. I-VIII (Helena, Montana, 1876-1917).

DAWSON, T. F., *Scrapbooks*, Vols. I-XIV, Colorado State Historical Society Library.

Iowa Journal of History and Politics, Vols. III-XXVIII (Iowa City, Iowa, 1905-1930).

Kansas Historical Quarterly, Vols. I-VII (Topeka, Kansas, 1931-1939).

Kansas State Historical Society *Collections*, Vols. I-XIX (Topeka, Kansas, 1881-1934).

Minnesota History Bulletin, Vols. I-V (St. Paul, Minnesota, 1915-1922).

Minnesota History—A Quarterly Magazine, Vols. VI-XVI (St. Paul, Minnesota, 1923-1935).

Mississippi Valley Historical Review, Vol. X (Cedar Rapids, Iowa, 1923).

Missouri Historical Review, Vols. I-XXXI (Columbia, Missouri, 1907-1937).

Missouri Historical Society *Collections*, Vols. I-VI (St. Louis, Missouri, 1880, 1931).

North Dakota Historical Quarterly, Vols. I-VII (Bismarck, North Dakota, 1926-1933).

Proceedings and Collections, Nebraska State Historical Society, Vols. I-XV (Lincoln, Nebraska, 1894-1907).

Proceedings of the Mississippi Valley Historical Association, Vols. VII, X (Cedar Rapids, Iowa, 1913-1914).

Publications, Nebraska State Historical Society, Vols. XIX-XXII (Lincoln, Nebraska, 1919-1936).

Reminiscences, North Dakota State Historical Society Library.

South Dakota Historical *Collections*, Vols. I-XVI (Aberdeen and Pierre, South Dakota, 1902-1932).

Transactions and Reports, Nebraska State Historical Society, Vols. I-V (Lincoln, Nebraska, 1885-1893).

Washington Historical Quarterly, The, Vol. XII (Seattle, Washington, 1920).

BIOGRAPHIES

ALTER, J. CECIL, *James Bridger* (Salt Lake City, 1925).

Autobiography of John Ball, Compiled by his daughters, Kate Ball Powers, Flora Ball Hopkins, Lucy Ball (Grand Rapids, Michigan, 1925).

BARROW, FRANK, *R. C. Barrow, His Life and Work* (Lincoln, Nebraska, 1892).

BLAIR, WALTER, and MEINE, FRANKLIN J., *Mike Fink, King of Mississippi Keelboatmen* (New York, 1933).

BUDGE, JESSE R. S., *The Life of William Budge* (Salt Lake City, 1915).

BURDICK, USHER L., *Life and Exploits of John Goodall* (Watford City, North Dakota, 1931).

CREIGHTON, EDWARD, "Biographical Sketch of Edward Creighton," *Nebraska History Magazine*, Vol. XVII.

DAVID, ROBERT BEEBE, *Finn Burnett, Frontiersman* (Glendale, California, 1937).

————, *Malcolm Campbell, Sheriff* (Casper, Wyoming, 1932).

DE BARTHE, JOE, *Life and Adventures of Frank Grouard* (St. Joseph, Missouri, 1894).

EL COMANCHO, *Old-Timer's Tale* (Place of publication not given, 1929).

EVANS, JOHN HENRY, *Charles Coulson Rich; Pioneer Builder of the West* (New York, 1936).

FAVOUR, ALPHEUS HOYT, *Old Bill Williams* (Chapel Hill, North Carolina, 1936).

GREER, WILLIAM ALLEN, *A Boy on the Plains and in the Rockies* (Boston, 1917).

HAGEDORN, HERMAN N., *The Magnate, William Boyce Thompson and His Time* (New York, 1935).

HOLCOMBE, THEODORE ISAAC, *An Apostle of the Wilderness* (New York, 1903).

LARPENTEUR, CHARLES, *Forty Years a Fur Trader on the Upper Missouri* (New York, 1898).

MULLENS, PATRICK A., *Biographical Sketches of Edward Creighton, John A. Creighton, Mary Lucretia Creighton, and Sarah Emily Creighton* (Omaha, Nebraska, 1901).

MUMEY, NOLIE, *The Life of Jim Baker, 1818-1898, Trapper, Scout, Guide and Indian Fighter* (Denver, 1931).

NIBLEY, PRESTON, *Brigham Young, The Man and His Work* (Salt Lake City, 1936).

PERKINS, JACOB RANDOLPH, *Trails, Rails, and War; the Life of General G. M. Dodge* (Indianapolis, 1929).

POND, SAMUEL WILLIAM, JR., *Two Volunteer Missionaries Among the Dakotas* (Boston, 1893).

ROBERTS, BRIGHAM H., *Life of John Taylor* (Salt Lake City, 1892).

SMITH, ELIZA R. SNOW, *Biography and Family Record of Lorenzo Snow* (Salt Lake City, 1884).

TANNER, J. M., *A Biographical Sketch of James Jensen* (Salt Lake City, 1911).

VICTOR, FRANCES FULLER, *The River of the West* (Hartford, 1870).

WALSH, RICHARD JOHN, and SALSBURY, MILTON S., *The Making of Buffalo Bill* (Indianapolis, 1928).

WARREN, ELIZA SPALDING, *Memoirs of the West, The Spaldings* (Portland, Oregon, 1916).

WEST, FRANKLIN LORENZO R., *Life of Franklin D. Richards* (Salt Lake City, 1924).

WHITNEY, ORSON F., *Life of Heber C. Kimball* (Salt Lake City, 1888).

YOUNG, JOHN R., *Memoirs of John R. Young, Utah Pioneer 1847* (Salt Lake City, 1920).

MISCELLANEOUS

BURDICK, USHER L., *Marquis de Mores at War in the Bad Lands* (Fargo, North Dakota, 1929).

JONES, LLOYD, "Pony Express," *Collier's Weekly*, September, 1910.

LOVE, CLARA M., "History of the Cattle Industry in the Southwest," *Southwestern Historical Quarterly*, Vol. XIX.

MERRIAM, LUCIUS S., "The Telegraphs of the Bond-Aided Pacific Railroads," *Political Science Quarterly*, Vol. IX.

"Missouri River Steamboating," *Nebraska History Magazine*, Vol. VIII, No. 1.

MUNSON, JUDGE LYMAN E., "Pioneer Life on the American Frontier," *Connecticut Magazine*, Vol. XI, Montana State Historical Society Library.

PACK, MARY, "The Romance of the Pony Express," *Union Pacific Magazine*, August, 1923.

PARSONS, EUGENE, "The Story of the Trapper," *The Trail*, July, 1911.

INDEX

INDEX

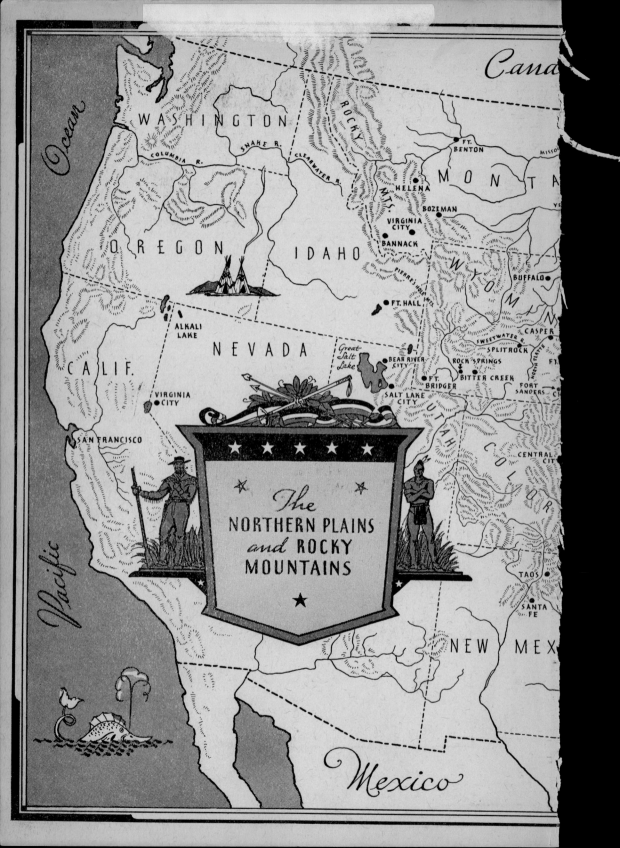